INSIGHT GUIDES
CHINA

APA PUBLICATIONS L
Part of the Langenscheidt Publishing Group

INSIGHT GUIDE
CHINA

Editorial
Project Editor
Tom Le Bas
Series Editor
Rachel Fox
Picture Manager
Steven Lawrence

Distribution

United States
Langenscheidt Publishers, Inc.
36–36 33rd Street 4th Floor
Long Island City, NY 11106
orders@langenscheidt.com

UK & Ireland
GeoCenter International Ltd
Meridian House, Churchill Way West
Basingstoke, Hampshire RG21 6YR
sales@geocenter.co.uk

Australia
Universal Publishers
1 Waterloo Road
Macquarie Park, NSW 2113
sales@universalpublishers.com.au

New Zealand
Hema Maps New Zealand Ltd (HNZ)
Unit 2, 10 Cryers Road
East Tamaki, Auckland 2013
sales.hema@clear.net.nz

Worldwide
Apa Publications GmbH & Co.
Verlag KG (Singapore branch)
7030 Ang Mo Kio Avenue 5
08-65 Northstar @ AMK
Singapore 569880
apasin@singnet.com.sg

Printing
CTPS – China

©2010 Apa Publications GmbH & Co.
Verlag KG (Singapore branch)
All Rights Reserved

First Edition 1990
Eleventh Edition 2010
Reprinted 2010

CONTACTING THE EDITORS
We would appreciate it if readers
would alert us to errors or outdated information by writing to:
**Insight Guides, P.O. Box 7910,
London SE1 1WE, England.
insight@apaguide.co.uk**

www.insightguides.com

ABOUT THIS BOOK

The first Insight Guide pioneered the use of creative full-colour photography in travel guides in 1970. Since then, we have expanded our range to cater for our readers' need not only for reliable information about their chosen destination but also for a real understanding of the culture and workings of that desti-nation. These days, when the inter-net can supply inexhaustible (but not always reliable) facts, our books marry text and pictures to provide those much more elusive qualities: knowledge and discernment. To achieve this, they rely heavily on the authority of locally based writ-ers and photographers.

This expanded eleventh edition of *Insight Guide: China* explores the world's oldest continual civilisation in depth. China is home to the world's longest recorded history, and its arts, crafts, literature and philosophy

inform those of most other Asian cultures today. The great cities of Beijing and Shanghai are among the most dynamic and influential in the world and, with its vastly expanded economy, this Asian giant is now playing a leading role in global economics and politics.

How to use this book
The book is structured to convey an understanding of China and its cul-ture, and to guide readers through its sights and attractions.

◆ The **Best of China** section at the front of the guide helps you to pri-oritise what you want to do.

◆ The **Features** section, with a pink bar at the top of each page, covers the country's history, geography and cul-ture in authoritative essays.

◆ The **Places** section, indi-cated by a blue bar, explores all the sights and areas worth seeing. The chief

LEFT: martial arts training at Shaolin Monastery. **BELOW RIGHT:** misty peaks at Huang Shan, Anhui province. **BELOW LEFT:** Confucius statue.

places of interest are coordinated by number with detailed maps. A selection of recommended restaurants appears at the end of each chapter.

◆ The **Travel Tips** section, headed by a yellow bar, offers a convenient point of reference for information on travel, accommodation and other practical aspects of the country. Information is located quickly using the index on the back-cover flap.

The contributors

This eleventh edition has been comprehensively updated and expanded by a team of writers commissioned by Managing Editor **Tom Le Bas**. New for this edition, Chinese characters are included for all featured sights in the text and maps, and in the lists of recommended restaurants and bars, now at the end of each Places chapter. Over 250 new images have been used to bring the book visually up-to-date, and there are also several additional maps. New photographic essays contribute a magazine-style visual guide to aspects of the Chinese world.

Adventure-travel writer and photographer **Brice Minnigh**, a longtime Asia resident, covered much of central and northern China, and provided new material on Henan, Hubei, Inner Mongolia, Shanxi and Shaanxi, as well as Tibet and Qinghai. Brice was also one of the principal photographers for this new edition of the book.

Chris Taylor, a China-based writer who has written or collaborated on some 30 travel guides to the region, updated the Yunnan and Sichuan chapters, as well as the History and Features sections, and wrote the new chapter on the Chinese economy.

The Shanghai, Jiangsu and Zhejiang chapters were overhauled by **Brent Hannon**, a Shanghai-based travel writer and journalist who has lived in Asia for more than a decade and contributed to *Business Traveller*, *DestinAsian*, *Discovery* and other publications.

Beijing resident and journalist **David Drakeford** has lived in China for five years; he updated the text on Beijing and its surroundings, the Northeast and Shandong province.

The southern provinces of China from Fujian to Guizhou were updated by British travel writer and photographer **Graham Bond**, who is currently based in Zhaoqing (Guangdong), and is the author of three China guidebooks. Insight regular **Andrew Forbes** updated the Silk Road chapter, with new material on Kashi and the southern Silk route.

Contributors to earlier editions include **David Bedford, Ed Peters** and **Manfred Morgenstern**.

Principal photographers include **David Henley, Brice Minnigh** and **David Shen Kai**. The guide was proofread by **Neil Titman** and **Sian Lezard**, and indexed by **Helen Peters**.

Map Legend

▬ ▪ ▬	International Boundary
▬ ▬ ▬	Province Boundary
▬ ▪ ▬	National Park/Reserve
▬ ▬ ▬	Ferry Route
✈✈	Airport
✝✟	Church (ruins)
✝	Monastery
∴	Archaeological Site
∩	Cave
★	Place of Interest
⌐	Beach
❊	Viewpoint
Ⓜ	Metro
🚌	Bus Station
❶	Tourist Information
☾	Mosque
✡	Synagogue
🕴	Statue/Monument
✉	Post Office

The main places of interest in the Places section are coordinated by number with a full-colour map (e.g. ❶), and a symbol at the top of every right-hand page tells you where to find the map.

Contents

Introduction

The Best Of China..................**6**
The New Superpower **17**
The Chinese **21**
The Lands of China **31**

History

Imperial China **37**
End of Empire to
    Modern Times **48**
Decisive Dates **60**

Features

The New China **67**
Beliefs and Religion................**74**
Traditional Medicine **84**
Chinese Literature.................**88**
Arts and Crafts **94**
Architecture.........................**100**
Cuisines of China.................**106**

Places

Introduction **121**
The North...........................**125**
    Beijing.............................**129**
    Outside Beijing **148**
    The Northeast **159**
    Inner Mongolia.................**166**
    Shanxi, Southern Hebei
        and Shandong **171**
    Xi'an, Shaanxi and Henan **183**
The Centre **205**
    Shanghai.........................**209**
    Nanjing, Jiangsu
        and the Grand Canal **227**
    Hangzhou and Zhejiang **243**
    Chang Jiang
        (Yangzi) Region **251**

The South **269**
    Hong Kong........................**273**
    Macau..............................**290**
    Guangdong, Hainan Island
        and Fujian **297**
    The Southern Interior **318**
The Southwest **329**
    Guangxi and Guizhou **331**
    Sichuan............................**347**
    Yunnan **359**
The West **377**
    Tibet and Qinghai..............**379**
    The Silk Road **397**

Insights

MINI FEATURES

Inventions and Technology **42**
Post-Imperial Leaders **50**
The Animal Trade **87**
Cinema in China **91**
Hutong **136**
Shaolin **192**
A Brief History of Shanghai....**212**
The Great Dam of China........**256**
The Overseas Chinese **316**

PHOTO FEATURES

The Bejing Olympics...............**72**
Chinese Festivals **82**
Chinese Opera.......................**92**
A Guide to Chinese Temples ..**104**
Building the Wall **156**
The Terracotta Warriors **198**
Ancient Treasures **200**
China's Sacred Peaks **264**
Chinese Wildlife....................**324**
Minorities of the Southwest ..**344**
The Silk Road **394**

LEFT: inspecting the crickets. **RIGHT:** Daoist priest. **BELOW LEFT:** road sign.

Travel Tips

TRANSPORTATION
Getting There **418**
Getting Around **421**

ACCOMMODATION
Choosing a Hotel **427**
Anhui **427**
Beijing **428**
Chongqing Shi **429**
Dongbei **429**
Fujian **429**
Gansu **430**
Guangdong **430**
Guangxi **431**
Guizhou **431**
Hainan Island **432**
Hebei **432**
Henan **432**
Hong Kong **433**
Hubei **434**
Hunan **435**
Inner Mongolia **435**
Jiangsu **436**
Jiangxi **436**
Macau **436**
Qinghai **437**
Shaanxi **437**
Shandong **438**
Shanxi **438**
Shanghai **439**
Sichuan **440**
Tibet **441**
Xinjiang **441**
Yunnan **442**
Zhejiang **443**

SHOPPING
What to Buy **444**
Bargaining **444**
Import and Export **444**
Where to Shop **444**

ACTIVITIES
Festivals **450**
The Arts **451**
Nightlife **452**
Outdoor Pursuits **452**
Tours and Agencies **453**

A–Z: PRACTICAL INFORMATION
Admission Charges **454**
Budgeting for your Trip **454**
Business Hours **454**
Climate **454**
Disabled Travellers **455**
Electricity **455**
Embassies and Consulates **455**
Emergencies **455**
Entry Regulations **456**
Gay Travellers **456**
Health and Medical Services **456**
Media **458**
Money Matters **459**
Photography **459**
Postal/Courier Services **459**
Public Holidays **459**
Public Toilets **460**
Religious Services **460**
Telecommunications **460**
Time Zone **460**
Tipping **460**
Tours and Travel Agents **461**
Useful Addresses **461**
Visitor Hotlines **461**
Weights and Measures **461**
What to Bring **461**
What to Wear **461**

LANGUAGE
Understanding the
  Language **462**
Words and Phrases **463**
Further Reading **468**

Maps
China **122**
Beijing **126–7**
Forbidden City **132**
Summer Palace **143**
Outside Beijing **151**
The Northeast **161**
Lower Huang He **172–3**
Qingdao **178**
Xi'an and Outside Xi'an **185**
Shanghai **206–7**
Nanjing **229**
Suzhou **234**
Jiangsu and Zhejiang **239**
Hangzhou **244**
Central China **252**
Chiang Jiang **254–5**
Wuhan **260**
Hong Kong **270–1**
Central, Wan Chai and
  Causeway Bay **274–5**
Kowloon **280**
Macau **292**
Guangzhou **298**
The South **306**
Xiamen **311**
Guilin **332**
Guangxi and Guizhou **334**
Sichuan **348**
Chengdu **350**
Kunming **360**
Yunnan **363**
Dali and Around Dali **365**
Lijiang and
  Around Lijiang **368**
Tibet and Qinghai **380**
Lhasa **383**
Silk Road **398**
Kashi (Kashgar) **410**

Inside front cover: China
End panel: Beijing and
Shanghai Metro systems
Inside back cover: China:
Political

THE BEST OF CHINA: TOP SIGHTS

The must-see sights of this vast country range from awe-inspiring ancient treasures to futuristic city skylines, timeless landscapes and fascinating old towns

▽ The glittering skyline of **Shanghai**, including the iconic Pearl Oriental TV Tower *(left)*, is the most compelling visual evidence of China's new-found prosperity. The city is bursting with life, and this, combined with its unique history and architecture, makes it a fascinating place to spend a few days. *Pages 209–23*

△ The magnificent landscapes that have inspired countless Chinese scroll paintings come to life along the Li River south of **Guilin**. Dreamlike rock spires tower above lush riverine scenery to stunning effect. *Pages 335–7*

▷ Built to keep the northern barbarians out of the Middle Kingdom, the **Great Wall** is a true wonder of the world, extending more than 6,400km (4,000 miles) across northern China from the east coast to the Gobi Desert. The section of Wall north of Beijing is both accessible and spectacular, writhing its way across a dramatic hilly landscape. *Pages 148–51, 156–7*

▷ Follow the **Silk Road** through the wide-open spaces of the northwest to experience a completely different side of China. Oasis towns strung along this conduit of trade and cultural exchange – such as Turpan and Kashi – have retained their exotic Central Asian flavour and are full of interest. *Pages 394–5, 397–413*

△ A visit to the beguiling riverside town of **Fenghuang** in Hunan province is a rare chance to see the old China, its wooden buildings and narrow streets representative of how much of the country looked in days gone by. *Page 323*

△ In the mountainous northwest of Yunnan province, the old town of **Lijiang** is one of the most popular destinations in China, with excellent tourist facilities, a relaxed atmosphere and superb scenery on its doorstep. *Pages 366–8*

◁ One of the world's most extraordinary historical sights, the **Army of Terracotta Warriors** was only discovered in the 1970s. Three large underground vaults house over 8,000 life-sized figures. *Pages 198–9*

△ Take a river cruise along China's longest river and marvel at the scenery in the **Yangzi Gorges**. *Pages 255–7, 425–6*

▽ **Huang Shan** in Anhui province is a fabulously scenic mountain with all the attributes of a classic Chinese peak: rocky crags, twisted pines and ethereal views over a sea of clouds. *Page 262*

▷ The **Temple of Heaven** in Beijing is perhaps the most accessible and beautiful of the country's A-list heritage sights. Set in a large park, the highlight is the circular Hall of Prayer for Good Harvests *(pictured)*. *Pages 137–8*

THE BEST OF CHINA: EDITOR'S CHOICE

Unique attractions, colourful festivals, urban highlights, fabulous landscapes, quiet backwaters, river cruises... here are our recommendations, plus some essential tips for travellers

TOP CITIES

● **Beijing** The great hub of power in China, past and present, with some unmissable sights. *See pages 129–45*
● **Shanghai** *see page 6*
● **Guangzhou** One of the best cities in China for eating out, this is a fast-paced boom town. *See pages 297–302*
● **Nanjing** With its broad avenues and placid canals, Nanjing is an attractive and relaxed city. *See pages 228–33*
● **Chengdu** The 2,000-year-old capital of Sichuan has kept some of its traditional feel, with colourful streets lined with tiny shops and tea-houses. *See pages 348–51*
● **Kunming** Capital of China's most diverse province, Yunnan, Kunming has an easy-going charm and a delightful climate. *See pages 360–2*

● **Qingdao** This northern port has a smattering of Teutonic architecture and sandy beaches. *See pages 176–7*
● **Xiamen** A port facing traffic-free Gulangyu island, full of eccentric European buildings. *See pages 310–2*
● **Xi'an** China's ancient capital has some major sights and the terracotta warriors nearby. *See pages 184–7*
● **Lhasa** At a dizzying altitude, the Tibetan capital is a fascinating city and now linked to the Chinese rail network. *See pages 381–4*
● **Hong Kong** Unique, vibrant and full of things to see and do, a perfect introduction to the Chinese world. *See pages 273–87*

TOP: delectable dim sum. **ABOVE:** Pingyao, one of China's best preserved old towns.

BEAUTIFUL TOWNS

● **Fenghuang** *see page 7*
● **Dali** With its beautiful setting, laid-back Dali is one of the most relaxing places in China. *See pages 364–6*
● **Pingyao** Wonderfully preserved small town in Shanxi province enclosed within Ming-dynasty walls. *See pages 175–6*
● **Suzhou** Historically prosperous Suzhou is famous for its silk and exquisite gardens. *See pages 233–7*

● **Chaozhou** Retaining the atmosphere and architecture of an ancient city, this is a southern Chinese gem. *See pages 306–7*
● **Quanzhou** A pleasant city that was once the world's busiest port. *See pages 312–3*
● **Kaifeng** One of the best-preserved old centres anywhere in China. *See pages 195–6*
● **Turpan** A Silk Road oasis deep in Central Asia, full of interest. *See pages 404–5*

ABOVE: dragon detail from a Chengdu temple.

MAGNIFICENT SCENERY

- **Guilin** *see page 6*
- **Huang Shan** *see page 7*
- **Longsheng rice terraces, Guangxi** The "Dragon's Back" terraces wind in huge layers 800 metres (2,600 ft) up the sides of a steep valley. The **rice terraces of southern Yunnan** are similarly spectacular. *See pages 337–8, 364*
- **Western Sichuan** Magical, sparklingly coloured lakes at Jiuzhaigou, and the panda reserve at Wolong. Further north are expanses of wild grassland. *See pages 356–7*
- **Xishuangbanna, Yunnan** This tropical region, home to rare birds, elephants and the Buddhist Dao people, has more in common with neighbouring Laos and Burma than the rest of China. *See pages 370–2*

- **The Three Parallel Rivers, Yunnan** Mighty gorges along the remote headwaters of three great rivers – The Nu Jiang, the Mekong and the Yangzi. *See page 370.*
- **Southern Hainan beaches** The white sands of Dadonghai and Yalong Wan are as close as China comes to a tropical paradise. *See pages 308–9*
- **Emei Shan** The Holy Mountain of Sichuan, with many Buddhist temples spread around its thickly forested slopes. *See pages 353–5*
- **Tai Shan** Another sacred peak, with stupendous views across the northern plains. *See page 179*
- **Tian Chi (Lake of Heaven)** A dazzling lake ringed by the snow-capped Tian Shan. *See page 408*
- **Wulingyuan Scenic Reserve** A magical landscape of limestone spires and forest. *See page 322*

ABOVE: rehearsing for a National Day parade, Shanghai.
LEFT: Sichuan panda. **BELOW:** Longsheng rice terraces.

FESTIVALS AND EVENTS

- With millions on the move, **Chinese New Year** is not a great time to be travelling in China; it is, nonetheless a special time, with dragon dances, parades and temple fairs. *See pages 82, 83, 450*
- Harbin's extraordinary **Ice sculpture festival** takes place in the depths of the northeastern winter. *See page 165*
- The **Dragon Boat festival** is an exciting event held all over eastern and southern China, with fiercely competitive races and plenty of noise. *See pages 82, 450*
- The **Miao and Dong festivals** of Guizhou province are some of the most colourful spectacles in the country. *See pages 340, 345*
- The **Birthday of Tin Hau**, the Goddess of the Sea (also known as Matsu and A-Ma), is marked in southern coastal regions with firecrackers and parades. *See pages 314, 451*
- **Buddhist festivals** include the birthdays of the Buddha and Guanyin, Goddess of Mercy. *See pages 83, 451*
- Moon cakes and lanterns make the **Mid-Autumn festival** a picturesque occasion. *See pages 82, 450*
- **National Day** is marked with parades and floral displays; as at Chinese New Year, most shops and businesses close for a week. It's a bad time to travel. *See page 82*

1 0

OFF THE BEATEN TRACK

• **Guizhou province**
Home to over 30 minority groups, each with its special culture – such as the Dong, builders of covered bridges, or the Miao, famed for colourful festivals. *See pages 339–42*

• **Beihai, Guangxi** A pleasantly relaxed port city near the Vietnamese border, with beaches and characterful old buildings from its days as a trading centre. *See page 338*

• **Lushan, Jiangxi** This hill town above the Yangzi plain was used as a summer retreat by western missionaries and, later, by Mao Zedong. *See page 320*

• **Kashi (Kashgar), Xinjiang** China's westernmost city, a Silk Road caravanserai surrounded by deserts and high mountains. *See pages 409–11*

• **Lanzhou, Gansu** Few tourists stay in this dusty city: there is little to see in terms of conventional sights and the air quality

is notoriously bad. Yet Lanzhou is unique: ranged along a Yellow River gorge, this long, narrow city has a Central Asian feel and some great food. *See page 397*

• **Inner Mongolian grasslands** A seemingly infinite expanse of grass and steppe, interrupted by a few lonely Buddhist stupas. *See pages 166–9*

• **Karakoram Highway** One of the world's most spectacular roads, between awe-inspiring peaks into Pakistan. *See pages 395, 412*

• **The Siberian far north** Vast pine forests and reed lakes – home to many rare birds – along the border with Russia. *See page 165*

• **Hainan's interior** The hills retain a few areas of tropical rainforest, and colourful minority groups. *See page 309*

• **Southwest Fujian** Yongding County is home to numerous Hakka round-houses. *See page 313*

ABOVE: Hangzhou's West Lake. **LEFT AND BELOW:** martial arts practice. **RIGHT:** temple incense.

CLASSIC CHINA

• **West Lake, Hangzhou** Celebrated by poets, this misty lake is ringed by woods and pagodas – the quintessential Chinese beauty spot. *See pages 244–5*

• **The Grand Canal** The ancient 1,800-km waterway, extended over 1,000 years, links a series of picturesque towns. *See page 237*

• **The Summer Palace, Beijing** One of the most complete classical Chinese gardens, with lotus pools between

lakeside pagodas. *See pages 143–4*

• **Yangzi River cruise** *see page 7*

• **Li River cruise** A placid trip through a spellbinding landscape. *See page 337*

• **Dayan Ta (Great Wild Goose Pagoda)** One of China's most striking pagodas, dating from the 6th century AD. *See page 186*

LEFT: Wulingyuan Scenic Reserve, Hunan province.

TEMPLES AND MONASTERIES

● **Wong Tai Sin Temple, Hong Kong** The "Fortune-tellers' Temple" is one of the most bustling, and most colourful, of Daoist shrines. *See page 283*

● **Yonghe Gong, Beijing** A beautiful Lamaist temple in the heart of Beijing. *See page 139*

● **Xuankong Si Temple** This "hanging temple" clings to the cliff-face on Heng Shan, one of China's sacred Daoist peaks. *See page 173*

● **Putuo Shan Island** A Buddhist holy mountain on a tranquil island near Shanghai, presided over by the Goddess of Compassion, Guanyin. *See page 249*

● **Shaolin** Famous worldwide as the great centre of Chinese martial arts. *See pages 192–3*

● **Labrang Monastery, Xiahe** The largest Lamaist monastery outside Tibet, with over 2,000 monks. *See page 400*

● **Baima Si Temple** The oldest Buddhist temple in China, founded in AD 68. *See page 191*

● **Qiongzhu Si Temple** Surreal sculptures of Buddhist saints in the hills above Kunming. *See page 362*

● **Kong Miao (Confucius Temple), Qufu** China's most important Confucian temple. *See page 180*

MAJOR HISTORICAL SIGHTS

ABOVE: the Leshan Buddha. **BELOW:** don't break the rules.

● **Terracotta Warriors** *see page 7*

● **Forbidden City, Beijing** History on a grand scale right in the heart of the capital, the emperors' city is a must-see. *See pages 130–2*

● **Longmen Caves** Amazing Buddhist carvings spread across a series of grottoes. *See page 191*

● **Leshan Buddha** This colossal 71-metre (230-ft) statue of Buddha was built to protect river traffic. *See page 355*

● **Mogao Caves** Over 490 caves lived in, carved and painted over 1,000 years by Buddhist monks, in a mountain on the edge of the Gobi Desert. *See pages 403–4*

● **Potala Palace, Lhasa** Symbol of Tibet, the immense 1,000-room palace of the Dalai Lamas dominates the city of Lhasa. *See pages 381–2*

● **Shaoshan** Mao's birthplace in Hunan province is now a museum-village, with his childhood home carefully preserved. *See page 321*

● **Tiananmen Square, Beijing** This vast square at the gates of the Forbidden City has witnessed momentous historical events. *See pages 133–5*

TRAVELLERS' TIPS

● **Tourist Information** Most CTS (China Travel Service) and CITS (China International Travel Service) offices exist to sell tours – rather than to impart free information to tourists. There are, however, a few exceptions. All CTS/CITS offices should be able to assist with tickets for air and rail travel.

● **Buying rail tickets** For overnight journeys, you should purchase your tickets 2–5 days in advance (5 days is usually the maximum), as they often sell out – more of a problem if you are joining the train a long way into its journey. The choice is either hard-sleeper or the noticeably more comfortable soft-sleeper. If you are told there are none left, it may still be possible to buy from a travel agent such as CTS. Railway stations in large cities usually have a dedicated ticket window for foreigners, with little queuing involved. *See page 422.*

● **Buses** Some long-distance buses (mostly between smaller cities) only set off once every inch of space is occupied. Tickets are usually easy to buy at bus stations on the day of travel. Most cities have several bus stations, but they are often miles apart.

禁止跨越
No striding

THE NEW SUPERPOWER

After 40 centuries of introspection, China is now
helping to define the world's future,
whether we're ready or not

China is a land of superlatives. The most populous country on earth and the third-largest nation after Russia and Canada, it can also claim the world's longest continuously recorded history: the precociously advanced civilisations of its distant past have given humanity some of its most significant scientific and technological inventions. After an extended period of decline and turmoil, China is rising once more, evolving into an economic superpower at a dizzying speed.

The name China, as used in the West, can be traced back to the Qin dynasty (221–206 BC), when the concept of a unified China became reality. The land was variously known as Tschin, Tschina or Tzinistan, and later Cathay, in the Indo-Germanic languages, while to the Chinese themselves it has always been, simply, Zhongguo – the Middle Kingdom.

In Beijing's Temple of Heaven a marble altar signifies the centre of the known ancient world, a place that only the emperor was allowed to enter. According to the world-view of ancient China, the Middle Kingdom lay precisely below the centre of the firmament. The further one was from the emperor's throne, the lower one was in the cosmic hierarchy. The unfortunate people and cultures living on the dark peripheries of the earth, especially to the gloomy north and the arid west, and to Europe beyond, were considered barbaric.

For centuries, Europeans similarly regarded China as near the edge of the known world; admittedly the Middle Kingdom was an empire of magnificence and cultural interest, but of little importance to the world scheme. Much later, Western analysts and pundits referred to China as a sleeping giant, or more lyrically, a sleeping tiger or dragon. Modern China, now wide-awake, is a global power helping to shape the new millennium.

Yet this role is not something with which the country is comfortable or experienced: for most of its existence China has turned its back on the world and focused inward, like a tai chi student seeking a centred stability. China may be learning fast, but the nation's emergence onto the world stage has not been without its difficulties.

PRECEDING PAGES: ice sculpture in Harbin; Dragon's Backbone Terraces, Guangxi. **LEFT:** Chinese opera. **TOP:** Buddhist monk at Putuo Shan. **ABOVE RIGHT:** ancient and modern in Shanghai. **ABOVE LEFT:** the Great Wild Goose Pagoda, Xi'an.

Since the end of World War II, the country's population has more than doubled to 1.3 billion people. Although only approximately 7 percent of China's land is suitable for agriculture, a fifth of the world's people must subsist on it. Finding employment for such a large section of humanity is a further headache: with the boom in the Chinese economy in recent years, the government has to do all it can to sustain employment levels in the new industries.

Travellers to China's large cities will see the results of accommodating the explosive demographic, and economic, growth: monochromatic, concrete cities veiled with the smoke of pollution, and legions of men from the countryside looking for work. Travellers will also see increasing affluence as the growth of the consumer society continues to eradicate the austerity of the past. The standard of living has improved exponentially for many in recent years, particularly in the prosperous coastal cities. The ruling Communist Party – the social and economic system is, of course, far from communist these days, yet the one-party state remains – is intolerant of political diversity or dissent.

Economics and politics aside, it is the land and peoples of China that enthral. A baffling hodgepodge of dialects unified by a common script, China is a fantastic and unique journey. From the mountain fastness of Tibet in the west to the affluent eastern coastline, from the dry northern heartlands to the resourceful and fertile south, China is a constantly engaging and challenging destination. "Seeing is easy, learning is hard" goes an old Chinese proverb. The insightful traveller must necessarily realise and acknowledge that China simply is China.

Notes about spellings and language

The romanisation system used in this book is *pinyin*, the modern standard and the official system used within the People's Republic. What was Peking is now Beijing, and it is now Nanjing, not Nanking. The founder of the Communist Party used to be Mao Tse-tung; now it's Mao Zedong. Most *pinyin* transliterations are straightforward and simple to pronounce – the main exceptions are the letters *q* (pronounced *ch*) and *x* (pronounced *sh*).

Mandarin uses suffixes to indicate many proper nouns, such as river *(-jiang or -he)*, temple *(-si or -ta)*, mountain *(-shan)*, or street *(-lu or -jie)*. In romanised or *pinyin* form, the suffix is sometimes integral with the root, sometimes not. We have chosen to separate the suffix to clearly identify the subject. Thus, the Tian Mountains are referred to as "Tian Shan". For the majority of temples and parks, we use the Chinese *pinyin* as the primary reference in bold type, followed by Chinese characters and English in parentheses. However, where a sight is more usefully identified in English – as in the case of most museums, or with well known sights with a familar English name such as the Great Wall or Moon Hill – we have the English in bold followed by Chinese characters and *pinyin*.

See pages 462–467 for an introduction to the Chinese language. Also see page 32 for a list of geographical suffixes – these can be useful when asking for directions. ❏

TOP: noodles with pork and vegetables. **ABOVE RIGHT:** a Miao *lusheng* festival in Guizhou province. **RIGHT:** *weiqi* (go), an ancient board game popular throughout China.

THE CHINESE

Around 1.3 billion people – almost one-fifth of the planet's population – live in China, and most are crowded into just one-fifth of the country's land area

The notion of being Chinese – that is, Han Chinese – is to some degree a cultural rather than an ethnic concept, an acceptance of Chinese values. Although over 90 percent of Chinese are considered ethnically Han, the distinction between them and other racial groups is not always clear-cut. The Han Chinese are, of course, derived from a distinctive racial background, but over the many centuries, their gradual migration southwards from their original homelands around the Huang He (Yellow River) has seen the absorption of numerous racial minorities.

The Han – the name relates to the Han dynasty (206 BC–AD 220), a pivotal period in Chinese history – have traditionally populated the eastern part of the country, leaving the empty west and north to the minority ethnic groups. But overpopulation in the east, coupled with the government's desire to bring minority areas in line with the rest of the country, along with financial incentives, has encouraged ever greater numbers of Han migrants to move to far-flung places like Xinjiang and Tibet.

China's vast population brings major advantages and disadvantages. A seemingly endless supply of cheap labour ensures a booming economy, but intense demand for food, fuel and other resources leaves the countryside exhausted and increasingly reliant on imports.

Only in Tibet does the indigenous group remain in the majority, despite frequent reports of population transfers that would seem to suggest the contrary.

LEFT: China's cultural scene is thriving.
RIGHT: ambitious infrastructure and other building projects have made construction workers in great demand across the country.

The Chinese today have more opportunities than they have ever had: more freedom to move around and travel overseas, more opportunities to seek better jobs and better education, and more chances to work and save money for a better future. The outlook has never been so good for so many people.

But at the same time, inevitably, huge problems exist. A wide gap separates rich from poor, and the gap is growing. In the cities, many people make relatively good money, but free access to schools, hospitals and housing, as well as other services which were taken for granted a generation ago, are increasingly threatened by privatisation, as China's Brave New World of market economics sweeps away the socialist past. Many of China's poor struggle just to survive. Farmers suffer from inflation and low prices for their crops, and some have been pushed off their land by developers.

Population headaches

Ninety percent of China's population lives on one-fifth of its land, mostly in the east and south. In contrast, the vast empty areas in the north and west are sparsely populated and often barely habitable.

China's population was counted for the first time about 2,000 years ago, in AD 4. By AD 742, during the Tang dynasty, the population was just over 50 million people. At the time of the invasion of Genghis Khan and the Mongols, the 100 million mark was probably exceeded for the first time. By the middle of the 18th century, the number had doubled; a century later, in 1850, the population had reached 400 million.

Shortly after World War II, there were half a billion people in China. Between the mid-1960s and the early 1980s, the population increased by over 300 million, more than the total population of either the United States or the former Soviet Union. According to official statistics, as of mid-2007, China was home to 1.32 billion people, nearly 20 percent of the world's total population. In recent years, China's population has increased by about 15 million annually.

TOO MANY PEOPLE, TOO FEW SURNAMES

When Genghis Khan was asked how he planned to conquer northern China, it is said that he replied: "I will kill everybody called Wang, Li, Zhang and Liu. The rest will be no problem."

With a population of well over 1 billion, it might be assumed that there would be plenty of surnames to go around in China. Yet of the 12,000 surnames that once existed in the nation, there remain today just 3,000. Nearly one-third of the population shares just five family names. In fact, nearly 90 percent of Chinese use just 100 surnames (the phrase *lao bai xing*, "old 100 names", is used to refer to the masses), with 90 million sharing the name Li, becoming by default the world's most common surname. In the US, by comparison, there are only 2.4 million people with the name Smith, the most common family name in the English-speaking world.

It is not surprising, then, that literally thousands of people in China can share the same full name, leading to many frustrating cases of mistaken identity. The possibility of a bureaucratic meltdown over the confusion caused by such a limited number of names is not far-fetched.

Much of the problem concerning the increasing shortage of surnames began centuries ago when non-Han Chinese, seeking to blend quietly into the dominant culture, abandoned their own names and adopted the common names of the Han Chinese.

In China it is usual to address someone using their surname rather than their first name, as a mark of respect.

The governing and administrative challenges of such a huge population are mind-boggling. Gathering statistics for over 1 billion people, much less analysing it, defies the imagination. Still, statistics reveal much about China's options. The numbers are chilling, considering that less than 10 percent of the world's agrarian areas are in China. For every 1,000 people, there are 21 births but just six deaths.

In 1979, the government began a one-child-per-family programme. In urban areas, the programme has been mostly successful, but in rural areas, where traditions die hard and larger families are needed for farming, the one-child policy has had limited success.

Skewing all population statistics, however, is the preference for male heirs. In China, family lines are passed on through the male child. Partly because of this, and because male offspring are more likely to support ageing parents, especially in rural areas, sons are preferred to daughters. Female infants in the countryside have fallen victim to infanticide. From 1953 to 1964, the sex ratios at birth were a little under 105 males for every 100 female infants. Ultrasound scanners, which allow the determination of the sex of foetuses, were first introduced to China in 1979. As their use became widespread, especially among the middle and upper classes, the ratio climbed (108 males to 100 females in 1982, 111 in 1990, close on 120 in 2007 and in certain areas as high as 135), and continues to climb, with official statistics indicating that by 2020 China will have 30 million more men than women. Doctors are officially banned from disclosing the results of ultrasound scans, but they can usually be persuaded to tell. Also, private businesses now offer the service.

Some factory owners pay wages just once a year, at Chinese New Year. Sometimes migrant workers then find that their pay packet is short of the promised amount.

China's population is increasingly difficult for the nation to sustain. Most Chinese experts have said China can comfortably support a population of only 800 million, a major reason for the great emphasis placed on birth control. Although its

original targets have proved excessively optimistic, the one-child policy has greatly reduced the rate of population increase. According to a recent estimate, the one-child policy had prevented 200 million births by 1993. The average Chinese woman had five or six children in the 1950s, but only around 1.7 by 2007.

Yet problems still remain. Thirty percent of births are not planned, despite widespread use of condoms. The State Family Planning Commission, a government agency, suggests several reasons. First, attitudes have not changed in rural areas. To a farmer, sons still provide the only security for old age. Second, sex education is still a taboo topic,

especially in conservative rural areas where the grandmother educates her grandchildren according to her own beliefs. In the cities, on the other hand, families actually prefer to have one child, as living space is restricted. Because living space in Shanghai or Beijing averages only 3.5 sq metres (38 sq ft), population-control measures are accepted.

Migrant workers

Contemporary China is the scene of a huge population movement, as tens of millions of migrant workers, lured by the sudden promise of wealth, have abandoned the still poor villages and towns of their home provinces in China's interior and western regions and headed for the coastal cities in search of opportunities.

LEFT: China's controversial one-child policy has had limited success in rural areas. **RIGHT:** polishing glassware at an upmarket Shanghai bar.

And what have they found? Better lives, mostly. Many are content living in dorms, working long hours, saving money. Most of the successful migrant workers are young, and often single. When conditions are favourable – reasonable hours, comfortable dorm rooms, decent working conditions and prompt payment of wages – this can be a good life. And the money they send home does a great deal to support the rural countryside, especially in the poorest provinces.

But the less fortunate migrants have found only struggle and hardship. The Chinese have a phrase, *chi ku*, to eat bitterness, that describes the lives of these unlucky ones. Many of them are older men,

guilty of many muggings, purse-snatchings and pickpocketings (bigger crimes, such as extortion, kidnapping and drug-smuggling, are usually the work of resident local gangs).

Perhaps the most serious problem for the migrant workers is non-payment of wages. With salaries paid only at Chinese New Year, migrants who discover that their pay packet is far short of what they expected, or in some cases does not materialise at all, have little legal recourse. Local officials are often in the pockets of the factory owners, and while the central government is concerned about their plight, resolving such issues can take months or years, and pursuing a case

often with families far away, who work in dangerous, dirty factory jobs, or on dangerous, dirty construction sites. They are everywhere in China, in the railway stations, on the streets, in the factories and on the building sites, always without helmets or safety goggles. With their dirty clothes, unkempt hair and ceaseless energy, they are easy to spot.

Like itinerant workers everywhere, the migrants of China face discrimination. With their provincial dialects – many don't speak *putonghua* (Mandarin), the national language – and grinding poverty, they make easy targets. Some of the native residents of the south have lost their jobs in struggling state-run factories, and blame the migrants for taking their jobs at lower wages. The migrants also get blamed for crime, and, indeed, they are

requires time and money. Lacking the means, most workers have little choice but to accept whatever deal their employers offer.

And profit margins for the factory owners and construction companies employing migrant workers are often paper-thin, as huge retail chains like Wal-Mart and Target, with their massive economies of scale, beat down prices to the last fraction of a penny. As wages rise throughout China – a trend that began in 2004 and has been accelerating ever since – margins are further squeezed.

The breakdown of the old system

In the old days, before market reforms and the lure of wealth changed everything, China was a place where lifetime employment was largely guaranteed, and people tended to remain in the same town or village for life. This stability was underpinned by the *hukou* system, whereby everyone in the country was registered at a particular address and which subsequently restricted movement as this required permission from the *danwei* (work unit). This has been breaking down since the 1990s, a process which has made it far easier for people to move around the country seeking work. (With more and more Chinese employed by private – or foreign – companies, the concept of the *danwei* has also broken down.)

Accompanying this freedom of movement is a growing lack of security. Migrant workers are

most, free housing is no longer provided, and for good medical treatment or schooling, payment is essential. These services are increasingly privatised, a process at the heart of a profound transition as China switches from a centrally controlled socialist system to a market economy.

The urban-rural divide

Farmers, who live far from media centres and big-city spotlights, are China's forgotten demographic. The migration from countryside to city is the largest movement in human history – so far, some 115 million people have relocated – and it is hollowing out the rural heartland. Many rural

rarely eligible for national health insurance, cannot afford private insurance, and their employers seldom provide it. Hospitals routinely turn away those who can't afford treatment, so an injury can mean the end of employment, or the end of a life. And then there is the lack of access to medical care and schooling.

It is important to stress, however, that it is not just the migrant workers who have suffered from the collapse of the state welfare system in matters of health, education and housing. Party workers benefit from free healthcare and schooling, but this is not the case for much of China these days. For

LEFT: communal exercise in a Beijing park. **ABOVE:** bemused by a modern art installation in Shanghai.

dwellers are lonely: ageing parents with sons and daughters working far away, families with absentee fathers, wives living without their husbands. Even in the richer areas of Beijing, Shanghai and its hinterland, Guangdong, Fujian, Zhejiang and Jiangsu, the farmers have their problems. As farmland gives way to industry and urban sprawl, they are often removed from their land. Compensation is supposed to be mandatory, but the amounts can vary according to the whims of local officials.

Farmers and poor rural residents have been fighting back, often by gathering in huge, hard-to-ignore protests. Sometimes the protests get violent, and sometimes, too, they get the attention of the rulers in Beijing, who generally side with the peasants. But the central government has limited power in the rural areas of China. Given the fact that farmers officially lease their land from the government *(see also page 70)*, this is a major political issue. Provincial, city and local officials all have much to gain by luring big-money projects to their districts, often in defiance of directives from Beijing. Local officials will usually green-light any project that delivers the cash, while the central government wants cleaner factories that produce higher-value goods. The tug-of-war between low-level officials and central government has become one of China's defining issues, with those in the middle – the rural poor – awaiting the outcome.

The urban middle class

In China, the middle class is clearly on the rise, growing in both numbers and general prosperity. These are the men and women who commute to work in the cities, the secretaries, salespeople, accountants and other service-sector workers. They tend to be educated, computer literate and sometimes English-speaking. They have disposable income and leisure time, they watch movies and go to restaurants, buy tailored suits, mobile phones, cars and watches. They travel, too, to domestic hot-spots like Hainan Island and Guilin, and overseas. Some are now seasoned travellers, and have visited cities in Europe and the US. On the negative side, the collapse of the state welfare system is a burden, and the rich cities on the eastern coast are

starting to experience many of the problems familiar to so many in the West: high property prices, crowded commutes and rising crime.

Family values

The Communist Revolution of 1949 and some of the movements that followed it – notably the Cultural Revolution, an assault on all Chinese traditions – along with the country's heady modernisation over the past two decades, have had a serious impact on the primacy of the family in Chinese society. Moreover, the one-child policy, which was introduced in 1979, has changed the traditional Chinese family structure – prior to the 1970s, families are thought to have averaged five children.

Even if the one-child policy has not been as effective as many outsiders imagine – and there are signs that it is gradually being loosened – some estimates indicate that the policy has now resulted in as many as 300 million fewer births nationwide, and combined with a swelling tide of urban migration, the outcome is a shortage of farmhands in rural China, where once the crops were tended by extended families. The policy is thought to have allowed a greater integration of women into the workforce, but on the downside it has put enormous strains on traditional family expectations. In times past, children were expected to support parents and grandparents in their old age, and as a result of the one-child policy a vast number of young Chinese face the burden of providing for two parents and four grandparents.

Problems such as these are being compounded by a generational fracturing. Young people speak the national language, *putonghua* (Mandarin), and sometimes even English, while their parents often speak only a local dialect. The older generation also knows nothing of the obsessions of China's

> It has been harder to implement the one-child policy in the countryside, where family ties remain strong. In villages common surnames traditionally identify membership of the extended family clan.

youth: mobile phones, video games, designer clothes, comic books and foreign fashions.

Thirty or 40 years ago, a city dweller's ticket to security was a job for life – the so-called "iron rice" bowl – with the Communist Party. On the farm, it was even simpler: plant the crops, work the fields and hope the elements were on your side. However, the new ticket to success is a college degree, proficiency in English and, more than anything else, youth. China's youth are drawn to the bright lights of China's coastal cities and don't want to work on the farms, and many of those for whom the bright lights are out of reach take jobs far away from home in the factories of the Pearl River Delta and the Shanghai hinterland. This has resulted in a generational gap unprecedented in China's history, with many young people feeling they have nothing to learn from their parents, and the parents themselves often feeling like they have nothing to teach. After all, the older generation was raised on a diet of Communist dogma that

Social life

The Chinese are far more communal than Westerners and like to eat and travel in groups, and group activities start young for the Chinese. Before their lessons begin, schoolchildren often "exercise" together. Taped music and a voice blare out from speakers. *Yi er san. One two three.*

Morning streets are crowded with commuters, and the armadas of cyclists that once poured through the streets have been replaced by motorbikes and private cars. Buses are always packed – people push their way on into the throng, stand crushed against their neighbours, watch in case a seat becomes free, then push their way out when

has very little place in China's freewheeling and effectively capitalist society, where money rules.

Women's status has improved immensely in recent years, and one, Wu Yi, is a State Council vice-premier, making good Mao's famous statement that "women hold up half the sky". Between 1990 and 2000 the number of women in the workforce rose from 280 million to 330 million, and they now account for around 46 percent of the total. But even Vice-Premier Wu Yi has admitted that women's role in politics was "far from satisfactory", and she has said that they "still faced discrimination in the workforce."

LEFT: urban underpass. **ABOVE:** the Beijing Olympics has inspired a generation of gymnasts.

they reach their destinations. Queuing is an introduced and foreign concept.

As their rich and varied cuisine reflects, the Chinese love to eat, and China's rise in living standards is apparent at mealtimes. City residents, to whom even pork was once a treat, now regularly consume beef, fish and shrimp. While meals in the home may be relatively simple affairs with a small selection of dishes from which to choose, restaurant meals can be veritable banquets.

This is especially the case if the meal is charged to entertainment expenses, or is being paid for by a businessman who wants to impress – the Chinese very rarely split the tab. For a banquet really to impress, it should include rare delicacies such as exotic fungi or, sadly and illegally, endangered wildlife. But whatever the offering, there should always be more food than the diners can eat, otherwise the host loses face. Dinner is the chief evening event, though with China's explosion of nightlife options in recent years the younger generation is likely to move on to bars and clubs later.

China's national and regional television stations are improving, and news reports in particular – while politically conservative – have become more daring. The production values in domestically produced sagas have improved greatly and they sometimes today rival foreign soap operas and dramas in popularity. More and more satellite dishes dot city rooftops, bringing MTV, Disney Channel and Star TV into Chinese homes (BBC and CNN can only be accessed in top hotels), and with China's profusion of internet access, more and more Chinese are downloading movies and TV shows from Hong Kong and Taiwan.

One indisputable phenomenon that can be attributed to China's new media is a sharp rise in nationalist sentiment countrywide. In the lead up to the Beijing Olympics anti-foreign sentiment was running at a high that had not been seen in decades. The main reason was a media blitz against perceived Western bias, occasioned by reports of protests in Tibet, and by news of the Tibet support groups disrupting the Olympic torch relay around

MEDIA AND POPULAR CULTURE IN TODAY'S CHINA

In their leisure time, the Chinese middle classes do what their counterparts do the world over: they watch TV. As Hong Kong industrialist Gordon Wu famously pronounced in the early 1990s: the people of China don't care about politics, what they want is to watch television in air-conditioned comfort. On one channel is Yao Ming playing basketball for the Houston Rockets, or coverage of a football match from England. On other channels are ever-popular historical costume dramas, or rather stiff news programmes, foreign films or TV shows from Japan, Korea or the US. But by far the most popular programmes are the *American Idol* clones, TV talent shows such as the wildly successful *Supergirl* contests.

The internet is also immensely popular. Chat rooms and websites hum with discourse, as millions of people weigh up the price of houses, the availability of jobs and the best schools, along with discussing television shows and shopping online. Internet usage in China jumped 30 percent in 2006, as 132 million people logged on. Naturally, the government is aware of this trend, and has erected the "great firewall of China" to monitor sensitive topics such as Tibet, Taiwan and democracy. Nonetheless, China is increasingly wired, and the technology has trickled down to migrant workers and farmers in the form of mobile phones. If a nearby factory raises its wages, for example, thousands of workers will instantly get the news via text message.

the world. But such sentiments had their precedent in anti-Japanese reporting in China over recent years – in some cases leading to anti-Japanese riots – and before that there was the demonisation of pro-independence Taiwanese politicians. The result is a new mood in China: one of extreme pride in the nation's recent achievements, notably winning and holding the Olympics, and any criticism is likely to be deemed anti-Chinese.

Minority groups

There are over 50 officially recognised minority groups living in China today, including those in Tibet and Xinjiang. Most of these minority groups live along China's strategic, sometimes troubled and usually sparsely populated international borders. Thus, when one of the minority groups needles Beijing, such as happens with Tibetans and Uighurs, the central government takes such deviations quite seriously. The minorities have often maintained close relationships with those of their group living on the other side of the border. As a result, central government cannot retain absolute control over some frontier groups.

In 2000, the central government announced its "Go West" campaign, aimed at opening up western China, especially to foreign investment, improving the infrastructure and, it can be surmised, trying to keep any nationalist sentiment in check. They are also encouraging ever more Han Chinese to relocate to these areas. The Qinghai–Tibet railway, completed in 2006, is encouraging this process.

The defining elements of a minority are language, homeland and social values. Around 8 percent of China's population is part of a minority group, with the largest being the 12-million-strong Zhuang, in southwestern China.

The constitution guarantees minorities certain rights and privileges. One of the most important is the right to use their own language. To grant these minorities the right to live according to their own beliefs and traditions is, in the eyes of the Chinese, a sign of goodwill, and the renunciation of the expansionism of the old regime. However, spoken and written fluency in standard Mandarin is the only way to become educated and improve social status. Schools for members of national minorities are rare, and universities teaching a minority language hardly exist. In reality, the slow expansion of the Chinese nation from its original heartland

around the Huang He is linked to an equally slow assimilation of non-Chinese peoples into the Han Chinese society, considered culturally and technically more advanced than the surrounding cultures.

In the autonomous region of Xinjiang in north-western China, Uighurs remain the largest existing ethnic group, but these days make up only 45 percent of the population. Only when grouped together with the Kazakhs, Kirghiz and others do Uighurs constitute an Islamic, Turkic-speaking majority. In the 1950s, 80 percent of the population fulfilled these criteria. But now, all the large cities (except for Kashi) have a majority of Han Chinese. Ürümqi, a city with over 1 million peo-

ple, is now more than 80 percent Han Chinese.

The Muslim Hui make up only one-third of the population in their autonomous region of Ningxia, and they usually live in the economically less privileged areas. Most Hui can only satisfy the criteria used to classify a Hui (Chinese-speaking Muslim) with great difficulty.

In Inner Mongolia, the Han have predominated for decades and now represent 80 percent of the population. Yet, surprisingly, more Mongolians live in this region than in the neighbouring country to the north – Mongolia. It is mainly the nomadic population who are Mongolian; almost all the settled farmers and people living in the towns are Han Chinese whose families have emigrated here from eastern China. ❏

LEFT: a TV audience at the vastly popular *Supergirl* show. **RIGHT:** Hui Muslims in Gansu province.

THE LANDS OF CHINA

China's vast territory extends from subarctic north to tropical south, from barren deserts and mountains in the west to intensive cultivation on the coastal plains

For many centuries, China's imposing geographical barriers created a natural border that both protected and isolated the Chinese from foreign contact. To the east and southeast is a coastline of about 18,000km (11,000 miles), and to the west are the Himalayas and the Tibetan plateau. In the north, contact with "barbarians" from Mongolia spurred the Chinese to build a series of walls over the centuries, collectively called the Great Wall.

China covers an area of 9,560,900 sq km (3,691,500 sq miles), with a border of 20,000km (12,500 miles). Its neighbouring countries are North Korea, Mongolia, Russia, Kazakhstan, Kyrgyzstan, Tajikistan, Afghanistan, Pakistan, India, Nepal, Bhutan, Burma (Myanmar), Laos and Vietnam. The distance from the northernmost town of Mohe, located on the northeastern border with Russia, to the south coast of Hainan Island on the South China Sea, is 4,000km (2,500 miles). East to west from the westernmost extremity in the Pamir Mountains to the easternmost point – the confluence of the Heilong Jiang and the Wusuli Jiang – measures 5,200km (3,200 miles).

China is the third-largest country in the world after Russia and Canada, and roughly the same size as the whole of Europe. It is slightly larger than the US.

On Hainan Island in the far south, winter is warm, while at the same time the northeast is paralysed by Siberian frosts and icy winds. Some parts of Tibet endure perpetual frost, while crops grow year-round in Guangdong and southern Yunnan.

LEFT: the Great Wall loops across the hills to the north of Beijing. RIGHT: bamboo grove.

Climate

Given China's size, it is not surprising to find a variety of climatic conditions. The varying elevation from the western mountain ranges to the eastern flatlands has an effect, but the main determining factor of China's weather is the country's position at the edge of the Asian continent next to the Pacific Ocean. In winter, frigid air masses form high-pressure zones in the heart of the continent which then move southward over China; this results in dry winters. An unpleasant aspect of this is the high dust content in northern China as the air blows the loess in from the Gobi Desert. In the summer, low pressure sucks in air from the Pacific bringing the rains from the ocean, with a rainy season lasting from May until September.

The northeast of China and northern Mongolia have relatively short but warm summers with some heavy rains, followed by long, cold winters. Immediately to the west lie the desert regions of Inner Mongolia and Xinjiang; they have hot and dry summers with occasional strong winds, and the winters are very cold and dry. On the Tibet-Qinghai Plateau, which is, on average, 4,000 metres (13,000ft) high, the winters are extremely cold and the short summers only moderately warm. In central China, summers are always hot, and rainfall is high; disastrous floods are not uncommon. Here, the agricultural growing season lasts for eight or nine months. Winters are cool and can be rainy. In

one percent of the nation's population. All the major rivers of China and Southeast Asia start in the Tibet-Qinghai Plateau. The Huang He (Yellow River) flows eastward from the remote wastes of Qinghai province, while the Chang Jiang (Yangzi) heads south and then east to bisect the country. The Nu Jiang (Salween) and Lancang (Mekong) flow south through Yunnan province, before coursing their way into Burma and Laos.

The second terrace is formed by plateaux with heights averaging between 1,000 and 2,000 metres (3,000–6,500ft) in central and northwest China. The third terrace is formed by the plains and lowlands on the lower reaches of the large rivers. It

the southern and eastern parts of China, winters are cool for the latitude (but warm in Hainan and in southern Yunnan), while summers are hot and wet. Typhoons periodically strike the coastline as far north as the Shanghai in late summer.

Topography

Two-thirds of China's territory is mountainous, hilly or high plateau. The terrain falls into three main regions, which can be thought of as topographical terraces.

The highest terrace is the Tibet-Qinghai Plateau, which rises 4,000 metres (13,000ft) above sea level and consists of Tibet, Qinghai and western Sichuan. Although the area is about a quarter of China's total land mass, it is home to less than

TERMS OF GEOGRAPHY

In Chinese, a suffix usually follows a name. In this book, most suffixes are separated from the proper name to make recognition easier. For example, we use Huang He (Huang River) rather than Huanghe.

shan, feng: 山, 峰: hill, mountain(s), peak	**bei**: 北: north
	nan: 南: south
he, jiang: 河, 江: river	**dong**: 东: east
pendi: 盆地: basin	**xi**: 西: west
hu, chi: 湖, 池: lake	**shi**: 市: city, municipality
hai: 海: sea	**xian**: 县: county
wan: 湾: bay	**sheng**: 省: province
xia: 峡: gorge	**zhizhiqu**: 自治区:
wenquan: 温泉: spring	autonomous region

rarely rises more than 500 metres (1,600ft) above sea level and runs along the east coast from the north of China down to the south. More than two-thirds of the population lives along this coastal stretch, and it is China's agricultural and industrial heartland.

This terraced structure is the result of massive tectonic movements beneath the Chinese land mass, which remain unsettled. Earthquakes continue to strike in many regions of China, particularly the northwest, southwest and northeast. The 1976 earthquake in Tangshan, 145km (90 miles) east of Beijing, claimed an estimated 250,000 to 665,000 lives. In May 2008, another

Still further north and again extending from west to east is the 4,000-metre (13,000ft) high Tian Shan range which, together with the Kunlun mountains, encloses China's largest desert, the Taklamakan. On the other side of the Tibetan Plateau are the Hengduan mountains running through eastern Tibet, western Sichuan and Yunnan. These remote ranges have, even in modern times, formed a largely insurmountable barrier between China and the lands lying to the west.

In the northeast, the relatively low Greater Xingan range forms a natural border between the Manchurian lowland and the Mongolian steppe. This is also China's largest wooded area and thus

massive earthquake hit Sichuan province and the neighbouring region, claiming 70,000 lives.

Rising above these terraces are the mountains. China has many of the highest peaks in the world. The Himalaya range, forming the southwest border of the country, is one of the youngest mountain ranges on the planet. On the border with Nepal is Mount Everest, the world's highest point at 8,850 metres (29,035ft).

Running parallel to the Himalaya range further north are the Kunlun mountains. In summer, the rivers that spring from the Qinghai Plateau are fed with frigid water from its melting glaciers.

LEFT: flatness of river and terrain, Xinjiang, in western China. **ABOVE:** climbing Everest.

> *The summit of Mount Everest, also known as Shengmufeng or Qomolongma, is shared by China and Nepal.*

an important watershed, with considerable influence on the climate. A similarly important climatic divide is the Qinling range, which reaches from the Gansu-Qinghai border all the way to Henan in central China. In summer, the Qinling acts as a barrier to the heavy masses of humid air brought by the monsoon: lands to the north are noticeably drier. In winter, the range effectively reduces the impact of the freezing winds streaming down from the Siberian steppes.

Great rivers

In historical terms, Huang He, the Yellow River, is undoubtedly the most important waterway in China. The region around the confluence of the Huang He and Wei rivers formed the cradle of Chinese civilisation. Yet, throughout the centuries, the river has also been known as "China's Sorrow". Given to radical shifts in its course and frequent flooding (a result of irregular rainfall upstream and heavy silt deposits), the Huang He has been a source of anxiety to generations of peasants living by the river.

Rising in the western province of Qinghai, the Huang He makes a sharp bend to the north near

built elaborate systems of dykes and levees that require constant maintenance because a breach in even one of the dykes can cause flooding for hundreds of kilometres around.

The lower channel of the Huang He has radically changed course several times. Between 602 BC and AD 1194, it flowed to the north of its present-day path into the Yellow Sea. From 1194 to 1853, it shifted south so that it entered the East China Sea, south of Shandong Peninsula. After some flooding, it shifted its course to flow north of the peninsula. In 1938, Nationalist troops smashed the dykes in Henan to divert the river and slow the advance of Japanese troops. An estimated 900,000

Lanzhou and then further on, near Baotou in Mongolia, it turns south again, forming the famous Huang He knee. Only as it passes through the central Chinese loess plateau does it fill up with the yellow earth that has suggested the river's name.

Due to early deforestation, the land erodes very easily. The Huang He transports more than 1 billion tons of sediment into its lower reaches every year. In fact, the water level in the estuary is so low that there is no shipping route to the sea. As the river bed widens in the lowland plain, the river deposits more than 4 million tons of silt.

Attempts to control the river go back almost as far as Chinese history itself. In 220 BC, Qin Shi Huangdi ordered dykes built and deepened the river's course. Over the centuries, peasants have

civilian lives were lost as a result. In recent years, however, the lower reaches of the river have repeatedly been dry.

The longest river in China, and third-longest in the world, is the 6,300km (3,900-mile) Chang Jiang, which rises in the Tanggula mountains of Qinghai province. Chang Jiang is the name commonly used for the middle reaches of the river, while the locals call the lower reaches, from Yangzhou to the estuary, the Yangzi. This is the name missionaries and colonialists became familiar with, and thus became established in Europe.

ABOVE: the Hukou Falls on the silt-laden Huang He (Yellow River). **RIGHT:** paddy fields in Guizhou. The traditional farming life persists in much of rural China.

The Chang Jiang has also caused considerable flood damage over past centuries. The most notable in recent history is the flood of 1931, in which 3 million people died. In 2003 the Three Gorges Dam, designed to control and subdue the mighty river, as well as generating electricity, began operating. Completed three years later, it is the largest in the world at 180 metres (600ft) high and 2.25km (1½ miles) long, and behind it there is now a reservoir over 640km (400 miles) long. Critics of the dam point to its high financial and social costs (close to 1.5 million people have been relocated) and warn of an ecological disaster in the making *(for more on the dam, see page 256)*.

Plans have been announced to build what will be the tallest dam in the world on the Lancang (Mekong) River in Yunnan province. It will be 292 metres (958ft) high, cause the relocation of 220,000 people, and have considerable environmental implications for the Mekong Delta area.

Resources

China is rich in natural resources. Coal exists in abundance, and China is among the world's top producers of gold, tin, mercury, aluminium, tungsten and barite. There are limited oil reserves in the northeast (wastefully exploited during the Mao era), Shaanxi and a few other places. China is now the world's largest importer of oil, and desperate to exploit potential oil- (and gas-) fields around the Spratly and Paracel islands in the South China Sea – a situation which has brought a long-running dispute with Vietnam and other Southeast Asian lands that also claim the territory.

Fertile soil is found in the south and east of the country. Despite being the world's largest pro-

ducer of rice and wheat, feeding a population of 1.3 billion is one of China's greatest challenges. Only 40 percent of the country can be used for agriculture or forestry, with only 12 percent of the total land suitable for farming. Deforestation and desertification are now two of China's biggest problems. In the past two decades, China has planted over 35 billion trees, increasing the area of forested land from 12 to 17 percent.

In 2002, an ambitious plan to divert water from the Yangzi Basin to north China was given the go-ahead. It involves three waterways from the upper, middle and lower reaches of the Chang Jiang, stretching more than 1,120km (700 miles) each. ❏

ENVIRONMENTAL ISSUES

China's overcrowded land has long been under intense pressure, with its forests, rivers and other natural resources heavily exploited for centuries to meet the needs of its vast population. More recently, there has been a reckless disregard for the environmental consequences of industrialisation, particularly during the Mao years but also with gargantuan schemes such as the Three Gorges Dam *(see above, and page 256)*. Poaching, logging and soil erosion have jeopardised wildlife habitats. Air and water pollution are appalling – five out of the world's ten most polluted cities are in China (the prevalence of coal power is partly to blame). Unrestrained consumption of water supplies has made North China increasingly arid in recent decades.

Despite the efforts of the State Environmental Protection Agency and various high-profile international agencies, the primary focus inevitably remains on economic development. This isn't to say that efforts have not been made, but all too often inadequate regulation of factories and other, often state-owned, polluters makes the task impossible. China's notorious corruption means it is all too easy to bend the rules: companies simply ignore expensive anti-pollution measures. Understandably enough, China also resents what is seen as the hypocrisy of Western nations which preach green policies but, at the time of their own industrialisation, gave no thought to the environment whatsoever. *For more on wildlife and conservation, see pages 324–5.*

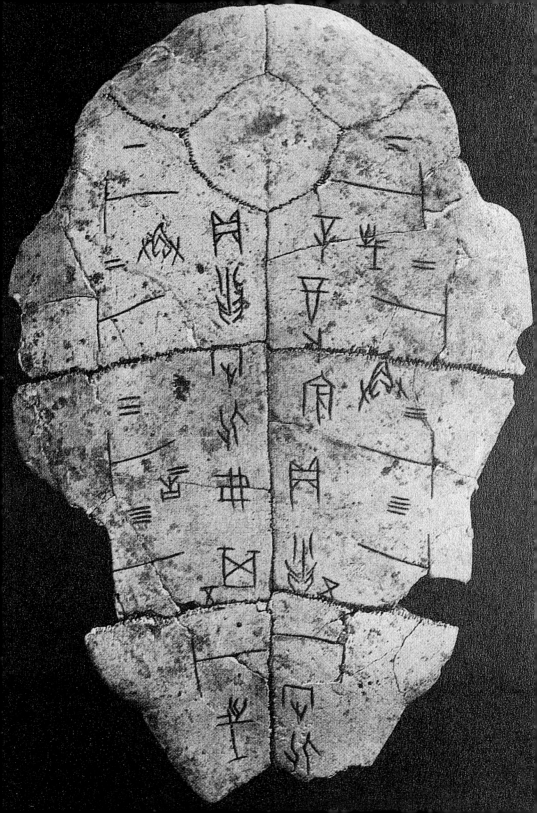

IMPERIAL CHINA

From the ancient Xia dynasty to the demise of the Qing in 1911, China's imperial history extends back over a period of 4,000 years

Historical legends remain a powerful symbol of the endurance and unity of Chinese cultural values. During imperial times, emperors claimed to follow the sage kings' examples as rulers; more recently, China's leaders have glorified the length of their history and its early achievements – even while condemning other aspects of the past – to foster unity and nationalism among the people.

Archaeological findings indicate that primitive people lived in the territory of today's China half a million years ago. In the early decades of the 20th century, archaeologists excavated a series of caves, one nearly the size of a football field, near a village just southwest of Beijing. Skulls, teeth and bones of more than 40 *Homo erectus* were uncovered, along with tens of thousands of stone tools dating from 200,000 to 400,000 years ago. Peking Man and Woman were hunter-fishergatherers who lit fires for warmth and for cooking animals like bear, hyena, sabre-toothed tiger and water buffalo.

Later discoveries indicate that early Chinese civilisation developed in a number of areas and possessed distinctive local characteristics as well as common features. Neolithic China (12,000–2000 BC) was characterised by the spread of agricultural communities, although people also hunted and fished for food; they raised pigs and dogs, and grew hemp to use for fabric. Silk was also discovered in this period, possibly as far back as 6000 BC. Clustered dwellings suggest kinship units, and pottery designs featured clan or lineage symbols, as well as pictures and images of animals and plants.

LEFT: early Chinese writing on a tortoiseshell oracle, Shang dynasty. **RIGHT:** government officials, 1901.

Of the early legendary dynasties – Xia, Shang and Zhou – the actual existence of the Xia remains in doubt for some. However, excavations in 1959 at Erlitou (near present-day Luoyang, in Henan province) unearthed palaces believed to have been of a Xia-dynasty capital.

Over the centuries the Chinese population migrated further south from their northern homelands, displacing the indigenous Austronesian aboriginals (related to similar groups in the Philippines and Indonesia) as they did so. Large parts of present-day Zhejiang, Jiangxi and Fujian provinces retained these communities well into historic times, and they still survive in parts of Taiwan. Other ethnic groups, such as the Miao peoples of the southwest, retreated into the hills.

Shang dynasty (16th–11th c. BC)

In 1899, scholars noticed pharmacists selling bones inscribed with archaic characters. By the late 1920s, these oracle bones had been traced to Anyang, in Henan province, where the last Shang capital was excavated. Shamans, serving the Shang kings, made divinations by applying a hot point to the shoulder-blade bones of animals to create cracks, which were then interpreted and the results etched onto the bone. Over 100,000 such oracle bones have been collected.

Oracle bones and inscriptions on bronze work, the excavation sites themselves, and the written records of the subsequent Zhou dynasty describe

the Shang as a remarkably stratified society. The elite hunted for sport and fought in horse-drawn chariots, while the peasantry lived in semi-subterranean dwellings. Ancestor worship was ritualised, and royal tombs contained valuable objects as well as animal and even human sacrifices. The mobilisation of mass labour for public works like city walls attested to the authority and power of the Shang aristocracy.

Zhou dynasty (11th c.–256 BC)

The primary structure of the Chinese state is considered to have emerged during the Zhou dynasty. The Zhou clan had long been vassals of the Shang, but eventually grew strong enough to defeat them in warfare in the 11th century. Their capital was

built at Chang'an (now called Xi'an), and the sons of Zhou rulers were despatched to preside over vassal states in a feudal-like system. A belief in heaven's mandate established a new basis for the legitimacy of rule. The idea of the mandate of heaven held that a leader's right to rule was based on his ability to maintain harmony between heaven and earth, himself and his officials, and the officials and the people.

The beginning of the Eastern Zhou period was marked by the eastward movement of its capital to Luoyang, in 771 BC. In the chaotic Spring and Autumn period (770–476 BC), aristocratic family-states formed shifting alliances and fought or absorbed each other until there were only seven large states remaining by the Warring States era (403–221 BC). Despite such political strife, social and economic advances included the introduction of iron, the development of infantry armies, currency circulation, the emergence of private land ownership, urban expansion and the breakdown of class barriers.

The foremost thinkers of the time were Confucius (551–479 BC) and his followers Mencius (c.370–300 BC) and Xunzi (c.310–215 BC). Perhaps in response to the anarchic times in which he lived, Confucius stressed the maintenance of tradition and the cultivation of personal morality and the moral accountability of the ruler towards the people. Peace and abundance were guaranteed if the ruler ruled fairly, preserved proper relationships in society and cultivated his own moral values.

Qin dynasty (221–206 BC)

The Qin state emerged as the most powerful state during the Warring States Period. Ruling by strict laws that supported agriculture and strengthened the state, it finally conquered the other states in 221 BC. The first emperor of the Qin dynasty, Qin Shi Huangdi, is considered to be the first ruler of a united China.

Weights and measures, currency and, most importantly, writing were standardised. Highways were constructed, and waterways and canals were

> *Early Chinese civilisations emphasised labour-intensive food production, which required a large population and a strict, hierarchical political system to build and control irrigation networks and maximise harvests.*

dug in the south to facilitate water transport. The archives of defeated states were burnt and hundreds of scholars critical of Qin rule were murdered. The immensity of the emperor's power and ego is illustrated by the discovery near Xi'an of over 7,000 life-sized terracotta warriors created to protect his elaborate tomb. Walls were built during these times, but the legend that the Great Wall was built by Qin Shi Huangdi is incorrect. While many dynasties built extensive walls for protection, the Great Wall visible today was mostly built by the Ming dynasty during the 16th century.

Qin Shi Huangdi's ruthless and perennial exploitation exhausted both the populace and

proper behaviour and personal integrity. It was during the Han dynasty that Confucianism became indelibly ingrained into Chinese politics, society and culture.

The stability of the Han period enabled China's population to grow to more than 50 million. Trade and industry developed, and communication and transportation systems improved, all of which fostered closer ties among China's far-flung and diverse regions. Cities attracted the educated and the wealthy from all over the country, becoming important cultural centres. People elsewhere, especially in areas of hardship, migrated to locations that afforded more opportunity.

DYNASTY PRIMER

For nearly 4,000 years, China was ruled by a Son of Heaven (the Xia dynasty is not recognised by some scholars). There were occasional periods of chaos when the empire fractured into separate parts.

Xia	21st–16th centuries BC
Shang	16th–11th centuries BC
Zhou	11th century–256 BC
	Spring and Autumn Period 770–476 BC
	Warring States Period 403–221 BC
Qin	221–206 BC
Han	206 BC–AD 220
	Three Kingdoms Period 220–581
Sui	581–618
Tang	618–907
Song	960–1279
Yuan	1279–1368
Ming	1368–1644
Qing	1644–1911

China's financial resources, and his empire rapidly fell apart after his death in 210 BC.

Han dynasty (206 BC–AD 220)

While repudiating the harsh rule of the Qin, the Han rulers built upon the established centralised bureaucracy. The important difference, however, was the way in which Han officials were drafted into service. By the 1st century BC, it was generally accepted that officials should be men trained in the Confucian classical texts, meaning they now had to reconcile their positions serving the emperor and state with the Confucian values of

LEFT: a bronze wine vessel from the Shang dynasty.
RIGHT: the Yellow Emperor, Qin Shi Huangdi.

In 180 BC, a new social class appeared at the imperial court for the first time: palace eunuchs, who were to maintain an important role all the way through until 1911. Originally hired to look after the emperors' wives and concubines, eunuchs soon became advisers, playing a significant part in palace intrigues and power struggles.

The Han dynasty reached its prime under the rule of Han Wudi (140–87 BC). The Chinese empire had long sought to control the troublesome nomadic tribes in the north and the west, and Wudi succeeded in defeating the Huns, a group that had established a strong empire in the north. Following this success, the empire stretched all the way west to what is now Xinjiang. This expansion encouraged numerous contacts with other cultures through traders from distant lands. From the 1st century BC, caravans had travelled along the Silk Road, bringing horses and gold in exchange for silk.

Buddhism was introduced to China from India during the late Han period; while Confucianism waned, Buddhist teachings and art made a lasting impression on Chinese culture in the north and the south. Buddhism was permitted to flourish by non-Chinese rulers of northern China, in part because it too came from outside the Chinese establishment that they were subsuming themselves.

Division and reunification

Regionalism and class distinctions grew after the fall of the Han dynasty around 220, as China split into the three rival states of Wei, Wu and Shu – a time known as the Three Kingdoms Period. Reunification and economic advance were achieved under the vigorous but short-lived Sui dynasty (581–618).

When the founder of the Sui took power, he rapidly established a new legal code, organised local governments and continued several institutions initiated by earlier kingdoms. Despite the unification and strengthening of the state, the depletion of the country's resources under the grand visions of the second Sui emperor led to the dynasty's downfall.

Tang dynasty (618–907)

The founders of the Tang dynasty – considered to have been something of a golden age – inherited the accomplishments of the Sui, including the large capital at Chang'an, now Xi'an. The Chinese bureaucracy continued to develop. During the Sui-Tang era, seven ministries were established – personnel, administration, finance, rites, army, justice and public works – as was a censorate, an agency responsible for inspecting and reporting on official and even imperial conduct.

Under the second emperor, Tang armies expanded east into Korea, south into northern Vietnam and west into Central Asia. This was the great era of the Silk Road, and as trade expanded along this route, contacts with the people and cultures of Central and West Asia increased and Chang'an developed into a great international metropolis. Between AD 600 and 900, no city in the world could compare in size and grandeur. People from Japan, Korea, Vietnam, Persia and West Asia seeking trade, Buddhist enlightenment or simply adventure injected their energy into Tang urban life.

The strength of the Tang nurtured a vigorous literary and artistic creativity. Later periods looked to Tang poetry in particular as a model of excellence. That the writing of poetry became a requisite in the civil service exams for higher qualifications and promotion can be credited to China's only female ruler, Empress Wu Zetian, who reigned from around 690 to 705.

The growing importance of the examinations in the late Tang period served to weaken powerful, aristocratic families of the north and presented greater opportunities for those from other areas to enter government. Scholar-officials – those who earned their rank through success in the examin-

> *The Tang dynasty is regarded as a golden age in Chinese history, with the arts – notably poetry and scroll painting – reaching new heights. The capital, Chang'an (Xi'an), was the largest city in the world, with a population of around 2 million.*

ations – started to become a minor elite within the imperial bureaucracy. The influence of great families became linked to the position of family members in high office; a powerful family could rapidly fall apart if two or three generations passed without a member attaining a high government position.

The height of Tang-dynasty splendour was reached under Emperor Xuanzong, who reigned from 713 until 755. Nevertheless, failings accumulated: military campaigns became overextended and expensive; powerful generals meddled in court politics; officials became involved in factional infighting, and the emperor increasingly turned to court eunuchs for support. In his old age, Xuanzong let his control deteriorate when he fell for a beautiful concubine.

A military rebellion weakened the throne but was put down; Tang rule was restored but its power never fully recovered. In 845, the emperor Wuzong ordered the repression of Buddhist monasteries that, by this time, had acquired large, tax-exempt estates with glorious temples housing

The Song dynasty was founded by the palace-guard commander of the last of the Five Dynasties in northern China, and is considered one of China's most creative and artistic eras. It is divided into two halves; the Northern Song (960–1127) and the Southern Song (1127–1279), the latter referring to the period after invaders took over northern China (to found the Jin dynasty there) when the imperial capital was moved from Kaifeng to Hangzhou.

Population growth promoted urbanisation, particularly in the capital. Coal and iron industries developed, and foreign trade was a large source of government revenue in the latter Song era, not to

thousands of monks. Thousands of monasteries were shut down, and Buddhism's decline was accelerated by the court's issuing of ordination certificates for monks. Subsequently, Confucianism experienced something of a revival, while Daoism also began to emerge. By this time, the population of the Tang empire had reached 80 million.

Song dynasty (960–1279)

Anarchy reigned during the final half century of Tang rule, but eventually regional states emerged out of the political and social chaos – called the Five Dynasties and Ten Kingdoms.

LEFT: a bronze storage jar dating from the Zhou dynasty. **ABOVE:** court ladies-in-waiting.

be matched again until the 19th century. Foreign trade decreased land tax and increased the use of paper money, a practice initiated in the late Tang period. China led the world in nautical expertise. Chinese ships could carry 500 men on as many as four decks, powered by a dozen sails on four or six masts.

The Song was the first society with books (paper had been invented in the 1st or 2nd century BC), key to the era's educational development. The government initially tried to control printing, but by the 11th century it was granting land and books to encourage the establishment of schools. The civil service examination system became a huge and elaborate institution crucial to upper-class life, until the structure's abolition in 1905. A majority of

Inventions and technology

China failed to capitalise on its early inventive genius; today it relies heavily on technology borrowed from the West

The Chinese were once world leaders in technology; monumental inventions such as paper and printing, magnetic compasses, gunpowder and irrigation were familiar to them hundreds of years before they were developed in Europe.

The belief that the emperor was the Son of Heaven led to the very early development of astronomical observation in China: Halley's Comet was first recorded in 467 BC, and a calendar of 360 days was in use by the 3rd century BC. By the 13th century there was a total of 17 different astronomical instruments at the Beijing Observatory, and Chinese astronomers had fixed the length of the year as 365.2424 days, very close to modern calculations.

The Chinese first made paper around AD 200, while printing evolved around eight centuries later – albeit with carved stamps rather than movable type. Imperial geographers were busy with the deviation of magnetic north from true north before Europeans were even aware that the earth had a magnetic field. More than a millenium ago iron foundries in China were producing quantities of iron and steel unmatched in Europe until the 18th century. Irrigation was in use by the 1st century AD, and the waterwheel 400 years later, again well ahead of Europe. In the 9th century, Daoist monks, searching for the elixir of life, mixed charcoal, saltpetre and sulphur and accidentally made gunpowder. The mixture was later used for fireworks and in bombs and grenades. The creation of porcelain is a famous example of Chinese technological superiority: fine glazed ceramics were being crafted in China from around AD 100, and later became highly prized in Europe (where it was, and is, known as "china"). It was not until 1708 that Europeans hit upon the elusive secret of its manufacture.

The Decline of Chinese Technology

Yet for all their precocious ingenuity, the Chinese inventions were the exclusive preserve of the uppermost echelons of society. This had the effect of restricting the further development of existing technologies, in sharp contrast with what was happening in Europe in the later Middle Ages.

The Chinese world was, above all, an insular one. Just when the rich and powerful Ming dynasty was poised to reach outwards and develop trade with Southeast Asia and beyond, an imperial edict – essentially the result of nothing more than a court squabble – banned foreign voyages by the Ming fleet, and at a stroke changed the course of Chinese history. Within 100 years, the first European adventurers were guiding their ships, equipped with guns developed from Chinese gunpowder technology, into the region, eventually to devastating effect. Before long, China was being subjugated and humiliated by the European colonial powers.

These days China is once again pursuing technology, this time with unprecedented rapidity. However, modern Chinese technology in fields such as the electronics and auto industries is in large part a result of copying or purchasing technical expertise from the West. ❑

LEFT AND ABOVE: the magnetic compass and gunpowder were among the many inventions of imperial China.

officials still gained office through nepotism, but the Song bureaucracy was staffed by more exam graduates than ever before. In theory, nearly any male could take the exams, but in reality it was generally only the wealthier families who could afford the time and money on tutors.

The expanding educational system revived the study of Confucianism and fostered its reinterpretation by a number of scholars, characterised by a Buddhism-inspired focus on individual self-cultivation.

Yuan dynasty (1279–1368)

The emperors of the Yuan dynasty were the descendants of Mongol leader Ghengis Khan, who had conquered most of Central Asia and parts of Eastern Europe in the early 1200s. By 1215, a part of northern China was under Mongol control, and in 1279 the Song dynasty finally fell to Ghengis's grandson Kublai Khan, who ruled China from 1271 until 1294.

Yuan officials set up a form of military administration that was soon dominating the Chinese-style bureaucracy. Most important posts throughout the empire were filled by Mongols or their non-Chinese allies; few Chinese rose to positions of authority except in cultural affairs. The Mongols were tolerant, however, of differing religions, reflecting the diversity of their multi-ethnic empire. During their rule, Tibet and Yunnan became part of China.

Trade along the Silk Road flourished. The Grand Canal between northern and southern China was repaired, as the new capital in Beijing (called Dadu) depended upon grains from the south. Domestic trade flourished, as did maritime trade from West Asia and India.

Ming dynasty (1368–1644)

After a long period of insurrections, the Mongols were overthrown by Han Chinese troops under Zhu Yuanzhang (Hongwu), who became the first emperor of the Ming dynasty in 1368.

Sponsored by Emperor Yongle (r. 1402–24) and under the command of the Muslim eunuch Zheng He, the Ming naval fleet made seven expeditions between 1405 and 1433 to Southeast Asia, India, the Persian Gulf and the east coast of Africa. Although some trade was conducted, the missions were mainly of a diplomatic nature, intended to

foster the tribute system whereby China granted large gifts to tributary states who in turn acknowledged China's supremacy and offered tribute (usually smaller gifts than they received from China). After Yongle's death in 1424, state support of overseas trade and diplomacy ceased, and the fleets of immense ships – larger than any European – were dismantled (see panel, opposite).

During the rule of the Ming, the first Christian missionaries came to China with the arrival at Guangzhou (Canton), in 1514, of Portuguese ships (see below). The danger to the Ming emperors' rule, however, continued to come from Northern and Central Asia. The Great Wall was

once again reinforced to protect China from the nomads, and the wars against the Mongols lasted into the 16th century.

Towards the end of the Ming period, intrigues of the palace eunuchs paralysed the court and sometimes its foreign policy, and the secret police suppressed even the slightest signs of opposition.

The coming of the Europeans

The first recorded account of Europeans in China appears to have been a visit of Northern European traders to Kublai Khan's court in 1261. Marco Polo is said to have travelled in China in the 1270s and 1280s, though some scholars now doubt he ever made it (he never mentioned the Great Wall, for example), suggesting he fabricated his writ-

RIGHT: Genghis Khan (1162–1227) united the nomadic tribes of Mongolia into a formidable force.

ings from other sources. In any case, his narrative in *The Travels* introduced the splendours of China to medieval Europe, particularly the sophistication of its urban life.

Early Catholic missionaries made their way to China during the Yuan dynasty (1279–1368), but large-scale commercial contact between China and Europe did not occur until the 1500s. Portuguese ships dropped anchor off Guangzhou in 1514, but the unruly behaviour of the crew onshore offended Chinese officials, who decided to contain them by leasing Macau to Portugal in 1553 as a trading base, from which the Portuguese could conduct business. In the early 1600s, Dutch

and English ships also arrived on China's south coast, reproducing the discourteous behaviour of the Portuguese.

China's early encounter with Jesuits, however, was positive, as these were educated men who could relate to Chinese scholar-officials on intellectual terms. While the Jesuits condemned Buddhism, they accepted most Confucian precepts, even conceding that the veneration of ancestors was a secular ritual.

Chinese scholars displayed interest in Jesuit expertise in astronomy, cartography, European clockworks and other sciences.The Italian Jesuit Matteo Ricci, who arrived in Macau in 1582, was probably the most important figure in Jesuit missionary activity. In 1598 he was introduced at

court in Beijing, and a few years later was granted permission to live there on an imperial stipend as a Western scholar.

Rival groups of Catholic missionaries in China, opposed to the Jesuits, regarded Confucian rites of ancestor worship as incompatible with the Christian faith and appealed to the Vatican for a decision. The papal authorities duly obliged, and from this time relations between Beijing and all missionaries deteriorated.

Qing dynasty (1644–1911)

In 1644 the Manchus, a non-Han Chinese people from Manchuria (the area of northeast China now known as Dongbei), continued the long tradition of attacking imperial China from the north and sacked the Ming capital at Beijing. The Qing dynasty was founded.

The Manchus had long been in contact with the Chinese and the Mongols. Although they were foreign conquerors, their rule did not break with Chinese traditions, unlike that of the Mongols in the Yuan dynasty. Instead, they adopted the terms, structure and ideology of Confucianism to support their political authority, promoting the veneration of ancestors and the study of the traditional Chinese classics, and accepting the Confucian theory that rulers ruled by virtue of their moral uprightness. The Manchu used a system of dual appointments in their civil administration, having both Han Chinese and Manchu in important positions and relying on civil service examinations. While the Manchu attempted to maintain their own identity and customs, they also promoted many Chinese traditions. The arts flourished, as did scholarship, and basic literacy was relatively high, even in rural areas.

Under the Qing, the Chinese empire would reach its greatest extent, controlling not just the whole of "classical" China, but also a vast area to the west encompassing Tibet, Xinjiang, all of Mongolia and a large slice of what is now Kazakhstan and Kyrgyzstan. In the mould of the later stages of its predecessor, however, it would develop as and remain very much a continental, land-based power, exercising little influence at sea.

Maritime challenges

While the Manchu carefully managed the inner frontiers, Western maritime powers were expanding and continuing to make their way towards East Asia. In China, all legitimate Western trade from 1760 to 1842 was regulated by what was called the Canton system, stipulating that Western traders must conduct all business in Guangzhou (Canton) under the supervision of Chinese merchants belonging to a guild called the Cohong. Western merchants were restricted to the city's river-bank area, but had to withdraw to the Portuguese settlement on Macau during the off-season. They were discouraged from learning Chinese, and they could not speak directly with government officials, but instead had to communicate through the Cohong.

The British and Dutch East India companies, established around 1600, were commissioned by their home governments to manage territories much more than woollen textiles from Britain, and China's low demand for imported goods eventually created a trade imbalance that forced the British to pay for goods in silver, rather than barter.

The British East India Company despatched James Flint, a Chinese-speaking trader, in 1759 to present complaints to the Qing court about restrictions on trade and corruption in Guangzhou. Emperor Qianlong at first seemed receptive, agreeing to send a commission of investigation to Guangzhou. Then, changing his mind, he had Flint apprehended and imprisoned for three years, charging him with violating regulations, improperly presenting petitions and learning Chinese.

The island of Taiwan was of little interest to the mainland Chinese until the 17th century, when it was used by the Ming loyalist Koxinga as a base to fight the new Qing dynasty. The rebels' defeat in 1683 brought Taiwan into the Chinese empire.

overseas and monopolise trade, essentially acting as the counterpart to the Chinese Cohong. The British bought large amounts of tea, silk and porcelain from China, but the Chinese did not buy

LEFT: Matteo Ricci, a Jesuit missionary, was influential in the Ming court. **ABOVE:** a Dutch engraving from 1665 showing Chinese peasants at work in the fields.

In 1792, Lord Macartney was sent by Great Britain's King George III to China as a special ambassador to the Qing court. Macartney arrived in Guangzhou in the summer of 1793, and was allowed to continue to Tianjin because he claimed to be honouring Qianlong's 80th birthday. He was accompanied by an entourage of nearly 100, and two escort vessels loaded with gifts meant to display British manufacturing technology. The gifts were deemed "tribute from England" and once ashore, he was escorted without delay to Beijing.

Lord Macartney requested the abolishment of the Canton system, the right to establish a British diplomatic residence in Beijing, the opening of new ports for trade, and fixed tariffs. Qianlong dismissed all of the requests, writing the famous letter to King George in which he praised the British king for inclining himself "towards civilisation", but informed him that "we have never valued ingenious articles, nor do we have the slightest need of your country's manufactures... You, O King, should simply act in conformity with our wishes by strengthening your loyalty and swearing perpetual obedience". Despite this unequivocal rebuff, a growing number of foreign traders continued to arrive in Guangzhou, and the Qing continued to enforce their previously established rules.

British traders, in particular, were becoming exasperated by the trade deficits that compelled them to make huge payments in silver for Chi-

official, Lin Zexu, recommended the strict suppression of the opium trade and the rehabilitation of addicts. He was despatched to the south, and upon arrival in Guangzhou immediately demanded that the foreign merchants hand over all the opium in their possession. In addition, he announced that all foreign merchants would be required to sign a bond promising never again to import opium. When the foreigners failed to take Lin seriously, he suspended all trade, blockaded foreign factories, and held 350 foreigners hostage, including the British Superintendent of Trade, Captain Charles Elliot.

Elliot commanded all British traders to surrender their opium to him, issuing receipts and taking

nese tea and luxuries. This trade imbalance motivated the British to ship opium from India to southern Chinese ports.

Despite the growing threat from outside, the Qing empire was at its peak during the reign of Emperor Qianlong (r. 1735–96), ruling virtually unchallenged over an area in excess of 13 million sq km (5 million sq miles), an area almost 40 percent larger than that currently ruled by the People's Republic.

The Opium Wars and the Taiping Rebellion

As the Chinese consumption of opium grew, so did the outflow of silver from China, to the exasperation of the Qing rulers. In 1838, a respected court

responsibility on behalf of the British government. Elliot then handed over the opium to Lin, who publicly destroyed it. Lin lifted the blockade, per-

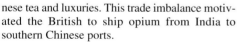

Emperor Qianlong's private life inspired many romantic stories. With two main wives and countless concubines and serving maids he sired 17 sons and 10 daughters.

mitted the resumption of trade and released the hostages.

Elliot and the entire British community left Guangzhou, and a Qing imperial edict was issued in 1839 that terminated trade between China and Britain. The British government decided that the only recourse to the termination of trade was war. Despite some attempts at negotiation, fighting began around Guangzhou in mid-1841, and after the British captured several coastal cities, the Qing agreed to binding negotiations.

The Treaty of Nanjing was signed in 1842. Its provisions included an indemnity to be paid by China to Britain, "equal relations" between China and Britain, four more ports opened to foreign trade with consuls and foreign residency, abolition of the Cohong monopoly, fixed tariffs and the surrender of Hong Kong to Britain in perpetuity. It was a devastating blow to Chinese integrity and independence.

By this time the Qing dynasty was in dire straits. A long, steady decline had set in from the early years of the 19th century, with poverty and official corruption sparking a series of increasingly violent uprisings across China. In 1851 a rising broke out at Jintian (today's Guiping) in Guangxi, when a 10,000-strong rebel force led by Hong Xiuquan defeated the Qing garrison forces. This was the beginning of the great Taiping Rebellion (1851–64), an uprising that would strafe southern and central China, causing at least 20 million deaths, and up to 50 million according to some estimates – the bloodiest conflict in the history of the world up to this time, and since superseded only by World War II. Several other rural rebellions across 19th-century China resulted in the deaths of millions more.

At the same time, tensions continued between the foreign communities in China and the beleagured Qing government. Minor incidents swelled into large-scale conflicts, which led to foreign intervention. Guangzhou was soon overrun by Anglo-French forces, who proceeded north to Tianjin. The Qing court yielded and the Treaties of Tianjin were signed in 1858. Ten new ports were opened, indemnities specified, and diplomatic residences established in Beijing.

Insisting on finalising the treaties in Beijing instead of Shanghai, as the Chinese wanted, the British occupied Beijing, then moved to the Summer Palace and completely destroyed it, forcing the emperor into exile.

The treaty was then reaffirmed, indemnities increased, and the Kowloon Peninsula ceded to Britain. Its terms effectively rendered parts of

China into European colonies, especially with the provision of extraterritoriality under which foreigners were liable to foreign, not Chinese, law.

The Boxer Rebellion

The Boxer Rebellion was a popular protest movement brought about by the combination of Qing misrule and foreign intrusion. In the plains of Shandong province, where the movement originated, years of floods and drought had left the people desperate. Germany's seizure of Qingdao in 1898 heightened anti-foreign sentiment and unrest. To protect their interests, Shandong peasants turned to secret societies such as the Boxers (*yihetuan*).

The Qing court initially backed the Boxer movement in the hope that it might succeed in expelling the foreigners. The rebels made their way to Beijing, where they killed a number of Christians and held missionaries, diplomats and other foreigners hostage in the Beijing legation quarter for eight weeks until an international army marched on the capital.

The Qing court retreated as the foreign troops approached, but soon arranged an agreement with the foreign powers, who had an interest in maintaining Qing rule – stability was good for foreign trade. The government was, nevertheless, compelled to pay a huge indemnity. The dynasty, and China's imperial tradition, was to survive for just one decade. ❑

FAR LEFT: British and Chinese officials negotiate, 1842. **LEFT:** Lord Macartney and Qianlong. **RIGHT:** US troops in Beijing after the Boxer Rebellion, 1901.

END OF EMPIRE TO MODERN TIMES

Much of China's 20th century was marked by civil
war and political intrigue, the turbulence and unrest
culminating in Mao's disastrous Cultural Revolution.
A change to pragmatic policies since then has
brought ever-increasing prosperity – to the point
that China is now a global economic power

When Westerners first began to intrude on China's sovereignty in the mid-1800s, China's rulers had to confront outsiders who would not conform to the Chinese view of the world. How to respond to the challenge and make China stronger became a top priority.

By 1901, the Qing court had realised reform was unavoidable. It despatched two official missions abroad in 1906 to study constitutionalism in England, France, Germany, the United States and Japan. The delegates returned recommending that a constitution, civil liberties and public discussion could in fact strengthen the emperor's position, as long as he retained supreme power.

The Revolution of 1911

Although institutional changes were moving rapidly, dissatisfaction grew more intense, driving the forces of revolution. Anti-Qing activists came from many quarters. There were Sun Yatsen's anti-Manchu Revolutionary Alliance, secret societies, disaffected military personnel, provincial leaders in government and business and intellectuals who wavered between advocating a constitutional monarchy and revolution.

In November 1911, representatives from 17 provinces gathered in Nanjing to establish the Provisional Republic Government under Sun Yatsen and a local military commander. To guarantee Manchu abdication, Sun was soon compelled to step down in favour of military strongman Yuan Shikai.

In 1912 Puyi, who had taken the emperor's throne after the death of Cixi in 1908, was forced to sign a declaration of abdication. Puyi continued to live in the Imperial Palace in Beijing until 1924, but the rule of the Sons of Heaven on the Dragon Throne, which had begun 4,000 years earlier, had come to an end.

A number of political parties formed and attempted to make an effective parliamentary system, but they were poorly organised and Yuan Shikai was intolerant of their criticism. He periodically dissolved the parliament and had the constitution rewritten, even attempting to make himself emperor in 1915. Yuan died the next year, but the violent opposition he incited helped create the conditions for the warlord period of 1916 to 1928.

Political awareness

A seminal event in the rise of Chinese nationalism, and still commemorated today, the May Fourth Movement was a major student protest that took place on 4 May 1919 in response to China's treatment in the Treaty of Versailles, following the end of

World War I. China had been told by the Allies that, upon Germany's defeat in the war, German territorial possessions in Shandong province would be returned. However, during the war, Japan had taken control of these territories (principally Qingdao) and, due to the Allies' inability forcibly to counter Japan at that time, the Japanese were not dislodged. The Versailles decision not to honour their promise was a major affront to Chinese national pride.

The events of 4 May served to broaden political awareness. The demonstrations of 1919 widened further the belief that protest is an honourable expression of people's concern with political events. It also reinvigorated the discussion of new

Civil war

China's increasingly politicised intellectuals were attracted to Marxist theory largely because it provided an explanation for China's hardships – imperialism and exploitation by the upper classes – and prescribed a way to order society that they believed could strengthen the nation. This led to the Chinese Communist Party (CCP) being founded in Shanghai in 1921. The Nationalist Party (Guomindang; also spelt "Kuomindang"), which under Sun Yatsen had ruled China in the immediate post-imperial period, was the Communists' main rival for power. In the 1920s, both parties were in contact with the leaders of the Soviet Union.

ideas, as disillusionment with the leaders' ability to govern effectively led to further questioning of political progress.

Between 1917 and 1923, political and social change, and the conception of modernisation, took on new dimensions. Young intellectuals denounced Confucianism and started socialist study groups, created political journals, travelled to the countryside to educate farmers, and initiated workers' organisations in the cities. Support for Chiang Kaishek's Nationalist Party was revived and an interest in Marxism developed.

LEFT: Puyi, the last emperor of China. **ABOVE:** Zhou Enlai addresses the troops at Zunyi during the Long March. **RIGHT:** Chiang Kaishek at a Nationalist rally.

Following Sun Yatsen's untimely death in 1925, Chiang Kaishek took over control of the Nationalists. With warlords still in control in the north, a long-planned "Northern Expedition" to unite

> *Following Sun Yatsen's death in 1925, Chiang Kaishek took over control of the Guomindang, consolidating his power by marrying Soong May-ling, the sister of Sun's widow.*

China under Guomindang control was launched, with the support of the CCP – but this did not last long. Chiang Kaishek, who distrusted his allies, seized an opportunity to use his criminal connections in Shanghai to attack the Communists, whose

Post-Imperial Leaders

Since the fall of the empire in 1911, China's leaders have overseen a series of turbulent and, at times, tragic events

Honoured as the father of modern China in both the PRC and Taiwan, **Dr Sun Yatsen** (in Mandarin, Sun Zhongshan) was born in 1866 near Macau in southern Guangdong province. Influenced by Christian and Western ideas, Sun plotted the

overthrow of the emperor and founded the republican Guomindang (Nationalist Party). With China divided, he set up a government in Guangzhou in 1920 that was to rival the military powers in the north, then reorganised the Guomindang with the Soviet Union's help. Sun died, aged 58, in 1925.

Chiang Kaishek (in Mandarin, Jiang Jieshi) was Sun's successor. Born in 1887, he underwent military training, then joined the Guomindang. After defeat by the Communists in the civil war, he fled to Taiwan, where his government was able to boost the economy with the help of the US. He died in 1975 without achieving his ambition of overthrowing the Communists and recapturing the mainland.

Chiang Kaishek's great adversary was **Mao Zedong**. No other figure had such an influence on

20th-century China. Born to a peasant family in Hunan province in 1893, Mao became co-founder of the Chinese Communist Party in 1921. During the Long March, he established himself as its leader, a position he retained until his death in 1976. Mao led the country out of its post-war economic misery, only to let it sink into chaos during the Great Leap Forward and the Cultural Revolution. A personality cult developed around "the Great Helmsman" during the Cultural Revolution.

Next in importance was **Zhou Enlai**, Mao's closest ally. Born in Huai'an, Jiangsu province, in 1898, Zhou was the son of a wealthy family. After studying in Europe in the 1920s, Zhou took a leading role Communist movement soon after his return to China. His special skill, diplomacy, soon became apparent, and he used his influence to curb some of Mao's worst excesses. Zhou's achievements in foreign policy are particularly significant – China emerged from isolation to become a member of the United Nations in 1971. There was widespread public grief after his death in early 1976.

Deng Xiaoping, born in 1904, was Zhou Enlai's right-hand man and close friend. Hailing from a peasant family in Sichuan province, Deng studied in France in the 1920s. After his return, he took part in the Long March and became a prominent politician. In 1973, he was appointed by Zhou Enlai as deputy prime minister, and was ultimately responsible for opening China's economy to the world as China's president. Despite some setbacks – most notably the suppression of the Tiananmen Square democracy movement in 1989 – Deng displayed finesse by steering China back into the global community. He died in 1997, last of the old leaders.

Deng's protégé, **Jiang Zemin**, became General Secretary of the Party during the demonstrations of 1989, and State President in 1993. He maintained Deng's policies of economic reform, oversaw the return of Hong Kong and Macau to China, and China's entry into the World Trade Organisation. Jiang was succeeded as party General Secretary in 2002 and later as State President in 2003 by **Hu Jintao** (see page 59). ❏

LEFT: Sun Yatsen is admired by both Communists and Nationalists. **ABOVE:** Zhu De and Mao posters, Yan'an.

power base was in the city. A brutal campaign, the White Terror, led to thousands of Communists and sympathisers being rounded up and executed.

The Guomindang forces continued northwards and took Beijing in 1927, ending the period of warlord rule. Chiang Kaishek established his capital at Nanjing and became the diplomatically recognised leader of the Chinese Republic.

Meanwhile, the CCP retreated to a remote stronghold in the hills of Jiangxi province, but under sustained Nationalist attack, its troops were forced out in 1934 and embarked on the legendary Long March. This epic journey lasted three years and involved marching to a new northern base at Yan'an in Shaanxi province. Of the 100,000 who set out, fewer than one-fifth survived the 10,000km (6,200-mile) ordeal. During this period, Mao emerged as the leader of the party.

Japan and World War

As early as 1931, Japan had annexed parts of northeastern China, where it founded a puppet state, Manchukuo, headed by Puyi, the last Manchu emperor, who had abdicated the imperial throne in 1912. The Japanese planned further conquests in China. Faced by this threat, Chiang Kaishek was unable to use his troops against the Communists. Also, those wishing to end the civil war and join forces with the Communists against the common Japanese threat were expressing criticism within his own party. They even "persuaded" Chiang to agree to an unlikely renewed alliance with the Communists.

By 1937, China and Japan were officially at war. Shanghai was bombarded and captured by the invaders, who are thought to have killed over 200,000 civilians in the brutal Nanjing Massacre. Chiang Kaishek retreated to Chongqing, in Sichuan province. The Communists fought a guerrilla war from their bases in the north, while Chiang's troops resisted the Japanese in the south. The two forces eventually stopped the Japanese advance. In part because of the drain on Japanese resources caused by the war in China, the Allies were able to gain military superiority over the Japanese in the Pacific after 1942.

The civil war began again in earnest following Japan's surrender in 1945. Chiang Kaishek, backed by the Americans, fought against Mao Zedong's Red Army, which was fighting mostly

on its own and with minimal Soviet support. The resumed four-year civil war was, for the most part, an easy victory for the Communists: the Guomindang was weakened when it demobilised large numbers of soldiers after 1945. Another decisive factor was that the Communists rapidly won the support of the Chinese people, exhausted by war and suffering from the Nationalists' mismanagement of the already extremely fragile economy.

After several campaigns, there was a decisive battle on the Yangzi, and Nationalist troops were so weakened that they were forced to retreat to the island of Taiwan, along with nearly 2 million refugees and most of China's gold reserves. The

civil war was finally over. On 1 October 1949 Mao Zedong stood on Tiananmen and pronounced: "The Chinese people have stood up!" And thus, a new nation was born.

The People's Republic

The initial public reaction after 1949 was one of euphoria. The CCP army was disciplined and polite, unlike the looting and raping Nationalist troops. Industries were nationalised and government administration taken over.

Land distribution had already taken place in many rural areas in the north before 1949; now it continued in the south. Mao's implementation of class struggle began in the countryside. After individual class status was determined, people were

RIGHT: Mao accompanies the Soviet First Secretary, Voroshilov, on a state visit, Beijing, 1957.

encouraged to "speak bitterness" against their former landlords. Up to 1 million landlords were dispossessed of their land, and many were killed.

A new marriage law made women equal to men and divorce possible. The liberation of women, in theory, seemed like true progress, but in reality women had to hold full-time jobs in addition to maintaining the home as before.

By the mid-1950s, Premier Zhou Enlai noted that political pressures had demoralised China's intellectuals and scientists. This led to the Hundred Flowers Movement: christened after the adage "Let 100 flowers bloom and 100 schools of thought contend", it was devised to allow open

Anti-Rightist campaign ensued (some believe Mao's motive for encouraging criticism was to search for enemies, but evidence is unclear). Limits to free discussion were now specified: any talk and debate must unite the people, benefit socialism and strengthen the Communist state. Thousands of intellectuals were persecuted and imprisoned and creativity was quenched, if not eliminated altogether.

The Great Leap Forward

Mao believed that China could be industrialised rapidly, fuelled by ideological motivation and the reorganisation of production. Rural and urban

criticism of the party. For several months in 1957, people were encouraged by statements from Mao and others to criticise the government and its policies. After some hesitation, many vented their

In 1960 relations with the Soviet Union, in trouble for some years, were terminated. Soviet advisers were expelled, to the detriment of Chinese industry and development, and Mao pursued increasingly isolationist policies.

dissatisfactions, with calls for more freedom of speech, independence of the judiciary and freer trade unions. Perhaps shocked by the level of discontent, the CCP reversed its policy and the

communities were encouraged to use their surplus labour and resources for heavy industries, especially steel production. Communes were established to increase the scale of production, while private enterprise was eliminated. "Backyard furnaces" were built to produce steel, but because of a lack of expertise, it turned out to be unusable – a perfect illustration of the period's misguided zeal. Agricultural production was expected to increase, and so local leaders falsely reported astronomical growth to advance their careers and avoid being labelled politically uncommitted or incorrect.

Between 1958 and 1961, the failure of the policies of the Great Leap Forward, combined with three years of bad weather, led to a famine in which up to 40 million Chinese died.

The Cultural Revolution

The final, bloody chapter of the period, the Cultural Revolution was an attempt by Mao – who had withdrawn into the background following the disaster of the Great Leap Forward – to prevent bureaucratic stagnation and to purge the party of what he saw as corrupt elements. He also wanted to consolidate his own power base.

Mao wanted to replace older leaders with younger ones, whose revolutionary zeal would be amplified by the act of toppling the establishment. He saw students as his activists and encouraged them first to turn on their teachers. The most chaotic phase lasted from May 1966 to late 1967.

tims. By 1968 there was widespread street fighting and virtual anarchy as rival Red Guard factions turned on each other. The army was called in to restore order, and millions of Red Guards were sent to the countryside to "learn from the peasants".

Transition to a new era

The chaos could not continue, and following Mao's death, the last two decades of the 20th century witnessed dramatic changes in the tempo and direction of Chinese society, government and economy. The convulsions of the Cultural Revolution spent, China set about rebuilding itself, and economic development, not political struggle, defined the era.

Students organised "Red Guard" units all over the country. Mao's slogan that "It is right to rebel" propelled their campaigns to destroy remnants of the old society. Brandishing Mao's "Little Red Book" of quotations, they destroyed temples and historic sites, and broke into private homes to smash and burn books, jewellery and art. Party leaders and other "counter-revolutionary" forces were denounced and subjected to mass trials.

Many died at the hands of the Red Guard, or, humiliated, committed suicide. Liu Shaoqi, Mao's chosen successor, was one of the first political victims.

LEFT: Red Guards, Shanghai, 1973. ABOVE: a Cultural Revolution-era march in Beijing. RIGHT: Mao figurines and other "maomorabilia", on sale all over China.

Zhou Enlai's death in 1976 went unmarked by the Chinese leadership; he had been under indirect criticism from party radicals since 1973, but his death caused widespread grief among the people. The Monument to the People's Heroes in the centre of Tiananmen Square was adorned with thousands of wreaths and poems in his honour, but overnight all of the wreaths were removed, sparking the first genuinely spontaneous demonstration since the founding of the People's Republic. The crowd of 100,000 clashed with police throughout the day, until the square was cleared early that evening. Deng Xiaoping, perceived to be siding with the less radical faction of the party, was dismissed from his posts two days later, and Hua Guofeng became premier and first deputy chairman of the party.

When Mao Zedong died on 9 September of that same year, Hua Guofeng succeeded him in key government and party positions.

Deng's new direction

The post-Mao era was the epoch of Deng Xiaoping, right up until his death in 1997. Although Deng was purged twice during the Cultural Revolution, he made a final comeback in 1978, acquiring positions and real power to set the political agenda. Deng began establishing his legitimacy by restoring the good reputations of many of those who had been politically persecuted during the 1950s and 1960s and during the Cultural Revolution.

Earlier, during autumn 1978, posters had appeared in Beijing calling for a fifth modernisation: democracy. The posters criticised the authoritarianism of Mao's time and appealed for free speech and institutional reforms. Initially tolerated by the leadership, the so-called Democracy Wall Movement was forcibly halted in the spring of 1979.

Relations with the United States were normalised in 1979 (although President Nixon's visit to China in 1972 had started the process). Deng travelled to the US a few months later, when he met President Carter and congressional and business leaders. Deng's policy of "opening" China to the outside was recognition that China needed

Within the party and government bureaucracy, many who held prominent and powerful positions had acquired them by demonstrating revolutionary zeal during the Cultural Revolution, rather than on merit through knowledge or ability. Reversing the pattern, Deng began promoting education and professionalism in government and party ranks.

In December 1978, Deng inaugurated what he called a "second revolution". He reiterated the "Four Modernisations" – in agriculture, industry, national defence, and science and technology – for Chinese development, first proposed by Zhou Enlai some years earlier. Mao had considered politics the key to China's progress. Deng defined China's modernisation to emphasise economic development.

> Deng Xiaoping was unable, or unwilling, to denounce Mao: to do so would have meant discrediting China's Communist Revolution. The solution was to divide Mao's rule into a "good" early phase and a "bad" latter phase.

technological expertise and capital from elsewhere. The Chinese political system, however, was not to be influenced by Western political systems or culture.

To modernise agriculture, Deng disbanded Mao's disastrous communes. Farmers could now sell excess vegetables, fruit, fish or poultry in private markets and keep the extra profits. Consequently, rural agricultural production rapidly increased in the 1980s, far outpacing population increase. Deng began reforming industry by upgrading outdated technology and managerial systems, implementing price reforms, advocating foreign trade and investment, revamping the banking system and encouraging private business. Promises of private profit for entrepreneurs and other non-government workers led to dramatic and sustainable production increases. It was a chaotic time, and it is a mistake to think that Deng had carefully planned every stage. There were still serious impediments to economic development. But he deserves credit for allowing private enterprise, stifled for so long, to flourish.

The Maoist emphasis on heavy industry shifted to light industrial goods for export. A new responsibility system in industry authorised managers, not party committees as in days past, to make decisions. The opening of foreign trade and investment led to the build-up of coastal cities formerly engaged in foreign trade, especially in the south. Special Economic Zones (SEZ) were set up, beginning with Shenzhen, right on the border with Hong Kong.

Protest and demonstrations

Despite the establishment of SEZs, for many Chinese – particularly the young educated elite – the opening up of the economy was not happening fast enough, and frustration at the tardiness of change was compounded by other issues such as official corruption and inflation. In April 1989, these problems came to a head and Tiananmen Square became the focus of the world's media as university students, later joined by workers, aired their grievances against the government in the largest demonstrations since 1949. The protests, which were prompted by the death of Hu Yaobang – one of the few high-ranking officials who offered the hope of political liberalisation – quickly developed into demands for democratic reform.

The protests gained momentum until, on 19 May, martial law was imposed. After several attempts to persuade the protesters to leave, the party lost patience. Through the evening of 3 June, soldiers and civilians clashed at various points in Beijing, and in the early hours of 4 June the student protesters were forced out of Tiananmen Square

---

LEFT: US President Gerald Ford and Deng Xiaoping, China's then-vice-President, at a state banquet in 1975. **RIGHT:** promoting family planning.

by tanks and guns. The soldiers were under express orders not to fire on anyone in the square itself, but several students were killed after exiting the square (most deaths occurred in Muxidi, west of Tiananmen Square, and at Liubukou). At least 300 people are believed to have died, although the government has never given a full account of what happened, and some witnesses and exiled leaders claim the number of deaths exceeded 2,000. In the following days, similar protests across the country petered out, most peacefully.

A nationwide hunt for the demonstration leaders – Wu'erkaixi, Wang Dan, Chai Ling and Han Dongfang – ensued. Thousands of demonstrators

were arrested and some executed, but many dissidents somehow managed to flee the country. Zhao Ziyang, reformist general secretary of the Communist Party, was ousted from office (immediately replaced by Jiang Zemin), and other reformers met similar fates.

A far-reaching consequence of the events of 4 June 1989 (known as *liusi* in Chinese) was to cripple the dissident movement. China's internal critics ended up in prison, went into exile abroad or were silenced. Meanwhile, the party became ever more vigilant in its campaign against dissent. The nascent China Democracy Party was rapidly demolished and its organisers jailed in the late 1990s as part of President Jiang Zemin's policy of quickly suppressing any organised opposition before it had time to grow. The quasi-Buddhist Falun Gong movement was outlawed in July 1999 after members demonstrated outside Zhongnanhai, Beijing's political nerve centre. Periodic Falun Gong protests were staged in Tiananmen Square, but the movement has been rigorously suppressed.

Not all protests are banned. After the NATO bombing of the Chinese embassy in Belgrade, police did little to prevent protesters stoning the US embassy in retaliation, but the most likely explanation for this is that the Chinese government is prepared to allow some public release of pent-up anger as long as the target is not the Chinese Communist Party itself, Another factor is that patri-

非典得到控制：曾經的恐慌漸行漸遠，但"滅薩尚未成功，抗非仍需努力".

otic and nationalistic sentiments are encouraged.

China has managed to become part of the modern economic world without commensurate political evolution. Access to information remains highly controlled, with the internet filtered for any undesirable content (eg BBC news online in Chinese), leaving Chinese citizens disengaged and disadvantaged. However, in recent years, the proliferation of blogs and of peer-to-peer downloading has alleviated the situation somewhat.

International issues

After Tiananmen, China was lambasted over its human rights record, particularly with regard to political prisoners and the situation in Tibet. Yet it soon became evident that Beijing cared little about world opinion of its internal affairs. As the economy continued to grow through the 1990s, and with the potential of the vast Chinese market rapidly becoming economic reality, foreign agents were increasingly likely to do business regardless.

China's most important relationship – with the United States of America – is fraught with distrust, but is not outwardly hostile. The US frequently rails against China's human rights abuses; China shrugs off the criticism. China desires good relations with the US so that it can continue to develop and modernise in peace and security; America views China's growing power and prestige as a threat to its influence in the Far East. Taiwan – which the US has pledged to defend against a Chinese invasion – is a particularly sharp thorn in relations. The collision in April 2001 between a US Airforce reconnaissance plane and a Chinese fighter jet incensed the Chinese, but no long-term action was taken.

Attempting to limit the supremacy of the US, China adopts a passive policy of fostering strategic alliances with countries such as Russia and Pakistan. Sino-US ties improved markedly, however, after the 9/11 terror attacks on New York and Washington in 2001. With the War on Terror dominating the agenda, China seized the opportunity to crack down harder on "splittist tendencies" amongst the Muslim Uighurs of Xinjiang Autonomous Region.

Relations with Japan remain tricky, largely due to Japan's bloody occupation of China and the refusal of the Japanese prime minister to offer a full apology for its imperial conquest. Among the common people (*laobaixing*), it is not rare to hear anti-Japanese remarks. Japan, however, remains a major investor in China and Beijing seeks to maintain the cash flow.

China's growing clout in the Far East has made its neighbours increasingly anxious. China claimed territorial sovereignty, for example, over islands far from its borders and closer to Vietnam, the Philippines and Indonesia. It offered two arguments: "historical" rights from centuries ago, when imperial ships sailed the South China Sea, and territorial rights, in fact applicable under international law only to true archipelagos like Indonesia and the Philippines. The islands involved – the Paracels and Spratlys, among others – sit on extensive petroleum reserves at a time when China is importing more and more oil to fuel its economic growth.

Having weathered the Asian financial crisis of the late 1990s, it is China, rather than Japan, that is seen by many as Asia's economic stabiliser in the 21st century. Whatever this century holds for Asia, China will have a major part to play.

Relations with Taiwan

Since 1949, a consistent aim of the Chinese Communist Party has been to reunite Taiwan and China. The Nationalists in Taiwan have carried the same banner, but with differing terms. With the issue of Hong Kong and Macau (returned by Portugal in 1999) resolved, China has focused on Taiwan, which it claims is a renegade province, not an independent state. The clumsy attempt to influence Taiwan's first direct presidential elec-

The election in 2000 of Taiwan President Chen Shuibian on a Taiwan independence agenda therefore incurred the wrath of Beijing. The election of Ma Ying-jeou to the presidency in March 2008, however, brought the Nationalists back into power and provides a stage for China and Taiwan to return to their former status quo – with Taiwan neither asserting its independence nor moving towards reunification with China. At the time of writing, direct flights were being inaugurated between China and Taiwan for the first time in nearly 60 years, among other moves to improve links. Even if this was not happening, most analysts predict the Chinese army currently lacks the

tions in 1996 – by conducting "missile tests" directly into Taiwan's two primary shipping lanes – cost Beijing considerable political capital. Afterwards, Taiwan's political and commercial contacts increased with several foreign governments.

Beijing has long expressed its determination to reunite Taiwan and China peacefully, while reserving the right to use force if necessary. China's avowed ambition is to adopt the "one country, two systems" structure to Taiwan in the same way that it has been applied to Hong Kong and Macau.

LEFT: the SARS outbreak caused panic in China in 2003. **ABOVE:** Beijing beats the competition to host the 2008 Olympic Games.

means to take Taiwan through conventional warfare, especially considering the US pledge to help defend Taiwan if an invasion occurred. Beijing's threat of using force has been widely interpreted as bluster and a way to influence negotiations, but the passing of an anti-secession law in March 2005, authorising the use of "non-peaceful means" if Taiwan formally declares statehood, increased nervousness on both sides of the straits, though the tensions were much diminished by the 2008 election of Ma Ying-jeou.

Changing ideology

During the industrialisation of China in the 1950s and 1960s, the Communist Party was the paramount touchstone in work and society, not only assuring ideological consistency among workers, but dictating industrial policy itself. Yet China's blossoming market economy (officially a "socialist market economy with Chinese characteristics") discourages intellectual conformity and rigid industrial policy. And the expanding sector dominated by non-industrial entities – securities and trading firms – is increasingly free of party influence (although the big four state banks are organs of the party). Those working in these areas are young, urban and increasingly as affluent as their counterparts in Japan and the West.

Ideology has been influenced by economic developments, and in March 1999 the NPC

Social tension

"Social disorder" is the biggest fear of the party, which is determined never to allow a repeat of the 1989 Tiananmen demonstrations. Anniversaries of the Tiananmen massacre have passed with little incident. Other issues have come to the fore, however. Large-scale interest in the prescriptions of Falun Gong pointed to the spiritual hollowness of contemporary life in China, after decades of Marxism were swiftly overturned by decades of mass consumerism. The Communist Party remains fearful of mass religious movements, perhaps recalling the devastating effects of rebellions such as the Taiping in the 19th century.

enshrined "Deng Xiaoping thought" in the constitution, giving Deng a status equal to Mao. The party publishes collections of his speeches and promotes slogans used by him, including the famous "To get rich is glorious." Deng's policies largely continued under President Jiang Zemin and his successor, Hu Jintao.

In November 2002, the 16th Party Congress marked a symbolic shift away from communist ideology, with significant changes to the wording of the constitution and membership of the party available to all, not just the "working class", while the 2007 National People's Congress saw the passing of the long-disputed property law, a significant step towards guaranteeing the right to the ownership of private property.

With the exponential rise of personal wealth and the expansion of consumerism in China, crime has mushroomed 10 percent annually since the early 1980s. Corruption is a serious problem, and the root cause of a rapid growth in the number of riots and demonstrations across the country. Government officials, from local mayors and cadres to senior party members, have been frequently implicated in a series of profiteering scandals, from the Henan Aids outbreak caused by contaminated blood supplies to the shocking case of the tainted baby milk powder in 2008.

Minority groups continue to present Beijing with issues that challenge its rule of this immense country. Buddhists in Inner Mongolia and Muslims in Xinjiang, as well as Tibetans, remain under close scrutiny following the recent rise in ethnic tensions in western China. During the lead-up to the 2008 Beijing Olympics, pro-Tibet activists interrupted the Olympic torch relay and Tibetans took to the streets in Lhasa. Of even more concern to Beijing were the violent riots that exploded on the streets of Ürümqi and Kashi in Xinjiang in the summer of 2009. Uighur lynch mobs went on the rampage, killing dozens of Han Chinese, who in turn retaliated. The situation has remained tense.

A further threat to stability is regional imbalance. China has achieved staggering economic growth over the past 25 years, but the fruits of reform have been unevenly distributed. The east and southern coastal cities grow rich while the rural areas of the interior lag ever further behind.

21st-century China

China entered the 21st century on an optimistic note. In 2001 it joined the World Trade Organisation – a hugely significant event that opened the world's markets to Chinese manufactured goods and the vast Chinese domestic market to foreign companies. Later in the same year Beijing succeeded in its bid to hold the 2008 Olympic Games. International companies continued to beat a path to China's door, and internal anti-government dissent had been effectively smothered. In 2002, Jiang Zemin handed over leadership of the Party to his deputy, Hu Jintao. Together with Wen Jiabao (who replaced Zhu Rongji as premier), Hu is seen to favour greater transparency and democracy.

Technological developments also proceed apace. As well as the Three Gorges Dam project *(see page 256)*, China became the third nation to achieve manned space flight in 2003, with the successful launch and return of the mission, and astronaut

China's huge demand for raw materials has had a major impact on the global economy, while friendly relations with resource-rich pariah states such as Sudan raises geopolitical issues and the ire of the US.

Yang Liwei. A first space walk followed in 2008.

Huge problems remain, however, and these were reflected in the issues discussed in the important 2007 National People's Congress, where the living conditions of China's some 800 million rural

LEFT: collecting scrap metal from a rubbish tip in Shanghai. China's huge appetite for raw materials has caused global scrap prices to rise. **RIGHT:** national flag.

dwellers were a prominent issue. Premier Wen Jiabao made a commitment to provide rural health insurance and free healthcare by the year's end, and also to abolish tuition fees for all rural children. Coupled with the new property law, the moves were widely seen as an effort by the Chinese government to abolish the widening wealth gap between the affluent cities and the countryside – a divide that has been leading to tens of thousands of mass protests every year.

The run-up to the 2008 Olympics proved a difficult time. The Tibetan riots and torch relay protests *(see above)* focused unwelcome attention on political and human rights issues. Then, in May, an

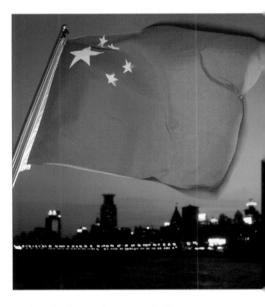

earthquake flattened towns and villages across central Sichuan province, killing tens of thousands.

Despite the challenges, and the global economic woes since 2008, the Chinese economy remains strong. In industry and manufacturing, technology has been bought – and sometimes stolen – from foreign rivals, enabling Chinese companies to produce an ever greater range of goods. Chinese manufactures, from clothes and footwear to electronics and toys, swamp the globe and drive down prices. Meanwhile, the insatiable demand for raw materials has had the overall effect of boosting commodity prices. As the Communist party marked the 60th anniversary of the People's Republic, China was impacting on the global economy as never before. *For more on the economy, see pages 67–71.* ❏

Decisive Dates

The Early Empire

c. 21st–16th century BC
Xia dynasty. Some scholars question whether this dynasty existed.

c. 16th–11th century BC
Shang dynasty, the first recorded dynasty. Ancestor worship is ritualised.

c. 11th century–256 BC
Zhou dynasty. Capital established at Chang'an (now Xi'an), later at Luoyang.

770–476 BC
Spring and Autumn Period. Consolidation of aristocratic family-states. Confucius (551–479 BC) stresses moral responsibility of ruler.

403–221 BC
Warring States Period.

Qin Dynasty (221–206 BC)

221 BC
Qin Shi Huangdi unifies China to found the first imperial dynasty. Weights and measures, currency and writing are standardised. Qin Shi Huangdi builds an immense underground tomb, including an army of thousands of terracotta warriors.

Han Dynasty (206 BC–AD 220)

206 BC
Han dynasty founded, with Chang'an (modern-day Xi'an) as its capital.

180 BC
Eunuchs are employed at the imperial court to look after the emperor's wives and concubines.

165 BC
Civil service examinations instituted.

AD 25
Capital moved to Luoyang.

105
Traditional date for the invention of paper. Paper may have already been in use for two centuries. Commerce between China and Asia/Europe thrives.

2nd century
First Buddhist establishments are founded in China.

220
Abdication of the last Han emperor. Wei, Jin, and Northern and Southern dynasties divide China.

Sui Dynasty (581–618)

581
Following nearly four centuries of division, Sui dynasty reunifies China. New legal code established.

589–610
Repairs of early parts of the Great Wall. Construction of a system of canals linking northern and southern China.

Tang Dynasty (618–907)

618

Sui dynasty collapses; Tang dynasty proclaimed. Government increasingly bureaucratised. Buddhism influences all sectors of society. Chang'an (Xi'an) grows into one of the world's largest cities by the end of the Tang dynasty.

690–705

Empress Wu (627–705) governs China as its first female ruler. Writing of poetry becomes a requisite in civil service examinations.

907–960

Fall of Tang dynasty. Five Dynasties and Ten Kingdoms partition China. Anarchy in much of China.

Song Dynasty (960–1279)

960

Northern Song dynasty reunites China; capital established at Kaifeng.

Top Left: Confucian scholars were persecuted by the Qin Emperor.
Above Left: Wei-dynasty tomb guardian. **Left:** most of the Great Wall dates from the Ming dynasty.
Above: a giraffe presented to Ming emperor Yongle. **Top:** a Yuan-dynasty battleship. **Right:** Kangxi.

1040

Invention of movable type, but not as efficient for printing pages of Chinese characters as woodblock printing. Development of Neo-Confucianism during 11th and 12th centuries.

1127

Beginning of the Southern Song dynasty, as invaders take over northern China and the Song capital is moved to Hangzhou, near Shanghai.

Yuan Dynasty (1279–1368)

1279

After nearly half a century of trying, Mongols led by Kublai Khan, grandson of Ghengis Khan, rout the Song court. Tibet is added to the empire. Trade along the Silk Road flourishes. Beijing is made the capital.

Ming Dynasty (1368–1644)

1368

Founding of the Ming dynasty after Han Chinese overthrow the Mongols.

1405–33

During the reign of Emperor Yongle, Muslim eunuch Zheng He (1371–c.1433) commands seven overseas expeditions to Southeast Asia, India and East Africa. Maritime trade is later abruptly curtailed as China turns inwards.

1514

The first Portuguese ships anchor off Guangzhou (Canton).

1553

Macau becomes a Portuguese trading port, and the first European settlement in China.

Qing Dynasty (1644–1911)

1644

A non-Han Chinese people, the Manchu, seize Beijing, beginning the Qing dynasty.

1661–1722

Reign of Emperor Kangxi.

1736–96

Reign of Emperor Qianlong.

1800

First edict prohibiting the importation and local production of opium.

1838

Lin Zexu, a court official, suspends all trade in opium. The following year, the Qing court terminates all trade between Britain and China.

1839–42

British forces gather off China's coast. Fighting begins in 1841 in the First Opium War.

1842
Treaty of Nanjing signed. More Chinese ports are forced open to foreign trade, and Hong Kong Island is surrendered to Great Britain "in perpetuity".

1851–64
Anti-Manchu Taiping Rebellion devastates large areas and results in tens of thousands of deaths.

1855–75
Muslim rebellions.

1858
Conflicts arise between European powers, mainly France and Britain, and China. Treaties of Tianjin signed, opening more ports to foreigners.

1860
British and French troops burn the Summer Palace in Beijing; Kowloon Peninsula ceded to Britain.

1894–5
Sino-Japanese War, which China loses.

1900
Boxer Rebellion seeks to remove foreign influences from China. Rebels take Europeans hostage.

1911
Republican Revolution: representatives from 17 provinces gather in Nanjing to establish a provisional republican government. Sun Yatsen is chosen president, but soon steps down.

1912
Forced abdication of the last emperor, Puyi.

Post-Imperial China
1912–20
Warlord Yuan Shikhai nominally rules much of China, but several provinces declare independence. After his death in 1916 China falls apart. Civil war amongst various warlords.

1919
On 4 May in Beijing, a large demonstration demands measures to restore China's sovereignty, thus beginning a nationalist movement.

1921
Founding of the Communist Party (CCP) in Shanghai.

1925
Sun Yatsen dies.

1927
Chiang Kaishek's Nationalist forces attack the Communists in Shanghai, take Beijing from warlord control and establish their capital at Nanjing.

1934–6
The Long March: Communists forced by Nationalists to abandon their stronghold in southern China.

1937–45
Following the Japanese invasion and the Nanjing Massacre in 1937, the Communists and Nationalists fight the Japanese – mostly separately – with American and British assistance.

1945
Japan defeated in World War II; full-scale civil war ensues in China.

People's Republic of China

1949
Mao Zedong declares People's Republic in Beijing on 1 October; Nationalist army flees to Taiwan.

1950–53
Chinese troops support North Korea in the Korean War.

1958–61
Great Leap Forward results in a mass famine.

1960
Split between China and the Soviet Union.

1966–76
Cultural Revolution brings chaos, destruction and death across China. The worst violence is in 1966 and 1967.

1976
Zhou Enlai and Mao Zedong die; the Cultural Revolution ends. Tangshan earthquake kills over 240,000.

1978
Deng Xiaoping becomes leader, instituting a policy of economic reform and opening China to the West.

1989
Tiananmen Square demonstrations; military crackdown ends with hundreds of deaths.

1997
Deng Xiaoping dies in February; Hong Kong reverts to Chinese sovereignty on 1 July.

1999
Anti-NATO demonstrations after the accidental bombing of the Chinese embassy in Belgrade. Macau reverts to Chinese sovereignty.

2001
China joins the World Trade Organisation.

2003
Shenzhou-V manned space mission. Hu Jintao becomes president. The Three Gorges Dam begins operating. SARS epidemic.

2006
The new railway to Lhasa, the capital of Tibet, is completed ahead of schedule.

2008
Anti-Chinese riots in Tibet. A huge earthquake in Sichuan kills tens of thousands. Beijing hosts the 29th Olympic Games.

2009
60th anniversary of the founding of the People's Republic. Major ethnic riots in Xinjiang as Uighurs go on the rampage against Han Chinese.

TOP LEFT: an opium den in the late 19th century. **FAR LEFT:** French troops in combat against Taiping rebels. **LEFT:** the Long March. **ABOVE:** Sun Yatsen, founder of modern China. **TOP:** revolutionary imagery. **RIGHT:** the Beijing Olympics' Aquatics Centre.

THE NEW CHINA

China's extraordinary economic transformation has brought unprecedented prosperity to millions. Yet growing inequality between rich and poor, environmental pressures and other issues present serious challenges

In 1992, Deng Xiaoping, who had gradually emerged as de facto leader of China after Mao's death in 1976, embarked on a tour of southern China, visiting Guangzhou and the two special economic zones (SEZs) of Shenzhen and Zhuhai. In the aftermath of the Tiananmen protests of 1989, leftist forces had been pressing to rein in the limited reforms of the 1980s and put China back on a more solidly centralised track. Deng's tour was, then, a deliberate intervention, and he took it as an opportunity to repeat the rallying cry with which he had jump-started rural reforms in 1982, "To get rich is glorious." Chinese needed to go into business "even more boldly" and "more quickly" to create a socialist market economy with Chinese characteristics, said Deng.

Deng's power had been greatly diminished since the Tiananmen protests, and his tour had little initial impact. Nevertheless, a series of articles he published in Shanghai's *Liberation Daily* under a pen-name won over local elites, and before long the calls for economic liberalisation began to become orthodoxy nationwide.

A large proportion of China's new business elite emerged during the chaotic years of the 1980s. Many of these people had been imprisoned under Mao but, following their release, seized the new opportunities created by Deng's reforms.

The result has been an explosion of economic growth unparalleled in human history. China's GDP growth has averaged more than 9 percent since Deng's tour, and it is now reckoned to be the

world's second-largest economy in terms of purchasing power parity (PPP) and fourth-largest in terms of gross domestic product (GDP). In 1985, foreign direct investment (FDI) inflows amounted to around US$2 billion, but by 2007 had exploded to around US$77 billion.

Meanwhile, China's share of world exports was around 7 percent in 2007, according to the World Bank, and that percentage is doubling every three years. The economy has gone from being exclusively state-owned, to one in which the private sector now accounts for 70 percent of tax receipts.

In the short space of some 20 years, China has carried out innumerable reforms that have collectively transformed its economy – and the changes continue to take place. Membership of the World

PRECEDING PAGES: a Shanghai shop. **LEFT:** keeping an eye on share prices. **RIGHT:** consumerism in action.

Trade Organisation since 2001 has had a major impact, effectively opening up the country to foreign trade, and the world's markets to Chinese manufactures. In 2005, China revalued its currency against the US dollar and pegged it against a basket of currencies, with the result that by 2008 the Yuan had gained 15 percent against the dollar.

Whatever the risks ahead, two decades of reforms have turned China into an economic powerhouse, with pundits variously predicting it will become the world's largest economy anywhere between 2012 and 2030 – giving it some room to deal with the occasional and inevitable setback (such as the global financial crisis that began in 2008).

The SEZs were all essentially harbour interfaces with the outside world, which had been long been kept at bay by the political Great Wall of the Mao era. Shenzhen was to become the most successful due to its proximity to that bastion of free trade and then British colony, Hong Kong.

Between 1978 and 1997, Hong Kong's manufacturing businesses relocated over the border into the so-called Pearl River Delta (PRD) region. Hong Kong's – and later Taiwan's – investment in the PRD is such that it has become common to call the delta "the world's workshop", though in recent years Shanghai and the Yangzi River Delta (YRD) have been catching up.

Reform beginnings

China first started to turn its back on the collectivised economy it had practised since the Communist Revolution of 1949 when it began to dismantle the agricultural commune system in the 1970s, allowing "village enterprises" to be established. In the early 1980s, it became possible for individuals to set up one-person enterprises, or *getihu*, while by the mid-80s families were permitted to establish businesses with up to seven employees. At the same time the government began to allow foreign investment, in the form of joint ventures, with the opening of 14 coastal cities to outsiders, and – between 1980 and 1988 – the establishment of Special Economic Zones (SEZs) in Shenzhen and other places.

For the first 10 years of China's reforms, the PRD led China into the global economic order via foreign-invested firms in Shenzhen, Dongguan and Guangzhou, and is today a leading global source for electronics, electrical and electronic components, textiles and garments, shoes, toys, watches and clocks, and everything from clothes hangers to cocktail mixers. Accounting for just 0.4 percent of China's total land area, the PRD is responsible for around 29 percent of the nation's total trade (imports and exports).

Regional competition

The PRD may have spearheaded China's economic rise, but in recent years it has been overtaken by competition from Shanghai and its Yangzi

River Delta (YRD) hinterland, and also faces competition from the so-called Bohai Sea Economic Zone, which includes the municipalities of Beijing and Tianjin, and the city of Qingdao in Shandong province. Exports from the YRD have grown at an average of 41 percent per year since the beginning of the new millennium, and it now accounts for 37 percent of China's total exports.

With annual GDP growth of 11 percent, it is calculated that Shanghai will overtake Hong Kong in less than 10 years. However, the rise of the YRD and other regional economies is placing a strain on the availability of the migrant workers – the low-cost labour pool that has powered China's

be closed within three years. China's key exporting provinces have been reacting to this by shifting gears toward the production of higher-value products, such as automobiles, electronics and computer chips. But, in the meantime, manufacturers of the products that made the PRD rich are tending to relocate to Vietnam and India rather than China's relatively undeveloped inland hinterland.

Recognising that growth has been overwhelmingly concentrated in four southeastern Chinese provinces – Guangdong, Fujian, Zhejiang and Jiangsu – which together account for some 60 percent of China's exports, in 2000 China adopted a Go West policy. The government has since spent

growth over the past decade. Despite the fact that around 150 million migrant workers have left their fields in the countryside to work in China's factories, in the past few years there have been consistent reports of labour shortages, and that is leading to rising labour costs.

Rising labour costs and the appreciation of the Chinese yuan against the US dollar are beginning to erode China's price competitiveness as a source for cheap manufactured goods, and a 2008 report by Credit Suisse estimated that if current trends prevail, a third of Guangdong's manufacturers will

around Rmb 1 trillion on infrastructure development in the interior, including the 1,140km (710-mile) railway to Tibet and a vast network of fast, efficient roads. But in terms of foreign investment, the fact remains that at present nine coastal provinces are the recipients of more than 80 percent of all of China's inward FDI, with the remaining 20 provinces receiving just 12 percent.

For many manufacturers, despite massive government investment in transport infrastructure, much of China's interior – home to some 700 million of the country's population – is simply too far from any port to run an economically viable business. This discrepancy in growth between the coastal areas and the hinterland is just one of many tensions that often bubble over into serious social

---

FAR LEFT: over 90 percent of Chinese households owns a mobile phone. **LEFT:** stock market dealers. **ABOVE:** migrant worker. **RIGHT:** toy factory in the PRD.

unrest, a problem that the central government is extremely concerned about, and which has led to a nationwide campaign for "social harmony."

Protests in a divided nation

In 2005, Beijing estimated there were some 85,000 uprisings nationwide, a 6 percent increase on the previous year, and approximately four times more than a decade earlier. Such uprisings are not happening in the relatively affluent areas that the vast majority of foreign tourists travel through, but in the huge swathes of rural China where as many as 80 percent of the population live and watch on as a small minority profit from

practice, and arresting or firing officials who are involved – has been a 14-years-in-the-making property law, which was finally passed in early 2007, and effective from October of that year.

The central clause of the law states that "the property of the state, the collective, the individual and other obligees is protected by law, and no units or individuals may infringe upon it". Critics of the law say that, because it has failed to address the issue of state ownership of land, it will do little to curb the confiscation of land from peasants in the countryside. But, even though it has not abolished the constitutional right of the government to own all land, it does offer new protec-

China's juggernaut acceleration towards economic superpower status. Triggering these protests are a host of factors, but chief among them are land and environmental issues.

Land is a particularly contentious issue in modern China because it is still state-owned, and in the countryside farmers have leases of 30–70 years. With real-estate speculation rife throughout the nation, this provides ample opportunity for corrupt officials to cooperate with developers, evicting rural dwellers from their properties with minimal compensation and allowing business to make handsome profits from housing developments, hotels, factories, and in some cases infrastructure build-outs. The response to this in Beijing – apart from issuing edicts banning the

tions for owners of private homes and for farmers with long-term leases on land.

The environment is another source of conflict, as China's race to the future has largely been run at the expense of massive environmental degradation. This is a problem that even relatively leafy, park-endowed Hong Kong has to endure. The explosion of manufacturing in the PRD has led to a situation where, on a bad day, visibility can be so poor it is barely possible to see across the harbour.

But if Hong Kong bemoans its environmental woes, the situation elsewhere in China is far worse. According to the World Bank, China is home to 16 of the world's 20 most polluted cities, and more than 400,000 premature deaths occur annually due to air pollution. In a rare admission in 2007, China's environment minister told the press that environmental issues were behind more than 50,000 protests and riots across the country in the previous year. Generally, very few of these are reported in the press, but a case in Zhejiang province that year involving thousands of villagers fighting for the closure of polluting chemical factories made headlines, and the villagers eventually succeeded in shutting them down. President Hu Jintao has sent increasingly conciliatory messages on the environment, however, pledging to invest in green technology and reduce emissions.

21st-century challenges

The reality is that, for all the talk of the coming China century, the rise of the world's most populous nation is a far more complex phenomenon than many commentators give credit to. A visitor who touches down in cosmopolitan, spectacularly affluent Hong Kong, and travels on to any of the innumerable five-star hotels in Beijing or Shanghai, could be forgiven for thinking China has "arrived". But lurking in the wings of China's success story is a host of problems that mostly impact on those who have not prospered from the past two decades of meteoric growth. After all, despite all the hype, the World Bank estimates that China's per-capita GDP, in terms of purchasing power parity, is only equal to that of Japan in 1950, when it was still a ravaged economy, struggling to recover from the catastrophic results of its World War II defeat.

Land and environmental issues usually top the lists of China's woes, but access to water, and failing health and educational systems, also deserve a mention. It is thought that some 300 million Chinese have no access to clean drinking water. In a

> Most observers and analysts believe that China will have to embark on some sort of political reform if its economic rise is to continue. Current prosperity is dependent on exports, rendering it vulnerable to protectionism – or recession – in the West.

country that has more than 200 cities with populations greater than 1 million (and an increasing number with populations over 10 million), urban development at a rate unprecedented in history is siphoning water away from rural hinterlands. Meanwhile, privatisation and reforms means that the state

LEFT: construction workers in Shanghai.
RIGHT: sign of the times; a fashion show in Beijing.

no longer provides free healthcare, and reportedly as many as 800 million people now lack access to even basic healthcare. These same reforms have also resulted in a largely pay-as-you-go education system that puts an enormous strain on the poor.

How successful China will be in resolving these issues remains to be seen, but there is no doubt that people in high places are aware of the urgency of addressing the problems. Premier Wen Jiabao has focused on the "Three Rural Isssues", or *san nong*: agriculture, rural areas and peasants. The idea is to provide funding for infrastructure and new technologies that would improve living standards for the more than 800 million rural dwellers who have

been increasingly left behind as the coastal cities boom. Other commitments included free basic healthcare for rural dwellers, the abolition of tuition fees for rural children and the provision of basic living costs for urban dwellers who had lost their jobs.

Since the end of 2008 the global downturn has impacted on China's economy, with yearly growth rates falling from over 10 percent to around 6 percent (still way ahead of most other economies), while domestic price inflation has risen sharply. Thus the government is faced with huge challenges: whilst ensuring that China can weather the economic storm, in the face of growing discontent it needs to ensure that the new-found prosperity is spread throughout the vast hinterland, and not limited to the southern and eastern cities. ❏

THE BEIJING OLYMPICS

The 2008 summer Olympic Games focused the world's attention on China as never before

Following its successful 2001 bid to host the 29th Olympic Games, Beijing launched an ambitious modernisation programme to present the city in the best possible light for the showpiece event. Part rallying point for national pride and part massive public relations exercise to showcase the New China, the Olympic host has seen a dizzying and painful transformation. Huge sums have been invested in infrastructure, with the subway system and airport expanded, streets widened and swathes of older housing demolished, a process which has involved the relocation of tens of thousands of people. No expense was spared, either, on the building of the main stadia and the upgrade of other existing facilities. What was a gritty, ancient capital is now a bona fide international metropolis boasting some of the world's most daring architecture, a comprehensive and efficient transport system, and a far higher international profile. A total of US$42 billion has been spent, making these by far the most expensive Games ever. Although the main event lasted for just 18 days, their legacy for Beijing will remain for decades.

The event itself was a big success. China led the medals table from the start, and finished with an impressive haul of 51 gold medals. There was a total of 43 new world records, with incredible performances of speed and stamina, notably in the athletics sprinting events and in the swimming. The stadia looked magnificent, too, particularly during the utterly spectacular opening and closing ceremonies.

LEFT: the now traditional global tour of the Olympic flame prior to the Games was the focus of protests against China's human rights record, particularly on the streets of London and Paris with regard to Tibet.

ABOVE AND RIGHT: Michael Phelps en route to his record-breaking eight gold medals in the Aquatics Centre. The plastic "bubbles" integral to the structure of the building give it a futuristic appearance and provide strength, while reducing the cost of heating and lighting – all linked with Beijing's commitment to provide a "green" Olympics. Five pools are open to the public.

ABOVE: in order to build a truly iconic stadium for the Olympics, Beijing spent a staggering US$423 million on a radical design of criss-crossing steel trusses by Swiss architects Herzog and de Meuron. Resembling a bird's nest, or perhaps a piece of cracked Chinese porcelain, the thatched exoskeleton leaves the building porous to its surroundings – wandering between the soaring columns is akin to a walk through a giant steel forest.

THE BACKGROUND: BEAUTIFICATION AND PROTEST

The moment the Olympics began, at 8.08pm on the 8th day of the 8th month of 2008, marked the culmination of years of intense preparation, inspired by the Chinese determination to show that their capital city, and their nation, is ready to participate fully on the world stage. The extraordinary efforts China went to in beautifying Beijing – ridding it of pollution, modernising and greening the urban landscape, and even "educating" its citizens on how to be the perfect hosts for foreign guests – is an indication of just how important the Olympics have been for national pride, and for the ruling Party to be seen in the best possible light.

On the other hand, the build-up to the Games acted as a beacon for protestors who deplore the Chinese government's human rights record, the situation in Tibet and the lack of democracy and accountability in Chinese politics. The Olympic torch relay attracted violent protests in London and in Paris, where someone managed to extinguish the flame.

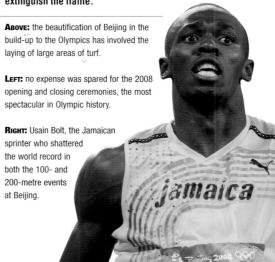

ABOVE: the beautification of Beijing in the build-up to the Olympics has involved the laying of large areas of turf.

LEFT: no expense was spared for the 2008 opening and closing ceremonies, the most spectacular in Olympic history.

RIGHT: Usain Bolt, the Jamaican sprinter who shattered the world record in both the 100- and 200-metre events at Beijing.

BELIEFS AND RELIGION

As diverse as the land and people, the beliefs and philosophies found in China reflect a historical depth and breadth existing nowhere else in the world

The "three teachings" of Confucianism, Daoism (Taoism) and Buddhism have traditionally dominated China's spiritual life. Of the two indigenous systems, Confucianism developed as a moral form of philosophy that taught ethical and pragmatic standards of behaviour, while Daoism had a religious as well as a philosophical dimension. Buddhism was imported from India in the 1st century AD, gradually evolving into a uniquely Chinese form as it was influenced by Daoism and Confucianism.

When the Communists came to power religion was deemed "counter-revolutionary", and during the Cultural Revolution there was widespread destruction of temples, mosques and churches. After Mao's death things became less repressive, and in 1982, freedom of religious belief was guaranteed by law – although what are deemed to be "cults", such as the Falun Gong movement, are seen as subversive and remain illegal *(see page 81).*

Apart from the fusion of Confucianism, Daoism and Buddhism that lies at the heart of Chinese religious belief, Islam is also practised, especially in the northwestern parts of China, and a small, but growing, Christian minority worships nationwide. Beyond philosophy or theology, the age-old traditions of lucky numbers, fortune-telling and geomancy naturally survive.

Fortune-telling and feng shui

Many Chinese take superstition, as distinct from organised religion, seriously. The idea of fate started in the feudal society, when it was believed that "the god" – that is, the emperor – decided one's destiny. With the Tang (618–907) and Song (960–1279) dynasties, society became more complicated, people were more concerned about fate, and fortune-telling became popular.

Following a fortune-teller's advice can mean shaving your head to appease the fortune god, or wearing a bright-red belt irrespective of your outfit. Carrying gold images around may bring good fortune, as may removing mirrors from the bedroom, or eating more mutton or less beef in the Lunar New Year period.

Fortune-tellers make predictions by reading faces and palms, or doing complicated calculations based on a person's name or the time and date of birth. The Chinese zodiac of 12 animal signs – rat, bull, tiger, rabbit, dragon, snake, horse, goat, monkey, chicken, dog and pig *(see page 83)* – was created during the Han dynasty (206 BC–AD 220). It divides people into the 12 categories according to the year they are born, and also tells their fortune and future by combining philosophy and numbers. At the end of every year, dozens of fortune-telling books are published.

Feng shui (wind and water) is a set of traditional spiritual laws, or geomancy, used to attract the best luck and prevent bad fortune. Those who take feng shui seriously consult a geomancer – a master of feng shui – to advise on designs of buildings, dates of important decisions, and layout of one's home and office. The most important tool in a feng shui master's bag is a compass-like device, which has eight ancient trigrams (bagua) representing nature, its elements and eight animals – horse, goat, pheasant, dragon, fowl, swine, dog and ox.

Feng shui theories are based mainly on the principle of *qi* – life's spirit or breath – divided into *yin* and *yang*, the female-passive and male-active elements of life. The concept of *wuxing* also has a prominent standing in Chinese philosophy, medicine, astrology and superstition. The term translates as "five elements", in which the five types of energy dominate the universe at different times. Water dominates in winter, wood in spring, fire in summer, metal in autumn, and earth is a transitional period between seasons.

Modern corporations in China often take feng shui extremely seriously. In Hong Kong's Central District, the angular design of the Bank of China tower is said to fling bad feng shui at just about every competing bank. The Hongkong and Shanghai Bank building, designed by Norman Foster, is supported on a series of giant pillars, making it possible to walk underneath the building. This satisfies the feng shui principle that the centre of power on the island (Government House) should be directly accessible from the main point of arrival (the Star Ferry).

The concept of lucky numbers played its part in the 2008 Beijing Olympics. The number 8 is considered auspicious and in view of this, the Games' opening ceremony kicked off at 8.08pm on the the the date 8.08.08.

Lucky (and unlucky) numbers

Even though most mainland Chinese – unlike their Cantonese neighbours in Hong Kong – tend to be somewhat dismissive of the idea that

some numbers are more auspicious than others, the connection between the pronunciation of Chinese numbers and possible bad- and good-luck associations with other Chinese words runs deep in Chinese culture. Chinese hotels and buildings of any sort, for example, often do not have a fourth floor, because the pronunciation – *si* – is a homonym for "death".

"Two" is generally considered a positive number because good things come in pairs, and for the Cantonese "two" has a particular resonance because it is pronounced *yat*, a homonym for "easy" – as in easy money. "Six" is not a major auspicious number, but it is liked by Chinese

because *liu* is a homonym for "to flow", and triple-six – the Number of the Beast in the West – is considered auspicious in China. "Eight" is the most auspicious of numbers, as it sounds similar to *fa*, or "to prosper", as in *facai*. "Nine" is regarded well by Chinese because it is a homonym for "long-lasting" – both are pronounced *jiu*.

Ancestor worship

Although the origins of ancestor worship are very ancient, Confucian notions of filial piety extending into the afterlife no doubt later conditioned it. By making offerings to the departed in the afterlife, the living show their respect and ensure that their ancestors will continue to take an interest in

LEFT: the *bagua* (trigram) mirror repels evil.
RIGHT: burning spirit money.

the fortunes of their descendants. One of the many superstitions that the revolutionary-era Communist Party attempted to banish from China, it is still a force in rural China, and Mao Zedong himself is subject to a form of ancestor worship – as the father of modern China – in public portraits and icons hanging over the dashboards of taxis and buses.

Ancestor worship has dwindled in importance in contemporary China. By contrast, it thrives in the Chinese communities of Hong Kong, Taiwan and even Singapore – communities that are in many ways more traditional than those of the mainland. Yet, even if it might seem to have no bearing on the lives of China's educated urban

elite, it is not unusual to see photographs of departed family members on the walls of rural family homes. Some Chinese still make a small shrine with offerings of fruit and burning incense for ancestors. In the traditional clan culture of rural China, ancestors could be traced back many, many generations, their names inscribed on plaques in clan temples where offerings could be made and ceremonies conducted.

Ancestor worship also manifests itself in popular holidays such as Qingming, popularly known in English as the Grave-Sweeping Festival, when traditional Chinese families go to the tombs of their ancestors, clean them up and make offerings of fruit, light incense and, particularly in Hong Kong and Taiwan, burn paper money.

Daoism (Taoism)

A central concept of Daoism is the *dao*, which means the way or path, but also has a secondary meaning of method and principle (by which the universe operates). Another important premise is *wuwei*, which is sometimes simply defined as passivity, or "swimming with the stream". The Chinese martial art of *taijiquan* is inspired by this concept. The notion of *de* (virtue) is another central tenet, as virtue that manifests itself in daily life when *dao* is put into practice.

Daoism perceives the course of events in the world to be determined by the forces *yin* and *yang*. The feminine, weak, dark and passive elements

are considered to be *yin* forces; masculinity, brightness, activity and heaven are seen as *yang* forces.

Laozi was the founder of Daoism, living at a time of crises and upheavals. He is traditionally thought to have been born in Henan province in 604 BC, into a distinguished family. Laozi was a contemporary of Confucius and ancient chronicles record that the two met. For a time, he held the office of archivist in Luoyang, which was then the capital, but later retreated into solitude and died in his village in 517 BC. According to a famous legend, he wanted to leave China on an ox when he foresaw the decline of the empire. Experts today still argue about Laozi's historical existence and legends swarm around his name. One of them, for instance, says that he was conceived by a beam of light, and that his mother was pregnant with him for 72 years and then gave birth to him through her left armpit. His hair was white when he was born and he prolonged his life with magic.

The earliest, and also most significant, followers of Laozi were Liezi and Zhuangzi. Liezi (5th century BC) was particularly concerned with the relativity of experiences, and he strived to comprehend the *dao* with the help of meditation. Zhuangzi (4th century BC) is especially noted, if not famous, for his poetic allegories. The Daoists were opposed to feudal society, yet they did not fight actively for a new social structure, preferring instead to live in a pre-feudalistic tribal society.

Ordinary people were not particularly attracted by the abstract concepts and metaphysical reflections of Daoism. Yet even at the beginning of the Han period in the 3rd century BC, there were signs of both a popular and religious Daoism. As Buddhism also became more and more popular, it borrowed ideas from Daoism, and vice versa, to the point where one might speak of a fusion between the two.

Both Daoists and Buddhists believed that the great paradise was in the far west of China, hence the name, Western Paradise. It was believed to be governed by the queen mother of the west, Xiwangmu, and her husband, the royal count of the east, Dongwanggong.

Religious Daoism developed in various directions and schools. The ascetics retreated to the mountains and devoted all their time to meditation, or else they lived together in monasteries. In the Daoist world, priests had important functions as medicine men and interpreters of oracles. They carried out exorcisms and funeral rites, and read special services for the dead or for sacrificial offerings.

The classic work of Daoism is the *Daodejing* (also written as *Tao Te Ching*), the "Way of Power". Although attributed to Laozi, it now seems certain that this work was not written by a single author.

Confucianism

While Laozi was active in the south of China, Kong Fuzi, known in the West as Confucius, lived in the north. For Confucius, too, *dao* and *de* were central concepts. For more than 2,000 years, the ideas of Confucius (551–479 BC) have profoundly influenced Chinese culture, which in turn coloured the world-view of neighbouring lands such as Korea, Japan and Southeast Asia. It is debatable whether Confucianism is a religious philosophy in the strictest sense, rather than a moral code for society. But Confucius was worshipped as a deity, although he was only officially made equal to the heavenly god by an imperial edict in 1906. (Up until 1927, many Chinese offered him sacrifices.)

Mencius, a Confucian scholar, describes the poverty at the time Confucius was born. "There are no wise rulers, the lords of the states are driven by their desires. In their farms are fat animals, in

their royal stables fat horses, but the people look hungry and on their fields there are people who are dying of starvation."

Confucius himself came from an impoverished family of the nobility who lived in the state of Lu (near the village of Qufu, in the west of Shandong province; *see pages 179–80)*. For years he tried to gain office with many of the feudal lords, but was repeatedly dismissed, so he travelled around with his disciples and instructed them in his ideas. All in all, Confucius is said to have had 3,000 disciples, 72 of them highly gifted individuals who are still worshipped today.

Confucius taught mainly traditional literature, rites and music, and is thus regarded as the founder of scholarly life in China. The Chinese

FAR LEFT: Buddha's birthday at Jing An Si, Shanghai.
LEFT: Taoist priest. **ABOVE:** Buddhist worship, Datong.

word *ru*, which as a rule is translated as Confucian, actually means "someone of a gentle nature" – a trait that was attributed to a cultured person. Confucius did not publish his philosophical thinking in a book, but his thoughts were recorded and collected together in the *Lunyu* (Analects) by his loyal disciples. The classic Confucianism canon also includes: *Shijing*, the book of songs; *Shujing*, the book of charters; *Liji*, the book of rites; *Chunqiu*, the spring and autumn annals; and *Yijing (I Ching)*, the book of changes.

Confucianism is, in a sense, a creed of law and order. Just as the universe is dictated by the world order, and the sun, moon and stars move accord-

ing to the laws of nature, so a person, too, should live within the framework of world order. This idea, in turn, is based upon the assumption that people can be educated.

Ethical principles were turned into central issues. Confucius was a very conservative reformer, yet he significantly reinterpreted the idea of the *junzi*, a nobleman, to that of a noble man, whose life is morally sound and who is, therefore, legitimately entitled to reign. Confucius believed that he would create an ideal social order if he reinstated the culture and rites of the early Zhou period (11th century–256 BC). Humanity *(ren)* was a central concept at the time, its basis being the love of children and brotherly love. Accordingly, the rulers would meet success if they gov-

erned the whole of society according to these principles. Confucius defined the social positions and hierarchies very precisely. Only if and when every member of society took full responsibility for his or her position would society function smoothly.

Family and social ties, and hierarchy, were considered to be of fundamental importance: between father and son (son must obey father without reservations), man and woman, older brother and younger brother, and a ruler and subject.

In the 12th century, Zhu Xi (1130–1200) succeeded in combining the metaphysical tendencies of Buddhism and Daoism with the pragmatism of Confucianism. His systematic

work includes teachings about the creation of the microcosm and macrocosm, as well as the metaphysical basis of Chinese ethics.

This system, known as Neo-Confucianism, reached canonical status in imperial China; it formed the basis of all state civil service examinations, a determining factor for Chinese officialdom until the 19th century.

Buddhism

Today, there are Buddhists among the Han Chinese, Mongols, Tibetans, Manchus, Tu, Qiang and Dai (Hinayana Buddhists) peoples.

The Chinese initially encountered Buddhism at the beginning of the 1st century AD, when merchants and monks came to China using the Silk

CONFUCIAN THOUGHTS

It is a pleasure to have friends come to visit you from afar.

It is these things that cause me concern:

failure to cultivate virtue,
failure to go deeply into what I have learned,
inability to move up to what I have heard to be right,
and inability to reform myself when I have defects.

A man of humanity, wishing to establish himself, also establishes others, and wishing to enlarge himself, also enlarges others.

He is the sort of man who forgets to eat when he engages himself in vigorous pursuit of learning, who is so full of joy that he forgets his worries, and who does not notice that old age is coming on. (Describing himself.)

Road. The prevalent type of Buddhism in China today is the Mahayana (Great Wheel), which – as opposed to Hinayana (Small Wheel) – promises all creatures redemption through the so-called Bodhisattva (redemption deities).

Two aspects particularly appealed to the Chinese: the teachings of karma provided a better explanation for individual misfortune, and there was a hopeful promise for existence after death. Nevertheless, there was considerable opposition to Buddhism, which contrasted sharply with Confucian ethics and ancestor worship.

Buddhism was most influential in Chinese history during the Tang dynasty (618–907). Several

gion. Only two schools have remained: Chan, or Zen Buddhism (associated with the Shaolin Temple – *see pages 192–3)*, and Amitabha-Buddhism, or Pure Land. The more influential is the Zen school, developed during the Tang dynasty, which preaches redemption through Buddhahood, which anyone can attain. It denounces knowledge gained from books or dogmas. The masters of Zen consider meditation to be the only path to knowledge.

In the 7th century AD, another type of Buddhism, called Tantric Buddhism or Lamaism, was introduced into Tibet from India. With the influence of the monk Padmasambhava (also known as Guru Rinpoche), it replaced the indigenous

emperors officially supported the religion; the Tang empress Wu Zetian, in particular, surrounded herself with Buddhist advisers. Late in the dynasty, however, for three years Chinese Buddhists experienced the most severe persecutions in their entire history: a total of 40,000 temples and monasteries were destroyed, and Buddhism was blamed for the dynasty's economic decline and moral decay.

In the course of time, 10 Chinese schools of Buddhism emerged, eight of which were essentially philosophical and did not influence popular reli-

LEFT: a statue of Confucius. **ABOVE:** Buddhist monk. **RIGHT:** a "thousand-armed" Guanyin sculpture at Shuanglin Si near Pingyao, Shanxi province.

Shaman Bon religion, while absorbing some of its elements. Tibetan monasteries developed into centres of intellectual and worldly power, yet there were recurring arguments. Only the reformer Tsongkhapa (1357–1419) succeeded in rectifying conditions that had become chaotic. He founded the sect of virtue (Gelugpa), which declared absolute celibacy to be a condition and reintroduced strict rules of order. Because the followers of this sect wear yellow caps, this order came to be known as Yellow Hat Buddhism.

The Gelugpas are led by the Dalai Lama and the Panchen Lama. The Dalai Lama represents the incarnation of the Bodhisattva of mercy (Avalokiteshvara; Guanyin to the Chinese), who is also worshipped as the patron god of Tibet. The

Panchen Lama is higher in the hierarchy of the gods and is the embodiment of Buddha Amitabha. The present 14th Dalai Lama, who was enthroned in 1940, fled to India from Tibet after an uprising in 1959, and has been living in exile since. The identity of the successor to the 10th Panchen Lama, who died in 1989, remains under dispute, and is a divisive political issue. The boy named as the successor by the Dalai Lama was removed by the Chinese authorities and is being held in Beijing. The Chinese government's choice was installed at Tashilhunpo monastery in 1995, but the majority of Tibetans do not recognise him as the new incarnation.

In Lamaism, a complex pantheon exists; apart from the Buddhist deities, there are numerous figures from the Brahman and Hindu world of gods and the old Bon religion. Magic, repetitive prayers, movements, formulae, symbols and sacrificial rituals are all means for achieving redemption.

Islam

Ten of the 56 recognised nationalities in China define themselves as Muslim: Hui, Uzbek, Uighur, Karach, Kyrgyz, Tatar, Shi'ite Tajik, Dongxiang, Sala and Bao'an – an estimated total of around 20 million people. The Hui are the only group who enjoy the special status of a recognised minority solely because of their religion: they are

mostly Han Chinese, and adhere to the teachings of the Koran less than most other Muslims.

Islam came to China via two different routes: one was the famous Silk Road, the other from across the sea to the southeastern coast of China. During the Yuan dynasty (1279–1368), the religion became permanently established in China.

Many of the policies of the Qing dynasty (1644–1911) were hostile to Muslims. In the 18th century, for example, the slaughtering of animals in accordance with Islamic rites was forbidden, and the building of new mosques and pilgrimages to Mecca were not allowed. Marriages between Chinese and Muslims were declared illegal, and relations between the two groups were made increasingly difficult.

The Cultural Revolution led to terrible persecution of Chinese Muslims, but by the 1980s Beijing's attitude to religions – particularly amongst the country's minorities – softened, and a more tolerant approach was adopted. Today, government figures indicate there are more than 35,000 mosques in China, and the religion has seen a resurgence, with Chinese Muslims taking the annual pilgrimage – or Hajj – to Mecca in increasing numbers – reportedly more than 10,000 in 2007. The events of September 11 in 2001, and the subsequent US War on Terror has, however, had negative effects for followers of Islam in China. Beijing has, in particular, cracked down on Xinjiang's population of Uighurs, who resent Chinese control of the province (and the large-scale influx of Han settlers) and harbour ambitions of independence.

Christianity

Christianity was first brought to China by the Nestorians, in 635, who disseminated their teachings with the help of a Persian called Alopen, who was their first missionary.

For a period, in spite of religious persecution, the religion spread to all the regions of the empire, and survived in some parts of the country until the end of the Mongol Yuan dynasty. At the same time, contacts were made between China and the Roman Catholic Church. The first Catholic church in China was probably built by a Franciscan monk from Italy, who arrived in Beijing in 1295. During the Ming period, Catholic missionaries began to be very active in China. A leading figure among the Jesuit missionaries, who played an important role, was an Italian, Matteo Ricci. When he died, there were 3,000 Christians in China.

The Jesuits used their knowledge of Western sciences to forge links with Chinese scholars, but other Catholic orders were more dogmatic and caused tension. The Chinese emperors, fed up with the squabbling, persecuted them all. In the early 1800s, Protestants began missionary activities using methods to convert people that were not always scrupulous.

The Vatican took a strong anti-Communist stance after World War II, and post-revolutionary China ordered Chinese Catholics to be no longer accountable to Rome. There has been a thaw in relations between the two in recent years, but the oft-predicted switch in relations from Taiwan to China has yet failed to materialise, with the Vatican maintaining its position that there is insufficient religious freedom in China to justify abandoning politically and religiously free Taiwan.

Religion in contemporary China

Despite the Vatican's views, there has been a significant loosening of control over people's right to worship in China, and amongst the increasingly affluent and educated elite a resurgence of interest in spiritual matters. Nevertheless, the Chinese Communist Party remains suspicious of organised religions, unless it can have a controlling hand in their appointments of clergy. This can be seen in Tibet, where there are deep divisions over Beijing-approved lamas and those approved by the Tibetan government in exile, and in the Catholic Church, which is divided between a Beijing-sanctioned order and an underground Church – the major sticking point in ongoing negotiations to normalise relations with the Vatican.

It can also be seen very clearly in Beijing's dealings with followers of the Falun Gong movement, a form of spiritual practice introduced to China in 1992 by Li Hongzhi. Based on meditative practices, Falun Gong aims to improve the

The Chinese tend to have a flexible approach to religion which is reflected in the long-running osmosis between Daoist and Buddhist faiths, as well as interaction with ancestor worship and more general superstitions.

characters of its followers through the principles of Truthfulness, Compassion and Forbearance. In 1998 the Chinese government estimated that the

movement had attracted as many as 70 million followers (the movement itself claims 100 million worldwide). Fearing it could become the kind of subversive millennial cult that plagued the closing years of the Qing dynasty, the Chinese government banned it in 1999. Since then there have been routine reports of followers being imprisoned and tortured.

In the meantime, however, Buddhist and Daoist temples have been renovated nationwide – and, in some cases, new temples constructed – partly to cater for China's fast growing tourism industry. But the proliferation of places of traditional worship in China has also resulted in a resurgence of

religious practice among ordinary Chinese unseen since the Communist Revolution. Increasingly, also, China's educated elite – particularly the creative elite – are turning to China's traditional faiths of Buddhism and Daoism, and in some cases Tibetan Buddhism, which is enjoying a resurgence of interest throughout China despite Beijing's opposition to the Dalai Lama.

It is, however, very difficult to ascertain just how many believers there are of any of China's major religions at present. China's most recent census, which was carried out in 2000, did not include questions on people's beliefs, and most Chinese are wary about providing such information due to previous crackdowns and the possibility of future ones. ❑

LEFT: there are an estimated 35,000 mosques in China.
RIGHT: a Catholic wedding in Shanghai.

CHINESE FESTIVALS

Traditional festivals in China have always served as a means of honouring the past. Many are specifically associated with ancestral worship

Most festivals in China are celebrated according to the Chinese lunar calendar: the first day of the lunar month is determined by when the moon is at its thinnest. These lunar months, of course, don't coincide with those of the Western calendar, so these festivals fall on different dates each year.

The biggest Chinese festival is the Spring Festival, or Lunar New Year, which falls in either January or February. Forget travelling and forget sightseeing during the Lunar New Year – the whole country comes to a standstill. Among the other better-known traditional Chinese festivals, the Qingming Festival on the 12th day of the third lunar month, in April, is an occasion to pay tribute to one's forebears. This festival is marked by visits to the graves of ancestors. Tombs are cleaned, hell money burnt, and food offered in honour of the departed.

The Dragon Boat Festival, on the fifth day of the fifth lunar month (usually July), commemorates the poet and loyal minister Qu Yuan, who in 278 BC drowned himself in despair and protest over his country's future. It is typically celebrated more in southern China and especially in Hong Kong, where dragon-boat races are held with much international fanfare, and celebrants eat *zong zi,* glutinous rice wrapped in lotus leaf.

The Mid-Autumn Festival, also known as the Moon Festival and occurring on the 15th day of the 8th lunar month (September or October), is celebrated today primarily by the eating of mooncakes. During the Yuan dynasty (1279–1368), when China was occupied by the Mongols from the north, the Han Chinese often communicated with each other by hiding messages inside mooncakes.

ABOVE: in July, elaborately decorated dragon boats race to the beat of loud drums. The frantic paddling represents the desperate actions of Qu Yuan's friends as they try to save him from drowning *(see left,*

RIGHT: beautifully decorated mooncakes for the Mid-Autumn Festival. Fillings vary but are usually a rich mixture of sugar, egg yolk and bean paste; they are best when accompanied by Chinese tea.

ABOVE: as well as national festivals, colourful local events are held throughout the country, such as those of the Miao people in Guizhou.
RIGHT: National Day on 1 October marks the founding of the People's Republic in 1949 with parades, fireworks and concerts.

BRINGING IN THE LUNAR NEW YEAR

The Chinese celebrate their new year according to the lunar calendar, the actual date in the Gregorian calendar falling in January or February.

In China, this festival is more popularly known as *chun jie*, or Spring Festival. It is by far the biggest and most important of Chinese festivals, and it is the only traditional festival to merit a public holiday.

Celebrations, which begin on the eve of the new year with a family reunion dinner, typically last four days, during which much of China shuts down. Tradition holds that the *cai shen* (fortune god) leaves for the heavens on new year's eve to give a report of a family's actions during the past year. He returns on the fifth day of the new year to bestow fortune, so many stores and businesses will reopen on the fifth day. *Hong bao* (red packets, known as *lai see* in Cantonese) filled with money are usually given to the young and old as people visit their relatives and friends to usher in the new.

Nowadays, the festive parades, dragon dances and fireworks are more common in the countryside and in Chinatowns around the world than in large cities in China. In Beijing, people celebrate by attending *miao hui* (temple gatherings), which are really social gatherings in a large park.

RIGHT: Chinese festivals can have a religious element, such as those honouring Guanyin, Goddess of Mercy and protector of women and children.

BELOW: the Spring Festival dragon dance in Hong Kong: the dragon is held aloft by a group of performers, who walk in set patterns so that the dragon appears to be flying.

TRADITIONAL MEDICINE

For millennia, the old-fashioned Chinese methods of caring for and treating the body have worked just fine. Can a billion people be wrong?

The mention of traditional Chinese medicine often conjures up images of magical needles, aromatic herbs and strange animal parts. Yet, despite its exotic stereotype, traditional Chinese medicine is increasingly gaining respect from both scientists and the general public in the West.

In China, scepticism and debate arose as to the value of traditional medicine during the first half of the 20th century. Intellectual and political groups, such as the Nationalists and Marxists, were particularly disapproving, and the medical establishment suffered greatly at their hands. After the founding of the People's Republic of China, competition between Western and Chinese medicine was eradicated for practical as well as ideological reasons, with an attempt to integrate the two systems.

This approach has persisted, and today medical care in China often consists of a mixture of both Western and traditional Chinese medicine, although Western-style medicine, or *xiyi*, tends to be domi-

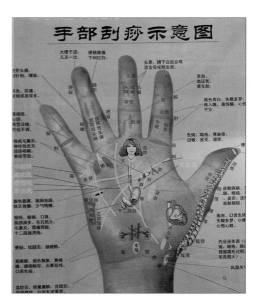

Yin-yang philosophy and the theory of five elements form a system of categories that explain the complex relationships between parts of the body and the environment.

nant. Large public hospitals *(renmin yiyuan)* in cities across the country offer both traditional Chinese and Western approaches to medical treatment. Hospitals dealing exclusively with traditional Chinese medicine, or *zhongyi*, tend to be smaller, less well equipped and harder to find.

The Chinese will usually visit a doctor trained in Western medicine if they feel that they are seriously ill and need to be treated quickly. If the problem is not too serious or urgent, the patient will most likely seek out a traditional doctor, who can better restore harmony to the body.

Historical roots

Traditional Chinese medicine, as practised today and in past centuries, is based upon an array of theories and practices from both foreign and native sources. Some argue that Chinese medicine can trace its roots back as far as 5,000 years to the time of Shennong, a divine farmer credited with the discovery of medicinal herbs. Historical writer Liu Shu reported that "Shennong tasted hundreds of herbs himself... some days as many as 70 poisonous herbs in one day". The validity of that statement is surely one to be debated, but *Shennong Bencaojing* (Shennong's Classic on

Materia Medica) describes the medicinal effects of some 365 herbs and is the earliest known text of its kind.

Another early text, which continues to be a cornerstone in the Chinese medical canon, is *Huangdi Neijing* (The Yellow Emperor's Canon of Interior Medicine). While authorship is unknown, its present-day version is believed to have been compiled between the 2nd century BC and 8th century AD, and later revised during the Song dynasty (960–1279). Over the centuries, volumes upon volumes of commentary have been written about this ancient text. Its influence remains important, as the main principles of Chinese medicine are still based on theories first set forth by it.

Key principles

Several main concepts are essential to understanding traditional Chinese medicine. Holism, or the concept that parts of a human body form an integral, connected and inseparable whole, is one of the main distinguishing features of traditional Chinese medicine. Whereas Western medicine tends to treat symptoms in a direct fashion, traditional Chinese medicine examines illnesses in the context of a whole.

The *yin-yang* philosophy is at the heart of Chinese medicinal practice. *Yin* and *yang* represent two opposite sides in nature such as hot and cold, or light and dark. Each of the different organs is said to have *yin* or *yang* characteristics. Balance between the two is vital for maintaining health. The five elements – earth, fire, water, metal and wood – are categories of characteristics into which all known phenomena can be classified. For example, just as water subdues fire, phenomena associated with water are said to control those classified under fire.

The pharmacy

A traditional Chinese apothecary has a unique smell made up of thousands of scents emanating from jars and cabinets stocked full of dried plants, seeds, animal parts and minerals. Among them are the well-known ginseng roots, dried or immersed in alcohol. You will also recognise the acupuncture needles and the cupping glasses made of glass or bamboo.

LEFT: diagram of the pressure points in the hand.
RIGHT: Chinese medicine store in Western District, Hong Kong.

One of the most famous Chinese apothecaries is the legendary Tongrentang pharmacy, in an old part of Beijing, which has been in business for over 300 years. It was once a royal dispensary during the Qing dynasty and still produces all the pills and secret concoctions once used by royalty. The size of this pharmacy is overwhelming, as is the selection of remedies: small and large eggs, snakes coiled in spirals, dried monkeys, toads, tortoises, grasshoppers, fish, octopuses, stag antlers, rhinoceros horns and the genitalia of various unfortunate – and sometimes endangered – animals. And then there are the myriad kinds of dried and preserved herbs, blossoms, roots, berries, mushrooms and fruits.

MEDICINAL FOODS

Diet is fundamental to the philosophy of traditional medicine. China's herbalists attribute medicinal value to various foods; indeed, the distinction between food and treatment is often blurred. Consider three traditional delicacies: shark's fin, abalone and bird's nest. These are exquisite parts of an extensive cuisine, eaten in part for their sensory delights. Yet each is claimed to have medicinal value. Shark's fin, for example, is said to benefit internal organs, including the heart and kidneys. Abalone calms internal organs; moreover, it regulates the liver and reduces dizziness and high blood pressure. Bird's nest, usually taken as a soup, cleanses the blood and assures a clear complexion.

Acupuncture

The popularity of acupuncture outside China has made it nearly synonymous for many Westerners with all traditional Chinese medicine. Not meant as a cure for everything, acupuncture has nonetheless enjoyed renewed interest in recent decades,

The Western medical community may still remain sceptical about the efficacy of Chinese medicine, but over a billion people, including increasing numbers in the West, find that it works for them.

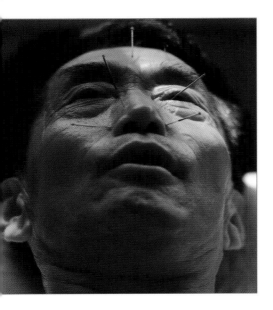

and is especially effective in controlling pain.

The practice of acupuncture is based on a theory of channels or meridians by which "influences" flow through the body. The flow of positive influences through the body is vital in maintaining health. Unhealthy symptoms are, in fact, manifestations of improper *qi*, the essence of life. The *Huangdi Neijing* describes 365 sensitive points used in acupuncture, in addition to 12 main conduits in the human body. Executed properly, acupuncture should be relatively painless.

Many countries are still somewhat reluctant to accept acupuncture as part of an alternative approach to medicine. However, it is increasingly accepted as a treatment by many Western physicians, particularly for pain relief. While Western-

ers may rely on drugs to moderate physical pain, the Chinese go to the acupuncturist. Many cases of back pain, for example, can be relieved by acupuncture. Chronic problems, however, require a longer healing process.

There is also a system of ear acupuncture, performed without needles. Small, round seed kernels are stuck onto certain points of the ear and massaged by the patient every so often. This method is not only very successful in the treatment of pain, but is also said to relieve some allergies, such as hay fever.

An acupuncture clinic often smells similar to a pharmacy. This is the typical smell of the *moxa* herb, or mugwort. It is considered especially helpful in the treatment of illnesses that, in Chinese medical terminology, are classified as "cold"; for example, stomach and digestive complaints without fever, certain rheumatic illnesses, chronic pains in the back, and cramped shoulders and neck. The mugwort is formed into small cones and placed on slices of fresh ginger; then it is allowed to grow slowly. The plant is then placed onto the acupuncture point in a process known as moxibustion.

Exercise

On any early morning in China, millions of people, most of them elderly, gather in parks to exercise. There are several types of traditional exercise that are regarded not only as ways to take care of one's body, but also as therapy.

The most common type of exercise is *taijiquan* (Supreme Ultimate Boxing), which is in fact a martial art. Another, perhaps less familiar to Westerners, is *qigong*, which is often translated as "breath skill". *Qigong*, in fact, plays a large part in the practice of *taijiquan*. With certain exercises, which may or may not involve conscious breathing, the patient learns to control *qi* – a person's vital energy – and to influence the course of an illness. It is claimed that those who have mastered *qigong* can walk outdoors in sub-zero temperatures without sufficient clothing and remain oblivious to the cold.

During the Cultural Revolution, *qigong* (along with many martial arts) was actually forbidden because it too closely resembled "superstitious" practices. Yet, in 1980, new *qigong* groups sprang up throughout the country. Today, an estimated 70 million people in China practise *qigong* on a daily basis, and the therapy has also developed a dedicated following in the West. ❑

LEFT: acupuncture stimulates pressure points.

The Animal Trade

Across the globe, respect for and patronage of Chinese medicine continues to spread, yet this growing interest has a darker side

The use of animal parts for medicine is not new. The Chinese have been using them for well over 1,000 years. The practice spread from China to other countries such as Korea and Japan, and to other parts of the world with significant East Asian populations.

The result is that some species, already suffering from the loss of habitat due to the intensive industrial and economic growth of many Asian countries, none more so than China itself, are now being pushed to the brink of extinction by the increased demand for their body parts.

The demand for tiger parts, for example, threatens the survival of the world's five remaining sub-species of this magnificent feline. Various parts of the tiger are employed in traditional medicine: eyeballs are used to treat epilepsy; the tail for various skin diseases; the bile for convulsions in children; whiskers for toothaches; and the brain for laziness and pimples. Yet of all tiger parts, it is the bones that are most valued; they are often used to treat rheumatism, weakness, stiffness or paralysis. Tigers have vanished from many of their natural habitats in Asia and, without radical intervention, they may disappear completely from the wild in less than a decade.

Tigers aren't the only victims on the trade in animal parts. Rhinoceros, bear and even shark populations are also rapidly shrinking. Rhinoceros horn has a reputation for being an aphrodisiac, and the

number of rhinoceros in the wild is falling. Without assistance, they too could be extinct within a decade or two. Bears from Asia and North America are also under threat, since their paws are believed to have medicinal value.

Shark's fin, though not used exclusively for medicine, is a highly sought-after delicacy. Served most commonly as shark's fin soup, this broth is believed to benefit the internal organs. In certain areas, the shark population – essential to the ecosystem, as the shark is the top predator – is on the decline.

Human populations and disposable incomes have increased dramatically in East Asia in gen-

eral, and in China in particular, along with a resurgence of interest in traditional cures. Use of certain traditional medicines is often seen as a status symbol, and as a way of holding on to traditional customs amidst the whirlwind of social and economic changes. While the effectiveness of these endangered animal products is still disputed, researchers today are confirming the benefits to health of the active ingredients present in many Chinese prescriptions. But as endangered animal populations contine to decline to the point of extinction, the use of their parts to feed an ever-growing demand is no longer sustainable. What is clear is that the trade in endangered animal parts for medicine must stop. This means finding an alternative to alternative medicine. ❑

ABOVE: medicinal ingredients come from a range of animals. **RIGHT:** there is a high demand for tiger parts.

CHINESE LITERATURE

The complexities of Chinese literature, beginning with the thoughts of Confucius in the 5th century BC, are challenging and inspiring. That is to be expected after 25 centuries of creativity

China has a long and venerable tradition in the written word. Whilst it is true that vernacular literature did not fully take shape as an art form until the 14th-century Yuan dynasty, the history of literature in the Middle Kingdom goes back to far earlier times, and sophisticated poetry was in evidence by the early Tang period (7th century AD). Perhaps the most famous of these ancient works are the thoughts of Confucius (551–479 BC), collected by his disciples into his famous *Lunyu* (Analects), a work that underpins the Confucian moral code – a long-lasting pillar of Chinese society.

Poetry

The earliest existing collection of poems is the *Shijing* (a book of odes). It is said that more than 3,000 songs were collected, of which Confucius selected 300, cutting out the saucier entries; he then compiled them in the *Shijing*. The contents of the odes are wide-ranging: love songs, songs

The writings of Confucius have profoundly influenced Chinese culture. Confucianism is more a moral code for society than a religious philosophy, though Confucius is sometimes worshipped as a deity.

about the land and songs glorifying outstanding personalities or personal qualities.

Poems in the lyrical or epic style play an extremely important part in Chinese literature. To be able to read and write poetry was part of the elementary education of the higher social classes. Students and civil servants of any rank or age were expected to be able to write a poem for any occasion. Girls and women who knew how to recite poems graciously were ensured the admiration of

the opposite sex. The *Chuci*, another collection of songs, comes from the south of China: its creation is attributed to the poet Qu Yuan (*c.* 322–295 BC).

The Tang dynasty (618–907) marked the golden age of Chinese poetry. No other period in history has produced such a great number of poets and epic works. *Quan Tangshi*, the vast collection of Tang poetry, contains nearly 50,000 compositions by 2,200 poets. One of the most famous wordsmiths of the time was Li Bai (699–762), who is said to have written his best-known poems in a state of total inebriation. The poet Du Fu (712–70) was a friend of Li Bai's, though his style is very different. He held office at the court for just a short time and was forced to flee due to political upheavals. He then led an unsettled, wandering life for a long time, eventually settling in Chengdu, where one can still visit the straw hut, Du Fu Caotang, that served as his home *(see page 350)*.

It is hard to say which of the two poets has better survived the passage of time. Li Bai was a natural talent, humorous, devoted to nature and close to the Daoists. Du Fu became a poet mainly through diligence. Bold and serious, his concerns about social issues were closely linked to Confucian ideas.

Fictional classics

Every child in China knows the novel *Journey to the West (Xiyouji* in pinyin) and its famous heroes: the monkey king Sun Wukong; a pig, Zhu Bajie;

A LI BAI SAMPLER

Li Bai, known to appreciate a good stiff drink, was the Tang dynasty's most beloved poet.

Moonlight gleams before my bed,
Like frost on the floor.
Lifting my head I see the bright moon,
Lowering my head I think of my old home.

At Yellow Crane Tower, I said goodbye to an old friend.
It was the third month, the season of flowers, when
you went down to Yangzhou.
Your solitary sail has become a
distant blue dot, and all I saw was the Yangzi flowing
into the sky.

We are but travellers on the world's horizons.
Meeting thus in a common fate, what does
acquaintance matter?

---

the river demon, Sha; and the Buddhist pilgrim and monk, Xuanzang. The novel recounts the adventures of the monkey king, who, together with the other characters, accompanies Xuanzang on a pilgrimage to India, in order to collect Buddhist scriptures. The story is closely tied in with Chinese popular religion, and includes Daoist and Buddhist deities. Its popularity can be explained by this familiarity and the fact that it combines exciting adventure with the themes of morality and spiritual purpose.

The *Shuihuzhuan* (The Water Margin, also known as Outlaws of the Marsh), whose origins are unclear,

---

LEFT: the ancient poet Qu Yuan, who lived in the 4th century BC. **RIGHT:** Shanghai's Library Biblioteca.

is a novel about thieves dating from the Ming period. The story is partly based upon historical facts about the robber Song Jiang and his companions, who wandered through what is now the province of Shandong around the end of the Northern Song dynasty (960–1127). Just like Robin Hood and his merry men, Song Jiang and his followers fought injustices according to their code of honour. They finally submitted to the imperial doctrine and fought against rebels who were threatening the state system.

The Water Margin is said to have been Mao Zedong's favourite book, although during the time of the Cultural Revolution, it was considered a negative illustration of capitulation.

Genre novels

The epitome of the genre novel is *Jinpingmei* (The Plum Blossom in a Golden Vase), written in the Ming dynasty. *Jinpingmei* portrays people as individual characters, realistically describing the many amorous adventures of its hero, Ximen. This novel conveys a very precise portrayal of social conditions in the 16th century. In 1687, Emperor Kangxi banned the book, yet it continued to be read, and in 1708 it was even translated into Manchurian. It was again censored in 1789 and once more in 1949.

Hongloumeng (Dream of the Red Chamber), written by Cao Xueqin in the 18th century, is considered to be the most complete genre novel. Its central character is Jia Baoyu, the amorous and

> *The oldest Chinese books were written on strips of bamboo, fixed together like a roller blind. This helps to explain why traditional writing runs from top to bottom and from right to left.*

sentimental son of a high-ranking official. The novel relates the rise and fall of the house of Jia, a distinguished Manchu family, in intricate detail.

Post-imperial literature

The political and cultural May Fourth Movement of 1919 heralded drastic social changes. Among other things, it aimed at reforming the use of clas-

sical language in literature, and prose literature became increasingly regarded as a means for social change. The leading proponent of this new vernacular prose was the writer Lu Xun, who believed China needed to modernise through revolution. His satirical novella *The True Story of Ah Q* is considered to be a masterpiece of modern Chinese literature. Ding Ling was one of a large group of women writers that emerged during the May Fourth Movement. In *Miss Sophia's Diary*, she evokes the lifestyle of her female contemporaries through the observations of an unhappy young woman.

The 1920s and '30s were a period of literary productivity in China. One of the most prominent writers of the time was Ba Jin. His best-known work, *The Family,* written in the tradition of *Hongloumeng*, relates the decline of a civil servant's family at the beginning of the 20th century.

Another key figure to emerge during the period was Guo Muruo (1892–1978), one of the founders of the Creation Society which championed a romantic style of writing. A dedicated Marxist, Guo went on to become an influential figure in the rise of communism in China – in fact he was one of many writers of the early 20th century sympathetic to the cause. Their literature became increasingly politicised, dealing with real rather than imagined events and glorifying communism. After Mao Zedong's speech on art and literature, in Yan'an in 1942, Social Realism was established as the only legitimate art form.

In 1956, during the Hundred Flowers Movement *(see page 52)*, liberalist writers and intellectuals expressed dissatisfaction with the policies of the Communist Party, protesting in particular against the lack of artistic freedom. They were branded as rightists, and their works labelled as "poisonous weeds". In the following decade the Cultural Revolution brought all literary endeavours to a halt: for a time, Chinese Opera was deemed the only acceptable form of cultural expression.

A new age

The end of the Maoist era in 1976 marked a resurgence of writing, focusing on the traumas caused by the Cultural Revolution. Lu Xinghua's work *Scar* gave the term "literature of the wounded" to this new literary form, itself part of the so-called New Realism, which typically looked at society's imperfections and the abuses of power.

The 1980s saw a burst of literary creativity in new writing techniques. Around 2,000 novels were published between 1979 and the early 1990s (compared with a total of 320 between 1949 and 1966). Today, however, writers still skirt issues that may draw criticism from the authorities, and much literary creativity is muffled by state censorship. Gao Xingjian, a Chinese writer in exile whose novel *Soul Mountain* won the 2000 Nobel Prize for Literature, has been cold-shouldered by Beijing. Other writers turn to safe topics, such as sentimental love stories and martial-arts sagas. Nevertheless, countless underground publishers and printers still thrive in China and the officially unapproved works of contemporary authors continue to circulate. ❏

LEFT: the Lu Xun Museum in Beijing.

Cinema in China

Over the past three decades, Chinese cinema has captured the imagination of film buffs around the world

ilm – literally "electric shadow play" in Chinese appeared in China in the early 20th century. The first silent movies, including the first "kung fu" films, were made in Shanghai, the centre of Chinese cinema. When the Communists took over, all films, apart from Socialist Realist propaganda, were banned. Then the Cultural Revolution brought film-making to a standstill, apart from a few socialist "model operas".

It wasn't until 1978 that the Beijing Film Academy re-opened its doors to students. A new generation of film-

makers, known as the Fifth Generation, developed individual forms of expression, moulded by the experiences of forced labour and political terror. Chen Kaige's debut *Yellow Earth* (1984) portrays the failure of those who rebel against authority and laments the failure of China's liberation through Communism. Other Fifth Generation films examined the destructive forces of power and tradition with landmark films like Zhang Yimou's

ABOVE: Gong Li in *Raise the Red Lantern.* **ABOVE RIGHT:** a scene from *The House of the Flying Daggers.*

Judou (1989) and *Raise the Red Lantern (1991)*, and Chen Kaige's *Farewell My Concubine (1993)*.

The subsequent Sixth Generation of film-makers have produced grittier, more realistic films, dwelling on urban desolation and the negative impact of China's economic growth. One of the movement's pioneers, Zhang Yuan, dealt with such taboo themes as homosexuality (*East Palace West Palace*, 1996), and he later achieved commercial success with the poignant *Little Red Flowers* in 2006. Other leading directors of this genre, often likened to Italian neo-realism, are Wang Xiaoshuai (*Beijing Bicycle*, 2001), Li Yang (*Blind Shaft*, 2003) and Jia Zhangke (*The World*, 2004 and *Still Life* – winner of the 2006 Golden Lion in Venice).

Chinese-language films are increasingly reaching mainstream audiences abroad. After the success of *Sense and Sensibility* (1995), Taiwanese director Ang Lee's went on to make *Crouching Tiger, Hidden Dragon* (2001), which was a big box-office hit around the world – despite being received rather poorly in China itself. His latest spy thriller *Lust, Caution* (2007) won him a second Golden Lion award.

Another dazzling martial-arts epic (the genre is known as *wuxia*), Zhang Yimou's *Hero* (2002) was met with rave reviews in the West. He followed it up two years later with *House of the Flying Daggers*. Most recently Yimou choreographed the lavish (and hugely expensive) opening ceremony of the 2008 Beijing Olympics.

Hong Kong cinema is known for its hard-man actors such as Chow Yun Fat and Jackie Chan, a household name the world over, and superstar Maggie Cheung. Apart from fast-action and martial-arts films, independent productions such as Wong Kar-wai's tender and violent *Chungking Express*, set in Hong Kong and starring Faye Wong, have found an international audience.

The Beijing Film Academy continues to turn out innovative film-makers such as Liu Jiayin, whose first film, *Oxhide* (2004), about the effect of China's fast-changing society on her family, won many plaudits on the international festival circuit. ❑

CHINESE OPERA

The emphasis in Chinese opera is on Confucian ethics and morality. Stories invariably have endings in which goodness is upheld and evil is punished

Although Chinese theatre in the form of skits, vaudeville, puppet shows and shadow plays has existed since the Tang dynasty (618–907), formal music-drama had its origins in the Yuan period (1279–1368), when scholars who were displaced from their government positions by the foreign Mongols turned to writing dramas in which songs often alternated with dialogue.

Since then, opera has evolved into one of the most popular forms of mass entertainment in China, and although there are reckoned to be more than 300 different styles, all share some general characteristics. Plots are based on legends or folklore with which audiences are familiar, and performances are a composite of different art forms – such as literature, song, dance and mime, as well as the martial arts. Costumes and make-up are symbolic, helping the audience to understand the various roles and personalities of the cast. Time is marked with the aid of a redwood clapper that produces a high-pitched clicking sound when struck. The flute, with its wide-ranging melodies, is the primary instrument.

Styles of regional opera include *chaozhou* (Teochew) opera, the puppet operas of Fujian, and the *bangzi xi* (clapper operas), which are popular in Shaanxi and the northern part of China, and which feature as their main accompaniment a datewood clapper struck with a stick.

By far the most popular Chinese opera, however, is the highly stylised *jingxi* (Beijing or Peking opera), which dates from the 1800s. The accompanying musical instrument in Beijing opera is usually the *huqin*, a Chinese fiddle, although cymbals are sometimes, but not always, employed in action scenes.

ABOVE: whether in soliloquies, spoken verse, songs or dialogue, the words used in Beijing opera are almost always colloquial – its intend audience has always been the common people. Performances often t place on streets and in market places and were a useful way for peop to learn about life beyond their day-to-day existence.

VISITING THE OPERA

A visit to the Chinese opera is a relaxed though occasionally quite noisy experience; formal dress is not the norm. Be warned, however, that this exotic art form doesn't appeal to everyone: once you've got over the visual spectacle of the elaborate costumes and startling make-up, you might find the strangled singing style, the atonal music and the complex plot too much to take for a whole performance – and performances can be long. Of course, a good grasp of the language enhances the experience (although some theatres provide subtitles in English). *See Travel Tips, pages 451–2, for a list of venues in major cities.*

ABOVE: the elaborate costumes are based on those of the court of the Han, Tang, Song and Ming dynasties, although they are symbolic rather than realistic. All actors must hone the fine body movements that are an essential part of every style of opera.

RIGHT: colours are highly symbolic. Red make-up on a male character indicates bravery and loyalty, while white denotes a powerful villain. Clowns have their own special make-up, often with a white patch on the tip of the nose to indicate wit or playfulness. The female role *(dan)* is usually played by a man wearing white make-up with various shades of carmine.

TOP: the epic tales of the Monkey King are one of Chinese opera's classic works. The adventures of the cunning, boisterous hero are brought to life with a dazzling display of acrobatics, music, puppetry and vibrant costumes.

BELOW: to get the most out of Chinese opera, it helps to know something of its conventions. Changes in time and place are evoked through speech, action and ritualised use of props. Walking in a circle symbolises a journey; circling the stage with a whip indicates riding a horse. English subtitles are provided in some theatres in Beijing and Shanghai.

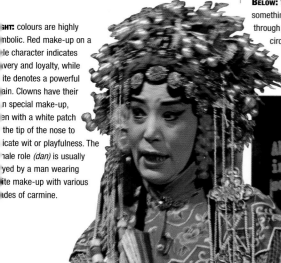

ARTS AND CRAFTS

With its long history and inward-looking tradition, China has developed and refined a resplendent catalogue of fine arts and exquisite crafts

From very early times, Chinese artisans dazzled the world with technical brilliance and innovation, and today, Chinese arts and crafts are renowned the world over. Since the 1950s, China has attempted to revive the traditional and native arts. Research institutes were established in craft centres to continue the tradition of the crafts, as well as to make further technical advancements. Promising young talent is recruited from around the country for training in specialised schools.

Painting and calligraphy

There has always been a close connection between Chinese painting and calligraphy. Ancient Chinese words started as pictograms, and while each has developed in a separate direction, there have nonetheless remained inextricable ties between the two. As a rule, classical Chinese painters have extensive training in calligraphy, while calligraphers have experience in painting. Both forms are created with the same brushes and are often present together in one piece of work.

In fact, what separated and elevated the status

Calligraphy has always been important to the Chinese as a marker of an individual's intelligence and social status. Mastery of the art form has always been closely linked with the attainment of knowledge.

of painting from other crafts was its similarity to calligraphy. Both calligraphy and painting are considered scholarly pursuits and have grand and esteemed traditions, but calligraphy has been held in higher regard. Literati painters, for example, judged works by their combination of painting, poetry and calligraphy. Success in all three areas

deemed paintings to be art. According to such standards, paintings and other art forms that lacked calligraphy were merely crafts, regardless of their level of technical brilliance.

For the Chinese, the written word is the carrier of culture, and the difficulty of learning written Chinese ensured the high social status of the scholar-gentry class. Mastery of writing and calligraphy was highly esteemed. Furthermore, despite the numerous spoken dialects in China, Chinese writing has maintained its single standard and style (apart from the presence of traditional, or

ABOVE: an example of the classic Chinese painting style. **RIGHT:** calligraphy brushes.
FAR RIGHT: a calligrapher at work.

full-form, Chinese characters in Hong Kong and Macau). This nationwide unifying and historically continuous script was therefore always more important than the spoken language.

Classical Chinese painting

Painting is learnt in much the same way as writing: by copying old masters or textbooks. Once developed, a particular painting style is rarely lost or abandoned, and is preserved in the painting canon.

Classical Chinese paintings can be grouped into six general categories: landscapes, portraits, flowers and birds, bamboo and stone, animals, and palaces or other buildings. Art connoisseurs later added four more groups: religious paintings, barbarians and foreign tribes, dragons and fish, and vegetables and fruits.

One of the most favoured painting forms in China since the Tang dynasty (618–907) is landscape painting. Called "mountain water paintings" in Chinese, this style features mountains and water most prominently, accented with clouds, mist and trees. By contrast, human figures are small specks in the landscape and lack the detail lavished on the vegetation, water and mountain. These proportions reflect Chinese philosophies on the relationship between individuals and the outside

TOOLS FOR THE JOB: THE FOUR TREASURES OF THE STUDY

Writing and painting utensils are referred to in China as the Four Treasures of the Study. They consist of the brush, ink, rubbing stone (or ink stone), and paper – tools held in high esteem by poets, scholars and painters.

Brushes are made with bamboo and various kinds of animal hair such as rabbit's fur, horsehair and even mouse whiskers, and come in a wide variety of sizes. Some brush tips are treated with glue to give them a stiff tip.

Ink was traditionally made from the soot of coniferous resin with the addition of glue. Ink in solid form, pressed into the shape of slabs, bars or prisms, is used both for writing and painting, and although liquid ink is now available, its use removes one of the more contemplative and ritualistic aspects of traditional Chinese painting, in which one first drips water onto a rubbing stone, then rubs the ink stick on it. The resulting ink is an intense black, but can be diluted to the lightest of greys as necessary. Ink of good quality has perfume added – musk in former days, but cloves are now commonly used.

Silk was once the standard of professional and court painters, as it gave better control over graded ink and colour washes, but scholar-painters preferred paper for its immediate response to the brush. Itself another ancient Chinese invention, developed by Cai Lun and used from the 2nd century AD onwards – paper is now produced in different qualities, offering the painter varying absorption and texture.

world. Unlike Western paintings, in which humans are central subjects and natural environments are rendered as backdrops, Chinese paintings show people as subservient to or a small part of their surroundings.

Chinese paintings are abstract and do not aim for realism. The best paintings successfully capture the spirit or essence of a subject. Furthermore, a painter is considered a master of his art when the necessary brush strokes for a bird, chrysanthemum or waterfall flow effortlessly from his hand. Chinese painting values quick execution. Indeed, the nature of the materials and brush techniques do not allow for careful sketch-

ing or repainting; mistakes cannot be hidden or painted over.

This strong emphasis on perfection quickly leads to specialisation by painters on particular subjects. In this way, for instance, Xu Beihong (1895–1953) became known as the painter of horses, just as Qi Bai-Shi (1862–1957) was famous for his shrimps.

A feature of the presentation of paintings is the scroll. After being painted on silk or paper, the painting is backed with stronger paper and mounted on a long roll of silk or brocade. Then a wooden stick is attached at the lower end (or left end, if the scroll is to be displayed horizontally). Typically, the picture was stored away rolled up and brought out only on special occasions, to be

slowly unfurled and revealing only parts of a scene that were pieced together in the mind of the observer, subtly drawing him into the picture. Whether vertically or horizontally, pictures were rarely displayed for long.

Silk

Calligraphy, painting, poetry and music are regarded in China as noble arts, the knowledge of which was required of any scholar. By contrast, applied arts such as silk and carving are considered merely honourable crafts, performed by craftsmen and gentlewomen. All the same, in the West these skilled crafts have always held a special fascination.

The cultivation of the silkworm is said to go back to the 3rd century BC. The planting of mulberry trees and raising of silkworms is credited to Fuxi, a legendary figure of prehistoric China. For centuries, silk held the place of currency: civil servants and officers as well as foreign envoys were frequently paid or presented with bales of silk. The precious material was transported to the Middle East and the Roman empire, mostly via the Silk Road.

The Chinese maintained a monopoly on silk until about 200 BC, when the secret of its manufacture became known in Korea and Japan. In the West – in this case the Byzantine empire – such knowledge was acquired only in the 6th century AD. The Chinese had long prohibited the export of silkworm eggs and the dissemination of knowledge of their cultivation, but a monk is said to have succeeded in smuggling – an offence punishable by death – some of the prized quarry to the West.

Today's centres of silk production are concentrated around the cities of Hangzhou, Suzhou and Wuxi, where silk can be bought at a lower price. Hangzhou has the largest silk industry in the People's Republic, while in Suzhou, silk embroidery has been brought to the highest artistic level.

Porcelain

The Chinese invented porcelain sometime in the 7th century. The history of Chinese ceramics, however, goes back to Neolithic times. Along the Huang He (Yellow River) and Chang Jiang (Yangzi), 7,000- to 8,000-year-old ceramic vessels – red and even black clay with comb and rope

LEFT: calligraphy for sale in a Lilichang shop, Beijing.
RIGHT: 18th-century turquoise-glazed vase.
FAR RIGHT: jade, China's most popular precious stone.

patterns – have been found. The Yangshao and Longshan cultures of the 5th to 2nd millennium BC developed new types of vessels in a diversity of patterns in red, black, and brown. Quasi-human masks, stylised fish, and hard, thin-walled stoneware, with kaolin and lime feldspar glazes, were created. Later, light-grey stoneware with green glazes, known as *yue* ware – named after the kilns of the town of Yuezhou – were designs of the Han period (206 BC–AD 220). During the Tang dynasty, Chinese porcelain was known in Europe and the Middle East.

The most widespread form of ancient Chinese porcelain was celadon, the product of a blending

of iron oxide with the glaze that resulted, during firing, in a green tone. *Sancai* ceramics, with three-colour glazes from the Tang dynasty, became world-famous. The colours were mostly strong green, yellow and brown. *Sancai* ceramics were also found among the tomb figurines of the Tang period in the shape of horses, camels, guardians in animal or human form, ladies of the court, and officials. The Song-period celadons – ranging in colour from pale or moss green, pale blue or pale grey to brown tones – were also technically excellent. As early as the Yuan period, a technique from the Near East was used for under-glaze painting in cobalt blue, commonly known as Ming porcelain (*Qinghua* in Chinese). Some common themes seen throughout the Ming period

were figures, landscapes and theatrical scenes. At the beginning of the Qing dynasty, blue-and-white porcelain attained its highest level of quality.

Once patronised by imperial courts, Jingdezhen (Jiangxi province) has been the centre of porcelain manufacture since the 14th century. Today, however, relatively inexpensive porcelain can be bought throughout China. Antique pieces are still hard to come by, as the sale of articles predating the Opium Wars is prohibited by the Chinese government.

Jade

Jade is China's most precious stone and one of the earliest art forms to reach a superior level of

achievement. According to a Chinese creation myth, when the god Pan Gu died, his breath became the wind and clouds, his muscles became soil, and the marrow of his bones jade and pearls. Chinese valued the stone for its beauty as well as for attributed magical powers. In early times, jade was used for ritual and religious purposes, but later it came to be used for ornamentation and other aesthetic purposes.

The oldest jades so far discovered come from the Neolithic Hemadu culture about 7,000 years ago. The finds are presumed to be ritual objects. Many small circular plates called *bi*, given to the dead to take with them, have been found. These round discs represent the harmony between heaven and earth. Even today, many Chinese wear these types of discs.

Jade was believed to have preserving powers and, consequently, burial suits were made with the precious stone. The Han dynasty probably saw an early peak in jade carving. During this time, the corpses of high-ranking officials were clothed in suits made of more than 1,000 thin slivers of jade sewn together with gold wire. The Hebei Provincial Museum in Shijiazhuang displays the jade suits of Prince Liu Sheng and his wife. It is said that jade glows with the vitality of the owner. If the owner became ill, for example, the jade would become tarnished. Jade ornaments were believed to impart good health, luck, and offer protection.

Jade is not a precise mineralogical entity, but rather comprises two minerals, jadeite and nephrite. The former is more valuable because of its translucence and hardness, as well as its rarity. Nephrite is similar to jadeite, but not quite as hard. Colours vary from white to green, but also black, brown and red. The Chinese value a clear, emerald-green stone most highly. Jade is an especially difficult material to shape due to its hardness.

In the jade-carving workshops of present-day China, there are thought to be as many as 30 kinds of jade in use. Famous among the jade workshops are those in Hetian (also called Khotan; Xinjiang), Shoushan (Fujian) and Luoyang (Hunan).

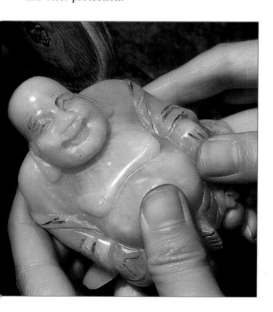

BUYING ANTIQUES IN CHINA

It is fairly standard practice to bargain when purchasing antiques in China, although don't try to bargain in the state-owned stores. It is essential to check that the official red seal of the shop is on the item, which allows it to be exported (antiques that date from before 1795 cannot be taken out of the country). Beware of fakes, as the fabrication of new "antiques" – and the official red seal – is a thriving industry. Avoid anything made from ivory or other illegal animal products. Apart from the moral issues, most Western countries ban imports.

In government shops, jade can be trusted to be genuine. On the open market and in private shops, however, caution is advised. Genuine jade always feels cool and cannot be scratched with a knife. Quality depends on the feel of the stone, its colour, transparency, pattern, and other factors. (If in doubt, a reputable expert should be consulted.)

Lacquerware

The oldest finds of lacquered objects date back to the Warring States Period (403–221 BC). At that time, lacquerware was an everyday material: bowls, tins, boxes, vases and furniture made of various materials (wood, bamboo, wicker, leather, metal, clay, textiles, paper) were often coated with a skin of lacquer. Emperor Qianlong (1735–96) had a special liking for carved lacquerware; he was buried in a coffin carved and preserved using this technique.

The glossy sheen of lacquerware is not only attractive but also strong and lightweight. The bark of the lacquer tree, which grows in central and southern China, exudes a milky sap when cut, which solidifies in moist air, then dries and turns brown. This dry layer of lacquer is impervious to moisture, acid and scratches, and is therefore ideal protection for materials such as wood or bamboo.

To make lacquerware, a base coat is applied to a core material, followed by extremely thin layers of

the finest lacquer that, after drying in dust-free moist air, are smoothed and polished. If soot or vinegar-soaked iron filings are added to the lacquer, it will dry into a black colour; cinnabar turns it red.

The contemporary art scene

Over the last several years, China has become the hottest thing on the international art scene, with pieces by Chinese artists – many of them still banned as late as the mid-1990s – fetching millions of dollars both in international and domestic auctions. Zhang Xiaogang was one of the first to

FAR LEFT: jade Buddha. LEFT: carved lacquer plate from the 18th century. ABOVE AND RIGHT: street and gallery art in Beijing's "798" district.

attract worldwide attention when his *A Big Family* sold for US$1.5 million at a 2006 Christie's auction in London, followed by US$2.3 million for *Tiananmen Square* in Hong Kong. In the same year, paintings that not long ago would have been deemed too controversial to be aired were selling for international prices in Beijing. A good example is that of Liu Xiaodong, whose *Newly Displaced Population* – a work critical of the resettlement of more than 1 million people to make way for the Three Gorges Dam – sold for US$2.75 million to a mainland Chinese collector.

Ground zero for the explosion of the contemporary Chinese art scene is Factory 798 in Beijing (see page 144), but it is rapidly being joined by other art centres, and has its Shanghai rival in 50 Moganshan Lu (see page 222), named after its address. For some, the surprise has been not that China can produce so much internationally well-received art, but that the censorship-prone Beijing government has been willing to tolerate the often politically loaded content. Most believe this is because Beijing has bigger fish to fry, and is more concerned with policing the domestic internet and other mass cultural outlets, while the high prices being fetched for contemporary art can only succeed in making China look good – a viewpoint borne out by the fact that some of the country's most controversial artists were included in the Olympics programme. ❏

ARCHITECTURE

In imperial China, architectural principles were dictated
by the cosmology defining heaven and earth. Across
the country, temples, palaces and pagodas are
imbued with these principles to create a
harmonious architectural legacy

The principles of traditional Chinese architecture reflect the twin philosophies of order
and authority. Careful layout applies not only
to residences and ceremonial buildings, but to
entire cities. The longevity and universal application of this approach also mean that classical
buildings across the length and breadth of China,
be they temples, pagodas or imperial palaces, tend
to exhibit similar characteristics.

Common features

Feng shui ("wind and water"), the traditional Chinese practice of placement to achieve harmony with
the environment, has been a significant factor in
the construction of buildings since records began.
The preferred orientation is north–south, with the
most important structures facing south, towards the
sun. A sheltered position, facing the water and away
from a hillside, is also considered auspicious.

One of the most characteristic aspects of Chinese architecture is the use of curving roofs –
more marked in the south of China than the north
– with ceramic tiles and circular end tiles, a style
dating back to the Warring States Period (403–221
BC). Overhanging eaves offered shelter from the
rain as well as keeping out the sun in summer, and
allowing it in during winter. Simple homes had
plain gabled roofs.

Surrounding and enclosing classical Chinese
residences, temples and palaces, is a wall. Walls
are very important to the Chinese; not only do
they provide protection and privacy, but they symbolise the containment and group mentality that
are such important aspects of Chinese society.
Cities were also surrounded by walls, their
entrance gates surmounted by watchtowers. Drum
and bell towers would announce the opening and
closing of the city gates.

From the earliest days, wood was favoured as a
building material as it was easily transported and
practical – although increasingly hard to come by in
most parts of China in more recent centuries. Residences were designed to be rebuilt, not to be permanent monuments. Brick and stone were only
used for important buildings intended to withstand
the elements for a prolonged period, such as imperial palaces, tombs, temples, ceremonial structures
and, occasionally, bridges.

Imperial architecture

Imperial buildings, mainly royal palaces and
temples, can be identified by the use of yellow-
glazed tiles on their roofs. Yellow was not only
reminiscent of the Huang He (Yellow River),

where Chinese civilisation is believed to have originated, but it also represented the element of earth that lay at the centre of the universe. In large palace complexes, the splendid Nine Dragon walls fulfilled the same function as spirit walls (a non-structural wall usually built behind entrances to bar the entry of evil spirits), while many pagodas, teahouses and other structures were approached by nine-cornered bridges – another anti-evil-spirit measure.

Chinese court architecture reached its apotheosis with the Forbidden City in Beijing, designed during the Ming dynasty. As with imperial buildings throughout China, its construction follows the fundamental principles of classical Chinese architecture, but on a very grand and opulent scale. The precise, geometric layout reflects the strict, hierarchical structure of imperial society, its fixed and ordered harmony an expression of cosmic order *(for more about the Forbidden City and its layout, see pages 130–32)*.

Pagodas and temples

Majestic and ornate, pagodas are an integral part of any romantic image of the Far East, and yet they are not indigenous to China. The concept originated in India where brick-built monuments, known as stupas, were used to enshrine sacred objects. During the first centuries AD, Buddhist missionaries from India preached the teachings of Buddha in China. Many Chinese monks later travelled the same route back to India, and in this way, reports of burial rites, religious art and impressive monastic and temple architecture filtered into China. Through the centuries, Chinese pagodas lost their religious associations and incorporated traditional Chinese architectural styles.

Much of China's historic architecture was lost during the vandalism of the Cultural Revolution. Most of what has survived – the old clan houses, ancient pagodas and traditional temples – is classical Chinese.

The oldest surviving pagoda, the Songyue Pagoda, stands near the old imperial city of Luoyang. Built in AD 523, this 40-metre (130ft) high, 12-sided structure has withstood the ravages of weather, natural disasters and revolutions for

over 1,400 years. At the nearby Shaolin Monastery, another rare sight is the Forest of Pagodas, a cemetery containing more than 200 stone funerary pagodas and the last resting place of monks.

Possibly the best-known pagodas in China are the two Wild Goose pagodas in Xi'an. Dayan Ta, the Great Wild Goose Pagoda, was designed by the monk Xuanzang, who, in the 7th century AD, undertook a long pilgrimage to northern India to collect Buddhist scriptures: the journey is the subject of the Chinese literary classic *Journey to the West*. After his return to China, he had a pagoda constructed to store the manuscripts he brought back with him. The Xiaoyan Ta, or Little Wild

Goose Pagoda, is smaller and more graceful than its monumental and somewhat clumsy counterpart.

Best-known for the Forbidden City, Beijing also contains many fine examples of Buddhist-inspired architecture. Rising majestically to the west of the imperial city, the White Dagoba is a massive bell-shaped structure set on a square base in the style of a Tibetan stupa *(chorten)*. It was built in 1651 to commemorate the first visit of the Dalai Lama.

Chinese temples, be they Buddhist, Daoist or Confucian, share the same design features, and are built to the same principles as palaces and wealthy traditional Chinese homes – laid out on a central north–south axis, with entrances facing the auspicious south and protected by a spirit wall. The main differences between them lie in decorative

LEFT: pagoda at Kaiyuan Temple, Quanzhou, Fujian.
RIGHT: pillar and ceiling inside the Hall of Prayer for Good Harvests, Temple of Heaven, Beijing.

details such as colour – the pillars of Buddhist temples are bright red, while Daoists use black – and the carvings of animals and deities. One of the most outstanding examples of temple architecture is the Temple of Heaven in Beijing, whose magnificent centrepiece is the Hall of Prayer for Good Harvests, with its highly unusual circular form. *(For more on Chinese temples, see pages 104–5.)*

Residential architecture

Chinese households traditionally centre around courtyards; the higher the rank of the occupant, the greater the number of courtyards. An important official might live in a large residence along

between the load-bearing columns could be easily removed. A spirit wall was usually built behind the entrance. Colour and construction styles varied according to the significance of the building and social status of the owner.

Certain areas are characterised by more individual buildings inhabited by ethnic groups such as the distinctive Hakka roundhouses found in western Fujian and eastern Guangdong provinces, designed to house an entire clan. Set in a circle around a central courtyard, the three- or four-storey structures were made of an innovative mix of clay, sand, lime, sticky rice and sugar, reinforced with wood or bamboo.

with numerous relatives and servants. The home of the head family is situated in the north of the compound, and faces south. The side buildings facing the central courtyard might belong to sisters and brothers, while more distant relatives might live around courtyards further south. In more modest homes, a similar layout prevails, with parents living in the main northern quarters facing south and children occupying the side quarters facing the courtyard.

Traditional timber-frame buildings were laid on elevated platforms made of beaten earth, brick or stone; the roof was supported by heavy wooden columns set in stone bases, often embellished with decorative carving. Inside, partition walls were made of light materials. In summer, the panels

The Dong minority areas of Guizhou province are famous for their unusual drum towers and wind-and-rain bridges (so called because they are covered), lovingly decorated by master carpenters. The Chengyang Wind-and-Rain Bridge in Sanjiang county is one of the best examples. Elsewhere in China, local architectural styles include the whitewashed, trapezoid buildings of Tibet, the ornate Buddhist temples of Xihuangbanna in southern Yunnan, the cave dwellings of the loess plateau in Shaanxi, and various forms of Islamic architecture in the northwest.

ABOVE: Tianxin Pavilion, part of the old city walls of Changsha, Hunan. **ABOVE RIGHT:** colonial architecture in Beihai, Guangxi. **RIGHT:** a Suzhou garden.

Colonial relics

It may be considered a shameful episode in China's history, but the colonial period did produce a scattering of architectural gems in the various Treaty Ports that provide welcome relief from the pervasive blandness of the modern urban landscape. The most notable concentrations are in Shanghai, Macau, Xiamen, Guangzhou (Shamian Island), Beihai and Qingdao, with a few remaining in Hong Kong, Shantou, Tianjin and Haikou on Hainan Island.

Shanghai has done a good job of preserving its architectural past, even if the famous buildings along the Bund are solid rather than elegant. In the former French Concession areas numerous English-style residences, complete with the occasional mock-Tudor building, create an unusual effect.

Despite the recent boom in casino-building, Macau has managed to preserve many of its colonial-era charms; it recently earned a World Heritage listing from Unesco for 29 key historical sites. Many of these Portuguese structures were the first of their kind on Chinese soil.

Xiamen, in Fujian province, was one of the busiest colonial enclaves in China in the late 1800s and early 1900s. Gulangyu Island, five minutes by ferry from the city. is home to dozens of examples of the large, graceful colonial-era structures that once served as consulates, residences and offices. Amid the colonial buildings are some equally well-preserved Chinese courtyard mansions.

Fifteen Western-style buildings in Beihai, on the coast of Guangxi, were recently included on a list for top state protection. The one-time German colony of Qingdao, further north on the Shandong coast, features a uniquely Teutonic city centre.

Modern architecture

Much of modern China is architecturally undistinguished, to put it mildly: a mass of residential towers and office blocks, mostly ugly and built on the cheap. Even many so-called "heritage" schemes have a dubious value. The Xintiandi area of Shanghai was flattened and rebuilt in a faux "old style" – but many other municipalities consider it a model for "cultural renovation". Tong Mingkang, deputy director of cultural heritage, commented that "it is like tearing up an invaluable painting and replacing it with a cheap print." Nonetheless, there are a few noteworthy modern architectural projects, mainly in Shanghai. ❏

GARDENS OF PHILOSOPHY AND EMPIRES

Classical Chinese gardens strive for a delicate balance between natural and artificial elements, reflecting the core Daoist principles of striving for harmony with nature. Philosophical concepts such as *yin-yang*, as well as literary and painterly themes, were used as the bases of garden design.

The art of gardens flourished during the Ming and Qing dynasties. Emperors – and the rich and powerful of the times – invested huge amounts of money and labour to build elaborate private gardens and retreats.

Two main types of gardens dominate: the imperial park and the scholar-official's private retreat. The best-known gardens of the first type are the Summer Palace and Yuanming Yuan (the Old Summer Palace), as well as Chengde (Jehol). Imperial parks were meant to suggest the riches and diversity of the empire. Chengde, the massive imperial park built by Emperor Qianlong northeast of Beijing, contains Tibetan

Buddhist-inspired architecture that was meant to assert the diversity of China.

Further south, in a historically prosperous region, the cities of Suzhou and Hangzhou offer numerous attractive examples of the scholar-officials' private garden hideaways, which sought to stir emotions by creating an intense microcosm of the natural world.

A GUIDE TO CHINESE TEMPLES

China's Buddhist, Daoist and Confucian temples are repositories of culture, and share many characteristics

By far the largest number of temples in China are Buddhist. As with all temples, halls are arranged on a north-south axis, with the main door facing south, and opening onto a courtyard. A so-called spirit wall may exist at the front entrance, barring evil spirits from entering. The first hall is where you usually encounter Maitreya, the rotund Laughing Buddha. Standing behind him is Weituo, protector of the Buddhist faith, often portrayed with a sword lying across his arms. The altar in the main hall supports three golden statues: the Buddha Sakyamuni (historical Buddha) flanked by the Buddhas of the present and the future. To the back of the main hall is a statue of Guanyin, the multi-limbed goddess of compassion, who often appears holding a small child.

Daoist temples share a similar layout to Buddhist temples, but can generally be distinguished by their black pillars (Buddhist temples normally use red), *bagua* symbols *(see picture, page 74)*, and prevalence of animal statues. The main hall is usually dedicated to Daoism's own holy trinity: Laozi, its founder; the Jade Emperor (Yuhuang Dadi); and the Yellow Emperor (Huangdi). Tianhou (Tin Hau), goddess of seafarers, and black-bearded Guandi, god of war, are also often celebrated. In parts of China, particularly in the south, Daoism and Buddhism fuse together, and some temples feature deities from both pantheons.

Confucian temples are fewer in number, and neither as colourful nor as vibrant as Daoist and Buddhist shrines. The main courtyard generally contains steles commemorating scholars, sometimes supported on the backs of *bixi*, mythical turtle-like dragons. Confucius himself is honoured with a statue at the entrance or by an effigy in the main hall, flanked by his disciples.

ABOVE: a typical Chinese temple entrance features a spirit wall inside the main doorway to block the path of evil spirits. The red lanterns also offer protection, as well as symbolising well-being and happiness.

LEFT: very conspicuous on palace roofs are ridge decorations: mythological beasts at the ends of the ridge are meant to protect the building from fire and evil spirits. The animals include a lion, dragon, phoenix, flying horse and unicorn, among others. At the front is often a man riding a hen – another common figure intended to protect the building and occupants against disaster.

MYTHOLOGICAL CREATURES

Traditional Chinese buildings are home to a veritable zoo of mythological animals. A pair of stone lions is often seen guarding the gates to temples and other buildings. On the left, the male is identified by a ball under his paw, symbolising control of the empire; to the right, the female has her paw on a cub, indicating offspring and continuation of empire. Not native to China, lions are associated with power and prestige, and the use of this beast was reserved for the court and officials of high rank.

Even more revered than the lion is the dragon, which reigns supreme over all animals. Dragons are believed to rise into the skies in the spring, and later plunge into the waters in autumn. As a creature between heaven and earth and symbolising the *yang* (male) energy, the dragon came to be identified with the emperor, thought to be the son of heaven. Together with the mythological phoenix, which represents the *yin* (female) force and is associated with the empress, the dragon appears frequently in decorative designs of imperial buildings. In combination, the dragon and phoenix can also stand for matrimonial harmony.

Other creatures include tortoises and cranes, which both represent longevity, and various beasts from the Daoist pantheon and the Chinese zodiac. Stylised fish on temple roofs (mainly in southern coastal regions) represent harmony and prosperity.

ABOVE: Guandi Temple in Quanzhou (Fujian province), its roof writhing with dragons, is dedicated to the Daoist god of war. As with many deities, this god is based on an actual historical figure, Guan Yu, from the Three Kingdoms period.

LEFT: Buddhist temples *(si)* feature large statues of the Buddhas of the past, present and future, normally beside each other.

RIGHT: incense burners, in various forms, are present at all temples. In ancient times the practice of burning sacrifices was thought of as a way of communicating with the spirits, and this has evolved into the idea that sweet-smelling incense smoke placates restless spirits.

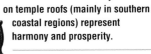

CUISINES OF CHINA

Cantonese cuisine, exported by generations of émigrés, is familiar around the world. Yet it is just one of the many distinctive regional cuisines of China. From the hot spicy dishes of Hunan and Sichuan to the more delicate flavours of the Yangzi region and the distinctive northern school, there is plenty to explore and enjoy

Few people in the world have a more passionate relationship with food than the Chinese. Food shortages over many centuries have forced the Chinese to be creative in order to utilise and conserve their relatively scant food supplies. The elite, meanwhile, have traditionally used a flamboyant approach to food as a way to flaunt their status. China's great geographical variety offers a wealth of different produce.

The Chinese preoccupation with food is reflected in China's philosophy and literature. Indeed, as depicted in numerous historical, literary and philosophical writings, more often than not scholars were also gourmands. Laozi, the founder of Daoism, said, "Handle a large country with as gentle a touch as you would cook a small fish." Another Daoist sage, Zhuang Zi, wrote a poem in which he advises an emperor to watch his cook: "A good cook needs a new chopper once a year – he cuts. A bad cook needs a new one every month – he hacks." Few will dispute the old saying that "appetite for food and sex is nature". This recognition of the importance of food has helped nurture a variety of healthy and delicious cuisines.

A traditional greeting amongst Chinese is "ni chi fan le mei yo?", which translates as "have you eaten rice yet?", emphasising the central importance of food in Chinese culture.

The old traditions are alive and well in Chinese cooking, yet – inevitably in a country as fast-changing as China – there are various new trends in evidence, too. Over the past two decades there has been a revolution in terms of dining options: scores of upmarket restaurants, the increasing popularity of Western cuisine in the cities, the arrival of fast-food chains, hot-pot chains, Korean barbecue and Japanese restaurants. And Chinese food itself is undergoing changes: restaurants are experimenting with fusion cuisines and paying greater attention to health issues – using less oil and natural flavours in favour of the once near-universal monosodium glutamate (MSG).

Technique

It is said that the four essentials in a Chinese kitchen are a cutting board, knife, wok and spoon. Historical fuel shortages made a reduced cooking

ABOVE: even the simplest meal can be presented with flair. **RIGHT:** steamed dumplings, a staple all over China.

time an early priority, and the proper preparation of ingredients is an important first step. Rapid, even chopping is a required trademark of any good cook. Faithful students of Confucius recorded that "he would not eat meat that was not cut properly, nor that which was served without its proper sauce". His pickiness made sense, since meat and vegetables cut to varying proportions result in unevenly cooked food.

The majority of Chinese dishes – generically known in Chinese as *xiao chao*, or "little fries" – are **stir-fried** fast and at a very high temperature in a wok. This not only saves fuel but also cooks meat thoroughly, while ensuring that vegetables have a crisp texture and retain their vitamins. **Steaming** is a technique used more in southern China than elsewhere – particularly for vegetables and fish – but it is used nationwide for cooking buns and dumplings. **Braising** is used throughout China, often for cooking pork and beef in stew-like dishes seasoned with aniseed and peppers. Very few Chinese homes – or restaurants for that matter – have ovens, and **roasting** is reserved for only a few speciality dishes, such as the famous Beijing Duck. Deep-frying is very rarely used in Chinese cuisine. **Hot pot**, in which meats and vegetables are placed in a simmering broth, is a Sichuan dish that has become enormously popular throughout China.

COMMON ITEMS ON THE MENU

English	pinyin	Chinese characters	English	pinyin	Chinese characters
Steamed rice	mifan	白饭	Soup	tang	汤
Fried rice	dan chao fan	蛋炒饭	Egg	jidan	鸡蛋
Noodles	miantiao	面条	Mineral water	kuangquanshui	矿泉水
Meat	rou	肉	Tea	chashui	茶水
Pork	zhu rou	猪肉	Coffee	kafei	咖啡
Chicken	ji rou	鸡肉	Beer	pijiu	啤酒
Duck	ya rou	鸭肉	Wine	jiu	酒
Beef	niu rou	牛肉			
Lamb	yang rou	羊肉	May we have the	Qing jie zhang/	请结帐 /
Fish	yu	鱼	bill/check, please	maidan	买单
Seafood	haixian	海鲜			
Vegetables	shucai	蔬菜	*For more menu items, see pages 465–7.*		

Ingredients

Chinese cuisines seek a balance of textures, flavours and colours within a meal, and few dishes feature any one ingredient exclusively. The harmonious blending of ingredients and balance in seasoning is important; common seasonings are soy sauce, ginger, garlic, vinegar, sesame oil, soybean paste and spring onions.

Rice is the staple food for most Chinese, although those living in the north traditionally eat food created from wheat flour, including noodles, dumplings and various steamed, deep-fried or griddle-fried breads. Soybean curd, both fresh and dried in either sheets or twists, provides important

bage and white radish are also salted or dried and used as seasoning, especially during the bitter winter months in the frozen north.

The use of monosodium glutamate (MSG) has had a significant effect on Chinese cooking, although it is a little less prevalent now than in the past. Called *wei jing* in Chinese, this miracle powder was introduced by the Japanese in the 1940s. Cooks discovered that it instantly added a meaty sweetness to the food, which could otherwise only be achieved by simmering stock for hours. Travellers who have an intolerance to monosodium glutimate can request that it not be used by saying *Bu yao fang wei jing*.

protein in a country where the majority of available land is given over to crops rather than grazing.

Cows and sheep, which require pasture lands, are not as common as poultry and the ubiquitous pig. Without doubt, pork is the most popular meat. In addition, both fresh- and saltwater fish are highly prized and usually well prepared.

Vegetables are of supreme importance, but are rarely eaten raw. This stems partly from hygienic considerations, as the traditional fertiliser was human waste. The range of vegetables cultivated in China is vast, particularly in the warmer south, and includes not only those known in the West, but other delights such as a huge range of leafy greens, bamboo shoots, water chestnuts, taro and lotus root. Some common vegetables such as cab-

THE REGIONAL CUISINES OF CHINA

With its vast range of climates and terrain, it is not surprising that distinct regional cuisines have developed in different parts of China. Experts argue endlessly over just how many exist, but it is generally agreed that there are four major styles. These include Cantonese, the food found in the southern province of Guangdong (and in neighbouring Hong Kong); the pungent, spicy food of the Sichuan Basin in western central China, particularly of the cities of Chengdu and Chongqing; the delicate flavours of Shanghai, Jiangsu and Zhejiang in eastern China, collectively known as Huaiyang cuisine; and northern cuisine, centred in Beijing but largely inspired by the province of Shandong, whose chefs monopolised Beijing's restaurants in the 19th century.

Increasingly considered a fifth major form of Chinese regional cuisine is the hot spicy food from Hunan province in central southern China. Somewhat similar to Sichuan cuisine, and sometimes even spicier, it is known in Chinese as *Xiangcai* and has become extremely popular across the country, partly due to the fact it is the home cuisine of Mao: Hunan restaurants often feature a portrait of the former Chairman.

Cantonese cuisine

Thanks to the large-scale emigration of Chinese from the southern province of Guangdong to the four corners of the Earth, Cantonese is by far China's best-known cuisine. Many claim that it is also the finest, and there's no doubt that the fertile south benefits from a benign climate and the widest selection of fresh produce anywhere in China.

Cantonese food is characterised by its great variety, and its delicate seasoning and freshness of ingredients. Cantonese chefs are renowned for their creativity and willingness to incorporate foreign ingredients. Chefs make abundant use of fruit and many types of vegetables, as well as seafood such as prawn, abalone, squid and crab.

Cantonese cooking methods are lacquer roasting, very quick stir-frying and steaming. Cantonese roasted chicken and pork are justifiably renowned. Seafood is typically seasoned first and stir-fried in hot oil, or else steamed.

The famous Cantonese array of titbits known as dim sum (or, in Mandarin, *dian xin*) is often served as brunch or a snack. Dim sum portions are usually dainty. Among the great variety of treats are dumplings of pork or seafood wrapped in transparent rice-dough wrappers; stuffed mushrooms or chilli peppers; deep-fried yam balls; and tiny spring

Chaozhou (Chiu Chow) cuisine is considered to be a branch of Cantonese. Centred on the city of Shantou in eastern Guangdong, it is best-known for its steamed crab, shrimp balls and steamed pork.

rolls. Self-serve trolleys arranged with small plates are wheeled through restaurants and teahouses. Although the Chinese do not normally eat dessert, two common offerings at a dim sum spread are custard tarts and cubes of almond-milk jelly.

LEFT: a happy chef in Hong Kong.
RIGHT: ingredients are chopped into small pieces.

Sichuan cuisine

After Cantonese, the cuisine of the southwestern province of Sichuan (formerly spelled as Szechuan) is perhaps the best-known to Westerners and the most emphatically flavoured in all of China.

Much of this emphasis comes from chillies, which appear in many guises: dried and fried in chunks, together with other ingredients; ground into a paste with a touch of added oil; as chilli oil; and crushed to a powder. Other ingredients important to Sichuanese cuisine are Sichuan "pepper" (the dried berry of the prickly ash or fagara), garlic, ginger and fermented soybean. The combination of chillies and the Sichuan pepper –

known in Chinese as *huajiao* – produces a flavour unique to Sichuan cuisine: *mala*, or, literally, "hot numb". Some writers claim that the Sichuan love of spicy, pungent food can be attributed to the humid climate, with its sticky summers and cold, clammy winters.

There are many superb Sichuan dishes, including duck smoked over a mixture of camphor and tea leaves, then deep-fried, and beancurd scrambled with minced pork and spicy seasonings. One of the best-known Chinese dishes, *mapo tofu* (or *doufu*), comes from Sichuan. Translated as "the pockmarked woman's tofu", the rather prosaic story relates how Mrs Chen, a pockmarked woman, created a spicy beancurd dish in the tavern she owned in the 19th century.

A now-famous Sichuan eating experience originated on the wharfs of Chongqing, where poor riverside workers prepared meals by tossing whatever they had available to eat into pots of boiling river water. More refined these days, when eating hot pot, or *huo guo*, diners sit around a table with a pot of seasoned broth heated by a gas fire (charcoal was used in the past). Each diner adds bits and pieces of prepared vegetable, meat, fish and beancurd. The food cooks very quickly and can be fished out of the broth using chopsticks or a special strainer, then dipped in sesame oil, peanut sauce or a beaten egg. Hot-pot chains are now ubiquitous in cities across China.

Huaiyang cuisine

The cuisine of the lower reaches of the Yangzi River, especially around Huaian and Yangzhou, gave rise to the term *huaiyang* to describe the food of China's eastern seaboard (it is also known as Jiangzhe cuisine, reflecting its origin in the north of Jiangxi and Zhejiang provinces, and sometimes as Shanghai cuisine). This fertile area, known as "the land of rice and fish", produces a wide range of crops as well as abundant fish, prawns and crabs. These aquatic foods are cooked simply, bringing out natural flavours. Huaiyang cooks often steam or gently simmer their food, rather than using the faster deep-frying style. Signature dishes include

Hunan cuisine

Hunan cuisine, the hottest of all Chinese regional styles, is something of a fusion of Sichuan and northern styles of cooking, although it also has some Muslim influences, which can be seen in skewers of lamb seasoned with cumin. Cumin is also used in another popular dish, *pingguo rou*, or "flat pot meat", in which the meat simmers on a bed of onion and vegetables over a low flame on the table where the diners sit.

Other popular Hunan dishes include Mao's favourite, red-cooked fatty pork, now usually referred to as *Maojia* or *Maoshi, hongshao rou* – Mao home or Mao clan red-cooked pork – often served with a dish of peanuts, and fish head cooked in a bright sea of chopped chilli peppers.

pork steamed in lotus leaves, Duck with Eight Ingredients, and Lion's Head Meatballs, all of which should be found in any good restaurant around Shanghai. Huaiyang cuisine places emphasis on soups, which come with every meal. In addition, "red cooking" (stewing meat in stock with soy sauce, star anise and other flavourings) and the heavy use of peanut oil and lard are characteristic.

Northern cuisine

The cuisine of northern China tends to be a rustic, home-style cooking that makes abundant use of onions and garlic, but is lacking in the variety of vegetables characterising the cuisines of China's more fertile regions.

Northerners eat wheat-based foods as a staple, not the rice found elsewhere in China. Indeed, one can find a wide variety of noodles; dumplings that are steamed, pan-fried or boiled; breads (once again, fried or steamed); and deep-fried lengths of dough, which are excellent with a bowl of sweet or salty soybean milk.

Most northern cuisine stems from Shandong province, but with some influences from Mongolian and Hebei cooking. Braised meat and poultry cooked in brown sauce, which form the base of much northern cuisine, are some of the most common dishes.

Although the indigenous food is relatively simple, Beijing benefited from its status as imperial capital. The emperors sought out the best chefs in the land, and the first among them could count on being given the rank of minister.

It was during these days that the most refined and complex dishes such as Peking Duck, Mandarin Fish, Phoenix in the Nest and Thousand-Layer Cake were created. Today, the ordinary citizen of Beijing (and, of course, visiting foreigners) can sample these palace dishes in special, but often expensive, restaurants.

No visitor should leave without a meal of Peking Duck. After the duck is slaughtered, air is pumped between the skin and the flesh of the duck, and then the skin painted with a mixture of honey, water and vinegar. The duck is dried, and then roasted in a special oven. The succulent, crisp skin is tucked into fine wheat-flour pancakes, painted with sweet black sauce and enlivened with spring onions. After this course, diners might enjoy the meat of the duck and complete the experience with a finale of duck soup.

For more information on local styles of cooking around China, see the restaurant listings at the end of each Places chapter.

THE PHILOSOPHY OF FOOD

For centuries, Chinese have regarded food as curative or preventative medicine: traditionally, food should not only be filling, but it should also have a healing effect. A Chinese meal is based on balance, even at the largest and most extravagant of banquets. Indeed, at times the relationship between food and medicine can seem quite

blurred. In fact, the word for recipe, *fang*, is the same as for prescription.

When planning a menu, the chef will want to consider the physical conditions of the diners and external conditions such as the weather. One of the most basic theories behind a balanced Chinese diet is that of "hot" and "cool" foods. Certain foods are believed to be either *yin* (cooling) or *yang* (warming); the ideal is to seek a balance between the two.

Internal heat is caused by eating "hot" elements such as coffee, meat and spicy food. Excess internal heat can cause unpleasant symptoms such as heartburn, rashes, cold sores and bad breath. Not

surprisingly, "hot" foods are popular in cold weather. Snake meat, for example, is considered to be fortifying and is therefore a popular winter dish

> The Chinese typically cherish a boisterous atmosphere when eating, filled with toasts and jokes and conversation. This is called *re nao* – hot and noisy – and is considered the hallmark of a good meal.

in some parts of the country. On the other hand, "cooling" foods combat excess internal heat. Low-calorie, bland vegetables such as watercress, bitter melon and white radish, as well as most fruits, are considered "cooling".

FAR LEFT: steamed rice, China's staple.
LEFT: the preparation of Peking Duck is a lengthy and complicated business. **RIGHT:** a traditional dish of noodle soup.

Symbolism and festivals

For all the attention and significance lavished on food by the Chinese, it is not surprising that Chinese food "language" developed to a level probably unparalleled by any other cuisine. Food can be endowed with symbolic meaning, and special occasions such as holidays or birthdays are observed with specific foods.

Chinese New Year is a particularly significant food event. As the most important holiday of the year, much care, planning and money is spent on celebrating this event with as sumptuous a feast as possible. Oranges and tangerines keep the sweetness of life, ducks represent fidelity

and joy, and fish represent prosperity, wealth and regeneration.

Birthdays are often observed by the serving of noodles, because the lengthy strands are said to represent long life. Another favourite is steamed buns shaped and coloured to look like peaches, as peaches also represent longevity. During the mid-autumn festival, also known as the moon festival, people eat heavy, round-shaped pastries called mooncakes. Round like the full moon, these cakes are usually filled with sweet paste and sometimes an egg yolk in the centre.

During the dragon-boat festival, people eat fragrant sticky rice wrapped in bamboo leaves or

ETIQUETTE PRIMER

Chinese table manners are quite different from those of the West. The Chinese slurp their soup (to cool it off on the way to the mouth), keep their elbows on the table, and lift their bowls. The usual way to eat a bowl of rice is to hold the bowl up with one hand and shovel the rice into the mouth with chopsticks – although you are unlikely to see people doing this in a top-class restaurant. Similarly, soup bowls can be held in one hand and the soup either sipped directly from the bowl or with a soup spoon. Be careful

not to stick your chopsticks upright into a bowl of rice. This is a very inauspicious sign as it resembles incense sticks burned for funerals or at shrines.

reeds, a treat called *zong zi*. The tradition commemorates the death of the poet and statesman Qu Yuan, author of the *Chuci*, who threw himself into a river and drowned. Townspeople threw *zong zi* into the river to feed the fish so that they would be distracted from eating Qu Yuan's body.

EVERYDAY EATING IN CHINA: WHAT TO EXPECT

Everyday meals are simple affairs. The Chinese tend to eat quite early, and lunch is often served in Chinese restaurants from 11am. (Hotels and restaurants catering for foreigners have, of course, adjusted to their preferences.) Away from the main centres you won't easily find a meal after 8pm, though this is somewhat different in the south, where social life continues until the late evening. Chinese meals are best eaten in a group, with diners sharing a variety of different dishes; Chinese restaurants are, on the whole, not well suited to individual diners.

Breakfast might consist of a bowl of rice, *baozi* steamed buns, or, in the south, with *zhou* (rice porridge) which comes with pickled vegetables and bits of meat, or perhaps hot soy milk and deep-fried dough sticks *(youtiao)*. For **lunch**, a noodle soup *(tangmian)* or a plate of rice with some meat and vegetables is common. A proper family **dinner** will normally consist of the staple rice or noodles, soup, and three or four freshly prepared hot dishes. The

ants, this will be served as a matter of course, and will generally be an inexpensive green tea. In more expensive establishments, however, diners are usually asked to choose from a selection of teas, the most popular being the semi-fermented varieties of Wulong and Tieguanyin, unfermented green tea, or *lucha*, and sometimes the popular Cantonese jasmine tea – *molihua*. If the tea is served in a pot, the correct etiquette when it's empty and you want it refilled with hot water is to leave the lid ajar.

When dining in groups, Chinese invariably also accompany their meals with alcoholic drinks. Sometimes this is simply beer (Tsingtao is the best-known brand internationally), but often it will be one of

soup is generally served at the end of a meal, except in Guangdong, where it is sipped throughout the meal. Although Chinese do not generally finish their meals with desserts, they will often – when it is available – eat fruit at the end of a meal, and in many restaurants, slices of watermelon or orange will be served.

Drinks

The Chinese almost always eat to the accompaniment of cups of tea. In regular downscale restaur-

China's very potent rice or barley wines – *baijiu* and *damaijiu*, though there are countless varieties. Several foreign joint-venture wineries now produce a variety of drinkable red and white table wines. It is impolite to take a sip of an alcoholic beverage without first toasting one of the other diners, and if you are toasted – and as a foreigner you will be, repeatedly – you are expected to down your drink in one go: the meaning the Chinese toast, *ganbei*, is "empty glass". If you are not particularly keen on drinking, or simply don't want to be inebriated at 7pm, it is sometimes possible to ward off the incessant toasts by declaring *suiyi* (which roughly translates as "drink as much as you want"); this gives you the freedom to respond to toasts with small sips rather than an empty glass. ❑

LEFT: street food in Hohhot, Inner Mongolia.
ABOVE: mooncakes are eaten at the mid-autumn festival. **ABOVE RIGHT:** tea is an essential accompaniment to a Chinese meal.

PLACES

A detailed guide to the entire country,
with principal sites clearly cross-referenced
by number to the maps

On early maps of China, only the scale of the coastline is correct; the further they extend into the interior, the more distorted becomes the cartography, or else it remains blank. One might have said the same about European understanding of China as a whole. Today the understanding has improved, but there is still a great deal of mystery and confusion about China and its people. And as before, the further one travels into the interior the more exotic and remote the landscapes and cultures become. Contemporary travellers will readily see that China is no monolithic culture. The influence of the Han Chinese may seem ubiquitous, but the rich Turkic culture of Xinjiang, the lively colours of Yunnan, or the lofty mantras of Tibet are also, often controversially, a part of China. Travellers may also come to recognise northern and southern differences amongst the Han themselves.

The northern part of China extends from Dongbei in the northeast – known to Westerners as Manchuria – across Inner Mongolia to the dusty lands around the Huang He (Yellow River), the cradle of Chinese civilisation. The terrain is often dry and infertile, freezing in winter, stifling in summer; yet the imperial capitals of China – Xi'an, Luoyang and Beijing – are all here, with a dazzling array of ancient sights.

The central belt of China follows the grandest of rivers, the Chang Jiang, or Yangzi to Westerners. This river divides China north and south before emptying into the sea close to Shanghai, China's fascinating 21st-century megalopolis.

Along the coast of southern China are the feisty, entrepreneurial regions centred around Guangzhou and Hong Kong, while parts of the inland south are home to colourful minority peoples and some beautiful scenery – notably around Guilin in Guangxi province. Yunnan province, in the country's southwestern corner, is an intoxicating mix of high mountains, tropical lowlands and ancient cities. The west of China is a land apart, and travelling to the remote landscapes and exotic cultures of Tibet and the Silk Road region of Xinjiang remains a rare adventure. ❑

PRECEDING PAGES: Lijiang, Yunnan province; the bright lights of Shanghai; Kazakh family and yurt, Xinjiang. **LEFT:** circular *tulou* dwellings in Fujian province. **TOP:** limestone spires at Wulingyuan, Hunan province. **ABOVE LEFT:** the Karakoram Highway.

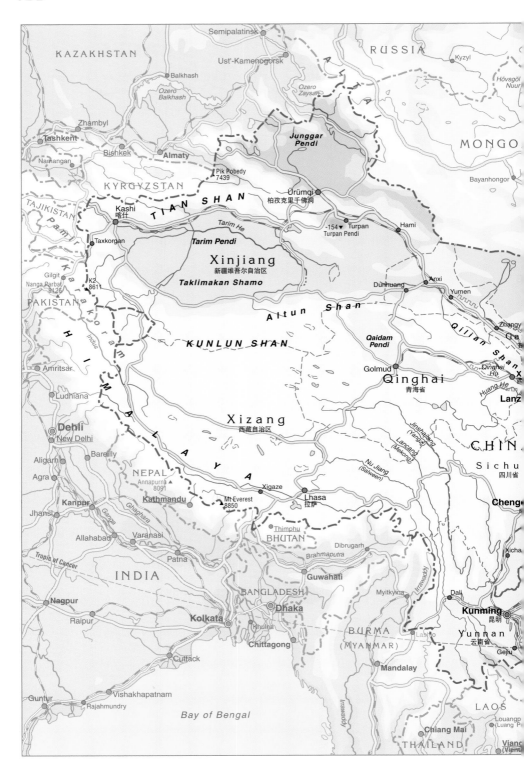

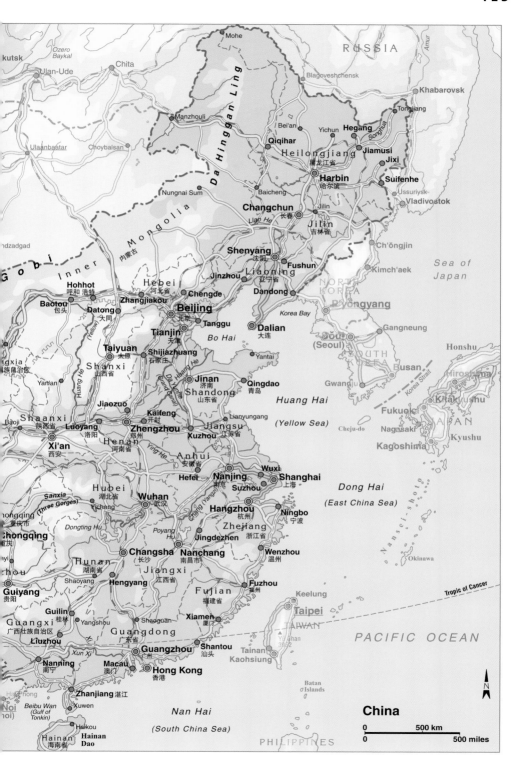

China

0   500 km

0   500 miles

THE NORTH

The north may be inauspicious in Chinese cosmology, but it was by the Huang He, the river that flows through the northern plains, that Chinese civilisation took root and flourished

Taking such a huge chunk of China and calling it "the North" leads to the suggestion of homogeneity, but this is emphatically not the case – the region is, after all, bisected by the Great Wall, emphatic dividing line between the civilised and the barbarian. Anchored by the great imperial cities of Beijing and Xi'an, this vast swathe of land stretches for thousands of miles across the wide open spaces of the northeast and Inner Mongolia to the dusty heartlands of ancient China around the Huang He (Yellow River).

Having successfully hosted the Olympics in 2008, Beijing has undergone a huge renovation programme but remains a fascinating jumble of ancient and modern, its 21st-century glass towers and gigantic 1950s architecture constrasting dramtically with the narrow hutong alleyways, imperial parks and classical Chinese buildings from an earlier time. Beyond the city, snaking westwards over the rocky hills and mountains, is the magnificent Great Wall. On the other side of the Wall is Dongbei – literally, East-North, but better known to the world as Manchuria – while reaching all the way west to Gansu and the Silk Road are the empty grasslands and deserts of Inner Mongolia.

To the southwest of Beijing are the regions where Chinese civilisation first flowered, and other ancient capitals; Xi'an, Luoyang, Anyang and Kaifeng. The silt-laden Huang He river loops through the Mongolian steppes and then heads south, flowing close to Xi'an, where the first emperor of a unified China, Qin Shi Huangdi, made ancient history. The starting point of the ancient Silk Road, Xi'an is famous today for the army of terracotta warriors discovered nearby.

Further east, the Daoist mount of Hua Shan invites pilgrims to attempt its slopes. In its lower reaches, the Huang He cuts through Shanxi – home of the Buddhist Yungang caves before traversing Henan, home to the awesome Longmen caves near Luoyang and globally renowned Shaolin Temple. Before emptying into the sea, the river passes through Shandong, home of Confucius, peerless Tai Shan and breezy Qingdao, the former German enclave on the shores of the Yellow Sea. ❏

LEFT: Chinese New Year in the northern snow. **TOP:** the terracotta warriors near Xi'an. **ABOVE LEFT:** Liulichang, Beijing. **ABOVE RIGHT:** the village of Cuandixia, Hebei province.

Zhonghua Minzu Yuan **37** Aolinpike Gongyuan (Olympic Park)
ese Ethnic Culture Park) 国家体育场
中华民族园

(Third Ring Road)

uan Zhonglu

Bahe

Wuhan Lu

Beisanhuan Zhonglu

Dashanzi Yishu Qu **35**
(Art District)
大山子艺术区

AOLINPIKE GONGYUAN
(OLYMPIC PARK)
国家体育场

Kehui Lu Kehui Lu
Beichen
Anli Lu

Hepingli Beijie

LIUYIN
GONGYUAN

Andingmenwai Dajie

Liufang China International
Exhibition Centre

Xianheyuan Lu
Dongzhimenwai Xiejie

Forest
Park
Beichen

deli Beijie Huangsi Dajie

DITAN
GONGYUAN

Hepingli Dongjie

Dongtucheng Lu

Xinyuan Dajie

Xilu
Olympic
Green

Olympic
Sports Centre

National
Indoor Stadium

Guojia Youyong
Zhongxin
(National Aquatics
Centre)
国家游泳中心

Guojia Tiyuchang
(National Stadium)
国家体育场

Ande Lu

QINGNIANHU
GONGYUAN

Ditan
(Altar of
the Earth)

Yonghegong

Andingmen Dongdajie

Dongzhimen
Bus Station

Second Ring Rd)

Xin Donglu

Sanlitun Lu

Datun Lu

Donglu

Olympic
Sports
Centre Stadium

Anli Lu

Beisihuan
Zhonglu

Beisihuan

CHINESE ETHNIC
CULTURE PARK

Dongdajie **Andingmen**
Zhonglou
(Bell Tower)
钟楼

Guozijian
(Imperial Academy)
国子监

18 Yonghe Gong
(Lama Temple)
雍和宫

20

Belouqu Xiang

19 Kong Miao
(Confucius Temple)
孔庙

Beixinqiao

21
Gulou (Drum Tower)
鼓楼

Gulou Dongdajie

Zhonghua Minzu

Xiongmaohuandao

TUCHENG GONGYUAN

dingqiao
ver Ingot Bridge)
银锭桥

Nanluogu Xiang

Gulou

Jiaodaokou

Dongzhimen
Nanxiaojie

Dongzhimenwai Dajie

0   800 m
0   800 yds

Di anmen Dajie

Di anmen Dongdajie

Zhangzizhonglu

Dongzhimen

ngshan
oujie

Nandajie

Dongsi Shitiao

Dongsishitiao

Gongren Tiyuchang Beilu

Gongtibeilu

JING SHAN GONGYUAN
(COAL HILL PARK)
景山公园

Mei Shu Guan
(China National
Art Gallery)

Nanxincang
(Imperial
Granaries)

DONGCHENG

Dongsi Beidajie

Chaoyangmen

Workers'
Stadium

TUANJIEHU
GONGYUAN

Yaojiayuan Lu

anqian Jie

Wusi Dajie

Dongsi

Chaoyangmennei Dajie

Chaoyangmenwai Dajie

Chaoyang Dajie

Hujialou

Third Ring Road

Sugong
故宫

Dong Si
Qingzhensi

Dengshikou

Chaoyangmennei
Nanxiaojie

Ritan
(Altar of
the Sun)

CHAOYANG

Chaoyang Lu

Guanghualu

in Cheng
bidden City)

SHAN
UAN
TSEN
园

4

Laodong Renmin
Wenhua Gong
(Working People's Cultural Palace)

Dongtang
(St Joseph's
Cathedral)

Mishitang
(Rice Market
Church)

RITAN
GONGYUAN

Guomao
(World Trade
Centre)

36
CCTV
Tower

Guo Mao

5

Tian'anmen 天安门
(Gate of Heavenly Peace)

16

WANGFUJING
王府井

Zongbu Hutong

Youyi Shangdian
(Friendship Store)
友谊商店

Xiushui
Shichang
(Silk Market)

Guanghua Lu

an'anmen
uangchang

6

Donghua'an Jie Wangfujing

Wangfujing

Oriental Plaza

Jiguomennei Dajie

17

Yong An Li

Jianguomenwai Dajie

Jianguomen

Jianguo Lu

Dong Tian'anmen

8 Mao Zhuxi Jiniantang
(Mao Mausoleum)
毛主席纪念堂

10

Zhongguo Guojia Bowuguan
(National Museum of China)

Qianmen Dongdajie

DONGDAN
GONGYUAN

Beijingzhan

15 Gu Guangxiangtai
(Ancient Observatory)
古观象台

Beijing Zhan
(Beijing)

Tonghui

Baiziwan Lu

Xidawang Lu

men

12

Dixia Cheng (Underground City)
地下城

Chongwenmen Railway Station)

Chongwenmen
Dongdajie

Baiqiao
Dajie

Guangqumennei Dajie

Qianmen Dajie

Beijing
Guihua Bowuguan
(Planning Exhibition Hall)
北京规划博物馆

Dongxinglong Jie

Huashi Dajie

Xindu Dajie

Guangqumenwai Dajie

Guangqu Lu

Shuagjing

CHONGWEN

Zhushikou Dongdajie

Ciqikou

Majuan
Bus Station

Dongsanhuan

Tiantan Lu

Tiantandongmen

Tiyuguan Lu

Jingsong Lu

Jingsong

tan Nanlu

Qinian Dian
(Hall of Prayer
for Good Harvests)
祈年殿

Hongqiao Shichang
(Hongqiao/Pearl Market)

Tiantan Donglu

Zuo'anmen Dajie

Longtan Lu

Ziran Bowuguan
(Natural History
Museum)

TIANTAN
GONGYUAN
(TEMPLE OF
HEAVEN PARK)
天坛

13

Longtan

LONGTAN
GONGYUAN

tan
re)

Zhai Gong
(Hall of
Abstinence)

Yuanqiu
(Altar of
Heaven)

Puhuangyu

Panjiayuan Shichang
(Ghost Market)
潘家园市场

14

men

Yongdingmen Dongjie

Yongdingmen Dongbinhelu

Zuo'anmen Xibinhelu

Tiantandong Lu

Fangzhuang Lu

Helawei Nanla

Zuo'an Lu

Beijing 北京

0   1 km
0   1 mile

Pufang Lu

Recommended Restaurants, Cafés and Bars on pages 146–7

BEIJING

Laid out in a grid according to feng shui principles, the Northern Capital and seat of political power is now a vast modern metropolis with an array of spectacular sights

Over the past 1,000 years, **Beijing** (北京) has served as the primary residence for three major dynasties. Under the rule of Kublai Khan in the 13th century, the city was known as Khanbaliq – the City of the Khan – and it was a magnificent winter residence for the Yuan-dynasty emperor. During the Ming dynasty, which replaced the Yuan, the Imperial Palace (Forbidden City) was built and Beijing acquired the layout that survives today. The Qing emperors surveyed their realm from the palace until the dynasty collapsed in 1911.

Traditional Chinese thought perceived the world not as the Ptolemaic disc of the West, but as a square. It was believed that a city, especially a capital city, should reflect this cosmic order and adhere to its geometrical definition, with a north–south and east–west orientation of roads and buildings *(see page 130)*. In no other Chinese city was this idea fulfilled as completely as in ancient Beijing. But the history of the area around the capital goes back much further: the discovery of the skull of *Sinanthropus pekinensis* (Peking Man), southwest of Beijing, proved that prehistoric humans settled here more than half a million years ago. Yet little more is known until 5,000 years ago, by which time Neolithic agricultural villages had been established.

The changing city

Beijing today is a mass of tower blocks, gargantuan flyovers and expressways. Construction sites are everywhere. Bicycles still throng the streets, but a huge knot of taxis, cars and buses brings traffic to a crawl. The successful bid for the 2008 Olympics propelled the Beijing authorities to start an ambitious regeneration plan. Massive investment in the subway and road networks, together with a beautification programme, has changed the face of the city. Overall the effects have been beneficial, although some question the exorbitant cost, while others bemoan the fate of historic *hutong* *(see page 136)* – many of which are falling prey to road-widening schemes.

Main attractions
FORBIDDEN CITY
TIANANMEN SQUARE
TEMPLE OF HEAVEN (TIANTAN)
YONGHE GONG (LAMA TEMPLE)
HUTONG ALLEYWAYS
HOUHAI / BACK LAKES AREA
NEW SUMMER PALACE (YIHEYUAN)

LEFT: the Hall of Prayer for Good Harvests at the Temple of Heaven.
BELOW: the opening ceremony of the 2008 Olympics.

BELOW RIGHT: a Qing-dynasty map showing the ancient layout of the city.

Most residents are hopeful the Olympic drives to reduce pollution from traffic and surrounding factories can be extended and more high-tech facilities and construction rolled out to complement the impressive Games venues.

The harsh northern climate brings long, hot summers and cold, dry winters. When sandstorms swirl through the city in spring, the fine dust forces its way through cracks and crevices in poorly insulated homes. Vehicle exhaust fumes, dust from construction projects, coal smoke and industrial emissions add to the pollution and pervasive greyness, even if it has been alleviated to a degree by the planting of lush grass by the roadsides.

Despite the rapid modernisation there remains plenty to see, including the unmissable Forbidden City and some of China's most spectacular temples and palaces, often set in beautiful gardens. To experience a more intimate side of the city, walk through its fast-disappearing *hutong*, alleys usually flanked by the gates and walls of traditional courtyard houses. By way of contrast, wandering around the vast spaces of Tiananmen Square surrounded by monumental buildings, or along the grand avenue of Chang'an Jie, gives a keen sense of recent history and centralised power.

The Forbidden City

At the heart of the teeming metropolis of modern Beijing, and unmissable on any city map at the centrepoint of the capital's grid layout, the **Forbidden City** ❶ (故宫; Gugong (Imperial Palace); summer 8.30am–5pm, winter 8.30am–4.30pm, ticket office closes an hour earlier; charge) is simply breathtaking. It is one of the world's best-preserved, and largest, historical sites – a vast labyrinth of interconnected halls, chambers and courtyards.

Following 17 years of construction, the Ming emperor Yongle moved into the new palace in 1421 *(see panel, below)*. It was to remain the imperial residence and centre of the Middle Kingdom for almost 500 years through the reigns of a total of 24 emperors, until the founding of the Chinese Republic in 1911.

Entrance was denied to ordinary mortals. Behind walls more than 10 metres (33ft) high enclosed within the 50-metre (165-ft) broad moat, life was dictated by the complex rules and rituals of the impe-

Geomantic Design

The third Ming emperor, Yongle, is credited with the planning of the city. In 1421, he moved his government from Nanjing to Beiping (Northern Peace) and renamed it Beijing (Northern Capital). His plans followed the principles of geomancy, the traditional doctrine of feng shui that strives to attain harmony between human life and nature. Beijing lies on a plain that opens to the south, an auspicious direction, as it is towards the south that the generosity and warmth of *yang* is thought to reside. All important buildings in the Old City face south *(nan)*, protected from harmful *yin* influences from the north *(bei)* – whether winter Siberian winds or enemies from the steppes.

A north–south axis centred on the Forbidden City divided the city, with important buildings and city features laid out as mirror images on either side. Ritan (Altar of the Sun), for example, has its equivalent in Yuetan (Altar of the Moon). Equally complementary were the eastern *(dong)* and western *(xi)* commercial quarters of Xidan and Dongdan. In the middle was the heart of ancient China and the centre of the physical world, the Dragon Throne, from which the emperor governed as the ritual mediator between heaven and earth. Outside it was the imperial city, again square, and crowded around this was a sea of mainly single-storey houses. This part of Beijing is still considered to be the inner city, or Old City.

Recommended Restaurants, Cafés and Bars on pages 146–7

rial court. The mandarins would arrive in their litters for the morning audience with the emperor, each shown to his place – arranged according to rank – where they listened to the emperor in respectful silence. Within the palace were more than 8,700 rooms in which some 8,000–10,000 people lived, including 3,000 eunuchs, as well as maids and concubines.

Preserved as a museum since the 1920s, and a Unesco World Heritage Site since 1987, the Forbidden City is usually entered from the south. From Tiananmen Square proceed through Tiananmen Gate (under the Mao portrait) and walk across the large courtyard, divided by another gate (Duanmen), to reach the 35-metre (117ft) high **Wumen** Ⓐ (午门; Meridian Gate), where the ticket office is located. There is also a ticket office just outside Shenwumen, the northern gate (same hours as the Wumen entrance).

Once beyond Wumen, one encounters the three great halls and courtyards of the outer area. The first and most impressive of these is the **Taihe Dian** Ⓑ (太和殿; Hall of Supreme Harmony), the largest building in the palace and fronted by an immense courtyard that could hold 90,000

spectators. In its centre is the ornately carved, golden **Dragon Throne** (龙椅), from which the emperor ruled. The most solemn ceremonies, such as the New Year rites or the enthronement of a new emperor, were held here. Behind Taihe Dian are **Zhonghe Dian** (中和殿; Hall of Complete Harmony) and **Baohe Dian** Ⓒ (保和殿; Hall of Preserving Harmony), completing a trinity that reflects the Three Buddhas and the Three Pure Ones of Daoism.

To the east of Baohe Dian is the splendid **Jiulongbi** Ⓓ (九龙壁; Nine Dragon Screen), representing the emperor as the indisputable son of heaven. On the other side of the Outer Court, to the north and separated from it by **Qianqingmen** (乾清门; Gate of Heavenly Purity), lies a labyrinth of gates, doors, pavilions, gardens and palaces. This is **Qianqing Gong** Ⓔ (乾清宫; Palace of Heavenly Purity), the residence of the imperial family, almost exclusively female as the emperor and eunuchs were the only men permitted to enter. The centre of this private section is formed by three rear halls

The Nine Dragon Screen, made of 1,773 glazed bricks. For the Chinese, dragons are friendly creatures with a protective function: the purpose of the screen is to repel evil spirits. Dragons are linked to the east – where the sun rises and rains originate – and symbolise emperors.

BELOW: the Court of the Imperial Palace.

The carved huabiao *pillars in front of Tiananmen Gate symbolised dialogue between emperors and their subjects.*

called the **Housan Gong** (后三宫). The politics of state business took place in the interlinked rooms to the left and right, where the scene was set for plots and intrigues as the more influential eunuchs and concubines vied for power and influence within the court.

The well in the northeast, just behind **Ningshou Gong** ❺ (宁寿宫; Palace of Peace and Longevity), was the place of one such grisly episode. In 1900, a concubine of Emperor Guangxu dared to oppose the fearsome Empress Dowager Cixi. As punishment, the concubine was rolled up in a carpet and thrown down into the shaft of the well by the palace eunuchs.

In the smaller halls to the east and west of the main halls are the exhibitions of the **Imperial Palace Museum** (故宫博物院; Gugong Bowuguan; separate charge applies). One highlight here is the **Hall of Clocks** ❻ (钟表馆; Zhongbiao Guan), where the exhibits include water clocks and various intricate, richly decorated European and Chinese mechanical timepieces.

At the end of the Forbidden City is **Yuhua Yuan** ❼ (御花园; Imperial Garden), composed of flower beds, cypress trees and mosaic walkways, before the northern exit, **Shenwumen** (神武门; Gate of Divine Might).

Outside the Forbidden City

Across the street from Shenwumen. on land that was formerly part of the palace grounds, is **Jingshan Gongyuan** ❷ (景山公园; Coal Hill Park; daily 6.30am–8pm; charge), the ideal place from which to view the palace complex. This artificial, pavilion-crowned hill was built with the earth dug from the palace moats in the early 15th century. The last Ming emperor, Chongzhen, hanged himself from a tree here in 1644, after killing his family and fleeing the besieged palace during a peasant uprising; the tree survives.

Back at the southern end of the Forbidden City between Tiananmen Gate and the ticket office at Wumen Gate are two areas of parkland. The western half, **Sun Yatsen Park** ❸ (中山公园; Zhongshan Gongyuan; summer 6am–9pm, winter 6.30am–8pm; charge), is a very relaxing landscaped park occupying the site of an old temple honouring the gods of the earth and of fertility. It was renamed after Sun Yatsen (1866–1925),

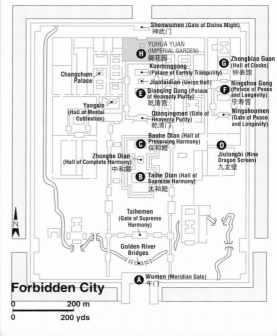

Shenwumen (Gate of Divine Might)
神武门

YUHUA YUAN
(IMPERIAL GARDEN)
❼ 御花园

Zhongbiao Guan
❻ (Hall of Clocks)
钟表馆

Kunminggong
(Palace of Earthly Tranquility)

Changchun
Palace

Jiaotaidian (Union Hall)

Ningshou Gong
❺ (Palace of Peace
and Longevity)
宁寿宫

Qianqing Gong (Palace
❺ of Heavenly Purity)
乾清宫

Yangxin
(Hall of Mental
Cultivation)

Qianqingmen (Gate of
Heavenly Purity)
乾清门

Ningshoumen
(Gate of Peace
and Longevity)

Baohe Dian (Hall of
Preserving Harmony)
❺ 保和殿

Jiulongbi (Nine
❹ Dragon Screen)
九龙壁

Zhonghe Dian
(Hall of Complete Harmony)
中和殿

Taihe Dian (Hall of
❷ Supreme Harmony)
太和殿

Taihemen
(Gate of Supreme
Harmony)

Golden River
Bridges

Wumen (Meridian Gate)
❶ 午门

Forbidden City

0   200 m
0   200 yds

Recommended Restaurants, Cafés and Bars on pages 146–7

GETTING AROUND BEIJING

Public buses are complicated to use without Chinese and extremely crowded during rush hours. Taxis are plentiful at almost all times and use a standard meter which starts at 10 Rmb and goes up 2 Rmb per km after the first four. Walking between some sights is feasible but be sure to check distances on a map as Beijing is vast. The city is laid out as a grid, so carrying a compass or paying attention to north (北; *bei),* south (南; *nan),* east (东; *dong*) and west (西; *xi) –* as well as centre/middle (中; *zhong)* – marked on street signs makes navigation quite easy. The ever-expanding metro system (www.bjsubway. com) is currently not extensive but easy to use and can take you directly to some major sites. There are stops at Wangfujing Shopping Street and Yonghe Gong (The Lama Temple) for example. Electronic tickets cost 2 Rmb for short journeys and have to be bought for each single-way journey on the day of travel. Having some 1 Rmb coins ready for automated ticket machines is advisable.

TIP

For entry to the Temple of Heaven and Summer Palace, it's best to buy an all-inclusive ticket *(tao piao),* otherwise you have to pay for entry to each building. However, the standard ticket for the Forbidden City gives access to all except a couple of galleries of the Palace Museum *(see page 132).*

revered founder of the Chinese republican movement. The triumphal arch near the southern entrance was originally set up in a different place in honour of the German foreign minister murdered during the Boxer Rebellion. Paddle boats can be hired for gentle cruises along the Forbidden City's moat.

To the east is **Tai Miao**, the former shrine of the imperial ancestors, now called **The Working People's Cultural Palace** ❹ (劳动人民文化宫; Laodong Renmin Wenhua Gong; daily, summer 6am–8pm, winter 6.30am–5pm; charge). The three imposing temple halls date from the Ming dynasty and housed the ancestral tablets of the imperial forebears, which the emperor was required to honour.

Tiananmen Square

On 1 October 1949, Mao Zedong, chairman of the Communist Party, proclaimed the founding of the People's Republic of China from the balcony of **Tiananmen Gate** ❺ (天安门; Gate of Heavenly Peace; daily 8.30am–6pm; charge to climb the tower to the viewing platform above the Mao portrait, free to pass through). The present structure dates from 1651, and was preceded by a

BELOW: Mao at Tiananmen Gate.

Mao's Portrait

The gigantic Mao portrait that gazes down from Tiananmen Gate measures 6 metres by 4.5 metres (20ft by 15ft) and weighs nearly 1.5 tons. The painting first appeared at the founding of the People's Republic in 1949 and became a permanent fixture during the Cultural Revolution – though a black-and-white version briefly replaced it after Mao's death in 1976.

Ge Xiaoguang, the latest of four artists who have maintained the image, has painted numerous giant portraits of the Great Helmsman. Each one takes about two weeks. The paintings are reinforced with plastic and fibreglass and have to be lifted into place by crane. Used portraits are apparently kept in case of demonstrations; in 1989 paint bombs added a touch of Jackson Pollock to Ge's work.

Beijing's Tiananmen, the gate from which Mao Zedong proclaimed the creation of the People's Republic of China, is perhaps the most iconic symbol of the country. Chang'an Jie ("Long Peace Avenue"), the boulevard which separates it from Tiananmen Square, is some 38km (24 miles) in length and is known as China's "first street".

wooden gate built in the early 15th century. When emperors left the Forbidden City to celebrate the New Year rites at the Temple of Heaven, they made their first offerings here. Five marble bridges lead to the five passages through the gate; the central one follows the imperial route and was reserved for the emperor. Since 1949 the gate has become the symbol of Beijing, and, indeed, of the whole of the People's Republic, and it is now the only public building in China to display the portrait of Mao on the outside.

Mao's giant image *(see page 133)* faces south across the expansive boulevard of Chang'an Jie to **Tiananmen Square ❻** (天安门广场; Tiananmen Guangchang). Quadrupled in size during the 1960s so that it could hold up to a million people, the square has been the venue for numerous political dramas, from Red Guards' rallies during the Cultural Revolution to the 1989 student demonstrations and subsequent blood-

shed. In the centre of the square stands the **Monument to the People's Heroes** (人民英雄纪念碑: Renmin Yingxiong Jinianbei), an obelisk unveiled in 1958. Immediately west of the square, **The Great Hall of the People ❼** (人民大会堂; Renmin Dahuitang; daily except when in session 9am–5pm; charge) is an imposing building in the Soviet neoclassical monumental style, where meetings of the People's Congress take place. A room of the hall is dedicated to each of China's 32 provinces and regions.

In 1977, a year after Mao's death, the **Chairman Mao Mausoleum ❽** (毛主席纪念堂; Mao Zhuxi Jiniantang; Tue–Sun 8–11.30am, Sept–May also 2–4pm Tue and Thur; free) was completed at the southern end of the square. People still come to pay their respects, filing past his embalmed body in its rose-hued glass enclosure, and queues can be lengthy. Just outside, visitors get to run a gauntlet of Mao busts, bags, badges and musical lighters playing "The East is Red".

Behind the Great Hall of the People is the city's most controversial building, the incongruous **National Grand Theatre ❾** (国家大剧院; Guojia Da Juyuan), a

giant glass-and-titanium dome rising out of its own moat. Unaffectionately nicknamed "The Egg" by locals, the Paul Andreu design breaks Beijing's age-old tradition of feng shui, and its proximity to the capital's heartland brought howls of consternation from conservatives. Once you get over the shock of its otherworldly appearance, however, the top-notch facilities inside cannot fail to impress.

Opposite the eastern side of the square, the National Museum is closed for renovation until 2011.

At the southern end of Tiananmen Square, the **Qianmen Gate** ❿ (前门) was once the southern entrance into the old Inner (Chinese) City from the Outer (Tartar) City and dates from 1421 during the reign of Yongle. The gate is in fact comprised of two separate structures; the stone Arrow Tower (Jianlou), which burnt down in 1900 and was reconstructed in 1903; and the main gate, the wooden Gate Facing the Sun (Zhengyangmen), just to the north, to which the city wall itself was connected. Just looking at the breadth of this gate gives you an idea of how thick the former wall once was.

South of Tiananmen

The old neighbourhood south of Qianmen Gate has undergone a controversial transformation as part of Beijing's modernising facelift. What was once a traditional and characterful collection of restaurants, opera houses, shops and brothels dating back to the Ming dynasty has become a modern retail development. Family homes and their occupants have been replaced by more than 300 shops with faux 1930s facades hawking international brands such as Adidas and Apple.

Nearby **Liulichang** (琉璃厂) ⓫ owes its name to a Yuan-dynasty workshop that produced the distinctive glazed tiles for the city's palaces and temples. It is now a renovated "culture street" featuring numerous shops for art supplies, calligraphy, trinkets and antiques, mostly reproductions, as well as a large amount of kitsch. It's still a good point from which to explore the maze of surrounding *hutong*.

To take in the vast sprawling grid of Beijing's urban construction all at once, the **Beijing Planning Exhibition Hall**

The National Grand Theatre, Beijing's first unorthodox modern building, may be controversial in appearance but as a venue it is a welcome addition to the city's cultural scene.

BELOW: the wide open spaces of Tiananmen Square looking towards the Great Hall of the People.

Hutong

For anyone keen to gain a sense of Beijing's past, a stroll through one of the city's old *hutong* neighbourhoods is essential

In a region formerly protected by the Great Wall, Beijing was also once hidden behind its own city walls. And within the city walls were its citizens, each with a wall built around their own homes and courtyards, or *siheyuan*.

Today, ring roads and walls of high-rise buildings have taken over the function of the city wall, itself a victim of town planning. In the city centre, the faceless buildings of the 1950s conceal a dwindling labyrinthine inner core of crumbling old grey alleyways, some dating back several centuries. These are the *hutong*, now disappearing to make way for roads, business parks and high-rises.

Old Beijing is a Mongol city. The nomadic conquerors who made it their capital brought their way of life and language with them. Horses were part of their lifestyle. Wells were dug and horse-troughs, *hut* or *hot* in Mongolian (as in Hohhot, the capital of the province of Inner Mongolia), were set up.

The people of Beijing turned these Mongol wells into the Chinese *hutong*.

Mongols or no Mongols, Beijingers could hardly leave their houses and homes lying unprotected amid the horse-troughs. All they had to do was close up the small spaces between the houses with a wall and privacy was restored. It was even simpler to build on to the wall of their neighbours, although no one was allowed to build so as to block another householder's route to water. In this way, the tangle of *hutong* grew, with space just wide enough to let a rider through.

The houses and courtyards, hidden away and boxed in, are themselves closed off with wooden gates that often have carved characters intended to bring good fortune to the house owner and to his trade. There will be a few trees, flowers and cacti. Three or four single-storey buildings overlook the courtyard. In the *siheyuan* of more affluent families, a second and third courtyard may adjoin the first.

The name of each *hutong* tells its story by describing the life it contains. Some indicate professions or crafts: Bowstring Makers' Lane, Cloth Lane, Hat Lane. Some lanes, if mostly populated by a single family, are named after that family.

Where to see *hutong*

The most popular area is around **Houhai Lake**, though other parts of the inner city can be equally rewarding. A large area of *hutong* remains east and southeast of the **Bell and Drum towers**. Historical **Xisi Nandajie** (西四南大街), north of Xidan shopping district, is surrounded by winding lanes full of communal life. **Zhuanta hutong** (砖塔胡同), leading off Xisi Nandajie, is said to be the city's oldest and takes its name from a 600-year-old brick pagoda built to house the remains of an eminent Buddhist monk. Once a bustling red-light district, it's now a relaxing spot to admire the original features of numerous *siheyuan*. Nearby **Baita Si** (White Pagoda Temple) fronts a warren of ancient alleyways including shady **Qingfeng hutong** (庆丰胡同). The *hutong* around Qianmen Dajie are disappearing fast. ❑

LEFT: in a traditional *hutong*. **ABOVE:** an aerial view illustrates the density of these old neighbourhoods.

(北京规划博物馆; Beijing Guihua Bowuguan; 20 Qianmen Dongdajie; Tue–Sun 9am–4pm) **⑫** includes a scale model of the city covering an entire floor. For another unusual view of the capital, **Underground City** (前门地下城; Qianmen Dixia Cheng; 62 Xidamochang Hutong, Qianmen; daily 8.30am–6pm; charge) gives you a glimpse of the mysterious subterranean tunnel network constructed by Mao to serve as an air-raid shelter for up to 40 percent of Beijing's citizens against the perceived threat from the USSR during the early 1970s.

The Temple of Heaven

Twice a year during imperial times, the emperor and a magnificent procession of some 1,000 eunuchs, courtiers and ministers would leave Gugong, the Forbidden City, for the **Temple of Heaven** (天坛; Tiantan; buildings: daily 8am–5.30pm, park: 6am–8pm; charge) **⑬**, 3km (2 miles) to the southeast of the Imperial Palace. Each time he would spend a night of fasting and celibacy in **Zhai Gong** (Hall of Abstinence) prior to the sacrificial rites the next morning. At the winter solstice, he expressed thanks for the previous harvest, and on the 15th day of the first month of the lunar year he begged the gods of sun and moon, clouds and rain, and thunder and lightning to bless the coming harvest.

Set in the middle of a park of 270 hectares (670 acres), the buildings in the Temple of Heaven complex form an outstanding ensemble of Ming-dynasty architecture. The park grounds are square, although the northern edge follows a curve, a symbolic expression of the fact that the emperor, in offering his sacrifices, had to leave the square-shaped earth for the round-roofed heaven.

The buildings are divided into two main groups: northern and southern, with the former centred around the **Qinian Dian** (祈年殿; Hall of Prayer for Good Harvests), one of the most famous sights in China. An exquisite example of Chinese wooden architecture and constructed without the use of a single nail, the round, 40-metre (130ft) tower has

three levels covered with deep-blue tiles that symbolise the colour of heaven. The roof is supported by 28 pillars: the four largest ones in the centre represent the four seasons, and the double ring of 12 pillars represents the 12 months, as well as the traditional divisions of the Chinese day, each comprising two hours. The Hall has been destroyed several times, and was last rebuilt in 1890.

The southern group of buildings includes a white, circular marble terrace, **Yuanqiu** (Altar of Heaven), the most spectacular of the city's imperial altars, consisting of a stone terrace of three levels surrounded by two walls – an inner round one and an outer square one. The lowest level symbolises the earth, the second, the world of human beings, and the last, heaven.

The nearby **Echo Wall** is famous for its acoustics – sound is transmitted along its length with remarkable clarity. The **Echo Stones** on the other side of Yuanqiu produce another peculiar effect: if you stand on the first slab and clap your hands, you will hear a single echo. On the second step you will hear a double echo, and on the third, a triple. The secret behind this

Vendors sell a variety of delicious snacks on Beijing's street corners: filled pancakes, known as xianbing, *are generally good and typically stuffed with spring onions and meat.*

BELOW: musician in the park at the Temple of Heaven.

The bright lights of Wangfujing. Partly pedestrianised, it remains the city's premier shopping street.

ingenious phenomenon has to do with the different distances at which each stone slab is placed from the wall.

The surrounding park is one of the best places in Beijing to watch early-morning enthusiasts of *taijiquan, gongfu,* calligraphy, ballroom dancing and badminton. Senior citizens gather to perform, and to listen to, Chinese music on traditional zithers and other instruments.

About 4km (2½ miles) to the east, past Longtan Park and close to the Third Ring Road, is **Panjiayuan Shichang** ⓮ (潘家园市场; Ghost Market; Huawei Lu Dajie), also sometimes known as the Dirt Market. It's a good place to buy antiques and souvenirs. Prices can be low if you bargain hard.

East of the Forbidden City

Head east from Tiananmen along Chang'an and Jianguomennei Dajie to reach **The Ancient Observatory** ⓯ (古观象台; Gu Guangxiangtai; Tue–Sun 9–11am and 1–4pm; charge). Chinese emperors were keen patrons of astronomy. An observatory was first built here in 1422, on what was then a tower in the city wall of the imperial capital. Its name changed several times – in the Yuan period it was the Terrace to Bring Down the Heavens, perhaps reflecting the Mongols' inclination to conquer. During the Ming, it was the Terrace for Watching the Stars. Seventeenth-century Jesuit-designed astronomical instruments are displayed on the roof of the tower. Exhibition rooms, set around a quiet garden that makes an excellent resting place for tired visitors, house rare instruments, scientific records, navigational charts and portraits of famous astronomers.

About 1km (⅔ mile) east of Tiananmen lies **Wangfujing** ⓰ (王府井), Beijing's premier shopping district, crowned by the glittering Oriental Plaza, a vast and impressive retail complex (sitting on the site of what was once the world's largest McDonald's). Occupying 100,000 sq metres (1,080,000 sq ft) of prime real estate, Oriental Plaza is Asia's largest commercial complex. Partly pedestrianised Wangfujing has a commercial his-

tory of several hundred years, and many long-standing brands can still be found such as Quanjude roast duck, Yongantang traditional medicine and Wuyutai tea. Set back off the northern part of Wangfujing is **Dongtang** (东堂; East Cathedral or St Joseph's; access for worship only), rebuilt after a fire in 1900, and one of the city's most prominent churches.

Further east again along Jianguomen-wai Dajie, beyond the Second Ring Road, is the souvenir-laden **Friendship Store** ⑰ (友谊商店; Youyi Shangdian; daily 9am–9pm). Its erstwhile neighbour, the well-known market at **Silk Alley** (秀水市场; Xiushui Jie) moved into a multi-storey building a few hundred metres to the east in 2006. Though looking a little more upscale these days, it still provides the same old selection of clothing, pearls, souvenirs and electronics, and is tied up in the same old international lawsuits over fake brand-name items. Sellers are used to dealing aggressively with foreign shoppers, so be prepared for hard bargaining.

North of the Forbidden City

The most elaborately restored sacred building in Beijing is **Yonghe Gong** ⑱ (雍和宫; Lama Temple; daily 9am–4.30pm; charge), a Lamaist (ie Tibetan Buddhist) temple in the northeast of the Old City, most easily reached by taking an underground train to the Yonghegong stop. Originally the private residence of Prince Yong, it was converted into a monastery when Yong became emperor in 1723. According to ancient Chinese custom, the former residence of a Son of Heaven had to be dedicated to religious purposes once he left.

From the mid-1700s, this was a centre of Lamaist religion and art, which at the same time offered the central imperial power welcome opportunities for influencing and controlling Tibetan and Mongolian subjects. The temple belongs, nominally at least, to the Yellow Hat sect, whose spiritual leader is the Dalai Lama – but given the ongoing tension between Tibetans and Chinese, it can hardly be considered a genuine working religious centre. Soaring aloft in the three-storeyed

central section of Wanfuge (Pavilion of Ten Thousand Happinesses) is a 26-metre (85ft) statue of the Maitreya, or Future, Buddha carved from a single piece of sandalwood.

Opposite Yonghe Gong, across Yonghe-gong Dajie, are **Kong Miao** ⑲ (孔庙; Temple of Confucius) and **Guozijian** (国子监; Imperial Academy; both daily 8.30am–5pm; charges), tranquil and now largely ignored former centres of scholarship. In its glorious past, Kong Miao was where emperors came to offer sacrifices to Confucius for guidance in ruling the empire. Built in 1306 during the Yuan dynasty, the temple's prize possession is a collection of 190 stelae inscribed with records of ancient civil service examinations. It is the second-largest Confucian temple in China, after that in Confucius's hometown, Qufu *(see page 180)*.

Now the Capital Library, Guozijian was the highest educational institution in the country. Thousands of students and

Yonghe Gong, the Lama Temple, is one of the city's best preserved sights. The temple was closed for three decades after 1949 and escaped damage in the Cultural Revolution.

BELOW: the number of bicycles has fallen in recent years, but cycle rickshaws are still easy to find.

Lotus Lane, on the shores of Qianhai Lake (a southern extension of Houhai), is a trendy – and relatively expensive – strip of bars, clubs and cafés.

BELOW: Bai Ta, the White Dagoba, at Beihai Park is a city landmark.

scholars came here to prepare for the imperial examinations, held once a year. A set of stelae commissioned by Emperor Qianlong records 13 Confucian classics. A total of 800,000 characters were engraved by a single scholar over a period of 12 years.

To the west of Kong Miao, **Zhonglou** ⑳ (钟楼; Bell Tower) and **Gulou** ㉑ (鼓楼; Drum Tower; daily 9am–5.30pm; charge) date from the Yuan-dynasty rule of Kublai Khan. The Drum Tower faces towards the Imperial Palace, 3km (2 miles) due south, and the Bell Tower is immediately north of the Drum Tower. They once marked the northern edge of Beijing, but were in the centre of the Yuan-dynasty city. Last rebuilt in 1747, the Bell Tower stands 33 metres (108ft) high. The Drum Tower once held 24 giant drums that were struck to mark the closing of the city gates and the passing of the night watches. There is a great view from the top over the surrounding area of traditional *siheyuan* courtyard houses which extends east to Houhai Lake.

Beihai Park

The area to the immediate northwest of the Forbidden City, in the grounds of today's **Beihai Park** ㉒ (北海公园; park daily 6am–9pm, closes at 6pm in winter; buildings 8am–5pm; charge), was the winter residence of the Mongol emperor Kublai Khan. Now, only legends remain of his former palace on Qiongdao (Jade Island), the site of **Bai Ta** (白塔; White Dagoba). A Buddhist shrine from 1651, Bai Ta is 35 metres (115ft) high, and was built in Tibetan style to commemorate the first visit to Beijing by a Dalai Lama. Other temples congregate on the northern shore of the lake, including the impressive Xitian Fanjing, not far from which is a spirit wall (designed to protect buildings from bad spirits), the glazed **Nine Dragon Screen**. Tuancheng (Round Town), in the southern part of the grounds, was once the administrative centre of the Mongol Yuan dynasty.

Zhongnanhai ㉓ (中南海; South and Central lakes), the site of the Politburo and State Council offices and grounds to the south, is known by many as the "New Forbidden City" and is strictly closed to the public. Mao Zedong and Zhou Enlai both lived and worked at Zhongnanhai. Its entrance is rather elegant, complete with a spirit wall.

Houhai Lake

Snaking north from Beihai Park (and just west of the Bell and Drum towers) are three man-made lakes – Qianhai, Xihai and **Houhai** ㉔ (后海) – which once served as the terminus of the city's canal network. The area was a gentrified locale during the Yuan dynasty and boasts some impressive courtyard houses and former residences, including those of Sun Yatsen's wife **Song Qingling** (宋庆龄故居; 46 Houhai Beiyan; daily 9am–4pm; charge) and Puyi's father **Prince Gong** (恭王府; 24 Liuyin Jie; daily 8.30am–4.30pm; charge). As tourists flock to the decreasing number of traditional *hutong* and Beijingers' thirst for nightlife grows, so Houhai has exploded into a frenetic, and profitable, free-for-all. Rickshaw drivers, masseurs and bombastic bar staff all

jostle for your custom, and chartering a vessel for some calming boating on the lakes may be the best escape. For a more casual stroll, **Nanluoguxiang** (南锣鼓巷), around 10 minutes walk east of Houhai, is a long renovated *hutong* packed with varied cafés, restaurants, backpacker hostels and some quirky and implausibly small shops.

The picturesque little bridge of **Yinding Qiao** (银锭桥; Silver Ingot Bridge), at the eastern end of Houhai, once marked the terminus of China's Grand Canal – the main artery between north and south *(see page 237)*. Here traders from as far as Hangzhou would unload huge shipments of grain for trading.

Western districts

Known as Wanshengyuan (Ten Thousand Animals Garden) when it was the personal menagerie of Empress Dowager Cixi, **Beijing Zoo ㉕** (北京动物园; Beijing Dongwuyuan; daily 7.30am–5pm; charge) is located between the Second and Third ring roads, some 7km (4 miles) west of Houhai. The animals' living conditions are often squalid, but the pandas remain a popular attraction and the aquarium (separate charge) is impressive.

On Suzhou Jie west of the zoo, **Wanshou Si** (万寿寺; Temple of Longevity; Tue–Sun, 9am–4.30pm; charge) dates from the 16th century and was originally built to store Buddhist sutras. The temple has undergone a major renovation, and features a museum collection, with a fascinating array of Buddhist statues and effigies displayed within the side halls of the complex.

Baita Si ㉖ (白塔寺; White Dagoba Temple; daily 9am–5pm; charge) is 3km (2 miles) southeast of the zoo. Established in 1096 and extensively rebuilt in Lamaist style in 1271, the temple is noteworthy for its fine collection of Tibetan Buddhist statuary, its collection of 18 ancient Luohan *(arhat)* terracotta figures and its white dagoba, a Tibetan stupa similar to that in nearby Beihai Park. To the west, close to the Second Ring Road, is the **Lu Xun Museum ㉗** (鲁迅博物馆; Lu Xun Bowuguan; Tues–Sun 9am–4.30pm; charge), displaying personal effects of the "father of modern Chinese literature". The area between the museum and Baita Si retains a sizeable proportion of its original *hutong*.

Yinding Qiao (Silver Ingot Bridge) at Houhai Lake's eastern end.

BELOW LEFT: Changlang, the Long Corridor, at the Summer Palace. **BELOW:** local youth.

The mosque at Niu Jie is one of the main centres for Beijing's 250,000-strong Muslim community. Some 10,000 Muslims – mainly Hui (ie Han Chinese followers of the faith) – live in the neighbourhood around the mosque.

BELOW: a tranquil vista across Kunming Lake.

Southwest of Baita Si, not far from Beijing West Railway Station, lies the serene **Baiyunguan** ㉘ (白云观; White Cloud Temple; daily 8.30am–4pm; charge), once the greatest Daoist centre of northern China. This former imperial palace was given by Genghis Khan as the headquarters of Qiu Chang Chun, a Daoist leader who had promised that "if the conqueror respects Daoism, the Chinese will submit". Today, a small group of monks lives here, and as headquarters of the China Daoist Association, White Cloud Temple also has a Daoist vegetarian restaurant and holds lively fairs at Lunar New Year.

Islam reached China during the Tang dynasty (618–907), and Muslims now live throughout the country. The **Ox Street Mosque** ㉙ (牛街清真寺; Niu Jie Qingzhensi; daily 9am–8pm; charge) was built in 966 and, although it has all the usual features of mosques found elsewhere in the world – minaret, prayer hall facing Mecca, Arabic inscriptions – the buildings themselves are distinctly Chinese. The neighbourhood surrounding the mosque is one of the main concentrations of hui Muslims in the capital (*see margin, left*), although many have moved elsewhere as the area has been redeveloped. It remains Beijing's largest and oldest mosque.

A further five-minute walk east is **Fayuan Si** ㉚ (法院寺; Temple of the Source of Buddhist Teaching; Thur–Tue 8.30am–4pm; charge), completed in 696 during the Tang dynasty to honour soldiers killed in battle. It is the oldest surviving temple in the city, though the current buildings are all from the 18th century. Today, the temple houses the Buddhist Academy, formed in 1956 and devoted to teaching Buddhist novices, who are then sent to monasteries across China. The academy has a library of more than 100,000 precious texts and an exhibition of Buddhist sculpture, some dating from the Han dynasty.

Summer palaces

The great aesthete Emperor Qianlong, who ruled from 1736 to 1795, fashioned a huge masterpiece of landscaping and architecture 16km (10 miles) northwest of the city centre: **Yuanming Yuan** ㉛ (圆明园; daily 7am–7pm, winter 8am–5.30pm; charge), now better-known to

Westerners as the **Old Summer Palace.** Construction followed the most lavish European styles, according to plans by the Italian Jesuit missionary and artist Giuseppe Castiglione and based upon models such as the palace at Versailles. During the Second Opium War (1856–60), the Western powers, led by British and French troops, pillaged the palace and reduced it to rubble. Amidst the picturesque ruins – crowned by the sublime ruins of the Great Waterworks – is a restored brick maze with a central pavilion.

A replacement for the devastated Yuanming Yuan was built nearby in the grounds laid out by Qianlong as a place of retirement for his mother. This new summer residence is associated with the notorious Empress Dowager Cixi, who fulfilled a wonderful, if rather expensive, dream in 1888. Using money intended for the building of a naval fleet, she constructed the **New Summer Palace** ❸❷ (颐和园; Yiheyuan; park daily 6.30am–7pm, until 6pm in winter, buildings 8am–4.30pm; charge), west of the Old Summer Palace.

As in every classical Chinese garden, water and mountains (usually represented by rocks) determine the land-scape. **Kunming Lake** (昆明湖) covers three-quarters of the total area; on its shore is **Wanshou Shan ⓐ** (万寿山; Hill of Longevity). Accessible via a series of bridges, stairs, gates and halls is the massive **Foxiangge ⓑ** (佛香阁; Pagoda of the Incense of Buddha), which crowns the peak of Wanshou Shan. In the eastern corner is a jewel of classical Chinese garden design, **Xiequ Yuan ⓒ** (谐趣园; Garden of Joy and Harmony), a picturesque copy of a lotus pool from the old city of Wuxi.

To make it more difficult for strangers to spy into the grounds, **Renshou Dian ⓓ** (仁寿殿; Hall of Benevolence and Longevity) was built right next to the eastern gate, **Dongmen ⓔ** (东门), now the main gate. Behind it lay the private apartments of Cixi, which today house a theatrical museum. Here, Cixi used to enjoy operatic performances by her 384-strong ensemble of eunuchs. Of light wooden construction and decorated with countless painted scenes from Chinese mythology, the impressive 784-metre (2,572ft) **Changlang ⓕ** (长廊; Long Corridor) runs parallel to the northern shore of the lake, linking the scattered

TIP

In the summer months a boat runs from behind the Beijing Exhibition Centre (just east of the zoo) to the (new) Summer Palace, following an old system of canals. Journey time is around 1 hour. Alternatively, take the subway to Xizhimen, then bus 375. Or cycle – around 90 minutes from the city centre. Once at the Summer Palace, it's possible to cross Kunming Lake by ferry from the pier by the Marble Boat, landing either on Nanhudao (Southern Lake Island), or on the neighbouring mainland.

TIP

To best way to get to Xiang Shan on public transport is to take bus 112 from Pingguoyuan (at the western end of subway line 1). Bus 360 from Beijing Zoo is another possibility. Bus 696 runs between Xiang Shan and the Old Summer Palace. All will drop you at a car park 10-minutes' walk from the park entrance.

palace buildings. It ends near **Qingyan-fang ⒢** (清晏舫; Marble Boat), an expensive folly in which Cixi took tea.

As with its predecessor, the Summer Palace was damaged by foreign troops – who were in China to fight the Boxer rebellion in 1900. Cixi had fled to Xi'an, and was said to have become apoplectic with rage when she heard that her throne had been flung into Kunming Lake. When she returned, some buildings were restored before her death in 1908.

Xiang Shan (Fragrant Hills)

One of the most popular destinations for Beijing's day-trippers, particularly when splashed with brilliant autumn colours, is **Xiang Shan ㉝** (香山; Fragrant Hills; daily 6am–7pm, until 6pm in winter; charge), 8km (5 miles) west of the Summer Palace. Clamber up the steps or jump aboard the cable car for views from the summit of Incense Burner Peak. **Biyun Si** (碧云寺; Temple of the Azure Clouds), near the North Gate, is well worth a visit. Among its several halls are the Hall of Arhats, containing 500 statues of Luohan (among which are two Qing emperors, Kangxi and Qianlong, repre-

sented as Luohan) and the Vajra Throne Pagoda, a stupa at the rear where the body of Republican leader Sun Yatsen was briefly interred.

To the east of Xiang Shan, the **Botanical Gardens** (北京植物园; Zhiwuyuan; daily 6am–8pm; charge) contain a large conservatory (separate charge) and pleasant grounds – best visited in May to catch the blossoming fruit trees. In the north of the gardens, **Wofu Si** (卧佛寺; Sleeping Buddha Temple; daily 8am–5pm; charge) is chiefly notable for its 54-ton reclining effigy of Sakyamuni (Buddha).

Haidian District

Though seldom on tourist itineraries, **Haidian ㉞**, Beijing's hi-tech and university district offers some cultural sites and an engaging look into the future of the capital. The campuses of Beijing's two most prestigious educational institutions, **Peking University** (北京大学; Beijing Daxue) and **Tsinghua University** (清华大学; Qinghua Daxue), date back over 100 years and are attractions in themselves. Peking University has a pleasant willow tree-lined lake, and you may be approached by friendly students keen to practise their English. Rarely visited, **Lidai Diwang Miao** (历代帝王庙; Temple of Emperors of Successive Dynasties; Fuchengmennei Dajie; 9am–4.30pm; charge) was built in 1530 during the reign of Jiajing as a place to pay homage to past rulers. Several huge buildings matching the imperial majesty of the Forbidden City are inside.

Zhongguancun (中关村) is China's answer to Silicon Valley, a major technology hub and home to several bustling electronics markets.

Dashanzi Art District

In the far northeast of Beijing, beyond the Fourth Ring Road and also known as just "798" after the German-built former arms factory-turned-gallery that serves as its symbolic heart, the **Dashanzi Art District ㉟** (大山子艺术区; Dashanzi Yishu Qu) is a thriving community of contemporary artists, shops, studios and galleries great and small. Under the threat of demolition

BELOW: Dashanzi, or "798", Art District.

for years, the district's future now seems secure as a government-sanctioned cultural zone. The numerous cafés are packed with art tourists earnestly discussing when the Chinese art bubble will finally burst, but for now the new talents keep emerging and prices of contemporary Chinese art make headlines around the world.

Though somewhat commercialised and a stopping point for tourist coaches, Dashanzi remains a collective of grassroots talents who still have the ability to surprise and even shock. The **Ullens Centre for Comtemporary Art** is an impressive multi-million-dollar exhibition space, **White Space Beijing** showcases established and up-and-coming artists and, for controversial shows, head to **Red Gate Gallery**. The easiest way to get here is to take a taxi to **Jiuxianqiao** (酒仙桥).

CCTV Tower

Across the Third Ring Road from the green expanse of Yuyuantan Park, the headquarters of state-run China Central Television, the **CCTV Tower** ⊛ is emblematic of Beijing's post-bid status as a playground for pioneering architects.

Rem Koolhaas's US$750 million masterpiece is an implausible Möbius loop design which creates a huge open space beneath the gravity-defying overhang viewable from a public observation deck.

The Olympic sites

Out beyond the Third Ring Road in the north of the city are the amazing stadia created for the 2008 Olympics. The main **Olympic Stadium** (国家体育场; Guojia Tiyuchang), known as the Bird's Nest, is flanked by the **National Aquatics Centre** (国家游泳中心; Guojia Youyong Zhongxin). Both will continue to function as sporting venues, with a shopping mall and hotel at the Olympic Stadium adding to the profit margins. *For more on the Olympics, see pages 72–3.*

Located just to the south, the **Chinese Ethnic Culture Park** ⊛ (中华民族园; Zhonghua Minzu Yuan; open daily 8.30am–6pm; entrance fee) is a large cultural theme park popular with school groups. Divided into two halves, it features a large number of fairly convincing reconstructions of buildings from all over China, as well as song and dance performances. ❑

En route to the airport, Dashanzi or "798" art district is an interesting area to look around. For more information, see www.798space.com

BELOW: Beijing's population (metropolitan area) was estimated to have reached 17.5 million in 2008.

RESTAURANTS, CAFÉS AND BARS

Restaurants

Prices for dinner for one (three dishes with beer in Chinese restaurants; a three-course meal with a half-bottle of house wine in Western-style restaurants):

$ = under Rmb 50
$$ = Rmb 50–100
$$$ = Rmb 100–150
$$$$ = Rmb 150–250
$$$$$ = over Rmb 250

Boasting more than 50,000 restaurants, cafés, kebab stands and snack shops, Beijing is now a highlight of any gourmet's travels. The embassy and nightlife area Sanlitun showcases an invasion of global cuisine, while Beijing's more traditional home-style cooking from its rapidly vanishing *hutong* can still be successfully found and digested. Gui Jie, or "Ghost Street" is a neon-lit all-night dining boulevard of spicy hot pots, deluxe private rooms and rowdy street life. The university district of Haidian offers minority restaurants catering to students from around China and throngs of inquisitive diners.

Peking Duck
Bianyifang 便宜坊
2 Chongwenmenwai Dajie, Chongwen District.
Tel: 6712 0505. **$$$**
Bianyifang has been serving up its own slow-oven-roasted style duck since 1855, although the Bianyifang name goes all the way back to 1416, and is considered the originator of Peking duck. It was also the first

restaurant in Beijing to offer take away – early telephone owners could phone for a home delivery service by bicycle.

Da Dong Roast Duck
大董烤鸭店
Nanxincang International Plaza, A22 Dongsishitiao, Dongcheng District.
Tel: 5169 0328. **$$$$**
Classy Peking duck and swish service. Located next to a restored imperial granary.

Qianmen Quanjude Roast Duck Restaurant
全聚德
32 Qianmen Dajie, Chongwen District.
Tel: 6701 1379. **$$$$**
Beijing's most famous and, some say, overrated restaurant.

Beijing Cuisine
Bai Family Mansion
白家大宅门食府
15 Suzhou Jie, Haidian District.
Tel: 6265 4186. **$$$$**
Qing-dynasty-style service and food in a secluded garden courtyard.

Jiumen Xiaochi
九门小吃
1 Xiaoyou Hutong, Xicheng District.
Tel: 6402 5858. **$**
A collection of traditional Beijing snack stalls recreated in a large courtyard.

Yuebin Restaurant
悦宾饭馆
43, 31 Cuihua Hutong, Dongcheng District.
Tel: 6524 5322. **$$**
Beijing's first post-1949 private-owned restaurant, offering authentic home-style cooking.

Sichuan
Feiteng Yuxiang
沸腾鱼乡
1 Gongti Beilu (Worker's Stadium North Road), Chaoyang District.
Tel: 6417 4988. **$$$**
Famous for various kinds of spicy-but-subtle water-boiled fish.

Kuan Xiangzi 宽巷子
306 Dongsi Beidajie, Dongcheng District.
Tel: 6400 3096. **$$**
Sichuan-styled "private home cuisine" in a cosy personal setting.

LAN Club 兰会所
4/F LG Twin Towers, B12 Jianguomenwai Dajie, Chaoyang District.
Tel: 5109 6012. **$$$$**
Glamorous, Philippe Starck-designed interior with impressive wine cellar and cigar lounge.

South Beauty 俏江南
1/F Tower A, Raycom Info-Tech Park, 2 Kexue Nanlu, Zhongguancun, Haidian District.
Tel: 8286 1698. **$$$$**
Sophisticated Sichuan cuisine with an emphasis on presentation.

Cantonese
Huang Ting 凰庭
B2/F The Peninsula Beijing, Wangfujing, Dongcheng District.
Tel: 8516 2888. **$$$$**
Flawless dim sum and Cantonese cuisine served amid Ming and Qing dynasty antiques.

Jin Ding Xuan 金鼎轩
77 Heping Xijie, just north of the Lama Temple, Dongcheng District.
Tel: 6429 6888. **$**

Popular dim sum joint famous for a characteristic, bustling atmosphere.

Guangxi and Guizhou
Miao Minority Restaurant 盛祥农家院
300 metres north of the west gate of Tsinghua University, Haidian District.
Tel: 6256 9150. **$$**
Watch nightly Miao dance performances to accompany adventurous dishes such as roast bullfrog and dog-meat hot-pot.

Three Guizhou Men
三个贵州人
West gate of the Worker's Stadium (above Coco Banana), Chaoyang District.
Tel: 5869 0598. **$$**
Hip, spacious restaurant offering authentic, spicy Guizhou food of reliable quality. Full picture menu and good milk tea.

Vegetarian
Though China can be tough for vegetarians, Beijing has a decent number of Buddhist restaurants which feature extraordinary meat-free creations such as vegetarian roast duck, abalone and snails.

Elaine's Vegetarian Restaurant and Bar
素心小筑
Luoma Lake, Shunyi District.
Tel: 8048 5088. **$$**
The place Beijing's vegetarians convert die-hard carnivores with a range of dishes and superior flavours.

Pure Lotus 净心莲
Inside Zhongguo Wen-lianyuan, 12 Nongzhanguan Nanlu, Chaoyang District.

Tel: 6592 3627. **$$$**
Buddhist monks serve
up the best and most
creative vegetarian
dishes in town.

Other Chinese
The East is Red
红色经典
266 Baijialou,
East Third Ring Road,
Chaoyang District.
Tel: 6574 8289. **$$**
Cultural Revolution-era
nostalgia and plenty of
kitsch. Nightly rousing
performances of com-
munist song and dance
and period fare.

Golden Peacock
金孔雀餐厅
16 Minzu Daxue Beilu
(Minority University North
Road), Haidian District.
Tel: 6893 2030. **$$**
Popular Dai minority
restaurant serving,
amongst other things,
tasty pineapple rice,
potato balls and fried
ribs.

Guoyao Xiaoju
国肴小居
58, Bei Santiao, Jiaodaokou,
Dongcheng District.
Tel: 6403 1940. **$$**
Small, relatively unknown
delight serving Tan family
cuisine.

Haidilao Hot Pot
海底捞火锅
A2 Baijiazhuang Lu,
Chaoyang District.
Tel: 6595 0079. **$$**
Popular hot-pot chain
famous for good service
and noodles handmade
at your table with a spe-
cial dance. English menu.

Huajia Yiyuan 花家怡园
235 Dongzhimennei Dajie
(Ghost Street),
Dongcheng District.
Tel: 6405 1908. **$$**
The perfect choice for
beginners, an impressive
traditional courtyard
restaurant with a compre-

hensive picture menu
detailing plentiful home-
style dishes.

Xinjiang Red Rose
新疆红玫瑰餐厅
7 Xingfu Yicun, opposite the
Worker's Stadium north
gate, Chaoyang District.
Tel: 6415 5741. **$$**
Hookah pipes, nightly
music, Uigher dancing
girls and excellent dapaiji
("big plate chicken").

Other Asian
Beijing is home to many
talented chefs from
Asia's five-star hotels
and restaurants. Excel-
lent Thai, Indian and
Japanese cuisine can be
found, but don't be afraid
to branch out.

Hatsune 隐泉日本料理
2/F Heqiao Building C, 8
Guanghua Lu,
Chaoyang District.
Tel: 6581 3939. **$$$$**
Award-winning Japanese
restaurant famous for
sashimi plates and
Californian-style rolls.

Purple Haze 紫苏庭
Opposite the Worker's Sta-
dium north gate,
Chaoyang District.
Tel: 6413 0899. **$$**
Provides reasonably
priced reliable Thai classics such as red chicken
curry and tom yum soup.

Taj Pavillion
泰姬楼印度餐厅
L128 China World Trade
Center, Chaoyang District.
Tel: 6505 5866. **$$$**
North Indian cuisine with
an emphasis on service
and quality.

Western
23 SALT 盐
1/F 9, Jiangtai Xilu,
Chaoyang District.
Tel: 6437 8457. **$$$$**
Contemporary, creative
cuisine and very reason-
ably-priced set lunches.

Annie's 安妮
A1 Nongzhanguan Nanlu,
Chaoyang Park,
Chaoyang District.
Tel: 6591 1931.
Child- and wallet-friendly
Italian. Puts service and
affordability ahead of
strict authenticity.

Blu Lobster 蓝韵
Shangri-La Hotel,
29 Zizhuyuan Lu,
Haidian District.
Tel: 6841 2211. **$$$$$**
Brian McKenna brings his
experience working in
Michelin-starred
restaurants to Beijing.
His "molecular gastron-
omy" includes foams,
jellies, a 42-ingredient
salad, chilli ice cream
and other implausible
wonders.

Mare 古老海
14 Xindong Lu,
Chaoyang District.
Tel: 6417 1459. **$$$$**
Offering a lengthy tapas
and wine menu for enjoy-
able lunches and roman-
tic evenings.

Cafés and Bars
Beijing's original Bar
Street is located next to
the **Sanlitun** diplomatic
area. It's packed full of
mediocre bars and
untrained staff, so
choose a reliable spot
before you head out. **The
Tree** (43 Sanlitun Beijie)
effects a traditional and
lively pub atmosphere;
more intimate is the
pub/microbrewery **Toper**
(2 Sanlitun Beixiaojie) or
try the friendly, well-run
Saddle Cantina (Nali
Studios East) for thirst-
quenching cocktails.
Sanlitun's bars spill
over into the **Worker's
Stadium** area. **Vics**

RIGHT: Beijing's Hard
Rock Café.

(Worker's Stadium north
gate) is the epitome of
Beijing's classy-but-vapid
club culture, although
memorable cocktail
lounge **Face** (just south
of the Worker's Stadium)
cannot fail to impress.
For a more local experi-
ence, once-tranquil lake
park **Houhai** has become
a neon-lit free-for-all with a
few nice spots such as
Lotus Blue (Lotus Lane,
Houhai) or the excellent
lake views at **Buffalo** (6
Lotus Lane, Houhai).
Nearby **Nanluoguxiang** is
now a bona-fide back-
packer area featuring
tranquil, pleasant **Pass
By Bar** (108 Nanluoguxi-
ang), which is well
stocked with travel books.
Starbucks and Chi-
nese equivalent **SPR Cof-
fee** can be found at any
major shopping centre for
reliable coffee and tea.
Beijing's blossoming café
district is the sprawling,
renovated *hutong* Nanlu-
oguxiang. Characterful
Xiao Xin's Café (103
Nanluoguxiang) is filled
with Beijing memorabilia
and excellent cakes. A
visit to the **798 Art Dis-
trict** would be incomplete
without a cappuccino
stop in one of its cafés.
Old Factory Café (4
Jiuxianqiao Lu) is suitably
sophisticated. Also worth
a visit is **Stone Boat
Café** (inside Ritan Park)
which is, quite literally, a
decorative stone boat.

OUTSIDE BEIJING

One of the wonders of the world – the Great Wall is a must-see on any Chinese itinerary. Further afield, the imperial summer residence of Chengde is a rewarding excursion

Main attractions
THE GREAT WALL AT BADALING
MUTIANYU
SIMATAI
THE MING TOMBS
CHENGDE
BEIDAIHE
SHANHAIGUAN

BELOW: the Great Wall snakes across the Western Hills.

The area surrounding Beijing is dotted with arresting sights that attract visitors hoping to escape the daily chaos of the capital. Transport by train or bus is possible, though for shorter trips such as the Great Wall at Badaling and the Ming Tombs, a pre-arranged tour or taxi is easiest; there are also regular tourist buses to Badaling from Qianmen in central Beijing.

The Great Wall

Punctuated by strategically located towers, the **Great Wall** (万里长城; Wanli Changcheng), winds its way for some 6,400km (4,000 miles) like an endless, slender dragon from Shanhaiguan on the Yellow Sea through five provinces, two autonomous regions, and deep into the Gobi Desert. It is a structure of over-whelming physical presence; a vast wall of earth, brick and stone topped by an endless procession of stout towers, rolling over craggy peaks and across deep ravines and barren deserts. It is massively symbolic of the tyranny of imperial rule, the application of mass labour, the ingenuity of engineers com-

Recommended Restaurants on page 155

missioned to work on the grandest scale, and the human desire to build for immortality. (Cynics may point out that some or all of these themes were also apparent at the opening ceremony of the Beijing Olympics.)

The earliest stages of the building of the Wall were in the 5th century BC, but the present course was mainly determined around 220 BC by Qin Shi Huangdi, the first Chinese emperor and founder of the empire. He linked up smaller, previously constructed sections, extending them northwards to ward off horse-riding nomads. However, the most impressive parts of the Wall seen today were built during the Ming dynasty. Vast numbers of soldiers and peasants from all parts of the country were conscripted, spending several years of their lives building this "ten thousand-*li* wall" – *wanli changcheng. For more on the history of the Great Wall, see pages 156–7.*

The Wall receives upwards of 5 million visitors a year. Badaling, the section that nearly all foreigners, and many Chinese, choose to visit is easily reached as a day trip from Beijing; other sections are also possible as a day trip.

Badaling

The most accessible and developed of all the Wall sites is at **Badaling ❶** (八达岭; daily 7am–6pm; charge; cable car extra), just 60km (38 miles) northwest of Beijing, which attracts an avalanche of visitors who stream past the tacky souvenir stalls before surging up the Wall. Despite the crowds, the views are breathtaking from the vantage points, where the mighty barrier climbs and descends across a fascinating mountain landscape.

The Wall here was strategically important and heavily fortified by the Ming emperors, the towers solidly built with high arrow slits. The way up on both sides of the valley leads to high beacon towers, from which you can see the northern plain and the Wall snaking across faraway hills. The western side is a steeper climb.

The majority of tourists visit Badaling as part of a tour, often taking in the Ming Tombs *(see pages 151–2)* en route and sometimes also stopping at **Juyongguan Fortress ❷** (居庸关堡垒; daily 6am–4pm; charge), built to guard the narrow, 20km (13-mile) long valley, and Beijing, against invading armies from the north.

Souvenir stalls at Badaling. The Wall's popularity as a tourist attraction among Chinese was given a considerable boost by Chairman Mao's comment to the effect, "If you haven't been to the Great Wall, you're not a real Chinese." The equivalent aphorism for foreign tourists is "If you haven't seen the Wall, you haven't seen China."

Although Beijing has been the capital for five dynasties, only the Ming Tombs are nearby. The Qing Tombs are 125km (78 miles) to the east, and as the Mongol rulers of the Yuan dynasty did not have burial rites, no Yuan tombs survive.

GETTING TO THE GREAT WALL

Tours: There are dozens of tours to sections of the Great Wall on offer by car, bus or bicycle. Most big hotels and tour companies in Beijing run their own excursions.

By bus: Public buses leave from Dongzhimen bus station to terminuses near different sections of the Wall. Tourist buses leave from around Tiananmen Square taking passengers to entrances of some sections, but may try to overcharge.

ELSEWHERE IN THE REGION

Tianjin: Super-fast bullet trains ("D" trains) run from Tianjin West Station to Beijing (1 hour), Qingdao (5 hours) and Nanjing (7 hours).

Chengde: Trains run to Beijing (5 hours), though buses (5 hours) are more frequent. Qinhuangdao (near Shanhaiguan) takes 5 hours by bus.

Beidaihe: Trains to/from Beijing take 2½ hours, and there are 7 daily. Frequent trains and buses run to Shanhaiguan (1 hour).

The Wall climbs steeply on both sides from the fortress.

Other Wall sites

The scenery at **Mutianyu** ❸ (慕田峪; daily 7am–6pm; charge; cable car extra) is similarly imposing, but located some 90km (55 miles) north of Beijing, this section of wall is far less touristy. A long section of restored Wall follows a high ridge, giving views over wooded ravine, and some sections remain as they were – not rebuilt – so visitors get a more authentic feel, although the walk is tir-

ing and quite tricky in places. Cable cars take visitors from the bottom of the hills almost to the Wall itself, though some may prefer to hike up the 1,000 steps.

The hike is even more strenuous at **Simatai** ❹ (司马台; daily 8am–5pm; charge; cable car extra), 110km (68 miles) northeast of Beijing, as the renovated section quickly turns into steep, dilapidated climbs. For the reasonably fit, the area makes for great hiking and camping, with panoramic mountain views.

A cable car is at hand at the east side of the reservoir. You can take this to a

BELOW: a restored section of Wall at Mutianyu. **BELOW RIGHT:** Badaling.

point 20 to 30 minutes' walk below the Wall, or make a longer excursion on foot. If you opt for the latter, from the car park you will see a small reservoir between two steep sections of Wall. Go through the entrance gate and take the path to the right (east) leading to the higher section of Wall. This is the most spectacular stretch.

Jinshanling (金山岭; daily 8am–sunset; charge), 10km (6 miles) to the west of Simatai, has been restored and is a bit kinder and easier to climb.

Once one of the main garrison areas guarding the capital, **Huanghuacheng ⑤** (黄花城; daily 8am–6pm; charge), lies 60km (38 miles) north of Beijing, the closest the Wall gets to the city. It once had few tourist facilities, but in recent years has become an unfortunate example of rapid overdevelopment. Climb up on either side from a small reservoir to the east of the road.

A relatively tourist-free section of the Great Wall, **Huangyaguan** (黄崖关; Huangya Pass; daily 8.30am–5pm; charge), lies east of Beijing, close to the Eastern Qing Tombs and 30km (17 miles) north of Jixian town. This was an important section of the Wall during the Qing dynasty.

The Ming Tombs

A visit to the Great Wall is normally combined with a trip to the **Ming Tombs ⑥** (十三陵; Shisanling; daily 8am–5.30pm; charge). Protected by an auspicious range of hills to the north, east and west, the tombs of 13 of the 16 Ming emperors lie in this geomantically favourable spot. Entry from the south on the valley floor passes through numerous gates of honour along the 7-km (4-mile) long **Shendao** (神道; Spirit Way), flanked with imposing stone figures of animals and officials (*see margin, right*).

Of the 13 tombs themselves, Chang Ling and Ding Ling are most often visited, as the others don't offer much in the way of historical or architectural interest. **Chang Ling** (长陵) is the final resting place of Emperor Yongle (died 1424), the third emperor of the Ming dynasty. Historians often look at Yongle's reign as ushering in a second phase of the Ming dynasty, as he made significant adjustments to the institutional

The 7-km (4-mile) Spirit Way at the Ming Tombs is flanked by a guard of honour: 12 pairs of stone lions, elephants, camels, horses and mythological creatures, followed by 12 human figures representing civil and military dignitaries and officials. The animals (half standing, half sitting) are said to change guard at midnight.

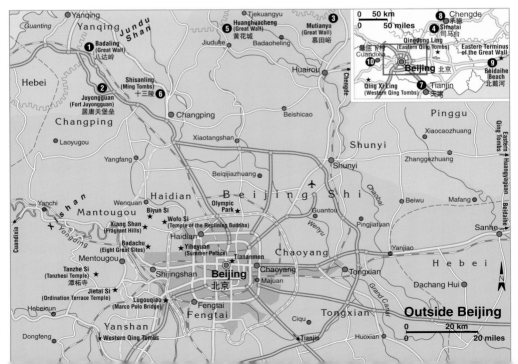

Outside Beijing

The Hall of Eminent Favours in Chang Ling, tomb of Emperor Yongle.

BELOW: stone guardian on the Spirit Way at the Ming Tombs.

forms of the state established by the founder of the Ming dynasty, his father Zhu Yuanzhang. Yongle usurped power from the chosen successor, his nephew, and moved the capital city from Nanjing to Beijing after reconstructing the city.

It was Yongle who chose the site of the tombs, and as he was the first to be buried here, his tomb is the largest and the most centrally located. Moreover, his tomb has served as the model for the other tombs that followed. The mound of the tomb has not been excavated, and the emperor and the empress still lie within the underground vaults today. Above are magnificent courtyards and ceremonial halls.

Ding Ling (定陵), the tomb of the 13th emperor, Zhu Yijun (died 1620), is the only Ming tomb to have been excavated. Take the wide staircase down to the entrance of the vaults, the underground palace, located 30 metres (100ft) below. The emperor's primary wife and one concubine were buried with him, although all you can see down there nowadays are some decorative chests and two stone thrones, placed for the sake of tourists.

The underground palace was sealed with a specially designed lock. The locking stone, which is still on display inside the entrance, fell automatically into place inside the vault when the doors were closed, making it nearly impossible to open them again. Unfortunately, grave robbers managed to gain access, and when the tombs were finally opened the vaults were nearly empty. The underground palace consists of three main halls. Two exhibition rooms above the vaults showcase rare relics belonging to the royals, although most have been moved to the museum at Chang Ling.

Tianjin

Some 140km (90 miles) southeast of Beijing and easily reached by train or bus, **Tianjin** ❼ (天津), with a population of 10 million, is the largest port city in northern China. A walk around town (by far the best thing to do in Tianjin) tells much about its history. If some of the city's colonial architecture and layout is suggestive of Shanghai, this is because Tianjin had a prosperous international community during the late 1800s. In 1860, Western powers, wanting to expand trade with China, turned it into a treaty port by landing troops in the city and forcing Beijing to parcel out the city to the various Western interests.

There are more than 200 concession-area buildings on **Diwu Dajie** (Fifth Avenue) alone, with French architecture prominent – especially on Chifeng Lu, which now serves as Tianjin's fashion district. Despite recent renovation lessening its authenticity, **Gu Wenhua Jie** (古文化街; Ancient Culture Street) in central Tianjin is a good place to look for books, porcelain, carpets, crafts and food, including the local speciality, *goubuli baozi* (steamed buns). It is also the location of the fine Daoist **Tianhou Gong** (天后宫; Tianhou Temple; 8.30am–4.30pm; charge), dedicated to Mazu, Goddess of the Sea.

Around 1km (⅔ mile) to the north is the Buddhist **Dabeichan Yuan** (大悲

禅院; Dabei Monastery; 40 Tianwei Lu; Tue–Sun 9am–4pm; charge), containing several impressive statues to Guanyin, the Goddess of Mercy. **Zhongxin Park** (中心公园; Zhongxin Gongyuan) is an attractive place to take in the ambience, and a stroll from here to Binjiang Dao via Chifeng Lu is one of Tianjin's most rewarding.

The impressive, Japanese-designed **Tianjin Museum** (天津博物馆; Tianjin Bowuguan; 31 Youyi Lu; daily 6.30am–4.30pm) houses priceless cultural relics including ancient calligraphy, paintings and ceramics – many from the imperial collections of Beijing and Chengde. Also worth seeing are the displays of local history on the top floor. For views across the sprawling city, the **Tianjin Zhi Yan** (天津之眼; Tianjin Eye; Yongle Qiao; daily; charge) is a 110-metre (360ft) diameter observation wheel on Yongle Bridge; on a clear day, it can provide views of up to 40km (25 miles).

Yangliuqing (杨柳青) is a pleasant old town situated about 15km (9 miles) west of the city, and known throughout China for its traditional Lunar New Year woodblock prints.

Chengde, imperial retreat

Chengde ❽ (承德), formerly known as Jehol, was the summer residence of the Qing emperors. A five-hour train ride 250km (150 miles) northeast of Beijing, it has retreated once again into the sleepy town it was before Qing-dynasty emperor Kangxi built his new summer palace in 1703. Summer temperatures are pleasantly cool compared with those of Beijing, and even though Chengde now has the ugly buildings and busy roads found everywhere in China, it has kept the feel of a summer resort.

For over 100 years, the emperors and their retinues passed the summer months here, spending their time on hunting excursions, equestrian games and other diversions, as well as on state business. Yet after 1820, when a bolt of lightning killed Emperor Jiaqing here, the resort was abandoned. Fearing that fate might deal them a second blow, the court stayed away, and the buildings and gardens fell into ruin.

What remains is the largest imperial residence in China that has survived in its original condition. The palace complex, the **Bishu Shanzhuang** (避暑山庄; Imperial Summer Villa; daily, park:

SHOP

BELOW LEFT: the Tianjin Eye.
BELOW: Putuozongcheng temple at Chengde.

BELOW: Cuandixia in winter sunlight.

5.30am–6pm, buildings: 8am–5pm; charge includes buildings in the park), is close to modern town of Chengde; its main hall, **Zhenggong**, built with valuable *nanmu* hardwood from Yunnan province, was where Emperor Xianfeng reluctantly signed the agreement with the British and French in 1860 which opened China to foreign trade. The main attraction, however, is the spacious grounds which extend north from the palace and are home to elegantly situated pagodas, halls and pavilions.

Outside the palace grounds, to the north and east, a total of 11 temples – mostly in the Tibetan style (a sign of the favour shown to the Lamaist religion by the Qing emperors) – were built. The **Waiba Miao** (外八庙; Eight Outer Temples; daily 8am–6.30pm, Oct–Apr until 5pm; individual charges) are of greatest interest, and the largest and most impressive of these is the dramatic, red-walled **Putuozongcheng** (普陀宗乘之庙; Shizigou Lu; daily 8am–6pm; charge), dating from 1771 and based on the Potala Palace in Lhasa, Tibet – indeed the temple served as a residence for high Tibetan dignitaries when they stayed at the Chinese imperial court. It is usually possible to access the roof for panoramic views across the entire complex.

Next door to the east is **Xumifushou** (须弥福寿之庙; daily 8am–5.30pm; charge), which was built in 1780 in honour of the sixth Panchen Lama's visit to Chengde for Qianlong's 70th birthday. It exhibits a blend of Han Chinese and Tibetan architecture. The Temple of Universal Peace, or **Puning Si** (普宁寺; Puning Temple; daily 8am–5.30pm; charge) houses a magnificent statue of the thousand-armed (actually there are only 42 arms) Guanyin, carved from five different types of wood and towering 22 metres (72ft) high.

There are several peaks in the immediate surroundings of Chengde, offering pleasant hiking opportunities in the summer and early autumn.

Seaside attractions

On the coast to the east of Beijing, **Beidaihe ❾** (北戴河) is a favourite summer destination for high-level party officials and several million tourists every year. The town has sandy beaches, some old Western-style villas, great

seafood, and bicycles can be hired in the summer months to explore the surrounding area.

East along the railway line from Beidaihe, the small, walled town of **Shanhaiguan** (山海关) marks the Great Wall's eastern boundary with the sea. Formerly an old garrison town, Shanhaiguan is crisscrossed with small, manageable streets similar to Beijing's *hutong*. The official highlight here is the **Tianxia Diyiguan** (天下第一关; First Pass Under Heaven; 7am–6pm peak season, 7.30am–5pm off season; charge), a stretch of battlements bombarded by music blaring from loudspeakers. Far more serene and impressive is the section of Wall at **Jiao Shan**, 3km (2 miles) north of town, where the Wall mounts its first range of hills. It may be tiring, but walking along the Wall is well worth the effort (there is also a cable car), and some fine walks are possible into the hills beyond. The potentially momentous **Lao Long Tou** (老龙头; Old Dragon Head), where the Great Wall meets the sea 4km (2½ miles) south of town, is actually an overpriced anticlimax, but access to the beaches on either side affords the same view for free.

Into the rural past

A tantalising glimpse of old-world China can be found at the village of **Cuandixia** ⑩ (爨底下村), 90km (55 miles) west of Beijing. Set in a valley not far from Zhaitang town, it is an enchanting jumble of traditional dwellings climbing the hillside. In total, there are over 70 courtyard houses dating from the Ming and Qing dynasties. The village is also notable for its collection of Maoist political slogans from the Cultural Revolution, which have been touched up and preserved.

Reaching Cuandixia by public transport is not easy; the best bet is to take the subway to Beijing's westernmost stop (Pingguoyuan) and then to take a taxi the rest of the way. Residents of the village also offer very cheap, simple accommodation for those who wish to stay overnight.

Either visited as you return from Cuandixia, or as a separate excursion, **Tanzhe Si** (潭柘寺; Mentougou District daily 7.30am–5.30pm; charge) is a vast Buddhist temple 45km (28 miles) west of Beijing that purportedly predates the city itself. The temple halls are arranged up the hillside in a glorious setting, and there is a sublime collection of stupas within the attached temple of **Talin Si** (塔林寺). ❑

Until recently the sandy beaches of Beidaihe were strictly demarcated, the best stretches being reserved for Party officials, and another area for foreigners. These days the restrictions are no longer in place, and the resort is crowded in the summer peak season when the shallow waters are pleasantly warm.

RESTAURANTS

Beidaihe
Haitian Yise Jiudian
海天一色酒店
56 Shandong Jie. **$$$**
Complement the speciality seafood with local or Cantonese dishes.

Chengde
Xin Qianlong 新乾隆酒楼
Dijingyuan Building, Xinhua Lu.
$$$$
Just 1km (⅔ mile) from the imperial resort, this luxury restaurant serves many cuisines including local dishes such as wild game.

Shangke Tang 上客堂
West side of Puning Temple. **$$**

A hall built for Buddhist monks visiting Chengde, this impressive hotel and restaurant serves a variety of food, including vegetarian cuisine.

Great Wall
Commune by the Great Wall 长城脚下的公社
Badaling Expressway, Great Wall exit 16.
www.commune.com.cn **$$$$**
This collection of outstanding Asian architectural projects near Badaling is worth a visit in its own right and boasts two high-class – and expensive – restaurants.

Tianjin
Goubuli 狗不理
77 Shandong Lu. **$**
Tianjin's most famous restaurant, serving juicy steamed dumplings made to a centuries-old recipe.

Laozhiqing Shaomai
老知青烧麦馆
Outside Binjiang department store, off Shandong Lu. **$**
This tiny, easily missable but popular place serves *shaomai* dumplings, congee and many other snacks.

Tianjinwei 1928
天津卫1928
1F Nuren Jie. **$$**

Local character, traditional food and performances including local comedy "cross-talk".

Huayun Bowuguan
华蕴博物馆
283 Hebei Lu. **$$–$$$**
A "museum" restaurant filled with hundreds of antiques and historical oddities. Local cuisine at a range of prices.

Prices for a meal for one, with one drink:
$ = under Rmb50
$$ = Rmb 50–100
$$$ = Rmb 100–150
$$$$ = over Rmb 150

BUILDING THE WALL

This astonishing project, conceived as the ultimate defence, took nearly 20 centuries to complete and involved millions of conscripted labourers

The Great Wall dates back more than two millennia, when a series of shorter walls were systematically linked during the Qin dynasty (221–206 BC) to protect China's northern borders. Centuries of gradual decline, and occasional repair, ensued before officials of the Ming court – fearing attack from the north – decided to rebuild the Wall into a formidable barrier, the "Ten Thousand Li Great Wall". The gargantuan project took over 100 years, but singularly failed to prevent the invasion of China by the Manchus in the mid-17th century.

The Ming-dynasty wall averages 8 metres (26 ft) high and 7 metres (21 ft) wide. Some sections are broad enough to allow five or six soldiers to ride side by side. Surveyors planned the route so that, where possible, the outer (generally north-facing) wall was higher. Countless parallel walls, fortified towers, beacon towers, moats, fortifications and garrisons completed a complex system. Local military units supervised construction. In a simple contract, officers and engineers detailed the time, materials and work required.

Many sections of the wall around Beijing were built on granite blocks, with some foundation stones weighing more than one ton. Elaborate wooden scaffolding, hoists and pulleys, and occasionally iron girders aided the builders. To speed up the construction process, prefabricated stone parts were used for beacon towers, including lintels, gate blocks and gullies.

BELOW LEFT: towers in remote areas were built close enough together to enable the beacon system devised in the Tang dynasty to function. When trouble was spotted, guards used wolves' dung to create smoke signals, which could be interpreted by neighbouring guard posts.

BELOW RIGHT: Ming-dynasty bricks were extremely heavy; pulleys, shoulder poles, handcarts, mules and goats were used to move them into place.

BELOW: the top part of the wall was built so that five or six horsemen could ride side by side. Crenallated walls, fortified towers, signal beacon towers and garrisons completed the defences.

A GUARD'S LIFE

From their small rooftop sentry boxes, Great Wall guards, though they kept their weapons and torches primed, saw no enemies for months on end. If an assault came, the guards' main function was not to defend the wall but to alert the nearest garrison using a complex system of torch signals.

Most guards lived in remote watchtowers shared with five to ten others. During the day, those not on lookout duty tilled small patches of farmland on the hillside, collected firewood and dried wolf and cattle dung, and sometimes hunted. They ground wheat flour in stone mortars and carried out minor repairs to the wall and towers. To supplement food supplies brought by road, migration of farmers was encouraged or enforced, and guards helped them construct irrigation canals and farmhouses.

The guards' crowded living quarters also served as storage for grain and weapons. Doors and windows had heavy wooden shutters to keep out the winter cold – the areas through which the wall passes regularly experience temperatures below -20°C (4°F) – and often guards shared a *kang*, a heated brick bed.

ABOVE: construction of the Great Wall varied according to the terrain and the perceived level of threat. With the aim of maximising its defensive capabilities, surveyors often chose unlikely routes across near-vertical hillsides. Engineers coped with the topography by using stretches of "single" wall, bridges, viaducts, and incorporating natural features.

ABOVE: the view from one of the thousands of watchtowers along the wall.

BELOW: to minimise transportation costs, brick kilns were constructed as close to the wall as possible. Brick-makers often recorded their names and the date of production on the bricks as a guarantee of quality. So far, some 50 brick kilns have been excavated. Archaeologists believe dozens – if not hundreds – more remain buried along the length of the wall.

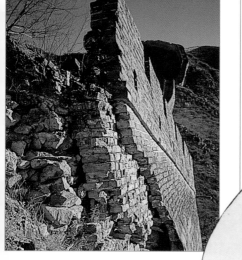

ABOVE: the 7-metre- (23-ft-) thick wall was constructed of an outer layer of brick and stone enclosing an inner core of earth, rubble and, legend has it, the bones of conscript labourers.

Recommended Restaurants on page 165

THE NORTHEAST

China's rugged northeast, known to the West
as Manchuria and to the Chinese as Dongbei,
has been shaped by conflict between China
and neighbouring Japan, Korea and Russia

Northeast of Beijing lie the three provinces of Liaoning, Jilin and Heilongjiang, collectively known as **Dongbei**, literally "East-North". The old name of Manchuria, still in use outside China, goes back to the fact that this was once the territory of the Manchu *(manzu)*, rulers of the Qing dynasty. With a blend of Chinese, Korean and Russian influences, this far-flung region has an unusual cultural identity. It was brutally occupied by the Japanese in the 1930s, and has long been the focus of conflict and power struggle. Recent fortunes have been mixed: the closure of state-controlled enterprises has caused difficulties in Dongbei's industrial heartlands – particularly in Jilin province – but some cities, notably Dalian, have thrived with the booming Chinese economy.

The Manchu rulers prohibited the settlement of Han Chinese in the region until the middle of the 19th century, when the pressure of an expanding population and the dislocations of the Taiping Rebellion forced them to change their policy. During the 1930s, the Japanese attempted to separate the northeast from China by setting up the puppet state of Manchukuo, under the rule of the former, and last, Chinese emperor, Puyi. The region was rapidly industrialised in the early Communist years, and the Manchu population became completely assimilated with the Han Chinese; in recent years, however, the special customs and traditions of the Manchu are once more being emphasised.

Shenyang

A busy transport junction and capital of Liaoning province, **Shenyang ❶** (沈阳) is one of the most important industrial cities in China. Formerly known by its Manchurian name of Mukden, it did not gain significance until the Song dynasty, when it became a centre of trade for nomadic livestock breeders. Shenyang's rise in status came during the Qing dynasty, when Liaoning was the home of the Manchu, the Qing emperors. Today, more than half of the Manchu *(manzu)* ethnic minority lives here. Formerly

Main attractions
IMPERIAL PALACE, SHENYANG
DALIAN BEACHES
CHANGBAI SHAN
   NATURE RESERVE
HARBIN
HARBIN ICE LANTERN FESTIVAL
THE FAR NORTH

LEFT: winter wonderland – ice and lights at the Harbin Ice Lantern Festival.
BELOW: keeping fit in the frozen north.

In the middle of the 1980s, Dalian became China's first certifiably rat-free city, following an intensive effort to rid the entire city of the rodents.

GETTING TO DONGBEI

Flights: Harbin has a small international airport with domestic flights to most major cities in China. Dalian and Shenyang also have airports.

By train and bus: Shenyang is a major transport hub, with extensive rail links and long-distance buses to cities across the northeast.

By boat: Dalian has a passenger ferry terminal with connections to Inchon in South Korea, also Shanghai (37 hours), Tianjin (13 hours) and Yantai (5–7 hours).

GETTING AROUND DONGBEI

Shenyang: The fastest trains go to Dandong (4 hours), Dalian (4 hours) and Jilin (5 hours).

Changchun: Frequent trains to Harbin (2 hours) and Shenyang (2 hours) make Changchun a useful rail hub. Bus journeys are an alternative such as to Jilin (1½ hours).

Changbai Shan: Yanji International Airport has infrequent flights to Dalian and Beijing. Erdao Baihe town has rail connections to Shenyang (13 hours via Tonghua).

called the Jurchen, they constitute the most populous non-Han minority in the northeast, and are also found scattered through Inner Mongolia. Now virtually indistinguishable from the Han Chinese, the Manchu once spoke an Altaic language unrelated to Chinese and used a separate writing system in existence since the 17th century. Today's Manchu population speak Mandarin and the Manchu tongue appears to have died out.

Shenyang's main tourist attraction is its **Imperial Palace** (故宫; Shenyang Gugong; 171 Shenyang Lu; daily 8am–5pm; charge), China's largest and most complete palace complex after the Forbidden City in Beijing. It was built in 1625, after the Manchu had declared Shenyang to be their capital, and it contains more than 300 buildings in an area covering more than 60,000 sq metres (650,000 sq ft). The palace was the residence of Nurhachi, the founder of the Qing dynasty, and his successor Abahai (Huang Taiji in Chinese), and it was maintained after the Qing emperors moved to the capital of Beijing. The main buildings – an amalgamation of Chinese, Manchu and Mongol architecture – are Chongzheng, Qingning Palace, Dazheng

BELOW: Dalian's sandy beaches attract the crowds.

and Wensu Pavilion. It is listed as a World Heritage site, and a large-scale renovation plan started in June 2008.

Of the three imperial Qing tombs in Liaoning province, two are in Shenyang. The Northern Imperial Tomb, **Bei Ling** (北陵; 12 Taishan Lu; daily 8am–5pm; charge), was built in 1643 for Nurhachi's son Abahai and is now in the centre of Beiling Park in the north of the city. The Eastern Imperial Tomb, **Dong Ling** (东陵; 210 Dongling Jie; daily 8am–5pm; charge), also known as Fuling, is the final resting place of Nurhachi and 8km (5 miles) outside the city. The third tomb, Yong Ling, built by Nurhachi for his ancestors, is in Xinbin district. Less visited, it is approximately three hours outside the city.

For those interested in the Japanese occupation of Manchuria, the **9.18 History Museum** (九一八历史博物馆; Qinhua Rijun Di 731 Budui Yizhi; 46 Wanghua Nanjie; daily 8.30am–4pm; charge) gruesomely details the period. The museum takes its name from the date the Japanese arrived in Shenyang – 18 September 1931. Public buses run to tourist spots from **Government Square**

(市府广场), and Shenyang's two train stations are also centrally located.

Boom town of the northeast

Anshan (鞍山) is a nondescript city 80km (50 miles) south of Shenyang, and the point of access for a pleasant visit to the scenic mountain of **Qian Shan** (千山国家公园), blanketed with ancient pines, pavilions, temples and monasteries dating from the Ming and Qing periods.

South from Anshan, the railway line passes broad fields of millet and soybeans to the tip of the Liaodong Peninsula and the dynamic city of **Dalian** ❷ (大连). This is an economic success story dubbed the "Hong Kong of the North", and one of the most attractive cities in north China. The ice-free harbour is the northeast's largest, a fact reflected in its repeated conquest: first by Japan in 1895 after the Sino-Japanese War, then for a short time by the Russians, until the Japanese regained control in 1905; they hung onto Dalian until it fell into the hands of the Soviet Union in 1945 before finally returning to China in the 1950s.

TIP

For a closer look at North Korea, take one of the daily boats from Dandong that goes out onto the Yalu River, the international border, and comes within 20 metres/yards of the Korean side.

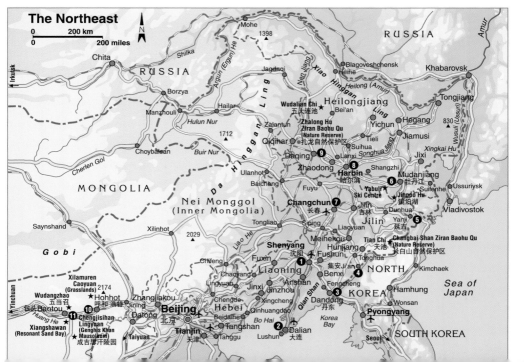

Dongbei is one of China's best areas for birdwatching, with several species of crane, including the red-crowned crane (also known as the Japanese or Siberian crane).

BELOW: Lake Tian Chi in Changbai Shan straddles the North Korean border.

The main impression of Dalian is of a busy port with broad streets and large squares planted with greenery. The period of foreign occupancy bequeathed the city an attractive array of European architecture, with the best examples ringing central Zhongshan Square – have a look at the Dalian Hotel and the old Bank of China Building. The city is also renowned for its extensive beaches, mild climate and excellent seafood restaurants.

Sections of the coastline offer dizzy views of plunging cliffs, especially at **Laohu Tan** (老虎滩; Tiger Beach). There is pleasant scenery and a sandy beach at **Bangchuidao Jingqu** (棒槌岛景区; Bangchuidao Scenic Area; Binhai Lu; charge), 5km (3 miles) southeast of the city centre. The sand-and-pebble beach at **Fujiazhuang** (府家庄; Xigang District; daily 6am–11pm; charge) is probably the best spot to swim or sunbathe away from the crowds. Using public buses is not particularly straightforward, but taxis are plentiful.

Korean borderlands

Southeast from Shenyang, or northeast from Dalian, is the city of **Dandong ❸** (丹东) and the mountainous vistas of **Dagu Shan** (大孤山), right on the North Korean border. From Dandong, the railway carries on into North Korea as far as its capital, Pyongyang. For those who want to say they've nearly set foot in North Korea, boats carry visitors to within only a few metres of the North Korean side on the Yalu Jiang River. Alternatively you can walk along the original bridge that linked China with North Korea until you reach the twisted wreckage created by American bombers and carefully preserved since by Chinese authorities.

East of Shenyang, the main road runs to the nearby industrial town of **Fushun** (抚顺)**,** where the last emperor, Puyi, was imprisoned from 1950 until 1959. Still further east is **Tonghua** (通化), a wine-producing town in the southeast of Jilin province. Accessible by train or bus from Tonghua, **Ji'an ❹** (集安) lies on the Chinese-Korean border, on the upper course of the Yalu Jiang. The numerous tombs in the vicinity (not all are open to the public) testify to the fact that Ji'an was once the capital of the Korean kingdom of Koguryo. Today it lies in the

middle of an autonomous region of China's Korean minority (there are about 2 million ethnic Koreans living in China, and more than 60 percent live in this region). The Yalu Jiang, separating China and North Korea, is only 30 metres (100ft) wide here, and in the summer months, women chat across the border while doing their laundry and children from both sides swim in the river together – although swimming to the opposite bank is not officially permitted.

The capital of this autonomous region is **Yanji 5** (延吉), where the Koreans also have their own university. The Korean influence is not restricted to this area alone. Some parts of Shenyang, Changchun, Jilin city and Mudanjiang, too, feel unmistakably Korean – people wear Korean clothing, signs are written in Korean, and Korean is the primary language of commerce. (In Shenyang, there is a cemetery dedicated to the memory of the Chinese who died in the Korean War.)

Between Tonghua and Yanji, the **Changbai Shan Nature Reserve** (长白山自然保护区; Changbai Shan Ziran Baohu Qu) follows the mountains along the China–North Korea border, one of the most diverse mountain-forest ecosystems in Asia and sanctuary for many endangered animals – leopards, Siberian tigers and bears amongst them. The easiest way to explore is to head to the **Changbai Shan Scenic Area** (长白山风景区; Changbai Shan Fengjing Qu; daily 7am–4.30pm; charge), which includes the Underground Forest and the Changbai Waterfall, or arrange a tour with CITS or a big hotel in Jilin. A highlight of this wild reserve is the beautiful **Tian Chi** (天池; Lake of Heaven), a volcanic crater lake high up in the mountains. Measuring 15km (9 miles) in circumference, the lake makes for a rewarding trip, but is only accessible between June and September; for the rest of the year the road is iced over and treacherous. Note that the lake straddles the North Korean border (which is not clearly marked), so don't walk all the way round. A creature akin to the Loch

Ness monster has allegedly been spotted lurking beneath the waters; the last sighting was in 1981. Water from the lake descends in an impressive waterfall, source of the Songhua Jiang.

Surrounded by beautiful scenery north of Yanji, in Heilongjiang province, is the town of **Mudanjiang 6** (牡丹江). The main attraction in these parts is **Jingpo Hu** (镜泊湖), a lakeside resort area surrounded by miles of virgin forest.

To the north

Connected to Yanji by road and rail, **Jilin City** (吉林) in central Jilin province is most famous for its winter display of ice-rimmed trees along the banks of the Songhua Jiang River. Other sights include the impressive functioning **Catholic Church** (天主教堂; 3 Songjiang Lu; Mon–Fri from 5am, Sat–Sun from 8am; free) and the **Wen Miao** (文庙; Wen Miao Hutong; Mon–Fri 8.30am–4pm, Sat–Sun 9am–4pm; charge), a temple built for imperial examination hopefuls to pay homage to Confucius.

The large provincial capital of Jilin, **Changchun 7** (长春) did not become an important city until the end of the 19th

Excellent ski facilities at Changchun play host to the annual Chinese Vasaloppet cross-country skiing competition.

BELOW: young children learning traffic policing skills.

In the early 1930s, Puyi, the last emperor of China, was made an emperor again by the Japanese, who set up a puppet empire in the northeast called Manchukuo. He was captured by the Russians in 1945 and later imprisoned by Mao before being "rehabilitated" by the Chinese Communist Party in his last years. He died in Beijing in 1964.

BELOW: ice art at Harbin's Taiyang Dao.

century, when it was the terminus of the Manchurian railway (built by skilled Russian labour). In 1932, the town, then known as Hsinking, became the seat of the government of the Japanese puppet state of Manchukuo. Nowadays, the town still shows signs of Japanese urban planning in its ruler-straight boulevards. This industrial university city of around 6.8 million people is also well known in China for its car-manufacturing works, and because of its large parks, it is sometimes known as the "town of woodland". At the **Weihuang Gong** (伪皇宫; Puppet Emperor's Palace; 5 Guangfu Lu; daily 8.30am–4.30pm; charge), you can peruse Puyi's living quarters and mementoes from the bizarre life of China's last emperor *(see margin, left)*.

Where China meets Russia

From Changchun, the journey continues north to **Harbin** ❽ (哈尔滨), the capital of Heilongjiang province, situated almost 1,400km (900 miles), and 13 hours by train, from Beijing. The city lies along the Songhua Jiang, which joins the Heilong Jiang, the river that defines China's border with Russia to the north (where it

is known as the Amur). Harbin has its industrial areas and newly built apartment blocks which stand in stark contrast to some of the older, European-looking architecture of Central Street (Zhongyang Dajie) downtown.

Russians first arrived in Harbin at the end of the 19th century with the railway, which passed through the city on its way from Vladivostok to Dalian. Large numbers of refugees followed after the Russian Revolution of 1917, and although most returned to the homeland after World War II, the city has retained the feel of a Russian outpost. The central **Daoli District** (道里区), in particular, has onion-domed churches, Russian restaurants and, following improved relations and easier travel between the two countries since the mid-1990s, increasing numbers of Russian traders and tourists, too. There are over a dozen Orthodox Christian churches, many of them built in neo-Gothic style, culminating in the restored **Cathedral**, formerly known as St Sofia's (圣索菲亚教堂; corner of Zhaolin Jie and Toulong Jie; 9.30am–5.30pm; charge). The district also offers some upmarket restaurants and hotels.

In the village of Pingfang, 30km (20 miles) south of Harbin, **Unit 731 Japanese Germ Warfare Experimental Base** was the site of the Japanese army's gruesome and inhumane medical experiments during the 1930s and '40s. the site is now open to the public as a **museum** (侵华日军地731部队遗址; Xinjiang Dajie; daily 8.30–11.30am, 1–4pm; charge). Denied by the Japanese government for decades after World War II, its existence eventually came to light after a Japanese scholar uncovered documented proof. Over 4,000 prisoners of war – Chinese and Allies – died from "medical" experiments involving cold, heat, chemicals, injections of viruses and plague, and live dissection.

Harbin is close to Siberia, and winters are extremely cold; temperatures regularly fall below –30°C (–22°F). The need for warm clothing cannot be exaggerated, especially considering the unmissable outdoor sights displayed every winter during the famous **Ice Lantern Festival** (冰灯节; Bingdeng Jie). The festival starts on 5 January and lasts for one month (though frozen sculptures often remain longer) and centres on **Zhaolin Park** (兆麟公园; Zhaolin Gongyuan; 5am–6.30pm; charge), which becomes home to dozens of extraordinary ice sculptures including animals, plants, mythical figures and famous buildings lit up from inside by coloured lights. On the north bank of the Songhua River, **Ice and Snow World** (冰雪大世界; 9am–10pm; Bingxue Da Shijie; charge) is a huge exhibition featuring the larger works. **Taiyang Dao** (太阳岛; Sun Island Park; 8am–5pm; charge) mainly displays incredible snow carvings whose detail and sheer size defy belief.

Several ski resorts can be reached by bus from Harbin, including **Yabuli** (亚布力滑雪旅游度假区; Xiangzhi City; Nov–Apr), China's best-equipped and largest ski centre, 200km (120 miles) southeast of the city.

The train from Harbin runs on to the northwest, towards the border with Inner Mongolia, passing through the oil town of **Daqing** ❾. The frenzied exploitation of these oilfields in the Mao era has led to their premature decline, and yields now dwindle year by year. With the demand for fuel rising rapidly across the country, China is having to import large quantities of oil to sustain its economic growth.

About 30km (20 miles) before the industrial sprawl of Qiqihar, the railway passes close to the **Lake Zhalong Nature Reserve** (扎龙自然保护区; daily 7am–5pm; charge), where the swampy terrain is home to rare red-crowned and white-naped cranes. The reserve can be reached by public buses leaving from Qiqihar's Number One Department Store or by tours organised by the CITS office. To the north, near Bei'an, is the volcanic area of **Wudalian Chi** (五大连池), with numerous hot springs and therapeutic mud baths.

In summer months, it is possible to journey north into "Chinese Siberia", a vast and remote region of endless birch and pine forests extending to the Heilong River (the Amur to the Russians). It is theoretically possible to cross into Russia from the town of **Heihe**, although a permit may be required from the Public Security Bureau *(gonganju)*. ❏

Russian influence is easy to see in Harbin.

RESTAURANTS

Changchun
Chufang Zhizao
厨房制造
Opposite entrance 2, Nanhu Park. **$$**
A pleasant park environment in which to enjoy snacks such as cakes made with durian or green tea.

Dalian
Wanbao Seafood Restaurant
万宝海鲜舫
108 Jiefang Lu. **$$$$**
Elegant place specialising in lobster and sea urchin.

Xiandai Shishang
现代食尚
59 Changjiang Lu. **$$**

Centrally-located at Zhongshan Square, this Dongbei restaurant strives for fashionable decoration and high-quality dishes.

Dandong
Donghai Yucan
东海渔村
42, Block E. Development Zone. **$**
Popular freshwater fish restaurant.

Harbin
Huamei Xi Canting
华梅西餐厅
112 Zhongyang Dajie. **$$**
Established in 1925 and claiming to be

the mainland's oldest foreign restaurant, this famous Russian spot serves borscht and other classics.

Xiangcun Dayuan
乡村大院
13 Dashun Jie. **$$**
Dongbei cuisine and raucous nightly Red Army song performances.

Prices for a meal for one person with one drink:
$ = under Rmb50
$$ = Rmb 50–100
$$$ = Rmb 100–150
$$$$ = over Rmb 150

INNER MONGOLIA

Main attractions
WUTA SI, HOHHOT
WUDANGZHAO
GRASSLAND TOUR
GENGHIS KHAN MAUSOLEUM
XIANGSHAWAN

BELOW: Mongolian children in national dress at the Genghis Khan Mausoleum, Dongsheng.

Stretching like a huge crescent across a vast swathe of northern China from the Siberian borderlands to the Gobi Desert, **Inner Mongolia** (内蒙古; Nei Monggol) is one of the world's emptiest places, a continuation of the endless grasslands and deserts of the independent Republic of Mongolia to the north.

Although the name Mongolia conjures up visions of Genghis Khan's horse-bound hordes and their phenomenal 13th-century military conquests – from a stunned imperial China right through the gates of eastern Europe – the cultural landscape of today is rather more subdued. As part of the People's Republic of China, the indigenous culture of today's Inner Mongolia has long been diluted by waves of Han Chinese settlers, with less than 15 percent of the population considering themselves ethnically Mongolian. But while Beijing's Sinification efforts are viewed as a model for more unruly regions such as Tibet and Xinjiang, far-flung pockets of traditional Mongolian life still flourish, and with a modicum of time and effort it is still possible for travellers to absorb some of these timeless nomadic rhythms. The industrialised population centred along the southern fringes may resemble that of most other large Chinese cities at first glance, but closer inspection reveals an undercurrent of Mongolian influence, whether through cuisine or custom. Finally, the mesmerising landscapes – from the sprawling grasslands in the northeast to the golden sand dunes of the southwest – represent a world-class attraction in their own right.

Hohhot

The most accessible part of Inner Mongolia is around the main cities of Baotou and Hohhot, where the Huang He (Yellow River) meanders through the dusty plains. Most visitors use **Hohhot** (呼和 浩特) ❿, the autonomous region's capital, as a base for organising summer trips to the well-trammelled grasslands within 80km (50 miles) of the city, but the town itself has several significant sights and is the most convenient place in which to get orien-

GETTING TO INNER MONGOLIA

Flights: Hohhot's Baita Airport, located about 14km (9 miles) east of the city centre, has flights to 28 Chinese cities, with daily service to Beijing, Xi'an, Xilinhot and Hailaer and frequent connections to Guangzhou and Shanghai. The only regularly scheduled international flight is to Ulaan Baatar.

By train and bus: Both Hohhot and Baotou are well connected by train to major northern Chinese cities, with daily services to Beijing, Datong, Taiyuan, Yinchuan and Lanzhou. The Trans-Manchurian and Trans-Mongolian railway lines running through Inner Mongolia make train travel to Russia and Mongolia possible. From Hohhot, there is a daily bus service to Beijing and Datong, while there are daily buses from Baotou to Yulin and Yan'an.

GETTING AROUND INNER MONGOLIA

Hohhot: There are several daily express trains to Baotou (2 hours), while buses depart every half-hour for Baotou (2 hours) and Dongsheng (3 hours).

Baotou: There are several daily express trains to Hohhot (2 hours), with buses leaving every 30 minutes for Hohhot (2 hours) and Dongsheng (1 hour).

Mutton is piled onto the altar at the Genghis Khan Mausoleum, 50km (30 miles) south of the city of Dongsheng, part of a sacrificial ceremony in honour of the great khan which takes place four times a year.

tated. It's largely a Han Chinese conurbation, although there is a palpable Mongolian presence in the old quarter as well as a visible and vibrant Hui (Chinese Muslim) community. A good, if somewhat overwhelming, venue for getting acquainted with the official Chinese version of Inner Mongolian history, culture and geography is the enormous new **Inner Mongolia Museum** (内蒙古博物馆; Nei Menggu Bowuguan; Tue–Sun, Oct–Apr 9.30am–5pm, May–Sept 9am– 5.30pm; free), housed in a capacious, multi-storey building (crowned by a rounded roof resembling a yurt and covered in *faux* grass). The museum, 15 minutes away by taxi in the eastern suburbs, has four floors holding 14 exhibition halls with limited English captioning.

Buddhist lamaseries

In the old Mongolian enclave in Hohhot's southwest corner is a cluster of Buddhist lamaseries, heavily Tibetan in both style

BELOW: endless grasslands.

Hohhot's Wuta Si is an unusual Indian-style temple. There are a total of 1,563 Buddha reliefs on the walls, as well as script and various arcane charts.

BELOW: traditional yurts *(ger)* are still used by the Mongolian nomads.

and substance, and clear reminders of the historic importance of Lamaist Buddhism to Mongolia. In their courtyards, young Tibetan and Mongolian monks mingle, keeping strong a special religious bond the cultures have shared for centuries – local lamas can often be spotted determinedly but clumsily reciting *sutras* in stilted Tibetan.

The largest and most active site is the Ming-dynasty **Dazhao** (大召; daily 8am–6pm; charge), tucked away on the west side of Danan Jie. First built in 1579, the original temple was itself a symbol of Mongolia's acceptance of Lamaist Buddhism, as it was founded by Altan Khan, who converted to Tibetan Buddhism after paying an official visit to Sonam Gyatso (who later became known as the third Dalai Lama) in Qinghai. It has been restored numerous times, including recently, and during the Qing dynasty it was expanded and dedicated to the Qing emperor Kangxi.

A short walk to the northeast across Danan Jie is another historic lamasery, the **Xilituzhao** (席里图召; daily 8am–6pm; charge), built in 1586 following a reciprocal visit to Hohhot by Sonam Gyatso. The lamasery's most distinguishing feature is its large, Tibetan-style stupa, which has a curious combination of Sanskrit script and Chinese and Tibetan motifs painted on its sides.

A 15-minute walk southeast of Xilituzhao is Hohhot's most intact example of historic architecture, the **Wuta Si** (五塔寺; Five Tower Temple; daily 8am–5.30pm; charge), a compact and rather unusual Indian-style stone structure comprising five pagodas. Originally built in 1727 as part of a larger complex, its walls are adorned with remarkably well-preserved reliefs of Buddhas, as well as an engraving of *sutras* in Sanskrit, Tibetan and Mongolian that extends the length of its perimeter. Inside the structure and around the back some intriguing Mongolian cosmological charts are etched into the stone walls.

Back onto Danan Jie and around 1km (⅔ mile) to the north, the **Qingzhen Dasi** (清真大寺; Great Mosque; free), with its mixture of Chinese and Arabic styles, is the main place of worship for Hohhot's sizeable Hui population. In the surrounding alleys are several Muslim noodle and kebab restaurants.

Baotou and Wudangzhao

The industrial town of **Baotou** ⑪ (包头), shrouded in smog from its numerous furnaces, lies two hours by train to the west of Hohhot. Though there is little to see in the city itself, it is the staging point for excursions to the handful of nearby attractions. The area's most historically significant sight is the captivating Tibetan-style lamasery of **Wudangzhao** (五当召; daily 8am–5.30pm; charge), about 70km (43 miles) northeast of Baotou. By far the largest and best-preserved lamasery in Inner Mongolia, the complex of white-washed temples and prayer halls stretches up the side of a hill and still houses numerous lamas. Founded in 1749, the lamasery was dedicated to the Yellow Hat Sect of Tibetan Buddhism, and its adherents still cling to the sect's tenets.

Genghis Khan Mausoleum

The **Genghis Khan Mausoleum** (成吉思汗陵园; Chengjisihan Lingyuan; daily 8am–5.30pm; charge), outside the coal-stained city of Dongsheng, about 110km (68 miles) south of Baotou, is very much revered by Mongolians from Inner and Outer Mongolia alike, and is one of the primary icons of their cultural identity.

Within the three distinctive cement buildings, constructed by the Chinese in the 1950s and representing Mongolian yurts, lie what are reputedly artefacts from the 13th century, While most experts do not believe the Great Khan was ever actually interred here, this does not deter thousands of ethnic Mongolians from converging on the grounds during the impressive sacrificial ceremonies that are held on the grounds four times each year. During these times, entire families of Mongolians (who travel great distances from across both Inner and Outer Mongolia), clad in colourful traditional dress, come to pay homage to their most influential historic figure. The main statue of the chieftain stands tall in the principal chamber of the three-domed mausoleum.

Resonant Sand Bay

Encroaching on the steppe about 45km (28 miles) south of Baotou is the spectacular **Xiangshawan** (响沙湾; Resonant Sand Bay), a sprawling sea of shifting sand dunes on the northern fringe of the Kubuqi Desert. The golden dunes, the highest of which are 110 metres (360ft), are an arresting sight, swallowing whole the surrounding patches of sparse grassland (it is in fact an illustration of one of the many serious environmental problems facing China – desertification as the Gobi Desert spreads southwards). A windswept section of the dunes has been made into a mini amusement park (open daily 8am–6pm; entrance fee) – accessible by cable car and offering camel rides and a sand slide – but a short walk will take you away from the tacky development and into a Sahara-esque dreamscape.

The entrance is 3km (2 miles) down a turn-off branching west from Highway 210, about halfway between Baotou and Dongsheng. Buses running between the two cities will let you alight at the turn-off, but from there you would need to walk to the dunes. Alternatively, CITS in Baotou offers day tours. ❑

TIP

Tours regularly depart from Hohhot to the **grasslands** beyond; many travellers find the tour-group atmosphere and paraphernalia intrusive, while others manage to appreciate the huge prairie to its full. Most visit the Xilamuren grasslands 80km (50 miles) to the north; other grassland tours (which typically last three to four days) head further afield to Huitengxile and Gegentala.

BELOW LEFT: feast-day gathering at the Genghis Khan Mausoleum.

RESTAURANTS AND MONGOLIAN FOOD

The Mongolian diet relies heavily on the grazing animals raised as part of the nomadic lifestyle – sheep, cattle and horses – either in the form of their meat (*hongshi* or "red food") or the dairy products (*baishi* or "white food") that they yield.

Sheep provide the staple meat: mutton (羊肉; *yangrou*), usually boiled but sometimes roasted whole or in sections. Out on the steppe, a favoured mutton speciality is *shouzhua yangrou*

(手抓羊肉), sheep legs boiled in a cauldron with a touch of salt. In Hohhot and Baotou, where the Chinese influence is strongly felt, the preferred mutton dish is *shuan yangrou huoguo* (涮羊肉火锅; thin slices of mutton in hotpot) boiled with cabbage, tofu and glass noodles and dipped in a spicy sesame sauce.

Hohhot

Malaqin Fandian
马拉沁饭店
34 Xinhua Dajie.
The most famous place for mutton hot

pot, where large groups come to share animated evening feasts.

The alleys off Daxue Xijie (大学西街), just south of the university in the southeast part of town, are full of small restaurants serving milk-based treats ("white food" – see above) such as *nailao* (奶酪; hardened white cheese) and *naipi* (奶皮; skin from boiled milk), all of which can be washed down with a steaming bowl of *naicha* (奶茶; milk tea).

Recommended Restaurants on page 181

SHANXI, SOUTHERN HEBEI
AND SHANDONG

The flood plains of the Huang He (Yellow River)
nurtured the birth of Chinese civilisation,
and the ancient sites strewn across the region
bear witness to five millennia of history

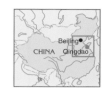

n a country famed for its rich cultural
heritage, the northern heartlands
encompassed by the modern provinces
of Shanxi, the southern part of Hebei and
Shandong (as well as Henan, covered in
the following chapter) are home to some
of the greatest historical and religious sites
– as well as being the homeland of three
of the most revered philosophers of
ancient China: Confucius, Laozi and
Mencius. These lands around the lower
stretches of the **Huang He** (黄河; Yellow
River) have been cultivated for at least
5,000 years, and several of China's earliest
states arose in this region. The great river
and its tributaries irrigated the soil, but regular floods and changes of course forced
people to work in close cooperation. Over
the centuries, the Huang He has changed
course numerous times, disrupting life and
agriculture and earning the sobriquet
"China's sorrow". Not until 1933 did it
find its present outflow to the ocean.

East of the river's long loop south from
the barren wastes of Inner Mongolia,
Shanxi (山西) province boasts a rich cultural heritage with the Buddhist caves at
Yungang, the extraordinary temple of
Xuangkong Si on the Daoist peak of
Heng Shan, and the sacred Buddhist
range of Wutai Shan. A picturesque relic
from a more recent era, the town of
Pingyao is a veritable museum of Ming-
and Qing-dynasty buildings.

The sights of **Hebei** (河北) largely congregate in the north of the province within
reach of Beijing (*see Outside Beijing,
pages 148–55*). The main attraction in

southern Hebei, which extends down
towards the Huang He, is the ancient town
of Zhengding, dotted with impressive
temple architecture.

The final stretch of the Huang He
passes through **Shandong** (山东). The
holy Daoist peak of Tai Shan, along with
Qufu, hometown of China's beloved
Kong Fuzi (Confucius), are a big draw
for visitors, while the former German
colony of Qingdao on the peninsular
coast is a further trump card with its
picturesque streets, beaches and excellent seafood.

Main attractions
YUNGANG SHIKU CAVES,
    DATONG
XUANGKONG SI
WUTAI SHAN
PINGYAO
TAI SHAN
QINGDAO – BEACHES AND
    COLONIAL ARCHITECTURE
QUFU

LEFT: Pusa Ding
temple at Wutai
Shan. **BELOW:** on a
film set in Pingyao.

SHANXI PROVINCE: DATONG

A seven-hour train ride west of Beijing, the brutal industrial sprawl of **Datong ❶** (大同) doubles as a tourism centre due to the diverse array of ancient religious structures and statuary left over from the succession of non-Han Chinese peoples who made it the seat of their dynasties. The precursor to the modern city first gained prominence when the Turkic Toba people moved the capital of their Northern Wei dynasty here in AD 386, and the sublime cave sculpture – China's oldest and best-preserved collection of Buddhist cave carvings – created by these devout Buddhists is the main reason to visit.

The sculptures are located 16km (10 miles) west of town at **Yungang Shiku** (云岗石窟; Cloud Ridge Grottoes; daily 8am–6pm; charge), a series of several dozen man-made caves forged into the side of a sandstone cliff and stretching for about 1km (⅔ mile). The grottoes, a Unesco World Heritage Site, are an impressive testament to the Buddhist fervour that began to grip the Northern Wei in the fifth century, and represent an intriguing blend of South and Central Asian Buddhist art with traditional Chinese styles. The caves were constructed from AD 453–525 by tens of thousands of labourers and artisans, many of them freshly returned from pilgrimages to western neighbours such as Afghanistan. Duly inspired, they frequently incorporated Indian and Central Asian characteristics into the smooth carvings that line the cave walls – this is particularly evident in the faces of the enormous Buddhas at the western caves (nos. 16–20), noteworthy for their sheer size and sharp facial features. The 14-metre (45ft) high Buddha at cave 20, in modern times exposed to the elements, is easily photographed and has become the complex's most iconic figure. Among the other highlights are the 17-metre (56ft) painted Buddha in cave five and the central sandstone pillar in cave six, replete with ornately carved Buddhas and Bodhisattvas.

Within Datong itself are a few historically significant sites, including the two temples that comprise the **Huayan Si** (华严寺; both daily 8.30am–5pm; separate charges), among the oldest remnants of the Mongol Khitan people's Liao dynasty which made the city its

Over the past 2,000 years, the Huang He has had 26 major changes in its course. It has also flooded at least 1,500 times in the same period, causing millions of deaths. Erratic rainfall upstream brings dramatic fluctuations in the volume of water; combined with the build-up of alluvial deposits around the great eastward bend, this makes it an extremely unpredictable river.

BELOW: big Buddha little Buddha at Datong's Yungang Shiku.

Recommended Restaurants on page 181

capital in 907. The more architecturally impressive **Upper Huayan Si** (上华严寺), first built in AD 1062, is distinguished by the soaring roof of its main hall, already elevated on a lofty platform. The most noteworthy feature of the **Lower Huayan Si** (下华严寺) is its main hall, Datong's oldest building and one of China's best examples of Liao-period architecture. Originally built in AD 1038, the hall's walls are lined with 38 wooden cabinets used for storing Buddhist scriptures. A few minutes' walk east of here is the **Jiulongbi** (九龙壁; Nine Dragon Screen; daily 8am–6pm; charge), a 45-metre (148ft) wall covered in colourfully glazed tiles and depicting nine whirling dragons to ward off malevolent spirits.

Heng Shan

Heng Shan ❷ (恒山), 70km (45 miles) south of Datong, is the most northerly of China's five sacred Daoist mountains (and not to be confused with the other Heng Shan, also Daoist but far to the south in Hunan province – *see page 321*). The hilly area is dotted with historic temples, hinting at its importance

as a spiritual retreat as long as 2,000 years ago. Though devout Daoists still flock here to worship at the temples and climb the highest peak, the vast majority of visitors come to see the gravity-defying **Xuankong Si** (悬空寺; Hanging Temple; daily 8am–6pm; charge), a former monastery perched high on a cliff face and supported only by wooden beams embedded into the rock. Originally constructed during the Northern Wei dynasty, the structure has repeatedly been rebuilt at successively higher locations after being swept away during flooding of the river that used to flow below it. Those with a head for heights can shuffle along the wooden walkways connecting the temple's main halls, which house shrines to Buddha and Confucius, as well as Laozi.

The elegant **Mu Ta** (木塔; Wooden Pagoda; daily 8am–5.30pm; charge) towers over the town of **Yingxian**, 30km (20 miles) west of Heng Shan, a solemn reminder of the architectural heights reached during the Liao dynasty. Built in AD 1056, and topping out at a lofty 67 metres (220ft), it is both the oldest and tallest fully wooden pagoda in China.

The Hukou Falls (Hukou Pubu) on the Huang He are an impressive sight, particularly in the spring and summer when the water is at its highest. Getting there is tricky, however: the main access point is the town of Linfen, 150km (90 miles) to the east and up to 6 hours away by bus or minibus. Linfen is 3 hours by train from Pingyao. The falls are pictured on the back of the Rmb 50 banknote.

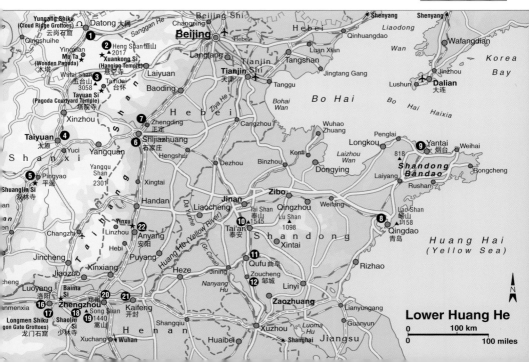

Lower Huang He

0   100 km
0   100 miles

Xuankong Si, the famous Hanging Temple clinging to the sides of Heng Shan, draws the crowds in the summer months – avoid if you suffer from claustrophobia and/or vertigo.

BELOW: the white pagoda of Taiyuan Si at Wutai Shan.

Originally constructed without any metal nails, its support beams are connected by clever interlocking wooden brackets that have helped the pagoda to survive numerous earthquakes.

Wutai Shan

South of Heng Shan, and a five-hour bus ride from Datong, lies **Wutai Shan ❸** (五台山; Five Terrace Mountain; overall charge, plus charge for each temple), one of China's four sacred Buddhist mountains and a major point of pilgrimage for Chinese and Tibetan Buddhists, who come in droves to worship at the three dozen or so temples that dot the hillsides. The five rounded peaks after which the area is named are believed by Chinese Buddhists to be the earthly domain of Manjusri ("Wenshu" in Chinese), the *Bodhisattva* associated with wisdom who is typically portrayed riding a lion and holding a manuscript. By the time of the Tang dynasty, there were over 200 temples in the Wutai Shan area; although many have not survived, a large concentration can be found in the tourist village of **Taihuai** (台怀), nestled in a

valley encircled by the mountains. The village has a cluster of small hotels and restaurants, frequent daytime bus connections to Datong (and Taiyuan to the south), and is only a short walk from some of the most revered temples.

Standing out from the rest is the **Tayuan Si** (塔院寺; Pagoda Courtyard Temple; charge), named after the white-washed Tibetan-style stupa that crowns its central courtyard. From here, a climb up a series of steps to the temple at **Pusa Ding** (菩萨顶; Bodhisattva Summit; charge) will yield sweeping views over the valley. About an hour's walk into the hills south of Taihuai is the **Nanshan Si** (南山寺; Southern Mountain Temple; charge), a sizeable complex first built in the Yuan dynasty and affording splendid views of the mountaintops to the north.

Taiyuan

The capital of Shanxi province, **Taiyuan ❹** (太原) is an industrial city whose origins as a settlement hark back to the fifth century BC. A convenient transport hub, most tourists use Taiyuan as a base from which to explore Wutai Shan and Pingyao just to the south, but the city

Recommended Restaurants on page 181

GETTING TO SHANXI

Flights: Taiyuan's Wusu Airport, 15km (9 miles) south of the centre, has regular connections to Beijing, Chongqing, Shanghai and Xi'an. Datong also has a tiny airport with daily flights to Beijing, three weekly to Guangzhou.

By train and bus: Taiyuan's railway station is conveniently located and has frequent connections to other points in Shanxi as well as long-distance services to cities such as Beijing, Chengdu, Luoyang, Shanghai, Xi'an and Zhengzhou. There are daily buses to Beijing, Luoyang, Xi'an and Zhengzhou.

GETTING AROUND SHANXI

Taiyuan: Buses are the most useful form of transport within Shanxi. There are regular buses from Taiyuan to Pingyao (1½ hours), Datong (4 hours) and the tourist village of Taihuai in Wutai Shan (5 hours). There are several trains daily to Datong (5½ hours) and Pingyao (2 hours), though for the latter these are often standing-room only unless you book well in advance.

Datong: There are frequent buses to Taiyuan (4 hours) and Wutai Shan (5 hours). Trains to Taiyuan take about 5½ hours. An overnight train leaves each night for Pingyao (9 hours).

Pingyao: Buses leave throughout the day to Taiyuan (1½ hours), as do trains to Taiyuan (2 hours). There are also daily trains to Linfen (3 hours) to the south, for the Hukou Falls.

Wutai Shan (Taihuai): Buses leave each day for Datong (5 hours) and Taiyuan (5 hours).

Fried dough sticks (youtiao), fried pancakes (youbing) and other doughy delights on sale in Pingyao.

itself has a handful of worthwhile sights.

Chongshan Si (崇善寺; Honouring Kindness Temple; daily 8am–5pm; charge) is a peaceful Ming-dynasty Buddhist sanctuary renowned for its collection of *sutras* printed in the Song, Jin, Yuan, Ming and Qing dynasties. Some of these, including a few in Tibetan, are on display inside the main hall. The "twin" pagodas of the **Shuangta Si** (双塔寺; Twin Pagoda Temple; daily 8.30am–5pm; charge), built in the early 17th century, are both just under 55 metres (178ft) in height. The 13 storeys of the slightly taller **Xuanwen Ta** can be climbed via a narrow, spiral stone staircase for outstanding views of the city.

Approximately 40km (25 miles) south of Taiyuan, on the right side of the road to Pingyao, is the **Qiao Jia Dayuan** (乔家大院; Qiao Family Compound; daily 9am–5pm; charge), the lavish Qing-dynasty courtyard house that film director Zhang Yimou used as the setting for his tragic masterpiece *Raise the Red Lantern*. The residence consists of six main courtyards with more than 300 rooms.

Pingyao

On the Beijing-Xi'an railway line around 100km (62 miles) south of Taiyuan, the idyllic town of **Pingyao** ❺ (平遥) is perhaps China's best-preserved ancient walled city and a highlight of many tourists' visit to the country. Although it has a 1,200-year history, Pingyao is mostly renowned for its largely intact Ming- and Qing-dynasty architecture, a result of its prominence as one of China's first banking centres and a subsequent decline that managed to protect it from the ravages of modernisation. A Unesco

BELOW: meditation at Wutai Shan.

While leisurely strolls along the town's myriad side lanes are a delight, it's possible to enter many of Pingyao's temples and traditional family homes.

BELOW: old China is at hand in Pingyao.

World Heritage Site, the town is surrounded by a 6km (4-mile) Ming-dynasty city wall (which you can walk around) complete with gates, enclosing the quaint streets in a grid-like pattern.

Though the entire town is filled with surprises, some of the best-kept architecture lies on **Ming-qing Jie** (明清街; Mingqing Street) and **Nan Dajie** (南大街; South Avenue), both filled with souvenir shops, restaurants and hotels. Many of the old buildings have been converted into atmospheric guesthouses with lovely courtyards and period furnishings, making Pingyao one of the most rewarding places to stay in China. You are entitled to enter various temples and even some family homes – as well as walk along the city wall – by purchasing an all-encompassing ticket *(tao piao)* that is valid for two days.

About 6km (4 miles) to the southwest of town, the **Shuanglin Si** (双林寺; Twin Forest Temple; daily 8am–6pm; charge) houses a large collection of original Buddhist wood-and-clay statuary,

each hall brimming with fantastic coloured figures – many of them crumbling, but retaining their original paintwork – dating as far back as the Song dynasty.

Shijiazhuang and Zhengding

Shijiazhuang ❻ (石家庄), Hebei's capital, is a modern creation, built on the back of the railways and only making it onto the map in the early twentieth century as a major junction town. The city's main attraction is the **Hebei Provincial Museum** (河北省博物馆; Hebei Sheng Bowuguan; Tue–Sun 8.30–11.30am, 2–5.30pm; free), which has some excellent exhibits, including the Han-dynasty jade burial suits of Prince Liu Sheng and his wife Douwan. There is also a reproduction Han-dynasty chariot and an extensive accumulation of funerary objects excavated in the region.

A short trip by train or bus 16km (10 miles) northeast of Shijiazhuang is the historic walled town of **Zhengding** ❼ (正定), with its rich complement of religious architecture. The most important shrine is the **Dafo Si** (大佛寺; Big Buddha Temple, also called Longxing Si; daily 9am–5pm; charge), with its 21-metre (69ft) Song-dynasty bronze effigy of Guanyin in the **Dabei Ge** (大悲阁; Great Mercy Pavilion).

SHANDONG PROVINCE: QINGDAO

At the end of the 19th century, an ambitious Germany was looking for a place in China to plant its colonial aspirations. After two German Catholic priests were killed by Boxer rebels in 1897, German troops were sent in to establish a presence at **Qingdao** ❽ (青岛). In true imperial style, the Chinese were quickly forced into an agreement to lease the surrounding Bay of Jiaozhou to Germany.

Before the first frigate moored in the bay, Qingdao had been a quiet fishing village. But German officers, sailors and traders were soon promenading up and down the Kaiser Wilhelm Ufer and dining in the seafront Prinz Heinrich Hotel. They drank beer from the Germania brewery, which later achieved fame in

Recommended Restaurants on page 181

many parts of the world under the name Tsingtao (the old Wade-Giles system of spelling Qingdao).

The success of the **Tsingtao Brewery Ⓐ** (青岛啤酒厂; 56 Dengzhou Lu; daily 8.30am–4.30pm; charge), guides tell visitors, is due not only to German expertise but also to the spring water collected from nearby Lao Shan. This is one of China's oldest and most successful export businesses, and Tsingtao is possibly its most famous global brand. The museum and visitor centre have an idiosyncratic "Willy Wonka" charm adorned with boozing cartoon animals and beer-bottle-shaped fountains.

Aside from beer, Qingdao is perhaps most famous for its beaches, although the city itself is also appealing with relics of the colonial past, including many 19th-century, **German-style buildings** whose red-tiled roofs, half-timbered facades, sloping gables and triangular attic windows lend the centre of town a unique Teutonic flavour. Most striking of all are the tall towers of **St Michael's Catholic Church Ⓑ** (天主教堂; Tianzhu Jiaotang; Zhongshan Lu; daily 8am–5pm; charge), the **Protestant Church Ⓒ** (基督教堂; Jidu Jiaotang; 15 Jiangsu Lu; daily 8.30am–5pm; charge) and the former **governor's residence Ⓓ** (迎并管; Ying Bingguan; 26 Longshan Lu; daily; charge), which has the air of a Prussian hunting lodge. St Michael's holds regular Sunday services, and some of the features have captions in English. The German presence lasted until 1914 – the beginning of World War I – when Japan conquered the colony. Liberated by the Chinese in 1922, Qingdao was reoccupied briefly by the Japanese in 1938.

There are a number of free parks dotted throughout the city including the coastal **May Fourth Square Ⓔ** (五四广场; Wusi Guangchang; 35 Donghai Xilu; daily 24 hrs), named after the nationwide anti-imperialist protest movement of 1919 that followed the ceding of Qingdao to Japan. **Zhongshan Park Ⓕ** (中山公园; Zhongshan Gongyuan; daily 6am–6pm) is a huge green space that includes the city zoo. Taiping Shan Park, its northeastern

section, is crisscrossed by numerous paths and a hill atop which a TV tower offers unparalleled views of the city.

Most of Qingdao's visitors come for the **white sand beaches**. strung out along a seafront that has benefitted from renovation prior to hosting the sailing events in the 2008 Olympics. No 6 Bathing Beach features a pier that extends some 350 metres (1,150ft) into the ocean and ends at the Huilian Pavilion with bracing sea views. The No. 2 Bathing Beach requires a charge and is somewhat quieter and cleaner. The best beach near the city centre is **Old Stone Man** (Shi Laoren), a long sandy strip named after a prominent rock outcropping said to resemble an old fisherman. Lao Shan Beach is located at the entrance to Lao Shan Park and has impressive views of the mountain range.

Lao Shan (崂山), a mountainous region 40km (25 miles) east along the coast from Qingdao, is famed for its Daoist fables and the spring water that finds its way into Tsingtao beer. The area is very scenic, with waterfalls, caves and (mostly ruined) Daoist temples. There are several winding routes up the mountain,

BELOW: sunset over St Michael's Catholic Church, Qingdao.

The Qingdao International Beer Festival held in August celebrates the city's brewing history with parades and performances. As a foreign visitor, it is likely you will be plied with free beer in the name of international friendship and cooperation.

GETTING TO SHANDONG

Flights: Qingdao has a modern airport with domestic flights from major cities and international flights from nearby Asian countries. Jinan Airport offers some domestic flights.

By boat: Qingdao has ferry connections to Japan and South Korea, also Dalian and Shanghai (seasonal). Yantai has ferry connections to South Korea and Dalian.

By train and bus: Jinan is the major rail hub. Shandong is well serviced by buses.

GETTING AROUND SHANDONG

Qingdao: Super-fast bullet trains ("D" trains)

go to Beijing (6 hours) and Shanghai (10 hours). Long-distance buses leave from south of the train station regularly to Yantai (3½ hours), Qufu (5 hours) and Jinan (4½ hours).

Yantai: Yantai has limited rail connections to Qingdao (4 hours) and Jinan (7–8 hours), a likely interchange station. Buses run from the train station and Qingnian Lu's long-distance bus station to all major cities.

Jinan: Regular bullet trains go to Qingdao (3 hours) and all major cities. There are several bus stations; the one opposite the main train station has services to Qufu (2½ hours), Yantai (5 hours) and Qingdao (4½ hours).

as well as a cable car. **Taiqing Gong** (太清宫; Palace of Great Purity; Laoshan Lu; daily 24 hrs; charge), which comprises three pavilions. The **Sanqing Pavilion** (三清店) houses a statue of Laozi, regarded as the founder of Taoism.

Yantai

Yantai ⑨ (烟台) is a port city sitting on the northern coast of the Shandong Peninsula, a quieter version of Qingdao with beaches and some colonial archi-

tecture. The **Yantai Museum** (烟台博物馆; Yantai Bowuguan; 257 Nan Dajie; daily 8am–5pm) is housed in the largest of the city's former guildhalls. The train and bus stations and passenger ferry terminal are all in the northwestern part of town.

The **Penglai Pavilion** (蓬莱阁; daily 7am–6.30pm; charge) is an attractive and unusual temple 70km (44 miles) west of the city. The legend of the Eight Immortals Crossing the Sea supposedly took

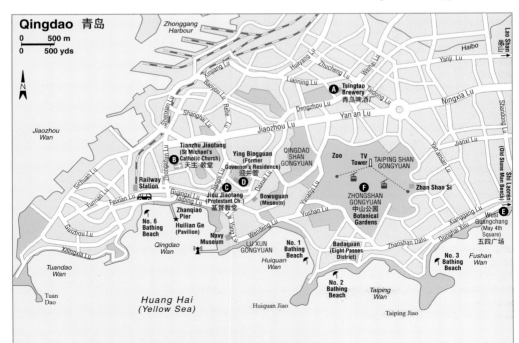

Map on pages 172-3

Recommended Restaurants on page 181

place here, and the place is famous for the "Penglai mirage", an optical illusion which appears every few decades.

Tai Shan

Considered to be China's most sacred Daoist mountain, **Tai Shan** ❿ (泰山) lies 300km (190 miles) west of Qingdao and 80km (50 miles) south of Jinan. Popular Chinese religion treats mountains as living beings: as well as creating clouds and rain, their stabilising power perpetuates the cosmic order. In ancient Chinese mythology, Tai Shan is said to have risen from the head of Pangu, the creator of the world. Shamans, and later emperors, have performed sacred rituals here for four millennia.

At the foot of the mountain, in the centre of the quiet tourist town of **Tai'an** (泰安), stands the magnificent **Dai Miao** (岱庙); daily 7.30am–6.30pm; charge), honouring the god of Tai Shan. This temple complex of more than 600 buildings was the venue for elaborate sacrifices and provided quarters for the emperor before he ascended Tai Shan. **Tiankuang Dian** (天贶殿; Hall of Heavenly Gifts), one of the largest classical temple halls in China, contains a fresco more than 60 metres (200ft) long.

A few hundred metres north of the temple, **Daizong Fang** (岱宗坊; Gate of the God) marks the starting point of a stone stairway to the 1,545-metre (5,070-ft) high summit. In earlier years, emperors and mandarins were carried up the 6,293 steps in litters. Modern pilgrims and travellers need a whole day for the round trip, or they can ride to a halfway point by minibus, then ascend by cable car almost as far as the summit. Of course, those who take the quick way miss the splendid variety of this open-air museum: temples, pavilions, shrines, stone stelae, inscriptions and waterfalls.

A little way off the main path, the text of a *sutra* has been engraved in a huge block of stone. The 1,050 characters, each 50 cm (20 inches) high, are considered a masterpiece of calligraphy. A more recent addition to the mountain's calligraphic works is Mao's "The most creative peo-

ple are the people now", penned in 1969.

Once past **Zhongtianmen** (中天门; Middle Gate of Heaven), the ascent becomes steeper. Passing **Wudaifu Song** (五大夫松; Pines of the Fifth Order of Officials), which, according to legend, were given this title by Qin Shi Huangdi after they sheltered the emperor from a thunderstorm, the path leads to **Nantianmen** (南天门; Southern Gate of Heaven). This is the entrance to the "realm of the immortals" on the summit, but first one must negotiate the earthly delights of **Tian Jie** (天街; Heaven Street), a Qing-dynasty parade of shops and restaurants. You can stay overnight here if you wish to join others in catching the famous Tai Shan sunrise: in clear weather the panorama can extend nearly 200km (125 miles) to the Yellow Sea.

Qufu

In 1919, Kong Linyu, a descendant of China's greatest philosopher, Kong Fuzi (Master Kong in English, Confucius in its Latinised form), died at the age of 76 during a visit to Beijing. According to tradition, Kong Linyu's two daughters could not continue the family line. All

According to one popular account, Confucius (Kong Fuzi) was born in a cave near Qufu. He taught in the area for many years, travelling to neighbouring states to try to influence everyday politics with his moral doctrines. Today, out of the 600,000 people who live in or near Qufu, 130,000 of them are named Kong.

BELOW: sunrise on Tai Shan.

Tomb at the Kong family cemetery in the Kong Lin (Confucius Forest) outside Qufu.

BELOW: the entrance to the Kong Miao (Confucius Temple), Qufu.

was not lost, as his concubine was in the fifth month of her pregnancy. Rival factions of the Kong clan posted guards outside the chamber of the pregnant woman, but the doors of the house remained open, to make it easier for the "wise ancestor" to find his way back for rebirth. In February 1920, Kong Decheng was born, representing the 77th generation after Confucius. Succession was assured, and the "first family under heaven" celebrated. But 17 days later, Kong Linyu's first – and childless – wife poisoned her rival, the mother of the heir.

The scene of this family drama was **Kong Fu**, or **Kong Family Mansion** (孔府; daily 8am–5pm; charge), in **Qufu** ⓫ (曲阜), the hometown of Confucius (551–479 BC), located 140km (90 miles) south of Tai Shan. Confucian ideology was given imperial status in the Han dynasty by Emperor Wudi, and subsequent emperors granted the great sage's descendants lavish titles and property. Originally built in the 16th century dur-

ing the Ming dynasty, the family mansion was home to the Kongs until 1948, when, with the Communist victory imminent, the last of the line left for exile in Taiwan. The outside of the residence looks rather plain, but it has around 500 rooms. Towards the end of the 19th century, the head of the Kong family was one of the wealthiest property owners in the country, presiding over his own judicial system and a private army. Inside many rooms are valuable works of art, calligraphy, articles of clothing and extensive archival material.

Confucius himself was buried under a simple grass-covered mound in **Kong Lin** (孔林; Confucius Forest; daily 7.30am–sunset; charge), the Kong family cemetery a short distance north of town. The way to the mound is lined with human and animal figures in stone, a custom otherwise reserved for emperors.

Reflecting this former glory is the size and splendour of **Kong Miao**, the Confucius temple (孔庙; daily 7.50am–4.30pm; charge) in the centre of Qufu. A temple is supposed to have been built on this site as early as 478 BC, one year after the death of Confucius. The view on the walk north, past ancient cypress trees and stone stelae, is dominated by the triple-roofed, 23-metre (75ft) high Kuiwenge (Pavilion of the Constellation of Scholars), first built in the 11th century. Passing the 13 pavilions in which stelae with imperial inscriptions are kept, the path leads to the 18th-century Dacheng Dian (Hall of Great Achievements), the main hall of the temple and once the venue for sacrificial rites in honour of Confucius. The 28 stone pillars supporting the roof of the hall have a total of 1,296 dragons carved on them. The yellow roof on the main hall – yellow was a colour reserved for temples and imperial buildings – again emphasises the traditional importance of the great philosopher.

In recent years, Qufu has developed its tourist facilities. One of the latest and most expensive is the **Confucius Six Arts City** (孔子六艺城; Kongzi Liuyicheng; 15 Chunqiu Lu; daily 9am–4.30pm; charge), a small theme park celebrating

six arts promoted by the great man, namely calligraphy, music, rites, archery, charioteering and mathematics.

Outside Qufu are several other noteworthy sites. **Zoucheng** ⑫ (邹城), 25km (16 miles) to the south, was home of the most famous follower of Confucius, Mengzi (or Mencius), and is where you can find the Meng Fu (the Meng family home), Meng Lin (Mencius Forest) and Meng Miao (Mencius Temple). **Shao Hao Ling** (少昊陵) is an unusual 6-metre (20ft) pyramid-shaped tomb faced with grey stone, situated 4km (2½ miles) east of Qufu. It is said to be the burial place of a legendary emperor, Shao Hao, who ruled this part of China around 4,000 years ago. ❑

Confucianism is best thought of as a moral code rather than a religion, one that stresses the obligations of leaders to set an example.

RESTAURANTS

SHANXI PROVINCE

Shanxi Province is renowned throughout China for its flour-based foods, especially noodles (面条; *miantiao*), which are some of the country's best. Noodle vendors are ubiquitous, and the sight of them twirling "hand-pulled" strips of dough or shaving off slivers of so-called "knife-cut noodles" is as common as that of locals eagerly slurping them down from steaming bowls. Other flour-based snacks such as *youtiao* (油条; deep-fried dough sticks), *youbing* (油饼; fried pancakes filled with chopped green onion) and *jiaozi* (饺子; fried dumplings), are perenially popular.

Datong

Datong is well endowed with street markets. A good one is just north of the Upper Huayan Si, on a side street running south from Da Xijie, the downtown area's main east–west thoroughfare. Look out for the local speciality, *shao-mai* (烧卖), steamed pork dumplings that are best dipped in vinegar.

Tonghe Dafandian
同和大饭店
11 Zhanqian Jie. $
Conveniently located across the train station square on the northern end (next to the Hongqi Dafandian), the Tonghe is another foreigner-friendly establishment with earnest staff and a picture menu (albeit in Chinese) that includes southern Chinese cuisine.

Yonghe Shifu 永和食符
Xiao Nanjie, near Shanhua Si. $$
This is Datong's most foreigner-friendly restaurant, with a range of northern and southern Chinese dishes (including extensive Cantonese options), helpful service and a useful English picture menu.

Pingyao

Practically all of Pingyao's many traditional guesthouses double as café-bar-restaurants, and eating out here is often simply a matter of popping into one for a drink and perusing their (often English) menu. While most of these can do rough approximations of Western food to cater to road-weary backpackers, it's worth asking about local specialities such as *tudou shao niurou* (土豆烧牛肉; fried beef with potatoes).

Pingyao International Financier Club 云锦成
64 Nan Dajie. $$
Located on the premises of the original guesthouse, this is by far Pingyao's poshest restaurant.

Sakura Café 樱花酒店
2 Dong Dajie. $
Like its affiliates in Dali, Lijiang, Kunming and Beijing, the Sakura aims to be the ultimate backpacker haven, with an extensive English menu of Western food, cold beer, cocktails, free internet and a constant supply of hip music.

Taiyuan

The provincial capital is fairly teeming with places to eat, but for the broadest selection it's best to head straight for Shipin Jie (食品街; Food Street), a pedestrian-only gauntlet of snack stalls and small restaurants northwest of Yingze Dajie, the city's main drag.

Taiyuan Mianshi Dian
太原面食店
5 Jiefang Lu. $
This is perhaps the best place in Shanxi for a crash course in the province's vast array of noodle dishes,.

SHANDONG PROVINCE

Shandong cuisine, one of the "Eight Great Traditions" of Chinese cooking, is noted for its unusual use of corn as an ingredient, as well as for its seafood. It has strongly influenced other northern styles, notably that of Beijing.

Jinan

Taisheng Fanzhuang
太生饭庄
13 Xiaodongxiang Beishou. $
Try Jinan's nutritious soups, fish and vegetable dishes in this inexpensive eatery.

Qingdao

Yunxiao Lu and Minjiang Lu are two dedicated food streets with excellent local, Korean and Japanese food. Seafood is big in Qingdao, with clusters of restaurants near St Michael's Church on Zhonghsan Lu and near the beach on Nanhai Lu.

Haixian Chufang
海鲜厨房
55 Yunxiao Lu. $$
Provides a menu wall of photos, tanks of live seafood and helpful staff.

Lao Zhuan Cun
老转村山东菜馆 转
112 Minjiang Lu. $$
Popular restaurant serving Shandong cuisine. Its specialities include a kind of local sausage.

Qufu

Queli Hotel Restaurant
阙里宾舍餐厅
1 Queli Jie. $$$
Centrally located hotel with Confucianism as its theme. Confucius was a notoriously picky eater; judge for yourself if the cuisine here deserves his name.

Prices for a meal for one, with one drink:
$ = under Rmb 50
$$ = Rmb 50–100
$$$ = Rmb 100–150
$$$$ = over Rmb 150

XI'AN, SHAANXI AND HENAN

Its ancestry traceable back to the foundations of the Chinese state, Xi'an's supreme attraction is its awesome Army of Terracotta Warriors. Close to Luoyang to the east are the spectacular Longmen Caves and the legendary monastery of Shaolin

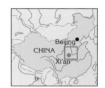

Xi'an, southern **Shaanxi** (勉县) province and neighbouring **Henan** (河南) form the heartlands of early Chinese civilisation, germinated by the abundant waters of the **Huang He** (黄河; Yellow River), which nourished the soil and encouraged the seminal settlements to which the Han Chinese trace their roots. As such, the entire region is brimming with antiquities – some excavated but the vast majority still doubtless underground – putting it on a par with the richest archaeological zones of ancient Mesopotamia, Egypt and Greece.

The capital of the Zhou dynasty, dating from the 11th century BC, was situated close to present-day Xi'an. It was here, too, that the state of Qin was founded, the first to unify the land and from whose name the English word for China is believed to have derived. The Silk Road, linking China to Central Asia and Europe, began here, attracting other cultures whose religions and art changed China for ever. And the Huang He's perennial volatility – frequently flooding and changing course – forced people to work in close cooperation.

Southern Shaanxi's brilliant past has bequeathed some truly spectacular sights. The dusty floodplains surrounding Xi'an are covered with imperial tombs, though none are as celebrated as that of Qin Shi Huangdi, with its underground Army of Terracotta Warriors. Bolstering the ample archaeological attractions is a formidable crop of museums and historic temples, further illuminating the region's long his-

tory. And within easy reach of Xi'an are several other worthwhile destinations, including the venerated Buddhist mecca of Famen Si, the revolutionary pilgrimage site of Yan'an and the sacred Daoist peaks of Hua Shan.

Far less famous than Shaanxi, Henan province to the east can nevertheless claim a history that rivals its neighbour in both scale and substance. Though now considered by many Chinese to be a rural backwater, for centuries Henan was the centre of the Chinese universe, its fertile plains sustaining a sizeable population

Main attractions
DAYAN TA (GREAT WILD GOOSE PAGODA), XI'AN
TERRACOTTA WARRIORS
HUA SHAN
YAN'AN
LONGMEN CAVES
SHAOLIN MONASTERY
SONG SHAN
KAIFENG

LEFT: a Terracotta Warrior at Bingmayong near Xi'an.
BELOW: an old street in Xi'an.

The giant bell at the Xiaoyan Ta (Little Wild Goose Pagoda) in Xi'an. The origin of the goose, after which the city's two famous pagodas are named, is something of a mystery – it possibly relates to an episode in the fable Journey to the West.

BELOW: Xi'an has a large Hui Muslim population.

and its cities serving a succession of dynastic capitals.

Religion flourished here, and the area was a major portal in the spread of Buddhism throughout China. As such, Henan has many of the country's oldest Buddhist sites, including the world-renowned Shaolin Temple – the original home of Chan (Zen) Buddhism and Shaolin boxing – and the White Horse Temple near Luoyang, considered by many to be China's oldest Buddhist sanctuary. Some of the world's most revered Buddhist statuary is carved into the cliff-side caves of the Longmen Shiku near Luoyang.

XI'AN

Xi'an ⑬ (西安), capital of Shaanxi province, lies in the protected valley of the Wei River, some 160km (100 miles) west of its confluence with the Huang He. It was from this irrigated valley that the emperor Qin Shi Huangdi unified China for the first time. Xi'an served as the capital for more than 1,100 years and 13 imperial dynasties; during the Tang years (618–907) it was the largest city in the world. Chang'an (Everlasting Peace), as it was called back then, was the destination

of thousands of foreign Silk Road traders and enjoyed unsurpassed prestige. Following the demise of the Tang dynasty, Xi'an's importance began to fade.

While Xi'an's centre retains its Tang layout, it is largely overwhelmed by modern buildings and heavy traffic. The Tang city stretched over 9km (6 miles) from east to west and nearly 8km (5 miles) north to south. All roads in the town itself were laid out in a classic Chinese grid pattern, running straight north–south and east–west, meeting at right angles. While the layout remains today, the plan of the ancient city is not identical to the modern one. Although the walls built during the Tang dynasty no longer exist, 14km (9 miles) of the Ming wall still surround the centre, and much of their length has been restored. In places such as **Nanmen** (南门; South Gate), it is possible to climb on top of these 12-metre (40-ft) thick ramparts. The moat outside the wall has also been reconstructed and integrated within a park.

In the heart of the city centre, where two main roads intersect, is the **Zhonglou** Ⓐ (钟楼; Bell Tower; daily late Oct–Mar 8.30am–5.30pm, Apr–late Oct 8.30am–

Recommended Restaurants on page 197

GETTING TO SHAANXI

Flights: Xi'an's airport is near the town of Xianyang, about 40km (25 miles) northwest of the city centre. It is well connected, with regular flights to all major domestic destinations as well as a few international ones.

By train and bus: Xi'an's railway station is one of China's busiest, with frequent connections to most major cities, including express services to Beijing and Shanghai. Onward train tickets should be booked a few days ahead of your anticipated departure. There are bus links to cities in neighbouring provinces, but most tourists choose to arrive and depart by train.

GETTING AROUND SHAANXI

Xi'an: The tourist sites to the east and west of Xi'an make for good day trips on dedicated tourist buses. Private buses to Hua Shan (2 hours) leave throughout the day from in front of the train station. To Yan'an, buses (6 hours) run all day, while there are two overnight trains (8–10 hours) daily.

Hua Shan: There are daily bus and train connections to Xi'an as well as destinations to the east such as Pingyao and Taiyuan in Shanxi province and Henan province's Luoyang and Zhengzhou.

Yan'an: There are daily buses (6 hours) and trains (8–10 hours) to Xi'an, as well as one daily bus each to Ningxia's Yinchuan (8 hours) and Taiyuan (3 hours) in Shanxi province. A couple of buses run each day to Yichuan (4 hours), the staging point for the Hukou Falls.

A lion statue outside the Xiaoyan Ta (Little Wild Goose Pagoda) in Xi'an. The irregularity on the upper section of the pagoda is the result of a 16th-century earthquake.

9.30pm; charge). This renovated 36-metre (118-ft) tower dating from 1384 was moved to its present site in 1582 and today is encircled by Xi'an's main shopping and commercial centre. East from Zhonglou runs Dong Dajie, with many shops and restaurants. Dong Dajie intersects with Jiefang Lu, which runs to the north and leads to the railway station.

A few minutes' walk to the northwest from Zhonglou is the not dissimilar **Gulou B** (鼓楼; Drum Tower; daily late Oct–Mar 8.30am–5.30pm, Apr–late Oct 8.30am–9.30pm; charge), also dating from the 14th century – although rebuilt after 1949. More than 60,000 Hui Muslims live in Xi'an, and the Drum Tower highlights the Muslim quarter to the

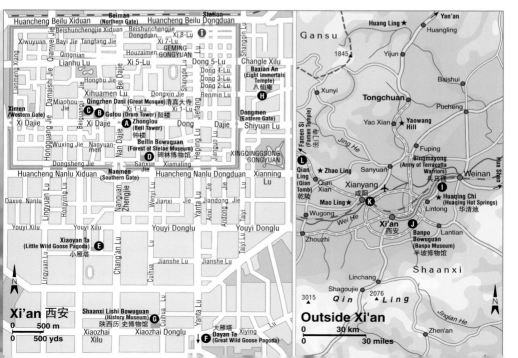

The 64-metre (210ft) Dayan Ta (Great Wild Goose Pagoda) is Xi'an's most famous landmark. It dates back to the 7th century.

BELOW: night view of downtown Xi'an from Zhonglou (Bell Tower).

west. Lined with souvenir shops, alleys winding through the Hui neighbourhoods lead to **Qingzhen Dasi** (清真大寺; Great Mosque; daily 8am–7pm; charge), a Ming-dynasty structure that has been skilfully renovated several times. As with other Chinese mosques, its halls and inner courtyards bear much architectural resemblance to those of a Chinese temple. The surrounding area is one of the most fascinating and diverse parts of Xi'an to explore on foot. Wander down an alley to get a sense of how the Hui live, or try one of the many food stalls selling dishes such as mutton-filled sesame rolls, or Xi'an's famous *yangrou paomo*, a concoction of mutton, noodles and flat bread cooked in a piping-hot broth.

Near **Nanmen** – the city wall's south gate – and in a former Confucian temple is the **Forest of Stelae Museum** (碑林博物馆; Beilin Bowuguan; daily 8am–5.30pm; charge), where 3,000 pieces of valuable stone tablets are preserved. There are exhibits in three main buildings. The first has a chronologically arranged exhibition of ancient Buddhist images from the early period of the Silk Road to the end of the Tang dynasty. The second, the museum's centrepiece, features a "forest" of stelae, or around 1,100 stone tablets on which ancient Chinese classical texts – including those of Confucius and Mencius – are engraved.

Outside the city walls and about 1km (⅔ mile) south of Nanmen, the 46-metre (151ft) **Xiaoyan Ta** (小雁塔; Little Wild Goose Pagoda; daily 8am–5.30pm; charge) was built in the early eighth century. Severely damaged during an earthquake eight centuries later and repaired in the late 1970s, it was again damaged in the early 1990s. You can climb up for views over Xi'an. Within the complex, and included in the admission price, is the new multi-storey **Xi'an Museum** (西安博物馆; Xi'an Bowuguan; daily 8am–5.30pm), housing an amazing collection of more than 130,000 historic and cultural relics, ranging from Neolithic artefacts to sublime Buddhist statuary and a wide array of calligraphic and landscape scrolls.

About 3km (2 miles) to the southeast is the 64-metre (210ft) high, seven-storey **Dayan Ta** (大雁塔; Great Wild Goose Pagoda; daily 8am–6.30pm; charge), anchoring the southern end of Yanta Lu. One of Xi'an's most recognisable structures, it was built in AD 652, at the beginning of the Tang dynasty, and was used to store Buddhist scriptures brought back to China in AD 645 by the eminent monk Xuan Zang. Xuan, whose adventures are recorded in the Chinese classic *Journey to the West*, had returned from a 15-year pilgrimage to India and spent his last two decades translating the Sanskrit *sutras* into Chinese. The pagoda was built as an add-on to the **Dacien Si** (大慈恩寺; Temple of Grace; daily 8am–6.30pm; charge), which had several hundred rooms when it was established in AD 647 but now consists of only a handful of buildings.

Just northwest of the Dayan Ta is one of the city's foremost attractions: the **Shaanxi History Museum** (陕西历史博物馆; Shaanxi Lishi Bowuguan; Tue–Sun late Oct–Mar 9am–5.30pm, Apr–late Oct 8.30am–6pm; free). More

Recommended Restaurants on page 197

than 3,000 historic artefacts are displayed here in chronological order and labelled in English. The collection ranges from tools and pottery from Palaeolithic and Neolithic times to bronze cooking vessels from the Shang and Zhou dynasties right on through to Ming- and Qing-dynasty ceramics. A select group of terracotta soldiers and horses is also prominently displayed.

Those planning to visit the sacred mountains of Hua Shan *(see page 188)* might warm up with a visit to the **Baxian An** ⓗ (八仙庵; Eight Immortals Temple; daily 8am–5pm; charge), Xi'an's largest Daoist temple and home to more than 100 monks and nuns. Inside the main hall stands a statue of the Green Dragon (to whose left is the White Tiger); the wall behind is painted with scenes from Daoist legends.

Outside Xi'an: The Eastern Tour

To the east of Xi'an lie several well-known attractions, some of which are routinely included in day tours organised by hotels and tour agencies. A highlight of any visit to China is Xi'an's most pop-ular site: **the Army of Terracotta Warriors** ❶ (兵马俑; Bingmayong; daily 8.30am–5.30pm; charge). This vast treasure, vying with the Great Wall and Forbidden City as China's most famous monument, lies 30km (20 miles) east of Xi'an and was stumbled upon in 1974 by peasants digging a well. *For more on this unmissable sight, see pages 198–9.*

On the way back to Xi'an are the **Huaqing Hot Springs** (华清池; Huaqing Chi; daily 7am–7pm; charge), in use for over 3,000 years and a favoured retreat for Tang-dynasty nobility. There are baths and pavilions in the park area. During the Tang dynasty, this is where the most famous concubine in China, Yang Guifei, bathed.

The **Banpo Museum** ❶ (半坡博物馆; Banpo Bowuguan; daily 8am–6.30pm; charge), 10km (6 miles) east of Xi'an, is dedicated to the Neolithic settlement that has been partially excavated near here. Relics, including ceramics, weapons and even infant burial jars from the matriarchal Yangshao culture, are on display here.

The Western Tour

Situated around 50km (30 miles) north-west of Xi'an, **Xianyang** ⓚ (咸阳) was

When the Terracotta Warriors were first uncovered from their earthen graves, their cheeks were rosy and they wore painted uniforms. Exposure to the air turned the statues black.

BELOW: a small section of the Terracotta Army at Bingmayong.

The large and impressive stone statues at Qian Ling represent dignitaries of the Tang court.

BELOW: the sacred peak of Hua Shan.

the capital during the reign of Qin Shi Huangdi, although few traces of the palaces said to have been built here are left. The **Xianyang Musuem** (咸阳博物馆; Xianyang Bowuguan; daily 8am–5.30pm; charge), situated in a former Confucian temple, contains artefacts from the Warring States Period and the Qin and Han dynasties. There is an impressive collection of 3,000 miniature terracotta horses and soldiers – each about 50 cm (20 inches) high – from the Han dynasty.

Further to the northwest is **Qian Ling** **ⓛ** (乾陵; Qian Tomb; daily 8am–5pm; charge), the joint burial place of the Tang emperor Gaozong and his wife, the empress Wu Zetian who succeeded him to the throne, becoming China's only female ruler in the process. The approach to the tomb – itself unopened – is guarded by a "spirit way" of large stone sculptures of animals and dignitaries. A group of 61 decapitated stone sculptures apparently represents foreign dignitaries. Peasants of the time are said to have knocked the sculptures' heads off during a famine, believing the "outsiders" were the cause of the food shortage.

Roughly 115km (70 miles) northwest of Xi'an, **Famen Si** (法门寺; Famen Temple; daily 8am–6pm; charge) is particularly sacred Buddhist site, for safeguarded and venerated at the temple are four of Buddha's finger bones. In 1981, during restoration work on the crypt that held the Buddhist relics, more than 1,000 long-forgotten sacrificial objects were discovered, now displayed in a museum next to the temple. The Famen Si, first established during the Eastern Han, has a history of about 1,800 years.

ELSEWHERE IN SHAANXI

Westernmost of China's five sacred Daoist peaks, **Hua Shan** **⓮** (华山; Flower Mountain; 2,160 metres/7,090ft; charge) looms 120km (75 miles) east of Xi'an and is one of China's most dramatic holy mountain climbs. As well renowned for its steep ascents and plunging drops as it is for its Daoist mysteries, hiking here can be gruelling and, on occasion, hair-raising. Some sections of steps dissolve into incisions cut from the almost vertical rock faces, with only a chain to hold for support. Courageous wayfarers make nocturnal ascents with

torches to arrive before dawn. For the less energetic, a cable car transports visitors to Bei Feng (North Peak), one of the four main summits. A trail along the Canglong Feng (Green Dragon Ridge) connects Bei Feng with Dong Feng (East Peak), Xi Feng (West Peak) and Hua Shan's highest point at Nan Feng (South Peak). If you are hiking, count on a minimum of two hours to reach Bei Feng via the steep path which winds underneath the cable car route. From Bei Feng, if you want to complete a circuit climbing the three other main peaks, factor in another six hours to do so comfortably. Spring and autumn are the best seasons.

A number of hotels operate in the village at the foot of the mountain, and a few basic guesthouses can be found on the mountain itself (useful if the weather worsens or you want to catch the sunrise).

Yan'an

The time-warped town of **Yan'an** ⑮ (延安), 270km (170 miles) to the north of Xi'an in the arid loess hills of northern Shaanxi, functioned as the Communist Party headquarters in the 1930s and 1940s. It was here that Mao Zedong's epic Long March *(see page 51)* finally came to an end in October 1935. During the Cultural Revolution and through the 1970s, Yan'an was, and to some extent remains, a national centre of pilgrimage, in the past as well known to Party officials as the Forbidden City in Beijing. It still attracts large numbers of patriotic domestic tourists.

The main attractions are the three former Communist Party headquarters sites, each simply maintained as if the revolutionaries themselves were still living there. The most popular of the three is the **Yangjialing Revolutionary Headquarters** site (杨家岭革命旧址; Yangjialing Geming Jiuzhi; daily 8am–5.30pm; free), about 3km (2 miles) northwest of the town centre. Here is the meeting hall where the first Central Committee meeting was held; banners of Marx, Engels, Lenin and Stalin still hang alongside those of Mao. The other two sites are **Wangjiaping** (王家坪革命旧址) and **Fenghuangshan** (凤凰山革命旧址; both

daily 8am–5.30pm; free). Mao's wooden bed and desk, letters and photographs are all on view.

The **Yan'an Revolutionary Museum** (延安革命纪　念馆; Yan'an Geming Jinianguan; daily 8am–5.30pm; charge) contains more than 2,000 documents and objects from the Yan'an period, which is still venerated by many older functionaries of the Chinese Communist Party as the "golden revolutionary era".

Perched on a hill in the southeast corner of town is **Bao Ta** (宝塔; daily 8am–5.30pm; charge), a pagoda which can be climbed for unparalleled views of the town and the cave dwellings that pockmark the surrounding loess hillsides.

HENAN PROVINCE: LUOYANG AND AROUND

A five-hour train journey east of Xi'an, **Luoyang** ⑯ (洛阳) was one of China's greatest ancient capitals, serving as the seat of power for numerous dynasties dating back to the Zhou, who made it their main capital in 770 BC. The city thrived during the Eastern Han dynasty (AD 25–220), as well as the Tang (AD 618–907) and Song (AD 960–1279) periods, before

The hills in and around Yan'an have been terraced and hollowed out for troglodyte houses.

BELOW: reminder of the past in Yan'an.

Between Zhengzhou and Luoyang are numerous homes burrowed in cliffs of dry loess, which is yellowish and quite soft, and an ideal building material. Though dark inside, these cave houses are naturally warmer in winter and cooler in summer than free-standing houses.

BELOW: ancient Buddhist rock carvings at the Longmen Caves.

GETTING TO HENAN

Flights: Zhengzhou's Xinzheng Airport, 36km (23 miles) southeast of the city, is reasonably well connected to China's other provincial capitals. There are daily flights to Beijing, Guilin and Shanghai, with less frequent links to Hong Kong and Singapore.

By train and bus: Straddling the north–south (Beijing–Guangzhou) line and the east–west (Shanghai–Xi'an) line, Zhengzhou is one of China's busiest rail junctions, with daily links to almost all major Chinese cities and tourist destinations – there are several trains each day to Beijing, Shanghai, Taiyuan, Wuhan and Xi'an. There are long-distance buses to cities in surrounding provinces, as well as to Beijing, but given the relative convenience and comfort of trains these are less popular with tourists.

GETTING AROUND HENAN

Zhengzhou: There are several trains daily to Anyang (2½ hours), Kaifeng (1 hour) and Luoyang (2 hours). Buses also run regularly throughout the day to Anyang (3 hours), Kaifeng (1 hour), Luoyang (2 hours), Dengfeng (1½ hours) and direct to the Shaolin Si (2 hours).

Kaifeng: There are frequent trains to Zhengzhou (1 hour) and Luoyang (3 hours). Buses leave throughout the day for Anyang (3½ hours), Luoyang (3 hours) and Zhengzhou (1 hour).

Dengfeng: There are regular buses to Luoyang (1½ hours) and Zhengzhou (1½ hours).

Luoyang: Trains depart throughout the day for Kaifeng (3 hours) and Zhengzhou (2 hours), while buses run frequently to Dengfeng (1½ hours), Zhengzhou (2 hours), Kaifeng (3 hours) and Anyang (4½ hours).

its importance was gradually eclipsed by that of the increasingly prosperous coastal towns. Heavy industrialisation has taken its toll on the modern city, and within its current confines there is little to suggest its former glory. But the environs are covered with long-forgotten burial mounds, and not far outside the city are two of China's most important Buddhist shrines: the time-worn Baima Si and the exquisite rock carvings of the Longmen Shiku. Some visitors also use Luoyang as a base for day trips to nearby Song Shan and the Shaolin Si.

Within the city itself, the only attraction worth visiting is the **Luoyang Museum**

Recommended Restaurants on page 197

(洛阳博物馆; Luoyang Bowuguan; daily 8am–5pm; charge), which houses four special collections of bronzeware, jadeware, ceramics and gold and silver artefacts, offering an overview of the area's development from the Neolithic period to the Song dynasty.

Some 13km (8 miles) east of downtown Luoyang is the venerable **Baima Si** (白马寺; White Horse Temple; daily 8.30am–5pm; charge), founded in AD 68 and considered China's first Buddhist temple. Now an active monastery, the name of the temple reflects the story of how its two founding monks – both Indians who were found in Afghanistan by special envoys despatched by the Eastern Han emperor – brought saddlebags of Buddhist scriptures to China on the backs of white horses. The temple was built in the monks' honour, and they lived here and translated the *sutras* from Sanskrit into Chinese. Both monks are interred inside the complex.

The Longmen Caves

The awe-inspiring **Longmen Shiku**  (龙门石窟; Dragon Gate Grottoes; daily 7am–7pm; charge), a Unesco World Heritage Site, are situated 12km (8 miles) south of Luoyang along the banks of the Yi Jiang. An elaborate ensemble of Buddhist statuary in stone, the remarkably varied carvings stretch for about 1km (½ mile) on both sides of the Yi and encompass the artistic toil of three dynasties: the latter period of the Northern Wei, the Sui and the Tang. The Turkic Toba, devout Buddhists, first set chisel to stone in AD 493 after moving the capital of their Northern Wei dynasty from Datong to Luoyang. For the next several centuries, grottoes and niches were dug out and decorated with ornate figures and reliefs, most of them sponsored by noblemen of the period.

There are said to be more than 2,300 grottoes and niches containing over 40 pagodas, some 2,800 inscriptions and over 100,000 statues and images. Regrettably, many of the most intricate sculptures were stolen or beheaded by collectors around the start of the 20th century, and are now in museums in the West. Another round of destruction took place during the state-sanctioned vandalism of the Cultural Revolution, when finely carved faces were crudely bashed in.

As well as the larger caves, the Longmen ensemble features thousands of small grottoes and niches carved into the soft rock. Signs in English help to enlighten visitors.

BELOW LEFT: the Longmen Caves are one of the most dramatic sights in China.

The Art of the Longmen Caves

As with the Yungang Caves in Shanxi province *(see page 172)*, work on the Longmen Caves was undertaken by the (non-Chinese) Buddhist Tuoba who ruled north China under the Northern Wei dynasty (AD 386–534). When the capital of the Northern Wei was moved from Datong to Luoyang, the stone carvers continued their creations at Longmen. Successive dynasties such as the Sui and Tang added to the worshipful enterprise, with most of the work taking place between the 5th and 8th centuries.

As Buddhist art is carved from stone (rather than wood or metal), much has survived to the present day, despite the sad preponderance of vandalised, headless Bodhisattvas. Some of the artwork was originally pigmented, but is now bleached by the elements, although flecks of paint survive on sheltered walls and ceilings.

The effigies number 100,000 in total and are in a variety of sizes: the largest of all measures 17 metres (56ft), the smallest just under 2cm (¾ inch). They depict a wide range of Buddhist deities, with the most popular being Avalokiteshvara (Guanyin), and the Maitreya and Amitabha Buddhas, while other carvings depict parables from the life of Sakyamuni. As the carving took place over a long period, a noticeable shift exists from the otherworldly Bodhisattvas of the Northern Wei to the more earthly Buddhas of the Tang dynasty.

Shaolin

Home of the martial arts, Shaolin is now cashing in by opening a commerical centre for training in its esoteric disciplines

The Shaolin Temple, in the Song Shan range near Luoyang, is the home of most East Asian martial arts. Be it *gongfu*, karate, taekwondo or judo, all are considered to have originated from ancient Chinese fighting techniques.

The origins of Shaolin's martial arts tradition are said to date back to the AD 527 visit of the Indian monk Bodhidharma (Damo). He realised that many of the Buddhist monks were unable to keep up demanding meditation exercises in complete quiet and concentration. Based upon observations of the movements of animals, the monk reputedly developed an exercise he described as a physical training method, which in turn became part of Shaolin boxing *(shaolinquan)*.

Wushu – the art of fighting – is the modern term for Chinese martial arts, whether involving weapons or empty-handed. The mastery of the various techniques once entailed very esoteric knowledge, which would only be passed on within a family or a monastery, or from master to pupil.

For an outsider, the variety of *wushu* styles is rather confusing. Sounding like a recipe for disaster, *zuiquan* (drunken boxing) imitates the stumbling gait and "soft" pliancy of a drunkard. Actually a brilliantly creative and deceptive boxing form, it can be highly effective. *Xingyiquan* (body mind boxing) aims to capture the fighting spirit of 12 animals, while also relying heavily on the use of *qi* energy. The movements are simple and quite easy to learn, although a lifetime is required for full mastery of the techniques. *Wuzuquan*, or five ancestors boxing, is a powerful Buddhist fighting art that relies heavily on breathing techniques and the cultivation of power through relaxation.

Taijiquan (supreme ultimate boxing) is a gentler method that aims to repel the opponent without the use of force, and with minimal effort. It is based on the Daoist idea that the principle of softness will ultimately overcome hardness. According to legend, it is also – just like Shaolin boxing – derived from the movements of animals, geared to breaking the momentum of an opponent's attack and letting it disappear into thin air. Originally a method of self-defence, in today's China it is mostly practised by older people for meditation and body-strengthening.

Like *xingyiquan*, *taijiquan* depends on the mastery and application of the life energy *qi*, which can be directed to all parts of the body with the help of mental training. *Qi* must flow and circulate freely in the body. The round movements of *taijiquan* are derived from this – they can be firm or loose, hard or soft, be directed forwards or backwards, but the movement must always be smooth and flowing. Through consistent practice of *taijiquan*, one eventually comes very close to the ideal of Daoism, namely *wuwei* – doing without a purpose.

In a wider sense, *qigong* (breathing technique) is also part of *wushu* and dates back 3,000 years. In *qigong*, techniques for regulating the breathing can bring about concentrated thinking and a state of inner calm.   ❑

ABOVE AND LEFT: martial arts training at Shaolin.

Recommended Restaurants on page 197

The most arresting part of the complex is the **Fengxian Si** (奉先寺: Temple for Worshipping Ancestors), with an exposed 17-metre (56ft) central Buddha statue (complete with 2-metre/6ft ears) surrounded by Bodhisattvas and heavenly guards. Completed in 676 during the reign of the Tang emperor Gaozong, the statue's face is said to be that of his wife, empress Wu Zetian *(see page 188)*, a powerful Buddhist patron.

Shaolin Si

Known worldwide for its pivotal role in the development of Chinese martial arts, **Shaolin Si** ⓲ (少林寺; Monastery of the Mount Shaoshi Forest; daily 8am–6.30pm; charge) is one of China's most famous tourist attractions. Located about 80km (50 miles) southeast of Luoyang, the monastery can be visited on a day trip from either city, or explored at a more leisurely pace from the nearby town of **Dengfeng** (登封).

Shaolin was first built in the 5th century AD but has been burnt down several times over the ages. Tradition holds that the Indian monk Bodhidharma lived here with the blessing of the emperor and introduced Chan (Zen) Buddhism to the resident Chinese monks. Once a remote and romantic retreat where the wisdom of the ages passed from master to novice, it is now a major tourist area as well as a place of pilgrimage for monks and lay Buddhists alike. A training hall, where many foreign martial arts enthusiasts come to study, has been built next to the monastery. For the typical tourist, however, the highlight of a visit is simply watching the hundreds of tracksuited, shaven-headed young students noisily running through their drills on the dusty fields near the monastery's entrance.

One of Shaolin's greatest treasures is the 18 *arhat* frescoes, painted in 1828, depicting monks in classic fighting poses that today's novices still emulate. In **Qianfo Dian** (千佛殿; Thousand Buddha Hall), the monastery's main hall, depressions in the stone floor serve as reminders of the tough combat exercises performed by the monks.

A short walk to the northwest of the monastery is **Talin** (塔林; Stupa Forest), an eerie resting place for expired monks comprising more than 240 brick-and-stone stupas, each containing the ashes of an accomplished monk. The oldest stupas are from the 9th century AD.

Song Shan and around

The several dozen mountain peaks stretching west from Shaolin Si comprise the holy range of **Song Shan** ⓳ (嵩山), forming the central axis of Daoism's five sacred mountains, as well as being sacred to Buddhists. Nestled in the hills surrounding Dengfeng – a town in the heart of the mountains, about 13km (8 miles) east of Shaolin – are some fascinating historic sights. The **Songyang Shuyuan** (嵩阳书院; Songyang Academy; daily 7.30am–6pm; charge), 3km (2 miles) north of Dengfeng, is one of China's four most influential ancient academies. Originally built in AD 484, during the Northern Wei dynasty, it was completely rebuilt in AD 1035. Among the highlights of the grounds are an enormous Tang-dynasty tablet carved in AD 744 and two giant cypress trees said to date back to 110 BC.

Shaolin is very popular with tour groups, and has become rather commercialised. Monks offer palm-readings and other fortune-telling services for a modest fee.

BELOW: Shaolin's eerie "Stupa Forest" (Talin).

The 13th-century Guanxing Tai observatory near Dengfeng was used to calculate the timing of solstices and other astronomical events.

BELOW: smile for the camera. **BELOW RIGHT:** an ancient statue of Confucius at Zhengzhou's Kong Miao (Confucius Temple).

To the northwest of the academy, 3km (2 miles) by road, is the **Songyuesi Ta** (嵩岳寺塔; Songyue Temple Pagoda; daily 8am–6pm; charge), originally constructed in AD 509 and considered China's oldest brick pagoda. About 2km (1¼ miles) before you reach the pagoda is the entrance to the **Taishi Shan Scenic Area** (太室山風景区; Taishi Shan Fengjing Qu; daily 8am–6pm; separate charge).

To the southeast of Dengfeng, near the town of Gaocheng, is the **Guanxing Tai** (观星台; Star Observation Platform; daily 8am–5.30pm; charge), an intriguing astronomical observatory which tourism officials claim is the oldest still standing in China. Built in 1276, it was at the centre of a network of 27 such Yuan-dynasty observatories.

One of the Dengfeng area's most impressive attractions is the **Zhongyue Miao** (中岳庙; Central Mountain Monastery; daily 6.30am–6.30pm; charge), a spacious Daoist monastery about 2km (1¼ miles) east of the city and accessible by green public bus no. 2. The extensive walled complex, originally founded around 220 BC but having undergone a complete restoration during the Ming dynasty, is an active monastery inhabited by a sizeable population of monks. The sprawling courtyards are filled with ancient cypresses and magnificently carved stelae, exposed to the elements and covered in moss.

Zhengzhou

The lively city of **Zhengzhou** ㉚ (郑州), about 80km (50 miles) east of Dengfeng and 20km (13 miles) south of the Huang He, is the capital of Henan province and an important railway junction straddling the crossroads of China's main east–west (Shanghai–Xi'an) and north–south (Beijing–Guangzhou) lines. There was a fortified settlement here as early as the Shang dynasty, some 3,500 years ago, but all that remains of that period are the high, packed-earth foundations of the **Shang-era walls** located in the southeast of the modern city. Locals of all ages climb to the top for a variety of recreational activities, making it an ideal place to observe daily life.

Another excellent place to people-watch is the **Kong Miao** (孔庙; Confucius Temple; 24 Dong Dajie; daily 8am–5pm; free), which effectively functions as an

Recommended Restaurants on page 197

after-school community centre, with halls doubling as study rooms and courtyards used for *taiji* training.

One block further north, at 2 Shang-cheng Lu, is the **Chenghuang Miao** (城隍庙; City God Temple; daily 9am–5pm; free), the most intact ancient building in the downtown area. Founded more than 600 years ago, during the Ming dynasty, its buildings have undergone a recent restoration and the walls of the main hall are adorned with freshly painted murals depicting the city gods of China's biggest urban centres.

Zhengzhou's most educational attraction is the cavernous new **Henan Provincial Museum** (河南省博物馆; Henan Sheng Bowuguan; 8 Nongye Lu; Tue–Sun 8am–5pm; charge), which features three floors of well-presented historic artefacts unearthed in the province – those on display are only a small percentage of the museum's total collection, a testament to Henan's archaeological wealth.

Kaifeng

An hour's bus ride east of Zhengzhou, **Kaifeng** ㉑ (开封) is one of China's most enduring ancient capitals, retaining enough historic sites to hint at its former glory yet largely resisting the indiscriminate modern development that now dominates most of its contemporaries. Although a settlement existed here during the Shang dynasty, dating as far back as 1000 BC, it was not until 364 BC that one of the Warring States declared it as a regional capital. Kaifeng served as a capital for six more dynasties, reaching its pinnacle in the Northern Song (AD 960–1127), when it was believed to be one of the world's biggest cities. Little remains of the great Song capital, however: due to its proximity to the temperamental Huang He, Kaifeng has been devastated by floods dozens of times, and almost everything from that era is buried under several metres of silt.

Still, most of the pounded-earth city wall survives, giving the ancient centre a quaint, compact feel. In Kaifeng's far northeast corner, just inside the city wall, is one of its only Song-period relics: the **Tie Ta** (铁塔; Iron Pagoda; daily 7.30am–6.30pm; charge), a 13-storey, 56-metre (184ft) brick structure soaring prominently in the middle of **Tie Ta Gongyuan** (铁塔公园; Iron Pagoda Park; daily 7am–7pm; charge). Built in AD 1049, the octagonal tower gets its name from the dark-brown glazed tiles that adorn its exterior, which from a distance looks like cast iron. Visitors can climb to the top via a narrow, winding stone staircase.

Kaifeng's oldest standing structure is the **Fan Ta** (繁塔; Fan Pagoda; daily 8.30am–5.30pm; charge), three storeys high and decorated with numerous carved Buddha figures in niches. Originally called the **Po Ta**, it is located outside the town wall to the southeast of the railway station.

In the city centre is the **Xiangguo Si** (相国寺; Prime Minister's Monastery; Ziyou Lu; daily 8am–6.30pm; charge), first built in AD 555 and for centuries an important Buddhist centre. Its golden age was during the Northern Song, when there were 64 halls in the complex. It was destroyed by flood in 1644 and most of the present buildings date back to 1766. The unassuming **Yanqing Guan** (延庆观; Yanqing Temple; 53 Guanqian Jie; daily

EAT

One of Kaifeng's main attractions – and its unquestionable culinary highlight – is the vibrant **night market** (开封夜市; Kaifeng Yeshi), one of China's biggest. Sprawling from the corner of Gulou and Madao streets, hundreds of mostly Hui Muslim vendors dole out kebabs and noodles; try the *xingren cha* (杏仁茶), a jelly-like porridge sweetened with powdered almonds and a host of berries.

BELOW: an offshoot of the Grand Canal in Anhui province.

Kaifeng's Yanqing Guan, a colourful Daoist temple in the heart of the old city.

8am–6pm; charge) is a Daoist sanctuary with only two halls; the first, the Jade Emperor Pavilion, is notable for its undecorated, high-domed ceiling. Also worth a visit is the **Shanshangan Huiguan** (陕山甘会馆; Shanshangan Guild Hall; 85 Xufu Jie; daily 8am–5.30pm; charge), an extravagantly decorated Qing-dynasty compound built by an association of merchants from Shanxi, Shaanxi and Gansu provinces to serve as a lodging and networking centre for visiting traders.

For an overview of the city's past, including some relics from the former Jewish community (see panel below), visit the **Kaifeng Museum** (开封博物馆; Kaifeng Bowuguan; 26 Yingbin Lu; daily 8.30–11.30am, 2.30–5.30pm; charge) on the other side of Baogong Lake from the Yanqing Temple.

Anyang

About 200km (124 miles) north of Zhengzhou, near the Hebei border, is the town of **Anyang** ㉒ (安阳), which marks the location of Yin – the ancient Shang-dynasty (1700–1100 BC) capital. Referred to in ancient Chinese annals, Yin was long forgotten until excavations in the

20th century yielded evidence of the vanished city. Visitors can see the remains of the settlement at the **Yin Ruins Museum** (殷墟博物院; Yinxu Bowuguan; daily 8am–5.30pm; charge), which has an excellent display of oracle bones unearthed at the site. The bones, mostly tortoise belly shells and ox shoulder blades, bear the primitive inscriptions upon which the Chinese writing system is based. There is also a new annex housing the intact remains of six chariots – complete with attached horse skeletons – excavated from nearby tombs.

In Anyang's old town is the curious **Wenfeng Ta** (文峰塔; Wenfeng Pagoda; daily 8am–5pm; charge), which – unlike most pagodas – is narrower at the base and gets wider towards the top. The tight squeeze up steep stone steps to the roof is worth it for the city views.

A relic from a more recent era, the **Hongqi Yunhe** (红旗运河; Red Flag Canal) draws visitors to **Linzhou** (林洲), 70km (45 miles) west of Anyang in the Taihuang Mountains. The canal, a testament to the ideological single-mindedness of the period, was engineered by hand during the Cultural Revolution. ❏

BELOW: Kaifeng once had a large Jewish community.

Kaifeng's Jews

Small enclaves of Jews are believed to have settled in northwest China as early as the Han dynasty (206 BC–AD 220), but those who migrated from Central Asia to Kaifeng during the Northern Song dynasty (960–1127) are widely considered the progenitors of China's longest-running Jewish identity. Only a few Kaifeng families still trace their lineage back to Jews and, on a cultural level, these claims are complicated by the fact that Chinese descent is patrilineal while Jewish heritage is matrilineal. But while the cultural debate continues, there is little disputing that the city once had a notable Jewish presence – a synagogue stood near the town centre until the late 19th century, and three stelae inscribed with imperial versions of their history are displayed on the first floor of the Kaifeng Museum (see above).

RESTAURANTS

SHAANXI PROVINCE

Shaanxi is known for a varied cuisine that reflects its long history as a trading crossroads, as well as its resulting ethnic diversity. In the countryside and far north, travellers can expect liberal doses of noodles accompanied by bowls of raw garlic – in keeping with rural tradition, locals routinely eat several cloves of garlic with meals. Urban areas typically feature a diverse mixture of foods from all corners of China, with a particular emphasis on Muslim fare.

Xi'an

Shaanxi's capital has a rich culinary heritage befitting its historic role as China's ancient capital. The city is saturated with places to eat, from simple street stalls devoted to a single speciality to fine dining establishments offering lavish, multi-course banquets. There is an interesting selection of restaurants in the city centre, especially along Dong Dajie just east of the Bell Tower.

Packing the alleys north of the Great Mosque are rows of Muslim street vendors selling inexpensive mutton and beef dishes as well as desserts and sweet porridges. Look out for the *roujiamo* (肉夹馍), fried lamb or beef in a pitta, as well as the standard *rouchuan* (肉串), skewered lamb or beef kebabs.

Beijing Zhengyamen
北京正鸭門
68 Youyi Xilu. **$$$**
A stylish and spotlessly clean Beijing Roast Duck restaurant, conveniently located just to the east of the entrance to the Small Wild Goose Pagoda, on the same side of Youyi Xilu.

Lao Sun Jia 老孙家
364 Dong Dajie. **$**
One of Xi'an's most famous restaurants, where Chinese and foreign tourists alike come to sample *yangrou paomo* (羊肉泡馍), a lamb stew filled with coin-sized chunks of flatbread – in keeping with a time-honoured ritual, diners themselves must tear the bread into tiny bits and pile them in their bowls before a meat-and-noodle-filled broth is poured over the top.

Shuyuan International Youth Hostel Restaurant
属院国际青年旅舍饭店
2 Shuncheng Xixiang Nan Jie. **$$**
A popular hangout for backpackers, the Shuyuan does competent, if slightly overpriced, Western standards.

Wuyi Fandian 五一饭店
351 Dong Dajie. **$**
Located on the ground floor of the May First Hotel, this cafeteria-style canteen serves northern Chinese food such as noodles, dumplings and steamed buns. Its streetside stalls sell skewers of barbecued meat, tofu and seafood.

Xi'an Roast Duck Restaurant 西安烤鸭店
369 Dong Dajie. **$$**
This no-frills, two-floor restaurant serves up generous portions of roast duck along with fine-sliced onion, plum sauce and thin crêpes in which to wrap it all. It fills up quickly at lunchtime.

Xiangzimen Youth Hostel Restaurant
湘子门国际青年旅舍饭店
16 Xiangzimiao Jie. **$$**
The best of Xi'an's youth hostel restaurants, with a fairly extensive English-language menu of Chinese and Western standards, delivered in a friendly environment. Open from early morning until late at night.

HENAN PROVINCE

Henan draws from its northern roots in producing some eminently palatable noodle dishes, and the ancient city of Kaifeng has one of the most vibrant night markets in all of China.

Zhengzhou

Henan's capital has no shortage of street food, with centrally located **night markets** surrounding Erqi Ta Square. Two blocks northeast is the **Guangcai Market** (光彩市场), with dozens of stands and outdoor restaurants.

Jingya Seafood Restaurant 净煨海鲜店
112 Chengdong Lu. **$$$$**
Directly across Chengdong Road from the Sofitel, this upmarket place specialises in exotic seafood dishes, especially Shandong and Cantonese delicacies.

Kaifeng
(see also margin note, page 195)

Xinsheng Restaurant
新生饭庄
66 Gulou Jie. **$**
An affordable venue with big, comfortable booths and a helpful picture menu with a nice range of standard Chinese favourites, the Xinsheng fills up quickly at lunch, so it's best to arrive early.

Luoyang

The area around the railway station has several cheap and convenient dumpling and noodle joints that are good for a quick breakfast or lunch. The best place to go for dinner is the **Nan Dajie Night Market** (南大街夜市), 3km (2 miles) southeast of the station, where you can snack to your fill on grilled lamb, beef and squid skewers and top it all off with some of the many dessert pastries filled with red beans and dates.

Tianxiang Restaurant
天香饭店
56 Jingyuyuan Lu. **$**
This modest restaurant serves spicy Sichuan cuisine and gets packed out with Chinese tourists during lunch and dinner.

The Terracotta Warriors

Vying with the Great Wall as China's most famous historical sight, this amazing, ancient army was only discovered in the 1970s

Located some 30km (20 miles) to the east of Xi'an, this singularly spectacular sight is just part of a grand mausoleum built by the emperor Qin Shi Huangdi in the 3rd century BC. Although the place is packed with tour groups of every nationality on any given day, and battalions of hawkers vie for your attention outside, it is well worth the effort to persevere through the crowds and linger awhile to admire the magnificent displays. Note that the signs prohibiting flash photography are routinely ignored by everyone, including the staff.

The site comprises three large vaults which have been surmounted with hangar-like structures: between them they house over 8,000 terracotta warriors. The main vault contains over a thousand figures, which can be viewed at close quarters from raised walkways, while at the rear lie the forlorn fragments of toppled and headless soldiers. The second and third vaults are smaller in size but the figures they contain feature a wider variety of poses. A spectacular pair of half-sized chariots, complete with terracotta horses, are on display in the small museum by the main entrance. This was discovered in 1980 and is similar to carriages used by Qin Shi Huangdi on his inspection tours, alive and above ground.

Most people will get more out of their visit by taking a guided tour or hiring an audio guide (both are available in English). There is also an informative film that screens in the on-site theatre.

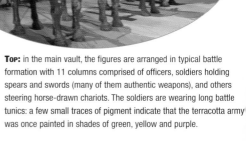

Top: in the main vault, the figures are arranged in typical battle formation with 11 columns comprised of officers, soldiers holding spears and swords (many of them authentic weapons), and others steering horse-drawn chariots. The soldiers are wearing long battle tunics: a few small traces of pigment indicate that the terracotta army was once painted in shades of green, yellow and purple.

Above: the half-sized models of bronze battle chariots feature some the hundreds of horse statues that accompany those of the main arm

Above and Right: each figure is about 1.8 metres (5 ft 10 inches) tall, and each head has been individually modelled with unique facial expressions.

THE GREAT NECROPOLIS

Excavation work at the Bingmayong site has continued since its original discovery in 1974. Archaeologists are excited by the prospect of unearthing new treasures on an even grander scale: according to historic surveys, a splendid necropolis depicting the whole of China in miniature is centred underneath Qin Shi Huangdi's tomb, its

ceiling purportedly studded with pearls depicting the night sky. It is thought that mercury may have been pumped in mechanically to create images of flowing rivers (trial digs have revealed a high mercury content in the soil). The entire complex may cover an area of up to 56 sq km (22 sq miles), but in order to excavate fully, 12 villages and half a dozen factories in the area would have to be relocated.

QIN SHI HUANGDI

Emperor Qin Shi Huangdi, ruler from 247 to 210 BC, bears all the hallmarks of a ruthless megalomaniac. Not only did he surround his tomb with thousands of life-sized statues of his personal army – a project that involved seven hundred thousand workers over 36 years – he is also thought to have buried alive thousands of Confucian scholars. It is possible that the emperor was so superstitious and fearful that he had the necropolis built as a decoy and is, in fact, buried somewhere else.

ABOVE: Qin Shi Huangdi, China's first great emperor and unifier of the country in 221 BC.

BELOW: the discovery of the terracotta warriors has done wonders for the regional economy. Huge numbers of tourists visit each year and the souvenir industry is a significant local employer.

ABOVE: the area surrounding this premium tourist site is crowded with souvenir stalls. Some (particularly within the site itself) are of reasonable quality, but beware pushy vendors – as well as overpriced food stalls.

ANCIENT TREASURES FROM THE ROYAL TOMBS

The royal tombs of ancient China offer a fascinating glimpse of the life, wealth, and beliefs of the early emperors and rulers

Almost all our knowledge of ancient China comes from the artefacts found in the tombs of princes and warriors. As early as 3000 BC, neolithic caves were elaborately carved and filled, but it was during the ascendancy of the Shang kings, around 1200 BC, that they were the most dazzling. The dynasty had had capitals at Anyang and Zhengzhou, and nothing was spared in the attempt to help Shang royalty reach the afterlife. Sacrifices were on an epic scale. Some 700,000 people laboured to build the tomb of the first emperor, and many of those who worked on the tomb were killed. Others simply died in the process. Courtiers and concubines were slaughtered in the death chambers, and both horses and charioteers perished in order to accompany their master (or mistress) into the underworld. Bureaucrats devoted their careers to overseeing the inventories of the tombs, which they prepared in great detail to present to the officials of the underworld, including deeds to prove the deceased owned the land he or she had been buried on.

The Shang tombs were constructed during the Bronze Age, and have yielded some remarkable bronze items, many of them showing vivid imagination and skill. Perhaps the most dramatic attire of the deceased was the jade suit *(see picture, right)*. The mineral is very hard and could not be carved – but had to be worn down to make the small rectangular squares that were then linked by gold or silver thread to fit the body. Jade suits were used from around 140 BC to AD 220; around 40 have so far been discovered.

ABOVE: one of a number of bronze heads covered with gold foil found at Sanxindui, from around 1200 BC. All the facial features are emphasised.

RIGHT: a vessel for food offerings, from the tomb of Lady Fu Hao, a warrior queen of around 1200 BC. Her tomb near Anyang contained 250 ritual bronzes.

ABOVE: this model of a storyteller who spoke, sung and danced tales, dates from around AD 25. There was a strong musical tradition in ancient China, and several tombs have yielded percussion and wind instruments.

MYSTERY FIGURE OF SANXINDUI

This life-size figure was discovered when two huge ancient burial pits were accidentally stumbled upon in Sanxindui, Sichuan province, in 1986. Barefoot and dressed in robes, it has massive hands that seem to be designed to hold something. It may represent a king or a priest, but there is no clue as to its identity. The find dates from the 12th century BC and it caused historians to re-think the way Chinese civilisation began. Up until the discovery, it was widely held that only the middle Yellow River (Huang He) valley supported civilisation at that time. The

pits also contained a treasure trove of charred elephants' tusks, bronzes, and jade blades unknown elsewhere, but no human remains. There was no evidence of writing, and nothing else is known of Sanxindui civilisation, or what became of it.

BELOW: this is the oldest root carving found in China, from the 4th–3rd century BC. Like a tiger on stilts, it has fierce red-and-orange eyes and shows extraordinary imagination. Small creatures can be seen running up and down its spidery legs, which are made of bamboo. It was found above the head of a woman in a tomb in Mashan, Jiangling County, and it was probably designed to be her guardian.

ABOVE: a fanciful bronze creature from the 5th-6th century BC sticks out its tongue. It may have been a stand for a musical instrument. The dragon had many variants down the centuries.

RIGHT: the jade suit of Liu Sheng (154–113 BC), Prince of Zhongshan. Knotted with 1,100g (40oz) gold wire, it took 10 years to make and has 2,498 jade plaques, which carefully follow this bon viveur's paunch. It was discovered in 1968 in a palatial underground warren together with some 4,000 burial items.

THE CENTRE

Linked by the mighty Chang Jiang (Yangzi River), China's green and densely populated heartlands are full of interest

The fertile land of central China, particularly the area around the eastern seaboard – "the land of rice and fish" – has long been the most prosperous and productive part of the country. Plentiful rainfall and mild winters make ideal conditions for rice cultivation, a labour intensive form of agriculture that has made the region home to the highest rural population densities in the world. Many of the important events that have shaped modern China over the past two hundred years have taken place here.

The great commercial centre of Shanghai, China's largest city, is its cornerstone for the 21st century: a glittering, high-rise, wealth-generating metropolis which is attracting migrant workers, entrepreneurs and business leaders from across China and the world. With China's best hotels, nightlife and shopping, some excellent museums, historic sights aplenty and mesmerising views, it has a lot to offer tourists too.

Close to Shanghai is the Grand Canal, the ancient conduit that linked north and south China, with picturesque cities and towns – Suzhou and Wuxi, amongst others – along its banks. Nanjing, upriver along the Chang Jiang, is a gracious, green city with deep layers of history. To the south, Hangzhou was once one of China's most important urban centres, marking as it did the southern terminus of the Grand Canal. The city's West Lake is considered by many Chinese to be the most beautiful place in the country.

Far off to the west, the Chang Jiang (Yangzi) surges through Chongqing, another boom town, from where cruise boats and ferries depart regularly for the famous Three Gorges – still awe-inspiring despite the effects of the gigan-

tic, and now completed, Three Gorges Dam. Boats continue downstream to the city of Yichang, with a few journeying onwards to Wuhan, capital of Hubei province. Both are within reach of scenic gems, including Shennongjia Forest Reserve and Huang Shan – in Anhui province – one of China's most idyllic mountains. ❏

PRECEDING PAGES: young gymnasts work on their technique. **LEFT:** Huang Shan, Anhui. **ABOVE RIGHT:** Hangzhou's West Lake. **ABOVE LEFT:** Shanghai skyline.

Shanghai Huochezhan
(Railway Station)
上海火车站 **7**

Shanghai
Railway Station **M**

JIAOTONG
GONGYUAN

Hengfeng Rd

Tianmu Road (W.)

Tianmu Road (W.)

Minli Rd

Datong Rd

Meiyuan Road

Gonghe Xin Road

Gonghe Road

Central Tianmu Road

Tibet (Xizang) Road (N.)

Xinjia

Yufo Si
(Jade Buddha Temple)
玉佛寺 **8**

Hengfeng Road

Hanzhong Road

Meiyuan Rd

Wuzhen

Xinjiang Road (N.)

Qufu

Wusong (Suzhou Creek)

Haifang Road

Hanzhong
Road **M**

Hanzhong Road

Datong Road

Chengdu Road (N.)

Xinzha Road

Central Tibet (Xizang

Jiangning Rd

Changping Road

Kangding Road (E.)

Xinzha Road

Shanghaiguan Road

Daian Road

Xinchang Road

Huangpi Road (N.)

Xinzha Road **M**

Xinzha Road (W.)

Kangding Road

Wuding Road

Xinzha Road

Beijing Road

NI CHENG QIAO

SHAANXI Road (N.)

JINGAN

Shimen No.2 Road

Beijing Road (W.)

Fengyang Road

Di Yi Baihuo Shange
(Shanghai No.1 Dept St
上海第一百货商

Jing An Si
(Jing An Temple)

Youtai Jiaotang
(Ohel Rachel
Synagogue)

Nanhui Rd

Beijing Road (W.)

Nanjing Road (W.)

Nanjing
Road (W.) **M**

Fengyang Road

Nanjing Road (W.) **15** 南京路

Nanjing Rd (W.)

Guoji Fandian
(Park Hotel)
国际饭店 **14**

Jinmen
Dajiudian
(Pacific Hote

RENMIN GON
(PEOPLE'S

People's
Square **M**

Shanghai Dangdai
Yishu Guan (MoCA)
上海当代艺术馆 **13**

人民公 **10**

Chengshi
Zhen

Westgate
Mall

Shanghai
Shangcheng
(Shangai
Centre)
上海商城 **16**

Plaza 66

CITC Square

Shanghai Meishuguan
(Art Museum)
上海美术馆 **12**

Shanghai
Zhengfu (

Shanghai Dianshitai
(TV Station)

Ming Tien
Guangchang
(Tomorrow Square)

Renmin G
人民厂

JC Mandarin

Weihai Rd

Shimen No.1 Road

Weihai Rd

Chengdu Road (N.)

Central
Plaza

Shanghai
Da Juyuan
(Grand Theatre)

Wusheng Rd

ShanghaiB
(Shanghai
上海博

Shanghai
Zhanlan Zhongxin
(Exhibition
Centre)
上海展 览中心

Tongren Road

Nanjing Road (N.)

Maoming Road

Huangpi
Rd (S.) **M**

Central Yan'an Road

Central Yan'an Road

Jinling Rd

YANZHONG
GONGYUAN

Huangpi Rd (S.)

Songsha

Hong

Hengshan
Male Bieshu
(Hengshan Moller Villa)

Julu Road

Rujin Road

Julu Road

Changle Rd

Shui On
Plaza

Cent
PM

Jinjiang Dickson
Centre

Lanxin Daxiyuan
(Lyceum Theatre)

Shaanxi Road (S.)

Changle Road

Changle Road

Chengdu Rd (S.)

Central
Plaza

Taicang Road

Xi
新 **19**

Julu Road

Changle Road

Huayuan
Fandian
(Okura Garden
Hotel)

Lao Jinjiang
Fandian
(Jinjiang Hotel)

Shimen No.2 Road

Central Huaihai Road

Isetan

Zhonggong Yidahuizhi
(Site of the First National
Congress of the CPC)
中共一大会址 **20**

TA

Xintia
新天 **21**

Xiangyang Road (S.)

Baisheng Gouwu Zhongxin
(Parkson Department Store)

New Hualian
Commercial
Building

Nanchang Road

Zhizhong

XIANGYANG
GONGYUAN

Shaanxi
Road (S.)

Sheng Nigulasi Jiaotang
(former St Nicholas
Church)

FUXING
GONGYUAN

LUWAN

Shanghai Tushuguan
(Shanghai Library)
上海图书馆

Xinle Road

Donghu Road

Central Huaihai Road 淮海路

Nanchang

Rujin No.2 Rd

Sun Zhongshan Guju
(former residence of Sun Yatsen)
孙中山故居 **22**

Sinan Road (S.)

Aigenisi Shimotejia Jinju
(Agnes Smedley's
former residence)

Central Fuxing Ro

Yinyue
Xueyuan
(Conservatory
of Music)

Xiangyang Road (S.)

Shaanxi Rd (S.)

Central Fuxing Road

Ruijin No.2 Rd

Zhou Enlai Guju
(former residence of
Zhou En-lai)

Chengdu Road (S.)

Hefei

Madang

Longhua Gu Si,
Xujiahui
龙华古寺 **23**

21

Shanghai Gongyi
Meishu Yanjiusuo
(Arts & Crafts Research
Institute)
上海工艺美术研究所

Wenhua Guangchang
(Cultural Square)

Ruijin
Binguan

Central Fuxing Road

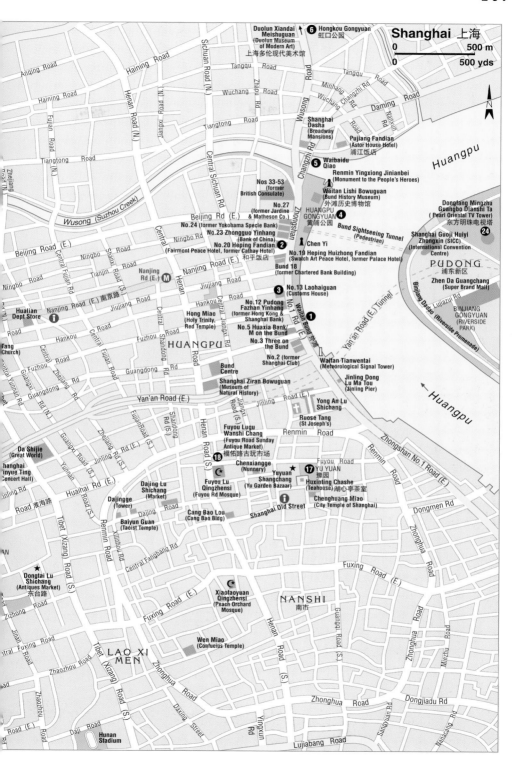

Duolun Xiandai
Meishuguan
(Duolun Museum
of Modern Art)
上海多伦现代美术馆

6 Hongkou Gongyuan
虹口公园

Shanghai 上海

0   500 m

0   500 yds

Shanghai
Dasha
(Broadway
Mansions)

Pujiang Fandian
(Astor House Hotel)
浦江饭店

Huangpu

5 Waibaidu
Qiao

Renmin Yingxiong Jinianbei
(Monument to the People's Heroes)

Nos 33-53
(former
British Consulate)

Waitan Lishi Bowuguan
(Bund History Museum)
外滩历史博物馆

Dongfang Mingzhu
Guangbo Dianshi Ta
(Pearl Oriental TV Tower)
东方明珠电视塔

No.27
(former Jardine
& Matheson Co.)

4 HUANGPU
GONGYUAN
黄浦公园

Bund Sightseeing Tunnel
(Pedestrian)

Shanghai Guoji Huiyi
Zhongxin (SICC)
(International Convention
Centre)

24

No.24 (former Yokohama Specie Bank)

No.23 Zhongguo Yinhang
(Bank of China)

No.20 Heping Fandian **2**
(Fairmont Peace Hotel, former Cathay Hotel)
和平饭店

Chen Yi

No.19 Heping Huizhong Fandian
(Swatch Art Peace Hotel, former Palace Hotel)

PUDONG
浦东新区

Zhen Da Guangchang
(Super Brand Mall)

Nanjing
Rd (E.) **M** 南京路

Bund 18
(former Chartered Bank Building)

No.13 Laohaiguan **3**
(Customs House)

BINJIANG
GONGYUAN
(RIVERSIDE
PARK)

Hualian
Dept Store

No.12 Pudong
Fazhan Yinhang
(former Hong Kong &
Shanghai Bank)

Hong Miao
(Holy Trinity,
Red Temple)

No.5 Huaxia Bank/
M on the Bund

No.3 Three on
the Bund

HUANGPU

Tang
Church

No.2 (former
Shanghai Club)

Waitan Tianwentai
(Meteorological Signal Tower)

Bund
Centre

Jinling Dong
Lu Ma Tou
(Jinling Pier)

Shanghai Ziran Bowuguan
(Museum of
Natural History)

Yong An Lu
Shichang

Da Shijie
(Great World)

Ruose Tang
(St Joseph's)

anghai
nyue Ting
Concert Hall)

Fuyou Lugu
Wanshi Chang
(Fuyou Road Sunday
Antique Market)
福佑古玩市场 **18**

Chenxiangge
(Nunnery)

17 YU YUAN
豫园

Yuyuan
Shangchang
(Yu Garden Bazaar)

Huxinting Chashe
(Teahouse) 湖心亭茶室

Dajing Lu
Shichang
(Market)

Fuyou Lu
Qingzhensi
(Fuyou Rd Mosque)

Chenghuang Miao
(City Temple of Shanghai)

Dajingge
(Tower)

Cang Bao Lou
(Cang Bao Bldg)

Shanghai Old Street

Baiyun Guan
(Taoist Temple)

Dongtai Lu
Shichang
(Antiques Market)
东台路

Xiaofaoyuan
Qingzhensi
(Peach Orchard
Mosque)

NANSHI
南市

Wen Miao
(Confucius Temple)

**LAO XI
MEN**

Hunan
Stadium

Zhongshan No.1 Road (E.)

Huangpu

Recommended Restaurants and Bars on pages 224–5

SHANGHAI

Eyed with envy by the rest of China, the rising star of stylish Shanghai – Paris of the East back in the glitzy colonial days – seems set to put even Hong Kong in the shade

n all of China, in all the world really, there is no other city like **Shanghai** (上海). This huge, sprawling beast of a metropolis has risen from the mud and silt of the Yangzi Delta, pushed aside its rivals and emerged as one of the liveliest and most exciting cities on the planet.

Shanghai has a reputation as a money-mad place, headlong and greedy in its single-minded pursuit of wealth, caring for nothing but the almighty red-backed Rmb. But this is only partly true; the dollar, the euro, and the yen are equally beloved, as are all the other foreign currencies that are driving the city's get-rich-quick mentality.

For better or for worse, modern Shanghai derives most of its energy from the ceaseless flow of money that swirls around the city, luring investment and talent from around the globe. Each year, more than US$10 billion in foreign cash flows into the city, where it is injected into the metropolis like a super-steroid, swelling the skyline with cutting-edge skyscrapers and modern mega-malls that sprout like bamboo shoots after a spring rain. Swirled together, these ingredients – the cash, the business zeal and the influx of people – have created a new world "fusion city" that is unequalled by anything else in China – or Asia.

At street level too, Shanghai pushes the envelope of the possible. Every week, it seems, another new nightclub pops into existence, hipper and groovier than its month-old rivals. On the restaurant scene, it's the same: no celebrity chef can be without a Shanghai flagship, while the siren song of modern Shanghai pulls in the deep-pocketed financiers, entrepreneurs, superstar designers, and large numbers of lower-ranking foreigners who make up the supporting cast.

It also, of course, attracts migrants from all over China. Labourers from the provinces are busy building the city, while earnest college students, young professionals and managers-on-the-go arrive from provincial capitals, adding their own unique brand of ambition to the ever-throbbing, ever-changing metropolis.

Main attractions

THE BUND, AND VIEWS ACROSS TO PUDONG
NANJING ROAD
PEOPLE'S PARK
SHANGHAI MUSEUM
YUYUAN GARDEN AND BAZAAR
FORMER FRENCH CONCESSION (XUHUI DISTRICT)

LEFT: the Pearl Oriental TV Tower, icon of modern China.
BELOW: Saturday afternoon on Nanjing Road.

BELOW: the
glittering city
skyline.

Brave New World

Meanwhile, the city government – which
enjoys provincial-level authority – has
fuelled the growth by launching a vast
number of ambitious infrastructure ventures. Every week, it seems, a glittering
new project is announced, or begun, or
completed.

The city is huge: the estimated population of the municipality reached 18.5 million in 2007, and the built-up area now
covers an area of 375 sq km (145 sq
miles). The population density is among
the highest in the world.

Administratively, Shanghai is a
metropolis without a province, made up
of surrounding rural districts and a dozen
city districts. Its provincial-level authority has given it enormous power to
remake itself, and it has done just that,
driving elevated highways through the
congested sections of the Old City, and
building the subway lines and bridges and
tunnels and other infrastructure that are
helping to ease the crowding and traffic.

The gateway **Pudong International
Airport** (浦东国际机场), connected to
the city by the world's fastest train,
opened a new passenger terminal in early
2008, and is building a third terminal,
plus another runway. A massive cruise
ship terminal-hotel-shopping complex is
taking shape on the banks of the
Huangpu River (黄浦江) north of the
Bund, and a couple more ferry docks are
popping up on the Pudong side. As ambitious as they are, none of those works
compares with the grandest scheme of
all: Expo 2010.

In 2007, the city began to level more
than 5 sq km (2 sq miles) of prime land
on both sides of the Huangpu, just south
of the iconic Bund. Sweeping away the
rusty factories and shabby warehouses
and derelict houses, the city planners are
erecting an exhibition for the ages, one
that they hope will sear the city onto the
global psyche in unforgettable fashion
when it opens in the spring of 2010.

All of these projects – subway lines,
cruise terminal, airport upgrade and
high-speed rails – are scheduled for completion by Expo 2010, and given Shanghai's can-do spirit, few doubt that the
deadline will be met.

Constant crowds are one of the most
evident aspects of Shanghai. Every street
corner, every sidewalk, every last train

Recommended Restaurants and Bars on pages 224–5

GETTING AROUND SHANGHAI

From the airport: The MAGLEV train whisks passengers from Pudong International Airport to a relatively remote eastern suburb, from where a taxi or the subway continue to downtown Pudong or downtown Shanghai.

Buses: Shanghai's buses are often slow and crowded, but for point-to-point travel they can still be useful, especially for short distances.

Metro: The Shanghai metro is fast and reliable, and the network is expanding rapidly, with eight lines open or partly open in 2008, and another five lines under way. Stored-value cards, which can also be used for taxis, buses and ferries, must be bought in convenience stores. They can be topped up at metro stations.

Taxis: During rush hours, taxis are very scarce, and if it rains (not uncommon), you'd better consider other options. Drivers are generally reliable, and pick-ups can be arranged in advance by telephone: Johnson Taxi tel: 6258-0000; DaZhong Taxi 96822; JinJiang Taxi 96961

Ferries: Regular pedestrian ferries cross the Huangpu River from Puxi to Pudong, from several docks south of the Bund, and the trip across the busy river is cheap and enjoyable.

Sold by street vendors all over Shanghai, xiao long bao *are small steamed parcels similar to* jiaozi *dumplings, filled with pork, seafood or vegetables in a small amount of soup. They are usually dipped in vinegar. Caution is advised – the filling can be scaldingly hot.*

station and eatery and ticket line, teems with people. Traffic tends towards the chaotic, taxis can be hard to find and buses, and the metro, are usually packed. Locals and outsiders agree on that: *ren tai duo* – there are too many people in China's largest city.

Like the Hong Kong Chinese, the residents of Shanghai have had longer to absorb the commercial instincts of the West, and they are considered some of China's most worldly, fashionable and open people. Like most Chinese, they are essentially regional, and speak a dialect that nobody else can fully understand, eat their own cuisine, and generally consider themselves to be light-years ahead of everyone else in the country.

Now the most expensive city in China, Shanghai's higher living standards, pulsating nightlife and cosmopolitan air can make even Beijing seem dowdy in comparison. This is truly the Chinese vision for the 21st century.

A Brief History of Shanghai

Not content with its meteoric rise from fishing village to commercial hub of China, Shanghai is now poised to become a global financial capital

Once upon a time, in fact just two centuries ago, Shanghai was nothing more than a silty corner of the Yangzi Delta. The city has no ancient history: while its neighbours Suzhou, Hangzhou and Nanjing took turns as the glittering capitals of China's imperial dynasties, Shanghai was nothing more than a drab gathering of farming huts and fishing villages.

Yet its location meant that it was a city waiting to happen, and happen it did, as successive waves of commerce crashed onto the muddy shores of the Huangpu River, each one bringing with it a new wave of streets and buildings and people and culture.

The first wave of development was modest: a few farmers and fishermen, and a handful of traders, settled on the banks of the Huangpu. In time, they erected a small village, which was immediately attacked, many times, by Japanese pirates. In response, the residents built a city wall, which surrounded the old city centre until 1912, just south of

the Bund in a circular area defined by Renmin and Zhonghua roads.

The next wave of development was a big one: in the aftermath of the Opium Wars of the 1840s, foreign concessions were established, and eventually occupied much of what is now central Shanghai, except for the old walled Chinese city. The British, French and Americans brought modern business to Shanghai: rule of law, customs houses, post offices, court rooms, electricity and the like, and for the next century, the city boomed.

In the latter half of the 1800s, attracted by the money-making opportunities in the foreign concessions, the Chinese flooded in. The city rapidly became the place to be – a growing metropolis with the liveliest culture, the most opulent dance halls, the largest volume of business, the tallest buildings. In time-honoured fashion, the foreigners cared more for commerce than morality, and licentiousness also thrived: opium dens, prostitution and gambling, inevitably accompanied by gangsters.

With the emergence of the Chinese Republic after 1912, new ideas flooded into the city, generating radicalism – another Shanghai tradition. The Communist Party was founded in the city in 1921. The 1920s and '30s, considered something of a golden age, saw the city boom still further – many of the familiar building on the Bund date this period. Shanghai had become a brash, cosmopolitan metropolis – seedy yet glamorous, obsessed with making money. Organised crime was everywhere.

The Japanese invasion, from 1937, spelt the beginning of the end, although it remained restricted to the Chinese parts of the city until the end of 1941 when the international community capitulated. After the Communist victory in 1949, Shanghai became a grey, sober city. Its renaissance began, slowly at first, in the 1980s, as the Chinese government began to allow commerce, and sparked by the reawakened entrepreneurial zeal of the Shanghainese, and by inflows of foreign cash, another wave of commerce, the biggest yet, flooded into Shanghai. ❏

ABOVE: 1930s cigarette promotion. **LEFT:** an old neighbourhood in Nanshi flanked by modern skyscrapers.

Preserving the past

Perhaps unexpectedly given the trends in modern China, once you move away from the commercial thoroughfares of Nanjing and Huaihai roads and the eternal construction sites of Pudong, Shanghai retains a significant amount of its former character. The old concession neighbourhoods *(see pages 221, 222)*, and the surrounding areas, are relatively quiet and peaceful, pleasant oases of cosy lane houses, plane trees and hidden villas surrounded by plantation-style lawns and gardens.

That's because Shanghai is not only about the new. The city had its salad days in an era of glorious architecture – the fabulous Art Deco era of the 1920s and 1930s. Back then, the world's top architects built hundreds of Art Deco classics in the city, from big hotels and breweries and warehouses to tiny apartments and out-of-the-way offices. Today, many of these buildings have been lovingly renovated, and they provide some of the classiest, calmest and most beautiful spaces in Asia. Others sit neglected, covered with wires and grime and satellite dishes, ageing but still graceful, waiting for the inbound flood of finance to give them a facelift.

The continued existence of these gentle giants is not entirely due to chance. The powers-that-be in Shanghai – government and investors – have taken a second look at the older parts of the city, and preservation efforts have gained momentum in the past few years. The city has restricted development, especially in the old concession neighbourhoods, while the commercial potential of the city's classic buildings has been rediscovered. And in Shanghai, as always, money talks.

That is the future of Shanghai: new millennium bells and whistles, state-of-the-art restaurants boasting celebrity chefs, design-heavy nightclubs, and some of the grandest infrastructure projects on earth, but also stately welcoming streets, peaceful old buildings and quieter, attractive neighbourhoods. As a blueprint for the future, this is a combination that is hard to beat.

On the waterfront: the Bund

Once the throbbing centre of commercial Shanghai, the **Bund** ❶ (外滩; Waitan) is now more of a tourist attraction.

TIP

All the prime buildings in Shanghai have guards, many of whom will deny entrance at first. Smile, be polite, conceal cameras, and tell them you'd like to "*kan yi kan*", or look around, and they'll usually let you in.

BELOW: an old revolutionary at the former Sun Yatsen residence.

TIP

Taking a river cruise is a highlight for many visitors to Shanghai. Tours vary from the hour-long Yangpu Bridge round trip to a full 3½-hour excursion to the mouth of the Chang Jiang (Yangzi). There are also luxury dinner cruises in the evenings. Most boats depart from Shiliupu Wharf on the Bund.

BELOW: a string of upmarket bars and restaurants – with panoramic views across the river to Pudong – occupy some of the upper floors of the Bund's 1930s blocks.

Its ponderous, stately buildings, many of them with classical columns, were long ago requisitioned by the Communist Party for its own use, although some banks and non-governmental institutions have now moved back in. The interiors are in various stages of renovation or decay, but the exteriors are in fine shape, and the Bund is beautifully illuminated at night. The curious term "Bund", meaning embankment, comes from Anglo-India.

Along the riverfront is a **promenade** that extends over 1km (⅔ mile) and is almost always packed with people. This walkway is ultra-popular with Chinese tourists, and no trip to Shanghai is considered complete without a souvenir snap with Pudong in the background. Here, in the early morning, the Shanghai day starts before dawn, with crowds of people practising tai chi, strolling the waterfront and flying kites.

In the spring of 2008, in a massive public project that is expected to take two years, the city government began to build a tunnel along the Bund, and eventually Zhongshan No.1 Road E, which runs in front of the famous Bund buildings, will move underground. That will further open the Bund to pedestrians, and elevate its iconic status among tourists, both foreign and Chinese.

Where Nanjing Road meets the Bund is the Fairmont **Peace Hotel ❷** (和平饭店; Heping Fandian), known as the Cathay Hotel in the old days and one of Shanghai's most treasured colonial buildings. It is the only Art Deco structure on the Bund, and with its Egyptian motifs, graceful vertical lines and signature peaked green roof, it is one of the most famous structures in China.

But the building went dark in 2007, as a dispute arose between the Chinese owners and the would-be foreign renovators, who wished to turn it into a world-class hotel. One of the problems is a big one: an errant bomb dropped by Chiang Kai-shek's Nationalist troops hit the building in the 1930s, causing expensive structural damage. As for when the famous building will reopen, that is anybody's guess; in China, such disputes can drag on for years.

With its superb views of glittering Pudong, and its wealth of fine old buildings, the Bund is home to a clutch of Shanghai's finest restaurants, along with a smattering of coffee shops, luxury vendors and the like. For sweeping views of the Bund and Pudong, the best of these is New Heights, which aside from its jaw-dropping location also serves the finest Martinis in all of Shanghai.

Just north of New Heights, which sits in the Three on the Bund building near the southern end of the Waitan, is the signature **Customs House ❸**, built in 1927, while next to that is the former Hongkong & Shanghai Bank, with its distinctive dome and impressive interior. This building was completed in 1923 by British architects Palmer and Turner, and their brief was a builder's dream: spare no expense and dominate the Bund. At night the Hongkong Bank building glows like a jewel, and by day it showcases a domed lobby encircled by magnificent mosaics.

Another notable Bund building is the former **Yokohama Specie Bank**, just north of the Bank of China: its dark doors open into a spacious gilded lobby filled with timeless details. And north of Yokohama Bank is the **Yangtze Insurance Building**, which leans toward Yokohama Bank like a talkative drunk, and like a drunk, it leans more with each passing year. Nor is Yokohama Bank the only leaning building in Shanghai; the city is built on silt, and subsidence is a problem that still challenges modern builders.

At the northern end of the Bund, across from the former British Consulate, is **Huangpu Park ❹** (黄浦公园; Huangpu Gongyuan), which features a drab concrete memorial. The **Bund History Museum** (外滩历史博物馆; Waitan Lishi Bowuguan; daily 9am–4pm; free) is situated within the park.

North to Hongkou

North of here, across **Suzhou Creek** (苏州河; Wusong Jiang), is **Hongkou** (虹口), a rapidly gentrifying riverfront neighbourhood that is set to become Shanghai's next boom district. The famous old **Waibaidu Bridge ❺** across Suzhou Creek, also called the Ironworkers' Bridge, has been towed away for renovation, and will be re-installed in 2010. This was the first bridge built by the British, and it connected the American and British districts until, in 1863, both merged into the International Settlement. From 1937 on, the bridge defined the border with the Japanese-occupied territory north of the Suzhou.

Hongkou is home to the new Hyatt on the Bund Hotel, and in the shadow of the hotel another of Shanghai's grand projects is rising: a cruise ship terminal and shopping complex that opened in 2007, but remains a work in progress, with final completion scheduled for 2010.

Despite all the development, this is one of those parts of Shanghai that has retained some of its old Chinese charm. As in much of the Old City and the former international and French settlements, laundry is draped from balconies on bamboo canes, and in the side streets, elderly people sit outside on stools to chat, chop vegetables, play cards or guard the bedding airing out in the street.

Hongkou is also a historical neighbourhood. It was home in the 1930s to a large population of Jewish refugees, and until 1941, China was one of the last countries open to immigrants, requiring

Tibetan women pose for the camera on the Bund's waterfront promenade. The famous skyline attracts tourists from all over China.

BELOW: the view along the Bund from the southern end of the waterfront promenade.

Shanghai has the best nightlife of any Chinese city. The main hotspots are clustered in an area to the west of downtown (see page 225 for details).

BELOW: part of the old city wall in Nanshi, the old city.

neither entry visa nor proof of financial means. A key building in Hongkou is the venerable **Pujiang Fandian** (浦江饭店), a lovely old hotel that now caters mainly to backpackers; visitors can stroll the teaklined corridors and highceilinged rooms. Various river cruises offer views of the Bund and the rapidly changing cityscape along the banks of the Huangpu.

At the edge of the northern part of Sichuan Road is **Hongkou Park 6** (虹口公园; Hongkou Gongyuan), one of the prettiest parks in Shanghai. Within the park is a museum and the grave of Lu Xun, China's most famous 20th-century writer. Well worth visiting is the writer's simply furnished **former home** (鲁迅故居; Lu Xun Guju; daily 9am–4pm; charge), where he lived from 1933 until his death in 1936.

Hongkou is also home to a relatively new tourist attraction, **Duolun Street** (多伦路). Formerly a lane filled with colonial-era houses, Duolun has transformed itself into a tourist getaway filled with bookstores, boutiques and cafés. The street is lined with statues of literary figures from days past, notably Lu Xun, a Shanghai native.

The key attraction is the **Shanghai Duolun Museum of Modern Art** (上海多伦现代美术馆; Shanghai Duolun Xiandai Meishuguan; Tue–Sun 10am–6pm; charge). This is a good venue for the display of cutting-edge Asian art, increasingly sought-after in the West. Just down the road is the **Old Film Café** (老电影咖啡馆; Lao Dian Ying Kafeiguan; daily 10am–1am), where they show old Chinese and Russian films from the 1920s and 30s, in an old-fashioned setting with some very modern touches, such as espresso and chocolate cake.

Over to the west is the **Shanghai Railway Station 7** (上海火车站; Shanghai Huochezhan), which lies in **Zhabei District** (闸北区). Here, the day begins even earlier than in the parks, with crowds of migrants from all over China camping out, either about to leave or having just arrived.

West of the train station, on the south side of Suzhou Creek on Anyuan Road, is **Yufuo Si 8** (玉佛寺; Jade Buddha

Recommended Restaurants and Bars on pages 224–5

Temple; daily 8.30am–4.30pm except Chinese New Year; charge), famous for its two Buddha statues made of white jade, brought to China from Burma (Myanmar) in 1882. The statues arrived in Shanghai in 1918, when the temple was completed. One effigy depicts the Sleeping Buddha, representing his entry into nirvana, but the other white-jade statue of the Seated Buddha – 2 metres (6ft 7ins) tall, decorated with jewels and weighing 1,000 kg (2,200 lbs) – is the more magnificent.

Nanjing Road and People's Square

Shanghai's key commercial street is **Nanjing Road** (南京路), which leads west from the Bund into the heart of the city. The stretch between Henan Road and People's Park is a pedestrian-only thoroughfare, one of the main focal points of the city – always filled with sightseers, tourists and shoppers. Shanghai is China's premier shopping city, and this is apparent after just a short stroll here: the amount of merchandise on sale is staggering, be it clothes, electronic goods, touristy tat, specialist items such as traditional theatre

props, musical instruments or art. Old state-owned food stores rub shoulders with the glitzy commercialism of new department stores and five-star hotels.

Halfway up the street from the Bund at the corner of Xizang (Tibet) Road is the store that sells everything – the state-owned **No.1 Department Store** ❾ (上海第一百货商店; Di Yi Baihuo Shangdian), a typical experience in Chinese domestic shopping.

Beyond Xizang Road is the large open space of **People's Park** ❿ (人民公园; Renmin Gongyuan). Once a part of a horse-racing course during the city's glory days, it is now the largest park in the city. The park is split into northern and southern halves by **People's Square** (人民广场; Renmin Guangchang), which for most people is the heart of Shanghai. The park and square feature three museums, a glamorous theatre and an underground shopping mall, along with the drab, Stalinist-looking Shanghai City Hall building.

The main highlight is the **Shanghai Museum** ⓫ (上海博物馆; Shanghai Bowuguan; Mon–Fri 9am–5pm, Sat 9am–8pm; free), in the southern part of

TIP

Pickpocketing is a problem in Shanghai, especially on buses, in the subway, and in busy tourist areas like the Bund. Bike theft is also endemic, so lock the bikes and zip the pockets.

BELOW: preparing *xiao long bao* (dumplings) is a laborious process.

The Shanghai Museum is one of the highlights of the city, and since 2007 admission has been free.

BELOW: early-morning badminton on Nanjing Road.
BELOW RIGHT: the Shanghai Grand Theatre.

the park. This facility, opened in 1996, offers an outstanding collection of Chinese art in a modern setting. Its 11 galleries house fine exhibits of paintings, bronzes, sculpture, ceramics, calligraphy, jade, Ming- and Qing-dynasty furniture, coins, seals and minority art. The bronze collection is one of the best in the world and the ceramics are superb, although its paintings collection is somewhat below par because many artworks fell victim to the vandalism of the Cultural Revolution. Information is well presented in English, and the audio guide is excellent. In 2007, the museum began to offer free admission, so expect big crowds.

In the middle of People's Square is the **Shanghai Urban Planning Centre** (上海城市规划中心; Shanghai Chengshi Guihua Zhongxin; Mon–Thur 9am–5pm, Fri–Sun 9am–6pm; charge), featuring entertainingly huge models of the city which help to make some sense of the scale of the recent building frenzy.

Nearby, on the opposite side of the park, the **Shanghai Art Museum** ⓬ (上海美术馆; Shanghai Meishuguan; daily 9am–5pm; charge) is housed in the former Shanghai Race Club – itself another striking classical building. This is Shanghai's finest collection of contemporary Chinese art, while atop the building, with superb views of People's Park, is Kathleen's 5 restaurant. The **Museum of Contemporary Art** ⓭ (上海当代艺术馆; MoCA), Barbarossa Lounge and the **Shanghai Grand Theatre** (Shanghai Da Juyuan) round out the attractions of People's Park.

A couple of noteworthy buildings flank the park. On the corner of Xizang and Hankou roads is the small, red-brick **Mu'en Tang** (沐恩堂; former Moore Memorial Church), worth investigating to get a feel for Christian architecture in Shanghai. North of the park on Nanjing Road West is the **Park Hotel** ⓮ (国际饭店; Guoji Fandian), designed by legendary Czech architect Ladislaus Hudec. The Park's striking glazed-brick exterior is intact, and so are the simple straight lines of its Art Deco design, featuring four narrow strips that rise to the roof, buttressing the tower and highlighting its vertical features. In any other city in Asia, the Park would be an archi-

Recommended Restaurants and Bars on pages 224–5

tectural superstar, but in Shanghai, it is just one of many dozens of buildings of similar size, beauty and pedigree.

Nanjing Road West and Jing An

A few hundred metres further west, Nanjing Road East morphs into **Nanjing Road West ⓖ**, an ultra-upscale shopping street that is home to the city's fanciest malls, all of them packed with famous designer brands, although actual shoppers are rather scarce, perhaps scared away by China's 30 percent retail tax on luxury goods. This is the **Jing An District**, Shanghai's most expensive shopping mecca: look for Plaza 66 and CITIC Square, the city's priciest malls.

Still further west on Nanjing Road West is the **Shanghai Centre ⓖ** (上海城; Shanghai Shangcheng). This busy complex houses the Portman Ritz-Carlton Hotel, two residential towers, a pair of multinational office buildings, and a shopping area that includes major airline offices, and Western stores and chain restaurants such as the Tony Roma's and Starbucks. Across the street from the Portman is the Soviet-built **Shanghai Exhibition Centre** (上海展览中心; Shanghai Zhanlan Zhongxin) – look for the 1950s-style Red Star atop the building – while further west, past more upscale malls and department stores, is the **Buddhist-Daoist Jing An Si** (静安寺; Jing An Temple).

Nanshi: the Old City

The edge of the **Old City**, formerly known as **Nanshi** (南市), begins where Henan Road intercepts Renmin Road. Combined with Zhonghua Road, this defines its circular limit. The city walls paralleled this small ring road until 1912, when they were knocked down and the moats were filled in. During the concession era, the Old City remained under Chinese law and administration, while much of the rest of central Shanghai was administered by foreign powers. Most of the residents in these old back alleys were Chinese, and eventually the area became notorious as a gangster-and-opium slum. Today, the vices are gone, but the tiny lanes, crowded but quaint neighbourhoods, and small houses still exist. Tourist-wise, the key features of this part of Shanghai are the Yuyuan Garden and the surrounding shopping streets, known collectively as Yuyuan Bazaar.

One of Shanghai's best-known sights, the Ming-dynasty **Yuyuan Garden ⓗ** (豫园; daily 8.30am–4.30pm; charge) is a classical Chinese garden with rockeries, pools, paths, and pagodas, similar to Suzhou's famous gardens. The traditional rock-and-tree landscape is filled with artificial hills, carp-filled ponds, dragon-lined walls, and pavilions connected by zigzagging bridges.

In the centre of Yuyuan is **Huxinting Teahouse** (湖心亭茶室; Huxinting Chashe), the city's oldest teahouse, which sits in the middle of a small bottle-green pond, with a famous nine-corner bridge that connects it to Yuyuan Garden proper. Dating from Qing times, the second floor serves some of the best – and priciest – tea in town. Despite the crowds, this is a peaceful spot that manages to preserve some of the flavour of Old China.

The area around Yuyuan bazaar is packed with shops and faux-Ming buildings.

BELOW: bargaining at Yuyuan Bazaar.

Ballroom dancing at Zhongshan Park. This form of sociable exercise remains popular all over China.

BELOW: in the heart of Xintiandi, Shanghai's upscale bar and restaurant neighbourhood.

Fuelled by the constant flow of tourists, the area around Yuyuan has become an ever-expanding bazaar. The complex, with its red walls and upturned tile roofs, has been a market-place and social centre since the 18th century, and it is replete with curios and tourist sou-venirs, as well as numerous food vendors. There is a pattern to shopping at Yuyuan: typical sou-venirs like fans, pearls, silk pyjamas, Terracotta Warrior stat-ues and Mao memorabilia are lined up along the main streets, while tucked away inside the courtyards and buildings are stalls that sell a variety of goods, such as beaded necklaces, Chinese medicines, children's toys, shopping bags of all sizes and shapes, wigs, yarn, women's purses, jewellery, clothes and so on – and on. It's a hotchpotch of a place – the words "fake" and "tacky" spring to mind – but it can be fun and rewarding. And it looks wonderful in the early evening, when the red lanterns lining the streets are lit, and the roofs of the faux-Ming buildings are outlined with fairy lights.

Just west of Yuyuan at Henan Road is the animated **Fuyou Road Sunday antique market** ⓲ (福佑路古玩市场; Fuyou Lugu Wanshi Chang), which sits inside an old factory. Hawkers come here as early as 4am to set up their stalls. The tiny lane bustles with people by mid-morning, by which time the best goods are usually sold. Similarly, at **Dongtai Lu** (东台路), further west beyond Tibet Road, shoppers will find an abundant and eclectic collection of antiques, including old maps of Shanghai, baskets and boxes, porcelain and old watches, antique lamps and light fixtures, plus some scattered modern goods and newly minted "Mao-morabilia".

Xintiandi

Due west of Nanshi, and south of People's Park, is **Xintiandi** ⓳ (新天地), the city's most upscale restaurant and bar district. Covering a large, two-square-block area, Xintiandi features elements of Shanghai's famous *shikumen* (stone gate) lane houses, although any claims of authenticity are bogus: much has been altered to make dining and drinking more convenient. Nonetheless, for first-timers

and strangers to the city, Xintiandi does gather together a variety of very pleasant bars and eateries, and a smattering of upscale shopping, in a pleasant, car-free area. More adventurous souls can explore genuine *shikumen* lane houses in other parts of the city.

Xintiandi is also home to the site of the **First National Congress of the Communist Party of China** ⑳ (中共一大会址; Zhonggong Yidahuizhi; daily 9am–5pm; charge). You can see the room where delegates founded the Party in July 1921. It remains in its original form, complete with a table set for 13 people, while waxworks of top party officials are also on view.

Huaihai Road and Xuhui

Leading west from Xintiandi is **Huaihai Road** (淮海路), Shanghai's number two shopping street, a thoroughfare that is bedecked with a predictable selection of department stores and small shops. Huaihai road leads directly to into the heart of **Xuhui District** (徐汇), which encompasses much of the old French concession and is one of the city's most charming neighbourhoods.

The pleasant tree-lined blocks of Xuhui are dotted with villas, rows of houses and other old buildings of various origin and use, including a scattering of beautiful 19th- and early-20th-century apartment houses. Most are semi-hidden from pedestrians, but these are the surprises that make these leafy streets such a delight. Here, an iron gate opens into a stately old villa or into the courtyard of an Art Deco apartment, and there, a small opening leads to a thriving neighbourhood of venerable detached houses or into a compound of graceful but run-down old mansions.

The old houses are of particular interest: these are East-West hybrids that incorporate traditional English elements with Chinese concepts of feng shui. The *shikumen* houses are larger than the new-style lane houses, with bigger gardens and wraparound courtyards featuring the signature stone gates. Most houses have tiny rooms for servants and for ancestral

The tree-lined streets of Fuxing, Wukang and other roads in the former French Concession make for a lovely walk, with their charmingly idiosyncratic old houses. Some of the buildings look as if they have been transported from a wealthy 1930s London suburb.

BELOW: urban planning.

Shanghai's Satellite Cities

Far from the eyes of tourists, nine unique architectural experiments are underway in the outskirts of Shanghai. This is the satellite city plan, or One City Nine Towns, wherein nine giant, brand-new residential villages, most based upon European patterns and designed by top-flight foreign architects, are being constructed in the remote suburbs.

The early results have unveiled some one-of-a-kind developments filled with eclectic homes. The German town of Anting (安亭德国小镇), for example, designed by German architect Albert Speer, includes winding streets, tiny courtyards, medieval plazas, and village-square fountains, and is meant to house 50,000 people. Similarly, Thames Town (泰晤士小镇) includes space for pubs, a town square, a village-style church and Olde England style shops.

The closest one to Shanghai – just 20 minutes by car – is Pujiang (新浦江城) Italian town, which combines European concepts of public space with traditional Shanghainese home styles, such as lane houses and villas. Small and workable, with housing for just 20,000 people, Pujiang is a genuine hybrid. The grandest of all is Linggang New City (临港新城), which, depending upon how well it sells, will house up to 800,000 residents. Linggang doesn't follow any national style; design-wise, it is breaking new ground.

A northern European town, along with Dutch, Spanish, American, and traditional Chinese villages, round out the offerings. Whether these experiments will become thriving suburban hotspots, or empty ghost towns, is hard to say. For the moment, almost all the propoerty owners in this brave new world are absentees – having bought up property solely for investment purposes.

TIP

Take one of the old **ferry boats** across the Huangpu River to Pudong – they leave just south of the Bund – and return on the shuttle train through the bizarre **Bund Sightseeing Tunnel** (open daily 8am–11pm). The latter is enlivened by surreal lighting displays, cut-out figures and scenes projected onto the walls – all to the accompaniment of a slightly disturbing soundtrack.

BELOW: contemplating art at the Shanghai Art Museum. **BELOW RIGHT:** even the body is a canvas for Shanghai's artists.

altars, both hallmarks of Chinese interior design. Most of the houses face south, as dictated by feng shui, with the gardens and biggest rooms always on the south. It is not uncommon, especially among the spider-web streets of Xuhui District, to see entire rows of houses set at crazy angles from the streets, so they can achieve a southerly aspect.

An excellent example of colonial architecture – just one of many – is the **Shanghai Arts and Crafts Research Institute ㉑** (上海工艺美术研究所; Shanghai Gongyi Meishu Yanjiusuo; daily 9am–5pm; charge). In this venerable old French mansion on Fenyang Road, visitors can watch artisans at work and purchase a variety of traditional Chinese handicrafts. Nearby on Huaihai Road is the **Shanghai Library** (上海图书馆; Shanghai Tushuguan; daily 9am–5pm), one of the largest in the world. Opened in 1996, the library features up-to-date information technology and holds a total of 12 million books. Many foreign consulates are located in the vicinity, and the surrounding neighbourhoods are perfect for leisurely exploration on foot.

The key tourist site in the area is the **Sun Yatsen Residence ㉒** (孙中山故居; Sun Zhongshan Guju; daily 9am–4.30pm; charge) on Xiangshan Road at Sinan Road, just south of Huaihai and near Fuxing Park. Mao Zedong and Zhou Enlai also lived and worked in this area.

Longhua and Xujiahui

In the south of the city, on the road with the same name, is **Longhua Gu Si ㉓** (龙华古寺), a temple and pagoda built in AD 242 and since destroyed and rebuilt several times. The temple site consists of seven halls that are again being used for religious purposes. Adjoining the temple, the Longhua Hotel was designed especially for Buddhist travellers and includes a vegetarian restaurant, although it welcomes all visitors.

To the northwest is **Xujiahui Catholic Cathedral**, an impressive French Gothic building dating from 1846. **Xujiahui** (徐家汇) is a bustling, mall-filled area that is fast becoming yet another key shopping zone, although it is more down-market that Nanjing or Huaihai roads, and more popular with teenagers and local shoppers.

Art District

Some inner-city neighbourhoods are dotted with art galleries, many of them good, but 50 Moganshan Road, off Suzhou Creek in the north of the city (west of Shanghai Railway Station) has emerged as the cutting-edge gallery district – an area of remodelled warehouses with a veritable treasure trove of galleries, some representing the city's best-known artists.

In modern Shanghai, two broad types of art have emerged. One is traditional and has attracted a Chinese audience: typical images are women with fans, men on bicycles, girls with birdcages, and lush, rich landscapes. The other is political pop art, which has attracted an overseas following. These works display overt messages about Chinese society, images of Mao and the military and such, and are often rendered in multimedia.

Pudong

Across the river from the Bund, on the eastern banks, is the remarkable **Pudong Xinqu** (浦东新区), or the Pudong New Area. Twenty years ago, Pudong (literally, east of the Huangpu River) was a rambling collection of warehouses, farms and small houses. Then in 1992 a magnificent plan was hatched, a plan that would turn Pudong into a global financial centre that would rival or even eclipse Hong Kong. The New Area is scattered over a whopping 522 sq km (200 sq miles) of land that contains a foreign trade zone, a high-tech zone, an export zone, a biotech zone, a tourist zone, a financial zone – you get the picture. Yes, Pudong New Area is one heck of an experiment.

Pudong remains a work in progress, and, as a quick trip up the shocking-pink **Pearl Oriental TV Tower** ㉔ (东方明珠电视塔; Dongfan Mingzhu Guangbo Dianshi Ta) illustrates, it is mostly unfinished, with vast patches of bare earth waiting for the erection of office buildings, residential towers, hotels and the like. In its current half-completed state, Pudong's best feature is modern architecture. Most public buildings in Pudong, and many private ones, are vaulting glass-and-steel designs that suit the ambience of New Area. But for the most part, with its wide-open, pedestrian-unfriendly streets, and its lack of street-level charm, Pudong lacks the appeal of Shanghai proper. Its distant location and empty spaces have even earned it the mocking nickname of Pu-Jersey.

The epicentre of Pudong, such as it is, sits at the base of the Pearl Oriental TV Tower. This tower is more than just a pretty face – it is a lightning rod for foreign investment. Pudong developers reckoned that a world-class attraction would lure the big bucks, and that's exactly what happened. The big balls are perfect places to view the work-in-progress that is Pudong. This area beneath the Pearl Tower is also home to an aquarium, and a pleasant riverfront park that features coffee shops, small restaurants, waterfront walks and wonderful views of the Bund. ❏

Acrobats and the Jin Mao Tower, superseded by the World Financial Centre as the city's – and China's – tallest building in 2008.

BELOW: Pudong's Century Park.

RESTAURANTS AND BARS

Restaurants

Prices for dinner for one (three dishes with beer in Chinese restaurants; a three-course meal with a half-bottle of house wine in Western-style restaurants):
$ = under Rmb 50
$$ = Rmb 50–100
$$$ = Rmb 100–150
$$$$ = Rmb 150–250
$$$$$ = over Rmb 250

Xintiandi has the city's biggest cluster of restaurants, including Chinese and Western, and the Bund also has several gourmet establishments. Food-wise, the native Shanghainese cuisine is dark, oily and sweet, a rich stickiness that shines through in the *hong shao* ribs and the lion's head meatballs. *Xiao long bao* dumplings are a famous local speciality. Note that not all establishments have a Chinese name. Characters in brackets indicate the specific branch we have featured.

Chinese (general)

Chang An Dumpling Restaurant 长安饺子楼
1588 Pudong Da Dao, Pudong
Tel: 5885 8416. **$**
The city's most famous dumpling house claims to have over 100 types. Open 6am–8.30pm.

Charmant
小城故事（徐汇店）
1418 Huaihai Rd (C)
Tel: 6431 8107/6431 8027 **$$**
Taiwanese food – oysters in black bean and scallion, taro cakes, pork rice and so on – in a convenient location.

Crystal Jade
翡翠酒家（新天地店）
Xin Ye St, Lane 123, Xintiandi
Tel: 6385 8752. **$$$**
Crystal Jade, of which this is one of several branches, represents a trend in Shanghai dining: a mixture of Shanghai and Cantonese offerings served in an upscale setting. Try the excellent *xiao long bao*, *dan dan mian* (spicy noodles in peanut sauce) or *jie lan* (a steamed southern vegetable).

Lost Heaven
花马天堂云南餐厅
38 Gao You Rd
(near Fuxing W Rd)
Tel: 6433 5126. **$$$**
Lost Heaven serves Yunnan folk cuisine, a combination of Burmese, Chinese and ethnic tribal flavours. The stunning décor and interesting food have made this one of Shanghai's trendiest restaurants.

Meilongzhen
梅龙镇（总店）
1081 Nanjing Rd (W)
Tel: 6253 5353. **$$**
Perhaps Shanghai's most famous restaurant, the Meilongzhen dates back to 1938. Serves regional and Sichuanese specialities.

Beijing Duck

Quan Ju De
全聚德（淮海店）
786 Huaihai Rd (C)
Tel: 5404 5799
547 Tianmu Xi Lu
Tel: 6353 8558. **$$**
Serves traditional rich, crispy, fatty, delicious Beijing Duck, wrapped in soft pancakes.

Cantonese

Fu Lin Xuan
富临轩（淮海店）
300 Huaihai Rd
Tel: 6358 3699. **$$**
Cantonese-style seafood. Dim sum brunch is available at weekends.

Wan Chai
湾仔（常熟店）
858 Ju Lu Rd
(near Changshu Rd)
Tel: 6248 5992. **$$**
Reliable Cantonese favourites such as steamed fish and stir-fried shrimp in a classy location.

Xian Yue Hien 申粤轩
Ding Xiang Garden,
849 Huashan Rd
Tel: 6251 1166. **$$**
Quality Cantonese and Shanghainese cuisine served in a pretty garden setting.

Shanghainese

1221 1221餐馆
1221 Yan'an Rd (W)
Tel: 6213 2441. **$$**
Run by a mother-daughter team from Hong Kong, these two restaurants serve Shanghainese food.

The Big Fan
大风车私家菜馆
1440 Hongqiao Rd
Tel: 6219 7514. **$$**
Shanghainese food in an Old-Shanghai setting.

The Grape 葡萄园
55 Xinle Rd
Tel: 5404 0486. **$**
A Shanghai stalwart. Two outlets have a bustling business of foreign and Chinese clientele, friendly service, great food and even better prices.

Jesse Restaurant
吉士酒家
41 Tian Ping Rd
Tel: 6282 9260. **$$**
This hole-in-the-wall serves some of the finest Shanghainese food in town, and is easily recognised by the clusters of people waiting outside.

Lubolang Restaurant
绿波廊（豫园路店）
115 Yuyuan Rd
Tel: 6328 0602. **$$**
A well-established and popular restaurant serving house specialities of *xiao long bao*, stewed ribs and lion's head meatballs.

Lulu
鹭鹭酒家（浦东店）
3/F 161 Liujiazui Rd (E)
Tel: 5882 6679. **$$**
This small and crowded place is the perfect spot in Pudong for Shanghai food, particularly seafood. A popular late-night place for Shanghai's fashionable crowd.

Xin Ji Shi 新吉士酒楼
（新天地店）
9 Xintiandi Complex
Tel: 6336 4746. **$$**
Xin Ji Shi has five outlets serving classic local cuisine: rich stewed pork ribs, crab-egg tofu, lion's head meatballs and all the rest. The Xintiandi branch is widely believed to be the best.

Sichuanese

Di Shui Dong
滴水洞（茂名南路店）
56 Maoming Rd, near the corner of Chang Le
Tel: 6253 2689. **$$**
This fiery favourite, with its rustic provincial décor

and boisterous atmosphere, really packs 'em in. The cumin-encrusted ribs are the signature dish. Reserve in advance.

Guyi Hunan
古意湘味浓（富民店）
No. 87 Fumin Rd
Tel: 6249 5628. **$$**
This sparkling little restaurant, with its mega-spicy food, is one of the best Chinese eateries in town. Reservations are a must at this popular place.

Sichuan Court 天府楼
Floor 39, Hilton Hotel
250 Huashan Rd
Tel: 6248 0000. **$$$**
Sleek, sky-high Sichuanese eatery at the top of the Hilton, with views over the city.

South Beauty 881
俏江南（延安中路店）
881 Central Yan'an Rd
Tel: 6247 6682. **$$**
Sharp, spicy Sichuan cuisine is served in a lavish century-old mansion and sprawling grounds. There is a rooftop lounge bar.

Yunnan
Southern Barbarian
南蛮子云南烧烤吧
Area E, 2/F Ju'Roshine Life Art Space, 56 Maoming South Rd, near Chang Le Rd
Tel: 5157 5510. **$$**
Not easy to find, but keep looking – its Yunnan cuisine is well worth the effort. Try the fried goat's cheese and the wild mushrooms.

Vegetarian
Gongdelin 功德林
445 Nanjing Rd (W)
Tel: 6327 0218. **$**
The Gongdelin has been serving vegetarian specialities for over 50 years. The "duck" and "beef" dishes look like the real thing, but are in fact made from tofu.

Western
A FuturePerfect
"AFP" (no Chinese name)
16, Lane 351 Hua Shan Rd
Tel: 6248 8020. **$$**
A small restaurant featuring a tree-lined patio back dropped by a lovely concession-era villa. The menu is continental, backed up by possibly the best bread in town.

Cucina 意庐
56/F Grand Hyatt Hotel, 88 Century Boulevard, Pudong
Tel: 5049 1234. **$$$**
Tuscan-style restaurant with great views of Shanghai.

Gourmet Café
(no Chinese name)
455 Shanxi Rd (N)
Tel: 5213 6885. **$$**
Serves the best hamburgers in town, by far.

Le Bouchon 勃逊
1455 Wuding Rd (W)
Tel: 6225 7088. **$$–$$$**
This small bistro/wine bar cooks up some highly authentic French food.

Leonardo's
李奥纳多达芬奇餐厅
Hilton Hotel, 250 Huashan Rd
Tel: 6248 0000 ext 1850. **$$$**
First-rate and sumptuous Italian cuisine.

M on the Bund
米氏西餐厅
7/F 5 Zhongshan East 1 Rd
Tel: 6350 9988. **$$$$**
World-class international cuisine with spectacular views of the Bund, the river and Pudong.

Mesa Restaurant & Manifesto Lounge 梅萨
748 Ju Lu Rd
Tel: 6289 9108. **$$$**
Epitomises modern Shanghai, from its central location and sunny terrace right down to the beautiful black-clad staff. Try the lamb chops or the Sunday brunch.

Moca Art Lab
摩卡艺术吧
Gate 7, People's Park, 231 Nanjing Rd (W)
Tel: 6327 0856. **$$**
A Mediterranean restaurant on the top floor of the Museum of Contemporary Art, in a former greenhouse now filled with art. The patio has wonderful views of the city.

New Heights Restaurant
新视角餐厅酒廊
7/F 3 The Bund
Tel: 6321 0909. **$$**
A global variety of dishes at reasonable prices, including Thai red curry, *char siu* ribs, five-spice duck breast, and bangers and mash. The outdoor terrace has fine views.

Indian
Jade on 36 翡翠36餐厅
36/F Pudong Shangri-La Hotel, 33 Fucheng Rd, Pudong
Tel: 6882 8888. **$$$$$**
The extravagant Jade on 36 serves elegant, super-stylish fusion delights in a must-see venue. Be sure to try the lemon custard dessert – it packs a real surprise.

The Tandoor
天都里印度餐厅
Jinjiang Hotel, 59 Maoming Rd (S)
Tel: 6472 5494. **$$$**
Many people call this restaurant the best in Shanghai. The food and service are superb and the décor magnificent.

Japanese
Meshi
器meshi石库门日本料理
37 Lane 248, Taikang St
Tel: 5465 2450. **$$$$**
A classy dining experience, from the beautiful ceramic plates and bowls to the exquisitely prepared, classical Japanese dishes. Try the lunch specials.

Korean
Gao Li
高丽烧烤（五原店）
181 Wuyuan Rd
Tel: 6431 5236. **$$**
Delicious Korean food and late opening hours.

Bars and pubs

One of the city's major nightlife areas is on Tongren Road, between Yanan and Nanjing West roads. This heady trawl of bars and clubs includes live music venues, pool bars and numerous "buy me a drink" bar girls.

Another lively area for bars is around Maoming (South) and Fuxing (Central) roads. Busy, ex-pat-y **Big Bamboo** (艺术家园), just off Maoming on Nanyang Road, is one. The nearby **Face Bar** (no Chinese name) in the Rui Jin Hotel on the corner of Ruijing Road, is in an attractive renovated villa. There are more bars south of Yanan Road, around Julu and Fumin roads – try **Manifesto** (魅莎) at 748 Julu for a cool ambience.

There are more bars around the eastern end of Hengshan Road and Dongping Road near the Pushkin Monument. **Oscar's Pub** (李香园) on the corner of Fuxing and Bao Qing roads is a lively English-style place.

For upscale bars with a view head for the Bund. The **Attica Shanghai** (爱奇多酒吧) on the corner of Jinling Road is one of several, but many restaurants such as **M on the Bund** and **New Heights** also serve drinks on their terraces.

Xintiandi is another major bar area: the **Paulaner Brauhaus** (宝莱纳餐厅) in the north block serves up large glasses of beer brewed on the premises.

Recommended Restaurants and Bars on page 241

NANJING, JIANGSU AND THE GRAND CANAL

The old southern capital of Nanjing is one of China's most habitable and pleasant centres, while Suzhou and other cities along the ancient Grand Canal are full of interest and atmosphere

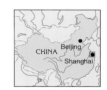

It is perhaps the greatest tourism slogan of all time: "Above is Paradise, below are Hangzhou and Suzhou." Then, as if that praise from Yuan-dynasty poet Yang Chaoying were not enough, along came Marco Polo, who supposedly visited Jiangnan (the rich delta area south of the Yangzi) in 1276. Polo piled further compliments on the area. Its cities, he wrote, "are the finest and most splendid in the world", and, thumbing through his 13th-century thesaurus, he went on to call them "great and noble, beautiful, magnificent and delightful," along with other flowery phrases too numerous to mention.

These celebrated lines may have amplified the appeal of the Jiangnan region, but even so, and even today, its cities and towns stand apart from the drab factories and dull architecture that typify much of eastern China. The bridges, canals and gardens that so impressed Marco Polo and the Yuan-era poet are still the area's signature highlights, and are among the most charming sights in China.

Cut by waterways and characterised by beguiling water towns, Jiangsu province has a prime location on China's prosperous eastern seaboard. Traditionally called "the land of fish and rice", the area is bisected by the mighty **Chang Jiang** (长江), or Yangzi River, which flows into the East China Sea north of Shanghai and is fed by a web of watercourses in its lower reaches.

The historic silk town of Suzhou is one of China's major sights – famed for its dreamy canal setting and classical gardens. And if Suzhou's charms whet your appetite, you will be drawn to the historic architecture of the other Grand Canal cities and towns – Wuxi, Tongli, Yangzhou, Hangzhou and many others. Meanwhile, the huge lake Tai Hu is ringed with sights, including Ding Shan, home of the distinctive Yixing pottery. And Nanjing, from the park-like setting of its famous university to the forested Zijin Shan (Purple Mountains) in the east, has a relaxed atmosphere that few modern Chinese cities can match.

Main attractions
NANJING MUSEUM
ZIJIN SHAN (PURPLE MOUNTAINS), NANJING
MINGXIAO LING (MING TOMBS), NANJING
SUZHOU'S GARDENS
TIGER HILL PAGODA, SUZHOU
GRAND CANAL WATER TOWNS

LEFT: the Humble Administrator's Garden, Suzhou.
BELOW: students at Nanjing University.

NANJING

Nanjing (南京) **❶** is one of China's more attractive big cities and subtly different from the other urban areas of the Yangzi Delta. For one thing, it isn't a rapid-fire commercial city, and the relative lack of investment – compared with the other regional boom towns – means that Nanjing is calmer, quieter and better-preserved than its neighbours. Like Hangzhou and Suzhou, it is a former capital and has a rich history, but it is also university town, home to some of China's top colleges, and it draws fewer tourists than the other cities. As a result, Nanjing is the most authentic and original large city in eastern China.

Nanjing can easily be reached by train, boat or plane, and regular express trains zip across from Shanghai in just over two hours. Arrival by train from the north is via the great **Yangzi Bridge** **Ⓐ** (南京长江大桥; Changjiang Daqiao), which opened in 1968 and has been a symbol of Chinese independence and national pride ever since. When relations between the former Soviet Union and China were severed in 1960, the Chinese constructed the bridge – which had been a Soviet-funded project until then – with their own design and resources. Its construction paved the way for numerous ambitious infrastructure projects that are so beloved by modern China. A stroll around the **Great Bridge Park** (大桥公园; Daqiao Gongyuan; daily 7am–6.30pm) alongside the structure affords excellent views.

A long history

The history of Nanjing dates back to the beginning of the Warring States Period (403–221 BC). Between the 3rd and 6th centuries AD, Nanjing was the capital of the Southern dynasties at a time when non-Chinese were in command in northern China. After various natural disasters and a peasant rebellion, the new Sui dynasty moved the imperial capital to Xi'an (AD 589) and destroyed Nanjing, along with almost all of its cultural and historical relics.

Nanjing regained national importance at the beginning of the Ming dynasty, when its first emperor, Hongwu (aka Zhu Yuanzhang), set up the seat of government here in the Southern Capital – a literal translation of the name Nanjing – until it

Nanjing has been a city of treaties. It was here, following the Opium Wars, that the first of several treaties was signed that opened China to foreigners. The same treaty also ceded Hong Kong island to Great Britain.

BELOW: walking along Nanjing's ancient city walls by Xuanwu Hu.

was transferred to Beijing in 1421. The well-preserved **city wall** dates from this period. This tremendous fortification had a circumference of over 30km (19 miles) and an average height of 12 metres (39ft). Several of the gates still stand today, including **Zhonghuamen B** (中华门) in the south of the city (a good reference point for navigating Nanjing), and **Zhongshanmen C** (中山门) in the eastern part of the wall.

Xinjiekou and Mochou Hu

The **Xinjiekou D** (新街口) roundabout marks Nanjing's modern city centre, and is packed with people, shops, vehicles of all descriptions, offices, banks and hotels. Here the 25-year-old **Jingling Hotel** (金陵饭店) stands out like a beacon, towering above the traffic; take the elevator to the top for a bird's-eye view of the city.

To the southwest of Xinjiekou is **Mochou Hu E** (莫愁湖), a lake named after the Mochou (Lady Without Sorrows), who is said to have lived here in the 5th century. The **Chaotian Gong F** (朝天宫; Chaotian Palace; daily 8am–5pm; charge) nearby dates back to the Song dynasty

(960–1279), a period known for Confucian revivalism. The palace is one of the area's best-preserved Confucian temples. A reminder of the temple's beginnings is the gate of Ling Xing (Spirit Star), a remnant of the Song dynasty and entrance to the complex. Immediately ahead is a maze of merchants selling bric-a-brac, antiques and magazines, some from the Cultural Revolution. Operas performed in the Jiangsu provincial tradition are held within the main courtyard. The three halls at the back of the complex contain fossilised human, buffalo and deer bones from the Neolithic period, as well as artefacts from the Ming and Qing dynasties.

Shitoucheng G (石头城), a partially preserved wall to the north of Mochou, is a reminder of Nanjing's turbulent history. There is a secluded, wooded walk that follows the path of the wall, and sections of the original stone wall are still clearly visible.

In the same area of town, close to the gate of **Jiangdongmen** (江东门), is the **Memorial to the Nanjing Massacre H** (大屠杀纪念馆; Datusha Jinianguan; daily 8.30am–5pm; charge), a sombre reminder of the horrors of the Japanese

The Yangzi Basin is notoriously prone to summer floods; in 2003 these were the worst for many years, with hundreds killed, millions made homeless and damage amounting to an estimated US$5 billion.

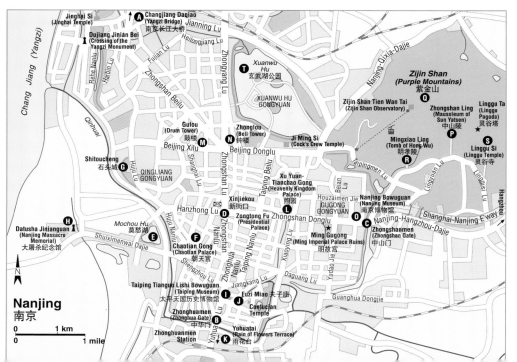

Nanjing
南京

Gulou, Nanjing's Drum Tower, dates from the 14th century, when the city was the largest in the world with an estimated population in excess of 450,000.

BELOW RIGHT: illustration of the Taiping rebels at the Taiping Museum, Nanjing.

invasion. Inside is a quiet exhibition of photographs, maps and eye witness accounts that document the arrival of Japanese troops in December 1937, the rapes, burning and looting of houses and historical relics, and the slaughter of some 300,000 Chinese that followed. Most silencing of all is a viewing hall overlooking a mass grave, one of the many *wan ren keng* (pit of ten thousand corpses) that the Japanese left behind.

South of Xinjiekou

In the southern part of the city, near Zhonghuamen gate, is a Ming-style garden residence housing the **Taiping Museum ❶** (太平天国历史博物馆; Taiping Tianguo Lishi Bowuguan; daily 8am–5pm; charge). The turbulent rise and fall of the quasi-Christian "Kingdom of Heaven", popularly known as the Taiping Rebellion *(see panel below)*, is well documented here in both Mandarin and English. Led by Hong Xiuquan, the Taiping captured Nanjing in 1853, making it the capital of their domain. The city was retaken by Qing troops in 1864 and

Hong's magnificent temple was levelled. Cannons, guns, swords and other weapons are displayed alongside photographs and paintings depicting the rebellion. In the official history, Hong's unique take on Christianity – he believed he was the younger brother of Jesus – has been erased, and he has been reinvented as a reformist fighter trying to overthrow the decaying Qing dynasty.

Two blocks to the west of the Taiping Museum is a lively market area known as **Fuzi Miao ❿** (夫子庙). A carnival atmosphere presides over this labyrinth of alleyways and small squares filled with souvenir and antique shops, and street stalls selling food. Within this maze is one lane that sells genuine articles: marble carvings, traditional clothing, tea sets and so on. At its heart is the site of a Confucian temple and ancient study centre, dating back 1,500 years. The temple and surrounding buildings were razed and rebuilt numerous times. The present buildings are Qing-dynasty renovations and recent additions built in the traditional Qing style.

South of Zhonghuamen gate is **Yuhuatai ⓚ** (雨花台; Rain of Flowers Ter-

The Taiping Rebellion

The Taiping Rebellion (1850–64), responsible for up to 20 million deaths, is a chapter saturated in blood. Led by the Hakka (Kejia) Hong Xiuquan, a failed civil service candidate who was convinced he was the son of the Christian God, the Taiping exploded out of south China in their campaign to exterminate the Manchu, overlords of the Qing dynasty.

Fired by evangelical zeal and a powerful sense of destiny, the Taiping swept through the provinces of Guangxi, Hunan, Hubei, Anhui and Jiangsu, taking Nanjing in 1853 and transforming it into the capital of their Heavenly Kingdom. Further expeditions against the Manchu in east and north China were abortive, however, and divisions appeared among the upper ranks of the Taiping faithful. Nanjing fell to Qing forces (bolstered by Western military training) in 1864, shortly after Hong Xiuquan's death.

With their radical egalitarian social framework and ethical edicts (for example, the outlawing of foot-binding and opium use), the fanatical Taiping are fêted by the Chinese Communist Party as revolutionary visionaries. On the other hand, the 1999 outlawing of the quasi-Buddhist Falun Gong movement also exposed the Chinese Communist Party's ever-present dread of religious mutiny against their monopoly on power. This paranoia is one way the Taiping Rebellion has left its mark on modern China.

GETTING TO NANJING/JIANGSU

Flights: Nanjing Lukou International Airport has overseas and numerous domestic connections, and is a quick 29km (18-mile) trip, on a new expressway, from downtown Nanjing. Wuxi Shuofang Airport is a thriving regional hub, well connected with the rest of the country. It is close to both Wuxi and Suzhou.

By train and bus: Trains from Shanghai, Beijing and elsewhere in China are cheap and plentiful, and bus services are frequent and often comfortable, depending upon the class.

GETTING AROUND JIANGSU

Nanjing: Trains are the best way to travel from Shanghai. The new China High-speed Rail (CHR) trains are clean, fast and comfortable, and the trip from Shanghai to Nanjing now takes just two hours.

Suzhou and Wuxi: Trains are again the best option from Shanghai, and the CHR trains reach Suzhou in just over 30 minutes. Suzhou station is north of the centre. From Hangzhou, buses or cars take a faster and more direct route to Nanjing.

Nanjing, together with Wuhan and Chongqing, is one of the "three ovens" of China, with summer temperatures soaring above 40°C (104°F).

---

race; daily 6am–7pm; charge), where in the 4th century, according to legend, the Buddha made flowers rain from the sky. Today there is a memorial in the park to the Communists and their supporters who died in 1927 at the hands of Nationalist troops. And if Zhongshan Lu with its right-angle turns at junctions seems confusing, there is a reason. From the docks on the Chang Jiang to the mausoleum, this is the route taken by the funeral entourage of Sun Yatsen (also called Sun Zhongshan) and is named after him.

North and east of Xinjiekou

Xu Yuan ❶ (煦园), 15 minutes' walk northeast of Xinjiekou on Changjiang Lu, is a pleasant, recreated Ming-dynasty garden, home to the **Tianchao Gong** (天朝宫; Palace of the Heavenly Kingdom; daily 8am–5.30pm; charge), once occupied by Taiping leader Hong Xiuquan.

Further northwest stand two reminders of the nascent Ming dynasty, **Gulou ⓜ** (鼓楼), the Drum Tower, and **Zhonglou ⓝ** (钟楼), the Bell Tower (both daily 8am–midnight; charge). Drum and bell

BELOW: Xinjiekou, the centre of modern Nanjing.

The tombs at Mingxiao Ling are a reminder that Nanjing was the national capital during the early Ming period (1368–1417).

BELOW: Shixiang Lu (Stone Statue Road) at Mingxiao Ling.

towers were common in all important imperial cities. The Drum Tower – whose purpose was to call the watch and warn the city of attack (the drums within it would signal the start and finish of the night watches along the city walls) – was completed in 1382, just 14 years into the reign of the first Ming emperor. The Bell Tower, completed six years later, was ceremonial.

The lively streets surrounding the leafy campus of Nanjing University are filled with lively student cafés, eateries and bookstores. In the eastern part of the city, next to Zhongshanmen gate, is the **Nanjing Museum O** (南京博物馆; Nanjing Bowuguan; daily 9am–5.30pm; charge). It has an extensive collection of ceramics, jade, lacquerware, textiles, bronzes, porcelain and stone figures from Nanjing and elsewhere in Jiangsu province. The collection covers 5,000 years of history, with many pieces dating from Neolithic times. The most important exhibit is a 2,000-year-old shroud from the Eastern Han dynasty (AD 25–220), made from 2,600 green jade rectangles sewn together with silver wire. A new museum building was opened in 1999, containing 10 gal-leries arranged around a central court-yard. The facilities are state-of-the-art, and well labelled in English.

Nanjing itself is like a living museum where each piece reveals another chapter in China's history. Southwest of the Nanjing Museum lie scattered the remains of the **Ming Imperial Palace** (明故宫; Ming Gugong) in **Wuchaomen Park** (午朝门公园). Erected by the first emperor of the Ming dynasty but reduced by war to a few scattered vestiges, some marble bridges and the ancient **Wumen** (午门) gate survive.

Sun Yatsen's Mausoleum

For most Chinese, the **Sun Yatsen Mausoleum P** (中山陵; Zhongshan Ling; daily 6.30am–6.30pm; charge) is Nanjing's main attraction. Known as the father of modern China, Sun helped found the Chinese Republic in 1911, and wrote many political treatises, which remain required reading in schools. Hailing from Guangdong province, Sun wanted his final resting place to be here, amidst the lovely **Zijin Shan Q** (紫金山; Purple Mountains). His desire was carried out four years after his death

Recommended Restaurants and Bars on page 241

when the mausoleum was completed in 1929. The size of this monument is staggering, covering 8 hectares (20 acres). At the end of the tree-lined avenue begins a climb of 392 granite steps leading up to the blue-tiled memorial hall. There are a few places to rest (alternatively take a sedan chair) and enjoy the view of Nanjing along the way.

Other sights around Nanjing

Ruins to the northeast of Nanjing, near Zijin Shan, offer a glimpse of the era of the Ming dynasty (1368–1644). Years before his death, the first Ming emperor, Hong Wu (1327–98), built his tomb known as **Mingxiao Ling** ❸ (明孝陵; daily 8am–5pm; charge). Unfortunately, it was plundered during the Taiping uprising in 1864, and only the yellow walls of the main structure remain. A "sacred path", known as the Shixiang Lu (Stone Statue Road) survives, and is lined with elegant stone carvings – soldiers on one side and animals, both real and mythical, on the other. Pause for a moment and admire the rich detail and evocative shapes and faces of these monumental works.

To the east of the tomb in Linggu (Valley of the Souls) is **Linggu Si** ❺ (灵谷寺; daily 8am–5pm; charge), a temple built at the end of the 14th century. Only the temple site of Wuliang Dian, which has been restored several times and built entirely from stone and without any wooden rafters, remains of the former large structure. Behind Wuliang Dian is the 60-metre (200ft) high **Linggu Ta** (灵谷塔), a pagoda built in 1929 in memory of the victims of the war between the warlords and Nationalists. There is a magnificent view of the surrounding landscape from the top floor. On the mountain stands an observatory, which has a museum containing astronomical instruments, old and new. The chair lift to the observatory provides a splendid view of the city, and is one of the lesser-known highlights of a visit to Nanjing.

The extensive park around **Xuanwu Hu** ❼ (玄武湖公园), a lake in the north of Nanjing, offers pavilions and small islands linked to the shore by dams and curved bridges. Understated in its beauty, it is a pleasant retreat. It is possible to walk along much of the well-preserved stretch of city wall that extends along the southern and western shore of the lake.

SUZHOU

If a tourist could see just one of China's smaller cities, a strong argument could be made for **Suzhou** ❷ (苏州). It has abundant history, and much of it is well preserved; the downtown area is filled with gardens, pagodas, silk works, waterways and ancient moats, while the Grand Canal itself slices through the middle of town. It is built around a lattice-work of 24 canals, home to small intimate garden spots tucked away behind houses and hidden between narrow streets.

In many ways, this small city captures the essence of modern China, typifying the tug-of-war between old and new that is taking place across the country. The tourist-friendly sections of Suzhou are only a small part of the whole; most of those sections are in the Old City, while surrounding them are a pair of high-

A silk brocade Mao-style jacket on display at the Suzhou Silk Museum.

BELOW: Suzhou's octagonal Beisi Ta pagoda, fronted by a large Buddha statue.

A quiet stretch along Suzhou's extensive network of canals.

TIP

Just 15 years ago, it took five hours to drive from Shanghai to Nanjing; today, it takes less than an hour to drive, and a trip on the new bullet train takes just 35 minutes.

powered industrial zones that are squeezing the downtown area from both sides.

To the east is the Suzhou Industrial Park (SIP), a thriving 180-sq-km (70-sq-mile) factory land that has also spawned a thriving tourism industry of shopping streets and restaurant strips, most notably the **Jinji Hu** (金鸡湖; Jinji Lake) area. The SIP was launched in the 1990s as a China–Singapore joint venture, but the local government borrowed the idea and launched an industrial park of its own, to the west of downtown. This is the Suzhou National High-Tech Industrial Zone, and while not as popular as the original SIP park, it is currently a construction-strewn playground for developers.

As much as any Chinese provincial city, Suzhou has benefited from the nation's new wealth. The main shopping street, pedestrianised and prosperous **Guanqian Jie**, is lined with clothing and shoe shops and fast-food restaurants. **Rainbow Walk** and **Li Gong Di** (李公堤) are both brand-new, pedestrian-friendly strips filled with dozens of upscale bars and restaurants, many of them branches of popular Shanghai venues. They are, however, somewhat off the tourist trail, being a 20–30-minute taxi ride east of the downtown area.

Across Jinji Hu, and visible from both Rainbow Walk and Li Gong Di, sits the shiny new Rmb 170 million (US$25 million) **Suzhou Science and Cultural Arts Centre** (苏州科技文化艺术中心), designed by French architect Paul Andreu. This swooping, soaring, metallic piece of modern architecture is the new home of the annual Golden Rooster awards, nicknamed the Chinese Oscars. In addition, Suzhou has new golf courses, an upscale marina bobbing with expensive yachts, and entire neighbourhoods filled with upscale bars and restaurants, just like those in Shanghai.

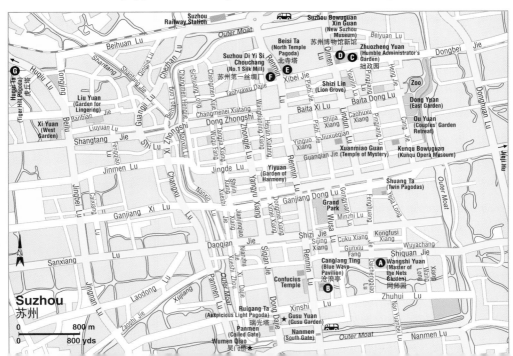

Suzhou
苏州

Recommended Restaurants and Bars on page 241

Successful though modern Suzhou is, its high-voltage economy is really only a reawakening of its traditional merchant heritage. Historically this has almost always been a rich city, a trading centre, a place of political prestige, and a popular domestic tourist destination.

It has a long and ostentatious history. Suzhou was the capital of the state of Wu during the Warring States Period (403–221 BC), albeit for a few years only, before flourishing as a trading and silk centre – especially from the early 6th century, when it was linked to other parts of eastern and northern China by the Grand Canal. The economy was at its prosperous peak during the Ming and Qing dynasties, when large numbers of officials, scholars and artists settled here, and local traders rapidly grew rich. This wealth was largely invested in some 287 beautiful gardens, of which 68 are still open to the public.

Its political supremacy may have long been hijacked by Shanghai to the east, but Suzhou retains its commerce and culture, and its historical relics have also been well preserved, and are a pleasure to visit.

Suzhou's gardens

The principles of Chinese garden construction – creating an illusion of the universe in a small space, and achieving a year-round seasonal balance of plants – are apparent throughout Suzhou. Water trickles between twisted, rocky crags; small islands are connected by canals and zigzag bridges; winding paths lead to tiny garden spaces with fountains, carefully manicured plants and fish ponds. A walk through the small alleys in the town, along the canals and through the gardens has a special charm in the misty mornings, when the tourists haven't yet arrived.

Wangshi Yuan ⓐ (网师园; Master of the Nets Garden; charge) is a delightful and compact garden that dates from the Southern Song period. Famous for its peony blooms in spring, the focus of the garden is its central pool around which cluster charming pavilions and walkways. A small slice of the Master of the Nets Garden has been recreated at the Metropolitan Museum of Art in New York, where it is called Ming Garden.

Also in the vicinity, the **Canglang Ting ⓑ** (沧浪亭; Blue Wave Pavilion)

TIP

Most of the gardens, temples and pagodas in and around Suzhou are open between 8am and 5 or 5.30pm, and charge a nominal fee.

BELOW: Zhuozheng Yuan (the Humble Administrator's Garden), in Suzhou, is the quintessential classical Chinese garden.

The smart New Suzhou Museum, designed by I.M. Pei, whose family hails from the town.

BELOW: display outside the Tiger Hill Pagoda.

is a beautifully arranged garden laid out next to a canal. Unlike the carefully manicured gardens elsewhere in Suzhou, the Blue Wave features a profusion of lush, untamed vegetation. The Panmen scenic area by the moat in the southwest of town is well worth exploring for its stretch of city wall, the delightful arched **Wumen Qiao** (吴门桥; Wumen Bridge) and the impressively restored **Ruiguang Ta** (瑞光塔; Ruiguang Pagoda).

The queen of Suzhou gardens, and one of the finest in all of China, is the wonderful **Zhuozheng Yuan** Ⓒ (拙政园; Humble Administrator's Garden), which covers an area of 4 hectares (10 acres). Wang Xiancheng, a retired court official, had it built in 1513 on the spot where the poet Lu Guimeng lived during the Tang dynasty. The name is something of a mistranslation: Zhuo really means silly or foolish, and is a reference that Wang made to himself, a high-ranking official who fell foul of the emperor and lost his lofty position.

His loss was Suzhou's gain, because Wang then built the Humble Adminis-

trator's Garden, a carefully balanced blend of vegetation, water and rocks. Each element of the garden has a layer of meaning: there are seasonal pagodas, where lotus, osmanthus, plum and bamboo bloom or leaf in different seasons, to provide year-round visual pleasure. There are paths with plum and phoenix tiles; to alternate steps on the tiles brings good fortune, according to the rules of Chinese wordplay. There is another area where Hong Xiuquan, the leader of the Taiping rebellion, set up temporary headquarters here, in the Dragon Head building. And those are only a few of the garden's attractions.

The New Suzhou Museum

Near the Humble Administrator's Garden is the long-awaited **New Suzhou Museum** Ⓓ (苏州博物馆新馆; Suzhou Bowuguan Xin Guan), which opened in late 2006 (daily 9am–5pm; free). Designed by the famous Chinese-American architect I.M. Pei, whose family is from Suzhou, the building displays many of his signature design features, such as squares, rectangles and pyramids, plus abundant use of natural light. It also uses Chinese elements such as a garden, a classical footbridge, moon-gate doors, and a traditional rock wall, along with replications of the whitewashed plaster walls and dark clay tiles that are the signature features of Old Suzhou. The exhibits are nothing special, however; the Nanjing and Shanghai museums have far better collections.

The area around the Suzhou Museum and Zhouzheng Yuan garden is as good a place as any to arrange a **boat trip** on the city's picturesque waterways. These trips can be arranged from several areas on the rectangular main canal, the broad waterway that embraces the Old Town like a moat. None of the boats are much of a bargain, but the bigger vessels work out less expensive if you don't mind waiting for them to fill up with tourists. The smaller boats, however, can explore the smaller waterways, so depending upon your budget, that's the choice. Most trips will last an hour or so.

Other sights in Suzhou

Further west is **Beisi Ta** **E** (北寺塔; North Temple Pagoda). The present octagonal pagoda dates from the Southern Song period, although two restorations occurred in the second half of the 17th century. A splendid view of Suzhou can be seen from the top of the 76-metre (250ft) high, nine-storey tower, and there is a teahouse with refreshments behind the pagoda (8.30am–5pm; charge).

Another highlight is the **Suzhou No. 1 Silk Mill** **F** (苏州第一丝绸厂; Suzhou Di Yi Si Chouchang; daily 9am–5.30pm; free), where tourists can see how ancient Suzhou's most sought-after luxury is made. This is no museum, but a real factory, and from mulberry leaves to worms, to cocoons, to thread, and on to the well-stocked gift shop, it ably guides visitors through the history of silk production in China. A key step is when the silkworm cocoons are steamed, then washed, and then the silk thread is pulled. The thread can sometimes measure almost 100 metres (110 yds) in length, and several threads are spun together into a rich, durable yarn. Many people in the area cultivate silkworms, usually as a profitable sideline.

On the western edge of the town, in the street of the same name, is **Liu Yuan** (留园; Garden for Lingering). It is aptly named: getting lost in the garden's many nooks and crannies is a pleasure. Liu Yuan is a good example of a southern Chinese garden of the Qing era (1644–1912), and thus belongs to the gardens protected as national cultural monuments.

Tiger Hill Pagoda **G** (虎丘塔; Huqiu Ta), in the far northwest of town, is one of Suzhou's finest attractions. And yes, it is leaning: at the top, the pagoda is 2.34 metres (7ft 8ins) out of kilter, and it has twice been stabilised: once during the Ming Dynasty, and a second time (unusually for the period) in 1961. The Ming effort was remarkable – it is the uppermost layer that straddles the top of the pagoda and sits off-centre, in an effort to rebalance the 48-metre (157ft) structure. The pagoda was finished in 961, and is made entirely of brick, a

TIP

The popularity of Shanghai's hip Xintiandi area has inspired a host of imitators, and Suzhou has two. One is called Xintiandi, but it is a little-visited amusement park rather than a bar-and-restaurant strip. A worthier imitator is Ligongdi: it has the same upscale restaurants as the real Xintiandi, and the same smattering of faux history, with imitation Ming- and Qing-dynasty arched bridges, pagodas and cobbled paths.

BELOW: the canal at Wuzhen.

The Grand Canal

Most people know about the Great Wall, but far fewer have even heard of ancient China's other great engineering feat: the Grand Canal (大运河; Da Yunhe). And while the Great Wall was a great failure – scarcely slowing the troops of Genghis Khan and other invaders –

the Grand Canal was a raging commercial success, and even today ships and barges carry cargo up and down the busy ancient waterway.

When the canal reached its peak during the Yuan dynasty, it was the longest man-made canal in the world, stretching 1,800km (1,100 miles) across the vast basin between Beijing and Hangzhou, and it joined together a pair of fabled rivers, the Yangzi and the Huang He (Yellow River). But the canal's importance went beyond its sheer length: it shifted China's centre of gravity from north to south, and it helped forge an empire. The rice-producing Jiangnan (south of the Yangzi) area became more important than the wheat-producing north, and a mass migration to the south began. The famous silks and teas and ceramics of Jiangnan also lured merchants and workers and immigrants to the south.

The customs tributes that were collected from the canals were transported to the capital via the waterway, as were rare wood and bricks used in the construction of the Imperial Palace in Beijing. During the Yuan period (1279–1368), when Beijing became the capital, the canal system was extended, connecting it directly with Hangzhou.

At the end of the 13th century, the waterway extended across the provinces of Zhejiang and Jiangsu, and connected four major river systems. Even today, a strong, steady flow of ships, barges and ferries runs through the Jiangnan sections of the canal, and it still forms an unbroken transport route between Hangzhou and the Yangzi, and as far north as Jining.

As a tourism resource, however, the Grand Canal is scarcely utilised. In the Jiangnan sections, pleasure boats are restricted to small stretches of the canal, to make way for commercial traffic. Some ferries ply the canal, but they run only during the night. Now, as then, transport is the main function of the Grand Canal.

The so-called water towns along the Grand Canal provide a glimpse of old China.

BELOW: the peaceful backwaters of Suzhou.

rarity in Chinese construction. Tiger Hill Pagoda is quite unusual, because unlike many of China's older sites, it has not been completely rebuilt, and the wonderful structure, aged and graceful, still evokes a strong sense of ancient China. The pagoda sits atop a much older site: the tomb of the original Duke of Wu, the founder of a small kingdom, who was buried here 2,400 years ago in a rocky cleft beneath the pagoda.

THE WATER TOWNS

The border between Jiangsu and Zhejiang provinces is sprinkled with water towns – small villages that thrived on the silk, tea, ceramic and rice trades – and six of them have been selected as Unesco World Heritage Sights. Those six – Luzhi, Nanxun, Tongli, Wuzhen, Xitang and Zhouzhuang – were once linked to Beijing by the Grand Canal, the watery highway that opened then up to global commerce (see page 237).

While differing in subtle details, the six water towns have certain features in common. They all thrived during the same era, the Ming and Qing dynasties, and they all provide the same tantalising glimpses of old China, with their cobbled paths, graceful arched bridges, labyrinthine canal networks and exquisite tiled roofs. Most are easily accessed from Shanghai and/or Suzhou.

Zhouzhuang ❸ (周庄), only an hour and a half by car from Shanghai, is small – just 400 sq metres (4,300 sq ft) – but it packs a lot of history into just a few blocks. Among the highlights are the houses of the rich. Zhang's House, built in the early 14th century, is a sprawling mansion with six courtyards, 70 rooms filled with antiques, and a canal running through the courtyards. Tucked in the rear is a sun-dappled patio, with a stone table carved into a chessboard.

Tongli ❹ (同里) is 20 minutes from Zhouzhuang by car, and two hours by boat. It is larger than Zhouzhuang, with wider canals, broader sidewalks and more trees. The pace is slower, and it

Recommended Restaurants and Bars on page 241

feels less crowded and more lived in. **The Garden of Seclusion and Meditation** (退思园; Tui Si Yuan) – a classic Chinese garden – is one of the highlights, and so are the canal-side tables at one of the local teahouses. Here, tourists can enjoy the aromatic herbal flavours of the local *longjing* tea, watch trained cormorants dive into the canal for fish, and listen as the evocative music of an *er hu* (a stringed instrument) floats along the cobbled streets. As night falls, red lanterns glow and ripple, reflected in the serene water of the canals.

Wuzhen ⑤ (乌镇), once the richest of the water towns, is two hours from Tongli. A wide canal bisects the centre of town and joins the Grand Canal itself, still a major commercial artery. A branch of the Grand Canal serves as the town's main street, and the houses have back doors that open straight onto the water. Wuzhen is famous for traditional crafts; some shops make wooden barrels and some spin cotton into cloth, while others make silk fans, rice wine, cotton slippers and brass buckles. In Wuzhen, all these products are made the old-fashioned way, just as they were 10 centuries ago.

This sense of preserved history is what makes the water towns of the Yangzi Delta worth visiting.

Wuxi and Tai Hu

Wuxi ⑥ (无锡), easily reached by train from either Suzhou (30 minutes) or Nanjing (90 minutes), or by boat from Hangzhou on the Grand Canal in about 13 hours, has a history that goes back more than 2,000 years. But the city's importance grew with the completion of the canal, and its wealth was achieved, as in the whole region, through agriculture, trade and silk production. The Grand Canal flows right through the centre of town, underneath elegant arched bridges.

Tai Hu ⑦ (太湖), China's third-largest lake, covers 2,420 sq km (934 sq miles) – although it is just 2.5 metres (8ft) deep, on average – and is peppered with 48 islands. The romantic landscape in green and blue, veiled with fine mist, has made this lake the subject of many poems. Not surprisingly, residents have a more pragmatic view of the lake: it provides them with fish, shrimp and hairy crabs, and they breed ducks and geese, as

To make the most of the canals you need to hire a boat. Be prepared to bargain – the first price you will be offered will be way over the odds.

well as grow lotus and water chestnuts on it. The distinctive rock found in all Chinese classical gardens comes from Tai Hu, and was an important family business in the past.

Tour groups tend to muster in numbers at the two main sights on Tai Hu outside Wuxi. Spring is the peak season at **Mei Yuan** (梅园; Plum Garden) overlooking the lake, when its many thousands of plum trees are in blossom. **Yuantou Zhu** (鼋头渚; Turtle Head Islet), a peninsula poking into the lake, is popular for its walks, pavilions and amusement parks. From Yuantou Zhu you can hop on a boat to the island of **San Shan** (三山岛; Three Hills). Finally, the attractive and unspoilt outcrop of **Dong Shan** (East Hill) projects into Tai Hu east of the island of Xi Shan (West Hill) and is easily reached from Suzhou.

Yixing County (宜兴县), on the western shore of Tai Hu, has a reputation for its ceramics – and in particular its teapots. Production is centred on the town of **Dingshan** ❽ (定山). Unglazed *Zisha* (purple sand) Yixing teapots absorb the flavour of the tea, and seasoned, well-used pots simply require the addition of boiling water – or so they say. The Ceramics Exhibition Centre allows you to appreciate the full range of Yixing's ceramic production and its historical importance.

Yangzhou

Two hours by bus from Nanjing, **Yangzhou** ❾ (扬州) dates back to the 5th century BC; it found prosperity in its prime position on the southern section of the Grand Canal. A salt monopoly further filled the coffers of this pretty canal town, but the Taiping rebels brought considerable destruction in the mid-19th century. **Daming Si** (大明寺; Daming Temple) in the northwest of town dates back to the 5th century AD, although it was razed by the Taiping and later rebuilt. The temple is chiefly notable for its Jian Zhen Hall, dedicated to a monk who failed five times to reach Japan to promote Buddhism, eventually succeeding on his sixth endeavour. Yangzhou's major scenic area is **Shouxihu Gongyuan** (瘦西湖公园; Shouxihu Park), looping south from Daming Si and marked by its **Wuting Qiao** (五亭桥; Five Pavilion Bridge). ❑

Silk and Silk Cultivation

Nobody knows when the first Chinese person decided to steam the cocoon of a silkworm, unroll it, and spin the resulting strands into one of the finest, softest, and most comfortable fabrics ever invented. According to legend, it happened some 5,000 years ago, when a princess accidentally dropped a cocoon into her tea, unravelled the thread, and hey presto! China had its most famous export.

Silk is made from the cocoons of mulberry silkworms, which thrive in the moist climate of the Yangzi Delta. The delicate worms need plenty of care: dust, rats and temperature changes can kill them. Silk-making remains labour-intensive: the cocoons are steamed to melt the resinous coating and kill the worm, then dipped in hot water to locate the end of the silk strand. Each strand is woven together with about 10 others and the resulting thread made into cloth.

That cloth – strong and durable, with an elegant soft lustre – has been in demand since the day the princess dropped the cocoon. Medieval Europeans, dressed in scratchy wool, couldn't get enough of it. The Silk Road became the most famous trade route in history, and even today, China still produces and exports most of the world's silk.

RESTAURANTS AND BARS

Restaurants

Prices for a meal for one, with one drink:
$ = under Rmb 50
$$ = Rmb 50–100
$$$ = Rmb 100–150
$$$$ = over Rmb 150

Restaurants in this part of China often feature the local Huaiyang cuisine, a light and mild cooking style that is famous for delicate soups, steamed dumplings and fresh seafood.

Nanjing

The pedestrian-friendly Lion's Bridge area (狮子桥) is the best place to find a good restaurant; it's a small area with a wide range of choices, from simple Chinese snack shops to upscale Western venues.

Blue Marlin Bar and Restaurant
蓝枪鱼西餐厅
8 Changjiang Rd, 1912 District. **$$**
Lively atmosphere and a good location make this a 1912 pub district landmark.

Hongxing Restaurant
红杏酒家
150 Fenghuang St (E). **$$**
For reliable servings of *ma la*-laden Sichuan specialties.

Jinling Fast Food
金陵快餐
Corner of Guanjia Qiao and Hanzhong Lu. **$**
Good steamed buns at great prices.

Jinying Dajuilou
金鹰大酒楼
9 Wangfu Dajie. **$$–$$$**
Classic south-of-the-Yangzi seafood in an upscale setting.

10,000 Buddhas Vegetarian Restaurant
毗卢寺万佛斋素菜馆
4 Han Fu St. **$$**
A dazzling array of food that looks and tastes like meat, but... isn't.

Xiao Fei Yang
小肥羊火锅城
48 Yunan Rd (N). **$$**
Convivial hot pot at one of China's favourite chains.

Suzhou

The main restaurant areas are at Ligongdi, on Jinji Lake, and around the shopping street of Guanqian Jie in the heart of the city.

Old Farm House
老农舍音乐餐厅
51 Ligongdi Rd. **$$$**
A German-Scandinavian pub-restaurant that serves reliable bread, cheese, beer and other Nordic favourites.

Hofbrau Suzhou
德国皇家啤酒
50 Ligongdi Rd. **$$$**
A genuine East-West hybrid with a Filipino band, home-brewed beer, thick sausages and a pleasant lakeside location.

In Restaurant
异料理餐
Hotel One,
379 Chang Jiang Rd. **$$**
A beautifully designed pan-Asian restaurant that serves fragrant, spicy curries in a warm and friendly atmosphere.

Tian Fu Zhi Le
天府之乐新区店
Wenhua Square, Shiquan St. **$$**
Mapo tofu, *gong bao* chicken and other reliable Sichuan classics.

Tomato Kitchen Café
番茄主义
56 Ligongdi Rd. **$$$**
A lakeside Italian eatery that is a firm local favourite. Reservations are a must.

Xinjiang Pamir Muslim Restaurant
新疆帕米尔餐厅
25 Shenxian St. **$**
Lamb, flat bread and other affordable Uighur specialities.

Wuxi

Wuxi Kaoya Guan
无锡烤鸭馆, or
中山路店
222 Zhongshan Lu. **$–$$**
Succulent roast duck wrapped in pancakes and served alongside local seafood dishes.

Bars

Nanjing

Castle Bar 古堡酒吧
9 Zhongyang Rd
Reliable weekend hangout.

Danny's Irish Pub
丹尼爱尔兰酒吧
4/F Sheraton Hotel, 169 Hanzhong Rd.
A tried-and-true formula still draws the crowds.

RIGHT: dipping a *xiao long bao* (dumpling) in vinegar.

HANGZHOU AND ZHEJIANG

Extolled by Marco Polo as the world's most
beautiful and magnificent city, Hangzhou is one
of China's six ancient capitals and the modern
hub of coastal Zhejiang province

One of the wealthiest provinces in China, **Zhejiang** (浙江), with its famous capital city of Hangzhou, spans a region whose geography ranges from canals, rivers and flat, fertile land in the north to hilly interiors and rugged seashores in the south and east. The long and fragmented coastline has several ports, such as industrious Ningbo and Wenzhou, that have played a decisive role in the area's historic prosperity.

Hangzhou is located in the north of the province at the lower end of the Grand Canal *(see page 237)*, and is one of China's most visited destinations. Its most cherished sight is the celebrated West Lake (Xi Hu), but the city and its environs are also renowned for their high-quality silk and fine tea. Nearby Shaoxing is a photogenic canal town.

Offshore, and reached by regular ferries from Hangzhou, Ningbo and Shanghai, is the sacred Buddhist island of Putuo Shan, with temples, panoramic sea views, sandy beaches, and Buddhist pilgrims from throughout China.

HANGZHOU

A fortified and prosperous town during the Tang period (618–907), **Hangzhou** ❿ (杭州) benefited greatly from its position at the southern end of the Grand Canal. At the beginning of the 12th century, the Chinese court was defeated in a battle against tribes from its northern borders, and fled south. In 1138, the newly formed empire of the Southern Song dynasty took the city as its tempo-

rary residence. The town flourished, with officials, writers and scholars moving there as the dynasty blossomed. During the Southern Song dynasty, Chinese culture reached a dramatic climax, and artworks from this era, particularly the richly detailed brush paintings, are considered to be among the finest works of art ever produced.

Hangzhou was the subject of poems even earlier than that, under the Tang dynasty, such as in the work of the poet Bai Juyi (772–846), who became governor of the town and had a dam built at

Main attractions
WEST LAKE (XI HU),
    HANGZHOU
LINGYIN SI MONASTERY,
    HANGZHOU
MOGANSHAN
PUTUO SHAN

LEFT: classical
Chinese scenery at
Hangzhou's West
Lake. **BELOW:**
crowds and tour
groups at West
Lake.

TIP

A gentle bicycle ride around West Lake is one of the best ways to enjoy China's most famous waterfront. Bicycles can be rented at many places; be sure to bargain. Incidentally, West Lake is the only National Scenic Area in China that is free of charge.

West Lake that still bears his name. During the Southern Song period the city's population increased from less than half a million to more than 1 million, making Hangzhou one of the largest cities in the world at the time. It was nearly wiped out in the second half of the 19th century, when Taiping rebels swarmed through, destroying much of its antiquity. Modernisation has also taken a toll, as the city walls and gates have disappeared, and the numerous old canals have been filled in and paved over.

Today, as in the past, Hangzhou is an important administrative centre in the middle of one of China's most prosperous regions. Its products include silk and **longjingcha** (dragon well tea), and its pharmaceutical industry and academy of

arts are well known throughout China. The population is now over 6 million.

While it is a good walking town, Hangzhou, and particularly West Lake, the main attraction, does become crowded with visitors, especially on weekends, as tourists and honeymooners arrive in the city from nearby Shanghai, on ever-faster trains that now take just 90 minutes.

It is said that every Chinese city has a **West Lake** (西湖; Xi Hu). In fact, although there are around 30 West Lakes in China, the one in Hangzhou is by far the most famous. The eastern shore is close to the town, while forested mountains, often shrouded in mist, surround the other shores, lending the landscape a romantic allure.

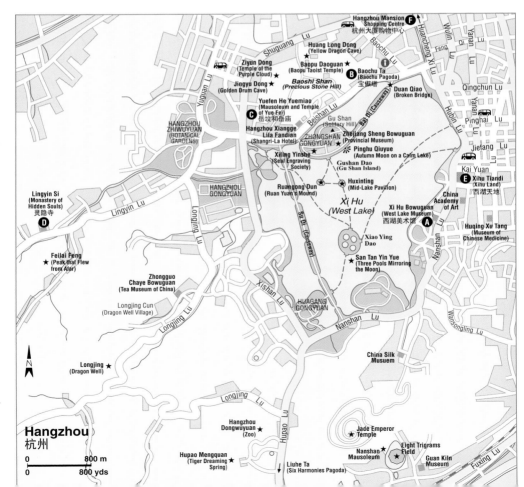

Recommended Restaurants on page 249

GETTING TO HANGZHOU/ZHEJIANG

Flights: Hangzhou Xiaoshan International Airport is less than 10 years old, but is already one of the busiest airports in China. The airport is 30km (19 miles) from downtown, and regular buses leave every 15 minutes or so. Passengers travelling to Shanghai must take a train or bus from downtown Hangzhou.

By train and bus: Hangzhou is well connected by rail and bus to many cities in China, particularly Shanghai.

GETTING AROUND ZHEJIANG

Hangzhou: Four different kinds of train connect Hangzhou to Shanghai, and the fastest one takes just 75 minutes.

Moganshan: The best way to reach Moganshan is by car, but it is possible to take a public bus to Wukang, and a 30-minute taxi ride from there. Another option is to ride a train to Hangzhou, and then take a bus to Wukang, or a taxi from the train station.

Ningbo: The awesome Hangzhou Bay Bridge, which opened to the public in 2008 and is the longest cross-ocean bridge in the world, has cut two hours from the travel time between Shanghai and Ningbo and other cities in southeastern Zhejiang province.

The beauty of West Lake is enhanced in summer by a carpet of water lilies.

The lake grew in stages: first in the early 800s with the Bai dyke, and then in 1090, when the famous poet and administrator Su Dongpo gathered thousands of labourers and dug out and extended the lake, a process that was repeated during the Ming dynasty. The most recent stage – a major one – was finished in 2003, when 80 hectares (200 acres) of lake were added on the western end. The **West Lake Museum** Ⓐ (西湖美术馆; Xi Hu Bowuguan), which opened in 2006, has some rare cultural relics and documents on display, all concerning the lake, and some displays about its history and importance.

In the northeastern part of West Lake, the pagoda at **Baochu** Ⓑ (宝俶塔) stands tall against the sky, a symbol of the city. It was originally built in 968, then later destroyed and rebuilt several times. The present pagoda dates from 1933 and is 45 metres (150ft) high. On the northwestern shore, the **Mausoleum**

BELOW: bridge and pavilion over the West Lake.

*Hangzhou's Lingyin
Si is one of China's
most famous and
picturesque Buddhist
monasteries. The
pillars are painted
black instead of
the red normally
associated with
Chinese Buddhism.*

BELOW: on the
streets of
Hangzhou. **BELOW
RIGHT:** a West Lake
pagoda.

of Yue Fei (岳坟和岳庙; Yue
Fen He Yuemiao) commemorates
the Southern Song dynasty general
who resisted the northern invaders,
but, in time-honoured Chinese
tradition, was falsely charged, executed and later exonerated.

In the west of the town, at the end
of Lingyin Lu and easily reached
by bus, is the beautifully situated
Lingyin Si (灵隐寺; Monastery
of the Hidden Souls; daily 8am–5pm;
charge). The Buddhist Indian Hui Li,
who thought the peak resembled part of
the Gradhrakuta Mountain in India,
founded the monastery in AD 326. Since
the second half of the 10th century, the
rock walls of the mountain have been
carved with about 300 Buddhist sculptures and inscriptions. The most popular
figure is at the foot of the mountain: the
fat-bellied Buddha from the Song period,
one of the most touched and photographed
figures anywhere; it is believed to bring
good luck. Up to 3,000 monks once lived
in the 18 pavilions and 75 temple halls
on the mountain peak.

Beyond these figures is the monastery,
one of the most famous Buddhist sites in
all of China. Behind the entrance gate to
the temple and two stone columns
inscribed with Buddhist texts is **Tianwang Dian** (天王殿; Hall of Heavenly
Kings), where another statue of the
Maitreya Buddha can be seen, guarded
by the two Heavenly Kings standing at
its side. The gilded statue of the Buddha
Sakyamuni, which is more than 20
metres (66ft) high and made of precious
camphor wood, is in Daxiongbao Dian
(Precious Hall of the Great Heroes).

Modern Hangzhou

In Hangzhou, as in the rest of China, the
old coexists with the new, side by side.
And Hangzhou, as one of the wealthiest
cities in China, has its share of the new.
Xihu Land (西湖天地; Xihu Tiandi),
was created by the same Hong Kong
developers that launched the Xintiandi
outdoor food-and-drink mall in Shanghai.
The Xihu Tiandi design is based on the
West Lake's landscaping and its surrounding historic architecture, but it is
mostly indoors, in brick-and-tile structures
that are linked to each other by stone paths,
with a scattering of villa-style buildings in
between. This area is home to large col-

lection of upscale bars and restaurants, both Chinese and international.

The **Hangzhou Mansion Shopping Centre ⑤** (杭州大厦购物中心) bristles with luxury goods shops selling the usual global brands, while the bar-and-nightlife zone is Nanshan Road, a lively strip that is home to beer gardens, nightclubs, live music and the like. It is also relatively lively during daylight hours.

Such developments are fuelled by the rising wealth of Hangzhou. Yet city residents don't regard themselves as money-mad; they prefer to boast of their quality of life and overall contentment, in contrast to their stressed-out neighbours in Shanghai. This sense of well-being is enhanced by the gentle beauty of their home. West Lake aside, the city is also ringed by mountains, adding to the overall charm and good feng shui.

Outside Hangzhou

To the west of Hangzhou is the village of **Longjing** (龙井村). Visitors here will be hectored to buy some of the Longjincha (Dragon Well) tea traditionally produced here. For the most part, the vessels used communally in the past for drying the tea leaves are now set in motion only when the tourist buses arrive.

An excursion to one of the surrounding villages, such as **Meijiawu** (梅家坞), about 20 minutes by car to the south of Hangzhou, is probably more worthwhile. The trip through the lovely landscape with its famous bamboo groves can be made by bicycle, hired in town. This village also grows tea, and the villagers, who have not yet been overrun by tourists, are hospitable and willing to explain tea production.

Heading west from town, Hangzhou Bay becomes the **Qiantang River** (钱塘江), which is called the Fuchun further upstream. By whatever name, the river is famous for its tidal bore, a surging wave of brown foamy water that roars up the river each day. The tide flows with extra vigour during the full moons of autumn, but very high tides can also be seen on about the 15th to 18th days of every lunar month, often around midday.

Further upriver is **Tonglu** (桐庐), home to the rather remarkable **Jiangnan Suspended Temple** (江南悬空寺; Jiang Nan Xuan Kong Si), built into a cliff face and supported by a series of pillars, which also support pathways and houses, all hugging the side of the cliff for dear life. Still further upriver is **Qiandaohu** (千岛湖; Thousand Island Lake), a popular place for boat trips.

ELSEWHERE IN ZHEJIANG

Shaoxing ⑪ (绍兴), 60km (37 miles) southeast of Hangzhou, is easily reached by train or bus. Famous throughout China for its culinary rice wine, the picturesque canal town is also notable as the birthplace of Lu Xun, the great modern writer. His **Former Residence** (鲁迅故居; Lu Xun Guju) and the **Lu Xun Memorial Hall** (鲁迅纪念馆; Lu Xun Jinianguan) both daily 8am–5pm; charge) stand on Lu Xun street in the south of the city. The best way to appreciate Shaoxing's charms

Dragon Well Tea Park in Longjing village near Hangzhou, home of the prized longjingcha tea.

BELOW: tea plantation in the hills south of Hangzhou.

is to amble alongside the town's canals. The **Bazi Qiao** (八字桥; Eight Character Bridge) is a historic 13th-century bridge named after its resemblance to the character *ba* (eight).

Moganshan

In the blessed green hills some 60km (38 miles) to the north of Hangzhou lies **Moganshan**  (莫干山; charge to enter the area), a cool, bamboo-clad oasis that draws weekend visitors from Shanghai and Hangzhou. Modern-day residents of Shanghai and Hangzhou are not the first to notice the airy charms of Moganshan, however. In the early 20th century, Shanghai's upper crust flocked to the mountain, where they built a variety of villas, plantations, clubs and other playgrounds, all made from the signature local stone. This was perhaps the closest thing in China to a colonial India-style hill station.

The notorious gangster Du Yuesheng also resided here, and the Guomindang likewise had a penchant for the hill resort. Later still, Communist bigwigs (including Mao) holidayed on the lush slopes. By the 1930s the area was dotted

Chinese rice wine – the best known from Shaoxing – comes in drinking and cooking varieties, the latter often being salted.

BELOW: bamboo forest on the cool slopes of Moganshan.

with more than 150 Western-style stone buildings along with churches and other colonial paraphernalia; many old villas remain and some operate as hotels. There is a Mao Museum – Mao slept here – and White Cloud Castle, where Chiang Kaishek honeymooned with Soong Meiling, and later met Zhou Enlai. Just for fun, compare the displays dedicated to Zhou with the ones dedicated to Chiang.

Some of the older buildings are in disrepair, and there they sit, patient structures in various stages of decay, which add enormously to the appeal of Moganshan. Even today, Moganshan is chiefly famous for three highlights: stylish old villas, soft white clouds and wild green bamboo. The mountain is laced with stone paths and steps and walkways, and hiking is mostly about serendipity: turn here, and find an old mansion or a quiet pond; turn there, and find a restful pagoda with fine views of the foothills. One exception is the **Sword Pond Waterfall** (剑池瀑布; Jianchi Pubu), a deep gorge sliced in the vertical rock and filled with ponds and patios, which is Moganshan's must-see attraction.

The relative peace and quiet of Moganshan may soon come to a crashing halt, however, as a brand-new superhighway is expected to reduce travel time from Shanghai from four hours to two, and is likely to bring with it a surge of renovations, visitors and investment.

Ningbo and Putuo Shan

Ningbo  (宁波), at the confluence of the Yuyao and Yong rivers, established itself as a prosperous trading port in Tang times, and later became China's most important port under the Ming. The city attracted both the Portuguese and the British, who established it as a treaty port in 1843. Its commercial importance was later comprehensively usurped by Shanghai, and these days tourists largely pass through en route to Putuo Shan offshore. Over Xinjiang Bridge and south of the ferry terminal, the 17th-century **Portuguese Catholic Church** is a well-preserved relic of the 19th-century European presence.

The easternmost of China's four sacred Buddhist mountains, **Putuo Shan** ⓮ (普陀山) is more of an island than a peak, but is a sacred domain nonetheless, and the island's holy ambience is enhanced by its isolation from the mainland. The reigning deity on this island is Guanyin, the Buddhist Goddess of Compassion, who is celebrated in several temples, the most famous of which is the **Puji Chansi** (普济禅寺; Puji Temple; daily 6am–9pm; charge). **Fayu Si** (法雨寺; daily 7am–5pm; charge), a substantial temple at the foot of Foding Shan, has a splendid thousand-arm Guanyin statue and a marvellous mountain backdrop. Visible from afar, a vast, bronze-plated effigy of the goddess – the 33-metre (108ft) high Nanhai (South Sea) Guanyin – rises up brilliantly on the southern tip of the island. Dotted with hotels, Putuo Shan can be reached by ferry from Ningbo in two hours (it can also be reached direct from Shanghai and from Hangzhou).

Southern Zhejiang

Pop into a Chinese restaurant in Paris or Venice and the owners and staff are very likely to come from **Wenzhou** ⓯ (温州). The citizens of this port city, at the southern end of the ragged Zhejiang coastline, have a great tradition of exodus from China to Europe. Those that return from abroad throw their weight behind the free-market bedlam that has gripped the city. There are not many sights in town per se, with the pleasant park on **Jiangxin Dao** (江心岛; Jiangxin Island) the main tourist diversion. Two churches (one 18th-century, the other 19th-century) survive in the city centre.

Some 80km (50 miles) from Wenzhou, the mountainous region of **Yandang Shan** ⓰ (雁荡山) is a stirring expanse of towering cliffs and peaks. The most famous sight is the dramatic 190-metre (625ft) **Dalongqiu Pubu** (大龙湫瀑布; Big Dragon Pool Waterfall), one of the highest falls in China. ❑

Photo opportunity on Putuo Shan, sacred island of Guanyin. The island becomes very crowded on Buddhist feast days.

RESTAURANTS

Hangzhou

Xihu Land on West Lake, and Nanshan Road both have sizeable concentrations of restaurants. The local cuisine (Huaiyang – *see page 110*) features fresh seafood and vegetables, lightly cooked, with mild flavours like ginger, salt and scallion. The signature dishes are freshwater shrimp with longjing tea, crab egg tofu, and steamed yellow croaker fish.

Butterfly Laguna 湖蝶
9A Xihu Tiandi,
147 Nan Shan Rd. **$$**
One of the fashionable restaurants in Xihu Tiandi, an area similar to Xintiandi in Shanghai. Surrounded by the beautiful scenery of the lake, the restaurant has nice views and is a good place for a relaxed afternoon gathering.

Elm Garden 榆园
1 Si Yan Jing, Man Jue Long Rd (near Hu Pao Rd). **$**
Located in a tourist spot famous for its sweet-scented laurel trees, this is a country-style restaurant with wooden tables and chairs and open-air dining. Simple, delicious Hangzhou cuisine with chicken, fish and seafood.

Gold Chino 金玲珑
149–2 Qing Chun Rd (corner of Zhong He Rd). **$$$**
Located in downtown Hangzhou, the Southeast Asian décor is matched by the high-quality food.

Jiang Nan Ah Er 江南阿二
31 Upper Mao Jia Bu Village. **$$**
In Mao Jia Bu village, where numerous small restaurants and local teahouses are located. The food is authentic and rustic.

Kui Yuan Guan 奎元馆
154 Jie Fang Rd (near Zhongshan Middle Rd). **$**
A traditional Hangzhou noodle restaurant, with many different varieties of noodles. Popular with visitors and locals alike.

Lin Yu Garden Restaurant 林语花园餐厅
6 Lin Yin Rd (corner of Yu Quan Rd). **$$$**
A quiet garden hidden in the trees, Lin Yu presents beautiful food of exquisite taste. A very pleasant dining experience.

Lou Wai Lou 楼外楼
30 Gu Shan Rd, Bai Di (Bai Causeway). **$$$**
This restaurant, with a good location near the West Lake, has a long history and serves authentic Hangzhou cuisine. Perenially popular with tourists.

Tsing-Teng Tea House 青藤茶馆
2/F Yuan Hua Plaza, 278 Nanshan Rd. **$**
This teahouse is a very typical and popular gathering place for locals. It offers a variety of tea, snacks, dim sum and other small dishes in a traditional Chinese setting, along with many kinds of Hangzhou tea.

Wei Zhuang 味庄
10–12 Yang Gong Di (Yang Gong Causeway). **$$**
A Chinese-style pavilion built on the West Lake, with a dream-like environment that duplicates an ancient royal palace.

Prices for a meal for one, with one drink:
$ = under Rmb 50
$$ = Rmb 50–100
$$$ = Rmb 100–150
$$$$ = over Rmb 150

CHANG JIANG (YANGZI) REGION

Better-known to Westerners as the Yangzi, the Chang Jiang slices through central China for 6,300km (3,900 miles), forcing its way through the dramatic Three Gorges to the plains beyond

The longest river in China (and the third-longest in the world) is called, appropriately enough, the **Chang Jiang** (长江) – Long River. Foreigners mistakenly refer to it as the **Yangzi** (扬子; sometimes spelled Yangtze); for the Chinese this term denotes the lower course from Wuhan to the sea. Meandering eastwards for some 6,300km (3,900 miles), this mighty river – which traditionally divides China's north and south – begins life on the slopes of Geladandong, the main peak of the Tanggula Shan range in remote Qinghai province. Its course ends just north of Shanghai, where a 13km (8-mile) wide mouth empties into Dong Hai, the East China Sea. Along the way, the river flows across nine provinces, with 700 main tributaries draining an area of nearly 2 million sq km (772,000 sq miles) – almost 20 percent of China's total geographic area, one-quarter of the country's arable land and supporting over one sixth of the world's population.

From the delta just north of Shanghai the river is navigable by ocean-going vessels as far as Wuhan, nearly 1,000km (620 miles) upstream. Its murky brown waters flow through many of China's important industrialised areas, not to mention centres of silk-weaving, embroidery, lacquer work and carving. This lower stretch of the river is also known as the Yangzi, its local name changing twice more upriver. When the early colonial powers arrived, they applied this name to the entire river.

One of the most ambitious engineering projects ever undertaken, the Three Gorges Dam was completed in 2006. The water level attained its targeted high of 175 metres (575ft) in 2008, and although tourist boats continue to ply the river, it is now wider and the surrounding cliffs are somewhat less dramatic.

CHONGQING

The vast city of **Chongqing ❶** (重庆) is the launching point for boat cruises *(see panel, opposite)* nearly 700km (435 miles) down the Chang Jiang, but more

Main attractions
YANGZI RIVER CRUISE
  (THREE GORGES AND
  THREE LITTLE GORGES)
SHIBAOZHAI
YUEYANG
HUBEI PROVINCIAL MUSEUM,
  WUHAN
WUDANG SHAN
SHENNONGJIA FOREST RESERVE
HUANG SHAN

LEFT: dramatic Three Gorges landscape.
BELOW: swimmers at the Qutang Gorge.

Two cable cars and an ever-growing number of bridges are rapidly phasing out the ferries that once carried city residents across the river.

notably in recent years it has earned itself the dubious distinction of having become the world's most populous municipality. Development is taking place at such a rapid pace that it is said that Chongqing is the fastest-growing city in the world. The actual population of the municipal area is disputed (anywhere between 4 and 10 million), though it is thought to be growing at an average of around 1,400 people a day, and in 2005 government statistics put the population of the municipality at just over 31 million.

The city sits at the confluence of two rivers, where the Jialing joins the Chang Jiang, a strategic location that has always guaranteed its place as an important trading centre. The location of the original core of Chongqing, on a rocky promontory hugging the river, is rare among Chinese cities; the steepness of its streets means there are no bicycles (when students from Chongqing make it to university elsewhere in China, they have to learn how to cycle, much to the amusement of fellow undergraduates).

During World War II and the Japanese occupation of large parts of the country, the Nationalist government under Chiang Kaishek retreated to Chongqing (then known in the West as Chungking) and made it their capital. Provincial status resumed after the war, although the city grew into an industrial powerhouse in the early communist years. The recent rapid development has led to the almost wholesale destruction of the architecture in the old city centre that was once one of the smoggy city's few redeeming qualities, and today it is indistinguishable from any other modern Chinese city.

What to see in Chongqing

The area around **Jiefang Bei** (解放碑; Liberation Square) is the heart of the city, and although much has been transformed into a pedestrian shopping centre, there are still some narrow, winding backstreets to explore. Steep steps lead from the tip of the peninsula down to the river banks, studded with moorings. At the tip of the peninsula is a small pavilion, **Chaotianmen** (朝天們; Door Facing Heaven). The flood level is marked here as a reminder of the great flood of 1982, which covered a large area and caused great devastation. Chang Jiang ferries arrive and depart from the busy Chaotianmen docks.

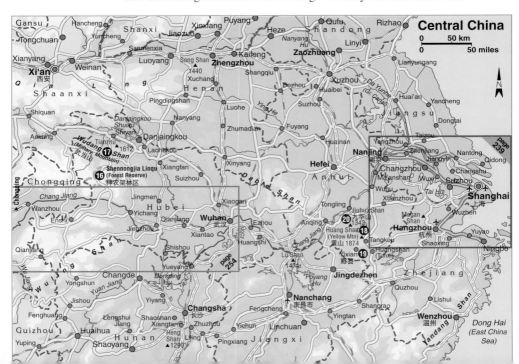

Recommended Restaurants on page 263

GETTING TO CHONGQING

Flights: There are frequent flights to most major cities in China.

By train and bus: There are daily trains to cities all over China including Wuhan (13 hours), Xi'an (16 hours) and Guiyang (12 hours). Buses are a better bet for travel to Chengdu and Yichang.

BOAT TRIPS ON THE CHANG JIANG (CHONGQING–YICHANG): Cruise boats, hydrofoils and regular passenger ferries depart daily from the Chaotianmen docks in Chongqing. Most are bound for Yichang (13 hours by hydrofoil, 48 hours by ferry), although a few continue on to Wuhan. *See page 425 for full details.*

"When the sun shines in Sichuan in winter, the dogs bark." This proverb is particularly apt for Chongqing, as on most days of the cool, clammy winter the town is shrouded in fog that rises from the rivers.

Back uphill, not far from Chaotianmen and hidden in a narrow side street, is a small Buddhist temple, **Luohan Si** (罗汉寺). Noted for 500 painted terracotta *arhat* sculptures, the temple has been restored in recent years, has a vegetarian restaurant and is worth a quick visit.

The **Great Hall of the People** (人民大会堂; Renmin Dahuitang) is a sprawling, classically inspired building constructed in 1951, and the architectural symbol of Chongqing. The adjoining **People's Square** (人民广场; Renmin Guangchang) laid with marble tiles, has a performance stage and is a popular spot for locals to practice ballroom dancing en masse in the evenings, weather permitting (often not the case in this rainy city).

Chongqing has a number of tourist attractions related to the Communist Party's war of liberation against the Guomindang. Probably the most interesting is the **former residence of Song Qingling** (宋庆龄旧居; Song Qingling Jiuju), which is just 100 metres (110 yards) south of the Hilton Hotel. One of the three Song sisters, Qingling married Sun Yatsen. She lived in this house – a German colonial-era residence – for the duration of the war of resistance against Japan.

Also of interest is the **Stilwell Museum** (重庆史迪威博物馆; Shidiwei Jiangjun Jiuju), housed in the former residence of General Joseph Stilwell, Commander-in-Chief of the US forces in China and Burma during World War II.

BELOW: modern Chongqing looms above the Chang Jiang.

TIP

Yangzi ferries and cruise boats are moored at Chongqing's Chaotianmen Docks, on the tip of the main peninsula. There is a ticket office for ferries at the end of Shaanxi Lu by the docks as well as numerous agencies selling cruises, but it is better to use the more reputable agents in town, such as CITS. Unpredictable water conditions, in part due to the construction of the Three Gorges Dam, mean that cruise schedules are often altered on a daily basis. *For more informaton see pages 425–6.*

On (increasingly rare) clear evenings there are good views across the city from **Pipa Shan** (琵琶山), about 2km (1½ miles) west of Jiefangbei. Further west into the suburbs, **Hongyan** (红岩; Red Crag Village; daily 9am–5pm; charge) was the site of important negotiations between Mao Zedong and Chiang Kaishek, an attempt to achieve an alliance to oppose the Japanese that ultimately resulted in failure.

Dazu

Before hopping on the ferry to drift through the Three Gorges (*see page 255*), take time to visit the Tang and Song grottoes at **Dazu** ❷ (大足), 100km (60 miles) west of Chongqing, now a Unesco World Heritage site. The predominantly Buddhist statuary (Confucian ideals also get a say) is divided into two reliquaries. At **Bei Shan** (北山; daily 8am–5pm; charge), north of Dazu's main street, around 1,000 carvings are segregated into numerous caves, including the noteworthy niche number 155, featuring the Peacock King. **Baoding Shan** (宝顶山; daily 8am–5pm; charge), 16km (10 miles) northeast of Dazu, has the

more impressive artwork, its highlight being a 30-metre (100ft) reclining Buddha *(wofo)* in niche number 11.

CHONGQING TO YICHANG

Fengdu ❸ (丰都), traditionally known as the Ghost or Devil Town for its celebrated demon statues housed in temples, has been almost completely submerged by the rising waters caused by the Three Gorges Dam. But the local authorities are turning deluge to their advantage by building "lakeside" resorts, and making Mount Mingshan – now effectively a peninsula – an attraction. The peninsula's demon temples, which date back to the Tang dynasty (618–907), can be accessed by cable car or boat.

Around 80km (50 miles) further downstream is **Shibaozhai** ❹ (石宝寨; Stone Treasure Fortress), a regular stop on the cruise boat itineraries. During the reign of Emperor Qianlong (1736–97), a temple was erected on top of a rock rising up 30 metres (100ft) from the river's edge. According to legend, there was a small hole in the temple wall from which enough rice trickled to feed the monks, thus the name, Stone Treasure. Because

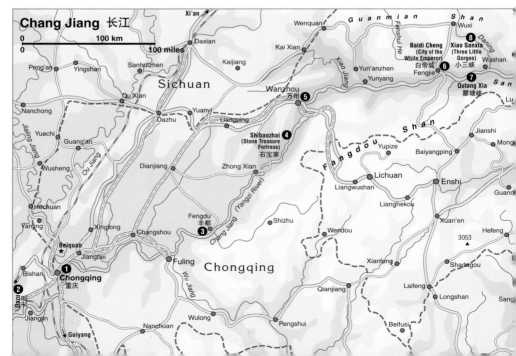

the ascent to the temple was tiring, a pagoda-shaped pavilion was built against the rock in the early 1800s, its 12 storeys reaching as far as the temple and affording easy access to it by means of a wooden staircase within. As of 2009, the rising waters mean that the Chang Jiang – now more lake than river – reaches close to the bottom of the pavilion. A wall is being built to protect the building.

The next large town downriver, Wanxian, has been renamed **Wanzhou** ❺ (万州). A long-established trading port on the Chang Jiang, most of the old city is now submerged, and a new town has been built to the north of the traditional waterfront centre to house displaced residents.

Baidi Cheng ❻ (白帝城; City of the White Emperor) is where the Three Gorges begin. Legend has it that a ruler of the Eastern Han dynasty (AD 25–220) saw a plume of white smoke in the shape of a dragon emerge from a well outside his palace; considering it a good omen, he henceforth called himself the White Emperor. In the main hall of the local temple, Baidi Miao, are the figures of two army generals of Shu from the Three

Kingdoms (221–63) period, Liu Bei and Zhuge Liang (whose exploits are related in the classic tale *Romance of the Three Kingdoms*). Baidi Cheng's hilltop location has saved it from submersion.

Sanxia (Three Gorges)

The entire length of **Sanxia** (三峡), the Three Gorges, is about 190km (120 miles). From west to east the individual gorges are Qutang Xia, Wu Xia and Xiling Xia. Although it is only 8km (5 miles) long and the shortest of the three, **Qutang Xia** ❼ (瞿塘峡) is probably the most fascinating. Perpendicular walls rise up from the river, pinching the gorge to a width of 100 metres (330ft) and making navigation through the one-way passage tedious.

Before Wu Xia is the town of **Wushan** (巫山), where the Daning He joins the Chang Jiang. Upstream along this tributary are the beautiful **Xiao Sanxia** ❽ (小三峡; Three Little Gorges); the journey involves transferring to smaller vessels which struggle against the Daning He's strong currents. The exquisite scenery, still

A cruise ship at the Sandouping locks.

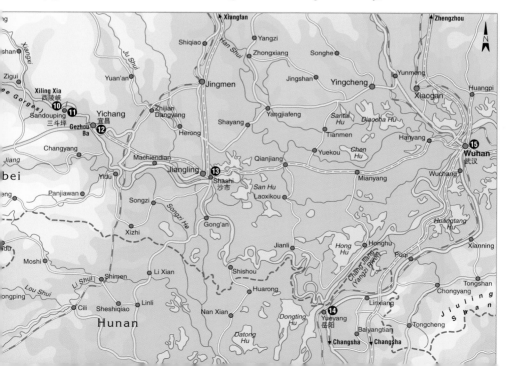

The Great Dam of China

The long-awaited Three Gorges Dam is now complete, harnessing the power of the Chang Jiang for China's ever-increasing energy needs

I n a land that conceived the Great Wall, China's current leaders are continuing a long Chinese tradition of marshalling manpower and resources into colossal and audacious projects. On 1 June 2003, 19 of the 22 sluice gates of the Three Gorges Dam were closed for the first time, and the water level behind the dam rapidly rose to 135 metres (440ft). With the maximum depth attained in 2009, the celebrated Three Gorges have become some 175 metres (575ft) less impressive.

First visualised by Sun Yatsen in 1919 for its huge power-generating capability, the scheme was shelved for four decades until championed by Mao Zedong in the late 1950s. The disastrous economic consequences of the Great Leap Forward followed by the chaos of the Cultural Revolution again mothballed the project. Strongly advocated by former Premier Li Peng, the National People's Congress ratified construction of the dam in 1992.

The Chinese Communist Party loves grandiose schemes. But the dam is more than a symbol of political power, and the ambitious endeavour has several pragmatic aims. Supporters argue that the devastating floods that have plagued the Chang Jiang region will be controlled, river-shipping tonnage will increase by 400 percent and the dam will generate enough power to illuminate half of China.

But the scheme has had many critics, who have argued that as well as destroying many sites of archaeological interest and damaging areas of scenic beauty, the dam would not even be an efficient way to generate power. Substantial silting would reduce its effectiveness at averting floods, the dam would interrupt navigation, and rival forms of power production would render the dam obsolete. Some of these claims have faded from the public agenda, but critics still oppose the dam on environmental grounds, despite the Chinese government's assertions that all is well.

Although allegations in some quarters that the dam had somehow triggered the Sichuan earthquake in 2008 have been widely dismissed (the dam was 700km/435 miles) from the epicentre), the wisdom of building the world's largest hydroelectric project in an earthquake zone continues to be questioned. Now that the dam and reservoir have been in operation for some time, its effects on the local area are beginning to be felt, and the signs are worrying. The Mayor of Chongqing claims that the banks of the reservoir have collapsed in scores of places, and that cracks have appeared in houses in the city. It is also considered likely that the 660-km (410-mile) reservoir behind the dam will become highly polluted as cities and industries discharge waste into it, causing untold damage to the river's ecosystem.

The dam's construction has involved the relocation of close to 1.5 million people, and the financial cost has been enormous. Time will tell if it is to be regarded as a milestone of engineering and an efficient energy source or a costly and embarrassing environmental disaster. ❑

ABOVE: the dam measures 2,335 metres (7,661ft) across. **LEFT:** the locks and bridge at Sandouping.

Recommended Restaurants on page 263

impressive despite the rise in water levels, is regarded by many as the highlight of a Chang Jiang cruise. At one point it is possible to spot wooden coffins tucked into a tiny ledge high up on a mountain. These coffins are said to belong to the Ba people, a lost culture from the Bronze Age that was absorbed by the Qin dynasty. The Ba placed the coffins containing their dead in tiny crevices on remote mountain tops.

Back on the Chang Jiang, the 45km (28-mile) long **Wu Xia** ❾ (武侠; Witches' Gorge) is relatively calm despite its name. The gorge, surrounded by 12 vertiginous peaks, is steeped in legend; in this case, troublesome dragons have been turned to stone by the goddess Yaoji.

The boat then passes **Zigui** on the northern bank, home of the famous poet Qu Yuan (330–295 BC), who, according to legend, drowned himself in despair over the occupation of his home state by the armies of the Qin empire (the Chinese world still celebrates the Dragon Boat Festival in his honour). The 1,400-year-old town is now underwater and its residents relocated, but the temple dedicated to Qu Yuan has not been affected.

The mouth of the Xiangxi (Fragrant River) on the northern bank, its green waters contrasting starkly with the brown Chang Jiang, signals the start of **Xiling Xia** ❿ (西陵峡). The last, longest, and traditionally the most dangerous of the Three Gorges, Xiling stretches for 66km (41 miles) and is itself made up of several smaller gorges. The peculiar shape of Niugan Mafei Xia (Horse-Lung and Ox-Liver Gorge) lent it its exotic name. Behind this is the 120-metre (400ft) long abyss of Qingtan (Blue Cliff). From the south, the river is overlooked by Huangling Miao (Yellow Hill Temple), whose main hall dates back to the Han dynasty.

The Three Gorges Dam is located at **Sandouping** ⓫ (三斗坪), a 10km (6-mile) stretch in the centre of Xiling Gorge, 35km (20 miles) west of Yichang. Most cruise boats will stop here to allow passengers to take in the immensity of the construction from the viewing platform. Beyond the dam, boats enter an enormous lock.

Yichang ⓬ (宜昌) is now a large and crowded city, as many people from the surrounding areas who were displaced by the construction of the Three Gorges

Water levels on the Chang Jiang have slowly risen over the years following the completion of the Three Gorges Dam.

BELOW: during the summer rainy season, the river's water turns yellow with silt.

GETTING TO HUBEI

Flights: Wuhan's Tianhe International Airport is one of the busiest in central China, with regular service to most mainland destinations. Internationally, there are daily flights to Hong Kong and weekly connections to Bangkok, Fukuoka, Macau and Seoul.

By train and bus: Wuhan is very well connected by rail, with daily services to Beijing, Guangzhou, Kunming, Lanzhou, Shanghai, Shenzhen and Xi'an. Trains arriving from the north typically stop at Hankou station, while those from the south usually call in at Wuchang station. There are several long-distance bus stations servicing destinations as far afield as Jiujiang, Nanchang, Nanjing and Shanghai.

GETTING AROUND HUBEI

Wuhan: There are daily slow trains to Wudang Shan (7 hours), while buses run regularly throughout the day to Xiangfan (4½ hours), from where you can catch onward buses to Wudang Shan. There are numerous daily buses to Yichang (4 hours).

Yichang: Frequent buses run to Wuhan (4 hours) and north to Xiangfan (3 hours), from where there are regular buses to Wudang Shan. There are also daily trains to Xiangfan (4 hours) and Wudang Shan (6 hours). It's possible to get to Shennongjia by a series of public buses, but it's faster and more cost-efficient to book a seat on one of the daily Chinese-language tour buses run by CITS

Shennongjia: For foreigners, the only legal route is from the south, making Yichang the main transit point *(see above).*

Wudang Shan: There are trains to Wuhan (7 hours) as well as daily connections to Yichang (6 hours) via Xiangfan (2 hours). Buses run daily to Wuhan (6½ hours) via Xiangfan (2 hours).

Dam have relocated here. A fast highway now connects it with Wuhan, and few cruise boats and passenger ferries continue downstream from here. Yichang is also an excellent staging point for trips further into **Hubei** (湖北) province, such as the Shennongjia Forest Reserve and Wudang Shan.

Downstream from Yichang

If you are continuing downriver from Yichang, you are likely to stop at **Shashi** ⑬ (沙市), 220km (140 miles) west of Wuhan. The ancient town of Jingzhou has an impressive Ming-dynasty city wall and a **museum** (Tue–Sun 8am–4pm; charge) where the fully preserved 2,000-year-old corpse of a Western Han-dynasty official can be seen.

The last stop downriver before Wuhan is the town of **Yueyang** ⑭ (岳阳) in Hunan province *(for other sights in Hunan see pages 320–3),* situated at the point where the Chang Jiang meets Dongting Hu lake. The lakeside waterfront is attractive, but the best-known sight is **Yueyang Lou** (岳阳楼; Yueyang Tower; daily 8am–6pm; charge), one of the region's most famous pavilion towers. Numerous songs have been composed about it since the Tang dynasty (618–907), although the restored building dates from the late 19th century. The tower is flanked on both sides by two pavilions, Xianmeiting (Plum Blossom of the Immortal Pavilion) and Sanzuiting (Three Drunks Pavilion).

BELOW: cruising through the Xiao Sanxia (Three Little Gorges).

Recommended Restaurants on page 263

WUHAN

The industrial and commercial city of **Wuhan** ⓯ (武汉), roughly halfway between Chongqing and Shanghai at the confluence of the Chang and Han rivers, is a major entrepôt through which many visitors to central China are likely to pass. A massive metropolis with more than 9 million inhabitants, Wuhan is actually an amalgam of three formerly distinct settlements: Wuchang, Hankou and Hanyang, all now municipalities in their own right, each spilling out from the banks of the rivers that divide them. Taking advantage of their privileged positions along the Chang Jiang as well as major rail and road networks, the cities together comprise one of the country's most important economic centres. Wuhan is also historically significant, perhaps most noteworthy for being the linchpin of the 1911 revolution that eventually brought down China's last imperial dynasty.

Colonial reminders

Of the three modern districts, **Hankou** Ⓐ (汉口) – on the Chang Jiang's northwest bank and north of the Han Jiang – is the most convenient for tourists, with efficient transport, abundant accommodation and a good variety of eating and nightlife options. It also has the greatest concentration of visible history, with an entire quarter of well-preserved colonial European architecture emanating from the waterfront – grandiose remnants of its role as a treaty port in the latter half of the nineteenth century. Though the former colonial sector encompasses several streets stemming northwest from the erstwhile Bund, or waterfront promenade (now named Yanjiang Dadao), the most complete segment is along the pedestrian-only **Jianghan Lu** (江汉路), now an immensely popular thoroughfare lined with a variety of trendy shops occupying the ground floors of giant European-style stone buildings.

Wuchang

Wuchang (武昌), on the Chang Jiang's southeast side and accessible via the Great Chang Jiang Bridge or regular public fer-

ries from Hankou, was an ancient port and administrative centre and, as such, has several historic sights. Most prominent of these is the 50-metre (164ft) **Huanghe Lou** Ⓑ (黄鹤楼; Yellow Crane Tower; daily Apr–Oct 7am–6.30pm, Nov–Mar 7.30am–5.30pm; charge), the grandest of the many towers along the Chang Jiang. Overlooking the city from atop **She Shan** Ⓒ (蛇山; Snake Hill), the tower – which can be climbed via internal staircases to the top floor – commands sweeping views of the river and its urban environs. The original tower was first built in AD 223, but after it burnt to the ground in 1884 a new one was constructed on a larger scale a few hundred metres away. Much of Snake Hill is covered with recently built classical-style Chinese buildings, including the shopfronts selling souvenirs along Ming Qing Jie, just inside the entrance to the complex.

Just east of here is the captivating **Changchun Guan** Ⓓ (长春观; Changchun Temple; daily 7.30am–5pm; charge), a multi-faceted Daoist temple compound with an annexed vegetarian restaurant that serves delicious mock meats and vegetable dishes. The temple's

Daoist ceremony at Wuhan's Changchun Guan Temple.

BELOW: kite-flying on the river bank at Yichang.

A vendor selling bamboo cages for keeping crickets. The tradition of cricket fighting, and associated gambling on the outcome, goes back at least as far as the Song dynasty. There are regular cricket-fighting events all over China; punters study the insect's form (fighting records are kept) and other attributes to make a qualified bet.

many halls are usually filled with incense-wagging worshippers, and resident Daoist monks regularly perform elaborate rituals, while others practise martial arts in the attached training area.

A further 1km (⅔ mile) to the southeast is the **Hong Ge ⓔ** (红阁; Red Chamber; daily 8.30am–5.30pm; charge), a colonial-style red-brick building which served as the headquarters of the Hubei Military Government leading up to the 1911 Wuchang Uprising. The structure now houses a museum showcasing the rooms filled with period furnishings and maps, as well as the military government's conference hall, dominated by a giant portrait of Sun Yatsen behind the stage. A bronze statue of the leader stands just outside the entrance.

Hubei Provincial Museum and Guiyuan Si

On Wuchang's far eastern fringe is **Dong Hu ⓕ** (东湖; East Lake), an expansive watery network situated within a huge park which makes for a pleasant retreat from Wuhan's suffocating summer heat. Nearby to the north is the **Hubei Provincial Museum ⓖ** (湖北省博物馆; Hubei

Sheng Bowuguan; Tue–Sun 9am–5pm; free), dedicated primarily to antiquities excavated from the tomb of Marquis Yi, who died in 433 BC during the Warring States Period. The exhibition is impressive and informative, with an extensive collection of well-preserved funerary objects displayed in an intuitive fashion and bolstered by English-language multimedia presentations. One of the highlights is a complete set of 64 bronze bells unearthed from the tomb, each of them still possessing perfect pitch and tone. Though the ancient bells themselves have only been played twice, concerts are regularly held in the museum auditorium using a duplicate set.

In Wuhan's third district, **Hanyang** (汉阳), on the Chang Jiang's northwest bank and south of the Han River, is the **Guiyuan Si ⓗ** (归元寺; Guiyuan Temple; daily Apr–Oct 7.30am–5.30pm, Nov–Mar 8am–5pm; charge), the city's biggest Buddhist monastery and a magnet for worshippers and tourists alike. To Chinese Buddhists, the monastery is renowned for preserving a complete, 7,000-volume set of ancient scriptures in its Sutra Collection Pavilion, which con-

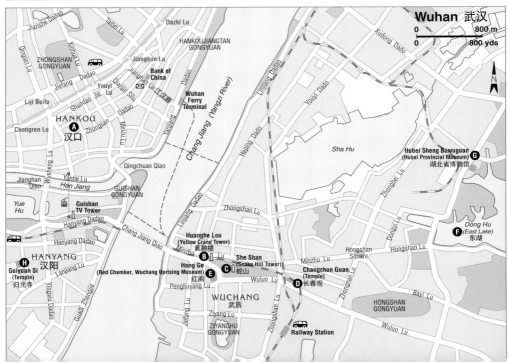

Recommended Restaurants on page 263

tains a graceful statue of the Sakyamuni Buddha carved in a Southeast Asian style from a single piece of Burmese white jade. More visually striking is the Hall of Arhats, built in 1850 and holding an intriguing collection of 500 life-sized clay sculptures of *arhats*, or pupils of Buddha, each with his own persona and in a different pose.

AWAY FROM THE RIVER

Further inland, Hubei province has some spectacular scenery, the most rugged of which lies within the **Shennongjia Forest Reserve** ⑯ (神农架林区; Shennongjia Linqu; daily 9am–4.30pm; charge), in the far northwest of the province about 200km (125 miles) from Yichang. The wild, mountainous preserve – the highest peak reaches 3,053 metres (10,016ft) – has for centuries been reputed for its rich diversity of flora, and is named after the mythical Xia emperor Shennong, who according to legend combed its mountains in search of medicinal plants. In the 20th century, the area has become known for alleged sightings of the Chinese "wild man" (*ye ren*), a giant, red-haired ape-like creature akin to

the yeti or bigfoot. Though visitors are unlikely to run across the Ye Ren, those making their way to **Xiaolong Tan** (小龙潭) – in the heart of the reserve – may be fortunate enough to spot a family of endangered golden monkeys.

The reserve is accessed via **Muyu Zhen** (木鱼镇), a small tourist village about 16km (10 miles) south of the entrance with several hotels and restaurants. It is possible to reach Muyu Zhen by public bus from Yichang, but a more convenient option would be to book a two- or three-day, all-inclusive tour with CITS in Yichang. Note that many parts of the reserve, including Shennongjia town, are considered off-limits to foreigners.

Hubei's far northwest: Wudang Shan

Tucked away in Hubei's far northwest are the multiple peaks of **Wudang Shan** ⑰ (武当山; Military Mountain; daily; charge), a misty, mountainous area of major importance to Daoists and martial artists alike. The tree-shaded mountainsides have for centuries been cloaked in Daoist temples, many of which have recently been restored amid a revival in

The Shennong Emperor Shrine at Shennongjia, dedicated to the mythical Xia-dynasty emperor (c.3000 BC). Also known as the Yan Emperor, he is credited with inventing agriculture in China as well as cataloguing hundreds of medicinal herbs.

BELOW: view of Wuhan from Huanghe Lou.

Map on page 252

TIP

Reaching Huang Shan is easy. Buses trundle to Tangkou at the foot of the mountain from Hefei, Nanjing, Shanghai and Hangzhou, while trains stop at Tunxi, 70km (43 miles) southeast, from where buses depart to the mountain. There are numerous hotels in Tangkou, or you can stay in lodgings on the trail to the peak and the summit itself. Pack warm clothing and a waterproof for the ascent, along with water and food.

BELOW: above the clouds on Huang Shan.

the area's popularity. But Wudang Shan is best known as the birthplace of a fighting style known as Wudang boxing, developed in these mountains by revered Song-dynasty monk Zhang Sanfeng and considered the essential precursor to *taiji*. As such, it is respected among martial artists as much as Henan province's more famous Shaolin Si, and fighters from all over the world come here to pay their respects to Zhang. For the average visitor, however, the main attraction is the chance to climb Tianzhu Peak, at 1,612 metres (5,249ft) the area's highest. The path to the top passes by numerous temples and shrines, but the most atmospheric are those inside the citadel at the top – especially the **Jindian Gong** (金殿宫; Golden Palace Temple; daily 9am–5pm; charge), which adorns the highest point and yields arresting views of the clouds sweeping through the pointed peaks below.

ANHUI

Anhui (安徽) province may be one of eastern China's poorest, but it lays claim to one of its foremost destinations and scenic wonders. It is to **Huang Shan** ⓲ (黄山; Yellow Mountain) – the mist-wreathed mountain immortalised in countless Chinese paintings – that travellers to Anhui naturally gravitate. Rising up south of the Chang Jiang, it may not be one of China's most sacred mountains, but merits a mandatory stop for its breathtaking mountain scenery. Along with Tai Shan in Shandong province, this is a mountain that all Chinese aspire to climb. It's a tough climb to the summit and the constant mob of tourists is trying, but in favourable weather the views can be mesmerising, with twisted pines, blooms of mist and sunlight-dappled bamboo.

Legions of travellers congregate on the summit area to witness the famed Huang Shan sunrise. The hiking trail up the mountain is divided into the eastern steps and the western steps. The eastern route (7.5km/4½ miles) is shorter than the 15km (9-mile) western route, but the only soft option is the cable car (or porter). A popular strategy is to ascend by the eastern steps and then descend by the western steps. But this is a mammoth undertaking and heavy on the joints. Many Chinese tourists alleviate the pain of the ascent and descent by availing themselves of one of the three cable cars that now ascend the flanks of the mountain.

The region around **Yixian** ⓳ (黟县), 60km (38 miles) northwest of Tunxi, is very attractive with small hamlets that are bastions of traditional Chinese architecture. The three villages of Xidi, Hongcun and Nanping (the latter was the setting for Zhang Yimou's classic film *Judou*) can be reached by taxi from Yixian town.

For those who find climbing Huang Shan a ridge too far, sacred **Jiuhua Shan** ⓴ (九华山; 1,342 metres/4,403ft) makes for a less exhausting ascent. The temple-covered mountain, around 50km (30 miles) northwest of Huang Shan, is one of China's four sacred Buddhist peaks. Jiuhua Shan may not be quite as scenic as Huang Shan, but makes up for this by being far less crowded. Hotels and restaurants can be found in the village of Jiuhuashan on the mountain and a cable-car is at hand for those whose stamina has deserted them. ❑

RESTAURANTS

Restaurants

Prices for a meal for one, with one drink:
$ = under Rmb 50
$$ = Rmb 50–100
$$$ = Rmb 100–150
$$$$ = over Rmb 150

Hubei's location in China's heartland alongside the country's busiest waterway is reflected in its varied cuisine – which hints at influences from southern and coastal provinces as well as the fiery fare of neighbouring Hunan and Sichuan. Time-honoured techniques of braising and steaming marine life have placed Hubei high on the list of China's most distinctive cuisines. Fish and other river life – such as eel and turtles – are primary components of the provincial diet, while the mountains in the north yield a huge variety of wild vegetables and herbs that routinely find their way into soups and steamed dishes. Sichuanese influences increase further west.

Chongqing

Chongqing – once part of Sichuan province – is well known for its fiery hot pot (huoguo). There are clusters of restaurants around Nanbin Lu on the south bank of the Chang Jiang (take the cable car) and in the downtown area around the Liberation Monument (especially Bayi Lu and Minzu Lu).

De Zhuang Hot Pot
德庄火锅
Qi Xing Gang. **$**

Allegedly Chongqing's first ever hot-pot restaurant – the city's most famous cuisine – many locals still consider it the title holder over innumerable competitors around town, many of which are also extremely good.

Little Swan Hot Pot
小天鹅
Liberation Monument (close to Luohan Si). **$$**
Little Swan is particularly popular with Chonqing's foreign residents, and is more accommodating to non-Chinese-speakers than most other hot-pot restaurants around town.

Tao Ran Ju 陶然居
15 Nanbin Lu,
Nan'an District. **$$**
Tao Ran Ju is probably the most popular restaurant in Nanbin Lu's already very popular Cuisine Street – very well worth exploring for other local specialities. Offering upscale, and very spicy unless requested otherwise, Sichuan cuisine in a traditional environment – its popularity can make it a bit noisy at times.

Waipo Qiao Fengwei Lou 外婆桥风喂楼
7/F Metropolitan Plaza, 68 Zourong Lu. **$$–$$$**
With its winning classical Chinese décor, this is an excellent place to sample a range of Chinese dishes, though largely with a Sichuan influence. Some of the more interesting entries on the menu are imperial court dishes from the Qing dynasty.

Wuhan

The city's widest selection of restaurants is in the Hankou District, particularly along Zhongshan Dadao and its many side streets – one of the best is Jiqing Jie, branching to the north. There is also a stretch of night-market stalls on Jianghan Yi Lu, which stems east from the pedestrian-only Jianghan Lu. The riverfront Yanjiang Dadao comes alive in the evenings with patio-seating hot-pot establishments and an interesting sprinkling of Western-style bars and cafés. Across the river in Wuchang District, the Shouyi Garden Snack Street has an eclectic array of snack stands specialising in tasty treats from all over China. There are also several restaurants here serving up spicy Hunan and Sichuan dishes.

Changchun Sucai Guan
长春素菜馆
145 Wulou Lu. **$$**
Part of the Changchun Guan Daoist temple complex, this delightful vegetarian restaurant exhibits a true mastery of making delicious mock-meat dishes from soybean and other vegetable products. The photo menu helps.

Man Qi Lou 满旗楼
136 Yanjiang Dadao. **$$**
This atmospheric riverfront avenue restaurant specialises in hot pot, with an emphasis on seafood. Outdoor patio seating is available when the weather cooperates.

Maojiawan 毛家湾
29 Shouyi Yuan. **$**
Cultural Revolution-era Communist kitsch is the theme here, with youthful waitresses in somber Red Guard attire serving spicy, home-style Hunan dishes that would no doubt meet the approval of the Chairman himself. It is tucked away on the north side of Shouyi Garden Snack Street, with no English sign.

Yuan Ming Yuan
圆明圆
6 Jianghan Lu. **$**
Dumplings of all shapes, sizes and substances are the main draw at this popular eatery, where locals order them by the dozens and chase it all down with the soup of their choice. Open daily 8.30am–2pm and 7.30–10pm.

Yichang

The main concentration of quality restaurants is a short walk from the waterfront promenade, near the intersection of Erma Lu and Fusui Lu, where there are also several bars and cafés.

Fuji Caiguan
福记菜馆
48 Fusui Lu. **$**
A well-located and clean restaurant specialising in authentic Hunan food, with friendly staff.

Wu Yue Wu Caifang
五月五菜坊
5 Erma Lu. **$**
A homey diner offering most Chinese standards, from rice and noodle staples to stir-fries.

CHINA'S SACRED PEAKS

If you want leg-stretching exercise, wonderful scenery, views and temple architecture, reach for the heights of China's sacred peaks

One of the best ways to get a feeling for China's enduring spirituality is to follow in the footsteps of the pilgrims and ascend one of its sacred peaks.

There are a total of nine holy mountains (five Daoist and four Buddhist) scattered across the land. The Daoist peaks include Tai Shan in Shandong province – probably the world's most climbed mountain. Perhaps the most dramatic, however, is Hua Shan in Shaanxi province, with its hair-raising ascents. The other Daoist peaks are Song Shan in Henan province, which attracts huge crowds, largely because the Shaolin Temple lies on its slopes, Heng Shan *(beiyue)* in Shanxi province and Heng Shan *(nanyue)* in Hunan province further south.

China's Buddhist peaks largely began as Daoist preserves, before becoming associated with the followers of Buddha *(fo)*. Perhaps the best known, Emei Shan in Sichuan province, inspires devotion in its legions of pilgrims. Putuo Shan, on a small island off the east coast, is also a major pilgrimage destination. Buddhist Jiuhua Shan in Anhui province may be overshadowed by nearby Huang Shan, China's most famous (non-sacred) mountain, but that makes it far less touristy. Noted for its dramatic scenery and fine temple architecture, Wutai Shan in Shanxi province is governed by Wenshu (Manjusri), the god of wisdom.

Climbing China's sacred mountains is considered a rite of worship, but you won't need crampons or ice axes as stone steps and guardrails line the route.

LEFT: a heavy load: building materials on China's sacred mountains have to be hauled up their steep slopes by hand.

ABOVE: Zhurong Daoist Temple on the icy 1,290-metre (4,232-ft) summit of Heng Shan, Hunan province.

RIGHT: a Daoist procession slowly makes its way up Wudang Shan (Hubei province), one of the lesser Daoist mountains. Zhang Sanfeng, the founder of tai chi, spent nine years here and it is a place of pilgrimage for Daoists and martial arts enthusiasts.

MOUNTAINS OF MYSTERY

To primitive man, the mountains were secret places, sources of cosmic energy inhabited by gods and spirits. Poets such as Qu Yuan celebrated the twilight world of witches and beings that populated the slopes of China's mountainous realm. These were places rife with superstition, magic and the unknown. Animists worshipped mountains such as Tai Shan even before the Daoists claimed it as their own.

The mountain is represented in the *Yijing (I-Ching; Book of Changes)* by the trigram *ken*, meaning Keeping Still. It is a place where life and death meet, a place of stillness, meditation and internal awareness.

China's Confucian tradition, dealing as it did with the world of man, temporal ritual and human relations, had no place here – hence the absence of sacred Confucian mountains.

Sacred they may be, but these peaceful peaks have become hostage to the tourist economy. Cable cars whisk those with little time or desire for contemplation up to the summit for a quick look at the view, and litter and noise can be a problem.

TOP: the steep paths up the slopes of Hua Shan are bedecked with red ribbons and engraved padlocks. Young couples attach the padlock to the guardrail and then throw the key into the mists below to ensure a long and happy marriage.

ABOVE: an image of the bodhisattva Dizang, saviour of damned souls and ruling deity on the Buddhist mountain of Jiuhua Shan. Jin Qiaojue, a Korean monk who died here in the 8th century, was said to have been a reincarnation of Dizang.

RIGHT: the gravity-defying Xuankong Si on Heng Shan contains 40 halls, fashioned from caves in the rock and covered with wooden facades supported on poles.

BELOW: China's sacred mountains have huge conservation as well as spiritual value: they are covered in dense forests which support a range of wildlife. Various species of monkey – including the rare golden monkey *(jinsi hou)* – can occasionally be seen on some of the central peaks, such as Wudang Shan.

THE SOUTH

Historically the most innovative and entrepreneurial
region of the country, the southern provinces are
at the heart of the Chinese economic boom

It was in the south of China, particularly along parts of the
southern coast, where Deng Xiaoping's economic modernisation programme germinated, took root and prospered. Over
two decades on, and the main focus of this innovation – the Pearl
River Delta around the city of Shenzhen – is well established as
the country's most prosperous neighbourhood, although Shanghai and its hinterland are catching up fast.

The idea of commerce is hardly an extraordinary notion in
southern China. Guangzhou, China's third-largest city, was
already an international port in the 9th century, and by the 1500s, when the
Portuguese arrived in a showy flotilla, the area had replaced the Silk Road as
the trade route of choice into China. Southeast China's other port of note
lacks the historical depth of Guangzhou, but has long had a remarkable
entrepreneurial zeal. As a British colony, Hong Kong became the definitive
capitalist free-market, no-holds-barred trading centre. Having weathered a
serious economic crisis following its return to China in 1997, it remains a fascinating and unique travel destination.

Off the coast of western Guangdong is the large island of Hainan, with
China's southernmost beaches – fringed by palms and bathed in year-round
warmth – now being aggressively marketed to tourists. Further east along the

coast, thriving Fujian province has, more than anywhere
else in China, looked out across the sea to make a living;
together with Guangdong, this is the major source of the
Chinese diaspora. The old European enclave of Amoy, now
called Xiamen, is one of China's most engaging cities, with
its enchanting island of Gulangyu decked out in colonial
era architecture and laced with lazy walks.

Inland are the provinces of Hunan and Jiangxi running north
to the Chang Jiang (Yangzi River), off most tourist itineraries
but encompassing some fabulous scenery (Wulingyuan, Heng
Shan and Lu Shan to name but three examples) and a scattering of charming old towns – none more so than Fenghuang,
photogenically perched on the banks of the Tuo River. ❑

PRECEDING PAGES: Fenghuang, Hunan province. **LEFT:** the coast east of Shenzhen.
TOP: Wulingyuan, Hunan. **ABOVE LEFT:** Fujian roundhouse. **ABOVE RIGHT:** Guangzhou.

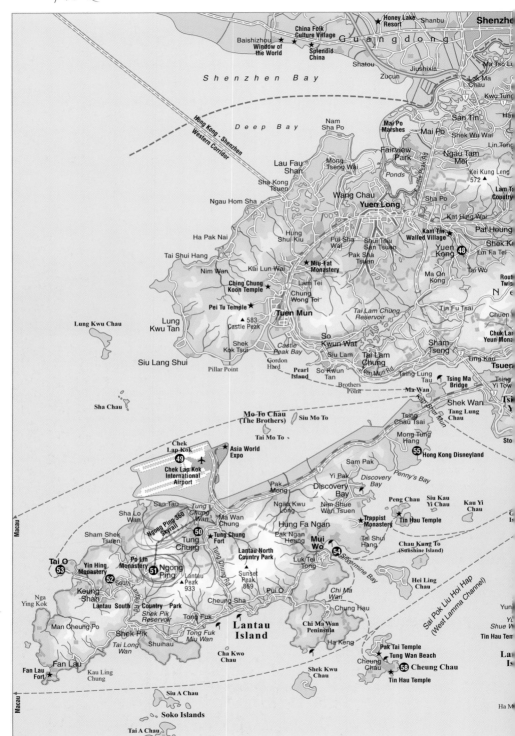

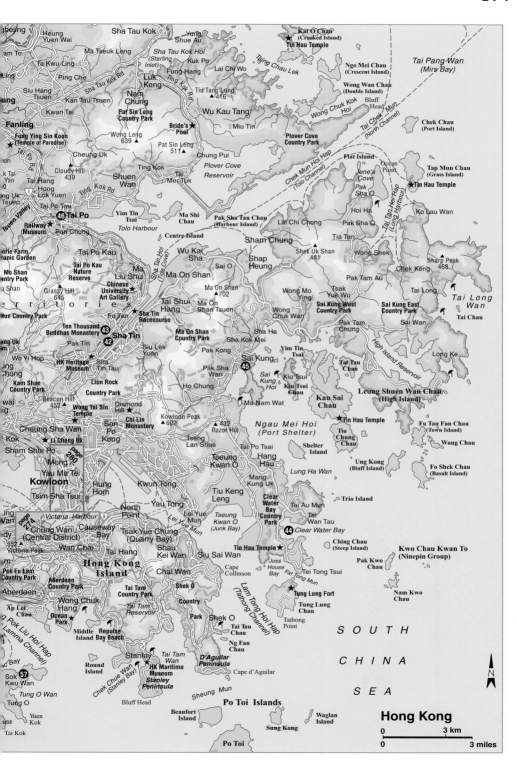

Hong Kong

0   3 km

0   3 miles

SOUTH CHINA SEA

HONG KONG

Taken from China during the Qing dynasty, Hong Kong – having returned to Chinese sovereignty – is as colourful, vibrant and appealing as ever

T he entry point into China for many tourists, Hong Kong makes a memorable introduction to the Chinese world. Glamorous, hectic, exciting and spectacular, with fabulous food, nightlife and shopping, this is a place like no other.

Archaeological evidence shows this part of the southern Chinese coast has been inhabited since the Stone Age. Han Chinese people began settling here in the Song dynasty (960–1279), but it remained a relatively obscure corner of Guangdong province until British opium merchants recognised the advantages of "annexing" 45 sq km (17 sq miles) of the best deep-water harbour in the region. Despite Lord Palmerston's famously contemptuous valuation – "a barren island with hardly a house upon it" – the colony quickly became a vital trading link between Europe and China, and by the time the British were compelled to hand it back to the motherland it had grown into one of the richest cities in the world.

Orientation

Since the return to China on 1 July 1997, Hong Kong has been a Special Administrative Region (SAR) with its own laws and administration. It can be divided into four parts: Hong Kong Island, Kowloon, the New Territories and the numerous outlying islands.

Hong Kong Island, its skyscrapers set against a spectacular mountain backdrop, is dominated by grand financial institutions, enormous, impressively futuristic buildings. It is also home to some of the SAR's oldest Chinese communities, beautiful walks and, on the southern side, some good beaches.

Across Victoria Harbour – just three minutes by the Mass Transit Railway, eight minutes by the venerable Star Ferry and less than 10 minutes by car through the three tunnels – the Kowloon Peninsula was ceded to the British in 1860, for better defence of the harbour. Most tourists see only its southern tip – the Tsim Sha Tsui District and its many hotels, bars and shopping centres. To the north past the Yau Ma Tei and Mong Kok

Main attractions
THE STAR FERRY AND HARBOUR VIEWS
CENTRAL DISTRICT
THE PEAK
TSIM SHA TSUI
SAI KUNG COUNTRY PARK
DISNEYLAND AND OCEAN PARK
SHOPPING AND MARKETS

LEFT: Central District's Legco Building dwarfed by tower blocks. **BELOW:** tai chi by Kowloon's Clock Tower.

The iconic green-and-white Star Ferry is old-fashioned, functional and reliable. A trip across the harbour between Central and Tsim Sha Tsui gives wonderful views of the famous skyline. Fares are very low – splash out an extra 50 cents to travel on the "de luxe" upper deck. The crossing takes seven or eight minutes (6.30am–11.30pm).

districts, Boundary Street marks the demarcation line between the old colony, granted to the British "in perpetuity", and the New Territories, which were leased in 1898 for a 99-year period. Surprisingly for a place known for its crowded urban areas, large areas of the New Territories, which include over 230 outlying islands, are almost devoid of people, and the empty, hilly countryside makes a pleasant antidote to the frenetic pace of life in the city.

HONG KONG ISLAND: CENTRAL DISTRICT

Central – still occasionally marked on maps as "Victoria", and Chung Wan in Cantonese – is Hong Kong's business and financial hub, at the heart of the incredible cliff face of high-rise buildings that extends along the north shore of Hong Kong Island. Squeezed between the harbour and the precipitous slopes of Victoria Peak, this is where the money is, the financial powerhouses, the glamorous high-end shopping malls, overlooked by the multi-millionaires' mansions on the Peak. And

in the midst of all the glitz, there are still strong elements of former days, with wayside hawkers dangling novelties and knock-offs, incense sticks smouldering by tiny shrines, and delivery boys pedalling serenely through red lights with a cargo of fresh meat balanced in their bike's cast-iron basket. It all adds up to one of the most fascinating areas of modern Hong Kong.

The best place to begin a tour is at the **Star Ferry Pier ❶**. The green-and-white Star Ferries have been shunting passengers across the harbour between Hong Kong Island and Kowloon since 1898, although the terminal relocated in 2006. Just to the west is the gigantic **International Finance Centre Two (IFC-2) ❷**, finished in 2003. Hong Kong's tallest building, it stands at a whopping 420 metres (1,378ft), is capped by a mass of curving spires, and dominates the famous harbour view.

Walkways connect the Star Ferry Pier and IFC to the rest of Central via **Exchange Square ❸**, home of the Hong Kong Stock Exchange and featuring a collection of sculptures by Henry Moore and Ju Ming in the adjacent plaza. Head

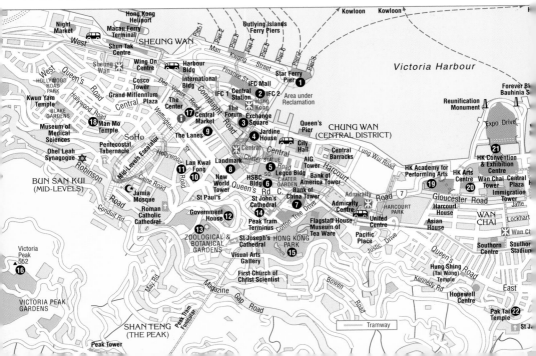

Recommended Restaurants and Bars on pages 288–9

GETTING AROUND HONG KONG

Hong Kong has an excellent public transport system. The **Mass Transit Railway** (MTR) is an extensive subway system linking the north shore of Hong Kong Island with Kowloon, Lantau and the New Territories. **Trams** are extremely useful for travelling along the north shore of Hong Kong Island. **Bus** services are good but less useful for tourists, except for the routes down to the south coast of Hong Kong Island. **Taxis** are cheap and plentiful. The outlying islands are linked to Central by frequent **ferries** *(see margin tip, page 286).* If you are staying more than a day or so, buy a stored-value Octopus card. *For more information see pages 418, 426.*

east along the walkway to **Jardine House** ❹, whose distinctive 1,700-plus round windows have inspired the nickname "House of a Thousand Orifices". Opened in 1973, it was for many years the tallest building in Hong Kong.

Back on street level and inland from the GPO, an underpass will take you to **Statue Square** ❺, on either side of Chater Road. On Sundays, throngs of Filipina maids gather here on their day off in a festive, chaotic outdoor party. The 143,000 Philippine nationals, most of whom work here as maids, now form by far the single largest foreign community living in Hong Kong.

This part of Central is the financial district, home to the headquarters of several major banks. Two of these are housed in iconic buildings: facing Statue Square is Norman Foster's US$1 billion **Hongkong & Shanghai Bank Building (HSBC Building)** ❻, the most expensive structure in the world when it was completed in 1985. Further east the sharp angles of the gleaming 368-metre (1,209ft) **Bank of China Tower** ❼, designed by Chinese-American architect I.M. Pei, point directly at the other banks, which makes for bad (or good, depending which side you're on) feng shui.

The former Supreme Court Building, now the **Legislative Council (Legco) Building**, is a rare survivor of classical architecture in amongst all the steel, glass and concrete.

Most taxi drivers in Hong Kong speak only a little English, but generally enough to understand where you want to go. If not they will radio through to a controller who will translate your request.

BELOW: merchandise for sale on Hollywood Road.

Central, Wan Chai and Causeway Bay

To get the most out of a walking tour of Central, visit on a weekday during working hours, as (Lan Kwai Fong/SoHo apart) this is not one of Hong Kong's after-hours locations – unlike Tsim Sha Tsui and Causeway Bay, many shops close by 7pm. Shops are open on Saturdays, but the energised atmosphere of the working week is lacking. Sundays are quiet, with shops shut, although the weekly Filipina get-together is in full swing.

BELOW: Central and Wan Chai from the Star Ferry.

Des Voeux and Queens roads

Heading inland from the Star Ferry/IFC on the elevated pedestrian walkways you will cross over the main east–west highway, Connaught Road, before reaching **Des Voeux Road**. The tram stop here, at the junction with Pedder Street, is one of Central's most photographed spots, a blur of traffic and people. Across the street, **The Landmark ❽** is a prestigious shopping mall dedicated to luxury brands. Five floors surround a vast atrium, around which walkways connect with neighbouring buildings such as **Chater House** and **Prince's Building**, flaunting a further abundance of marble and relentlessly upmarket shops.

The next east–west road away from the harbour, **Queen's Road Central**, marked the waterfront before land reclamation began in the 1850s. Running between its shops and emporia and those of Des Voeux Road are two narrow alleyways, **Li Yuen Street East** and **Li Yuen Street West** – also known as **The Lanes ❾**, lined with stalls and outlets selling clothing, fabrics and counterfeit designer fashion accessories. The atmosphere is a complete contrast to the smart high-rises on the larger avenues nearby, and bargaining is still expected.

Lan Kwai Fong and beyond

Behind Queen's Road Central the terrain rises steeply. D'Aguilar Street leads up to **Lan Kwai Fong ❿**, which together with neighbouring SoHo is a prime nightlife area. Modern cuisine, bars, clubs, English pubs and tiny snack shops bring in the crowds, and late-night revellers can get everything from pizza to sushi in the wee hours. At weekends many bars stay open until 5am or later.

At the top of Lan Kwai Fong, winding Wyndham Street is becoming an extension of the trendy bar zone, leading on to **Hollywood Road ⓫**, packed with shops selling top-dollar antiques. Beyond is **SoHo** (SOuth of HOllywood), accessed via the handy Central–Mid-Levels Escalator, full of small quirky bars and restaurants, mostly cheaper and less modish than those of Lan Kwai Fong.

Colonial relics

The higher up one gets on the Island, the more desirable the property and the higher the rents – a pattern established

in the early colonial years, when the upper slopes were considered less prone to malarial mosquitoes.

Just above Lan Kwai Fong on Upper Albert Road, the rarefied air is immediately apparent at **Government House** ⑫, grand home of the former colonial leaders of Hong Kong and now the official residence of the Chief Executive. The mansion dates from the 1850s but during World War II was remodelled by the Japanese, who added a tower with a vague Shinto look. There is a clear view of the building through the wrought-iron gates, which are opened to the public only a couple of times a year, usually in spring and autumn (no set dates).

Opposite Government House are the **Zoological and Botanical Gardens** ⑬ (daily 6am–7pm; free), a lush tropical area housing a small assortment of wildlife. It opened in 1864 and still retains elements of its original Victorian gentility, with the added Eastern spirituality of elderly Chinese performing their tai chi exercises each morning. From here it is just a short stroll to the Victorian Gothic **St John's Cathedral** ⑭, consecrated in 1849 and the city's oldest

Anglican church. In nearby **Hong Kong Park** ⑮, **Flagstaff House** is another example of bespoke architecture. It is home to the **Museum of Tea Ware** (Wed–Mon 10am–5pm; tel: 2869 0690; free) and completed in 1846. The building – of more interest than the museum – is reputedly Hong Kong's oldest surviving colonial structure.

The Peak

Make your way along to the **Peak Tram terminus** on Garden Road to ascend Hong Kong's most notable natural landmark, properly though rarely called **Victoria Peak** ⑯ (Shan Teng in Cantonese). "The Peak" is the residential aspiration of most of the population. The upper tram terminus at the **Peak Tower** is shaped like a wok, and is for many people one of the ugliest buildings in Hong Kong. Of course, the main reason for coming up here is to marvel at some of the world's finest vistas. Many find the night-time views even more incredible, a vast glittering swathe of electric light, most spectacular immediately below in Central and Wan Chai as the buildings attempt to outdo each

Until the completion of the Peak road in 1924, the tram was the only public transport up the hill. The vertiginous tram, which runs from 7am to midnight, ascends to 396 metres (1,299ft) above sea level in just seven minutes. In addition to transporting the majority of the Peak's estimated 3 million annual visitors, it is also used by commuters.

Hollywood Road is the place to look for antiques.

BELOW: the view south to Shek O from the Dragon's Back, Hong Kong Island. **BELOW RIGHT:** Aberdeen's floating restaurant.

other in their eye-catching displays. The **viewing platform** has been raised 30 metres (100ft) to the top of the "wok" for a 360-degree panorama. Attractions inside the tower include Hong Kong's own **Madame Tussaud's** waxworks (daily 10am–10pm; charge). The area around the Peak Tower is in fact Victoria Gap, whereas the summit of Victoria Peak itself (552 metres/1,811ft) lies to the west.

Western District

As its name suggests, the area is located just to the west of Central, but, although there has been much recent development here, it is still worlds apart from the ultra-modern financial district, offering instead a glimpse of the more traditionally Chinese Hong Kong. Western is known as a last refuge of the Hong Kong Chinese artisan, unseen by most visitors, where there are mah-jong-makers, herbalists and craftsmen. The area begins at Possession Street and sprawls west to Kennedy Town, but its atmosphere begins to emerge around the purpose-built **Central Market ⓲**, the starting point for the Central–Mid-Levels Escalator. Up the

hill, on the western stretch of Hollywood Road, **Man Mo Temple ⓲** (daily 8am–6pm) is still one of Hong Kong's most atmospheric temples, dimly lit and thick with incense smoke.

Wan Chai and Causeway Bay

To the east of Central, Wan Chai and Causeway Bay are among the territory's most crowded and active districts, revealing the authentic flavour of modern Hong Kong. Despite its reputation, **Wan Chai** has lost much of its former risqué character, although there's still a lively bar and restaurant scene. **Causeway Bay** is one of Hong Kong's premier shopping districts. The tram line (which was on the waterfront when it was built at the beginning of the 20th century) runs right the way through these districts, and provides cheap and convenient transportation.

Close to the Wan Chai waterfront are the **Academy for Performing Arts ⓲** and the **Hong Kong Arts Centre ⓴**, two of the most popular venues for theatrical and cultural performances in Hong Kong. Right on the harbour is the futuristic **Hong Kong Convention and**

Exhibition Centre ㉑, which underwent a HK$4.8 billion extension in order to serve as the venue for the formal handover ceremony in 1997. Elevated walkways lead south from the convention centre to **Lockhart Road**, a lively neighbourhood of bars and restaurants. To the south is a far more "Chinese" part of town, Queen's Road East, which traces Wan Chai's original waterfront. The Hung Shing (Tai Wong) Temple (1860) and the old Wan Chai Post Office (1912) recall an earlier era, while the picturesque **Pak Tai Temple** ㉒ is nearby in Stone Nullah Lane.

Inland is **Happy Valley** ㉓, home of the Hong Kong Jockey Club's Happy Valley Racecourse. During the September–July racing season, it attracts over 50,000 punters on Wednesday race nights. The **Hong Kong Racing Museum** (Tue–Sun 10am–5pm, 10am–12.30pm on race days; charge) is at the Happy Valley Stand, providing a background to Hong Kong's obsession with racing. Opposite are the Colonial and Parsi cemeteries.

Causeway Bay actually was a bay until the 1950s, when it disappeared into a land-reclamation project. The present-day "bay" is occupied by the **Royal Hong Kong Yacht Club** ㉔ on Kellett Island (which also was once a real island before land reclamation), and the Typhoon Shelter.

The south side

In contrast to the intensely built-up northern part of the island, the southern coast is lined with beaches and countryside. **Aberdeen** has a character unlike any other town in Hong Kong, and is famous for its bustling harbour, a natural typhoon shelter crowded with fishing boats, houseboats, pleasure junks and tiny sampans, rounded off by a rather theatrical floating seafood restaurant.

A short bus or taxi ride away is **Ocean Park** (daily 10am–6pm; charge), a fun theme park with a spectacular cable-car ride overlooking the South China Sea, a 3,000-seat marine-mammal theatre, the world's largest reef aquarium and numerous adventure rides.

The beach at **Repulse Bay**, widened to several times its original size, can get extremely crowded at weekends. Nearby

Betting on the horses contributes around 12 percent of Hong Kong's annual tax revenues. As well as Wednesday nights at Happy Valley, there are weekend (daytime) races at Sha Tin in the New Territories which attract even larger crowds.

BELOW LEFT: Nathan Road neon. **BELOW:** Hong Kong has one of the world's highest population densities.

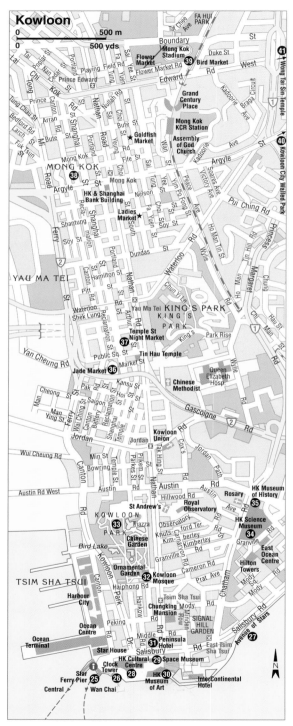

Stanley was the site of the largest indigenous settlement in Hong Kong when the British first set foot here in 1841. The main attraction is **Stanley Market**, which draws thousands in search of the perfect souvenir or clothing bargain. Also in Stanley, on the ground floor of elegant Murray House, the **Maritime Museum** (Tue–Sun 10am–6pm, Sat until 7pm; charge) explores the territory's long relationship with all things marine.

KOWLOON

The Kowloon Peninsula is in many ways very different from the glittering island across the harbour, more down to earth and more Chinese. Yet, somewhat paradoxically, Tsim Sha Tsui – its southern tip – is the location of the majority of Hong Kong's tourist hotels. Nathan Road is host to the quintessential Hong Kong image of gaudy neon signs and hundreds of small electronics shops. Save for the waterfront views, it is not an especially attractive place. But few can deny the electricity that charges life here, especially at night.

Lacking the steep mountainsides that hem in the north shore of Hong Kong Island, Kowloon sprawls. Until Kai Tak Airport closed in the late 1990s, regulations restricted its buildings to a modest height. Now they shoot skywards as never before, a process most obvious above Kowloon station on the West Kowloon Reclamation, where the Union Square development is to include a 484-metre (1,588-ft) skyscraper. This sister building to the IFC tower across the harbour will usurp its sibling as the city's tallest when completed in 2010. The reclaimed area itself is set to become the "West Kowloon Cultural District", with hi-tech arts and cultural venues in place by 2011.

Tsim Sha Tsui

Kowloon Peninsula starts at **Tsim Sha Tsui**. The waterfront promenade from the **Star Ferry Pier 25** to Tsim Sha Tsui East offers spectacular views of the harbour and Hong Kong Island. The **Railway Clock Tower 26**, erected in 1915

Recommended Restaurants and Bars on pages 288–9

next to the ferry terminal, is the final vestige of the historic Kowloon-Canton railway station, the Asian terminus of the old *Orient Express* to London.

From the Star Ferry Pier eastward along the harbour, a **waterfront promenade** provides a great vantage point for viewing the north shore of Hong Kong Island. At 8pm each night the promenade is the place to be for watching the Symphony of Lights, the world's largest sound and light show, which lights up the glittering skyline more than ever. The promenade itself – dubbed the **Avenue of Stars ㉗** – is decorated with tributes to the famous and less so of Hong Kong and Chinese cinema, with Hollywood-style stars set in the pavement.

Next to the Clock Tower, the **Hong Kong Cultural Centre ㉘** is a minimalist structure with an impressive concave roof spoilt by ugly tiles. It caused a great deal of controversy in 1984, as it was designed without windows on the prime harbour site. The Centre stages local and international opera, classical music, theatre and dance. The complex abuts the igloo-like **Hong Kong Space Museum ㉙** (Mon, Wed–Fri 1–9pm, Sat–Sun 10am–

9pm; tel: 2721 0226; charge, but free on Wed), with IMAX movies on space travel and exhibitions of Chinese astronomical inventions. The **Hong Kong Museum of Art ㉚** (Fri–Wed 10am–6pm, closed Thur; tel: 2721 0116; charge, but free on Wed).

Across Salisbury Road is the venerable **Peninsula Hotel ㉛**, built in 1928, where people used to stay before boarding the *Orient Express*.

At the bottom of **Nathan Road** – the start of Hong Kong's famous Golden Mile tourist belt – hundreds of small shops lie tightly crammed together: tailors' shops, jewellers and electronics stores. Less than a kilometre (about ½ mile) north on Nathan Road, in the southeastern corner of Kowloon Park, are the four minarets and large white marble dome of **Kowloon Mosque ㉜**. The pleasant expanse of **Kowloon Park ㉝** lies beyond.

From the mosque, streets lined with discount clothing stores lead eastward to Chatham Road. **Carnarvon** and **Kimberley** roads are both stuffed with clothing and electronics shops, while nearby **Knutsford Terrace** hosts numerous bars

> "*Kowloon was a delightfully peaceful place when I arrived. No lorries, a few small buses... only 12 private cars... Nathan Road was lined on both sides by large trees. Beyond that it continued to Mong Kok through rice fields, not far from the sea.*"
>
> Marjorie Bird Angus

BELOW: crowds of Saturday shoppers in Mong Kok.

TIP

The Chinese are generally relaxed about tourists visiting temples, but it's polite to bear in mind some rules of etiquette regarding photography. There is usually a sign to indicate if taking photographs of the interior is banned, but, nonetheless, it is considered disrespectful to take pictures of people worshipping unless you have their permission.

BELOW:
worshippers at Wong Tai Sin Temple.

and restaurants. On the other side of Chatham Road, **Tsim Sha Tsui East** is home to two of the best museums in Hong Kong. The **Hong Kong Science Museum** ㉞ (Mon–Wed, Fri 1–9pm, Sat–Sun 10am–9pm; tel: 2732 3232; charge, but free on Wed) displays more than 500 scientific and technological interactive exhibits.

Just opposite is the **Hong Kong Museum of History** ㉟ (Mon, Wed–Sat 10am–6pm, Sun and public holidays 10am–7pm; tel: 2724 9042; charge, but free on Wed), charting the 6,000-year story of Hong Kong from Neolithic times right up to the handover.

Yau Ma Tei and Mong Kok

Continue north on Nathan Road, and left onto Kansu Street, to the **Jade Market** ㊱ (daily 9am–6pm), packed with stalls selling ornaments and jewellery. Dealers offer jade in every sculptable form – from large blocks of the raw material to tiny, ornately carved chips. Remember that not everything on offer is genuine.

North from here is **Yau Ma Tei**. Shanghai Street continues north into an area once famous for its temples, but now renowned for the **Temple Street night market** ㊲ that lights up after dusk. Palmists, physiognomists, and a fortune-teller whose trained bird selects slips of paper to predict the future, vie to reveal your destiny. This area has numerous open-air restaurants, where oysters, prawns, clams, lobsters and fish are laid out on beds of ice to tempt diners.

Mong Kok ㊳ is one of the most crowded, noisy and lively districts in the territory. In the early days of British rule, *gweilos* (foreign devils) seldom ventured past Yau Ma Tei, and even today, despite a certain amount of gentrification around the edges, Mong Kok is notorious for Triads, illegal gambling dens and sleaze. It is also known for several colourful street markets: the **Ladies Market** (noon–10.30pm), selling a mixture of clothes and souvenirs, the **Goldfish Market** (10am–6pm), and the factory outlet shops on Fa Yuen Street, offering fashion bargains galore. Further north is Hong Kong's premier **Flower Market** (10am–6pm), at the end of which you will find the Yuen Po Street **Bird Market** ㊴ (7am–8pm), with hundreds of songbirds and beautiful birdcages for sale.

Across Boundary Street

Just to the north of these markets is Boundary Street, the old demarcation between British Hong Kong and the New Territories, leased to Britain for 99 years in 1898. The area between Boundary Street and Lion Rock (the mountain that hems in Kowloon from the north) is known as **New Kowloon**.

Near the eastern end of this thoroughfare, and close to the old airport, is the **Kowloon City Walled Park** ⓭. The infamous Walled City was a small area of the New Territories excluded from British control due to a legal loophole. The area deteriorated into a semi-lawless enclave which was left to its own governance. After World War II, low-rise blocks built without authority and lacking proper foundations sprang up on the site, resulting in a multi-storey squatter area with unauthorised electricity and water supplies. In 1987, with China's consent, 35,000 residents were resettled in housing estates, and the entire block was razed to the ground. The park that replaced it, modelled on the Jiangnan garden style of the early Qing dynasty, has exhibits on the Walled City.

Due north, one of Kowloon's most colourful and popular places of worship, the **Wong Tai Sin Temple** ⓫ (daily 7am–5.30pm; donation expected) on Lung Cheung Road, sits opposite an MTR station bearing the same name. The temple hosts a row of fortune-tellers who can divine your future via the I Ching (Yijing) and other arcane Chinese oracles. East of Wong Tai Sin Temple and near Diamond Hill MTR station is the **Chi Lin Nunnery** (Thur–Tue 9am–4pm; donation expected), a reconstructed Buddhist temple complex.

THE NEW TERRITORIES

The buffer between the urban area of Kowloon and the boundary with Shenzhen and Guangdong province, the New Territories are an odd mixture. Nobody is ploughing with water buffalo any longer, but there are corners where time seems to have not so much stood still as gone into reverse. Conversely, other areas are as

modern as anywhere else in Hong Kong, notably the New Towns such as Sha Tin and Yuen Long. There is scenic beauty aplenty, with calm beaches to seek out and lofty mountains to hike.

Sha Tin ⓬ is one of Hong Kong's fastest-growing New Towns, with massive housing projects occupying what was once an area of rice paddies. The **Ten Thousand Buddhas Monastery** ⓭ (daily 9am–5pm; free) is reached by climbing 431 steps up the hillside above the Sha Tin railway station. There are 12,800 small Buddha statues on the walls of a main altar room, and huge, fierce-looking guardian deities protect the temple. Further up the hill is another series of temples.

In Tai Wai, south of Sha Tin, is the impressive **Hong Kong Heritage Museum** (Mon, Wed–Sat 10am–6pm, Sun 10am–7pm; tel: 2180 8188; charge) displaying a range of cultural exhibits relating to the ex-colony.

East of Sha Tin lies the New Territories' most attractive area. In summer, **Clear Water Bay** ⓮ is dotted with revellers on corporate junks, and the beach is jam-packed with sunbathers. Branching

Bamboo chim *sticks at Wong Tai Sin Temple are used for fortune-telling. People shake the container until a single* chim *falls out. Each has a number that is later interpreted, for a fee, by a fortune-teller at one of the rented stalls.*

BELOW: rural life in the New Territories.

A Disneyland ticket gives a full day in all four themed parks. You can buy tickets online or collect them from HK Disneyland Ticket Express at Hong Kong MTR station.

BELOW: hiking in Sai Kung Country Park.

off Clear Water Bay Road, the highway leads down to **Sai Kung** ㊺, a seaside town known for its Chinese seafood restaurants, and a kicking-off point for exploring the natural beauty of **Sai Kung Country Park**. While the fringes of the town have fallen prey to development, Sai Kung still remains very much a fishing community. The most interesting part of the town is hidden behind the Tin Hau temple, off Yi Chun Street. A maze of narrow alleyways leads past traditional herbalists and noodle shops interspersed with ordinary family homes.

To the north is **Tai Po** ㊻, meaning "buying place". Once a small market community, this is now a booming new town. Two sites worth visiting here are the 19th-century Man Mo Temple and the Hong Kong Railway Museum (Wed–Mon 9am–5pm; charge).

The western side of the Kowloon Peninsula has been reshaped by huge land-reclamation and construction projects that have redrawn the map, most notably for the road and rail links that connect to Hong Kong International Airport on Lantau Island. **Tsuen Wan** ㊼ is another new town, although the Chinese presence

seems to have begun about the 2nd century AD. A historical remnant in the centre of town is the **Sam Tung Uk Museum** (Wed–Mon 9am–5pm; free) a 200-year-old walled Hakka village complete with period furniture. Just northeast of Tsuen Wan, the main hall of the multi-faith **Yuen Yuen Institute** is modelled on the Temple of Heaven (Tiantan) in Beijing.

In **Tuen Mun**, east of 583-metre (1,900ft) **Castle Peak** and adjacent to the Ching Chung light-rail station, is the huge **Ching Chung Koon** temple, which serves as a repository for many Chinese art treasures, including 200 year-old lanterns and a jade seal over 1,000 years old. The library, which holds 4,000 books, documents Daoist history.

Just outside **Yuen Long** ㊽ are the walled villages of **Kam Tin**. The most popular for visitors is the Kat Hing Wai village, which stands rather incongruously across the road from a supermarket. There are 400 people living here, all with the same surname: Tang. Built in the 1600s, it is a fortified village with walls 6 metres (20ft) thick, guardhouses on its four corners, slits for the arrows used in fighting off attackers, and a moat. The authenticity of the village may seem spoilt by some of the commercialism; inside, one street is lined with vendors' outlets.

THE OUTLYING ISLANDS: LANTAU

Hong Kong's international airport opened in 1998 off Lantau's northern coast on a tiny island called **Chek Lap Kok** ㊾, with reclaimed land connecting it to Lantau. While this part of the island has undergone considerable development, together with the northeast (Disneyland) much of Lantau – with twice the area of Hong Kong Island – has escaped the worst excesses of development for now, and most of the island remains rural.

On the northern side of Lantau, pay a visit to **Tung Chung** ㊿, an old fortress near a bay that curves around the pointed southern tip of little Chek Lap Kok island. On a hill overlooking this harbour is the old fort, constructed in 1817. Its thick ramparts are still standing, as are

Recommended Restaurants and Bars on pages 288–9

six old cannons dating from the 19th century which guarded the town and bay from smugglers and pirates.

Up on the mountainous central spine is the island's best-known attraction, the brightly painted red, orange and gold **Po Lin Monastery** ⑤ (daily 6am–6pm; free), where the world's largest outdoor bronze statue of Buddha (24 metres/79ft high) was consecrated in 1993. The huge statue is a popular tourist attraction, but also a major site of pilgrimage for Buddhists. The monastery also has a large and popular vegetarian restaurant. A cable car, **Ngong Ping 360** (Mon–Fri 10am–6pm, Sat 10am–6.30pm, Sun 9am–6.30pm; charge), links Tung Chung with the monastery, offering stunning panoramic views. West of Po Lin, in the direction of Tung Chung on Lantau's north coast, is an excellent walking path that traverses mountain ridges and small canyons en route to Lantau's **Yin Hing Monastery** ⑤, a haven rich with traditional Buddhist paintings and statues.

Offshore from Lantau's principal town, **Tai O** ⑤, on the west coast, the island's Tanka "boat people" have built rickety homes on stilts over parts of a creek, where waters rise during tide changes. Efforts to entice them into new government-built flats have proved largely unsuccessful.

Lantau is also popular for its many long, smooth and often empty beaches. The finest are on the southeast coastline that arcs from Cheung Sha south of Silvermine Bay to Tong Fuk. The most popular and crowded beach (easiest to reach, but with poor-quality water) is **Silvermine Bay Beach** ⑤. Take a ferry to Mui Wo, where you can catch buses and taxis to South Lantau Road. Keen hikers can cover most of Lantau's sights on the 70km (43-mile) **Lantau Trail**, a wild trail across the island that begins and terminates at Mui Wo.

Hong Kong Disneyland

After years of wrangling over costs and various delays, **Hong Kong Disneyland** ⑤ (daily 10am–7, 8 or 9pm; charge includes all rides) opened in 2005 in Lantau's northeastern corner. Partly owned by the government, the theme park has proved a major draw for visitors from mainland China, although visitor numbers have not been sustained. To get there, take the MTR Tung Chung line from Hong Kong Island or Kowloon to Sunny Bay

One way to reach the central Lantau heights is by taking the Ngong Ping 360 Skyrail cable car from Tung Chung (a short walk from the MTR station). Once at the top, stroll through Ngong Ping's gardens to the Big Buddha.

BELOW LEFT: the Big Buddha at Po Lin.
BELOW: resident monk.

TIP

Ferries run from the Outlying Districts ferry piers in Central to Silvermine Bay (Mui Wo) on **Lantau** approximately every 30–50 minutes throughout the day on weekdays, and every 40–60 minutes at weekends. To **Cheung Chau** departures are every 30 minutes daily. **Lamma** ferries are run by Hong Kong and Kowloon Ferry Ltd (HKKF) – services run at 20–60-minute intervals to Yung Shue Wan, less often to Sok Kwu Wan.

BELOW: Hung Shing Ye beach, Lamma.

station, then cross the platform for the three-minute ride to the Victorian-themed Disneyland Resort station. The trains are brightly coloured with Mickey Mouse-shaped windows.

The 126-hectare (310-acre) theme park features four themed "lands" similar (but smaller) to those at other Disneyland parks, and has been built with an emphasis designed to make it more relevant to Asians. **Main Street USA** is an evocation of 19th-century small-town America, and City Hall is the central information centre where you can exchange currency, make dining reservations and pick up guide maps; you can jump aboard a log-raft and drop anchor at Tarzan Island in **Adventureland**, cross the moat to Sleeping Beauty's castle in **Fantasyland** and rocket to stratospheric heights on Space Mountain in **Tomorrowland**. There are also daily parades and nightly fireworks.

Two new hotels have opened up in the complex, **Hong Kong Disneyland Hotel**, a luxury Victorian-style hotel set on the shore of Penny's Bay, and **Disney's Hollywood Hotel**, Art Deco-styled, which has all the movie glitz of a bygone age of Hollywood. Both hotels have been built in

keeping with the principles of feng shui. There is no fourth floor in the 400-room Disneyland Hotel (the number four is pronounced like the word 'death' in Cantonese and considered unlucky). In the Chinese restaurant a real waterfall with projections of goldfish swimming upstream represents wealth and prosperity.

Lamma

The third-largest of the outlying islands, and less well known both to visitors and to locals, is **Lamma**, associated with some of the earliest settlements in Hong Kong. Although just over 13 sq km (5 sq miles) in size and home to a prominent power station, Lamma is rich in grassy hills and beautiful bays and is renowned for its seafood restaurants. There are no high-rise buildings and no roads. The town of **Yung Shue Wan** 56, at the north end of Lamma, is one of two ferry gateways to the island (Sok Kwu Wan is the other). The village, popular with expatriates and Chinese keen to get away from the crowds of the city, has streets lined with small restaurants and bars. Yung Shue Wan's Tin Hau Temple is dedicated to the Queen of Heaven and the Goddess

of the Sea. The 100-year-old temple is guarded by a pair of stone lions. Inside, behind a red spirit stand (to deflect evil spirits) is the main shrine with images of the beaded, veiled Tin Hau.

A well-maintained concrete pathway runs much of the length of the island to Yung Shue Wan's sister village of **Sok Kwu Wan** ⑰, about an hour to an hour and a half away. Heading south, the path passes the haphazard housing of the village outskirts, fields and trees until it reaches **Hung Shing Ye**, a pleasant beach. The route then leads steeply up and down across hills and valleys, treating hikers to sweeping views out across the sea and back to the apartment buildings of Aberdeen and the south side of Hong Kong Island. Sok Kwu Wan is famous for its seafood restaurants – most visitors stop here for a meal before catching the ferry back to Central.

Cheung Chau

Cheung Chau ⑱ island is much smaller than Lamma, and is urbanised in a charming "Old China" way. This dumbbell-shaped isle, with hills at either end and a village nestled in the middle, is so narrow at its narrowest point that you can walk from Cheung Chau Harbour on its west side to Tung Wan Harbour on the east in just a few minutes. Cheung Chau is a fishing island, its curving harbour filled with boats of all sizes, shapes and colours, including Chinese junks and sampans. They compete for space with the ubiquitous *kaido*, the small boats used as motorised water taxis. The colourful **Pak Tai Temple**, around 300 metres/yds north of the pier, is the island's most interesting shrine.

Cheung Chau is famous for its four-day **Bun Festival**, which usually takes place in May and is one of Hong Kong's most colourful events. It originated many years ago after the discovery of a nest of skeletons, believed to be the remains of people killed by pirates. The island was subsequently plagued by a series of misfortunes; to placate the restless spirits of the victims, offerings were made once a year. During the festival, giant bamboo towers covered with edible buns are erected in the courtyard of Pak Tai Temple, while colourfully clad "floating children" are hoisted up on stilts and paraded through the crowds. ❏

The Cheung Chau Bun Festival originated when offerings – including buns – were made to the restless spirits of people killed by marauding pirates.

BELOW: the Pak Tai Temple on Cheung Chau.

RESTAURANTS AND BARS

Prices for a three-course dinner per person with one beer or glass of house wine:
$ = under HK$150
$$ = HK$150–300
$$$ = HK$300–500
$$$$ = over HK$500

Hong Kong Island's main eating-out and nightlife areas are around Lan Kwai Fong and SoHo in Central, around Lockhart Road in Wan Chai, and also – in less concentrated form – in Causeway Bay. Over in Tsim Sha Tsui (Kowloon), most of the action is focused on the cluster of streets south of Kowloon Park, and also around Mody Road a little further to the east. There is a lively strip of bars and restaurants on Knutsford Terrace.

Hong Kong Island
Cantonese
Dynasty
3/F Renaissance Harbour View Hotel, 1 Harbour Rd, Wan Chai.
Tel: 2802 8888.
Open: L & D daily. $$$
Dynasty's palatial dining hall, with its tasteful décor and selected antiques, is the setting for a truly exceptional dining experience. The kitchen excels in all areas. Look for seasonal delicacies like snake soup.

Luk Yu Teahouse
24–26 Stanley St, Central.
Tel: 2523 1970.
Open: L & D daily. $$
This traditional

Cantonese teahouse in the heart of Central is legendary for its bad-mannered management. Despite that, chauffeurs tend the lined-up Mercs outside while tycoons and criminal kingpins in dark glasses take their yum cha. Tourists take second place, but the food is excellent.

Mak's Noodles
77 Wellington St, Central.
Tel: 2854 3810
Open L & D (closes 8pm) daily. $
If wonton noodle soup is Hong Kong's national dish, this is the place to sample it. Pale-pink, prawn-filled pillows of pastry float on a nest of noodles in a beef tendon broth tinged with fermented shrimp paste. Better by far than its imitative neighbours.

Victoria City
2/F Sun Hung Kai Centre, 30 Harbour Rd, Wan Chai.
Tel: 2827 9938.
Open: D daily. $$
Victoria City is seafood heaven for local Cantonese. One of the best for daily dim sum.

Yung Kee
32–40 Wellington St, Central.
Tel: 2522 1624.
Open: L & D daily. $$
A true Hong Kong institution, the Yung Kee has a rags-to-riches history spanning seven decades. Justly famous for its roast goose and the obligatory 1,000-year-old eggs. Also a great place for dim sum.

Other Chinese
Chuen Cheung Kui
108–120 Percival St, Causeway Bay.
Tel: 2577 3833.
Open: L & D daily. $$
Long-standing Hakka cuisine specialists famous for chicken cooked in salt and served with a pungent garlic and scallion sauce. The main restaurant is on the first floor.

Red Pepper
G/F 7 Lan Fong Rd, Causeway Bay.
Tel: 2577 3811.
Open: L & D daily. $$$
Long-established Sichuanese restaurant serving up authentically fiery dishes.

Yellow Door
6/F 37 Cochrane St, Central.
Tel: 2858 6555.
Open: L & D Mon–Fri, D only Sat. $$
Owned by one of Hong Kong's best-known artists – obvious from the simple but inventive interior. High-quality Sichuanese and Shanghainese menus are served at lunch and dinner respectively.

French
Le Tire-Bouchon
45a Graham St, Central.
Tel: 2526 5965.
Open: L & D Mon–Sat. $$$
This long-standing French restaurant has the feel of a subterranean wine cellar. A traditional menu offers rich, tasty and satisfying food and vintages from a comprehensive cellar.

Indian
Tandoor
1/F Lyndhurst Tower, 1 Lyndhurst Terrace, Central.
Tel: 2845 2262.
Open: L & D daily. $$
Classy Indian restaurant featuring a top-notch lunchtime buffet.

Indonesian
Indonesia 1968
G/F 28 Leighton Rd, Causeway Bay.
Tel: 2577 9981.
Open: L & D daily. $
Serving up favourites like gado gado, sambal rending and nasi goreng since 1968, this Indonesian restaurant has smartened up its décor to meet the high quality of its food – but remains good value.

International
Harlan's
Shop 2075 IFC-2, Central.
Tel: 2805 0566.
Open: L & D daily. $$$$
Brash and moneyed, Harlan's aims to attract Hong Kong's jet set and succeeds. High-class "modern Western" cooking featuring fine ingredients prepared with panache.

M at the Fringe
1/F 2 Lower Albert Rd, Central.
Tel: 2877 4000.
Open: L & D Mon–Fri, D only Sat–Sun. $$$
A perennial favourite with a unique atmosphere and a dedicated clientele. The satisfying modern Oz menu overflows with French and Middle Eastern influences. The rooftop bar

above is a great place
for a drink.

Peak Lookout
121 Peak Rd.
Tel: 2849 1000.
Open: L & D daily. $$
This historic building on
Victoria Peak is like an
Alpine hunting lodge trans-
ported to the tropics.
Vivid, lively and colourful,
with great views.

Italian
Di Vino
73 Wyndham St, Central.
Tel: 2167 8883.
Open: L & D Mon–Fri, D only
Sat. $$
Smooth and savvy wine
bar and restaurant
operated by a trio of
charming Italians.
Always has an interest-
ing menu, and serves
tapas-style appetisers
gratis to guests.

Kowloon
Cantonese
Hoi King Heen
B2 Grand Stanford
InterContinental Hotel,
70 Mody Rd, Tsim Sha
Tsui East.
Tel: 2731 2883.
Open: L Mon–Sat, D daily.
$$$
Endlessly creative
Cantonese fine dining,
adapting novel ingredi-
ents into classic Can-
tonese cooking. A quality
operation.

T'ang Court
1/F Langham Hotel,
8 Peking Rd,
Tsim Sha Tsui.
Tel: 2375 1333.
Open: L & D daily. $$$
Among the most stylish
Cantonese restaurants in
town. The lush interior
brims with sumptuous
opulence, but don't let
that distract you from a
menu that dotes on
shark's fin, bird's nest
and abalone.

Other Chinese
City Chiu Chow
East Ocean Centre,
98 Granville Rd, Tsim Sha
Tsui East.
Tel: 2723 6226.
Open: L & D daily. $$
A great place to sample
Chiu Chow specialities
like cold crab, *e-fu*
noodles or chicken in
chin jiu sauce.

Hutong
28/F 1 Peking Rd,
Tsim Sha Tsui.
Tel: 3428 8342.
Open: L & D daily. $$$
Serious Sino-chic featur-
ing an intoxicating mix of
the antique and up to
date. The menu offers
classic northern Chinese
cuisine with a contempo-
rary twist.

Peking Restaurant
1/F 227 Nathan Rd,
Jordan.
Tel: 2730 1315.
Open: L & D daily. $
The Peking Restaurant is
a nostalgic blast from the
past, manned by white-
gloved geriatrics with limited attention spans. The
Peking menu features
good-quality roast duck
and traditional accom-
paniments.

Spring Deer
1/F 42 Mody Rd,
Tsim Sha Tsui.
Tel: 2366 4012.
Open L & D daily. $$
Always busy, so reserve
ahead at this classic
restaurant. Peking Duck
with pancakes, and shred-
ded beef are highlights.

French
Gaddi's
The Peninsula,
Salisbury Rd,
Tsim Sha Tsui.
Tel: 2315 3171.
Open: L & D daily. $$$$
The historic Peninsula
Hotel's French haute-

cuisine legend is a high-
society magnet, serving
flawless food in splendid
surroundings. Jacket and
tie required. The
chandeliered dining room
exudes opulence.

Japanese
Aqua
29/F 1 Peking Rd,
Tsim Sha Tsui.
Tel: 3427 2288.
Open: L & D daily. $$$
Panoramic vistas and
a glamorous interior
design, with high-quality
Japanese (Aqua Tokyo)
and Italian (Aqua Roma)
cuisine.

Hibiki
15 Knutsford Terrace,
Tsim Sha Tsui.
Tel: 2316 2884.
Open: L & D daily. $$
Neo-Japanese temple to
tempura, sushi, sashimi
and Kobe beef. Dark
wooden textures and
subdued lighting promote
a cosy atmosphere.

Bars

Hong Kong Island
Carnegie's
53–55 Lockhart Rd,
Wan Chai.
Tel: 2866 6289.
Rowdy bar, packed and
boisterous at weekends
and fun most nights.

Club 97
9 Lan Kwai Fong, Central.
Tel: 2810 9333.
Long-running but still one
of the hippest in town.

Club Feather Boa
38 Staunton St, SoHo,
Central.
Tel: 2857 7156.
Like a regency drawing
room; amazing, eclectic
and very SoHo.

Dublin Jack
1/F 40 D'Aguilar St,
Central.

Tel: 2543 0081.
Lively Irish bar in Lan
Kwai Fong. Plenty of Irish-
style comfort food, Guin-
ness and screens for
sports.

Fringe Club
2 Lower Albert Rd,
Central.
Tel: 2521 7485.
Live bands downstairs,
or a relaxing beer garden
on the roof. Along with
reasonable drinks
prices, this place is a
rare gem.

Mes Amis
83 Lockhart Rd,
Wan Chai.
Tel: 2527 6680.
Open-fronted bar on the
corner of Luard and Lock-
hart roads.

Staunton's
10 Staunton St, SoHo,
Central.
Tel: 2973 6611.
Long-running bar next to
the Mid-Levels Escalator.

Vodka Bar
13 Old Bailey St, SoHo,
Central.
Tel: 2525 1513.
Hip bar and gallery.

Kowloon
(Tsim Sha Tsui)
Aqua Spirit
1 Peking Rd.
Tel: 3427 2288.
Amazing views of the sky-
line in this trendy, expen-
sive bar.

Chillax Bar & Club
G/F The Pinnacle,
8 Minden Ave.
Tel: 2722 4338.
One of the livelier of sev-
eral bars and clubs on
Minden Avenue.

Rick's Café
53–59 Kimberley Rd.
Tel: 2311 2255.
Loud basement bar/club,
usually packed.

MACAU

Following in the steps of Hong Kong, Macau has become a Special Administrative Region of China. Its Portuguese colonial ambience and rapidly expanding resort status offer a unique experience in China

Main attractions
SÃO PAULO
FORTALEZA DO MONTE
MUSEUM OF MACAU
BARRA PENINSULA
GUIA FORTRESS AND LIGHTHOUSE
VENETIAN CASINO
COLOANE VILLAGE

BELOW: the facade of São Paulo.

I
n 1557 the Portuguese established the first European colony on Chinese soil in Macau, almost 300 years before the British claimed Hong Kong. For much of its recent history this was a sleepy outpost, playing second fiddle to its high-profile neighbour on the opposite shore of the Pearl River. But things have changed quickly since Lisbon returned the enclave to China in 1999. Macau is being developed into a leisure destination with luxurious Vegas-style resort and casino complexes, luring ever greater numbers of tourists, particularly from mainland China.

Yet away from all the glitz, glamour and mega-developments the old Macau survives – graceful old buildings redolent of southern Europe, overlooking cobbled streets shaded by ancient banyan trees. Drive from the gargantuan Venetian Macau on the new Cotai strip to Coloane village for lunch in one of the restaurants on the square, and you could be on the Iberian Peninsula rather than in the heart of the Orient.

The historic centre

The obvious place to start any foray into this old city is the **Largo do Senado** ❶ (Senate Square), Macau's largest piazza, paved with a bold wave-pattern mosaic. A handy tourist information centre is situated on the square (daily 9am–6pm).

Across the main road (Almeida Ribeiro) is the **Leal Senado** ❷ (Loyal Senate; daily 9am–9pm) building, regarded by most as the best example of Portuguese architecture in Macau. At the northern end of the square is **São Domingos** ❸ (St Dominic's), on the site of a chapel established here in 1597 by Spanish Dominicans newly arrived from Mexico. The current yellow-walled church dates from the 17th century. The white building on the eastern side of the square is **Santa Casa da Misericórdia** ❹ (Holy House of Mercy).

From São Domingos follow the pavement north along one of Macau's main shopping streets before turning uphill to the ruins of **São Paulo** ❺ (St Paul's; open access). The site must have bad

Recommended Restaurants and Bars on page 295

GETTING TO MACAU

Macau's airport is linked to several Asian cities and cities across China. Jetfoils operate every 15 minutes (7am–1am) from the Shun Tak Centre on Hong Kong Island. Journey time is 1 hour. *For more details see page 426.* For those in a hurry, helicopter flights from the Shun Tak Centre depart every 30 minutes (9am–10.30pm). Journey time is 20 minutes.

GETTING AROUND MACAU

The city streets are notoriously congested these days, and taxis can be hard to come by. It is hardly worth bothering with buses.

Take an elevator to the top of the Macau Tower for panoramic views – a good way to appreciate the scale of Macau's programme of reclamation and construction.

feng shui. After the first church on the site was destroyed by fire in 1601, Japanese Christians (fleeing persecution in Nagasaki) crafted the classical facade between 1620 and 1627. In 1835 another fire destroyed São Paulo, the adjacent college and a library. In 1904, efforts were made to rebuild the church, but little progress was achieved. Nonetheless, it remains Macau's most enduring icon.

Overlooking São Paulo are the massive stone walls of the **Fortaleza do Monte ❻** (Tue–Sun 7am–7pm; free), often simply called Monte Fort, built in the early 1600s. When Dutch ships attacked and invaded Macau in 1622, the half-completed fortress was defended by 150 clerics and African slaves. A lucky cannon shot hit the powder magazine of the Dutch fleet's flagship and saved the city. The **Museum of Macau** (Tue–Sun 10am–6pm; charge) on the site of the fortress has well-captioned exhibits that chart the history of the enclave.

A short stroll to the west will take you to picturesque **Camões Grotto ❼**, where Luís de Camões, the celebrated Portuguese soldier-poet, is said to have composed part of the national epic, *Os Lusíadas* (The Lusiads).

South to Barra

Several UNESCO historical sites lie along an easy-to-follow route from Largo do Senado to the southern tip of the Macau Peninsula. Among several notable buildings around the Largo de Santo Agostinho square is the Baroque-style

BELOW LEFT: a quiet lane in old Macau.
BELOW: on the battlements of Monte Fort.

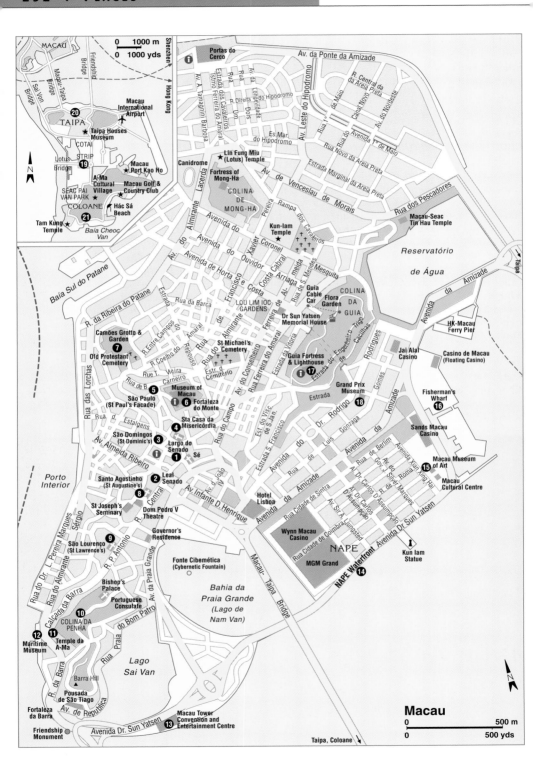

MACAU

Friendship Bridge

Macau-Taipa Bridge

Sai Van Bridge

0   1000 m
0   1000 yds

Shenzhen

Hong Kong

Portas do Cerco

Av. da Ponte da Amizade

R. Central da da Areia Preta

Av. A. Tamagnini Barbosa

Estrada dos Cavaleiros

Istmo Ferreira do Amaral

Rua Direita Carlos Eugenio

Longuidade Dois

Rua Dois

Es.Mar. do Hipodromo

Av. Leste do Hipodromo

Av. do Nordeste

Canal Novo do Nordeste

de Maio

Rua do Avenida 1 de Maio

Rua Nova do Areia Preta

Estrada Marginal da Areia Preta

Rua dos Pescadores

20 TAIPA

Macau International Airport

★ Taipa Houses Museum

COTAI

19 COTAI STRIP

Lotus Bridge

Macau ★ Port Kao Ho

A-Ma Cultural Village

Macau Golf & Country Club

SEAC PAI VAN PARK

COLOANE

21

Tam Kung Temple

Hác Sá Beach

Baía Cheoc Van

Baía de Van

Canidrome

Lin Fung Miu (Lotus) Temple

Fortress of Mong-Ha

COLINA DE MONG-HA

Lacerda

Almirante

Xavier Coronel

Av. de Venceslau de Morais

Kun-Iam Temple

Macau-Seac Tin Hau Temple

Pereira

Rampa dos Cavalros

Costa Cabral

Av. de S. Mendes Mesquita

Reservatório de Água

Baía Sul do Patane

Avenida do

Avenida de Horta e Costa

Ouvidor

Francisco de

R. da Ribeira do Patane

R. da Barca

LOU LIM IOC GARDENS

Costa Arriaga

de Almeida

Guia Cable Car

Flora Garden

Dr Sun Yatsen Memorial House

COLINA DA GUIA

Amizade

HK-Macau Ferry Pier

R. da Ribeira do Patane

Estrada

R.Entre Campos

Amaral

Ferreira do Amaral

Engenheiro Trigo

Cacilhas

Rodrigues

Jai Alai Casino

Casino de Macau (Floating Casino)

Camões Grotto & Garden **7**

Old Protestant Cemetery

R.Coelho do

Rua de B. **5**

Rue T.

Vieira

Carneiro

São Paulo (St Paul's Facade) **5**

Museum of Macau **6**

Fortaleza do Monte

Sta Casa da Misericórdia **4**

St Michael's Cemetery

Rua da

Estrada da Vitória

Av. do Consulheiro

Estr. d. Cemiterio

Guia Fortress & Lighthouse **17**

Grand Prix Museum **18**

Fisherman's Wharf **16**

Sands Macau Casino

Rua das Lorchas

Rua d. Estalagens

São Domingos (St Dominic's) **3**

Largo do Senado **1**

Sé

Est. de Visc. de S.Jan.

Estrada S.Francisco

Dr. Rodrigo

Estrada

Luis Gonzaga

Gomes

Amizade

Macau Museum of Art **15**

Macau Cultural Centre

Porto Interior

Santo Agostinho (St Augustine's) **8**

St Joseph's Seminary

Leal Senado **2**

Dom Pedro V Theatre

Governor's Residence

Av. Infante D. Henrique

do

Rua

Avenida

da

Amizade

Av. Dr. Carlos D'Assumpção

Av. do Dr. Rodrigo

Av. Dr. Carlos D'Assumpção

Hotel Lisboa

Rua Cidade de Sintra

Rua de Berlim

Rua de

Av. de Roma

Gov. J. Silvel Marques

Av. Xian Xing Hai

São Lourenço (St Lawrence's) **9**

R. P. Antonio

Fonte Cibemética (Cybernetic Fountain)

Bahia da Praia Grande (Lago de Nam Van)

Wynn Macau Casino

MGM Grand

NAPE

Rua Cidade de Coimbra

Av. Sir A. Lijungstec

Av. Dr. Sun Yatsen

NAPE Waterfront

Kun Iam Statue

14

Bishop's Palace

Portuguese Consulate

COLINA DA PENHA

10

11 Temple da A-Ma

Maritime Museum **12**

Barra Hill

Pousada de São Tiago

Fortaleza da Barra

Friendship Monument

Lago Sai Van

Macau Tower Convention and Entertainment Centre **13**

Avenida Dr. Sun Yatsen

Macau-Taipa Bridge

Taipa, Coloane

Taipa

Macau

0   500 m
0   500 yds

N

Recommended Restaurants and Bars on page 295

Santo Agostinho ❽ (St Augustine's). Further south on Rua de São Lourenço is the elegant pale-yellow church of **São Lourenço** ❾ (St Lawrence's), raised up above street level and surrounded by a small garden.

Take a detour up **Colina da Penha** ❿ (Penha Hill) for sweeping views and to visit the Chapel of Our Lady of Penha. The chapel and Bishop's Palace next door were important centres of Roman Catholic missionary work. Heading down to the foot of Barra Hill to Largo do Barra is **Temple da A-Ma** ⓫ (daily 7am–6pm), the oldest temple in the territory, said to date back 600 years to the Ming dynasty. It is dedicated to Tin Hau, the patron goddess of fishermen and called A-Ma in Macau. Close by is the **Maritime Museum** ⓬ (Wed–Mon 10am–5.30pm; charge, but free on Sun), tracing the history of shipping in the South China Sea.

New Macau

The 338-metre (1,110ft) **Macau Tower** ⓭ features an observation deck (daily 10am–9pm; charge) with 360-degree views of Macau; a look through its glass floors is not recommended for vertigo sufferers. Thrill-seekers can "skywalk" around the edge of the clear handrail-free platform, climb all the way to the top of the mast or even leap off in a controlled bungee jump.

Across Nam Van Lake (also called the Baia da Praia Grande), a series of brash new casinos are the glistening landmarks of Macau's burgeoning skyline. The copper-coloured **Wynn Macau**, the gold-and-silver **MGM Grand**, the 34-storey **StarWorld Casino** and the golden **Sands Macau** symbolise the new breed of Vegas-style gambling palaces for which Macau is becoming famous. Bounded on the north by the Avenida da Amizade, the rectangle of reclaimed land on which they sit is known as the **NAPE**.

In addition to the casinos, the area is also home to a growing number of small restaurants, cafés and bars. The **NAPE waterfront** ⓮ is marked by the bronze statue of Kun Iam, designed and

São Lourenço (St Lawrence's), originally built in the 1560s then rebuilt in the mid-19th century, is one of Macau's most attractive Portuguese churches.

BELOW AND BELOW LEFT: the Venetian casino.

Macau's Casinos

Macau's premier entertainment rumbles to the rattle of the roulette ball with the speed of a croupier shuffling a deck of cards. Gambling – or gaming as the industry would have it – is Macau's principal revenue-earner, fleecing the pockets of millions of Chinese and other nationalities every year, but equally sending a few on their way with riches beyond the dreams of avarice. With over 30 casinos open and plenty more on the way, "Asia's Las Vegas" has overtaken the original in terms of gaming revenue.

The casinos fall into two groups: the older, relatively low-rent establishments, owned by local gazillionaire Stanley Ho and epitomised by the original Lisboa; and the often spectacular new breed of Vegas-style palaces and resorts such as the Sands, Wynn, Grand Lisboa and Venetian, which have been taking over since the law was changed in 2002 to allow foreign investment and ownership into the lucrative business.

China's newly flush punters are streaming in. Revenues grew by more than 30 percent between 2005 and 2007, and Macau is set to become the world's no. 1 gambling destination by 2010.

The 17th-century Guia Lighthouse is the oldest on China's coast.

BELOW: lunchtime at Fernando's.

crafted by Portuguese artist Christina Reiria. The **Macau Cultural Centre** is located at the far end of the NAPE and has two auditoria that host a regular programme of performances. Next door, the **Macau Museum of Art** has spacious art galleries over five floors (Tue–Sun 10am–5pm; charge), which houses a permanent collection of over 3,000 works of Shiwan ceramics, calligraphy and art from Macau and China.

Further east towards the ferry terminal, an artificial volcano marks the entrance of the **Fisherman's Wharf** entertainment area.

North to the border

The hill of **Colina da Guia**, the highest point in Macau, rears up in front of the Hong Kong ferry terminal and is home to the **Guia Fortress and Lighthouse** (daily 9am–5pm; free), a 17th-century Western-style construction. A cable car links the hilltop with a pleasant small park and aviary at **Flora Garden** below (daily 7am–6pm).

Every year, in the last weekend of November the streets of Macau are taken over by the Macau Formula 3 Grand Prix and the Macau Motorcycle Grand Prix. Learn more about the "Guia Race" history of these exciting road races at the **Grand Prix Museum** (Wed–Mon 10am–5pm) at 431 Rua Luis Gongazaga Gomes in the basement of the Tourism Activities Centre. Next door, the **Wine Museum** (Wed–Mon 10am–5pm) tells the story of Portuguese wines.

At the northern end of Macau is the modern border gate between the Special Administrative Region and the city of Zhuhai in mainland China.

Taipa and Coloane

What were until recently the two outlying islands of Taipa and Coloane are now melded together by the **Cotai strip** , 620 hectares (1,550 acres) of reclaimed land either side of the 1.3km (¾-mile) road that used to link the two. Cotai is the focus for Macau's drive to become Asia's leisure capital, and home to the colossal **Venetian casino**, complete with a vast hotel, shops, gondolas and a campanile.

In **Taipa Village** a few bits and pieces of Old Macau survive. The **Taipa Houses Museum** (Tue–Sun 9.30am–5pm; charge) consists of five beautifully restored houses, while local history and developments are explained in the three-storey, mint-green **Museum of Taipa and Coloane History** (Tues–Sun 10am–6pm; charge).

The relatively quiet island of **Coloane** is a retreat from Macau's new-found bustle, traffic and casinos. Peaceful **Coloane Village** lies in the southwest of the island, its petite Portuguese-style village square alive with restaurant tables and festivities at weekends and holidays. It's a great place to sit with some Portuguese wine and Macanese food and watch the world go by. The village back-streets have a few furniture shops, cafés and the odd temple.

Over on the quiet eastern side of Coloane is **Hac Sa Beach**, famous for its black sand and Fernando's restaurant *(see opposite page).* ❏

RESTAURANTS AND BARS

Restaurants

Prices for a three-course dinner per person with one beer or glass of wine: (MOP$ = patacas)
$ = under MOP$150
$$ = MOP$150–300
$$$ = MOP$300–500
$$$$ = over MOP$500

Macau is a great place for eating out. It's cheap, and the local cuisine features elements from the far-flung Portuguese colonies of old, with African, Brazilian, Goan and Chinese influences combining with those from the European homeland.

Portuguese/ Macanese
A Lorcha
289 Rua Almirante Sérgio.
Tel: 2831 3193.
Open: L & D Wed–Mon. **$$**
One of the best of Macau's Portuguese restaurants, serving pork with clams, *feijoda* (pork-and-bean stew) and seafood rice.

A Petisqueira
15A & B Rua São João, Taipa.
Tel: 2882 5354.
Open: L & D Tue–Sun. **$$**
Fish and seafood are a must here: prawns, seafood salads, sea bass and Portuguese-style cod dishes.

Clube Militar de Macau
975 Avenida de Praia Grande.
Tel: 2871 4009.
Open: L & D daily. **$$$**
Former officers' mess dating from 1870, Clube Militar still attracts the cream of the city's Portuguese and Macanese society. Truly Portuguese cuisine and an excellent wine list.

Fernando's
9 Praia Hac Sa, Coloane.
Tel: 2888 2531.
Open: L & D daily. **$$**
At weekends, and on many weekdays, scores of diners queue for tables at this beachfront institution on Coloane Island. Crispy African chicken, prawns in clam sauce and casseroled crab are all excellent, and even the salad is exceptional.

Nga Tim Café
8 Rua Caetano, Coloane Village, Coloane.
Tel: 2888 2086.
Open: L & D daily. **$$**
Eat alfresco on Coloane village square at Nga Tim. It satisfies its many regular customers with a straightforward menu of Portuguese and Macanese classics, like African chicken and garlic prawns.

O Manuel
90 Rua Fernão Mendes Pinto, Taipa.
Tel: 2882 7571.
Open: L & D Thur–Tue. **$$$**
This unassuming but popular restaurant fully deserves its reputation. Portuguese treats include cod fishcakes, grilled sardines and calde verde (Portuguese vegetable soup).

O Porto Interior
259 Rua Almirante Sérgio.
Tel: 2896 7770.
Open: L & D daily. **$$–$$$**

Enjoy fine Macanese classics in an attractive restaurant decorated with interesting prints and artefacts.

Cantonese
Tung Yee Heen
1/F Mandarin Oriental Macau, Avenida da Amizade.
Tel: 2879 3821.
Open: B, L & D daily. **$$–$$$**
Classic Cantonese fare with dim sum available all day. Well worth trying are deep-fried prawns with garlic chilli sauce.

French
La Bonne Heure
12A & B Travessa de São Domingos.
Tel: 2833 1209.
Open: L & D Thur–Tue. **$$**
French cuisine prepared by chef who trained under Robuchon. Cosy bistro has art exhibitions and stays open for post-dinner drinks and music until 1am Friday nights.

La Comédie Chez Vous
Avenida Xian Xing Hai, Edificio Zhu Kuan (opp. Cultural Centre) Tel: 2875 2021.
Open: B, L & D daily. **$–$$**
The ground-floor café, serving memorable crêpes, is popular for breakfast (8am–noon). Lunch or dine in the upstairs restaurant.

Robuchon A Galera
3/F Hotel Lisboa,
2 Avenida de Lisboa.
Tel: 2857 7666.
Open: L & D daily. **$$$$**
Joel Robuchon, lauded by the Parisian media as "chef of the century", chose the Lisboa Hotel as the location for his first establishment out-side France. Fiendishly expensive for dinner; good value for lunch.

Italian
Antica Trattoria
40–42 & 46 Avenida Sir Anders Ljuungstedt, NAPE.
Tel: 2875 5103.
Open: L & D daily, closed 2nd Tue each month. **$$**
One of three restaurants run by different members of the same Italian family, Antica Trattoria serves up great pasta, pizza and Italian snacks.

Pizzeria Toscana
Calcada da Barra, 2A Edificio Cheong Seng.
Tel: 2872 6637.
Open L & D daily. **$$**
A Macau institution in the Barra area near the Moorish barracks. Clam linguine and the giant profiteroles are recommended. Great value.

Bars

In addition to its many casinos, Macau has a lively nightlife scene. The NAPE is one of the main areas; good bars here include **Bex**, a trendy lounge bar on Avda Xian Xing Hai, **Casablanca**, **Oparium** and the loud **MP3**, all on Avda Sun Yatsen. **Al's Diner** on nearby Fisherman's Wharf is a well-known Hong Kong bar. There is also a range of upmarket hotel bars – try **Vasco** at the Mandarin, and the **Whisky Bar** at the Star World Hotel on Avda da Amizade. There are a few older-style bars scattered about, too, such as the **Old Taipa Tavern** in Taipa Village.

GUANGDONG, HAINAN ISLAND AND FUJIAN

Many of the West's important historical encounters with China occurred down south; today the region remains dynamic, outward-looking and far removed from Beijing's influence

The southern provinces of **Guangdong** (广东), **Hainan** (海南) and **Fujian** (福建) are – particularly in their coastal areas – among the wealthiest and most forward-thinking in China, with a tradition of looking out across the South China Sea to the tropical regions beyond for trade and settlement. Indeed most overseas Chinese *(huaqiao; see pages 316–17)* hail from these parts, and what the Western world knows as "Chinese" food is almost without exception the distinctive cuisine of Guangdong. The region is also decisively set apart from the Chinese heartland by language: Cantonese and Fujianese are dialects with a rich linguistic heritage, and most southerners are more at ease speaking their mother tongue than they are the national language, Mandarin. Even on a physical level, locals differ markedly from their northern relations, who are typically taller, stockier and fairer-skinned.

In recent times Shenzhen and the Pearl River Delta have developed at breakneck speed to become China's largest manufacturing zone, pulling in migrant workers by the million from the poorer hinterland. Meanwhile, Hainan Island has been busily promoting itself as China's very own tropical beach paradise.

GUANGZHOU

The provincial capital of Guangdong, **Guangzhou ❶** (广州; Canton) has long been at the core of China's economic reforms. Close to the mouth of the Zhu Jiang (Pearl River), the city is thought to

have been founded in 214 BC as an encampment by the armies of the Qin emperor Qin Shi Huangdi. By the Tang period (AD 618–907), it was already an international port, and it was the first Chinese city to come into contact with European maritime power after a Portuguese flotilla arrived in 1514. These pioneers were, of course, followed by the British and a chain of events that would eventually lead to the Opium Wars and the opening of China to foreign trade. Over the years, close contact with overseas Chinese ensured the continuation of

Main attractions
SHAMIAN ISLAND, GUANGZHOU
SHENZHEN THEME PARKS
ZHAOQING
CHAOZHOU
HAINAN ISLAND BEACHES
GULANGYU ISLAND, XIAMEN
MARITIME MUSEUM, QUANZHOU
HAKKA ROUNDHOUSES, FUJIAN
WUYI SHAN

LEFT: Hakka roundhouse in Fujian province.
BELOW: a view of Guangzhou from Liurong Si temple.

Jogging in Yuexiu Park in central Guangzhou, the city's largest open space.

Guangzhou's openness to the world and a desire for reform. This, in turn, would eventually spawn revolutionary zeal *(see page 301)*.

Mao earmarked Guangzhou as China's principal international port. While the rest of China was isolated from the world, Guangzhou did business with the West at the biennial Canton Fair, which runs to this day. In the post-Mao era, the city has remained a centre for business and trade: it is still one of the richest cities in China and continues to expand with bold new engineering projects like the Zhu Jiang New City, soon to be home of a huge new museum and opera house.

Around 7 million people live in the main urban area, with a total of over 12 million in the sprawling conurbation.

Shamian Island and old Guangzhou

In the southwest of the city, the island of **Shamian** Ⓐ (沙面岛; Shamian Dao) is a preserved relic of the colonial past and the most picturesque spot in the city. Originally a sandbar on the north bank of the Zhu Jiang (Pearl River) before it was

reclaimed and expanded, the small island – just 1km by 0.5km (⅔ mile by ⅓ mile) – was divided in 1859 into several foreign concessions, primarily French and British. At night-time, Chinese were kept off the island by iron gates and narrow bridges.

Rather than feeling like an artificial enclave for tourists, Shamian is a thriving community, with century-old mansions forming an attractive backdrop, and antique cannons pointing out over the river as a reminder of more turbulent times. The more significant buildings sport plaques outlining their antecedents, while statues are dotted about depicting rickshaw pullers, tradesmen and – rather daringly – a trio of women from down the ages, the most recent of whom wears tight shorts and gabbles on her mobile phone.

Shamian is possibly the only part of this ever-changing city that feels genuinely timeless. The only significant change to the island in recent decades came in 1983 when the jarring, 34-storey White Swan Hotel was built, along with an elevated driveway. Despite the architecture being at odds with the surroundings, its presence scarcely affects Shamian's true character. Perhaps a more serious threat is the

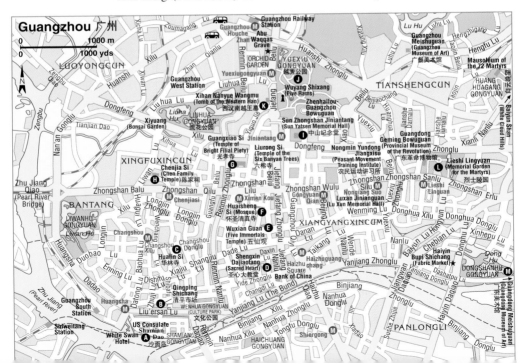

government's plan to revert the island to its former usage and offer colonial buildings up to foreign companies as boutique office space. **Shamian Gongyuan** (沙面公园; Shamian Park), a few steps from the White Swan, is chock-a-block with people most hours of the day, performing tai chi, ballroom dancing, kicking feathered quoits back and forth, playing mahjong and generally revelling in their own mini-island resort.

Opposite Shamian on Qingping Lu is **Qingping Shichang B** (清平市场), a market occupying the side alleys north of Liu'ersan Lu. This district has flourished since the economic reforms of 1978 and, always busy with shoppers, has a carnival feel. It was one of the first places to develop under China's gradual adoption of market economics, and for years it was a capitalist oddity. Qingping was once notorious for selling every imaginable animal for sustenance, including dogs, cats, owls and a variety of insects. Now, however, many stalls have moved inside and the exotic animals have all but disappeared in various beautification and hygiene campaigns.

The immediate area is notable for its old world ambience and pre-revolution architecture, although you need to get off the main roads and head into the side streets to find most of the market stalls and musty old antique shops selling jewellery, timepieces, Mao paraphernalia and antique porcelain reproductions. Just north are the pedestrianised shopping streets of Dishipu, Xiajia Lu and Shangji-ulu (collectively refered to as "Shangxia-jiu"). A little further on, spilling out either side of Changshou Lu, is Guangzhou's most famous jade market.

Xiajiu Lu leads north to the famous three-storey Guangzhou Restaurant. Founded in 1935, it's the city's oldest. Behind it, located in a narrow side alley named Shangxia Jie, is **Hualin Si C** (华林寺; daily 8am–5pm; free). This temple is said to have been founded by an Indian monk in 526, although the existing buildings date from the Qing period. There are 500 statues of *luohan* – pupils of the Buddha – in the main hall.

Along the waterfront

Beside the bridge that connects the eastern end of Shamian with the mainland is **Renmin Daqiao** (人民大桥), the oldest steel bridge across the Zhu Jiang, built in 1933. About 100 metres (110 yards) to the east is a memorial to the Chinese demonstrators who died in a hail of bullets fired by foreign troops guarding the foreign quarters in the mid-1920s. Stretching further east from here is the so-called Guangzhou "Bund", a moderately elegant strip of 19th-century waterside buildings which shares more than just a name with its more famous Shanghai namesake. Here, on Yanjiang Xilu, are some of the city's trendiest restaurants, bars and clubs. Just to the north are the 50-metre (165ft) double towers of **Sacred Heart Church D** (圣心大教堂; Shengxin Dajiaotang), the Catholic cathedral. Completed in 1888, it was left to decay after 1949 but following restoration in the 1980s it now holds services under the auspices of the Patriotic Catholic Church – which finally received papal approval in 2007 after long-running disputes between Beijing and the Vatican.

TIP

Every month, thousands of migrant workers pour into Guangzhou looking for work – often unsuccessfully. As a result, you may encounter more crime, such as pickpocketing, here than elsewhere in China. Be especially careful near the train station and on the metro.

BELOW: Shamian island: harmonious architecture and shade-giving banyan trees.

BELOW: the Pearl River flows through the heart of the city.

North to Zhongshan Lu

About 500 metres (550 yards) north, the Daoist **Wuxian Guan** Ⓔ (五仙观; Five Immortals Temple; daily 9am–noon, 2–5pm; charge) dates back to the 14th century and marks the place where the mythical five rams (who founded Guangzhou, according to legend) appeared. A 5-ton Ming-dynasty bronze bell in the tower at the rear remains silent; its ringing is traditionally associated with catastrophe for the city.

South of Zhongshan Lu in Guangta Lu, one can spot the onion dome of **Huaisheng Si** Ⓕ (怀圣清真寺), a 7th-century mosque founded by a trader who was said to be an uncle of the Prophet Mohammed. Arab traders were frequent visitors to China at that time, so the legend may contain some truth, although it does not give sufficient evidence for an exact date of the mosque's origins. The 25-metre (82ft) minaret, **Guang Ta** (Naked Pagoda), rises up among Guangzhou's high-rise skyline, and the mosque – the buildings of which are of recent construction – acts as a cultural centre for the city's sizeable Muslim community.

Three temples

To the north of Zhongshan Lu, a narrow street leads to **Liurong Si** (六榕寺; Temple of the Six Banyan Trees; daily 8.30am–5pm; charge), and within its grounds is **Hua Ta** (Flower Pagoda), built in 1097 and a symbol of the city. The pagoda appears to be nine storeys high, each level with doorways and encircling balconies, but in fact it contains 17 levels. There is a good view from the top.

A few minutes' walk to the northwest is **Guangxiao Si** Ⓖ (光孝寺; Temple of Bright Filial Piety; daily 6am–5pm; charge), a Buddhist temple preserved during the Cultural Revolution on orders from Premier Zhou Enlai. Local legend has it that the temple is older than the town, dating from around AD 400. Some of the present buildings were, however, built after big fires in 1269, 1629 and 1832. At the entrance is a brightly painted laughing Buddha *(Milefo)*, and in the main courtyard, a huge bronze incense burner fills the air. The main hall is noted for its impressive ceiling of red-lacquered timbers, and the back courtyard contains some of the oldest iron pagodas in China. The Indian monk Bodhidharma, founder of

Chan (Zen) Buddhism and Shaolin boxing, visited the temple.

Restored after the Cultural Revolution, **Chenjia Si**  (陈家祠; Chen Family Temple; daily 8am–5pm; charge) dates from 1894 and lies further west, near the intersection of Zhongshan Qi Lu and Kangwang Zhonglu. It has six courtyards and a classic layout, with the rooftops and walls decorated with wooden and stone friezes. The largest frieze stretches 28 metres (92ft) across the roof of the central hall and depicts scenes from the epic *Romance of Three Kingdoms*, with thousands of intricate figures against a backdrop of ornate houses, flourishing gates and pagodas. Families with the name Chen, one of the most common in Guangdong province, donated money to build the temple.

North of Dongfeng Lu

After the overthrow of the Qing dynasty in 1911, Guangzhou became the centre of the movement led by Sun Yatsen and the headquarters of the Guomindang (Nationalists), the first modern political party in China. Sun Yatsen is still revered today as the founder of modern China,

and to the northeast of the intersection of Jiefang Lu and Dongfeng Lu, the blue roof tiles of the **Sun Yatsen Memorial Hall** ❶ (中山纪念堂; Sun Zhongshan Jiniantang; daily 8am–6pm; charge) stand out strikingly within the setting of a formal garden. The hall, built after Sun's death in 1925 and completed in 1931, houses a large theatre and lecture hall that can seat several thousand people.

Guangzhou's largest park, **Yuexiu Gongyuan** ❶ (越秀公园), due north, is attractively landscaped with artificial lakes, hills, rock sculptures and lush greenery. It is dominated by **Zhenhailou** (镇海楼; Tower Overlooking the Sea), built as a memorial to the seven great sea journeys undertaken by the eunuch Admiral Zheng He. Between 1405 and 1433, Zheng travelled to east Africa, the Persian Gulf and Java. Today, the tower houses the **Municipal Museum** (广州市博物馆; Guangzhou Shi Bowuguan; Tue–Sun 9.30am–4pm; charge), with relics relating to the city.

Nearby is the **Sun Yatsen Monument** (孙中山纪念碑; Sun Zhongshan Jinian

The Sun Yatsen Memorial Hall is easy to spot with its eye-catching blue-tiled roof.

BELOW: Liurong Si temple from the Hua Ta pagoda.

There is a famous Chinese idiom: in Beijing one talks, in Shanghai one shops and in Guangzhou one eats. Without a doubt, Guangzhou is best-known for its eclectic food – from insect omelettes to dim sum. The latter, also known as yum cha, consists of delicate dumplings (such as the har gow*, pictured), pastries and noodle dishes.*

BELOW: the Tianhe Centre in eastern Guangzhou.

Bei), built of marble and granite and sitting on a hill above Sun Yatsen Hall. Cimb to the top for a great view of the city. Yuexiu Park also features some recreational facilities, including a golf driving range, bowling alley and swimming pool.

Opposite the park to the west on Jiefang Bei Lu is the **Xihan Nanyue Wangmu** Ⓚ (西汉南越王墓; Tomb of the Western Han; daily 9.30am–5.30pm; charge), the burial site of the Emperor Wen Di, who ruled the Nanyue kingdom, a vast swathe of southern China and what is now northern Vietnam from 137 to 122 BC, discovered when bulldozers were clearing the ground to build new apartments in the 1980s. The museum houses the skeletons of the emperor and 15 courtiers, including concubines, guards, cooks and a musician, who were buried alive with him. One part of the museum recreates the setting of the tomb so that visitors can walk downstairs into the actual chambers, though the highlight is the exhibition building, slightly up the hill, where thousands of funerary objects are displayed, including the suit of jade that the emperor was buried in.

Eastern districts

In the eastern part of the city, on Zhongshan Lu, is the former Confucius Temple, which lost its religious function during the "bourgeois revolution" in 1912. In 1924, the **Peasant Movement Training Institute** (农民运动讲习所; Nongmin Yundong Jiangxisu) opened here, and in effect became the first school of the Chinese Communist Party. During a period of cooperation between the Guomindang and Communists, Mao Zedong and other prominent party members worked and taught at the Institute: Mao's quarters can be viewed. This is where he developed his theory of peasant revolution.

After the collapse of a workers' uprising in 1927, the Communists were forced to retreat for a time from the cities. A park and memorial, **Lieshi Lingyuan** Ⓛ (烈士陵园; Memorial Garden for the Martyrs), was created in 1957 in memory of the uprising and its 6,000 victims.

Further east, on Er-sha Island, is the **Guangdong Museum of Art** Ⓜ (广东美术馆; Guangdong Meishuguan; 38 Yanyu Road; Tue–Sun 9am–5pm; charge). Its dozen exhibition halls display some of the more avant-garde examples of Chinese art, with frequent exhibitions of work by local students as well as special events celebrating artists from overseas. There is also an outdoor sculpture area.

SHENZHEN AND THE PEARL RIVER DELTA

Shenzhen ❷ (深圳) is a frenetic Special Economic Zone (SEZ) on the border with Hong Kong, an economic miracle and magnet for overseas investors. For the typical overseas tourist venturing into mainland China for a day or two from Hong Kong, it provides a decidedly unrepresentative, but fascinating, glimpse of "the other side". Culture may be at a premium, but Shenzhen makes up for it with bargain shopping, wild nightlife and no less than five US-style theme parks.

Shenzhen is a sprawling city. Bounded by its eponymous river to the south (marking the border with Hong Kong), it has spread from its historic centre in the

Recommended Restaurants on page 315

GETTING TO SHENZHEN
Hong Kong–Shenzhen
Trains: 3 per hour (5.30am–11pm) from Kowloon to Lo Wu (43 mins).
Ferries: There are numerous departures from Hong Kong/Kowloon and Hong Kong Airport to Shekou (50 mins).
Buses: Frequent shuttle buses from downtown Hong Kong and the airport.

Shenzhen–Guangzhou
Trains: 3–5 express per hour (55–70 mins), plus slower trains (1½–2 hours).
Buses: frequent buses (1½–2 hours). Good bus and train links across Guangdong, plus ferries to Delta ports.

GETTING TO GUANGZHOU
Hong Kong–Guangzhou
Trains: 7 daily between Kowloon and Guangzhou East (1¾ hours).
Ferries: Hydrofoils (2 departures daily) take 2½ hours, and arrive at Nanhai port, 20km (12 miles) south of the city centre.
Buses: frequent (2½ hours).

GETTING AROUND GUANGDONG
Trains from Guangzhou: Shaoguan (frequent, 2½ hours); Meizhou (3 daily, 6 hours); Chaozhou/Shantou (2 daily, 6½/7 hours); Zhaoqing (10 daily, 2 hours).
Buses from Guangzhou: Frequent to Zhuhai (2–2½ hours), Qingyuan (1½ hours), Kaiping (2 hours), Zhaoqing (2 hours), Meizhou (8 hours) and Chaozhou/Shantou (5–6 hours).
Chaozhou/Shantou: Guangzhou trains (2 daily) take 6½ to 7 hours. There is also an overnight train to Shenzhen (10 hours). Buses take 5½ hours to Guangzhou and 4 hours to Shenzhen.
Kaiping: Buses to Guangzhou (2 hours) run every 20 mins or so. There are also buses to Shenzhen, Zhuhai and Zhaoqing.
Shaoguan: The city lies on a major north–south rail route and trains from Guangzhou (1½ hours) are frequent. Guangzhou buses take around 4 hours.

Luohu District across every inch of land up to the border with Hong Kong, and north into the hilly green hinterland.

If you are coming up from Hong Kong on the train, you will arrive at **Luohu** (罗湖; Lo Wu when transliterated from the Cantonese). After disembarking at Lo Wu station in Hong Kong, it's simply a case of walking across the border (indoors) to emerge into a large concrete plaza on the Chinese side. The **Lo Wu Commercial City** (罗湖商业城; Luohu Shangye Cheng) is to your right. This is one of Shenzhen's largest – and cheapest – retail centres, selling a vast array of electronics, leather goods, jewellery and a medley of other merchandise that is packed layer upon layer.

Opposite is the railway station, with frequent trains to Guangzhou and various

BELOW: shopping in Guangzhou.

Window of the World brings Europe to China. Some sights are smaller than others... the 108-metre (354ft) Eiffel Tower being the largest.

BELOW: Shenzhen, boom town.

PRD destinations, and the metro, which can whisk you north to the downtown area (around 2km/1¼ miles north), on to Futian District – a major nightlife and shopping area – and beyond, to the cluster of theme parks around 15km (9 miles) west of town.

The most popular of these parks is **Window of the World** (世界之窗; Shijie Zhichuang; daily 9am–10pm; charge), a sort of global Lilliput which showcases scale models of everything from Thai palaces to Japanese teahouses – to say nothing of the Eiffel Tower, one of the area's most prominent landmarks.

Nearby **Splendid China** (锦绣中华; Jinxiu Zhonghua; daily 9am–6pm; charge) is a good option for anyone without the time to travel the entire country. For here are the Terracotta Warriors, the Great Wall, the Old Summer Palace, the Forbidden City and much more besides, all replicated in miniature, spread over 30 hectares (75 acres) and doable in a couple of hours. The adjacent **China Folk Culture Village** (民俗文化村; Minsu Wenhua Cun; daily 9am–9.30pm; charge) recreates the homes and lifestyles of the country's ethnic minorities.

The ubiquitous OCT development company opened its most ambitious project, **OCT East** (东部华侨城; Dongbu Huaqiao Cheng), in 2007. Set around a man-made lake in eastern Shenzhen's hills, the 890-hectare (2,225-acre) site has been crafted as a facsimile of Interlaken, Switzerland, complete with ski chalets, mineral baths and Chinese "Fräulein" girls in braids. It's an impressive, albeit slightly plastic, reproduction. To the south are Shenzhen's two best **beaches**, **Dameisha** (大梅沙; free) and **Xiaomeisha** (小梅沙; charge). The sandy strands and resort developments give visitors an interesting glimpse into China's slightly prudish beach culture. Just don't expect to do much sunbathing or swimming.

Around the Delta

While international trade is all the rage in the Pearl River Delta, early attempts by Western traders to introduce opium to China in the 19th century met with stiff official resistance, commemorated at both a park and a museum in the town of **Humen** (虎门), north of Shenzhen's airport. It was at here that Commissioner Lin Zexu contaminated several thousand chests of opium with quicklime in 1839, then deposited the haul in the so-called opium pits on the shore to the south of town. The British retaliated, sparking the First Opium War. Much is made (and rightly so) of the immorality of foreign merchants in the **Opium War Museum** (鸦片战争博物馆; Yapan Zhanzheng Bowuguan; daily 8am–5.30pm; charge) in Zhixin Park. On the coast 5km (3 miles) south of Humen town, the original **opium pits** and the **fortress of Shajio** (沙角炮台; Shajiao Potai) are worth a visit (8am–5pm; charge).

Some 25km (16 miles) southwest of central Guangzhou, **Foshan** (佛山; Buddha Mountain) is famous for its venerable **Zu Miao** (祖庙; Ancestral Temple; daily 8.30am–7pm; charge). Dating back to the 11th century, the Zu Miao's main effigy is a 3-ton statue of Beidi (Pak Tai in Cantonese), a Daoist deity in charge of the waters whom the locals sought to vener-

The Rise of the Pearl River Delta

Building on its glorious trading history, the Pearl River Delta (PRD) was the first part of China to be prised open in the reforms of the 1980s and it has revelled in economic success ever since. Huge industrial estates now dominate areas where, a generation ago, there were only paddy fields and fish ponds.

The statistics are arresting: the PRD's thousands of factories generate a GDP of US$113 billion – an average increase of 11 percent per year since the 1980s; if it declared independence from China it would still be the world's 11th-largest trading economy; it attracts almost half of the total foreign investment in China; and it is the world leader in light manufacturing – churning out vast quantities of everything from hi-tech electronics to garments, footwear and toys. Shenzhen itself is the second-richest city in China. Per capita income is around eight times the national average, and the population has risen from 700,000 to 11 million in 25 years. On the negative side is a serious pollution problem, worker exploitation and increasing competition from elsewhere in China, notably in the Yangzi Delta.

Recommended Restaurants on page 315

ate in this flood-prone region. Note the distinctive ceramic figures on the roof tiles made in the adjacent town of **Shiwan** (石湾; Stone Bay), one of China's leading ceramic centres and home to the **Nanfeng Ancient Kiln** (南风古灶; Nanfeng Guzao; daily 8am–6pm; charge), two early-Ming-dynasty kilns which have remained in constant use for around six centuries.

Heading south towards Zhuhai and Macau, the countryside is less developed. **Shunde** (顺德) is home to **Qinghui Yuan** (清晖园; Qinghui Garden; daily 8am–5.30pm; charge), a classical Chinese garden with a series of fish ponds, bamboo groves and fanciful engravings.

Zhongshan ❸ (中山) is one of the more attractive cities in the region, and has become popular with Hong Kongers as a weekend retreat. The nearby village of **Cuiheng** (翠亨村), where Sun Yatsen was born in 1866, lies to the southeast. The man most frequently described as the Father of Modern China spent only part of his childhood here, and the original house was demolished in 1913. However, it has since been reconstructed and turned into the **Dr Sun Yatsen Residence Memorial Museum** (孙中山故居; Sun Zhongshan Guju; Cuiheng Dadao; daily 9am–5pm; charge), standing as a suitable testament to his life as well as an illuminating depiction of rural existence in pre-revolutionary days.

ELSEWHERE IN GUANGDONG

One of Guangdong's more agreeable cities and a favourite destination for Hong Kongers and mainland tourists, **Zhaoqing** ❹ (肇庆) sits on the Xi Jiang River, 110km (68 miles) west of Guangzhou. The town is famous for its **Qixing Yan** (七星岩; Seven Star Crags), a range of limestone peaks that rise from a man-made lake in the north of town. Extravagant comparisons with Guilin are inaccurate, but the crags are picturesque in the right light conditions and set in pleasant surroundings. The Ming-dynasty **Chongxi Ta** (崇禧塔; Chongxi Pagoda; daily 8am–5pm; charge) affords long views over the river to the south and

across to two further pagodas rising up on the opposite bank. It's also possible to walk on the pleasingly unrestored sections of the Song-dynasty city wall. Access is off either side of Renmin Nanlu, close to the river. The forested reserve of **Dinghu Shan** (鼎湖山), 20km (12 miles) to the northeast, is a lovely range of pathways, temples, woodland, waterfalls, streams and pools.

South from Zhaoqing, **Kaiping** ❺ (开平) is famous for its *diaolou* towers. These multi-storeyed defensive village houses, built from the early 17th century to the 1930s, display an ornate fusion of Chinese and Western architectural styles. The remaining *diaolou* – more than 1,800 in all – are scattered over a wide area, some hidden beside duck ponds in the backstreets of Kaiping, but most in the villages around the city. Twenty of the most outstanding examples were collectively given Unesco World Heritage listing in 2007, but the area still receives relatively few foreign visitors.

Eastern Guangdong

This corner of Guangdong is historically one of the main centres of emigration

Originally intended as fortifications for villages, Kaiping's diaolou watchtowers evolved into showpieces of wealth and style, as locals who had made their fortunes overseas returned home. Many display Western European, Greek and even Arabic influences in their architectural details.

BELOW: Zhaoqing's Seven Star Crags.

Doorway at the Kaiyuan Temple in Chaozhou. The symbol confers good fortune and longevity.

from China, and contains three of its best-known cities – Shantou, Chaozhou and Meizhou. The last two are traditional homelands to their respective ethnic groups – the Chiu Chow (Teochew) and the Hakkas.

Nearing the border with Fujian province and one of China's original SEZs, **Shantou** ❻ (汕头) is a port city that was opened to foreign trade after the Second Opium War. The crumbling colonial quarter on the knob of land poking into the harbour is a fascinating – albeit slightly melancholy – area, where locals reside amid decaying European architecture. **Shipaotai** (石炮台; Stone Fort Park; daily 7.30am–6pm; charge) preserves a moated fortification built in 1879 for coastal defence. The fort is squat and

solid, its 5-metre (16ft) thick outer wall made of a surprising blend of granite, glutinous rice, brown sugar and crushed seashells. Atmospheric arched tunnels run around its base, with chambers on either side. Enter the circular central courtyard to see the wave-like steps which allowed cannons to be rolled up to the battlements. A total of 18 cannons face the harbour. Nearby is the marvellously restored **Tianhou Gong** (天后宫; Tianhou Temple), dedicated to the Queen of Heaven.

Chaozhou ❼ (潮州), 40km (25 miles) north of Shantou, is a historic trading town, its attractive centre full of narrow lanes and a section of Ming-dynasty wall bordering the Han Jiang river. The Guanyin Pavilion, inside the

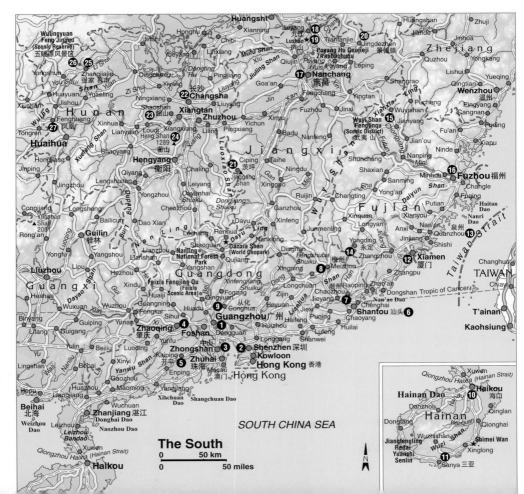

Recommended Restaurants on page 315

expansive Tang-dynasty temple **Kaiyuan Si** (开元寺; daily 6am–6pm; charge), is notable for its arrangement of Guanyin effigies representing the various earthly manifestations of the goddess. The temple complex features some ancient stonework and several venerable old trees. Directly east from the square in front of the temple you'll find a long section of the **Old City Wall**, the largest remaining in Guangdong. The nearest opening is **Guangji Gate** (广济门; Guangji Men); you can climb steps here to reach a three-storey watchtower on top of the wall. Opposite, the **Guangji Bridge** (广济桥; Guangji Qiao), a medieval trading link between Guangdong and Fujian, stretches across the wide Han Jiang.

Further inland, and bisected by a loop of the Mei Jiang, is the small city of **Meizhou** ❽ (梅州), considered the home of the Hakka people (although the ancient origins of this migratory ethnic group are likely to have been in central China). Hakkas have spread all over China and are found in Overseas Chinese communities worldwide; around 95 percent of these are from the Meizhou area (*see pages 316–17*).

Northern Guangdong

Forming part of a near-continuous line of hills that stretch right across southern China and relatively unknown to tourists, the northern parts of Guangdong are a world away from the booming coastlands.

The **Feixia Scenic Area** (飞霞风景区; Feixia Fengjing Qu) is an attractive riverside site of hills and temples an hour by bus north of the town of Qingyuan. Two to three hours northeast of Guangzhou by bus is the town of **Conghua** ❾ (从化), home to **Conghua Hot Springs** (从化温泉; Conghua Wenguan), a well-known destination famous for lychees and popular for its clean air and serene setting.

The city of Shaoguan is the access point for the **Nanling National Forest Park** (南岭国家森林公园) and the **Chebaling National Nature Reserve** (车八岭国家自然保护区), where the last remaining South China tigers may just survive. Around 50km (30 miles) northeast of Shaoguan, **Danxia Shan** (丹霞山; Danxia Shan World Geopark; 6.30am–7pm; charge) is an area of high eroded peaks of red sandstone, sculpted by time and water into a variety of odd shapes.

The red sandstone cliffs at Danxia Shan. Nearby Chebaling reserve has some of the best-preserved forest in southern China and is an important sanctuary for birdlife.

BELOW: Hakka women.

Taking it easy on holiday in Hainan. At the end of the 1990s, the island was little-known outside China, but since then a strong marketing campaign has raised the profile of "China's Hawaii" and there are now over half a million foreign visitors annually – many from South Korea and Russia.

BELOW: a southern Hainan beach.

HAINAN ISLAND

Historically and geographically out on a limb, for centuries shunned as a miserable place of exile battered by typhoons, **Hainan Island** (海南岛) has come into its own as a tropical resort destination with Chinese characteristics. It basks in year-round warmth, and there are plenty of palm-fringed beaches on which to take advantage of that fact, particularly in the south around Sanya – the only stretches of sand in China really worth packing a beach towel for.

The island's capital, **Haikou** (海口), is a pleasant city, with an unmistakably laid-back ambience. The Old Quarter in the north of the city centre is attractive, and features a promenade extending along Changdi Lu past clipped lawns and the banks of the Haidian River.

The real reason to come to Hainan, though, is to voyage down to the surf and sun at the island's southern extremity. These days most people fly straight to Sanya, the southern hub, but if you are travelling from Haikou along the east-coast highway, places of interest en route include some fine beaches around the village of **Qinglan** (清澜), and Hainan's surfing centre at **Shimei Wan** (石梅湾; Shimei Bay) near the town of Xinglong – also home to the beautiful **Xinglong Tropical Botanical Garden** (兴隆热带植物园; Xinglong Redai Zhiwuguan).

Sanya and the beaches

Sanya ⓫ (三亚) itself was originally one of several fishing villages on the southern tip of Hainan, and fishing docks still occupy a focal point at the town's hub. The Sanya River divides the town from north to south, with the original settlement lying to the west. It's all pleasantly relaxed; shabbiness now rubs shoulders with a form of gentrification – several good restaurants have opened and there is a trend for upmarket teahouses.

The rocky **Luhuitou** (鹿回头) Peninsula, immediately south of Sanya, is dominated by a giant sculpture depicting the legend of a hunter and a deer. The statue is located in a hill park in the north of the peninsula, with superb views of Sanya City, Dadonghai Bay and other nearby beaches available from the highest point.

GETTING TO HAINAN

Haikou and Sanya airports are both well connected with mainland cities. Hainan's new railway links with the mainland rail network via the ferry, which the train itself actually boards. There are direct services from Sanya to Guangzhou (3 daily, 13 hours). Sleeper buses run between Haikou and Guangzhou (daily, 12 hours), and there are ferries from Shenzhen (Shekou; daily except Sat, 18 hrs).

GETTING AROUND HAINAN

Haikou: Trains to Sanya via Dongfang take just under 3 hours, with 6 services daily. Buses to Sanya take 3 hours.
Sanya: Trains and buses (far more frequent) to Haikou take approximately 3 hours. Wenchang is 3½ hours away. Minibuses ply the routes between the south-coast resorts.
Tongzhi: There are plenty of buses to Haikou (3 hours) and Sanya (1½–2 hrs).

GETTING TO FUJIAN

Fuzhou and Xiamen are the main airports. Overlanding from Guangdong is easier by bus, as rail links are slow (14 hours Guangzhou–Xiamen). Rail is better between Fujian and Jiangxi or Hunan.

GETTING AROUND FUJIAN

There are no train services between Xiamen, Quanzhou and Fuzhou.
Xiamen: Trains to Yongding (2 fast trains daily, 3 hrs), Wuyishan (3 daily, 13½ hrs) and Nanchang (4 daily, 17 hours). Frequent buses to Fuzhou (3 hours), Quanzhou (2 hours) and Yongding (5 hrs).
Fuzhou: Trains to Wuyishan (6 daily, 5½ hours) and Nanchang (11 daily, 12–13 hrs). Frequent buses to Xiamen (3 hours), Quanzhou (2 hrs), Wuyishan (6–8 hours).
Quanzhou: Thre are frequent buses to Xiamen and Fuzhou (both 2 hours), as well as Yongding and Wuyishan.

Five minutes southeast of the city centre by road, or a 45-minute walk, lies the long fine-sand bay of **Dadonghai** (大东海). The whole of its beachfront has been developed, with mostly high-end hotels and villa resorts. Off the main drag, side streets are wall-to-wall with seafood restaurants and beachwear and souvenir knick-knack shops; it's all fairly laid-back, with little hard sales pressure.

Palm-tree shade is a little scarce, although it's possible to rent chairs and tables under parasols. The water is clean, but deceptive currents mean that it's not suitable for children or weaker swimmers. **Yalong Wan** (亚龙湾; Yalong Bay), 20km (12 miles) to the east, is a gorgeous 7km (4½-mile) strip of pale, powdery sand; warm sunshine throughout the winter high season attracts the crowds, and activities include scuba-diving, deep-sea fishing and paragliding. Further proof, if it were needed, that Yalong Bay represents one of China's most successful gentrification operations is the raft of new, internationally managed resorts – Marriott, Sheraton and Hilton included – that line the seafront. Backpackers beware.

Hainan's island culture is best typified by the livelihood of its minority Li and Miao peoples. Several Li and Miao villages can be reached around the town of **Wuzhishan** (五指山市; also called Tongza and Tongshi) in the highlands north of Sanya, which has a very interesting **Minority Nationalities Museum** (民族博物馆; Minzu Bowuguan; Tue–Sun 8am–5pm; charge) dedicated to the culture of the Li and the Miao. The **Jianfeng Ling Primeval Forest Reserve** (尖峰岭热带原始森林自然保护区; Jiangfengling Redai Yuanshi Senlin Ziranbaohuqu), 110km (68 miles) northwest of Sanya, is a striking mountainous area that has been successfully reforested and welcomes visitors.

BELOW: Jackie Chan at a Miss World event in Sanya.

*Typically grand
architecture on the
peaceful island of
Gulangyu, Xiamen.*

FUJIAN PROVINCE

Historically linked to Taiwan by proximity and a common tongue *(minnanhua)*, Fujian province has, like its neighbouring provinces of Guangdong and Zhejiang, spearheaded the emigration of Chinese overseas. Thanks to Taiwanese investment and an expedient maritime footing, it is one of China's wealthiest provinces. Seldom visited by foreign tourists, it offers enough history, spectacular scenery, folk traditions and other attractions to rank alongside some of the country's more lauded destinations. On a gloomier note, the province is permanently earmarked as an ideal launch pad for any (however unlikely) mainland invasion of Taiwan, and bristles with missiles. The islands of Chinmen and Matsu, in the waters just offshore from Xiamen and Fuzhou, remain in Taiwanese hands.

Xiamen

One of China's most engaging cities, the port of **Xiamen** ⑫ (厦门) has an attractive old centre and an utterly beguiling offshore haven, the island of Gulangyu. Formerly known in the west as Amoy, it became wealthy during the expansive maritime trading years of the Ming dynasty. The port was opened to foreign trade after the Opium War, and the offshore island of Gulangyu became a foreign enclave, complete with the full array of colonial trappings. In 1980, Xiamen joined the likes of Shenzhen in becoming a Special Economic Zone, and its economy thrived amid a raft of economic incentives and tax-relief measures. It continues to attract a disproportionate number of economic migrants and is today one of southern China's wealthiest and most tastefully developed cities.

Xiamen is an island, linked to mainland Fujian by a 5km (3-mile) causeway. The **Old Town** Ⓐ is focused around the lower (western) end of Zhongshan Lu, and is a pleasant place to wander around, although lacking in any notable sights. On Siming Nanlu, about 2km (1¼ miles) south, lies the **Overseas Chinese Museum** Ⓑ (华侨博物馆; Huaqiao Bowuguan; Tue–Sun 9.30am–4pm; charge), its outstanding collection of pottery and bronzes gathered with the help of donations from members of the huge overseas Fujianese community. There is also a section on the diaspora itself.

Xiamen's most famous temple is **Nanputuo Si ⊙** (南普陀寺; daily 8am–5pm; charge), north of the university in the southeast of town. The Tianwang Dian (Heavenly King Hall) at the entrance is home to the Bodhisattva Milefo, Weituo and the awesome Four Heavenly Kings. The name of the temple echoes Putuo Shan *(see page 249)*, and, unsurprisingly, effigies of the goddess Guanyin are in abundance.

Along the shore south of the temple is the **Huli Shan Fort ⓓ** (胡里山炮台; Huli Shan Paotai), a gun emplacement established on a hill. The impressive cannons, originally imported from Germany in 1891 to defend Xiamen against pirate attacks, were used a few decades later to sink a Japanese battleship and are still in place on the firing platform.

Gulangyu Island

Occupied by colonial powers until World War II, the island of **Gulangyu ⓔ** (鼓浪屿) is Xiamen's main attraction, a laid-back, hilly retreat accessed by ferry *(see margin, right)* from the city, and a museum piece of colonial architecture. Peace and quiet is a big part of the appeal

– there are no cars, motorbikes or even bicycles allowed, although electric trains now trundle slowly along the pleasant leafy lanes. The island measures just 2 sq km (¾ sq mile) in area, so even if you get lost (most people do), it's easy to retrace your steps.

Close to the pier, in the main restaurant and shopping area and rather at odds with the rest of Gulangyu, is **Xiamen Undersea World ⓕ** (海底世界; Haidi Shijie; 9.30am–4.30pm; charge), a well-equipped aquarium. Turn left from the pier to reach the huge **Koxinga statue** (郑成功铜像) at the easternmost point of the island. Xiamen became a hive of anti-Manchu resistance after the Qing took control of China in 1644. Led by Koxinga (Zheng Chenggong), the Ming rebels fought a losing war against the northern invaders. Koxinga is claimed by politicians on both sides of the thorny Taiwan question. To the Chinese, he's unambiguously presented as a great military patriot, partly for his reclamation of Taiwan from Dutch colonialists. However, his fierce Ming loyalties saw him flee to Taiwan and establish his own kingdom in opposition to the new Qing

TIP

At the terminal just north of Zhongshan Lu, ferries cross the narrow channel to Gulangyu every 10–15 minutes from 5.30am until 9pm, and then every 20–30 minutes until 12.20am. The journey time is 5–7 minutes. It's also possible to take a 30-minute boat tour that circles Gulangyu, before dropping you off on the island.

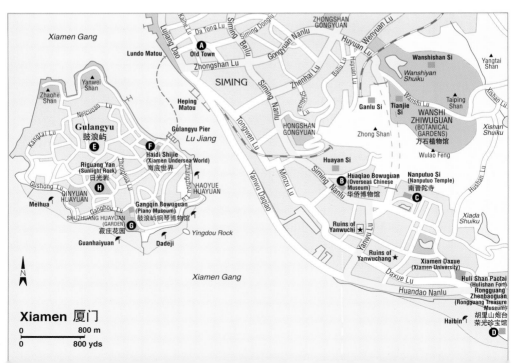

Xiamen 厦门

The lack of vehicles makes Gulangyu one of the most relaxing places in China.

BELOW: inside one of the communal Hakka roundhouses.

court. Accordingly, some view him as a forefather of Taiwanese separatism.

Continue walking along the coast to reach one of the most picturesque places on Gulangyu, the **Shuzhuang Garden** (菽庄花园; Shuzhuang Huayuan; daily 6.30am–8pm; charge) in the southeast, with its zigzag bridge that enables you to believe that you "walk on water" at high tide. Beyond the garden, the pleasant sandy beach extends along much of the island's southern coast.

The leafy sanctuary at Shuzhuang was the pet project of Lin Er Jia, who is believed to have brought the first piano to Gulangyu, starting a musical tradition that continues to this day – the island has its own concert hall, where the Xiamen Philharmonic Orchestra occasionally gives performances. With the absence of any vehicles it is still possible to hear the tinkling scales and trills that still cascade out of many an open window around the island. The **Piano Museum** (鼓浪屿钢琴博物馆; Gangqin Bowuguan; daily 8.15am–5.15pm; charge) at Shuzhuang Garden includes numerous antique pianos from Austria, Germany, France, the UK and the US.

Sunlight Rock (日光岩; Riguang Yan; daily 6.30am–8pm; charge), a favourite photo opportunity and the highest point on the island at 93 metres (305ft), is to the north. The charge includes a cable-car ride to the summit. Just below it within the same park is the **Koxinga Memorial Hall** (郑成功纪念馆; Zhengchenggong Jinianguan; daily 8am–5pm; admission included with Sunlight Rock), with a mixture of 17th-century artefacts and a large dose of Taiwan-related propaganda.

Some of the most interesting buildings on Gulangyu are situated in the area immediately uphill from the main ferry pier – on Fujian Lu, Lujiao Lu and Long-tou Lu (the latter is also a good bet for restaurants). A little further west is the long-closed **Xiamen Museum** at 43 Guxin Lu, whose beautiful cupolas are visible from most points on the island.

Quanzhou and the southwest

A thousand years ago **Quanzhou** (泉州) was arguably the world's most significant port, with a lucrative position at the centre of the maritime silk trade. It

Tulou: Hakka Roundhouses

The Hakka (*kejia* in Mandarin; literally "guest people") are a Chinese people whose distinctive earthen houses – *tulou* – can be found in the borderland counties where Guangdong, Jiangxi and Fujian provinces meet. Communal entities, *tulou* are fortified against marauding bandits and generally made of compacted earth, bamboo, wood and stone. They contain many rooms on several storeys, so that several families can live together. The small, self-contained design is a common characteristic of Hakka dwellings (eg the Hakka walled villages at Kam Tin in Hong Kong's New Territories). *Tulou* come in a variety of styles, and can be circular, triangular, rectangular, octagonal or other shapes. The extraordinary round earth houses range in size from the small scale (around 12 rooms) to the large (up to 72 rooms). Most are three storeys high, but the largest have up to five storeys. Some *tulou* stand independently, while others cluster

into groups. The *tulou* located in Hukeng near Yongding in southwest Fujian include the circular Zhenchenglou and a Five Phoenix House (Wufenglou), among others. Five Phoenix buildings tended to belong to Hakka officials and are more palatial than typical *tulou*.

prospered enormously during the Song and Yuan dynasties, when it was visited by Marco Polo (the port was known as Zaytoun then) and played host to thousands of Arab merchants, many of whom made fortunes introducing Chinese inventions such as gunpowder and printing to the West. The port fell into irreversible decline following the restrictions on maritime trade imposed by the Ming emperors in the 15th century. Yet it has retained its heritage remarkably well by Chinese standards, and all new buildings must follow height and design standards to keep them in harmony with the past.

The **Ashab Mosque** (清净寺; Qingzhen Si; daily 8am–6pm; charge) on Tumen Jie dates from 1009, and its presence stands as testimony to Quanzhou's heyday as a cosmopolitan city, home to many thousands of Muslim traders. It is said to be the only mosque in Han (ie eastern) China built along traditional Islamic, rather than Chinese, lines. English-language signs help to bring alive the past for the (rather rare) foreign visitor.

Islam was not the only foreign religion to reach Quanzhou, as you soon realise on the ground floor of the **Maritime Museum** (海外交通史博物馆; Haiwai Jiaotongshi Bowuguan; daily 8am–6pm; charge) on the northeast side of town. Nestorian crosses, carved fragments from Hindu temples, stones bearing the star of David, Arabic inscriptions and even remnants of a 7th-century Manichean shrine compete for attention in this fascinating display. On the upper floor you will find a masterly survey of China's seafaring history and a sizeable display devoted to the remarkable expeditions of Admiral Zheng He. Imaginative layout and lively exhibits make this one of China's best museums, fully worthy of its Unesco sponsorship. All labels are translated into English.

Kaiyuan Si (开元寺; Kaiyuan Temple; daily 8am–5pm; charge) is Quanzhou's largest Buddhist temple, and one of China's most beautiful. The temple dates back to the late 7th century, but its two pagodas were later additions, constructed in the 13th century. They have managed to survive largely as they are built of stone, not wood.

Yongding ⑭ (永定) in southwest Fujian near the border with Guangdong is unremarkable in itself, but there is an

The traditional Islamic design of the Ashab Mosque in Quanzhou is unusual: most Chinese mosques are almost indistinguishable from Chinese temples.

BELOW: Hakka roundhouse at Yongding County, Fujian.

The Fujian coast – specifically Meizhou Island north of Quanzhou – is where the legend of Tin Hau (Matsu), protector goddess of the fishermen, originated. The story goes that a young girl (Tin Hau) dreamt that her brothers were about to be shipwrecked, but managed to save them in her dream. Her birthday is marked with festivities across southern China (see page 451).

BELOW: Wuyi Shan.

unusual attraction northeast of town. A large Hakka earthen roundhouse called Zhenchenglou is located north of the village of Hukeng *(see panel, page 312)*.

Wuyi Shan

In the isolated northwestern corner of Fujian, **Wuyi Shan** ❶ (武夷山) is a Unesco-listed World Heritage Site with towering peaks and dense forest cradling a rich and unique ecosystem. Several trails head into the peaks, and this is prime hiking territory. However, despite the remote location, a nearby airport facilitates the passage of a huge number of Chinese tour groups, and a fairly unappealing new town has sprung up to cater to their needs. Wuyi Shan has an unfortunate reputation as one of China's foremost tourist traps. The price hikes and aggressive vendors can mar what is, otherwise, one of the most spectacular parts of southern China. Spring or autumn is the best time to visit to avoid the crowds (winters are cold and often wet).

The entrance to the reserve is just 10km (6 miles) southwest of Wuyishan City, and there are frequent minibuses between the two. These take you to the

resort area around the confluence of the Chongyang Stream and Jiuqu River (Nine Bend Stream).

Most visitors climb up to some of the most famous vantage points and strange rock formations. The Heavenly Tour Peak, Tiger Roaring Rock, Thread of Sky, Water Curtain Cave and King Peak will occupy a couple of half-days. The extraordinary "hanging coffins", mostly made from whole trees, are wedged in caves high up on cliff faces. Carbon dating has revealed that they are more than 3,000 years old, but no one has yet explained how or why they were installed in such seemingly inaccessible locations.

Rain or shine, the raft trip down **Nine Bend Stream** (九曲溪; Jiuqu River; Jiuqu Xi) is an essential part of the Wuyi experience. Throughout the 80-minute trip you are likely to be regaled by tales of the curious rock formations and anecdotes about celebrities who have taken the trip.

Fuzhou

The provincial capital, **Fuzhou** ❶ (福州), is of limited interest. It's a clean and well-maintained sort of place, but there is little in the way of sights.

Directly behind the Mao statue is the modest **Jade Hill** (玉山; Yu Shan), and on its western flank stands the 10th-century **Bai Ta** (白塔; White Pagoda), commanding views over the city. Further west, beyond the major shopping thoroughfare of Bayiqi Zhonglu, is **Wu Shan** (乌山; Black Hill), crowned with the corresponding **Wu Ta** (乌塔; Black Pagoda), an ancient granite structure dating back to the 8th century.

Xichang Temple (西昌寺; Xichang Si) is the city's largest and oldest temple, dating back to pre-Tang times, although it has been much restored in recent times thanks to donations from prosperous overseas residents. Situated off Gongye Lu some 1.5km (1 mile) west of the centre near the Min River, the buildings epitomise Fujian style at its most flamboyant.

To the east of the city are the wooded slopes of **Gu Shan** (鼓山). Horrendously crowded at weekends, it makes for a pleasant escape at other times. ❏

RESTAURANTS

Restaurants

Prices for a meal for one, with one drink:
$ = under Rmb 50
$$ = Rmb 50–100
$$$ = Rmb 100–150
$$$$ = over Rmb 150

Guangzhou

Guangzhou is the home of Cantonese cuisine, the most celebrated culinary genre in China, and there are hundreds of good restaurants in which to sample it. Other Chinese and foreign cuisine is well represented, too. Restaurants are spread out across the city; two popular areas are Shamian Island and the streets north of Qingping Market.

Cantonese and other southern Chinese
Guangzhou Restaurant
广州酒家
2 Wenchang Nanlu, near Xiajiu Lu. **$$**
Signature dishes at this famous establishment include Wenchang chicken and double-boiled shark's-fin soup with black chicken. Very popular with local residents for dim sum.

Seafood (Chinese)
Hongxing Seafood Restaurant
鸿星海鲜酒家
276 Huanshi Zhonglu, Tianhe District. **$$**
Downtown and downright excellent. There are non-seafood choices, but regulars sing the praises of the stuffed giant crabs.

Northern Chinese
Dong Bei Ren 东北人
36 Tianhe Nanerlu. **$$**

Dong Bei Ren is renowned for its *jiaozi* and its sweet red wine.

Muslim
Nur Bostan
诺尔波士顿餐厅
43 Guangta Lu. **$**
Uighur-style halal food – with lamb predominating – at this inexpensive reminder of the city's sizeable Islamic population.

Thai and Vietnamese
Cow and Bridge
牛桥泰菜
2/F Xianglong Huayuan, 175–181 Tianhe Beilu. **$$**
Serves top Thai dishes to very satisfied customers on sleepy Shamian Island.

Lemon House 月茗苑
Ground Floor, 11 Jianshe Liu Ma Lu/507 Huifu Donglu. **$$**
There are some Thai dishes on the menu, but concentrate on the Vietnamese, especially the range of *pho*.

International
1920 1920西餐
183 Yanjiang Zhonglu. **$$$**
A charming riverside café that's just the place for lunch, or somewhere to kick back and watch the world go by of an evening. It's also a good place for drinks.

Shenzhen

Regional Chinese cuisines are especially well represented, and the downtown area around Jianshe Lu/Shennan Zhonglu and Heping Lu. Futian's shopping areas further west have plenty more and lots of bars.

Cantonese
Phoenix House 凤凰楼
2/F The Pavilion Hotel, 4002 Huaqiang Beilu, Futian. **$$**
Great for dim sum, with a very good ambience.

Indian
Spice Circle 印度餐厅
Tianjun Mansion, Dongmen Nanlu Xnr Jiabin Lu. **$$$**
This is the Mumbai chain's first restaurant in mainland China. The chefs are from the subcontinent, so it's authentic.

International
360 at the Shangri-La
360度餐厅
Shangri-La Hotel, 1002 Jianshe Lu, Luohu. **$$$$**
The views are top-notch, ditto for the cuisine, to say nothing of the wine list and décor at this world-class venue.

Around Guangdong

Chaozhou (Chiu Chow) restaurants are found in Chinatowns the world over, with cuisine primarily based on seafood – but also featuring vegetarian dishes. Hakka cuisine features dried and preserved ingredients: fermented tofu, fried pork and preserved vegetables.

Shantou
Chaozhou Restaurant
潮州菜馆
2 Changping Lu. **$**
One of the best places for Chiu Chow specialities.

Hainan Island

Haikou
Reasonably priced noodle and congee restaurants abound, while Jinlong Road has become known as "Food Street".

Lu Zhi Hai Xien Mai
吕记海鲜美食城
Tze Chen, 38 Hai Xiu Donglu. **$**
Bang in the centre of the city, with local seafood.

Sanya Area
The numerous live-aquarium eateries of Dadonghai are good. Yalong Bay's restaurants are only in the resorts, but are invariably top draw.

Fujian Province

Fujianese cuisine features strong, salty flavours and lots of seafood.

Quanzhou
Ho An Por (Rou Zong Dian) 侯阿婆 (肉粽店)
4, Block 19, Liu Guan Lu. **$**
Anywhere in Quanzhou's food street is a sure bet; Ho An Por is famous for its leaf-wrapped, steamed rice dumplings.

Wuyishan
Lao Zi Hao
老字号农家宴
Wuyishan National Tourist Resort. **$**
In this rustic restaurant visitors dine on local produce in a straw-roofed bamboo hut. Wild game and local mushrooms are available in season.

Xiamen
Lujiang Restaurant
观海餐厅
Lujiang Hotel, 54 Lujiang Dao. **$$**
Rooftop dining – either indoors or alfresco – in the heart of the city, with great views over the harbour and Gulangyu. Good dim sum available all day, plus Cantonese buffet and Fujian specialities.

The Overseas Chinese

The millions of Chinese who have left their home country to escape poverty represent one of the great success stories of international migration

China has a long history of emigration that has spawned Chinese communities in virtually every country in the world. As far-flung as Peru, Italy and Mauritius, Chinese people are living in their adopted countries, some first-, second-, third-, and even fourth- or fifth-generation.

There are about 34 million people of Chinese descent living in more than 130 countries outside China, Taiwan and Hong Kong. Yet the vast majority of this number originated from the two southern coastal provinces of Guangdong and Fujian, and even within those provinces, from a limited number of districts and villages.

The Chinese populations have adapted well to life in their host countries and achieved a good degree of economic success. Despite years of living away from home, there is an underlying "Chineseness" that resonates throughout the diasporic community and maintains its affinity to China.

The early migrants

China's history of emigration has been characterised by three significant waves marked by economic and political change. The first phase came during the Ming dynasty between 1405 and 1433, when the intrepid navigator and admiral Zheng He set sail with a huge fleet of 300 ships and 28,000 men bound for Southeast Asia and the Indian Ocean, in search of trading opportunities and to flaunt the superiority of Chinese power.

Following in the wake of these pioneering voyages, a fairly modest number of peasants and villagers looking to escape the hardship and poverty of life in rural China (they were mainly from the poorest districts of Guangdong and Fujian) began to emigrate overseas with the ultimate intention of returning home with their new-found wealth. They became some of the first Chinese settlers in Thailand, Malaysia, the Philippines and Indonesia. Migration took place despite imperial edicts forbidding foreign travel, laws established by Ming emperors who feared those disaffected by Chinese rule would be pushed outside China's borders, thus laying the empire open to invasion from rebel armies. So entrenched was the paranoia that these edicts remained in force until the 19th century.

The second wave

A new, and far more significant, surge of migration from China took place in the 19th century during the European colonial period, when millions of Chinese were transported across the globe on European ships. They can be considered economic migrants, fleeing poverty and famine in China. The Qing rulers were now compelled to permit emigration by the European powers, hungry for a cheap and plentiful labour supply for the colonies. As "coolie" labour, the Chinese were put to work in mines, plantations and railroads across the globe. Records show that between 1848 and 1888, more than 2 million people departed, and like their forefathers, many originated from the provinces of Guangdong and Fujian.

Those that survived the perilous journeys and working conditions settled, usually unable to afford the fare back to China. Once free from the shackles of their exploitative employers, and unable to return their homeland, the Chinese – wherever they found themselves – adapted well to what was available to them. Despite some discrimination, overall they prospered through hard work and a flair for business, and became respected members of the wider community. In Southeast Asia, many of the big tycoons and political figures of the past century have come from humble Chinese beginnings.

It is not surprising that today Southeast Asia has the largest population of people of Chinese origin. Estimates place more than 23 million ethnic Chinese in the region, which adds up to fully 80 percent of the world's Overseas Chinese. Although – with the exception of Singapore – they are minorities in their adopted countries, they are a universally significant group in terms of their economic contribution.

Recent emigration

The most recent wave of migration has followed the series of political upheavals in the 20th century. With the opening up of the economy in the 1980s and a newly open attitude towards the outside world, China's citizens were able to take advantage of greater mobility, and increasing numbers moved abroad. In 1989, the situation was brought to a head with the Chinese government crackdown in Tiananmen Square. The international outrage at the strong-arm tactics used by the government opened the doors of many Western nations to Chinese students, with the United States taking on the largest portion, granting 80,000 green cards to students already on US territory under the Chinese Student Protection Act. There followed a steady outflow of migrants, some fleeing the political situation, but the majority taking advantage of the economic and professional opportunities of living in the West.

This episode of Chinese migration continues today, with the preferred destinations being North America, Europe and Australasia. The Chinese communities in certain North American and European cities in fact date back to the second wave of migration – well-known examples being San Francisco and New York in the United States, Vancouver and Toronto in Canada, and Liverpool and London in the United Kingdom. Therefore, these Chinese communities tend to be comprised of a mix of earlier Cantonese- and Hokkien-speaking immigrants

with those fresh out of China who speak the official language, Mandarin, and are just as likely to come from the north of the country, and who are usually highly educated and highly skilled.

Links with the motherland

The spread of Chinese people across the globe has done little to diminish their ties with their ancestral homeland. In fact, the Overseas Chinese *(Huaqiao)* have been assiduous in giving back to the places whence they came. Donations are collected and given on an informal basis through family connections, temple networks or community organisations, which then go on to contribute towards the development of the area. So prolific is this practice that some counties in Guangdong and Fujian (known as the *Quaoxiang* – Overseas Chinese counties) have been transformed. Through the donations, hospitals, schools, ancestral halls, bridges and roads have been built to better the home villages, and the family clans (denoted by the surname) are noted on tablets or by the naming of the place.

This allegiance to China has also drawn many to return to explore their cultural and family roots, an extension of the Confucian practice of filial piety. Migrants return to pay homage to their ancestors and to validate their identities and histories as part of the fabric of China's long history. ❏

LEFT: Chinatown in Vancouver. **ABOVE LEFT:** indentured Chinese labourers arrive in 19th-century Singapore. **RIGHT:** most overseas Chinese retain close ties with their ancestral villages.

THE SOUTHERN INTERIOR: JIANGXI AND HUNAN

Best-known in China for their revolutionary past and fiery cuisine, these relatively poor inland provinces contain some sublime scenery and interesting old towns

Main attractions
LUSHAN
MAO'S HOME, SHAOSHAN
HENG SHAN
WULINGYUAN SCENIC RESERVE
FENGHUANG

BELOW: the
limestone crags at
Wulingyuan.

The subtropical provinces of Jiangxi and Hunan are on few tourist itineraries, although their associations with Mao and the early years of the Chinese Communist Party ensure a steady stream of Chinese tour groups to places such as Shaoshan and Jinggangshan. Nonetheless, there is plenty to see here, not least some pockets of beautiful scenery, and a scattering of attractive towns and villages – notably Fenghuang, in western Hunan.

JIANGXI

Jiangxi (江西) province is one of China's most neglected areas, a forgotten backwater through much of Chinese history. This landlocked province, south of the Yangzi, found a modicum of importance after the Grand Canal was constructed in the 7th century AD in neighbouring Zhejiang. Suddenly Jiangxi found itself on part of a complex trading route that linked prosperous Guangdong with northern China. However, its star faded with the advent of coastal shipping which made it quickly overshadowed by the more prosperous provinces to the south and east. The 20th century saw Jiangxi mired in conflict, initially between competing warlords and then caught up in the Communist–Nationalist civil war. In recent years it has been playing catch-up with its neighbours.

Nanchang

Jiangxi's capital, **Nanchang** ⑰ (南昌), until recent years known primarily for it role in Chinese communism's history, is now at the forefront of another revolution: the rapid economic upsurge of China's so-called "second-tier" cities, many of them capitals of interior provinces that are now benefiting from the spread of investment inland from the more developed coastal areas such as Guangdong and Fujian.

The premier historic site in town is the impressive nine-storey **Tengwang**

GETTING TO JIANGXI

By train and bus: Nanchang has rail connections with Fujian and Hunan, and north to Wuhan, Nanjing and Shanghai. Buses run to Changsha, Wuhan, Shanghai, Xiamen, Guangzhou and other cities.

GETTING AROUND JIANGXI

Nanchang: The fastest trains to Jiujiang (12 daily) take 2½ hours, while buses take 2 hours. Trains and buses to Jingdezhen (several daily) both take 4 hours. There are frequent buses to Lushan (1½ hours), and 3 daily to Jingganshan (5–8 hours).

Jiujiang: Trains to Nanchang (12 daily) take 2½ hours. There are frequent buses to Lushan (1 hour), and hourly to Jingdezhen (2 hours).

Lushan: There are buses every 40 minutes or so from Nanchang (1½ hours). Similarly frequent buses run from Jiujiang (1 hour).

Jingdezhen's pottery was once one of China's principal exports. The Chinese were crafting porcelain from as early as AD 100, and it became highly sought after in the Middle East and, later, in Europe. The secret of its manufacture was not discovered in Europe until the early 18th century.

Pavilion (滕王阁; Tengwang Ge; 7 Yanjiang Bei Lu; summer 7.30am–7pm, winter 8am–4.30pm; charge), which towers majestically over the Gan Jiang River. At night, a multicoloured array of lights brings its graceful flying eaves to life. It is surrounded by a garden of elegant pavilions and gently weeping willows.

Around 2km (1¼ miles) to the east off Minde Lu, Nanchang's main commerical and nightlife thoroughfare, is **Zhu De's Former Residence**, (朱德旧居; Zhu De Jiuju; 2 Huayuanjiao Jie; daily 8am–5.30pm; charge). Together with Mao and Zhou Enlai, Zhu De led 30,000 Communist troops in the abortive 1 August 1927 rebellion against the Nationalist forces. Despite its calamitous failure, the uprising is considered the first major conflict of the Chinese Civil War, and, as such, 1 August *(bayi)* has come to be celebrated as the anniversary of the People's Liberation Army's formation. The **1 August Uprising Museum** (八一纪念馆; Bayi Jinianguan; 380 Zhongshan Lu; daily 8am–5.30pm; charge), situated a short distance to the south on Zhongshan Lu, covers the events more fully, but the grandest tribute to the uprising is without doubt **1 August Square** (八一广场; Bayi Guangchang), China's largest public square after Beijing's Tiananmen.

BELOW LEFT: handicrafts made from forest nuts, Fenghuang. **BELOW:** Mao befriends the peasants in this Socialist Realist painting.

Socialist Realist art on sale in Fenghuang.

BELOW: the "Little Red Book", quotations from the Great Helmsman.

Elsewhere in Jiangxi

Tucked between the Yangzi's southern bank and the northern fringe of Poyang Lake is the rambling port of **Jiujiang** ⑱ (九江), a pleasant town with a scenic walkway offering the chance to stroll along the Yangzi.

In addition to being a crucial overflow reservoir when the Yangzi bursts its banks, the large lake of **Poyang Hu** (鄱阳湖) provides a wetland habitat for several endangered species of waterfowl. The large **Poyang Lake National Nature Reserve** (鄱阳湖国家级自然保护区; Poyang Hu Guojieji Ziranbaohuqu), situated around the village of **Wucheng**, is considered by many birdwatchers to be one of Asia's supreme avian spectacles, attracting six species of crane each winter.

Rising up west of Poyang Hu (Poyang Lake) in the north of Jiangxi, **Lushan** ⑲ (庐山) offers respite from the steamy summers along the central plains. It was singled out as a retreat for missionary and expatriate families in the 19th century, and their European-style stone dwellings, later occupied by Nationalists and Communists alike, survive; some now operate as charming hotels. The resort is

surrounded by pleasant mountain scenery, and there are numerous hiking trails to explore.

Jingdezhen ⑳ (景德镇), in the northeast of the province, is a historic kiln town and the manufacturing base of celebrated Jingdezhen porcelain. Several museums detail the history of the town, which fashioned imperial porcelain and overseas export ware, and pottery factories and workshops are open to the public.

Celebrated as the cradle of the Chinese Revolution, the rugged mountains of **Jinggangshan**, along Jiangxi's southwestern border with Hunan province, provided essential shelter for the embryonic Chinese Red Army divisions during fierce fighting with the Nationalists in the late 1920s and early 1930s. The village of **Ciping** ㉑ (茨坪) served as a base for Mao Zedong and Zhu De after they united their divisions to form the Fourth Red Army in 1927. The **Former Revolutionary Headquarters** (革命旧居群; Geming Jiujuqun; Nanshan Lu; summer 7.30am–6pm, winter 8am–5.30pm; charge) houses a collection of restored mud houses where some of the Communist leaders lived and planned their battles in 1928.

Just north of here, atop Beishan (North Hill) is a vast Soviet-style complex centred on the **Monument to the Revolutionary Martyrs** (烈士纪念堂; Lieshi Jiniantang; daily 8am–5pm; charge). Spanning the entire hillside, the circuit of monuments draws legions of flag-waving Chinese tourists and makes for a fascinating hour's walk.

HUNAN

The large province of **Hunan** (湖南) is famed for its cuisine, a fiery brew of chilli and spices, and as the birthplace of Mao Zedong. This is one of China's main rice-growing regions, and the landscape is dominated by paddy fields, but there are some scenic mountain areas, too, including Heng Shan and the reserve of Wulingyuan.

Changsha

Located on the main Guangzhou–Beijing rail line, the provincial capital, **Changsha**

The Cult of Mao

The cult of Mao was a pervasive, propaganda-fuelled phenomenon that etched the leader as a deity in the minds of most Chinese. In the bad old days of the 1960s his image was everywhere, dominating didactic posters emblazoned in red. Workers and students alike wore badges with his portrait, and after the 1966 publication of *Quotations from Chairman Mao* – the "Little Red Book" – even his words were on the lips of every student and soldier. Mao's increasing paranoia encouraged him to harness the power at his disposal to launch the disastrous Cultural Revolution in 1966.

Following his death in 1976, the power of the personality cult rapidly waned, but even today the Chairman's image is China's most prevalent, adorning the country's banknotes, staring down from classroom walls and swinging from taxi-drivers' rear-view mirrors. Despite espousing scorn for traditional superstitions during his lifetime, Mao is regarded as "lucky" by many Chinese. Anyone who visits his hometown of Shaoshan will be able to see for themselves how old habits die hard.

Recommended Restaurants on page 323

㉒ (长沙), is by far the largest city in Hunan, with a population of over 6 million. While at first sight it is not the most enticing of places, further investigation reveals a city with a fair amount to offer. The **Hunan Provincial Museum** (湖南省博物馆; Hunansheng Bowuguan; 50 Dongfeng Lu; daily Apr–Nov 8am–6pm, Dec–Mar 8.30am–5.30pm; charge) stands out as the main sight in town. The first settlements in the Changsha area date back 5,000 years, and the gigantic concrete museum housing more than 110,000 artefacts is rightly famous for its 2,100-year-old Western Han tombs, corpses and coffins, as well as Shang- and Zhou-era bronzes discovered in the region.

The must-see for those on the Mao trail is the **Clearwater Pool** (清水潭; Qingshui Tang; daily 8.30am–5pm; charge) on Bayi Lu. The site contains the first Chinese Communist Party provincial headquarters, established by Mao in 1921, as well as a house where the future leader lived for two years.

Mao's homeland

Mao's childhood home in **Shaoshan** **㉓** (韶山), 90km (55 miles) southwest of Changsha, is a place of pilgrimage for students of the Communist Revolution and Maoist iconography. The intensity with which Mao is still venerated here is a throwback to an earlier time, and a phenomenon in itself *(see panel, opposite)*. Nothing can prepare you for the old-world propaganda and tack that lies in store in this otherwise peaceful area of Hunanese countryside – something of an eye-opener in China's fast-changing society.

The mud-walled **Former Residence** (毛泽东故居; Mao Zedong Guju; daily 8am–5.30pm), where Mao was born on 26 December 1893 and brought up with his two brothers, is surprisingly large. Inside are detailed descriptions in both Chinese and English of every section of the house, including the rooms of his brothers Mao Zemin and Mao Zetan, who both died fighting for the Communist cause.

Slap bang in the middle of the village is the **Bronze Square**, where, in something reminiscent of Turkmenistan or North Korea, tour groups line up to bow. Across from the Mao statue is the **Museum of Comrade Mao** (毛泽东纪念馆; Mao Zedong Jinianguan; daily summer 7.30am–5.30pm, winter 8am–5pm), which gives visitors a quick rundown in timeline fashion of the life of the Great Helmsman. Next to this is **Mao's Ancestral Temple** (毛氏宗祠; Maoshi Zongci; daily 8am–5.30pm; charge), which traces the family ancestry back to a Ming patriot who fought the Mongols.

Heng Shan

Hunan's religious dimension is provided by the southernmost of the Daoist sacred mountains, **Heng Shan** **㉔** (衡山), 120km (75 miles) south of the provincial capital, Changsha. The mountain, the highest part of a range that stretches from Hengyang northwards all the way to Changsha, is accessed on foot from the town of **Nanyue** (南岳), rising just to the north: allow around five hours to reach Wishing Harmony Peak (Zhurong Feng), the highest point, and another three hours to descend back to Nanyue: in all it's a full day's hike. Alternatively, there are frequent minibuses which travel all the

BELOW:
on the heights of Heng Shan.

Wulingyuan has a sizeable population of rhesus monkeys, the most common of China's primates.

BELOW: Fenghuang.

way to the summit, or a cable car to the top of an adjacent peak from approximately halfway up.

Frequently misty, the route up the 1,290-metre (4,232ft) mountain passes several temples, including the Nanyue Damiao at the start of the climb, and the nearby Zhusheng Si; at the peak is the Zhurong Dian (Zhurong Hall).

The far northwest

Prosperous **Zhangjiajie City** ㉕ (张家界市; Zhangjiajie Shi) is the regional hub of the far northwest of Hunan, and lies some 33km (21 miles) south of the fabulous scenery at Wulingyuan *(see below)*. A short taxi ride south of Zhangjiajie City brings you to what is purported to be the world's longest **cable-car** run (daily 8am–5.30pm), which climbs the spectacular face of **Tianmen Shan** (天门山) – a vertiginous panorama of rock shards festooned in forest and often shrouded in mist. The cable car runs for a distance of 7.5km (4½ miles), rising 1,300 metres (4,260ft) in elevation.

A one-hour bus ride from Zhangjiajie City (last bus at 6.30pm) lies **Zhangjiajie Village** (张家界村; Zhangjiajie Cun), the

most popular springboard for exploring principal **Wulingyuan Scenic Reserve** ㉖ (五陵源风景区; Wulingyuan Feng Jingqu; charge). From this entrance there is a stunning 5.7km (3½-mile) stroll along the valley floor, as well a handful of trails which climb the valley walls. Another climbing option, which should not be missed, is the **Bailong Lift**. Tacked onto a sheer cliff face, it's cited in the *Guinness Book of World Records* as being the largest outdoor elevator in the world. It whisks guests up 326 metres (1,070ft) in under two minutes and provides jaw-dropping views.

Wulingyuan Reserve protects a magnificent landscape, with mature forests, crystal-clear lakes, limpid streams and, rising above all, the karst topography: the 3,100 precipitous quartzite sandstone crags are simply breathtaking. The area shelters a remarkable variety of plants (over 3,000 species, including more than 500 species of tree) and some rare animals – including a few clouded leopards, various monkeys, and 1-metre (3ft) long giant salamanders. Unfortunately it is often flooded with noisy tour groups, and parts of the park are littered with their

GETTING TO HUNAN

By train and bus: Hunan lies on the main Guangzhou–Beijing line, and rail connections with Guangdong, and north to Wuhan, Nanjing and Shanghai, are frequent. Buses run to Guangzhou, Wuhan and other cities.

GETTING AROUND HUNAN

Changsha: There are frequent buses to Shaoshan (2 hours), regular trains to Zhangjiajie (6 hours, 7 daily; note that some take much longer) and also trains to Shaoshan (3 hours, 1 daily).

Yueyang: There are frequent trains and buses to Changsha (1½–2 hours) and one daily bus to Zhangjiajie (7 hours).

Shaoshan: There are frequent buses to Changsha (2–3 hours). One train per day departs for Changsha (3 hours).

Zhangjiajie: Buses depart for Fenghuang (4 hours, 2 daily). There are trains to Changsha (6 hours, 7 daily).

Fenghuang: There are regular buses to Jishou (1 hour) and Haihua (2 hours). Jishou and Haihua are both well connected by train with Changsha (8–9 hours).

Fenghuang's tourist facilities have developed quickly but are still relatively modest – although quantity is not a problem: there are plenty of cheap restaurants and guesthouses.

detritus. The entrance ticket is also one of the most expensive in China. A final sucker punch is the highly volatile weather, which often leaves the peaks smothered in clouds and mist.

Fenghuang

In the far west of Hunan, close to the border with Guizhou, is the ancient riverside town of **Fenghuang** ㉗ (凤凰), home to Miao and Tujia minorities. The Tuo River runs through the old district (the town dates back to 248 BC), surrounded by the red-sandstone city walls and grand old gateways, while Ming- and Qing-style architecture lines up along the elegant intersecting stone-paved streets. It all

adds up to one of the most attractive places in China, and Fenghuang has woken up to its tourist potential: in recent years it has become very popular with tour groups.

The focus for tourism is pedestrianised **Dongzheng Jie** (东正街), which runs from the centrepiece covered bridge of Hongqiao, past the 18th-century **Dongmenlou** (东门楼; East Gate Tower) and into the thicket of low-rise buildings southwest of the river. The Tuo River is straddled by several bridges, and its depth is sufficiently shallow to allow two sets of **stepping stones**, opposite where Wenxing Jie meets the riverside city walls, to provide an alternative means of crossing. ❑

RESTAURANTS

Jiangxi is part of China's spice belt, and chillis feature heavily in local cuisine. In the Yangzi region of the north, fish is more prevalent.

Hongni Shaguo 红泥砂锅
Tengwang Pavilion, South Gate.
Tel: 0791 670 4888. **$**
This friendly establishment, situated next to the Tengwang Pavilion, is one of the best places to try the Jiangxi take on delicacies such as savoury *hongshao*

ruyu (soy-braised mullet).

Hunan Wang Caiguan
湖南王菜馆
99 Supu Lu.
Tel: 0791 623 8433. **$**
Facing Bayi Park, this immensely popular restaurant has some of Jiangxi's most authentic Hunanese cuisine.

Hunan is famous for its fiery food, and local restaurants indulge in a liberal use of chillis with pretty much everything. Similar to

Sichuanese cuisine but even hotter, it has become popular across China, and there are Hunanese restaurants in all large cities.

Huogongdian 火宫殿
93 Wuyi Donglu.
Tel: 0731 412 0580. **$**
A great place to sample a wide range of local specialities, with appetising Hunanese morsels served on dim sum-style trolleys. Make sure you try the cured chilli beef. Mao himself praised the smelly tofu

when he dropped by in 1959.

The riverside streets on both sides of the Tuo River are full of small restaurants, bars and cafés, and there's a cluster of street-food stalls around the Hong Qiao bridge.

Prices for a meal for one, with one drink:

$ = under Rmb 50
$$ = Rmb 50–100
$$$ = Rmb 100–150
$$$$ = over Rmb 150

CHINESE WILDLIFE

China is the world's third-largest country and its varied habitats endow it with a bountiful biodiversity

China's vast territory encompasses practically every climate and habitat on earth, from frigid Siberian *taiga* to tropical rainforest. Central and southern China's location at the boundary of the temperate and tropical zones ensures that there is also an abundance of endemic species, with 17 percent of mammals and 36 percent of reptiles found nowhere else on earth. However, centuries of population pressure compounded by rapid economic growth and a cavalier attitude towards the natural bounty (particularly during the Mao years) has put the landscape under intense pressure, destroying many habitats and threatening the survival of numerous species. The demand for animal parts from the Chinese medicine trade *(see page 87)* and the local penchant for eating anything that moves have also contributed to the decline. Some faltering progress has been made to preserve the country's biological diversity *(see opposite)*, but the challenge remains enormous.

Much of China is mountainous, and it is in the remote montane forests that some of the most spectacular wildlife survives. Western Sichuan is home to the giant panda (a few also survive in the Qin Ling Shan further east), and its smaller relative, the red panda. Snow leopards prowl at higher elevations throughout the Himalayan zone. Further south, a few clouded leopards, black bears and golden takin remain in the wilder parts of Yunnan, while the tropical south of that province still shelters wild elephants. A handful of South China tigers may remain in the forests of northern Guangdong; the larger, paler Manchurian tiger is endangered in the far northeast. The wide open spaces of western China are home to herds of Tibetan antelope and wild Bactrian camels. Numerous species of monkey thrive in southern and southwestern areas, including the rare golden monkey.

Other star species include the giant salamander and Chinese alligator, although the Yangzi dolphin *(baiji)* may already be extinct. Birdwatchers are drawn to some of China's lakes and wetlands, stopping off points for various species of crane on their migration between Siberia and tropical Asia. Colourful tragopans can be seen in the forests of the southwest.

ABOVE LEFT: giant salamanders can reach 1.8 metres (6ft) in length.

ABOVE: less well known than their black-and-white cousins, red pandas thrive in the sub-Himalayan forests of Yunnan and Sichuan.

RIGHT: Tibetan macaques are common on Emei Shan in Sichuan.

ABOVE: a snow leopard. A few thousand of these magnificent creatures live in rocky habitats at altitudes of 3,000–6,000 metres (10,000–20,000 ft) throughout the Himalayas and Tian Shan Mountains.

CONSERVATION

China's State Environmental Protection Administration works hand in hand with international agencies such as the WWF, the Wildlife Conservation Society, Wetland International and the National Geographic Society in a bid to protect species such as the giant panda *(xiongmao)*, the giant salamander *(wawayu)* and the golden, or snub-nosed, monkey *(jinsi hou)*. Some nature reserves are also Unesco World Heritage Sites, a status that brings in much-needed investment and useful experience in management. Since the establishment of Dinghushan Nature Reserve in Guangdong province in 1956, China has created over 700 nature reserves, and fully 8 percent of China's land is now protected.

China is also party to the Convention on Biological Diversity, the Convention on International Trade in Endangered Species (CITES) and other international conventions protecting the environment. But lack of experienced personnel and under-investment in nature reserves and other conservation schemes remain serious problems. There is still a great need for increased scientific research on specific conservation issues and exploratory surveys to catalogue wildlife populations and locations.

ABOVE: the endangered status of the giant panda is only in part due to man's impact on the environment; their principal food is the arrow bamboo, which periodically dies off across large swathes of forest leaving the pandas having to make do with an alternative, omnivorous diet. Some weaker individuals cannot cope with the change and starve to death.

LEFT: blood pheasants live in the forests of northwestern Yunnan. Together with their close relatives, the tragopans, they are some of the most spectacular of Chinese birds.

RIGHT: Tibetan antelope (*chiru* in Tibetan) are under threat from poachers who can make big profits from the animals' fine wool. Population numbers are thought to remain over 70,000, however, so it is not classified as an endangered species.

THE SOUTHWEST

From Guilin to Chengdu, tropical Xishuangbanna to snowy Himalayan peaks, there is a huge amount to see in China's fascinating southwestern corner

The southwest is many travellers' favourite part of China, and it isn't hard to understand why. In terms of scenery and cultural diversity, this region is hard to beat, and exploring its riches gives a greater sense of adventure, a more complete "travel experience". Many parts of the southwest lie outside the mainstream Han Chinese world, and therefore look and feel quite different from the rest of China.

Guangxi is less known for its cultural aspects than for its incredible scenery. The Li River winds its way lazily through an astonishing landscape around the city of Guilin, familiar to anyone who has set eyes on a classical Chinese scroll painting. To the north, a scenic route leads via the stunning Longsheng rice terraces to Guizhou, one of the poorest parts of China, populated by a colourful array of minority groups with exotic architecture and festivals. The landscape across much of the province is wild and mountainous and travel is often rough, with poor accommodation and terrible roads, but can be extremely rewarding for the hardy.

The large province of Sichuan, famous for its spicy food, is split between the  densely populated east and south, centred around the pleasant city of Chengdu, and the wild mountains and forests of the largely Tibetan west and north, which provide a habitat for pandas and an array of other wildlife. The holy Buddhist mountain of Emei Shan and the stupendous Buddha statue at Leshan south of Chengdu, are further attractions.

Finally, much of southern Yunnan feels more like Laos or Thailand than China, with elaborate Buddhist temples, jungles and minority peoples. Beyond the pleasant provincial capital, Kunming, the land rises to the easternmost ridges of the Himalayas. Here you will find the magical cities of Dali and Lijiang, both set against dramatic mountains and within easy reach of some of the best trekking in China. The far northwest around Zhongdian is culturally part of Tibet, and marketed as "Shangri-la" to tourists seeking adventure. ❑

PRECEDING PAGES: limestone formations on the Li River. **LEFT:** the Jade Dragon Snow Mountain from Lijiang. **TOP:** Miao festival dancers in Guizhou province. **ABOVE LEFT:** the giant Buddha at Leshan. **ABOVE RIGHT:** the Stone Forest in eastern Yunnan.

GUANGXI AND GUIZHOU

The provinces of Guangxi and Guizhou are
endowed with extraordinary limestone
landscapes, spectacular rice terraces and a
colourful array of minority peoples

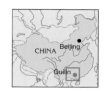

"The river is like a green silk belt, and the hills are like turquoise jade hairpins." So wrote the Tang-dynasty scholar and writer Han Yu (768–94), becoming the first prominent voice to immortalise the landscape around Guilin in **Guangxi** (广西; the full name is Guangxi Zhuang Autonomous Region). Nowadays, tourists swarm from all over the world to sample the magical scenery. Together with Beijing, Shanghai and Xi'an, Guilin is one of China's foremost destinations.

The Guilin area owes its exquisite beauty to geological disruptions over 300 million years ago. Limestone formations pushed through an ancient seabed, then the wind and rain eroded the hills and peaks into innumerable shapes, leaving behind labyrinthine caves and grottoes within them. With some peaks rounded and some sharply pointed, perpendicular cliffs and trees that sprout from the cracks to bend skyward, this is a dreamlike landscape, familiar to anyone who has looked at a Chinese scroll painting, and which has long lured travellers to the area.

China's southwest is also where Han uniformity runs up abruptly against a constellation of non-Han ethnic tribes. The largest ethnic minority in China, the Zhuang comprise about one-third of Guangxi's 46 million inhabitants, dominating its eastern half. Another 5 percent belong to 10 other minorities, such as the Yao, Miao, Dong and Yi, living primarily in the western and northern mountains of Guangxi. Longsheng, with its immac-

ulate terraced slopes, and the famous covered wooden bridge at Sanjiang in northern Guangxi, are testament to the industrious, rustic existence of these tribes that is so distinct from the prevailing Han culture.

Guizhou (贵州) province to the north is also home to a particularly colourful patchwork of ethnic groups, notably in the picturesque southeastern region around Kaili. There are some beautiful old villages here, and if you are lucky enough to witness one of the numerous festivals *(see page 340)* then any travel hardship in

Main attractions
JINJIANG PRINCES PALACE, GUILIN
YUZI PARADISE
LI RIVER CRUISE
YANGSHUO AND SURROUNDINGS
LONGSHENG RICE TERRACES
MIAO AND DONG MINORITY VILLAGES, GUIZHOU
ZHENYUAN
HUANGGUOSHU FALLS

LEFT: Li Jiang and limestone spires.
BELOW: a street in Xingping village.

Guilin, a perennial favourite of tour groups, has excellent transport links with cities across China.

accessing this remote area will have been worthwhile.

GUILIN

The tourist hub for the amazing limestone region of Guangxi, **Guilin** ❶ (桂林) literally means "cassia tree forest", named after the local cassia or osmanthus trees, whose scent wafts through the city in autumn. Historical records put Guilin's founding at 214 BC, during the reign of Qin Shi Huangdi, the first emperor of a united China, when he ordered the construction of the Ling Canal to connect the central plain of China with the south and with Southeast Asia, via the Yangzi, Li and Zhu rivers. The canal, one of the world's longest, still exists and can be easily seen at Xing'an, 65km (40 miles) northwest of Guilin.

Guilin has been a significant political and cultural centre since the Tang dynasty (618–906), but its golden years arrived during the Ming dynasty (1368–1644), after Zhu Shouqian, the son of the founding Ming emperor who was appointed ruler of this part of China, set up his court in Guilin.

Being so far from Beijing, Guilin and Guangxi have a tradition of sheltering refugees. In 1647, the fleeing Ming court established a temporary residence here in their flight from the Manchus. Three centuries later, as the Japanese army swept into China, hundreds of thousands of northerners sought safety in Guilin. In 1949, it was one of the last Guomindang strongholds to fall to the Communists.

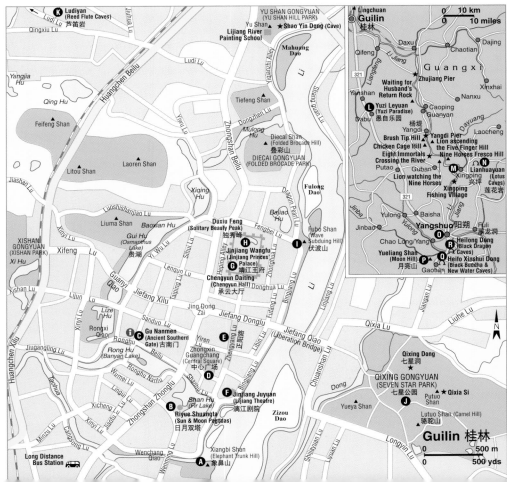

Recommended Restaurants on page 343

GETTING TO GUANGXI

By air: Guilin and Nanning are well connected with cities across China.

By train and bus: Guangxi lies on the Beijing–Hanoi railway, with other long-distance routes between Guangzhou and Yunnan crossing the province. Guilin is a major rail hub. Sleeper buses run from Guilin (and Yangshuo) to Guangzhou, Changsha and other cities.

GETTING AROUND GUANGXI

Guilin: There are regular bus services to Yang-shuo (1–1½ hours, every 20 minutes), Long-sheng (1½ hours, hourly) and Nanning (4–4½ hours, every 15 minutes). There are trains to Nanning (4–6 hours, 10 daily).

Yangshuo: There are frequent minibuses to Guilin (1–1½ hours). The nearest railway station is at Guilin.

Longsheng: Buses depart every 15 minutes to Guilin and take 1½ hours. Guilin is the nearest railway station.

Pingxiang (Vietnam border): There are bus services to local towns, and trains to Nanning (3½ hours, 6 daily).

A trip on a bamboo raft is the best way to appreciate Elephant Trunk Hill.

At first glance there is little to see of Guilin's rich history – almost the entire city was razed by the Japanese army in 1944. When it was rebuilt, there was little to distinguish it from any other mid-sized Chinese city – apart from the unusual sight of limestone peaks in the city centre. As one of China's premier tourist sights, the city is typically swamped with visitors, but Guilin remains attractive. Parks and osmanthus trees mottle the urban landscape, and a few limestone peaks, such as Xiangbi Shan (Elephant Trunk Hill) and Fubo Shan, rise above the buildings. The Li Jiang River cuts through the town, and many small restaurants offer river cuisine, such as fish, eel, frog, turtle, snail, shrimp and snake.

City Sights

Guilin's landmark **Xiangbi Shan** Ⓐ (象鼻山; Elephant Trunk Hill) is a good place to start a walk around the city. Located slightly south of the centre on the river bank, the hill distinctly resembles a limestone elephant. If you have the energy, climb the 200-metre (650ft) hill and catch your breath inside the Pux-ian Pagoda, which was built more than 500 years ago.

At night the colourful lights of the 40-metre (130ft) **Riyue Shuangta** Ⓑ (日月双塔; Sun and Moon pagodas; daily; charge) cast glittering gold and silver reflections on Shan Hu (Fir Lake), just to the north of Xiangbi Shan.

To the northwest, beside an 800-year-old banyan tree on the northern bank of the Rong Hu Lake, is an authentic remnant of the Old City. The **Gu Nanmen** Ⓒ (古南门; Ancient Southern Gate), was built during the Tang dynasty and expanded in Ming times, when Guilin became the provincial capital. It was once part of the city walls, so the oldest part of the gate is a modest stone tunnel. A Ming-style single-storey building now sits on top of the wall. From here the lakeside promenade turns westward, and

BELOW: Riyue Shuanta (the Sun and Moon pagodas) in Guilin.

BELOW RIGHT:
Olympic souvenirs
in Guilin.

then north, along Yiwu Lu following the banks of Baoxian Hu, the former moat that forms the western border of the Old City and runs parallel with the Li River.

Further north, as you enter the middle section of the city's grid layout, the lakeside fairy lights give way to neon lights, and Guilin is suddenly indistinguishable from any medium-sized Chinese city. The main hub of activity is the area around **Central Square ⓓ** (中心广场; Zhongxin Guangchang), built in 1999 south of the intersection of Jiefang Lu and the city's other main thoroughfare, Zhongshan Lu. In this downtown area department stores, stalls and restaurants are open until late. Between Central Square and the Li River, pedestrianised **Zhengyang Lu ⓔ** (正阳路) runs south from Jiefeng Lu to Nanhuan Lu. Popularly referred to as "walking street", this area is geared towards tourists, with a selection of restaurants, bars, galleries and fairly kitsch souvenir stalls.

On the waterfront thoroughfare, Binjiang Lu, the **Lijiang Theatre ⓕ** (漓江剧院; Jinjiang Juyuan) has a changing programme of evening shows that often feature Guangxi's minorities.

Evening boat trips along the city's restored waterways, and other tours, can be booked at the numerous agents along Binjiang Lu, or through hotel tour desks.

The most historic area of Guilin is the **Jinjiang Princes' Palace ⓖ** (靖江王府; Jinjiang Wangfu; daily 8.30am–5pm; charge), a short stroll north of the city centre. Its walls, gates and halls follow the classic lines of a Ming-dynasty city. Tour guides will always stress that it was built 34 years before the larger Forbidden City, but unlike Beijing's palace, most of what you see today has been reconstructed in the last 20 years.

First built in 1372 as the palace of Zhu Shouqian, the palace was home to the next 12 generations of Jinjiang princes until the end of the dynasty in 1644. When the Ming court fled south, they tried to establish a Southern Ming dynasty from here, but in 1650 the Manchus drove them out of Guilin and the city was destroyed.

Parts of the original city walls are still in place, and some original stone carvings and balustrades have been recovered and restored. The main palace in the centre of the complex, **Chengyun Hall** (承云大厅; Chengyun Daiting), houses a

Recommended Restaurants on page 343

small exhibition about the 14 princes who lived here down the centuries.

Guilin's ancient city within a city has its very own karst mountain inside its walls (included in charge). **Duxiu Feng** Ⓗ (独秀峰; Solitary Beauty Peak) rises up above the Ming buildings, and climbing the 300 or so steps to the pagoda at the top rewards you with the delightful view enjoyed by princes and poets over the centuries. At the western foot of the peak is the entrance to **Pingshiku** (平石窟; Peace Grotto; included in charge), a network of caves and passages where the princes once worshipped their ancestors.

To the east lies **Fubo Shan** Ⓘ (伏波山; Wave Subduing Hill; daily 7am–7pm; charge). A short, steep climb up the steps takes you to a small viewing platform on the summit, from where you can see the hills of **Diecai Shan** (叠彩山; Folded Brocade Hill; daily 8am–6.30pm; charge), which at 220 metres (720ft) in height are the tallest in the city and so called because when this group of hills catch the changing daylight they are said to resemble piles of folded fabric.

Across the Li River from the city centre and reached via Liberation Bridge (Jiefang Qiao) lie the scenic peaks of **Qixing Gongyuan** Ⓙ (七星公园; Seven Star Park; daily 7am–7pm; charge). The park within which they are set allows you to sample all the city's natural attractions in one manageable 40-hectare (100-acre) site. It is a pleasant mix of landscaping, caves and temples set amid the seven peaks, which lie in the shape of the Big Dipper constellation.

The **Ludiyan** complex Ⓚ (芦笛岩; Reed Flute Caves; daily 8.30am–4.30pm; charge) is located about 7km (4 miles) northwest of the city centre and is considered to be the most dramatic of Guilin's cave systems.

South of Guilin

The extraordinary beauty of the countryside south of Guilin is no secret, and a steady stream of riverboats make the scenic journey along the Li River between Guilin and Yangshuo. The landscape in this region is dominated by the outlandish limestone pinnacles rising sheer from

It may be mainly for the benefit of tourists these days, but using cormorant to catch fish has a long history in this part of China.

BELOW: Qixia Temple at Qixing Gongyuan (Seven Star Park).

A summer rainstorm in Yangshuo. Northern Guangxi is one of the rainiest parts of the country.

BELOW: bamboo raft trips are a popular way of seeing the river.

the otherwise flat terrain of paddy fields. Farmhands in conical hats work the rice terraces, while on the river villagers fish from bamboo rafts using trained cormorants. This is the classic Chinese landscape familar from so many scroll paintings, and for many visitors, this region represents a quintessential taste of China.

On the road to Yangshuo, 30km (18 miles) south of Guilin, the mountains make an inspired setting for the sculpture park at **Yuzi Paradise** (愚自乐园; Yuzi Leyuan; daily 8.30am–6pm; www.yuzi-paradise.com; charge). Large contemporary sculptures are spread over 60 hectares (150 acres) in a landscape of winding paths, lakes, modern architecture and the odd karst outcrop. It's a fascinating place to explore for a few hours.

If you opt to travel between Guilin and Yangshuo by road, it is also possible to join a boat at **Xingping** for a short river trip. From Yangshuo, there are local

buses every 20 minutes for the one-hour journey to Xingping, which was the main town in the area 400 years ago. Surrounded by seven peaks on the east side of the river, it is worth allowing some time to stroll through the oldest part of Xingping, where traditional houses line narrow, unpaved footpaths.

Three km (2 miles) outside Xingping are the caves of **Lianhuayan** (莲花岩; Lotus Caves; daily; charge). The entrance includes a guide, who will turn on the multicoloured lights within the 600-metre (2,000ft) underground passageway and point out a multitude of hard-to-discern animal shapes.

Yangshuo

The town of **Yangshuo** (阳朔) lies amid stupendous scenery on the west bank of the Li, 60km (37 miles) downstream from Guilin. It has long enjoyed a prime position on the backpacker trail, although these days it is crammed with foreign and domestic tourists of all budgets, and fills up even more in the afternoons when visitors disembark from the Guilin boats.

Despite all this, Yangshuo somehow manages to retain a riverside country town

feel, and for most tourists remains one of the most enjoyable destinations in all of China. The great appeal is the opportunity it provides to slow down, bike or hike and explore the Chinese countryside that is otherwise only glimpsed from trains and buses. It is certainly one of the easiest places in China to spend time. There's a good selection of reasonably priced accommodation in the town, a wide choice of clean, inexpensive restaurants with foreigner-friendly food, cheap beer and excellent Yunnan coffee.

Xi Jie (西街; West Street) is the centre of the tourist scene. Most visitors arrive either at **Yangshuo Quay** (阳朔码头) at the bottom of the street, or at the bus station on the corner of Diecui Lu and Pantao Lu. Chengzhong Lu has a few pavement cafés and small guesthouses, and there are more hotels along Binjiang Lu, some with great river views.

Around Yangshuo

Try to hire a bike in town (*see margin page 338*) and pedal out into the countryside. The 10-km (6-mile) journey to **Yueliang Shan ❷** (月亮山; Moon Hill) southwest of town is fabulous and highly recommended; the view from the summit of the hill (a reasonably tough clamber) is spellbinding.

Nearby are two popular cave complexes that rely less on coloured lights for effect and more upon the visitor's sense of adventure. The **Heifo Xinshui Dong ❸** (黑佛新水洞; Black Buddha New Water Caves) were discovered in 1991, and the 1½- or 3-hour tours will involve some scrambling along ladders and wading through mud. About 3km (4 miles) down the road, the **Heilong Dong ❹** (黑龙洞; Black Dragon Caves) can be explored by boat or by kayak if you arrange your tour with a guide or agent in Yangshuo in advance.

Yangshuo has become one of China's foremost adventure-sport capitals in recent years. Rock-climbing, boating and ballooning trips can all be organised from operators in town. All three pursuits offer spectacular new perspectives on the landscapes around Yangshuo. Rafting around

Yulong Qiao (玉龙桥; Jade Dragon Bridge) is a particular highlight.

If you are staying overnight in Yangshuo, don't miss the amazing **Impression Liu Sanjie** show. This beautifully choreographed musical extravaganza takes place in an open-air venue on the Li River, close to Yangshuo, with the karst peaks providing an inimitable backdrop to the performance.

North to the Guizhou border

To the northwest of Guilin and nearing the border with Guizhou province are the counties of **Longsheng** (龙胜) and **Sanjiang** (三江). This region's traditional architecture, terraced hills and ethnic costumes (the Miao and some Yao groups are famous for their embroidery skills) make it an excellent introduction to southwest China's minorities. **Longsheng ❷**, although unspectacular itself, is the access point to an enchanting surrounding landscape. To the southeast of town is the region's most famous attraction, **Longji Titian** (龙脊梯田; Dragon's Backbone Terraces), the evocative name given to a series of steep hills layered with rice terraces. The effect is extraor-

Shopping can easily consume many hours in Yangshuo, with shops selling a vast range of souvenirs, minority handicrafts, embroidery, textiles, art and jewellery. Surprisingly, urban offerings include Asian-inspired interior design, CDs and DVDs. Yangshuo's clothes shops offer everything from Beijing 2008 T-shirts, tie-dye and minority batiks to branded sports shoes and designer clothing.

BELOW: cruising on the Li river.

Li Riverboat Trips

A boat trip on the Li River is a highlight of a trip to China. The most popular journey is to sail the 80km (50 miles) from Guilin down to Yangshuo, through the heart of the incredible karst scenery which has made the region famous. For most of the year, boats leave from the tourist port at Zhujiang Pier, 20km (12 miles) south of central Guilin; tickets include transport to the pier from the city centre. Shorter trips are also possible, as well as trips starting in Yangshuo and Xingping.

The cruise passes the endlessly fascinating limestone spires that shoot up from the flat plains. It's a relaxing way to take in the peaks and catch a glimpse of life along the river bank. En route, guides will intermittently point out the names that the poets have bestowed on the peaks: Waiting for Husband's Return; Lion Ascending the Five Finger Hill; Chicken Cage Hill; Eight Immortals Crossing the River. As you approach the town of Xingping, fellow passengers will pull out Rmb 20 notes to compare the real thing with the peaks that appear on the back of the note. The journey takes three to five hours, depending on the water level, with lunch and transport back to Guilin by bus included in the (hefty) ticket price.

BELOW: the Dragon's Backbone Terraces at Longsheng.

dinary, and highly photogenic. Basic accommodation can be found in Ping'an, a small Zhuang village positioned amid the terraces and within range of other minority villages.

Sanjiang ❸ (三江), the scruffy capital of the Sanjiang Dong Autonomous County 165km (100 miles) northwest of Guilin, is of no particular interest in itself; the reason to visit is the wooden **Chengyang Wind-and-Rain Bridge** (程阳风雨桥; Chengyang Fengyuqiao) 18km (11 miles) north of town. There are over 100 such bridges in the county, but the Chengyang bridge is celebrated as the finest – 78 metres (255ft) long and 20 metres (66ft) high, it straddles the Linxi River and was completed by the Dong people in 1916 with such precision that it did not require the use of a single nail. Simple accommodation and restaurants are available on the other side of the river in Chengyang itself, and several other minority villages dot the area.

Southern Guangxi

As one approaches the southern coastal areas of Guangxi, the landscape assumes a more tropical feel. Guangxi's capital of **Nanning ❹** (南宁), southwest of Guilin, is an affluent metropolis of over 1 million people. Among its attractions are the **Provincial Museum** (省博物馆; Sheng Bowuguan; daily 8.30am–noon and 2.30–5pm; charge), with its fine bronze drum collection, and the adjoining cultural centre, where architectural examples from the Dong, Miao, Yao and Zhuang minorities have been recreated in an open-air museum. Just 5km (3 miles) southeast of the city, in Qingxiu Park, stands the highest pagoda in Guangxi.

The port of **Beihai ❺** (北海) on the south coast still sports 19th-century European buildings that recall its history as a treaty port (the best examples are near the waterfront); the town is also known for its beaches. **Silver Beach** (北海银滩; Beihai Yintan) is a pleasant enough stretch of sand, although it does get very crowded at times. Be aware that the water is not especially clean.

Some 200km (125 miles) southwest of Nanning en route to the Vietnamese border, the country town of **Ningming ❻** (宁明) is the jumping-off point for a boat trip along the scenic **Zuo River** (左江).

It's worth visiting the **Friendship Pass**

(友谊关; Youyiguan) on the Vietnamese border 30 minutes south of Pingxiang by taxi or pedicab, even if you're not crossing into Vietnam. Graced by two imposing landmarks – a colonial French customs house and a ceremonial Chinese gateway – the crossing straddles a narrow pass between tall, misty mountains. Cracked stone steps lead up to vantage points on either side. Inside the French-era building, faded photographs show Mao Zedong trading jokes with Ho Chi Minh; friendship hasn't always been in great supply: within 15 years the two neighbours were at war with each other.

GUIZHOU PROVINCE

Guizhou (贵州), one of China's poorest provinces, is a little-known backwater that rewards exploration. Situated on the eastern section of the Yunnan-Guizhou plateau, its hilly landscape is both tricky to cultivate and soaked with persistent rain, but this authentic slice of the Chinese countryside is populated by an intriguing ethnic patchwork of minorities (including Dong, Miao, Bouyei, Sui, Hui and Zhuang, plus picturesquely named sub-groups such as the Small

Flowery Miao and the Long-Horned Miao High in the west, Guizhou drops off sharply towards the east; there is an area of limestone karst scenery in the south central region.

Although the Han Chinese have penetrated the province for over two millennia, infertile land and tribal resistance to Han rule traditionally made the province an insignificant region of the Chinese empire, until a large influx of Chinese arrived during the Qing dynasty. Guizhou is perhaps most often associated in the Chinese mind with both rural poverty and *maotai*, a potent and high-priced liquor fermented from sorghum, considered the *ne plus ultra* of Chinese *baijiu* ("white spirit").

Guiyang

Guizhou's modest capital, **Guiyang** ❼ (贵阳), right in the centre of the province, has little to entice visitors, and largely acts as a transit point. The **Provincial Museum** (贵州省博物馆; Tue–Sun 9–11.30am, 1–4pm; charge) on Beijing Lu has displays relating to the province's ethnic tribes, and Qianling Shan Park to the west is a pleasant,

Cable-cars on Qianling Shan, Guiyang.

BELOW: Jiaxiu Lou (Jiaxiu Pavilion) on the Nanming River, Guiyang.

The covered wind-and-rain bridges in some of the Dong minority villages of southern Guizhou and northern Guangxi are a striking sight.

BELOW RIGHT: a Miao *lusheng* festival.

wooded area of hills topped by the attractive Buddhist **Hongfu Si** (弘福寺; Hongfu Temple; accessed by steps or cable car).

Eastern Guizhou: the Miao and Dong areas

Many tourists come to Guizhou with one target in mind: the tribal reaches in the province's east and the Miao and Dong Autonomous Prefecture, an area home to a fascinating variety of minority groups.

Just across the border from Guangxi, the far southeast of the province is home to the Dong minority, known for their construction of wooden towers and bridges, and indigo-dyed clothing, also seen over the border in Guangxi province at Sanjiang (*see page 338*). The town of **Zhaoxing ⑧** (肇兴), the Dong's main centre, is utterly entrancing, with five impressive drum towers and five wind-and-rain bridges. Almost all other buildings in the town are of traditional wooden three-storey design.

The regional capital, **Kaili ⑨** (凯里), connected to Guiyang by train and encircled by minority hamlets reachable by minibus, is a functional base equipped with hotels, banks, restaurants and internet cafés. Ask at your hotel in Kaili or at CITS in the Yingpanpo Binguan (Yingpanpo Hotel) for maps and details of the local festivals and markets in surrounding villages – it's best to coincide your exploration with festival dates if possible; tours can also be arranged at CITS. The lovely Miao hamlets of **Matang** (麻塘), **Chong'an** (重安) and **Shibing** (施秉) to the north and **Xijiang** (西江) to the southeast are among the many intriguing settlements spread across the hilly countryside around Kaili.

Zhenyuan ⑩ (镇远) is ranged photogenically along the deep, green valley of the Wuyang River a short train journey (1 hour 40 minutes) northeast of Kaili. Its **Heilong Dong** (黑龙洞; Black Dragon Cave; daily 6.30am–7.30pm; charge) is in fact a collection of Buddhist and Daoist temples and pavilions that cling to the rock face on the opposite side of the river from the historic Old Town. The complex, dating from 1530, gives good views of **Zhusheng Qiao** (竹生桥; Zhusheng Bridge) on which sits **Kuixing Lou** (魁星楼; Kuixing Pavilion). Beside

Miao Festivals

The Miao are famous for their festivals, with hundreds taking place around Guizhou during the course of a year. The most famous are the *lusheng* **festivals**, at which young girls don their traditional costumes and dance to the music of the *lusheng* pipes (long reed pipes made from bamboo). These festivities mainly occur from October to April, particularly in January and February when agricultural work is at a minimum. Often accompanied by bullfights, they are held at a designated site called a "flower ground", which could be anything from the local basketball court to a picturesque natural setting, and are real community events: the gatherings are traditionally an opportunity for young people to find suitable marriage partners – the Miao call this "fishing".

A more ritualised courtship takes place from the 15th to 17th days of the third lunar month at the **Sister's Meal festival**, with the symbolic exchange of sticky rice and other gifts between prospective partners. It is centred around the Miao villages of Shidong and Taijiang to the northeast of Kaili. Shidong is also the best place to catch the **Miao Dragon Boat festival**, commemorating the slaying of a dragon that once terrorised the local population, while **Miao New Year** takes place over a five-day period around the end of the 10th lunar month.

GETTING TO GUIZHOU

By air: Guiyang airport has regular connections with most large cities in China.

By train and bus: There are several daily trains between Guiyang and Kunming (12–15 hours), Guilin (2 daily, 16 hours), Changsha (3 daily, 14 hours), Chongqing (5 daily, 12 hours) Chengdu (3 daily, 19 hours) and Guangzhou (5 daily, 24 hours). There are 2 daily buses (one of which is a sleeper bus) to Guilin, taking around 10 hours.

GETTING AROUND GUIZHOU

On the whole, it is better to use buses rather than trains in Guizhou.
Guiyang: There are frequent buses to Anshun (1½ hours), Kaili and Zunyi (both 2½ hours). Trains to Kaili take 3 hours, to Zunyi 5 hours and to Anshun 2 hours.
Kaili: Frequent buses to Guiyang take 2½ hours, and there are erratic bus services to surrounding villages. Trains to Guiyang take 3 hours.
Zunyi: Buses to Anshun (3 daily, 5½ hrs) and Guiyang (2 daily 2½ hrs).

Mao befriends the peasants, Zunyi Conference Hall Revolutionary Museum.

the bridge, on the edge of the Old Town, a steep climb up a paved path provides even better views. At the top, the old city walls seem to offer less protection than the karst mountains on which they were built. Following a path to the left and then down the hill leads to the small temple of **Sigong Si**, from where a descent back into the town is possible. The Han Dragon Boat racing festival (on the fifth day of the fifth lunar month) is the town's major festival.

For more water-based activities a cruise along the **Wuyang River** (舞阳河; Wuyang He) is recommended. They can be arranged at the large town of **Shibing** (施秉), 40 km (19 miles) west of Zhenyuan.

Tongren, near the border with Hunan to the east, is the access point to the mountain and forest reserve of **Fanjing Shan ⑪** (梵净山), renowned for its diverse fauna and flora. Home to several rare species including the golden, or snub-nosed, monkey *(jinsi hou)* and the giant salamander *(wawa yu)*, the preserve also sustains a huge array of trees and medicinal plants. At 2,494 metres (8,180ft), the climb up to the summit is hardly a stroll (allow at least a day up and a day down), and climbers should be prepared for chilly weather in the upper reaches. Fanjing Shan, literally "Buddhist Pure Mountain", doubles as a Buddhist mountain; a monastery near the summit can offer basic accommodation so you can stay overnight and catch the sunrise.

Zunyi and the north

Zunyi ⑫ (遵义) would be an undistinguished industrial blob 165km (102 miles) north of Guiyang were it not lauded by Communist Party cadres for its historic revolutionary credentials. Dragging itself into Zunyi in January 1935 halfway along the Long March, the Communist army held a meeting here that paved the way for Mao Zedong to assume control of the Chinese Communist Party (CCP), and approved his strategy of promoting rural revolt among the peasantry. The event is memorialised at the **Zunyi Conference**

BELOW: rural life in much of Guizhou has changed very little.

Birdwatchers flock to Caohai Hu to catch the winter migratory period, when a plentiful array of rare birds, including black-necked cranes, stop over here.

Site (遵义会议址; Zunyi Huiyizhi; daily 8.30am–5pm; charge), laid out with 1930s period furnishings, while the **Long March Museum** (长征博物馆; Changzheng Bowuguan; daily 8.30am–5pm; charge) brings you up to speed on the circuitous route followed by the weary army.

Around 10 hours by bus northwest of Zunyi, the small town of **Chishui** ⑬ (赤水) is set in an impressively remote region of subtropical forest on the Guizhou-Sichuan border. The **Shizhang-dong Pubu** (十丈洞大瀑布; Shizhang-dong Falls) 40km (25 miles) south of town is uncluttered by tourism and makes for an enjoyable escape; trails through Sidonggou, closer to town, open up the remarkable landscape to exploration.

Western Guizhou

In a karst region 100km (60 miles) south-west of Guiyang, the unkempt town of Anshun is primarily a place from which to reach the Huangguoshu waterfalls and the Longgong Caves, although the hilltop Ming-dynasty **Xixiu Shan Ta** (西秀山白塔; Xixiu Mountain Pagoda) is worth a mention. Minibuses regularly depart Anshun for the regional drawcard,

Huangguoshu Pubu ⑭ (黄果树瀑布) waterfalls, 45km (28 miles) to the south-west; many tours also take in the flooded **Longgong Dong** (龙宫洞; Longgong Caves; where boats tour China's longest underground river) en route. There are charges for both sites. Huangguoshu is but one of many falls in the area, but is the most impressive (and most commercialised). Watch the water crashing into Rhino Pool and its consequent huge bloom of spray or access the tunnel behind the curtain of water. Time a trip to the 68-metre (223ft) falls during the summer rainy season, when the flood-waters are at their most forceful. Accommodation options exist in the park.

Around 90km (55 miles) northwest of Anshun, in an area of striking limestone scenery, the karst cave network of **Zhijin Dong** (织金洞; Zhijin Caves; daily 8am–5pm; charge) is famed for its scale, extending into the hillside for several kilometres.

Further west in the mountainous Wumeng Shan region near Yunnan province, **Caohai Hu** ⑮ (草海) is a beautiful freshwater lake and part of a celebrated nature reserve.   ❑

RESTAURANTS

Restaurants

Prices for a meal for one, with one drink:
$ = under Rmb 50
$$ = Rmb 50–100
$$$ = Rmb 100–150
$$$$ = over Rmb 150

GUANGXI PROVINCE

Guangxi cuisine lacks a clear identity – there is a strong Cantonese influence in the east and south, while things get increasingly spicy further inland. Guilin has a reputation for outlandish zoological delicacies.

Beihai

Tommy's Bar
来来汤米吧
Block D, Yuenan Jie, Waishadao.
Tel: 0779 208 7020. $
Tommy's Place, a two-storey venue behind the seafood restaurants on the north shore, has its own micro-brewery and an East/West menu which includes steaks and pan-Asian dishes. Outdoor seating completes the picture.

Guilin

Restaurants are clustered around Central Square (Zhongxin Guangchang) and along Zhongshan Zhonglu heading south from the square.

Forest Gump 阿甘酒家
3 Yiren Lu.
Tel: 0773 286 3038. $
Modest Chinese restaurant with branches across the city – and no apparent connection to the film of the same name. Good choice of dishes and friendly staff.

Left Bank Café
滨江左岸
18 Binjiang Lu.
Tel: 0773 288 2259. $$
An ambitious range of offerings includes steaks, burgers, pizzas and fried rice served in a dimly lit dining room. On the river, with views of Seven Star Park.

Natural Café 闻莺阁
24–25 Yiren Lu.
Tel: 0773 283 8866. $$
Large restaurant offering Western staples, Chinese dishes and curries.

Two Pigs Asian Fusion
二豚餐厅
Hotel of Modern Art (HOMA), Yuzi Paradise, Dabu Township, Yanshan District.
Tel: 0773 386 9172. $$
Immaculately presented fresh food in this arty modern restaurant with noodles, Thai, sushi and burgers all available.

Zhengyang Tang Cheng
正阳汤城
54 Zhengyang Lu.
Tel: 0773 285 8553. $
Popular local restaurant whose range of dishes includes a few local specialities.

Nanning

V-Touch Restaurant
水沙莲餐厅
43-12 Xinmin Lu.
Tel: 0771 263 6388. $
V-Touch Restaurant has a helpful picture menu and English-speaking staff. The house special is hot pot, and there are vegetarian options.

Yangshuo

Most of the action is along Xi Jie (West Street).

Café Too
自由人旅店餐厅
7 Cheng Zhong Lu.
Tel: 0773 882 8342. $
Serves a satisfying choice of local dishes, and there's an extensive menu of Western food. Breakfast, pages long in all its permutations, is good value.

Drifters 旅行者
58 Xi Jie.
Tel: 0773 882 1715. $
Australian-owned bar-café with a long menu of filling meals.

Le Vôtre 乐得法式餐厅
79 Xi Jie.
Tel: 0773 882 8040. $$
A restored Ming-dynasty building with a large outside terrace houses something unusual in provincial China – an upmarket French restaurant serving salade niçoise, croissants and chocolate mousse.

7th Heaven Café
桃源饭店
2 Cheng Zhong Lu.
Tel: 0773 882 6101. $
All the Yangshuo café favourites, plus the added bonus of a selection of medicinal Chinese soups. Friendly service.

GUIZHOU PROVINCE

Food in Guizhou is hot and spicy. In the towns and cities and at festivals, kebab, noodle and hot-pot stalls provide cheap and interesting dining opportunities.

Most restaurants have neither English signs nor menus. Therefore, hotel restaurants are easier to locate. KFCs and various other foreign-based impostors can be found in the main cities.

Guiyang

For local fare try walking from the railway station along Zunyi Lu: there are plenty of stalls along the side streets.

Howard Johnson Plaza Hotel:
Western Restaurant
瑞迪那西餐厅
Chinese Restaurant
怡园厅
29 Zaoshan Lu. Tel: 0851 651 8888/810 8888. $$
If you are pining for those back-home foods, the "all you can eat international buffet" in the ground floor restaurant should satisfy, providing great value in a 5-star setting. The à la carte menu is comprehensive and reasonably priced. There is also a Cantonese restaurant on the third floor.

Merrylin Restaurant
美林阁
1F Motel 168,
2 Guiyang Shi Shenghu Lu
Tel: 0851 821 7692. $$–$$$
An upmarket establishment offering good-quality Chinese and Japanese fare and a comprehensive selection of Chinese wine.

Zhaoxing

The Haixing Pub
海湘酒吧
Zhaoxing Street. $
Situated in a two-storey Dong house, this is a great place to watch rustic life go by. Good local food as well as the only pizza you are likely to find outside Guiyang.

THE MINORITIES OF SOUTHWEST CHINA

The minority groups of southwestern China, with their magnificent costumes and colourful festivals, have retained their identity and traditions into the present day

The swathe of southern China from western Hunan province through Guizhou, parts of Guangxi and much of Yunnan is home to a sizeable concentration of minority peoples, remnants of a larger population that has been displaced by the Han Chinese over the course of many centuries and retreated to remote highland regions (a trend accelerated by persecution following the rebellions of the 19th century). This isolation has created a strong sense of identity and tradition, which makes a visit to a minority village – particularly at festival time – a fascinating experience.

The largest minority group is the Zhuang of Guangxi and eastern Yunnan, although they are more integrated into mainstream Chinese life than the other main groups – the Miao (numbering over 8 million, most of whom are concentrated in Guizhou), the Yi (Yunnan), Dong (southern Guizhou), Dai (southern Yunnan), Bai (Dali region) and Naxi (Lijiang region). There are dozens of smaller groups scattered around the region.

All China's minority populations are now guaranteed freedom to retain their language and customs by the Chinese constitution. That isn't to say that they are on an equal footing with the Han, although this is perhaps less to do with discrimination than the fact that it is difficult for these tradition-bound communities to break the cycle of rural poverty.

RIGHT: a Khampa horseman from the remote plateaux of eastern Tibet.

TOP: Miao men playing *lusheng* pipes at festival time. The dyeing and weaving of their indigo robes is an important cottage industry.

BELOW: like most of Yunnan's minority groups, the Bai are predominantly Buddhist, but with influences from a wide range of other religions, including Daoism and even Christianity.

LEFT: the well-known Naxi orchestra in Lijiang performs music dating back to the Song Dynasty. The Naxi people of northwestern Yunnan are a matriarchal society and one of the few southwestern minorities to have a written script.

MINORITY COSTUME

The Miao and other minority groups (such as the Dong, pictured right) are known for their colourful festivals – a time when the community comes together, with the people (mainly the women) resplendent in traditional costume. Most striking of all are the remarkable silver headdresses worn by Miao girls at the *lusheng* festivals. There are several Miao subgroups, each of which has its own distinctive costume. The Small Flowery Miao specialise in extravagant bouffant hairdos, while the Long-Horned Miao tie their hair around wooden horns projecting from the sides of the head. The Dong wear splendid indigo-dyed garments. These forms of dress are not merely ornamental; they are an assertion of a cultural identity distinct from mainstream China and the relentless consumerism that continually erodes the minorities' way of life.

BELOW: Bai dancers at the foot of the Three Pagodas in Dali. As well as being skilled architects, the Bai people are known for their dance, music and lacquer work. White is their preferred colour for clothes, and their name means "white people".

Recommended Restaurants on page 357

SICHUAN

Isolated from the rest of China by a ring of
mountains, Sichuan is famous for its fiery cuisine
and the world's biggest Buddha. The remote
western forests provide a refuge for the
endangered panda

Isolated from the rest of China by a series of mountain ranges, **Sichuan** (四川) is the country's third-most populous province. Most of its 87 million people are crowded into some of the world's highest rural population densities in the flatlands of the Red Basin, south and east of the provincial capital, Chengdu. A large chunk of what was eastern Sichuan was cleaved off the province in 1997 to form Chongqing Shi; this area is detailed in the Chang Jiang chapter *(see pages 251–4)*. Sichuan is famous for its cuisine, often spelled "Szechuan" or "Szechwan" in the West.

Sichuan has a long history. The two kingdoms of Shu and Ba have been dated back to the 9th century BC, and were part of present-day Sichuan under the first emperor of a united China, Qin Shi Huangdi. The character for Shu survives as the official abbreviation for Sichuan. Around AD 1000, during the Northern Song dynasty, four districts were created to facilitate administration. They were called Chuan Xia Si Lu (four districts of Chuanxia), and were later abbreviated to the modern name Sichuan.

Today, Sichuan is one of inland China's richest provinces, but its economy and infrastructure took a serious setback in 2008, when on 12 May, a magnitude 8.0 earthquake struck the town of Wenchuan, 80km (50 miles) northwest of Chengdu. At the time of writing the quake was estimated to have killed more than 69,000 people, with a further 18,000 listed as missing. Chengdu got off very lightly –

locals reported cracked residential buildings, but no buildings collapsed – and the worst-affected areas were parts of Sichuan that see next to no foreign tourist traffic.

The lay of the land

The heart of Sichuan is the fertile Red Basin, surrounded by mountains to the north, south, east and west, with a climate very favourable to agriculture: this is one of China's major rice-growing areas, and the warm summers, mild winters and high humidity allow cultivation throughout the year. Even during the cold months

Main attractions
WUHOU SI TEMPLE, CHENGDU
CHENGDU TEAHOUSES
WOLONG NATURE RESERVE
EMEI SHAN
LESHAN BUDDHA
JIUZHAIGOU NATURE RESERVE
LANGMUSI
HAILUOGOU GLACIER
LUDING BRIDGE

LEFT: the gigantic Buddha at Leshan.
BELOW: synchronised tai chi in a Chengdu park.

TIP

Chengdu's teahouses, *chadian*, have long been centres of activism and free discussion. They were shut down during the Cultural Revolution, but are back again. Try the teahouse in Renmin Park.

of January and February, the markets are filled with fresh fruit and vegetables.

In complete contrast, the western half of Sichuan is wild and mountainous. The expansive forests are rich in fir and deciduous trees, and shelter rare wildlife. This is the home of the giant panda, forced into ever higher mountain regions by human encroachment, and now threatened with extinction despite great efforts to save the species.

The mountain areas are home to 15 recognised ethnic groups, including a sizeable Tibetan population: much of western Sichuan lies within the traditional Tibetan lands of Kham. They have suffered less friction with the Han Chinese than in Tibet (Xizang province), thanks to a long history of peaceful relations and a lack of contention over territorial sovereignty, although there was some anti-Chinese violence in the town of Aba in the build-up to the Beijing Olympics.

CHENGDU

Sichuan's easygoing capital, **Chengdu** ❶ (成都), lies on the western edge of the Red Basin. The city, which is more than 2,000 years old, now has a population of around 3.3 million in the city proper, and around 10.2 million in greater Chengdu, making it China's fifth-largest city. In contrast to some other Chinese urban centres, and despite raging redevelopment, it has managed to preserve an atmosphere that evokes a sense of history.

As the centre of the kingdom of Shu, Chengdu was already the political, economic and cultural centre of western Sichuan by 400 BC. During the Five Dynasties period (AD 907–60) numerous hibiscus trees were planted on the city walls, beginning a tradition of tree-planting that has continued over the centuries and resulted in the city having particularly attractive parks.

Built on flat terrain, Chengdu can easily be explored on foot or by bicycle. It has almost a southern aspect, with pleasantly colourful old streets lined by scores of small, traditional shops and restaurants, and walkways that remain crowded until late with traders, buyers and people just out for a stroll. The commercial centre is concentrated around Dongfeng Lu and Dong Dajie, southeast of the large Mao statue and the Exhibition Hall, and Tianfu Square subway station.

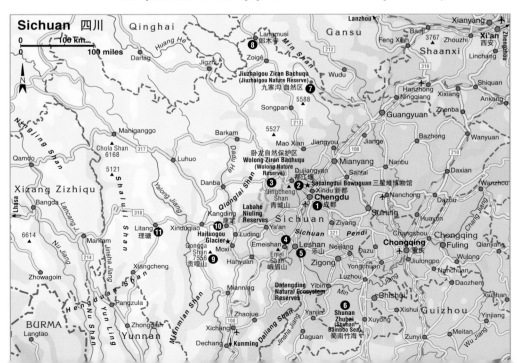

Recommended Restaurants on page 357

GETTING TO SICHUAN

Flights: Chengdu has domestic flights to all major cities in China. The province has 10 other airports, but only Jiuzhaigou and Panzhihua are likely to be used by foreign travellers.

By train and bus: Chengdu is a major transport hub, with extensive rail links and long-distance buses to cities throughout China. Rail connections include Lhasa (48 hours), Beijing (24 hours), Guangzhou (32 hours), Xi'an (13 hours), Guilin (25 hours), Shanghai (36 hours) and Chongqing (4½ hours).

GETTING AROUND SICHUAN

Chengdu: There are frequent buses to Emei Shan (5 hours), Dujiangyan (1½ hours), Leshan (5 hours), Jiuzhaigou (36 hours), Songpan (8 hours), Kangding (14 hours), Yibin (8 hours) and Zigong (6 hours). There are regular trains to Emei Shan (2–3 hours), Panzhihua (12 hours) and Xichang (11 hours). Jiuzhaigou is most easily reached by a daily flight from Chengdu.

Emei Shan: There are frequent buses to Chengdu (5 hours), Xichang (10 hours) and Ya'an (3 hours), while trains connect Emei with Chengdu (2–3 hours), Panzhihua (11 hours) and Xichang (5 hours).

Leshan: Buses depart for Chengdu (4 hours), Emei Shan (1½ hours), Yibin (6 hours) and Ziigong (3½ hours).

Yibin: There are buses to Chengdu (8 hours), Ziigong (2½ hours) and Gongxian (2½ hours).

A Chinese bulbul atop a pillar, Wenshu Yuan, Chengdu.

One could eat one's way through the region's countless specialities by visiting the snack bars or **teahouses** *(chadian)*, which often have free performances of Sichuan opera or other instrumental pieces to entertain guests as they sip their jasmine tea. These teahouses are popular gaming hangouts, particularly for older men playing *weiqi* (played with black-and-white stones on a 19 by 19 line board), or Chinese chess. To sample this thriving teahouse culture, take a walk around **People's Park** Ⓐ (人民公园; Renmin Gongyuan), a short distance west of Tianfu Square. For some visitors, particularly during the hot summer months, the sprawling park leaves the most lasting impressions of the city, with its crowds at leisure, sipping tea in wicker chairs, playing cards and Chinese chess,

BELOW:
Tianfu Square in downtown Chengdu.

Relics, including a series of wells, from the Tang dynasty at Du Fu Caotang (Du Fu's Thatched Cottage).

and as evening approaches perhaps practicing ballroom dancing en-masse.

Kuan Xiangzi (宽巷子; Kuan Alley), around five minutes' walk northwest of Renmin Park, has been restored to its Qing-dynasty glory, and while there is something somewhat artificial about its appearance – as is the case in China's many other historical restoration efforts for tourism, such as Lijiang and Shangri-la in Yunnan – it is also difficult not to be impressed by this small pocket of old Chengdu, which elsewhere is very much a Chinese 20th-century city. There are no notable attractions, but it makes for an interesting stroll, and there are restaurants and tea shops to linger in.

Temples and other sights

Chengdu has several attractive temple complexes. **Wuhou Si B** (武侯祠; Temple of the Duke of Wu; daily 8am–5.30pm; charge), southwest of the city centre, was built by the king of the Cheng empire in the last years of the Western Jin period (AD 265–316), and named after the Three Kingdoms military strategist Zhuge Liang. The temple site as seen today was rebuilt in the Kangxi era of the Qing dynasty, in the late 1600s. There are more than 40 sculptures of famous personalities from the Shu and Han periods, as well as numerous memorial stones, scrolls and sacral implements.

Don't forget to explore the alleys that crawl around either side of the temple walls. At first sight, they make look to be something of a tourist trap, but they hide away some charming tea shops (which serve Sichuan's little-known equivalent to Guangdong's dim sum), several relaxing bars with balcony views, and a host of souvenir stalls. To the south is the Tibetan part of town, with its own distinct atmosphere and some interesting shops.

Further out towards the western suburbs is an attractive park containing **Du Fu Caotang C** (杜甫草堂; Du Fu's Thatched Cottage; daily 9am–5pm; charge). Du Fu *(see page 88)*, who lived in the 8th century and is possibly China's most famous classical poet, fled an official post in Chang'an (now Xi'an) and sought refuge in Chengdu with his family. He built a straw hut on the property of a helpful friend, and lived there for

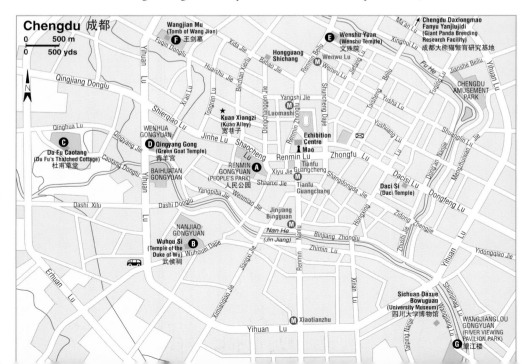

Chengdu 成都

Recommended Restaurants on page 357

three years in very modest circumstances. He wrote more than 240 of his popular poems here. The memorial to Du Fu has been renovated or rebuilt several times during the subsequent dynasties, and even today there is an active Chengdu Du Fu study society.

Another temple of note is the nearby **Qingyang Gong ❹** (青羊宫; Green Goat Temple), a fascinating complex dedicated to Laozi, the founder of Daoism. You can compare its more sober mysteries with the **Wenshu Yuan ❺** (文殊院; Wenshu Temple), in the north of town halfway between the Mao statue and the railway station; this is Chengdu's largest and busiest Buddhist temple, and home to one of the city's most popular teahouses.

It is worth visiting **Wangjian Mu ❻** (王剑墓; Tomb of Wang Jian; daily 9am–5.30pm; charge), in the northwest. Wang Jian was a general during the last days of Tang emperor Lizhu's rule in the early 10th century, and was the first ruler of the newly founded state of Shu in present-day Sichuan province. The building has three burial chambers. The centre chamber contains a sarcophagus between two rows of stone figures.

Southeast of the centre

Wangjianglou ❼ (望江楼; River Viewing Pavilion Park; daily; free) stands on the southern bank of the Jin Jiang River, in the southeastern part of Chengdu. It was built during the Qing dynasty in memory of Xue Tao (AD 768–831), a famous Tang-dynasty poet. Today, this area is a public park with several towers and pavilions. The Chongli Pavilion, which is 30 metres (100ft) tall and has four floors, is particularly noticeable because of its striking ornaments, green-glazed tiles and red-lacquered columns. More than 100 varieties of bamboo, including such rare varieties as spotted and square bamboo, have been planted here in honour of Xue Tao, who is thought to have loved the plant.

Very close to the pavilion, heading back in the direction of the city centre, the **Sichuan University Museum** (四川大学博物馆; Sichuan Daxue Bowuguan; daily 9am–6pm; charge) is worth a visit for its eclectic collection of Sichuan-related artefacts, some of them Tibetan.

Panda centre

Head northeast of town for 6km (4 miles) to the **Giant Panda Breeding Research**

TIP

The area around Wenshu Yuan is one of the most enjoyable parts of Chengdu for exploring on foot, with a network of renovated alleyways lined with an array of traditional shops. As well as the famous teahouse within the temple grounds, there is a sprawling teahouse area immediately to the east.

BELOW: the recently renovated area around Chengdu's Wenshu Yuan.

The giant panda first came to European notice in the 1860s. There are perhaps only 1,000 or so individuals still living in the wilds of China, clustered in two or three dozen groups in northern Sichuan, and also in the Qingling mountains of southern Gansu and Shaanxi provinces.

BELOW: a typical Sichuan landscape of flooded paddy fields.

Facility (成都大熊猫繁育研究基地; Chengdu Daxiongmao Fanyu Yanjiujidi; tel: 8351 6748; daily; charge), far preferable to the city zoo as a natural environment for both the giant and lesser (red) pandas. There are more than a dozen pandas living here, and the facility includes excellent exhibits and a museum.

The museum in particular makes the facility worth visiting as much as a glimpse of the pandas themselves. Covering an area of some 7,000 sq metres (75,000 sq ft), US experts were hired to help develop bilingual interactive exhibits that explain how the panda lives, its habitats and the efforts that are being made to protect the species from human encroachment.

Outside Chengdu

There are several places of interest easily reached by bus from Chengdu. Some 18km (11 miles) north of the city, in the town of **Xindu** (新都), is the Buddhist monastery **Baoguang Si** (宝光寺; Pre-

cious Light Monastery; daily 8am–6pm; charge). It is thought to have been founded during the Eastern Han dynasty, providing housing for more than 3,000 monks in the 10th and 11th centuries. The oldest structure is the 30-metre (100ft) tall Sheli Pagoda; the 500 well-preserved Qing Luohan *(arhat)* effigies are impressive.

Qingcheng Shan (青城山), 64km (40 miles) west of Chengdu, is a Daoist peak providing excellent hiking opportunities in a mountainous landscape of temples, caves and lakes. To the north is **Qingcheng Hou Shan** (青城候山), a further expanse of rambling walks and trails. There is a steep but not too strenuous hike to the summit, where it's possible to shelter in temple tea gardens and take in the views.

It is worthwhile making the effort to visit the **Sanxingdui Museum** (三星堆博物馆; daily 8.30am–5.30pm; charge), a mysterious collection of archaeological discoveries 40km (25 miles) north of Chengdu. A farmer digging a ditch in 1929 unearthed the first of the finds here, but later systematic digging revealed a host of ancient relics dating back 3,000 years and more, some of them looking

more Mayan than anything else that belongs to ancient Chinese history. The official explanation is that they belong to the ancient Shu civilisation of Sichuan, isolated from the central Yellow River plains where Chinese culture was long thought to have evolved. But the artefacts remain something of an enigma, and further ongoing digs elsewhere in the region suggest that a non-Han Chinese civilisation may have flourished in the region thousands of years ago.

Dujiangyan ❷ (都江堰), on the upper course of Min Jiang and 55km (34 miles) northwest of Chengdu, is a town famous its 2,000-year-old irrigation project. Built between 306 and 251 BC, the network of water channels was capable of irrigating an area of 200,000 hectares (500,000 acres). Today, the farmland is still supplied with water from the system, although capacity has been considerably enlarged by the addition of dams and pumping stations. A 3-metre (10ft) 1,900-year-old stone statue of Li Bing, the original builder, stands in Fulongguan (Pavilion of the Dragon's Defeat), while the Daoist Erwang Miao (Two Kings Temple) was built in his honour. Dujiangyan was close to the epicentre of the 2008 earthquake, but the irrigation system has survived.

The **Wolong Nature Reserve** ❸ (卧龙自然保护区; Wolong Ziran Baohuqu), a 200,000-hectare (500,000-acre) preserve of the giant panda some 140km (85 miles) northwest of Chengdu, is three hours by bus from Dujiangyan, or four hours direct from Chengdu. At the time of writing, unfortunately, the pandas had been evacuated from the reserve due to threats of landslides and other hazards from the aftermath of the 2008 earthquake. The reserve is likely to reopen in 2009, when the 20-odd captive pandas will again be on view. Don't come expecting to see pandas in the wild, but the scenery and hiking trails make the reserve a very worthwhile trip. The remote, pristine forests are a sanctuary for exotic wildlife such as snow leopards and golden monkeys, as well as pandas.

Around 40km (25 miles) south of Chengdu and easily reached by bus, **Huanglongxi** (黄龙西) is a well-preserved old riverside town, its winding streets lined with ramshackle shops and temples dedicated to Guanyin.

EMEI SHAN

Daoists began erecting temples around the mountain of **Emei Shan** (峨眉山) in the 2nd century AD, but as Buddhism gained popularity from the 6th century onwards, the mountain became a sacred place of Buddhism. It has been a major pilgrimage centre for centuries, and although buses and cable cars now ascend the heights, the old-fashioned method of walking up is well worth the effort. Beautiful scenery abounds, and the protected forests shelter rare animal and bird species, as well as an abundance of butterflies.

The Emei mountain range lies to the southwest of the Red Basin some 160km (100 miles) from Chengdu. **Emeishan** ❹ town, 7km (4 miles) from the start of the trail, can be reached either by bus or train (around two hours from Chengdu; it's possible to get off the Kunming–Chengdu train here). There are minibuses between

TIP

Lodging on Emei Shan is simple and cheap at the many monasteries along the way. Arrive before 5pm, when it's easier to get a bed in a separate room, rather than sleeping on the floor in the temple halls with many other hikers. A growing number of guesthouses on the slopes and on the Jinding summit provide a more comfortable alternative.

BELOW: Wannian Si on Emei Shan.

Sage advice on the slippery slopes of Emei Shan.

BELOW: Tibetan macaques are common on Emei Shan. Note they can be aggressive if provoked. **BELOW RIGHT:** on the summit.

the town and the main access point to the beginning of the trail at **Baoguo Si** (报国寺), a 16th-century monastery around which there is a range of accommodation, making it a convenient base for day trips up the mountain. The temple is set on a slope and comprises four halls, built one above the other. There are also various exhibition halls with artefacts, calligraphy and paintings.

Steps lead all the way from Baoguo Si to the summit, although many people start the hike from Wannian Si *(see following page)*, 500 metres (1,640ft) further up and reached by cable car from Jingshui village (itself reached by bus from Baoguo Si). Alternatively, buses wind up to **Jieyin Dian** (接引殿), a pavilion at an altitude of 2,670 metres (8,760ft). From here the summit can be accessed by a cable car, or via a two-hour hike. Just below the summit is **Jinding Si** (金顶寺; Golden Peak Temple), with a 20-metre (66ft) bronze hall.

The peak of Emei Shan is a lofty 3,099 metres (10,167ft), and in favourable weather conditions a remarkable natural phenomenon can be experienced here. If the sun is in the right position, an observer's shadow is cast onto the clouds below the peak, and an aura of pastel rainbow colours forms around the silhouette (one can also see this phenomenon from an aeroplane above the clouds). Buddhist pilgrims interpret this as a special sign, and in the past, some would throw themselves from the peak into their shadow, imagining that this led directly to the longed-for nirvana.

Most hikers choose to descend the mountain on a different route, while others take the easy option: bus or cable car up and hike back down. The trail from Jieyin Dian pavilion runs down to **Xixiang Chi** (洗象池; Elephant Bathing Pool), a relatively large temple built against a rock, offering a lovely view of the surroundings. According to legend, this is where the elephant of Bodhisattva Samantabhadra (Puxian; the patron deity of Emei Shan) took his bath. Below this point, the descent divides into a relatively steep but shorter path to Wannian Si or a longer route to Qingyinge.

Further along the Wannian Si path is a small gorge, **Yixiantian** (一线天; Thread of Sky), through which winds a stream lined with lush vegetation.

Recommended Restaurants on page 357

Wannian Si (万年寺; Temple of Eternity) stands at the lower end of the steeper path. It was built in the 4th century and once consisted of seven halls, but today only one 16-metre (52ft) high hall remains. The square structure, with a domed roof and made of bricks without rafters, is typical of Ming-dynasty architecture. It contains a bronze figure, of Samantabhadra on a white elephant, dating back to around 920.

According to some of the many folk tales relating to the mountain, this Bodhisattva came to Emei Shan riding on the white elephant. The northern and southern paths join again at Qingyinge (Pavilion of Pure Sound), where the two streams Black Dragon and White Dragon also join – the source of the pure sounds. The pavilion is now a rest house that also serves meals.

Leshan

Around 50km (30 miles) east of Emei Shan, the town of **Leshan** ❺ (乐山) is famed for its colossal 71-metre (233-ft) seated statue of Buddha *(dafo)*. Recently completed large-scale restoration work has done much to improve the appearance of the statue, which had suffered from centuries of erosion and, more recently, pollution. The giant figure overlooks the confluence of two rivers, the Dadu He and Min He, and despite the simple artistic rendering, is astonishing in scale. Believing the effigy would protect boats on the river, the monk Haitong began work on the Herculean task in 713; it took 90 years to complete. Equipped with a sophisticated elaborate drainage system to combat weathering of the sandstone, *dafo*'s heights can be scaled along steps in the rock. There are several temples in the hills around, linked by paths through the woods.

The Bamboo Sea

In the southeastern corner of Sichuan, close to the border with Guizhou, is the remarkable **Shunan Bamboo Sea** ❻ (蜀南竹海; Shunan Zhuhai). Often used as a film set, its vast forests of 12-metre (40-ft) bamboo are accessed by an extensive network of paths, It's a very out-of-the-way place – easiest access is from the city of **Yibin**, 75km (47 miles) away.

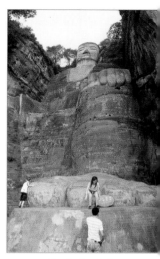

The Leshan dafo is the world's largest Buddha statue.

BELOW AND BELOW LEFT: buddhas at Wuyou Si, just south of the Big Buddha.

NORTH AND WEST SICHUAN

The rugged mountains of Sichuan's northwestern half begin immediately to the west and north of Chengdu. This is a wild, remote area with fabulous scenery, including some of China's largest remaining forests, much of it lying within the historic boundaries of Tibet. The mountainous terrain makes access to many areas extremely difficult.

Jiuzhaigou and northern Sichuan

In the northwest of Sichuan close to the border with Gansu province, about 500km (300 miles) from Chengdu, **Jiuzhaigou Nature Reserve ❼** (九寨沟自然区) is a natural wonderland. The park was opened in 1978, and abounds with lush montane forests, grassy steppes, fantastically clear blue lakes, rivers and waterfalls, all framed with high mountains and peaks covered with eternal snow. The Tibetan people in the region have a legend about the creation of Jiuzhaigou. An immortal called Dage and a fairy called Wunuosemo lived deep in the mountains and fell in love. One day, Dage gave Wunuosemo a mirror as

a present, which he had polished to a high shine with the wind and the clouds. Unfortunately, she dropped the mirror and it broke into pieces, which transformed into the 108 lakes of the Jiuzhaigou.

Many travellers spend a few days horse-trekking in the hills around the town of **Songpan** (松潘). The town itself is nothing special (although its old stone gates remain), but the treks can be exhilarating, passing mountain lakes and waterfalls. Guides operate from Songpan, and finding them is no problem.

Continuing on towards Gansu province, on the route between Chengdu and Xiahe, is the remote village of **Langmusi ❽** (郎木寺), with its population of Tibetans, Goloks and Hui Muslims as well as Han Chinese. Surrounded by dramatic grassy mountains, Langmusi has the feel of an untouched traditional Tibetan village, and is becoming popular with tourists. This is an excellent area for hiking, and is one of the few places outside Tibet where visitors can witness a traditional Tibetan sky burial (although remember to keep a respectful distance and avoid photography if you see such a

The intense blue of Jiuzhaigou's lakes is caused by calcium deposits. The reserve has become enormously popular in recent years; some find the crowds overwhelming.

BELOW: grassland and mountains near Langmusi.

burial). From Langmusi the rough roads continue across expansive grasslands to the beautiful Labrang Monastery at Xiahe *(see page 400)*.

The road to Tibet

Travelling through mountainous western Sichuan is fascinating, and the region itself becomes more markedly Tibetan in character the further west you penetrate. At the time of writing, however, crossing into Tibet through western Sichuan remains officially illegal. This is as much to do with the dangers presented by the treacherous road conditions as political sensitivities. Visitors to the **Hailuogou Glacier** (海螺沟) can stop at the nearby town of **Luding** (泸定) to see the Luding Bridge, famous for a Communist victory over Guomindang troops on the Long March. More spectacular, though, is the glacier itself and the breathtaking mountain scenery on **Gongga Shan** ❾ (贡嘎山; 7,556 metres/24,790ft). You can hire guides from the nearby village of Moxi (accessible by road from both Leshan and Emeishan) for return treks up to the glacier, which take around three days.

The Tibetan presence becomes stronger at **Kangding** ❿ (康定; 2,560 metres/8,400ft), capital of Ganzi Tibetan Autonomous Prefecture, which is effectively a border zone between Han Chinese and Tibetan Sichuan, with a sprinkling of Qiang and Yi minorities. There is little to do in this town, which resounds to the sound of a raging river that intersects it, except lounge in the town square with the locals or take a cable car to a mountain monastery overlooking it, but Kangding's remoteness will be appealing to some.

For Yunnan-bound travellers, the route from high and remote **Litang** ⓫ (理塘; 4,000 metres/13,100ft), home to a Tibetan monastery, south through Xiangcheng takes you to Zhongdian *(see page 370)* – now popularly known as Shangri-la. This in one of China's most scenic road journeys, and it is not as time-consuming as many people seem to imagine. Litang to Xiangcheng is around five hours by bus – weather permitting – while the road from Litang down to Zhongdian, enjoying wonderful mountain views en route, is around eight hours.   ❏

Damage from the 2008 earthquake will take many years to repair. In the meantime some of the routes into the mountains west and north of Chengdu are even slower and more circuitous than usual.

RESTAURANTS

Sichuanese food is famous for its fiery flavours, and is one of the most popular of Chinese cuisines.

Chengdu

Perhaps more than any other city in China, Chengdu has a strong sense of self-identity that is reflected in the pride that it takes in its food. Fiery Sichuanese dishes such as *kung pao* chicken *mapo dofu* are generally excellent in the city restaurants. Other cuisines are less reliable, and for international cuisine the best bet is to stick to hotel restaurants.

8trees Wine Bar 倮樹
9 Ping'an Alley

(off 25 Xihuamen Jie). **$$**
This poised establishment, with an extensive selection of international wines, offers a somewhat eccentric mix of dishes, switching from pan-fried tuna to "bangers and mash", but ordering selectively will not disappoint.

Gongguan Cai 公官菜
41 Qinghua Lu. **$$**
Close to the northern entrance to Du Fu's Cottage, Gongguan Cai translates as "official's food", and is a very well-respected place in Chengdu to eat quality Sichuan cuisine.

Huangcheng Laoma
皇城老媽
Erhuan Lu, Section 3. **$$**
Quite possibly the king of Chengdu's hot-pot restaurants – though the name means "mother of the imperial city" – this four-storey restaurant not only takes hot-pot cuisine to a new level, it also has impeccable Chengdu-themed décor.

Peter's Tex Mex
彼德西餐
117 Kehua Beilu. **$**
Popular with expats living in Chengdu, this homesick-themed restaurant serves up southern US-stateside cuisine and is a good place to meet people, over

burgers, burritos, enchiladas and other familiar fare.

Shunxing Old Teahouse
順興老茶館
3rd Floor, Chengdu International Exposition Centre, 258 Shawan Lu. **$$**
This atmospheric Sichuan tea shop offers sets of Sichuan's little-known answer to the Cantonese dim sum in period décor, and with traditional performances. Bookings are essential.

Prices for a meal for one, with one drink:
$ = under Rmb 50
$$ = Rmb 50–100
$$$ = Rmb 100–150
$$$$ = over Rmb 150

Recommended Restaurants on page 373

YUNNAN

With exotic Burma, Laos and Vietnam on one side and Tibet on the other, culturally diverse and ethnically rich Yunnan is one of China's most fascinating regions

China's southwestern province of Yunnan (云南) lies at the threshold of Southeast Asia, and no place in China offers the traveller as much diversity, both geographical and cultural. From the tropical south to the Himalayan northwest there is an abundance of interest in the form of ancient cities, colourful minorities and wonderful scenery. Yunnan is also one of the few parts of the country where travel is possible and enjoyable throughout the year.

Some history

Historically isolated at the furthest edge of the empire, Chinese troops first marched into Yunnan in the 4th century BC. When political reversals cut them off from their homeland, they stayed on and created the Kingdom of Dian, near present-day Kunming. The Han dynasty (206 BC–AD 220) later tried to reassert control over Dian to protect newly established posts on the southern Silk Road, but overall Chinese control of Yunnan remained intermittent, and by the Tang dynasty (618–907) the area was divided into several small princedoms. The prince of one of these made the long journey to Chang'an (Xi'an). When the Tang emperor asked from where he came, the prince replied he was from far away to the south, beyond the clouds of rainy southern Sichuan. So the emperor named the prince's homeland Yunnan, or South of the Clouds.

In the 8th century one of the princes seized power in central Yunnan and founded the Nanzhao Kingdom, which fought a century-long, three-sided war with Tibet and China for control of the southwest. Yunnan remained beyond China's jurisdiction until Kublai Khan conquered Nanzhao's successor, the Kingdom of Dali, in 1253. Even as the Han Chinese finally became a majority of the population, rulers and officials of the imperial court continued to regard Yunnan as wild, dangerous and culturally deprived – in other words, the perfect place to send malcontents and political troublemakers to start life over as pioneers on the frontier.

Main attractions
KUNMING MUSLIM QUARTER
QIONGZHU SI
WESTERN HILLS
STONE FOREST
YUANYANG RICE TERRACES
DALI AND SURROUNDINGS
LIJIANG AND SURROUNDINGS
TIGER LEAPING GORGE
LUGU LAKE
ZHONGDIAN
JINSHA NIGHT MARKET, JINGHONG
SANCHAHE NATURE RESERVE
TROPICAL BOTANICAL GARDENS, MENGLUN

LEFT: Dali pagodas.
BELOW: Bai women.

> *You arrive at the capital city, which is named Yachi (Kunming) and is very great and noble. In it are found merchants and artisans, with a mixed population consisting of idolators, Nestorian Christians, and Saracens...*
>
> Marco Polo

The land

The heart of the province lies on the Yunnan-Guizhou Plateau, at an average altitude of 2,000 metres (6,500ft). Mountains comprise a significant part of the landscape, with the ranges in the sub-Himalayan northwest the highest. The northern half of Yunnan has temperate-zone flora and fauna, with clearly marked seasons that guarantee spring flowers and bright autumn colours. In the lower-lying south, tropical vegetation dominates: year-round temperatures here are higher than anywhere else in China.

Some of the greatest rivers in Asia pass through Yunnan on their journey south and east from the Tibetan Plateau. The Chang Jiang (the Yangzi, known as the Jinsha Jiang in Yunnan) weaves its way across the north, while the Yuan Jiang (Red River), Nu Jiang (Salween) and Lancang Jiang (Mekong) all flow southwards before crossing into Vietnam, Burma and Laos respectively.

Yunnan is home to 25 recognised minority nationalities. Their lifestyles and local ecosystems vary almost as much as their colourful costumes. Altogether they form one-third of Yunnan's population.

KUNMING

Yunnan's capital, **Kunming** ❶ (昆明), sits at 1,900 metres (6,200ft) above sea level off the northern shore of Dian Chi Lake. Despite its development as a business centre for China's burgeoning economic links with Southeast Asia, the city retains a degree of its old-fashioned charm and atmosphere. The altitude makes the climate pleasantly cool in the summer months, and winter days are sunny and mild. There are also some beautiful walks and temples in the nearby hills.

Kunming did not become an important centre until the Yuan dynasty (1271–1368), when the Mongols made it the provincial capital, replacing Dali. Nonetheless, the city's most ancient landmarks, the two 13-tier pagodas **Xisi Ta** Ⓐ (西寺塔; West Pagoda) and **Dongsi Ta** Ⓑ (东寺塔; East Pagoda) in the southeast quarter (both 9am–8.30pm; charge) date back earlier to the Tang dynasty.

Head directly north from Xisi Ta and you'll pass through the city's traditional Muslim quarter, under strain from the pressures of modernity but retaining a certain character and a fair-sized community – a number of Hui restaurants still remain.

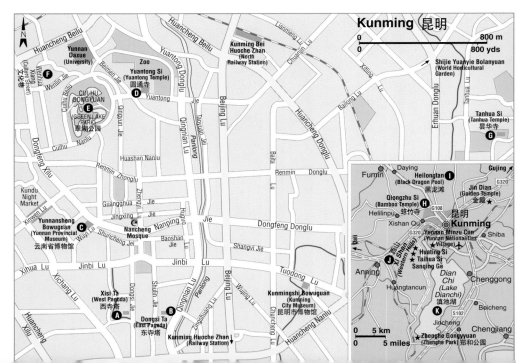

GETTING TO YUNNAN

Kunming is an important regional centre and is connected with most cities in China, as well as to Thailand. Dali, Lijiang and Jinghong also benefit from good air connections. There are trains linking Kunming with Beijing, Shanghai, Chengdu, Xi'an, Guilin and Guangzhou.

GETTING AROUND YUNNAN

Kunming: Buses to Hekou run twice daily (12 hours) and to Yuanyang three times daily (6–7 hours). The Stone Forest is 2 hours away by bus.

Dali: There are 3 or 4 daily flights between Dali and Kunming. Overnight trains from Kunming take 8–9 hours, frequent buses 7 hours. Frequent buses to Lijiang take 3 hours, to Ruili 10–12 hours.

Lijiang: There are several daily flights to/from Kunming (and elsewhere in China), and buses to Dali (3 hours) and Zhongdian (5 hours).

Jinghong: There are 4–6 flights per day between Kunming and Jinghong. Sleeper buses to/from Kunming depart every 30 minutes (4–8pm), journey time 10 hours. Jinghong to Dali by bus takes 17 hours and Ruili 24 hours.

A street market in Kunming. The best places to look for souvenirs are the shops along Dongfeng Lu and Beijing Lu.

Continue north to reach the heart of what was once the Old Quarter. The **Yunnan Provincial Museum** ⓒ (云南省博物馆; Yunnansheng Bowuguan; daily 9am–5pm; charge) on Wuyi Lu has an extensive collection of local bronzeware and exhibitions on Yunnan's minority cultures.

Yuantong Si ⓓ (圆通寺; daily 8am–5pm; charge), in the northern part of town, has been Kunming's most important Buddhist temple for more than 1,000 years. It was greatly expanded in the 14th century to encompass today's ornamental gardens. A short walk west from here lies **Cui Hu** ⓔ (翠湖; Green Lake), with ornate boats on the water and bright pavilions on its shores. The grounds form the city's major park, occupied every morning with Chinese *taiji* enthusiasts, as well as those practising their ballroom dancing. Yunnan University is located nearby; youthful crowds are catered for at the shopping and dining precinct of **Wenhua Xiang** ⓕ (文化巷), or Culture Street. Weekends are particularly lively, and when the weather

BELOW: downtown Kunming.

Looking down to Lake Dianchi from the Dragon Gate (Longmen) in the Western Hills.

BELOW: *luohan* figures at Qiongzhu Si.

is fine many of the restaurants set up tables and chairs alfresco.

Kunming's most arresting historical attraction is **Tanhua Si** (昙华寺; daily 8am–5pm; charge), a lofty pagoda located approximately 3km (2 miles) east of the city centre down Renmin Lu. An active Buddhist place of worship dating back to 1634, it is named after a species of magnolia tree that grows in its front courtyard – another popular spot for communal exercises. A climb to the seventh floor provides splendid views across the city.

Outside Kunming

With the beautiful Western Hills (Xi Shan) and Dianchi Lake right on its doorstep, there are numerous possibilities for day trips from Kunming.

Qiongzhu Si (筇竹寺; Bamboo Temple; daily 8am–6pm; charge) lies 13km (8 miles) northwest of the city. It is a famous hall of 500 idiosyncratic 19th-century statues of the *luohan* (Buddhist

saints and disciples), each uniquely sculpted to embody a Buddhist virtue. The surreal, grimacing figures surf amid a foaming frenzy of sea monsters, or reach upwards with super-extended limbs.

Heilongtan (黑龙潭; Black Dragon Pool; daily 8am–6pm; charge), 11km (7 miles) north of the city, is more conventional. It is flanked by a Ming-era Daoist temple, and the nearby botanical garden has a collection of camellias, rhododendrons and azaleas.

Atop Phoenix Song mountain, 7km (4 miles) northeast of Kunming, stands **Jin Dian** (金殿; Golden Temple; daily 8am–5pm; charge), which is actually furnished with walls, columns, rafters and altars made of bronze – about 300 tons of it – rather than gold. A cable car links with the **World Horticultural Garden** (世博园; Shiboguan; daily 8am–5pm; charge), with masses of colourful local blooms, rare species of tree, a tea plantation, some peculiar topiary and a themed area relating to ethnic minorities.

The Western Hills (西山; Xishan), which rise to 2,350 metres (7,700ft) west of Kunming and Dianchi Lake, have three temples of note, though the crowds can be overwhelming, particularly during Chinese holidays.

The hike to the temples provides some great viewing opportunities across **Lake Dianchi** (滇池湖). At 340 sq km (130 sq miles), this is one of the largest freshwater lakes in China, extending for 40km (25 miles) end to end. Instead of signing up for a tour from Kunming, consider taking a taxi to **Huating Si** (华亭寺; Huating Temple; daily 8am–6pm; charge) at the base of the hills and then hiking uphill from there. The original structure at Huating is thought to date back to the 1300s, but it has been through several reconstructions since. Some of the statuary here is notable, with impressively large gilded Buddhas in the main hall.

From Huating, a forest path snakes upwards to the Chan Buddhist **Taihua Si** (泰华寺; Taihua Temple; daily 8am–6pm; charge), although the way is easier to find by the road. The Taihua complex features a pond and a pavilion for viewing Lake

Recommended Restaurants on page 373

Dianchi, making it a perfect place to rest for a while, before continuing up the more than 1,000 steps to **Sanqing Ge** (三清阁), a Daoist temple with tremendous views.

There is a chairlift, and a tram, to the highest lookout point at **Dragon Gate** (龙门; Longmen). The walk afterwards involves negotiating your way through a series of vertiginous corridors and grottoes that were chipped from the cliff face by Qing-dynasty monks – if you are claustrophobic, scared of heights or don't like crowds, it is best avoided.

The chairlift also rattles downhill to the lakeside **Yunnan Nationalities Village** (云南民族村; Yunnan Minzu Cun; daily 8am–7pm; charge), featuring all 25 of Yunnan's minorities in traditional dress, dancing and singing. Most foreign visitors find it tacky, though it is a staple on the Chinese tour-bus circuit.

The Stone Forest

Some 126km (78 miles) southeast of Kunming and reached by frequent minibuses is the region's most famous tourist attraction, the **Stone Forest** ❷ (石林; Shilin; daily 8.30am–7pm; charge). So famous, in fact, that many

visitors complain that the "forest" of bizarre limestone rock formations has become a circus, with cheek-by-jowl crowds, designated walking trails and Sani minority tour guides and souvenir-sellers hiding behind every rock. To a certain extent, this is true. The crowds can be maddening, but the otherworldly rocks – some of which tower more than 30 metres (100ft) high – are still a sight to behold, particularly early in the morning and late in the afternoon.

Around 10km (6 miles) to the north is the **Black Stone Forest** (乃古石林; Naigu Shilin), somewhat less spectacular – but with far fewer tourists.

South to Vietnam

It is a 12-hour bus journey from Kunming south to the Vietnamese border, but if you have time on your hands it's worth breaking up the trip with overnight stays at Jianshui and Yuanyang. The route passes through the old city of **Tonghai** ❸ (通海) at the southern end of the central Yunnan lakes region, with its 2,000-year-

The Stone Forest is Yunnan's most popular tourist sight after Lijiang. From Kunming, minibuses run every 30 minutes between 8am and noon and take two hours. Minibuses on the return journey to Kunming leave in the afternoon when full.

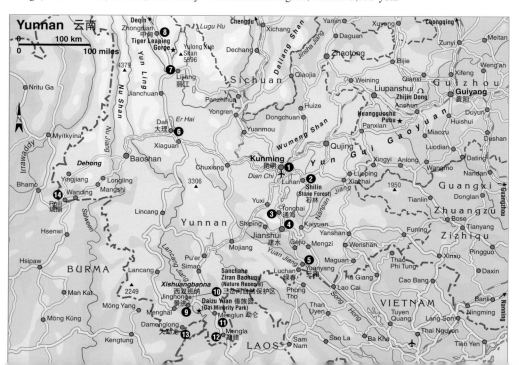

The recently built temple behind Dali's Three Pagodas, with the snow-flecked Cang Shan Mountains in the distance.

BELOW:
at the junction
of Fuxing Lu and
Renmin Lu, Dali.

old **Xiu Shan Park** (秀山公园; Xiu Shan Gongyuan). A half-hour bus ride away is **Xinmen** village (薪门). More than 750 years ago one rampaging Kublai Khan passed through this settlement and founded a garrison whose descendants are still much in evidence.

The ancient city of **Jianshui ❹** (建水), a further 80km (50 miles) south of Tonghai, is one of the best-preserved cities in southeastern Yunnan, famous for its old walls. From here, the road to Vietnam heads east, then southeast, taking a little over half a day by bus. It's a picturesque journey.

Another scenic road from Jianshui runs south to **Yuanyang ❺** (元阳) along vertiginous ridges and mountains of rice terraces, with villages perched on the lofty slopes. Continuing on to **Luchun** (绿春) brings some of the very best scenery in all of southern Yunnan, with a series of awesome landscapes of terraced paddy fields rivalling those in northern Guangxi.

DALI

Dali ❻ (大理) is an ancient walled city some 400km (250 miles) west of Kun-

ming, and one of the most picturesque destinations in all of China. Mountain scenery, the beauty of Er Hai Lake, a mild climate and the presence of the traditionally garbed Bai people and their Yi neighbours all combine to make Dali a favourite stop for foreigners as well as Chinese tourists – and there is a good range of accommodation, shops and restaurants to cater to their needs. Note that the old town lies some 18km (12 miles) north of "new Dali" (Xiaguan) – an endless source of confusion amongst travellers *(see margin opposite)*.

The ancient town is a legacy of the Nanzhao Kingdom *(see page 359)*, which began to coalesce in the 5th and 6th centuries AD. Yunnan's centre of power shifted west from Kunming during this period to a collection of six *zhao*, or kingdoms. At the height of its power in the 8th century, Nanzhao extended north into Sichuan, west into Burma and south into Vietnam. Internecine conflict brought its swift demise two centuries later.

City sights

It is possible to get a glimpse of some Nanzhao historical treasures at the small

Dali Museum Ⓐ (大理博物馆; Dali Bowuguan; daily 8am–5.30pm; charge) on Cangping Lu. The museum was also the headquarters of Du Wenxiu, an ethnic Hui Muslim who led the Panthay Rebellion (1856–73) against the Qing dynasty and was executed for his efforts.

The nearby **South Gate** Ⓑ (南门; Tonghaimen; also called Nanmen) is the best-preserved section of the old city walls. The gate is largely a reconstruction, as the original walls were badly damaged in the Panthay Rebellion, and restoration efforts did not begin until the 1990s.

All four city gates and the walls that link them are worth a look; the walls themselves feature a total of 45 battlements, while the **North Gate** Ⓒ (北门; Anyuanmen, also called Beimen) has some surviving woodcarvings. Not far from the South Gate, straddling **Fuxing Lu** (复兴路) – now a very busy tourist street, chock-a-block with souvenir shops – is the Qing **Wuhualou** (五华楼), or Tower of Five Glories.

Further north along Fuxing Lu is **Yu'er Park** Ⓓ (玉耳公园), a tranquil garden. Two blocks on and to the left, on Pingdeng Lu (Equality Street) is a small

Catholic church, a legacy of early – and largely unproductive – proselytising efforts by missionaries bent on converting the Buddhist Bai.

Dali's most spectacular and famous attraction is the San Ta Si, more commonly known as the **Three Pagodas** Ⓔ (三塔寺; daily 8am–7pm; charge), which are around 1km (⅔ mile) north of town. Well over 1,000 years old, the exact date of construction of the fluted towers is uncertain, but they are known to be of Nanzhao provenance. The central tower (Qianxunta) is 69 metres (230ft) tall and has 16 tiers, while its two flanking structures have 10 tiers and stand at 43 metres (141ft). The pagodas were restored in 1979, after miraculously surviving earthquakes and the vicissitudes of nature for centuries, although the Chongsheng Monastery they once stood guard over is long gone. It has been replaced by a new and sprawling monastery complex that draws tour-bus crowds of Chinese daily.

Although the Three Pagodas are the picture-postcard scene most associated with Dali, there are a couple of other Nanzhao-era pagodas still standing. West of the South Gate is the **Lone Pagoda**

TIP

Confusingly, there are two Dalis. The old walled town, where almost all foreign visitors stay, is known as **Dali Gucheng** (大理古城; Dali old city), while the newer, larger Dali, around 20 minutes south of the old city by road, is usually marked on maps as **Xiaguan** (下关), but sometimes as just Dali and sometimes as Dali Shi (Dali City). Whatever it is called, it's a less than charming urban sprawl. Most buses from Kunming and Lijiang terminate at Xiaguan rather than Dali Gucheng, but taxis are available for the final leg at around Rmb 30.

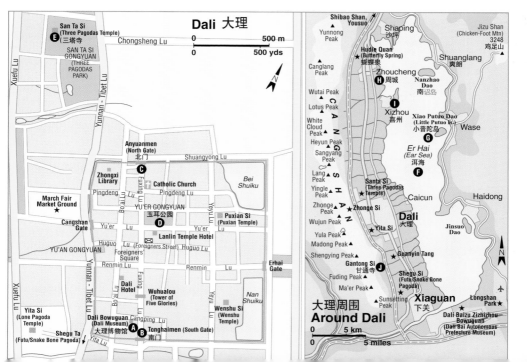

TIP

Numerous outlets in Dali can organise tickets for the Er Hai Lake tour boats, which leave from Taoyuan Pier. An alternative is to head to the wharf just east of town at Caicun village (彩村) and charter your own boat. The most popular destination is the village of Wase (挖色) on the eastern side of the lake (there used to be a daily ferry from Caicun to Wase but it runs infrequently these days). Anyone who wants to explore the other side of the lake should bring a bicycle to the wharf.

BELOW: the Three Pagodas.

(一塔寺; Yita Si), another 16-tiered tower. Further south, **Futu Pagoda** (蛇骨塔; Shegu Ta) also goes by the name of the Snake Bone Pagoda – which recalls the legend of a local hero who died in battle with a huge python that once preyed on the inhabitants of Dali.

Around Dali

Dali's most obviously compelling natural attraction is **Er Hai** (洱海), or "Ear Sea", a 250-sq-km (100-sq-mile) lake. On the kind of sunny day that is commonplace during Dali's pleasant spring and autumn months, the lake is a profound shade of aquamarine, and when the weather turns colder it is crowned from the far side by the snow-frosted peaks of the Cang Shan mountains.

Not so long ago, the only boats that traversed the Er Hai were fishing vessels and small ferries plying the waters in coordination with local market days in nearby villages. Times have changed, and most of the lake traffic today can be accounted for by sightseeing boats (*for details on boat trips, see margin, left*).

Over on the eastern shore of the lake is the picturesque Bai village of **Wase**, and just offshore is **Little Putuo Island** (小普陀岛; Xiao Putuo Dao), which derives its name from the mythical mountain home of Guanyin, the Chinese goddess of compassion. There is a small statue of the goddess – who is said to guard the lake's waters – in a temple on the crown of the small island.

A few kilometres north is the fishing village of **Shuanglang** (爽朗), which has perhaps the best views of the lake and the mountains on the far side. **Nanzhao Island** (南诏岛; Nanzhao Dao) is a tacky adjunct to the Er Hai boat cruises, and best avoided.

Rounding the northern tip of the lake, the road passes **Hudie Quan** (蝴蝶泉; Butterfly Spring), once a charming pond shaded by an acacia tree and locally famed for its butterflies – now an obligatory stop on the tour-bus lake circuit, and awash with souvenir stalls.

Nearby **Zhoucheng** (周城), a more authentic Bai village that looks much as Dali did three decades ago, is a far more enticing prospect. The women still sport traditional red vests and bonnet-like headwear, and the buildings are also traditional – mostly in *sanfang*, or courtyard style, with upturned eaves, and fronted by cobbled streets. Continuing in the direction of Dali, the road passes **Xizhou** (喜州), another traditional Bai village, and a renowned southern Silk Route trading town during the Ming dynasty.

The beautiful **Cang Shan mountains** (苍山) flank the western side of Er Hai Lake, providing a splendid backdrop to the Dali area. The Nanzhao-era temple of **Gantong Si** (甘通寺) is the chief attraction, accessed via an 11km (7-mile) trail. The site is very picturesque, with tremendous views, although only one hall remains of what was once a huge 36-hall Buddhist place of worship.

LIJIANG AND THE NORTHWEST

The diversity and scenery for which Yunnan is famous reaches its high point in the northwest, both in terms of culture and – literally – in terms of geography. The Naxi and Tibetan "minorities" form the majority in these parts, and have

recorded their significant cultural and historical achievements in their own written languages. The landscapes are magnificent: the southeasternmost corner of the Tibetan Plateau extends into the area, and the surrounding Himalayan peaks reach altitudes of over 6,000 metres (22,000ft).

The prime draw is the beguiling town of **Lijiang** ❼ (丽江). With its backdrop of snow-capped mountains, rich local culture, twisting cobblestone lanes and vaulted stone footbridges crossing rushing canals of clear water, it's not hard to see why it has become China's No. 1 tourist attraction, and improved infrastructure (including a new airport) has ensured that it can cope. As appealingly old-world as Lijiang is, however, bear in mind it is actually an expanded recreation of the original Old Town, most of which was levelled by an earthquake in 1996.

The settlement here has flourished for centuries as a caravan stop for those travelling to and from Tibet. It was Kublai Khan who gave the town its name ("beautiful river") when his troops passed through here in 1253, and the Khan also introduced Chinese music to the Naxi,

initiating a unique musical tradition which still flourishes today.

The Old Town

Tourists flock to the 750-year-old Naxi district of Lijiang, known as **Dayan** (大研). The most logical place to begin a walking tour is on its northern edge at **Yu He Square** Ⓐ, noted for its large waterwheels. Head south from here and take Xin Yi Jie, which runs to the east of Dong Da Jie (the main drag). This smaller street crosses Wuyi Jie, which climbs into the more tranquil eastern section of the Old City. Tiny food shops and small groceries are built into the fronts of the old Naxi homes, with carved wooden doors leading into central courtyards of intricate tile work. Massive wooden posts frame the scene, and stairways wind to the latticework balconies.

To complete the 3-km (2-mile) circuit, turn right onto Wen Hua Xiang and walk through a quiet residential neighbourhood before turning right onto Chongren

Lijiang's old town is one of the largest and best preserved in China.

BELOW:
Lijiang's old market square (Sifang Jie).

The waterwheels on Yue He Square of Lijiang's old town. Lijiang was built around an extensive canal system which supplied drinking water.

Xiang, then right again onto Qi Yi Jie. The second street on the left, Guangyi Jie, leads to the entrance of the **Mu Family Mansion B** (木府; Mufu; 8.30am–6pm; charge) a recreation of a Ming-style palace commemorating the rule of the Mu family, who governed Lijiang in the name of the Yuan, Ming and Qing emperors from 1254 until 1723. This series of six large pavilions in a walled compound was financed by the World Bank and constructed soon after the earthquake in 1996.

While the recent changes to overcome Lijiang are undeniable, they have strengthened a Naxi cultural revival which flourishes in the arts, particularly music. The 23 Tang-dynasty songs which Kublai Khan bequeathed to the Naxi were lost elsewhere in China but have survived here. Performances of this music, augmented with original Naxi folk music, take place at the **Naxi Orchestra Hall C** (纳西音乐厅; Naxi Yinle Ting), opposite the Dongba Palace on Dong Da Jie.

A short walk north of the square, following the stream, is the **Black Dragon Pool Park D** (黑龙潭公园; Heilongtan Gongyuan; 6.30am–8.30pm; charge). This park, where willow and chestnut trees line pathways which meander around a small lake, is home to some architectural treasures, notably the **Five Phoenix Hall E** (五凤楼; Wufeng Lou), built in the 17th century and recently moved here from the Fuguosi Temple outside Lijiang. It is one of the best places in town to admire the view of Yulongxue Shan (Jade Dragon Snow mountain), whose jagged snowy profile is reflected in the water of the lake.

Outside the rear gate of the park is the **Dongba Research Institute** (东巴文化研究室; Dongba Wenhua Yanjiushi; 8.30am–6pm; charge), with collections of the ritual clothing and accoutrements used by the Naxi shamans, as well as a collection of painted scrolls and manuscripts written in their pictographic script.

Around Lijiang

The high plains (2,400 metres/7,850ft) around Lijiang are dominated by the **Jade Dragon Snow Mountain F** (玉龙雪山; Yulongxue Shan), 5,596 metres (18,359ft) in altitude and the best-known massif in

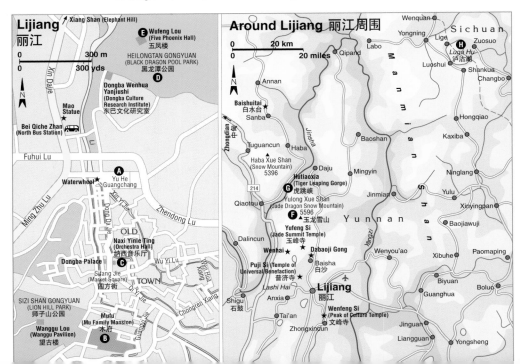

the province. First climbed in the 1960s, its 13 peaks are mantled with permanent snow. Yulongxue Shan is home to half of Yunnan's 13,000 plant species, including 400 species of tree and one-third of China's known medicinal herbs and plants. Its many ravines, creeks, cliffs and meadows all have Naxi names and are settings for the myths and legends of these people, who have made the plain their homeland for 1,000 years. Still heavily forested, the mountain bursts into bloom every spring when the camellias, rhododendrons and azaleas start flowering. Herders take their cattle, goats, sheep and yaks to graze on its slopes.

For closer views of the mountain, travellers can travel north to **Baishuitai** (白水台), or White Water Creek. From here, take a pony ride or cable car up the steep slope to Yunshanping, a delightful meadow at 3,300 metres (10,830ft). Further north, the 5,400-metre (17,720ft) high Haba peak towers beside Yulongxue Shan. The 16km (10-mile) narrow valley between the two massifs, cut by the surging waters of the Jinsha Jiang, is **Tiger Leaping Gorge G** (虎跳峡; Hutiaoxia), so named because at its narrowest point a fleeing tiger is supposed to have escaped a hunter by leaping across the 30-metre (100ft) gap to safety *(see margin, right)*.

North to Lugu Lake

On the border between Yunnan and Sichuan, 240km (145 miles) by road from Lijiang, **Lugu Lake H** (泸沽湖; Lugu Hu) is a beautiful body of water dotted with small islands and surrounded by mountains. Log cabins are the dominant architecture to be found along the shore. The countryside around is home to the Yi minority, easily recognisable by the women's long tri-coloured skirts and large black hats.

The Mosuo people, who live in the area of Lugu Lake and Yongning Basin, have a true matrilineal society. Property and land passes from mother to daughter, and all children remain permanently attached to their mother's household.

The far northwest

The road into northwest Yunnan climbs up onto the edge of the Tibetan Plateau, at 3,500 metres (11,500ft). **Zhongdian**

The hike through Tiger Leaping Gorge is a popular expedition, and there are numerous guesthouses en route. In the rainy season from July to August hiking can be dangerous due to landslides.

BELOW: Lijiang's Naxi orchestra preserves a unique musical tradition.

BELOW: scenery north of Zhongdian.
BELOW RIGHT: Lugu Lake.

❽ (中甸), 200km (120 miles) north of Lijiang, exhibits all the traits of Tibetan culture: barley cultivation, yaks, lamas and active monasteries, butter tea and prayer flags. As a marketing gimmick, it has, however, been re-branded by the tourism authorities as **Shangri-la** (香格里拉; *see panel, below*).

The **Old Town** – which, like Lijiang, has mostly been built in recent years – is located on the southern edge of Zhongdian, and is full of new restaurants and cafés, souvenir emporia and rustic guesthouses. Muddy alleys have become cobbled lanes, and Tibetan folk dancing takes place around a central square in the evenings, with visitors enthusiastically joining the circle. On a hill behind the Old Town, a 23-metre (70ft) **golden prayer wheel** is pushed by locals, launching their prayers heavenwards. Beside the spiritual benefits, the spot offers a fine view over the old town.

About 5km (3 miles) north of town, in the village of **Songzhanling** (松赞林), lies **Songsenling**, (松赞林寺; Sumtseling Gompa in Tibetan; daily 7am–4pm; charge), a sprawling monastery of the Gelugpa (Yellow Hat) sect.

The road from Zhongdian to **Deqin** (德钦) consists of 190km (115 miles) of fantastic mountain scenery. Reaching altitudes of 4,000 metres (13,200ft), with sharp curves and precipitous drops, it is an incredible engineering feat and an unforgettable journey.

XISHUANGBANNA

Down in Yunnan's deep south is China's little slice of Southeast Asia, a tropical nugget cushioned between Laos and Myanmar (Burma). The region is known as **Xishuangbanna** (西双版纳), a name derived from the Thai *Sip Sawng Panna*, meaning 12 rice-growing districts, and is populated by 14 minorities. The most populous group is the Dai, who speak a language closely related to Thai and account for around one-third of the autonomous prefecture's 830,000-strong population. Most of the Dai are Theravada Buddhists, and their exotically shaped pagodas add to the overall sense of being in Southeast Asia rather than China, further compounded by the palm trees, year-round heat and, in a few areas, tracts of tropical jungle. There are even a few wild elephants.

Shangri-la

In 2001 the State Council, a lofty arm of the Chinese bureaucracy, announced that new research had proven that James Hilton's 1933 novel *Lost Horizon*, set in a remote and idyllic Himalayan valley, was in fact based on the area surrounding the town of Zhongdian. They declared that the area was now known officially as Shangri-la, and a campaign of tourist promotion followed. In fact, Hilton never saw the Himalayas, and the name of his hidden valley is probably based on the Tibetan word *shambala*, meaning paradise.

Nonetheless, this bold re-branding exercise, aided by a new airport with direct flights to Beijing and Shanghai, and the creation of a new "Old Town", has proved to be a dramatic success. Tourist arrivals have increased tenfold, and the cobblestone streets of the "Old Town" are filled with shops and guesthouses. After years of repression, the local Tibetans are encouraged to revel in their culture and religion, and despite some misgivings the locals generally consider tourism less of a threat than the alternatives of mining and logging.

Jinghong and around

Once a sleepy town lining the Mekong River (known locally as the Lancang Jiang), the regional capital **Jinghong** ❾ (景洪) is today a rapidly expanding city of close to half a million inhabitants. The main reason to visit is to explore the surrounding minority villages (bike trips are a good option), but the city itself is not without appeal.

The **Tropical Flower and Plants Garden** (热带花卉园; Redai Huahuiyuan; also known as the Botanical Gardens; daily 7.30am–6pm; charge) off Jinghong Xilu has more than 1,000 examples of Xishuangbanna's native flora. About 1km (⅔ mile) southwest of the centre is the **National Minorities Park** (勐巴拉纳西公园; Mengbalanaxi Gongyuan; daily 8.30am–6pm, Wed and Sat until 11pm; charge), which is avoided by most foreign tourists due to its somewhat ersatz song-and-dance performances. Nonetheless, the lush park makes a very pleasant setting.

The **Jinsha Night Market** (金沙夜市场; Jinsha Yeshichang), underneath the new Xishuanbanna Bridge, is a lively place in the evenings, with numerous food stalls and even an outdoor massage area. Just north of Manting Park is **Wat Manting** (曼听佛寺; Manting Fosi; charge), Xishuangbanna's largest Buddhist monastery. Red and gold predominate colour-wise in this giant temple, with traditional Thai-style sloping roofs and large dragon statues protecting the entrance.

Travelling out of town, you will encounter minority villages everywhere, some within walking distance. Exploring on your own can be fun, but hiring a guide to visit a Dai village will provide a more intimate glimpse of village life, as most of the guides (check first) speak Dai. Guides can be hired in Jinghong at the Mei Mei Café or the Forest Café.

Better-known locally as Wild Elephant Valley, the **Sanchahe Nature Reserve** ❿ (三岔河自然保护区; Sanchahe Ziran Baohuqu), some 50km (30 miles) north of Jinghong, is one of Xishuangbanna's most popular attractions – 359 hectares (887 acres) of tropical rainforest, with a cable-car ride, herds of wild elephants, a small zoo and some touristy performing elephant shows. One of the highlights is the cable-car trip over the jungle, which lasts for around 40 minutes.

There are still a few wild elephants in the jungles of southern Yunnan.

BELOW: a remote Xishuangbanna village in the wet season.

Experience an unusual perspective on the jungle from the Bupan Aerial Walkway near Yaoqu.

BELOW: the golden pagoda at Ganlanba's Dai Minority Park.

Ganlanba (橄榄坝; also known as Menghan) is a nondescript town on the Mekong around an hour southeast of Jinghong. It is situated in the heart of a fertile plain that has long been an important agricultural zone for the Dai people. The chief attraction is the **Dai Minority Park** (傣族园; Daizu Yuan; 24 hours; charge). The mornings are peaceful, and it is possible to walk around the five villages undisturbed. In the afternoon the place is flooded with crowds of tourists on golf carts, and the daily shows of singing and dancing and water-splashing are in full swing. The largest of the temples in the cultural village – **Chunman Dafo Si** (春满大佛寺) – is well worth a visit, as it has been renovated in fine style, with a gold-leaf stupa. In each of the five villages are guesthouses, offering an inexpensive opportunity to overnight and dine with a local Dai family.

Menglun ⓫ (勐仑), 90km (55 miles) east of Jinghong, is home to the splendid **Tropical Botanical Gardens** (热带植物园; Redai Zhiwuyuan) down by the Luosuo River (daily 8am–midnight; charge). The largest garden of its kind in all China, it features more than 3,000 examples of the local flora labelled in both Chinese and Latin.

The route south to **Mengla** ⓬ (勐腊) traverses one of the wilder parts of Xishuangbanna, an area which has retained plenty of its forest cover. A quiet road runs north from Mengla through picturesque forested scenery to Yaoqu; some 25km (16 miles) along the way is the **Bupan Aerial Walkway** (补蛙望天树空中索道; Bupan Wangtianshu Kongzhong Suodao), strung between the trees approximately 40 metres (130ft) above the ground, allowing for close-up views of the forest canopy.

A road heads west from Jinghong to the small town of **Damenglong** ⓭ (大勐龙), close to the Burmese border – the 70km (43 miles) taking anywhere from three to five hours hours by bus or car. The chief attraction in the vicinity is the **Bamboo Shoot Pagoda** (曼飞龙笋塔; Manfeilong Sun Ta), nestled beside Manfeilong village about 30 minutes' walk from downtown Damenglong. Founded in 1204, and the most famous stupa in Xishuangbanna, it is said to commemorate a visit to the region by the Sakyamuni Buddha, and an oversize footprint in a niche on the stupa is said to be his.

The far west (Dehong)

The Dehong region lies to the west of Xishuangbanna and is most easily accessed by road from Dali. The lively town of **Ruili** ⓮ (瑞丽), a short hop from Burma, enjoys a multi-ethnic, borderland frisson that comes from thriving trade (much of it illegal). It may be seedy, but it's a different world (especially at night) from the political conformities in Beijing. The main attraction for Chinese tourists is the sprawling **Jade Market** (珠宝街; Zhubao Jie) – said to be among the busiest in the world, and no place to spend money unless you really know your jade. Bicycles are available for hire inexpensively in the city centre, and it is possible to cycle out to several Dai Buddhist temples.

The small border town of **Wanding** (畹町), to the east on the Shweli River, is the official access point (over the bridge) to Burma. ❑

RESTAURANTS

Restaurants

Prices for a meal for
one, with one drink:
$ = under Rmb 50
$$ = Rmb 50–100
$$$ = Rmb 100–150
$$$$ = over Rmb 150

Yunnanese cuisine fea-
tures a diverse range of
flavours reflecting influences from Indo-China
and Burma as well as
Sichuan and the Hui
Muslim community. Many
dishes are sour/spicy
combinations. The most
famous is "crossing-the-
bridge" noodles (guoqiao
mian), a hot noodle soup.

Kunming

There is a large number
of restaurants and cafés
around the Camellia
Hotel on Dongeng
Donglu. Wenlin Jie, close
to Yunnan University, is
another popular eating-
and-drinking district.

1910 La Gare du Sud
火车南站
8 Houxin Jie. **$$**
A colonial-style restaur-
ant with a garden area
serving Yunnan special-
ities and Chinese cuisine
staples. An English menu
is available, and prices
are reasonable. It's best
to go by taxi (ask for
huoche nanzhan canting),
as it is difficult to find
even with a map.

Belvedere International
Restaurant 翠湖宾馆
Greenlake Hotel,
6 Cuihu Nanlu. **$$–$$$**
With lakeside views, the
24-hour Belvedere is the
perfect place for a blow-
out Western meal. There

is also an "open kitchen"
rice/noodle centre serv-
ing Yunnan noodles.

The Brothers Jiang
将兄弟
1 Jinbi Qianjie (corner of
Jinbi Lu and Shulin Jie).
$–$$
The speciality of the
house is crossing-the-
bridge noodles, which
you order by buying a
ticket at the front door.
Note that the army of
plates that turn up at
your table are not nibbles
but, along with the noo-
dles, are meant to be
mixed into the broth
when it arrives. One of
several branches scat-
tered around town.

Guangyi 广义
68–70 Beimen Jie. **$$**
This Yunnan Minorities
restaurant has a trad-
itional setting, with a
lovely courtyard area. One
of the favourite dishes is
the Naxi hot pot.

Salvador's
萨尔瓦多咖啡馆
76 Wenlin Jie, Wenhua
Xiang. **$$**
Salvador's is a foreign-
run café and restaurant
with excellent Tex-Mex
cuisine, home-made ice
cream and free internet.

Dali

Dali has no shortage of
restaurants catering to
backpackers, but very
few regional Chinese
restaurants. On upper
Renmin Lu, though, there
is a profusion of kitchen-
style eateries – many of
these don't even have
menus (or English
names), but a little cre-

ative pointing and gestur-
ing can result in a superb
meal at a bargain price.
In the evenings, on the
corner of Fuxing Lu and
Huguo Lu, a collection of
stalls offer barbecued
lamb, chicken and beef.

An Caife Beag
休闲咖啡
215 Renmin Lu. **$**
This cosy café (the name
is Gaelic, and translates
as "a small cafe") on
lower Renmin Lu serves
Dali's best breakfasts,
and also has a selection
of Chinese dishes.

King's Park Kitchen
竹园
5 Huguo Lu. **$$**
In a courtyard at the far
end of Huguo Lu, King's
serves up the best Can-
tonese cuisine in town,
though it is a good idea
to call by in advance if
you want fish dishes.

Tower Café 钟楼
44 Foreigner's Street
Square. **$$**
It may be slightly difficult
to find (make a right
halfway down Foreigner's
Street, walking east, and
then make another right
on the square), but the
Tower has Dali's best
Western cuisine.

Lijiang

There is a wide choice
of Chinese and inter-
national restaurants and
cafés in the Old Town.

Le Petit Lijiang Book
Café 小丽江
50 Chongren Xiang,
Qiyi Jie. **$**
Feast on the Western
and Chinese dishes

either seated in the
courtyard or inside this
old Lijiang home. A
knowledgeable Belgian-
Chinese couple also
offer travel services.

Sakura Café 樱花园
123 Cuiwen Xiang. **$$**
Located on one of
Lijiang's canals, the spe-
ciality here is Korean
food, and both the hot
pots and Korean barbe-
cue are good. Japanese,
Chinese and Western
dishes also served.

Xishuangbanna

In southern parts of Yun-
nan you are likely to
encounter fresh fish
roasted with lemongrass,
chicken boiled with sour
bamboo shoots, and pork
cooked in bamboo tube.

Jinghong
Mei Mei's 美美咖啡
Manting Lu. **$**
The original backpackers'
hangout, with all the refer-
ence material you could
wish for on getting around
Xishuangbanna, plus
standard banana-pancake
fare. Internet access and
books in English.

Night Market 金沙夜市
Mekong Bridge. **$**
Just to the north side of
the new bridge, this is
the finest dining experi-
ence in Jinghong. Select
the freshest of produce
which is then typically
cooked to Dai traditions:
in other words heavy on
the lemongrass and a ver-
itable taste explosion.
Don't miss the rice in a
hollowed-out pineapple.
Get here before 9pm to
sample the best produce.

THE WEST

The vast expanses of western China, from the Roof of the World to the Silk Road oases of Xinjiang, encompass some of the most extreme terrain on earth

China's breathtaking western region, comprising Tibet, Qinghai, Gansu and Xinjiang, occupies a mind-boggling swathe of remote territory inhabited by a variety of peoples and cultures. This region lies at the edges of Chinese consciousness and on the road less travelled, and the sheer physical distances involved are daunting – the city of Kashi (Kashgar) is closer to Baghdad than it is to Beijing.

Tibet (*Xizang* in Chinese) comes to us with high expectations – fabulously remote, exotic and other-worldly. Chinese political control and a huge influx of Han migrants has changed the character and appearance of Lhasa and other towns, a process accelerated now that the new railway from Golmud is complete, but Tibet's unique landscape and high altitude environment still exercise a powerful hold on the imagination, and the idiosyncratic religious culture still casts an undeniable spell. To the north, and culturally part of Tibet, Qinghai is an immense swathe of mountain and desert largely devoid of people.

Emerging from the city of Xi'an, the legendary Silk Road soon passes into Gansu, the province that bridges the gap between classical Han China and the remote west. Lanzhou, its capital, has the feel of a frontier town, an enticing glimpse of what is to come. Labrang Monastery at Xiahe, to the south, is one of the most magical places in China, and the best place to see Tibetan culture outside Tibet itself, while in the far west are the magnificent Mogao Caves.

From Gansu the route leads westwards to Xinjiang before dividing into two strands, one north and one south of the formidable Taklamakan Desert. This trade link from China to the shadowy barbarian lands beyond brought wealth and worldliness to the remote oasis towns. Xinjiang, once known as Chinese Turkestan, is a gigantic expanse of glaciered mountains, waterless basins and intoxicating emptiness. Highlights include the wonderfully atmospheric desert cities of Turpan and Kashi (Kashgar), and – in contrast to the rest of the region – the lush mountains to the east of Ürümqi. ❑

PRECEDING PAGES: sand dunes near Dunhuang. **LEFT:** scenery on the road to Pakistan. **TOP:** Lhasa's Potala Palace. **ABOVE LEFT:** Tibetans. **ABOVE:** desert transport.

Recommended Restaurants on page 393

TIBET AND QINGHAI

Visiting the fabled Roof of the World remains one
of the great travel adventures of our times.
Modernisation and change are inevitable,
but the vivid Tibetan culture survives,
albeit in a diminished state

nown as **Xizang** (西藏) in Chinese, Tibet has, for the most part, long been hidden from the rest of the world, isolated and impenetrable beyond the world's highest mountains. For centuries, this mysterious land was the dream of innumerable explorers and adventurers. The mystery and allure remain, and since opening to tourism in the 1980s, the Land of Snows has been the goal of both backpackers and well-heeled travellers intent on seeing the top of the world. To the north of Tibet is **Qinghai** (青海), a vast, empty stretch of wilderness, much of which lies within the boundaries of the ancient Tibetan lands of Amdo.

Visiting Tibet is a unique and unforgettable travel adventure, even if the erosion of the traditional culture in the face of a huge influx of Han Chinese is a cause for sadness. Lhasa has rapidly become a modern Chinese city, with garish new office blocks and apartments replacing the older Tibetan buildings. Some of the monasteries are almost empty. The railway link to Golmud in Qinghai province opened in 2006 *(see page 387)* and can only accelerate these changes. Yet this is still one of those rare places that inspires a feeling of wonder. The extreme altitude makes the air sparkle with clarity; the dramatic mountains cast deep shadows across colossal camel-coloured landscapes; the strange, gloomy temples, their exotic deities dimly lit by pungent yak-butter lamps, seem to belong to another world.

A brief history

Ethnologists believe that the Tibetan people are descended from a nomadic race who migrated southeast from Central Asia. The first named king of Tibet, Nyatri Tsenpo, was the first of a long line who practised the shamanist Bon religion. In the 7th century, Songtsen Gampo created a powerful military state, conquering a vast territory, and even threatening the Chinese capital as well as India and Nepal to the south. Songtsen Gampo's Chinese and Nepalese wives brought Buddhism to Tibet, which flourished until the 9th

Main attractions
POTALA PALACE
THE JOKHANG
NORBULINGKA
SAMYE MONASTERY
GYANTSE
TASHILHUNPO MONASTERY,
    SHIGATSE
EVEREST BASE CAMP
MOUNT KAILASH
XINING MARKETS

LEFT: Tibetan pilgrim in Lhasa.
BELOW: prayer flags on a remote mountain pass.

century, when the pro-Bon Langdarma came to power. Tibet then broke up into numerous small vassals. Influenced by the Indian scholar Atisha, Buddhism was gradually revived, and in the 1100s, the abbots of the larger monasteries became powerful enough to challenge the worldly rulers. In 1207, the first Mongol armies invaded Tibet, and later Kublai Khan gave secular powers to the powerful abbots of the Sakya Monastery.

In the 1300s and 1400s, the great reformer Tsongkhapa (1357–1416) further revived Buddhism and established new monasteries that became centres of both religious and secular power. He founded the Gelugpa (Virtue) sect – known as the Yellow Hat sect after the colour of the monks' hats – which was to become the dominant religious and secular power. Indeed, its highest representatives became the Dalai Lama and the Panchen Lama, incarnations of the highest gods of Tibet. The Great Fifth Dalai Lama founded the theocracy of the Yellow Church, supported by the Mongol Khan Gusri, who benevolently governed the Tibetan kings and followers of Tibet's ancient Bon religion.

Chinese rule over Tibet began in the 18th century. In 1720, the Qing emperor Kangxi chased the Dsungar invaders out of Tibet and took control. Chinese functionaries, so-called Ambane, headed the local government. Finally, in the late 19th century, the British began to penetrate into Tibet, and the country quickly became a centre of great-power conflicts. In addition to the British, the Chinese and Tsarist Russians also made claims on the country. China, torn by war and revolution in the early 1900s, lost control of Tibet until 1950, a year after the Communists came to power, when the Chinese army invaded and took control.

Hopes for meaningful autonomy were quickly crushed. In 1959, a Tibetan uprising was brutally repressed before the Cultural Revolution of the late 1960s and early 1970s resulted in vigorous suppression of religious life. Conditions improved after Mao's death in 1976, and the first tourists were allowed in from the early 1980s. But while Beijing continually states that the Tibetans are happy and grateful for the benefits brought by their rule, there continue to be periodic anti-Chinese outbursts. Violent demon-

Recommended Restaurants on page 393

GETTING TO TIBET

Flights: Lhasa's Gongkar airport, 90km (55 miles) southwest of the city, has daily flights to/from Chengdu as well as several connections weekly with Xi'an, Xining, Kathmandu, Kunming, Chongqing and Zhongdian.

By train and bus: Express trains *(see page 387)* run to Lhasa via Golmud daily from several cities including Beijing (47 hours). Buses operate between Lhasa and Kathmandu and Golmud.

GETTING AROUND TIBET

Lhasa: There are regular minibuses from Lhasa to destinations outside the city, including the Drepung and Sera monasteries. There are at least a dozen buses daily between Lhasa and Shigatse (6 hours), from where there are onward buses to Gyantse (1.5 hours). For most other destinations in Tibet, it will be necessary to hire a Land Cruiser and driver through a Lhasa-based travel agency, which will also arrange all the required permits.

Tibetan prayer wheels (chokhor) contain printed mantras: spinning the wheel equates to saying the prayers, although a verbal recitation of the relevant mantra is considered necessary while spinning. Some prayer wheels are even equipped with electric motors.

BELOW: outside the Jokhang, Tibet's holiest temple.

strations occurred in the late 1980s and into the 1990s, and the spring of 2008 saw the entire region – including Tibetan areas of Gansu, Qinghai and Sichuan – explode in violence that led to a bloody crackdown on Tibetan dissidents and temporary restrictions on tourism.

LHASA AND THE TIBETAN HEARTLANDS

The only sizeable city in Tibet, and centre of Tibetan Buddhism, **Lhasa ❶** (拉萨) lies at a dizzying altitude of 3,680 metres (12,070ft) on the banks of the **Lhasa He**, (Kyichu) and a tributary of Yarlung Tsangpo Jiang. While its name conjures up lofty and romantic images, Lhasa has increasingly assumed the cast of a Chinese city, with ugly concrete buildings, polluting traffic, and even satellite links to the Shanghai Stock Exchange.

The Dalai Lama's residence

Crowned by golden roofs visible from far and wide, the **Potala Palace ❹** (布达拉宫; Budala Gong; daily 9am–6pm; charge) is a huge, dramatic building, symbol of Tibet and residence of the Dalai Lamas from its completion in the 1640s until 1959.

BELOW: the Potala Palace. **BELOW RIGHT:** a weather-beaten Tibetan.

The section known as the White Palace (Potrange Karpo) was built first; the smaller Red Palace (Potrang Marpo), which houses almost all the items of interest, was completed 50 years later. The entire palace covers an area of almost 400 metres (1,300ft) from east to west, and 350 metres (1,150ft) from north to south. The 13 floors hold almost 1,000 rooms, with ceilings supported by more than 15,000 columns.

Within the Red Palace are the great ceremonial halls, 35 small chapels, four meditation halls, and eight vaults for deceased Dalai Lamas. The most splendid and valuable vault is for the fifth Dalai Lama, decorated with 4 tons of gold, and innumerable diamonds, turquoise, corals and pearls. In the northeastern part of the palace is the chapel of Avalokiteshvara, considered the oldest part of the structure and said to have been preserved from the original palace of King Songtsen Gampo. The chapel contains a statue of the king with his Chinese wife, Wen Cheng, and his Nepalese wife, Bhrikuti. There is a tremendous view down into the valley and the Old City from the roof of the Red Palace.

Tibet's holiest temple

Holiest of all Tibetan religious sites, the **Jokhang** Ⓑ (大昭寺; Dazhao Si; daily 8am–8pm; charge for inner temple) is at the epicentre of the Tibetan world and the heart of Lhasa, the destination for devout pilgrims from across the land. The pilgrims constantly prostrate themselves in the dust outside the temple; others continuously turn their prayer wheels and chant mantras.

Enter the incense-filled interior by walking through a prayer hall supported by red columns. The main building, built on a square mandala foundation, dates all the way back to the 7th century, when it was built as a shrine for a Buddha statue that the Chinese princess Wen Cheng brought to Lhasa as a wedding gift from the Chinese emperor. This Buddha, called Jobo in Tibetan, gave the temple its name: Jokhang, the hall of the Jobo Buddha. Four gilded roofs mark the holiest halls: the chapels of the Jobo Buddha, Avalokiteshvara and Maitreya, and the chapel of Songtsen Gampo.

The golden Jobo statue is richly decorated with jewels and usually covered with brocade and silk bands. At the feet

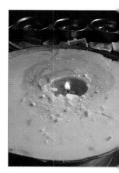
of the Buddha, lamps made of heavy silver and filled with yak oil burn continually. It is not certain whether the statue is actually the original from the 7th century, since other artefacts were destroyed during the Cultural Revolution and later replaced with copies.

From the roof of the Jokhang is a view of Potala Palace and of the **Barkhor ⑥** (八角街; Bajiao Jie), the sacred ritual path that surrounds the site, crowded with pilgrims and traders. There used to be a longer ritual path, the Lingkhor, which surrounded the town, but it has been broken up by new buildings.

At the entrance of the Jokhang temple, along the Barkhor, a willow tree planted in 1985 marks the spot where, in 641, a Chinese princess originally planted another willow as a friendship symbol. A floor tile in front of the temple entrance has an inscription of a Tibetan-Chinese friendship treaty, from 821.

North of the Barkhor is **Ramoche ⑩** (小昭寺; Xiaozhao Si; daily 9am–6pm; charge), probably the oldest monastery in Lhasa. It is said to have been constructed in the first half of the 7th century and served as a shrine for a statue brought to

Tibet by the Nepalese wife of King Songtsen Gampo. Later, after the arrival of the Chinese princess Wen Cheng, the Jobo Buddha was housed here before it was transferred to the Jokhang.

The Dalai Lama's summer residence

About 7km (4 miles) west of the city centre and set in pleasant grounds, the **Norbulingka ⑤** (罗布林卡; Luobulinka; daily 9am–12.30pm, 2.30–6pm; charge) was built on the orders of the seventh Dalai Lama in the second half of the 18th century. Since then, it has served as a summer residence for the Dalai Lama. The New Summer Palace, which was built for the 14th Dalai Lama and completed in 1956, is the best-preserved of the whole site. On the top floor of the building, which is decorated with numerous wall murals, is an audience hall with paintings from the history of the Tibetan people. Also open are the meditation room and bedroom of the Dalai Lama.

The Big Three

Three great monasteries near Lhasa are considered to be important centres of the

Enter a Tibetan monastery or temple and you will immediately notice the unusual odour produced by the butter lamps.

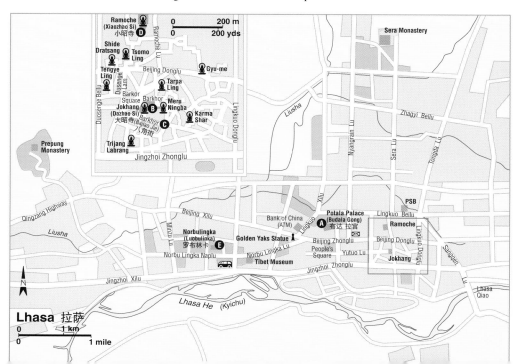

Yellow Hat sect and pillars of the theo-cratic state: Sera, Drepung and Ganden.

Just 5km (3 miles) north of Lhasa, at the foot of the chain of mountains dominating the Lhasa Valley, **Sera Monastery ❷** (色拉寺; Sela Si; daily 9am–noon, 2–4pm; charge) was built in 1419 by a pupil of Tsongkhapa, at a place where his great master had spent many years studying and meditating in a small hut. During its most active period, almost 5,000 monks lived here, and it had a bril-liant reputation because of its famous academy. Today, Sera is home to around 300 monks.

En route to Drepung Monastery and 10km (6 miles) west of central Lhasa is the small **Nechung Monastery** (乃穷寺; Naiqiong Si), which used to house the Tibetan state oracle. Both monks and lay people could become oracle priests. Before important state decisions, the ora-cle was consulted after the priests had put themselves into a trance. The last oracle priest went into exile in India with the Dalai Lama.

Drepung Monastery ❸ (哲蚌寺; Zhe-bang Si; daily 9am–6pm; charge), built in 1416, was for a long time the political

headquarters of the Yellow Hat sect. The predecessors of the Great Fifth Dalai Lama lived here before moving to the Potala. The tomb stupa of the second, third and fourth Dalai Lamas are housed in Drepung. Probably the largest monastery in the world at the height of its power, nearly 10,000 monks are said to have lived within its walls. The lower part of the site is occupied by hermitages for the monks, along with numerous storerooms. Further up are prayer halls and *dukhang*, which contain valuable statues and documents.

The third big monastery of the Gelugpa sect is **Ganden ❹** (甘丹寺; Gandan Si; daily 9am–noon, 2–4pm; charge), 40km (25 miles) northeast of Lhasa. The monastery, which was founded in 1409 by Tsongkhapa, is one of the most sacred places of Tibetan Buddhism. It once housed 5,000 monks, making the almost total destruction of the site during the Cultural Revolution even more tragic. Hardly any of the monastery's treasures were preserved, and the buildings were torn down to their foundations. Only in 1985 was the reconstruction of the monastery finally completed, and that was limited to the most important build-ings, including the mausoleum of Tsongkhapa, recognisable from a distance by its red walls. Since then, several hun-dred monks have returned.

The Yarlung Valley

A two-hour bus ride east from Gonggar Airport south of Lhasa is **Tsedang ❺** (泽当; Zedang). From here, one can undertake excursions to the Yarlung Val-ley and the Tibetan kings' graves, and to the ancient monasteries of Samye and Mindroling. The town of Tsedang is said to have been built on the spot where Bodhisattva Avalokiteshvara (wor-shipped in China as Guanyin) descended from heaven in the shape of a monkey and, with the help of a female demon, produced the first Tibetan.

Some 7km (4 miles) south of Tsedang is **Trandruk Monastery** (also called Khrabrug), one of the first Buddhist monasteries in Tibet and said to have been built under the rule of King Song-

The Tibetans are thought to be the descendants of Turan and Tangut tribes from Central Asia, who reached Tibet from the north, settled in the Yarlung Tsangpo Valley, and mixed with the local population.

BELOW: monks enjoying animated theological debate at Sera Monastery.

tsen Gampo. After the Cultural Revolution, the site was used as a farm.

A further 5km (3 miles) south into the Yarlung Valley heartlands is the ancient and spectacular site of **Yumbulakhang** (雍布拉康; daily 8am–6pm; charge), which looks as if it grew out of the peak of a hill. Home of the Yarlung kings (AD 627–842), it is thought to have dated from a much earlier period, possibly around 130 BC and the first Tibetan king, Nyatri Tsenpo. Sadly, it was reduced to ruins in the Cultural Revolutiuon and most of what stands today is a 1980s reconstruction. There is a superb view across the valley below, whose fields have been cultivated for over two millennia.

In the neighbouring valley to the southwest is **Chongye**, burial place of Yarlung kings, although the tombs are only discernible as small mounds of earth. The biggest mound, which has a small temple built upon it, is claimed to be the burial ground of Songtsen Gampo.

Samye Monastery

Tibet's oldest monastery, **Samye** ❻ (桑木耶寺; Sangmuye Si; daily 9am–12.30pm, 3–5pm; charge) makes a fas-

cinating trip from Tsedang. Part of the appeal is the ferry across the Yarlung Tsangpo River from a point 35km (20 miles) west of Tsedang; on the opposite bank, a lorry carries travellers to the monastery in about 30 minutes.

Samye was founded by the Indian teacher Padmasambhava around AD 770. Considered to be the founder of Tibetan Buddhism, he is said to have succeeded in winning over the demon gods of the Bon religion – many of the demon gods in Tibetan monasteries refer back to such Bon gods. The site has been built on a mandala foundation and reflects the cosmic view of Tibetan religion. The main temple stands in the centre and symbolises the mythical Buddhist peak of Mount Meru, while four smaller chapels were erected on the four cardinal points of the compass.

About 60km (37 miles) west of Tsedang is **Mindroling Monastery** ❼ (敏珠林寺; Minzhulin Si; daily 9am–5pm; charge), which can also be visited on an excursion to or from Lhasa. Built in 1676, it is a monastery of Nyingma, the oldest order founded by Padmasambhava.

Towering over the historic Yarlung Valley, Yumbulakhang is one of the most spectacularly situated Tibetan temples.

BELOW: pilgrims on the Tsangpo ferry to Samye Monastery.

Tibetan temples are liberally adorned with images of protector deities, fearsome creatures who protect people's souls from straying off the path to enlightenment.

BELOW: the ruined fort *(dzong)* at Gyantse.

THE ROAD TO NEPAL

The journey from Lhasa, via Gyantse and Shigatse to the high Himalayas and then over the border into Nepal is a bona fide travel adventure, taking in some of Tibet's grandest scenery and its largest monasteries.

Between Lhasa and Shigatse there are two options, northern and southern, but the latter is far more interesting. This route winds along the banks of the Yarlung Tsangpo before climbing up to the 4,800-metre (15,750ft) pass of **Kampa La**. Looking south from here are the turquoise waters of **Lake Yamdrok** (羊卓雍错; Yangzhuo Yongcuo), around whose shores the road continues for about 30km (19 miles). From the opposite shore, a hairpin road hewn into the steep mountain face leads up to the next pass, the 5,000-metre (16,400-ft) **Karo La**.

Gyantse

West of Lake Yamdrok the route passes small villages, fertile valleys, cattle herds and many yaks. **Gyantse** ❽ (江孜; Jiangzi), which lies by the northern bank of the Nyangchu River, 265km (165 miles) southwest of Lhasa, is the third-largest of the old Tibetan towns. Its location on the route to India, Sikkim and Bhutan made it one of the most important trading centres. In 1910, an English diplomat compared the market of Gyantse – where one could buy Scotch whisky and Swiss watches, amongst other things – with Oxford Street in London. The **dzong**, a fortification on a hill visible from some distance away, was attacked and pointlessly destroyed in 1904 by Colonel Younghusband's military expedition from British India.

The main Tibetan structure in Gyantse is **Palkhor Chode Monastery** (白居寺; Baiju Si; Mon–Sat 9am–noon, 3–6pm; charge). The circular site, enclosed by a wall, once housed several monasteries belonging to different sects. The 32-metre (105-ft) **Kumbum** dagoba in the centre of the complex is a unique example of Tibetan architectural skill. Built in the shape of a three-dimensional mandala, it symbolises Mount Meru; the central structure at the tip is a chapel for the original Buddha. Again, there are four chapels at the four cardinal points of the compass. Other shrines are located on the four floors. The path to the centre is thus

Recommended Restaurants on page 393

a symbol of the spiritual path of salvation. The stupa was erected in the first half of the 17th century.

Shigatse

Shigatse ❾ (日喀则; Rikaze; also spelled Xigaze), 360km (224 miles) west of Lhasa on the southern bank of Yarlung Tsangpo, is Tibet's second city and the seat of the Panchen Lama, the second head of Tibetan Buddhism. In ancient Tibet, this was the provincial capital of Tsang. The Great Fifth Dalai Lama bestowed the title of Panchen Lama on his teacher from Tashilhunpo Monastery. While the Dalai Lama is said to be an incarnation of the Tibetan deity Avalokiteshvara, the Panchen Lama is worshipped as the reincarnation of the Buddha Amithaba, and is therefore higher up in the heavenly hierarchy. This latent conflict of hierarchy was constantly manipulated by the Russians, British and Chinese in their colonial rivalries.

The residence of the Panchen Lama, **Tashilhunpo Monastery** (扎什伦布寺; Zhashilunbu Si; daily 9am–noon, 3.30–5pm; charge) is one of the most impressive religious centres in Tibet. The site

dates from the 15th century but was substantially expanded during the 17th and 18th centuries. Nearly 4,000 monks once lived here; today, there are around 600. The most important building is without doubt the **Maitreya Temple**, a chapel built in 1914 by the ninth Panchen Lama. A 26-metre (85ft) tall golden statue of Maitreya, the Buddha of the Future, is housed in the red-stone building.

The memorial of the fourth Panchen Lama is also worth seeing. Erected in 1662, it is decorated with 85 kg (187 lbs) of gold, 15 tons of silver and innumerable precious stones. The gilded roofs of the chapels for the deceased Panchen Lamas tower over the entire site. On feast days, huge *thangkas* (scroll banners) are hung. To the west of the town, in a large park, is the palace of the seventh Panchen Lama. The Panchen Lama controversy *(see margin, right)* has made the resident monks somewhat wary of tourist visits.

Sakya

About 145km (90 miles) southwest of Shigatse is **Sakya** ❿ (萨迦; Sajia),

Tashilhunpo, home of the Panchen Lama, is at the centre of an ongoing controversy. After the 10th Panchen Lama died in 1989, the Chinese authorities invited the Dalai Lama to help in the search for his successor, but then disagreed with his choice and installed their own child. The Tibetans' successor is currently detained in Beijing.

BELOW: the railway to Tibet.

Railway on the Roof of the World

To hasten Tibet's development, China has built the world's highest railway linking Lhasa with the Chinese rail network. China says the 1,142km (710-mile) rail line, which opened ahead of schedule in July 2006, will bring unprecedented economic opportunities to a perennially poor region, but critics maintain that the central government will use it to strengthen its political grip on the Tibetan people.

The railway has allowed for a dramatic increase in tourist numbers to Tibet, both foreign and domestic Chinese. The train carriages are pressurised and feature individual oxygen tubes that can be inserted into passengers' noses in the event that altitude symptoms are felt. Beijing has hailed it as an engineering marvel, the latest in a long line of colossal Chinese construction projects – roughly half of the line has been built on permafrost, with bridges spanning the most unsta-

ble sections of frozen ground. In areas prone to melting, cooling pipes have been embedded into the ground to ensure it remains frozen and to stabilise the tracks. The project cost about Rmb 26 billion (US$ 3.2 billion).

At its highest point, the Tanggula Pass, the tracks climb to 5,072 metres (16,640ft), making it the world's highest rail crossing. The chosen route has caused concern over its potential impact on the fragile environment of this area, but Beijing has pushed aside these worries, stating that the railway avoids certain nature reserves. The train also passes through an earthquake zone, raising other safety issues.

Other critics worry that the railway will lead to increased settlement of Tibet by Han Chinese, further swamping Tibetan culture and mirroring the transformation of parts of Xinjiang. *For more details see page 423.*

reached via a road that crosses two mountain passes – on most days you can see Mount Everest from here. The **monastery** (Mon–Sat 9am–noon, 4–6pm; charge) at Sakya has a special place in Tibetan history. Its foundation in 1073 saw the creation of a new order, the Sakyapa school. Since 1247, when the Mongol Khan Göden made the abbot Pandita of Sakya vice-king of Tibet, the Sakya Trizin, an incarnation of the Bodhisattva Manjusri, ruled over most of the region to the west of Shigatse.

The Sakya Monastery buildings are striking because of their dark-grey colour and the white horizontal stripes under the roof, as well as the red vertical stripes on the corners. While the southern monastery was left alone during the violence of the Cultural Revolution, the northern monastery was almost completely destroyed. Some buildings have since been rebuilt.

World-record heights

Heading on Highway 318 towards Nepal, southwest of Lhatse and about halfway between Shekar and Dingri, a newly sealed road branches directly south into the **Mount Everest** (珠穆朗玛峰; Qomolangma) region, from where ascents of the world's highest peak are staged each year. From late spring to early autumn it is possible to visit the Everest Base Camp and the nearby **Rongbuk Monastery** (絨布寺), at 4,980 metres (16,339ft) the highest monastic dwelling on earth. Only 200 metres (650ft) lower in elevation than the base camp itself, the monastery often affords monumental views across the Rongbuk Valley onto the north face of Everest, towering far above all else, its snow-crowned summit catching the first and last light of every day. The monastery was founded in 1902, though ascetics had already inhabited the mountain area for a few hundred years – the hillsides around the complex are dotted with caves once used for meditation. There is a bare-bones guesthouse with mostly dorm-style accommodation nearby, and it is also possible to camp here if you have your own tent.

About 8km (5 miles) further south is **Everest Base Camp** (珠峰大本营; Zhufeng Dabenying), which lies at 5,180 metres (16,995ft) and consistently yields

The Himalayas are the youngest folded mountains in the world. Before the southern Indian land mass began to shift northwards about 40 million years ago, one of the largest oceans in the history of the earth occupied the area.

BELOW: the view south to Everest from Dingri.

superior views of the mountain than can typically be had from the base camp on the southern, Nepalese side. During the usual climbing seasons in late spring and early autumn, the camp is filled with brightly coloured tents sheltering the climbing parties ahead of their ascents. In recent years, and partially thanks to the improved road conditions, visitor numbers here have increased markedly, leading to a slight improvement in tourist amenities while also negatively impacting on the once-pristine environment. In warmer months, there are spartan tent guesthouses offering an ample supply of blankets to stave off the nightly chill, but the minimal food available is basic and extortionately priced.

On to Nepal

Back on the Friendship Highway and about 50km (31 miles) south from the Everest turn-off is the Tibetan village of **Dingri** (定日), a convenient stopover on the road to Nepal that boasts sweeping views across the dusty plains to Everest and neighbouring mountains such as Cho Oyu, Shishapangma and Gyachung Kang – all among the world's fifteen tallest

peaks. The best vantage point is from the derelict ruins of the fort on the hill overlooking the main village, from where a host of other ruins – the result of a devastating 18th-century invasion by Nepalese Gurkhas – can be seen scattered across the arid landscape. Dingri has a couple of modest hotels and guesthouses as well as a few tiny restaurants.

Heading southwest, the road gradually climbs for the next 80km (50 miles), topping out at the exposed passes of Lalung La (5,050 metres/16,568ft) and Thong La (5,120 metres/16,798ft), both offering unfettered vistas of the Himalayas, and especially the mighty peak of Shishapangma. The road then switches back tightly on the descent to the village of **Nyalam** (聂拉木), and with the elevation loss comes a gradual increase in vegetation as well as temperature. From here, it's another 35km (22 miles) of switchbacks to the border town of **Zhangmu** (樟木), a curiously sordid amalgam of Chinese, Tibetan and Nepalese influences

Tibetan pilgrims prostrate themselves en route to the Jokhang temple in Lhasa while reciting mantras.

BELOW: Zhangmu, on the border with Nepal.

Apart from a handful of major routes, most Tibetan roads are unsurfaced, making a four-wheel-drive vehicle essential.

BELOW: the blue waters of Lake Manasarovar.

near the border crossing, and the 9km (6 miles) of no-man's land to Kodari, on the Nepalese side.

THE WILD WEST

The inhospitable high country of **Western Tibet** is one of the world's most isolated places, its barren, sparsely populated plains and windswept mountain passes making the Tsangpo River (Brahmaputra) Valley region through which the Friendship Highway winds seem positively benign in comparison. While much of Eastern and Southern Tibet is identified with monks and monasteries, the far-flung western territories are known for their unadulterated wilderness, lands where the endless vistas are punctuated only by raging melt-water torrents and the occasional soot-stained canvas of a nomad's tent. But for all its remoteness and inaccessibility, the wild west is considered by Tibetans to be an extraordinarily sacred place, with holy lakes and mountains that easily rival the importance of man-made monuments such as the Jokhang and

Potala in the Tibetan psyche. And though independent and organised travel through this area is challenging at the best of times, the few travellers who dedicate the time and effort to getting here invariably find it a transforming experience.

The most scenic and rewarding artery through the west is the so-called "southern route", via lonely Highway 219, which extends northwest from the fork just after Lhatse on the Lhasa–Nepal route. This road, which runs in an arc parallel with the Himalayas, is crossed by freezing rivers throughout most of each summer, making for slow progress. The main goals for most visitors to this area – foreign or Tibetan – are the adjacent holy sites of Lake Manasarovar and Mount Kailash, near the sources of Asia's greatest rivers.

Three holy pilgrimage sites

Some 900km (560 miles) northwest of Lhatse, well past the tiny settlements of Saga and Zhongba, lies **Lake Manasarovar ⓫** (瑪旁雍錯; Mapang Yongcuo; Mapham Yutso in Tibetan), at an average elevation of 4,550 metres (14,928ft) the world's highest freshwater lake. Celebrated as the holiest of all lakes by both Tibetan Buddhists and Hindus, it is an important place of pilgrimage for adherents of both faiths. For Tibetan devotees, the four-day, 88km (55-mile) clockwise circuit around the lake is considered sacred, and during warmer months pilgrims come to pay their respects at the handful of temples and monasteries along its shores. For their part, groups of Indian Hindus come here each year to purify themselves by bathing in and drinking from the lake's icy waters, which are frozen throughout the winter months. Hindu mythology holds that the lake was first conceived in the mind of Lord Brahma, and it is also revered because some of the subcontinent's major rivers – such as the Brahmaputra, the Indus, the Ghaghara and the Sutlej – originate near here.

The area's most famous attraction is **Mount Kailash ⓬** (冈仁波齐峰; Gangrenboqi Feng; Kang Rinpoche in

Recommended Restaurants on page 393

Tibetan), the legendary Trans-Himalayan hump that is considered holy by Hindus, Jains, Tibetan Buddhists and Bon believers. Dominating the skyline about 30km (19 miles) north of Lake Manasarovar, Kailash has drawn worshippers for thousands of years – it is believed that circumambulating it will bring good fortune, and thousands of pilgrims arrive each year to complete the circuit, or *kora*, that winds for 58km (36 miles) through a series of river valleys at the mountain's base. Hindus and Tantric Buddhists navigate the route in a clockwise fashion, while Jains and Bon adherents circle it anticlockwise; Westerners tend to walk in a clockwise direction in deference to the Tibetan Buddhist majority here. Some pilgrims attempt to complete the entire course in one long day, while others – mostly Tibetan Buddhists – cover the distance by performing the requisite sequence of body-length prostrations, a physically demanding process that usually takes several days. As the watershed of the major rivers feeding South Asia, Kailash is believed to have geomantic energy, and climbing on the mountain itself is considered strictly taboo. The route is accessed via the small town of **Darchen** (塔青; Taqing), which has a guesthouse, a store with food supplies and a Swiss-established medical clinic.

About 70km (44 miles) north of Darchen is another popular point of pilgrimage, the **Tirthapuri Hot Springs** (札达不若温泉, Zhadaburuo Wenquan), where pilgrims come to soak their feet in the shallow pools, often after completing the circuits just to the south. Near the springs is a small temple built around a cave where Padmasambhava and his Tibetan consort Yeshe Tsogyel are said to have meditated – inside is a pair of granite stones with indentations believed to be their footprints. The springs are about 6km (4 miles) southwest from the turn-off at Montser.

Remains of Guge: Toling and Tsaparang

Further north are all that remains of the 10th-century kingdom of **Guge**, then located near the main Indo-Tibetan trade routes of the day and largely responsible for bringing Buddhism to the heart of Tibet. The temples and religious buildings of the monastery at **Tholing**  (托林寺; Tuolin Si), most of them built from 1014–25, are considered to be the finest surviving examples of the Guge style of Buddhist art, which incorporated Indian, Tibetan and Nepalese influences. In the complex are monks' quarters, halls containing well-preserved murals and an impressive row of 108 earthen pagodas. The turn-off is 131km (81 miles) north of Tirthapuri at Namru, from where it is a further 144km (90 miles) over a mountainous road to Tholing; the final descent yields intoxicating views of the ruins scattered across the valley, framed by the snow-capped peaks of the north Indian Himalayas.

The sprawling ruins of the citadel at **Tsaparang** (阿里土林; Ali Tulin), where the later Guge kings moved their capital, lie 26km (16 miles) west of Toling. Prior

Yaks are the main domesticated animal in Tibet.

BELOW: Mount Kailash, sacred peak for Buddhists, Hindus and Jains.

Ta'er Si Monastery near Xining, birthplace of Tsongkhapa.

to its decline, Tsaparang was a thriving religious and commercial centre, located near the crossroads of several Silk Road trade routes.

QINGHAI

Bordered by Tibet, Xinjiang, Gansu and Sichuan and occupying the northeastern fringe of the Tibetan Plateau at an average altitude of 4,000 metres (13,100ft), **Qinghai** (青海) is one of China's least visited and poorest provinces, a place for which the term "back of beyond" is unusually apt. Named after the huge Qinghai Hu (Green Sea Lake), the province is a swathe of mountains and plateaux and home to several hardy minority groups, including Hui, Tibetans, Mongols and Kazakhs. Geographically part of Tibet and historically a distant region that for centuries solely supported nomadic herdsmen – mostly Tibetans and Muslims – it was taken over by the Communists in 1949 and later found fame as a far-flung gulag where intellectuals and political prisoners were carted off for re-education

through forced labour. Qinghai has been one of the last provinces to benefit from the government's drive to develop China's western reaches, but in recent years there has been increased investment in its main cities of Xining and Golmud, and tourist numbers are on the rise, although most of these only make brief stopovers on their way into Tibet proper.

Xining

The gateway to the province is its capital and largest city, **Xining ⑭** (西宁), which principally serves as an access point to the chief attractions of Ta'er Si and Qinghai Hu but also has some historically significant sights of its own. The **Dongguan Great Mosque** (东关清真大寺; Dongguan Qingzhen Dasi; daily 8am–8pm; charge), in the downtown area on Dongguan Dajie, features an intriguing blend of Arabic and Chinese architectural styles, with green-tiled domed towers flanked by Chinese-style archways. Its sprawling inner courtyard can get packed out with worshippers during prayer times. Just north of the city is the **Beishan Si** (北山寺; North Mountain Temple; daily 7am–7pm; charge), originally a series of Buddhist grottoes carved into the cliff face during the Northern Wei dynasty but now functioning mostly as a Daoist place of worship. After climbing a lengthy set of steep steps to the base of the cliff, some of the 18 grottoes can be accessed by interconnecting wooden walkways embedded into the rock.

Birthplace of Tsongkhapa

The sizeable **Ta'er Si** (塔尔寺; Kumbum Monastery; daily 8am–6pm; charge), 25km (15 miles) southeast of Xining, is one of the most important Tibetan religious centres outside of the Tibetan heartlands. Construction began in 1560 to mark the birthplace of Tsongkhapa, but many of its once-exquisite halls bore the brunt of legalised vandalism from Red Guards during the Cultural Revolution. Extensive restoration work has resulted in the complex returning to fully functioning monastic life, with several hundred resident monks. The entrance

ticket provides access to nine temples, the most renowned of which is the Hall of Butter Sculpture, replete with reliefs fashioned from yak butter portraying Tibetan myth and Buddhist parables.

China's largest lake

The immense **Qinghai Hu** ⑮ (青海湖; Green Sea Lake; originally called by its Mongolian name Kokonor) is China's biggest lake, covering an area greater than 4,500 sq km (2,800 sq miles). Famous for its birdlife (*see margin,*

right), it forms part of the **Qinghai Lake Natural Protection Zone**, which limits visitors to two main viewing areas (daily 9am–5pm; charge). The lake's eastern fringe is only about 150km (90 miles) west of Xining, but to see any concentration of birds you will need transport to the northwest side; CITS in Xining offers one-day bus tours that often ply the lake's entire perimeter. Alternatively, casual observers can see the lake from the bus or train while travelling between Xining and Golmud. ❑

Qinghai Lake is a spring and summer stopover for countless migratory birds en route to or from the Siberian Arctic, including various species of cranes, geese, gulls and swans. The "Bird Islands" at its northwest corner offer the best vantage points.

RESTAURANTS

Tibet
The traditional Tibetan diet is sparse, drawing mostly from the meat and milk of the yak – and to a lesser extent the sheep. A constant source of sustenance is the ubiquitous butter tea (酥油茶; *suyou cha* in Chinese), a bitter concoction of tea, yak butter and salt with an unmistakable aroma that will greet you at monasteries. Another staple is *tsampa*, or roasted barley flour, which Tibetans typically stir in with their butter tea and then roll the mixture into doughy balls. Yoghurt and cheese are also common, while yak meat is comparatively scarce but is sometimes added to *thukpa*, a noodle soup. In towns and cities it is possible to find *momos*, dumplings filled with ground yak meat or mutton. Tibetans' favoured tipple is *chang*, a sweet, beer-like beverage made

from fermented barley. Most foreign visitors find these staples to be, at best, an acquired taste, and hold out for the Chinese- and Western-style food that can be found in Lhasa.

Lhasa
Lhasa has a reasonable variety of food, with Tibetan, Chinese and Western-style fare as well as Nepalese and Indian curries. For the best *momos* and *thukpa* in Tibet, try one of the tiny noodle joints near the Tromzikhang Market, just north of the Jokhang. The busy night market on the northern segment of Dosengge Lu, just west of Ramoche Monastery, is popular with both Chinese and foreign tourists. The section of Beijing Donglu to the north of the Jokhang has several Western-style places, as well as some Sichuanese restaurants.

Dunya Restaurant
100 Beijing Donglu. **$$**
This popular foreign-run place has a wide-ranging menu, from home-baked breads and daily soups to excellent Nepalese and Indian curries and a good breakfast buffet.

Namtso Restaurant
8 Beijing Donglu. **$**
On the rooftop of the Banak Shol Hotel, this restaurant has a diverse menu ranging from yak burgers to kosher and vegetarian specialities and also does a cracking English breakfast.

Tashi II
105 Beijing Donglu. **$**
Located in the Kirey Hotel, this inexpensive restaurant caters to budget travellers and is a good place to try hygienic *momos* and *bobis* – unleavened flatbread topped with cream cheese and fried meat or vegetables.

Qinghai Province
Xining
For Muslim food, try the restaurants on Dongguan Dajie (东关大街), near the Great Mosque, most serving noodles and tasty mutton dishes. For cheap Muslim street food, take a stroll down the narrow lane that runs south from the front entrance to the Dongguan Great Mosque.

More street food is available at the huge downtown Shuijingxiang Food Market (水井巷食品市场, south side of Xi Dajie). Try the vegetable and meat kebabs, hot pot and *shaguo* (砂锅), a claybowl hot pot filled with meat and vegetables.

Average price for a meal for one, with one drink:
$ = under Rmb50
$$ = Rmb50–100
$$$ = Rmb100–150
$$$$ = over Rmb150

THE SILK ROAD: CHINA'S ANCIENT LINK WITH THE WEST

Conduit for religious and scientific ideas as well as merchandise, the Silk Road has shaped Chinese culture

The ancient Silk Road flourished for much of the first millennium AD, reaching its prime during the Tang dynasty. From the 15th century, land trade between China and the Middle East was beginning to wither away, superseded by new maritime routes between Europe and Asia, and by the 18th century, the Silk Road had largely ceased to function.

In its heyday, it was more than simply a conduit for silk and other trade goods. As well as the merchants, there were invaders, travellers, pilgrims and missionaries using the road and, crucially, spreading their ideas. The scientific knowledge, inventions, religions, philosophies and even the food that passed along the route transformed isolated regions into an interdependent global community. This made it the first and perhaps the most important of all information superhighways, helping to lay the foundations of our modern world – and instrumental in shaping Chinese culture and society.

From Chang'an (modern day Xi'an), the Silk Road headed westwards into the Hexi corridor – westernmost outpost of the Chinese empire – to reach the fortress town of Jiayuguan, and on to the oasis town of Dunhuang before splitting into a northern and a southern route which relinked at Kashgar (Kashi) on the threshold of Central Asia.

ABOVE: the classic fable *Journey to the West* describes the travels of the Buddhist monk Xuan Zang. The Silk Road was instrumental in the spread of Buddhism – and Islam – into China from other parts of Asia.

BELOW: Kuqa's Jama Masjid (Great Mosque).

ABOVE: silkworm on a mulberry leaf.

LEFT: as with all trade routes, the Silk Road acted as a conduit for ideas – religious and cultural exchanges between east and west, north and south. Buddhism, for instance, reached China from India via Afghanistan. This unusual Buddha image – it is in Greek garb – from northern Pakistan illustrates the point.

ABOVE: a 13th-century illustrated manuscript of Turkish origin depicts a Silk Road bazaar. From left to right are a jeweller, a herbalist, a butcher and a baker.

ABOVE: the Silk Road extended for approximately 8,000 km (5,000 miles). Silk would normally take several months, even years, to reach the Mediterranean from the orchards of eastern Cathay.

MODERN SILK ROAD TRAVEL

The break up of the Soviet Union and the opening of the Ürümqi–Almaty railway in the 1990s ushered in a new era for Silk Road travel, at least in terms of tourism. These days it is possible to travel without undue difficulty (by train or air-conditioned bus) from the cities of Xinjiang to their counterparts across the Tien Shan in Central Asia: Tashkent, Samarkand and Bukhara, all in Uzbekistan, can be reached as long as your papers are in order. Note that onward visas should be arranged either in your home country or from Beijing – they are not generally available at borders.

There are overland crossings between Xinjiang and Kazakhstan at Korgas and Tacheng, as well as a rail link at Alashankou to Druzba and on to Almaty in Kazakhstan. Two roads lead to Kyrgyzstan, the relatively easy Irkeshtam Pass to Osh and the less-frequented Torugart Pass to Naryn and Bishkek. The Karakoram Highway leads to Baltit (Hunza), Gilgit and Islamabad in Pakistan.

There are fascinating possibilities further north, too, across the Altai region from the far north of Xinjiang, then by train north to Siberia through some of Central Asia's lushest scenery.

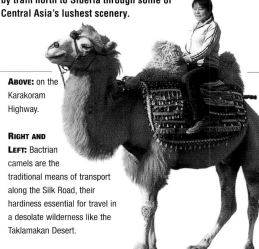

ABOVE: on the Karakoram Highway.

RIGHT AND LEFT: Bactrian camels are the traditional means of transport along the Silk Road, their hardiness essential for travel in a desolate wilderness like the Taklamakan Desert.

Recommended Restaurants on page 413

THE SILK ROAD

For centuries the main conduit of commerce and culture between China, Central Asia and Europe, the Silk Road passed through the heart of what is now China's fascinating northwestern region

C hina's vast northwestern region, known in earlier times as Chinese Turkestan, is accessible to travellers along the classic Silk Road. In AD 200, this transcontinental route linked the Roman empire in the west with the imperial court of China, while foreign traders who belonged to neither of the two old empires conducted trade along the route.

Before the discovery of the sea route from Europe to India in the 16th century, the Silk Road was the most important connection between the East and West. It experienced its last great era during the 13th century, when the entire route from China to the Mediterranean lay within the Mongol empire. This ancient trade route began in the old capital of Xi'an (then called Chang'an), reached the Huang He (Yellow River) at Lanzhou, then headed westward through deserts and mountains before dividing into two routes at the oasis of Dunhuang.

The northern route went via Hami, another oasis, before running to the south of the Bogda Shan range to the oasis of Turpan. It then reached Ürümqi, ascended several mountain passes through the Tian Shan range to Korla, and on to Kashi (Kashgar) from where it continued west into Central Asia. The southern route led from Dunhuang to Khotan, Yarkand and Kashi, holding a course between the river oases on the northern slopes of Kunlun Shan and the notorious Taklamakan Desert. *For more on the Silk Road, see pages 394–5.*

EASTERN GANSU: LANZHOU

Lanzhou ❶ (兰州) is the largest city and provincial capital of **Gansu** (甘肃) province. Due to its strategic location astride the Huang He (Yellow River), set in a long and narrow defile dominating all traffic between central China and the northwest, it has long been a vital garrison town that has expanded rapidly in recent decades to a major city of more than 3 million people. With an economy based on heavy industry and petrochemicals, Lanzhou suffers from appalling pollution and isn't the most obviously

Main attractions

LABRANG MONASTERY, XIAHE
JIAYUGUAN
MOGAO CAVES, DUNHUANG
TURPAN
TIAN CHI (HEAVEN LAKE)
KASHI
KARAKORAM HIGHWAY

LEFT: taking a rest at the Dunhuang oasis. **BELOW:** Uighurs in Ürümqi.

Lanzhou's strategic position on the Huang He has made it an important transport town and garrison with a long history.

appealing city. Yet it is a very cosmopolitan place, with a noticeable Hui Muslim presence and a strong flavour of Central Asia.

As well as good hotels and restaurants, Lanzhou has a few attractions to appeal to visitors, including the fast-flowing Huang He, already a major river though still some 1,500km (900 miles) from the East China Sea. Take the cable car across the chocolate-coloured, loess-rich waters up to **Baita Shan** (白塔山; White Pagoda Hill; daily 6.30am–8.30pm; charge), where fine views across the city can be enjoyed together with a cold drink and a snack.

Close to the cable-car station, by the river bank and facing symbolically westward towards Central Asia, stand the **Journey to the West Statues** (西游记; Xiyouji) featuring the celebrated Buddhist monk Xuan Zang and his legendary companions, Monkey, Pigsy and Sandy *(see pages 89, 101, 406)*. Nearby is **Waterwheel Park** (水车园; Shuicheyuan; daily 6.30am–8.30pm; charge), where two giant reconstructed waterwheels turn in the powerful current. Introduced as an

irrigation technique from Yunnan in the 16th century, these two wheels are all that remains of an estimated 250 used in the area in the early 20th century.

Also in the same downtown area, the Daoist **Baiyun Guan** (白云观; White Cloud Temple; daily 7am–5.30pm; charge) offers a tranquil and attractive retreat from the city bustle. Close to the West train station, the **Gansu Provincial Museum** (甘肃省博物馆; Gansu Sheng Bowuguan; Tue–Sun 9am–5pm; charge) is definitely worth visiting for its unsurpassed collection of Silk Road artefacts including, most famously, the "Flying Horse of Gansu" discovered at Wuwei in 1969, and a 2nd-century silver plate showing Dionysus, the Greek God of Wine, found near Lanzhou but clearly originating far to the west and carried overland to China during the early Silk Road era.

South of Lanzhou

Linxia (临夏), formerly known as Hezhou, is a little-visited but prosperous trading town on a southern spur of the Silk Road leading to the Tibetan Plateau and Lhasa. Nowadays a city of 300,000, it is home to an Islamic majority popula-

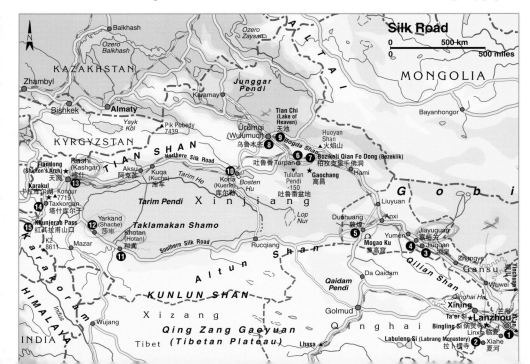

GETTING TO THE REGION
Lanzhou and Ürümqi are the main transport hubs, with frequent trains and flights to Beijing, Xi'an, Guangzhou and Shanghai. Ürümqi is also linked by air with Tashkent and other Central Asian cities, and by train to Almaty.

GETTING AROUND THE REGION
Lanzhou: Trains going west stop at Jiayuguan (11 hours), Liuyuan/Dunhuang (14 hours), Daheyan/Turpan (22 hours) and Ürümqi (24 hours). There are 3 direct buses daily from Lanzhou to Xiahe (6 hours); more frequent buses travel via Linxia.
Dunhuang: Train departures from Dunhuang

include Jiayuguan (6 hours), Lanzhou (11 hours), Turpan (11 hours), Ürümqi (14 hours), Xi'an (24 hours) and Yinchuan (18 hours).
Ürümqi: There are flights to Lanzhou and Kashi; there are also daily train departures to these cities (25 and 23 hours respectively). Trains also leave daily for Kuqa (14 hours). Buses go to Turpan, Kuqa and Kashi.
Turpan: Buses to the nearest train station (Daheyan) run every 30 minutes. There are buses to Ürümqi (2½ hours), Kuqa (15 hours) and Kashi (26 hours).
Kashi: There are bus connections between Kashi and Ürümqi (24 hours), Turpan and Taxkorgan (6 hours).

Gansu is among China's poorer provinces, traditionally plagued by drought, famine and earthquakes. In 1920 a strong quake killed an estimated 180,000 people, and was followed by another 12 years later which killed around 70,000. Housing construction standards have since greatly improved.

tion comprising Chinese-speaking Hui Muslims, Mongol-speaking Dongxiang Muslims and Turkic-speaking Salar Muslims who are believed to have originally migrated from distant Uzbekistan.

The town is an important Sufi centre for Muslim mystics (recognisable by their six-cornered hats), as well as a cultural meeting point for Han Chinese, Hui Muslims, Tibetan Buddhists and Dongxiang Mongols. There's not a great deal in the way of sights, but it's a convenient place to stay overnight if travelling between Lanzhou and Xiahe. There are several good hotels, and it's easy to find cheap and delicious Muslim food – *lamien* noodles, lamb and beef kebabs, toasted *bing* flat breads and the like – at the night market on central **Nationalities Square** (民族广场; Minzu Guangchang).

The **Bingling Si** (炳灵寺; Thousand Buddha Caves; daily 9am–5pm; charge)

BELOW: statues in Lanzhou depict Xuan Zang and his companions on their *Journey to the West.*

Xiahe, which has grown up around Labrang Monastery, is one of the largest Tibetan cultural centres outside of Tibet proper (Xizang province).

BELOW: Labrang Monastery at Xiahe.

are located 80km (50 miles) west of Lanzhou and comprise Buddhist grottoes carved into a 60-metre (200ft) cliff face. The caves are decorated with Buddhist sculptures, frescoes and statues. Most celebrated is the striking 27-metre (89ft) high statue of Maitreya, the future Buddha. Entry into the more interesting caves is expensive and getting to Bingling Si on one's own can be a hassle, but local travel agencies run day trips that involve travel by both bus and boat.

Xiahe

Highly recommended is a trip to **Xiahe** ❷ (夏河), a dusty town 280km (175 miles) to the southwest of Lanzhou, reached by direct bus (6 hours) or by changing buses at Linxia. Here, attached to and effectively supported by the predominantly Tibetan town of Xiahe, stands the awe-inspiring **Labrang Monastery** (拉卜楞寺; Labuleng Si; daily 8am–7pm; charge). The surrounding grasslands and mountains where one can hike amid Tibetan nomads are another powerful draw.

Labrang Monastery is the second-largest of the six major Gelug "Yellow Hat" monasteries in Tibetan Buddhism, and a major pilgrimage centre attracting Tibetans from as far afield as Lhasa and even Dharamsala – the Dalai Lama is a member of the Yellow Hat order, though of course he cannot visit, at least for the present. It is a major centre of learning, containing six academic institutes and 10,000 books of Tibetan scripture, as well as important Buddhist cultural relics.

Established in 1709, Labrang once held as many as 4,000 monks, though the monastery suffered grievously during the Cultural Revolution. Today numbers of monks are once again approaching 2,000, the temple buildings have been largely restored, and crowds of Tibetan pilgrims throng the prayer-wheel corridors in their colourful clothing. In an interesting – if ironic – sign of the changing times, increasing numbers of Han Chinese visitors come to worship at the temple, some even painfully completing the full 6-km (4-mile) pilgrimage circuit *(kora)*, constantly prostrating themselves full length as they go.

The monastery complex is large and completely dominates the western part of town. The white or ochre walls and gilded roofs are predominantly Tibetan

in style, though the occasional Chinese dragon also graces some eaves. In all there are 18 halls, six colleges, the **Gongtang Ta** (贡唐塔), a magnificent golden stupa bearing gilded bas-reliefs of the Goddess Tara, and miles – literally – of covered prayer-wheel corridors.

The modern town of Xiahe, where some surprisingly good restaurants are to be found, lies to the east. It's here that the Han Chinese and Hui Muslims have their shops. In a commercial endeavour that clearly indicates the pragmatism of local Muslims, many Hui shopkeepers and pedlars make a good living by selling all kinds of religious paraphernalia, including Buddha images and prayer wheels, to visiting Tibetan Buddhists. Accommodation can be found in the Tibetan area west of the monastery as well as in the newer town.

From Xiahe a fascinating overland route runs southwards across high-altitude grasslands into Sichuan, passing through the Tibetan towns of Langmusi, Zoige and Songpan *(see pages 356–7)*, before eventually reaching Chengdu.

NINGXIA

To the northeast of Lanzhou is the diminutive **Ningxia Hui Autonomous Region** (宁夏回族自治区; Ningxia Huizu Zizhiqu), China's second-smallest province and home to a large population of Hui, Chinese Muslims descended from Middle Eastern traders who arrived in China along the Silk Road. The Hui constitute around 30 percent of the population of Ningxia.

Situated close to the Huang He, the source of irrigation that sustains the region, **Yinchuan** (银川) was formerly the capital of the non-Chinese Xi Xia dynasty, obliterated by Genghis Khan. The **Ningxia Museum** (宁夏博物馆; Ningxia Bowuguan; daily 8am–5pm; charge) on Jinning Nan Jie has wide-ranging displays on the Xi Xia dynasty and Hui culture. In the courtyard stands **Xi Ta** (西塔; West Pagoda; same hours; charge), which you can climb for views over town.

The land around Yinchuan is rich in interest, with the fascinating **Xi Xia**

Wangling (西夏王陵; Western Xia Tombs; daily 8am–6pm; charge) just 20km (12 miles) to the west. Near Qingtongxia, 80km (50 miles) south, the **108 Dagobas** (青铜峡 一百零八塔; Qingtongxia Yibailingba Ta; daily 8am–6pm; charge) are an otherworldly collection of stupas arranged in rows. The town of **Zhongwei** (中衛) in the west of the region is famed for its multi-faith Gao Miao (Gao Temple), originally constructed in the 15th century. The Huang He can be visited at **Shapotou** (沙坡头), and fragments of the Great Wall snake to the north along the fringes of the Tengger Desert.

WESTERN GANSU

From Lanzhou, Gansu province extends northwestwards in a great arc to the border with Xinjiang. The varied loess landscape and the diverse desert moods make the overland journey between Lanzhou and Jiuquan, an ancient crossroads and garrison town, truly extraordinary. In the south, the distant snow-covered peaks of Qilian Shan flank the railway line. The train reaches a flat, 800km (500-mile) long corridor when it arrives at the old admin-

TIP

Most of the people of Gansu speak a dialect of Mandarin Chinese. In outlying areas, Tibetan, Mongol, Kazakh and Salar – the last a Turkic language – are also spoken, but Mandarin, also called *putonghua* or "common speech", is understood by just about everyone.

BELOW: Muslim street food in Linxia.

BELOW:
Jiayuguan fort.

istrative and garrison town of **Wuwei** (武威). The famous "Flying Horse", an Eastern Han-period bronze statue, was excavated nearby in 1968 *(see page 398).*

The next point of interest, **Zhangye** (张掖), lies 140km (87 miles) to the west. Founded in 121 BC as a garrison town, its most notable sight is China's longest reclining Buddha, a supine 35 metres (115ft), housed in the **Dafo Si** (大佛寺; Big Buddha Temple; daily 7.30am–6.30pm; charge). Zhangye's wooden pagoda (Mu Ta) dates from the Tang period; its first six floors are made of brick.

Jiuquan ❸ (酒泉), a thriving industrial town 200km (125 miles) further west, was founded in 111 BC as a garrison outpost. Between 127 and 102 BC, the Han emperors relocated nearly a million peasant families here, including at least 700,000 victims of a devastating flood in Shandong. Today, the Old Town Quarter around the drum and bell towers is changing: small alleys are being torn down and modern buildings erected. Out in the desert, China's ambitious commercial space programme launches Long March rockets into the heavens *(see margin, left).*

Jiayuguan

Some 30km (20 miles) further on is **Jiayuguan ❹** (嘉峪关), a historic fortress town close to the western end of the Great Wall – almost 5,000km (3,100 miles) from Beijing – built to guard the pass between the Qilian Shan and Hei Shan mountain ranges.

Completed in 1372, just four years after the rise of the Ming dynasty, the **fort** (daily 8.30am–5.30pm; charge) was historically the last bastion of imperial China. Beyond it lay the barbarian lands. The structure comprises a square inner courtyard enclosed by walls and two gates. On top of the 10-metre (33ft) high, 640-metre (2,100ft) long wall are 17-metre (56ft) high watchtowers from the late Ming and the early Qing periods. The wall was first restored around 1507, again during the Qing period, and again in recent years for the benefit of tourists. The structure, which dominates the landscape and is particularly impressive when approached from the west, can also be viewed from a distance on the train bound for Liuyuan.

A monument with the inscription "Strongest Fort of the World" has stood outside the western gate since 1809,

while at the southern entrance is an elevated pavilion-like stage: dignitaries used to watch plays from the pavilion opposite on the right-hand side. Within the complex is the **Great Wall Museum** (entrance included with fort admission).

Some 8 km (5 miles) northwest of the fort is the last section of wall, known as the **Overhanging Great Wall**, most of which has been restored in recent years. There are sweeping views of the landscape from its battlements.

Weijin Bihua Mu (魏晋壁画墓), eight tombs from the Wei (AD 220–65) and the Jin (AD 265–420) dynasties, are 20km (12 miles) to the northeast of Jiayuguan. They contain wall murals with scenes from daily life, but only one of the eight tombs is open to visitors. Consequently, few foreign tourists make it out here.

Dunhuang

The town of **Dunhuang** ❺ (敦煌), in an irrigated cotton-producing oasis, is on many people's itineraries as it is the base for visiting the magnificent Mogao Caves. The 2006 opening of a new branch line connecting with the main Lanzhou–Xinjiang railway has made it far more accessible.

About 40km (25 miles) before Dunhuang, near the road, is a well-preserved watchtower dating from 1730, an example of the type of communications used at that time. By daylight, flag signals were given from the top platform; at night, fire signals lit the skies. After crossing the drained plain of Shule He, remnants of the Great Wall from the Eastern Han period are visible.

Between cotton fields and threshing areas at the edge of the town, Baima Ta (White Horse Dagoba) is reminiscent of Beijing's White Dagoba. Baima Ta is where the white horse of the famous travelling Indian monk Kumarajiva (AD 344–431) is said to have died. The Dunhuang Xian Bowuguan (County Museum; daily 9am–5pm; charge) has some local finds, visual displays and models of the oasis, reflecting the historic significance of this settlement, as well as a few manuscripts from the Mogao Caves.

Mogao Caves

The most important attraction in northwest Gansu and the main reason most Silk Road travellers and Buddhist pilgrims visit Dunhuang, are the **Mogao Caves** (莫高窟; Mogao Ku; daily 8.30–11.30am, 2.30–6pm; charge). Located about 25km (16 miles) southeast of the town centre and readily accessible by taxi or minibus *(see margin tip, page 404)*, the caves were cut into the soft rock face of the **Mingsha Hills** (鸣沙山; Mingsha Shan) over a period of more than 1,000 years, from the 3rd to the 14th centuries. They represent China's most extensive collection of Buddhist statuary, paintings and manuscripts, though many of the original materials are now in foreign museum collections, especially in Europe and Japan. Mingsha Shan itself is a mountain range of pure sand, imposingly etched against a cloudless blue sky. Watching the sunset from the top is an unforgettable experience.

Having suffered many depredations at the hands of robbers, warlords, iconoclastic Muslims and Red Guards over the years (but none so damaging to the Mogao Caves, at least, as their late 19th–early

The impressively restored Overhanging Great Wall extends northwest from Jiayuguan Fort.

BELOW: the oasis of Dunhuang flanked by the imposing Mingsha Shan (Singing Sand Dunes).

TIP

To get to the Mogao Caves you can take a regular bus, minibus or taxi for the 30-minute journey. From the centre of Dunhuang it's easy enough to find transport. Once you reach the caves you are obliged to join a guided tour to see a selection of the caves – there is no alternative.

BELOW: the entrance to the Mogao Caves.

20th-century discovery by archaeologist-explorers like Aurel Stein and Paul Pelliot), the cave complex is now extremely well cared for. Visitors cannot enter without a guide, photography is strictly forbidden, and generally the only illumination available will be the guide's flashlight – to prevent the murals fading over time.

Almost 500 caves survive, set back against and cut into the cliff face, and connected by a series of ramps and walkways. Not all the caves are open to the public – even accompanied by an obligatory guide – and it may be necessary to make special arrangements (and payment) with the Mogao authorities to explore further such off-limits grottoes. An estimated 45,000 sq metres (484,000 sq ft) of murals and more than 2,000 painted stucco figures can be seen, though it would take considerable dedication and several days to try to visit all of them.

The years of darkness have kept the generally pastel colours fairly bright, and it is a wonderful experience, even to the lay person with limited knowledge of Buddhist art, to wander through the caves as the torchlight reveals image after image derived, variously and distinc-

tively, from South Asian, Gandharan, Turkic, Tibetan and Chinese traditions. A well-presented museum in front of the caves features examples of the astonishing number of scripts found on manuscripts and other documents preserved at the caves, including writings not just in Chinese and Sanskrit, Tocharian and Tibetan languages, but also in various Turkic dialects, Persian and even Hebrew.

The grottoes show an uninterrupted history of Chinese painting, particularly of landscapes, over a period of nearly 1,000 years. One of the most beautiful caves (no. 323) shows an Indian Buddha statue made from sandalwood being presented to the reigning emperor. Most impressive is a 35-metre (115ft) high statue of Maitreya Buddha carved into the cliff face.

WEST TO XINJIANG

China's Central Asian backyard, the autonomous region of **Xinjiang** (新疆) is a huge expanse of desert and mountains bordered to the north by Mongolia, to the south by Tibet and to the west by the ex-Soviet republics of Kazakhstan, Kyrgyzstan and Tajikistan. It is predominantly Islamic, with the Muslim Uighur people accounting for approximately 45 percent of the total population. The proportion of Han Chinese, however, has increased from 8 percent in 1940 to almost 50 percent today, with migrants lured by financial incentives offered by the government. As in Tibet and Inner Mongolia, the Han are concentrated in the larger cities; smaller oases and nomadic areas are still dominated by Uighurs and Kazakhs.

Turpan

One of the most rewarding cities in the region is **Turpan ⑥** (吐鲁番; Tulufan), a remote Silk Road oasis and the first place of significance reached on the route west from Gansu. It is 11 hours by train from Dunhuang and five hours by bus from Ürümqi, although access is not straightforward as the nearest railway station is at Daheyan, 60km (37 miles) from the town.

Turpan is atmospheric, although only a handful of old buildings have been pre-

Recommended Restaurants on page 413

served. **Sugong Ta** (苏公塔; Emin Minaret), built with clay bricks in 1777 and finished in 1788, and the sparsely furnished mosque next to it are the symbols of the town, and have been designated a historical monument. Sugong Ta's 72 steps leading to the top are closed to visitors. The mosque, the largest in Turpan, can hold up to 3,000 people and is used only during important Muslim festivals.

In an ancient and fantastic underground irrigation system – the Karez wells – snowmelt from the mountains is channelled to the oasis over long distances underground (to prevent the water from evaporating) using the force of gravity. The subterranean canal system is over 3,000km (1,860 miles) long.

To the northeast of town, **Putao Gou** (葡萄沟; Grape Valley; daily; charge) is the most celebrated of Turpan's extensive vineyards and a must on every tour-group itinerary. Turpan has been cultivating grapes for almost two millennia, and today more than 100 varieties are grown, accounting for around 90 percent of China's seedless grape produce. In times past the most valued variety of grape, known as *manaizi* or "mare's nipple"

grapes, formed part of Turpan's tribute to the Chinese court at Xi'an and later Beijing. Today the grape harvest contributes substantially to the wealth of the oasis and its people, and vines are cultivated just about everywhere they can be grown, for fruit, wine and indeed shade. To celebrate this bounty, an annual **Turpan Grape Festival** is held each August–September at the end of the harvest.

Around Turpan

Turpan lies within the **Turpan Basin** (吐鲁番盆地; Tulufan Pendi), some 150km (93 miles) long from east to west and, at 150 metres (490ft) below sea level, second in the low-altitude stakes only to the Dead Sea in Israel. The exact low point is Aydingkol Hu (Moonlight Lake), a salt lake in the basin that is drying up and is 154 metres (500ft) below sea level. In summer, the temperature here can rise to 47°C (117°F).

Stretching 100km (60 miles) to the east, the **Huoyan Shan** (火焰山; Flaming Mountains) are a range of bare sandstone mountains rising up to 1,800 metres (5,900ft), which achieved fame in the novel *The Journey to the West*.

Turpan's Emin Mosque and Minaret.

BELOW: empty highway of the western desert.

Bactrian camels, a mainstay of Silk Road transport, have been domesticated for around 2,500 years. They can survive for five days without water, carry heavy loads and move surprisingly quickly. They also produce milk and wool, and their dung can be used as fuel for fires.

BELOW: vineyard in the oasis village of Tuyok near Turpan.

Some 45km (28 miles) to the southeast of Turpan is the ruined city of **Gaochang** (高昌), the ancient Karachotcha or Khocho. Founded as a garrison under the Han emperor Wudi (140–86 BC), during its heyday the town had 30,000 inhabitants, over 3,000 monks and more than 40 Buddhist monasteries. Today, one can see the division of the town into a centre with sacred buildings and suburbs with bazaars and housing estates.

The **Astana Ancient Tombs** (阿斯塔那古墓; Asitana Gumu), 6km (4 miles) to the northwest, are a burial ground for Gaochang's dead. There are over 500 tombs, although only three are open to visitors, and with many archaeological remains having been carted off to museums, few visitors make the effort to visit.

To the north of Gaochang is the ancient cave monastery of **Bezeklik** ❼ (柏孜克里千佛洞; Bozikeli Qian Fo Dong; daily 8am–4pm; charge). The trip through the canyon leading to Bezeklik begins at a watchtower dating from the Qing period (around 1770), located opposite the cave monastery site Samgin

(Murtuq), used from around 450 to the 1200s. The caves of Bezeklik – there are around 80, of which only five can be visited – have been carved into the cliff face some 80 metres (260ft) above the western bank of the river.

The plunder of valuable paintings by German and British archaeologists damaged the pictorial representation of the Buddha and Bodhisattva (redemption deities) in several caves. After 1860, Islamic fanatics destroyed most of the facial depictions, a legacy of destruction that continued with the Cultural Revolution in the late 1960s. What remains in the caves is underwhelming, but the caves themselves are still an impressive sight, and the setting is superb.

About 30km (19 miles) southeast of Bezeklik and 70km (43 miles) east of Turpan, near the eastern rim of the Turpan Basin, the traditional Uighur village of **Tuyoq** (吐峪沟; Tuyugou; daily; charge) offers a fascinating opportunity to visit a remote and traditional Uighur community set in a narrow valley in the southern flanks of the Flaming Mountains. There is only one road into the village, and tourists have to pay a fee to enter.

There are numerous caves set high into the steep mountainside above the village, but they are all but inaccessible, and such artistic treasures as they once held have mainly either been destroyed or dispersed to museums in China and Europe. Yet the appeal of Tuyoq is less these caves than the village's idyllic setting and bucolic charm. Mud-brick houses and courtyards surrounded by lush grapevines cluster in the valley around the green-and-white mosque, while a locally revered shrine surmounted by a green dome, the Tomb of the Seven Sleepers, dominates the hillside above the settlement. The local Uighur people, amiable but shy, do not permit non-Muslims to enter either the shrine or the dusty cemetery that abuts it.

Predating even Gaochang is the ruined city of **Jiaohe Gucheng** (交河故城), which in the past was called Yariko or Yarkhoto. Lying 10km (6 miles) to the west of Turpan, it was founded in the Han period and served as the centre of a kingdom until the 5th century. Jiaohe lies on a plateau on a sharp curve of a river – a natural fortification. Civil wars and lack of water at the time of Mongol rule in the early 13th century brought the

town to ruins. The central sacred site and the remnants of Buddhist monasteries and stupas in the northwest, which are most prominent among the ruins, are still well preserved. The remains of underground dwellings, which offered protection from the summer heat and the arctic winter, are of special interest.

Ürümqi

The road from Turpan to Ürümqi leads westwards across the lunar-like Turpan depression before reaching the Baiyang He, a pass which leads to a completely different landscape. The route travels along the richly forested valley of the Baiyang He (White Poplar River) and then through pastures along the northern slope of Tian Shan before arriving in Ürümqi (186km/116 miles from Turpan).

The capital of Xinjiang autonomous region, **Ürümqi** ❽ (乌鲁木齐; Wulumuqi) is a large city 186km (116 miles) west of Turpan and 900 metres (2,900ft) above sea level. It has the dubious honour of being the world's most continental city – situated further from the sea than any other. Over 80 percent of its 2.8 million population are Han Chinese. The city has

Hami is famous for its deliciously sweet melons (Hami Gua).

BELOW: the sands of the Taklamakan Desert.

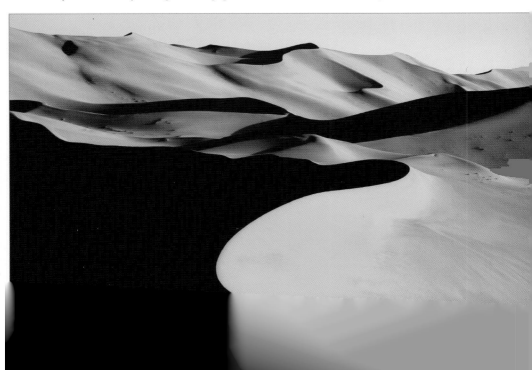

TIP

Ürümqi was the scene of violent ethnic riots in the summer of 2009 *(see page 59)*, and at the time of going to press the atmosphere has remained tense in the city, as well as in Kashi. It is worth checking the situation before travelling.

little ethnic character, and industrial proliferation has resulted in high levels of pollution, particularly in the freezing winter.

The **Xinjiang Sheng Bowuguan** (新疆省博物馆; Regional Museum; daily 9.30am–7pm; charge) is worth a visit. Apart from significant archaeological finds, it also exhibits life-sized models of the houses and tools of the nationalities in the region. The highlight, however, is the display of some 3,000-year-old mummies of European, Kashmiri and East Asian ancestry found in Xinjiang (one academic even postulates a Celtic connection after an analysis of the weave and dye of their clothing).

In the town, there are numerous small mosques and bazaars full of activity. A pavilion in the style of a Chinese garden lodge and a small pagoda, both symbols of the town, are located on **Hong Shan** (红山), which also offers a good view of the town. The town itself has modern highrises and wide, tree-lined streets. Older buildings, marked by sterile exteriors, date from the time of the Soviet presence and influence. It is possible to take a train from Ürümqi across the border into Kazakhstan. *For more details, see page 420.*

Heavenly Mountains

Definitely worthy of exploration is the breathtaking **Tian Chi** ❾ (天池; Lake of Heaven), some 110km (68 miles) east of Ürümqi on the slopes of **Tian Shan** (天山), at the foot of the high Bodga range. The road between Ürümqi and Tianchi passes through some ravishing scenery. The lake has a developed tourist arrival area, but trails and walks into the surrounding hills get you away from the hubbub. It's a great idea to stay the night here: some travellers intend to visit for a couple of days and end up staying for weeks in lakeside yurts where local Kazakh families dwell.

Silk routes to Kashi

The long journey from Ürümqi and Turpan west to Kashi (Kashgar) was historically one of the most treacherous on the Silk Road, a brutal stretch of desert infested with bandits and plagued either by intense heat or extreme cold. There were in fact two principal routes: a northern road, from Korla to Kashi via Kuqa and Aksu; and a southern, starting from Dunhuang and running along the northern edge of the Kunlun Shan via Khotan

BELOW: Tianchi (Lake of Heaven).

Recommended Restaurants on page 413

and Yarkand. Both routes pass along the edges of the notorious Taklamakan Desert (whose name is popularly mis-translated into "he who goes in does not come out"). As elsewhere on the Silk Road, the predominant theme is barren landscapes punctuated by the irrigated fields and poplar trees of the occasional oasis.

Korla ⓾ (库尔勒; Kuerle) is an important transport hub and something of a boomtown, with a high proportion of Han Chinese. **Kuqa** (库车; Kuche) was formerly an important staging post on the Silk Road. The area around this Uighur town is rich in ancient pre-Islamic city ruins; to the west are the **Kezier Qianfodong** (克孜尔千佛洞; Kizil 1,000 Buddha Caves), although only a few are open to tourists. A relatively short distance west, the industrial city of **Aksu** (阿克苏) is of limited interest, although it makes a good stopping point en route to Kashi, with a good range of hotels and restuarants.

The southern route has long descended into obscurity, but at one time the settlements along its barren length were thriving centres of commerce. The most significant was **Khotan** ⓫ (和阗; Hotan/Hetian), centre of an early Buddhist empire in the 3rd century BC, when the eldest son of the Indian emperor Asoka is said to have settled there. The city was for a time one of the greatest on the Silk Road, famed for its jade and its carpets, and is claimed to have been the first place outside Han China to have cultivated silk. There is little of the Old City remaining, but it remains an atmospheric place, largely Uighur in identity.

A long trawl further west, **Yarkand** ⓬ (莎車; Shache) has retained a picturesque charm and is one of the least modernised cities in China.

Kashi (Kashgar)

On the Tumen River in the middle of an irrigation oasis that nurtures cotton and other crops, **Kashi** ⓭ (喀什; Kashgar) lies closer to Islamabad, Delhi, Kabul, Tehran and even Baghdad than it does to Beijing, with the borders of Kyrgyzstan, Tajikistan, Afghanistan and Pakistan close by.

One of the most famous of all the Silk Road towns, today Kashi is changing fast. Once ringed by crenellated walls and staunchly Uighur, it is becoming increasingly Chinese, as waves of settlers from the east follow the newly constructed railway (completed in 1999) from Turpan and Ürümqi to seek their fortune in China's "Wild West". Large parts of the Old City have been demolished in recent years, although the authorities have now belatedly recognised that the **Old Town** (老城; Altyn Shahr/Laocheng; daily; charge) is a valuable tourist asset and should be preserved.

Old Kashgar is best seen to the west of **Id Gah Square** (艾提朵尔广场; Aitikaer Guangchang) – where parts of the ancient city wall are still extant to the west of Seman Lu; another section of the Old Town has been preserved to the east of Id Gah Square and is now actively promoted as a tourist attraction. The square itself is teeming with snack bars, teahouses, craft shops, workshops and numerous small stores selling everything from flowers to cameras. There has also been a proliferation of modern shopping centres blaring out loud Uighur music.

The ancient city of Khotan retains the flavour of the old Silk Road with a lively market and some beautiful old wooden architecture.

BELOW: desert oasis: an avenue of poplars near Kashi.

Best visited on a Sunday, the huge Animal Market (Mal Bazaar/Dongwu Shichang) is great fun and uniquely Uighur. Located in the southeast of town, some distance beyond the confines of urban Kashgar, it's packed with local men buying and selling livestock of all kinds, from fat-tailed sheep to horses, camels and yaks.

Id Gah Mosque (艾提朵尔清真寺; Aitika Qingzhensi) has been renovated many times and is China's largest mosque, able to hold 6,000 worshippers. Although paint is peeling off its central dome and two flanking minarets, the building, dating from 1442, still dominates its surroundings. Behind the gate are tree-lined squares for prayer. Some 100 metres (330ft) behind is the Great Prayer Hall, open only for Friday prayer. The steps in front of the side walls are a popular meeting place, particularly for the elderly. On religious feast days, up to 50,000 worshippers come for Friday prayer.

To the north of the mosque and square runs an extremely lively bazaar street of barber shops, book and fur traders, blacksmiths, bakers, tailors and, directly by the mosque, dentists. The covered bazaar has just about anything for sale.

The most important weekly event is the *basha*, or **Sunday market** (Xingqiri Shichang or Yekshenba Bazaar – not to be confused with the Mal Bazaar animal market, *see margin*), still held by the banks of the Tumen River. Tens of thousands of visitors and buyers and sellers come to this market from all around, giving it a cosmopolitan atmosphere.

Another major Uighur site is the **Tomb of Yusup Has** (哈斯哈吉南墓; Hasihaji Nanmu; daily 10am–7pm; charge for non-Muslims), around 2km (1½ miles) southeast of Id Gah Square. Yusup Has was the author of the Uighur text *Qutatu Bilik* or *Benefical Lore*, one of the greatest works of Uighur literature, and together with Mahmud Kashgari remains among the most respected and revered of Uighur intellectuals.

About 5km (3 miles) northeast of town is **Xiangfei Mu** (香妃墓), the Abakh Hoja mausoleum, dating back to the 16th century and renovated in 1980 and again in 1997. All the buildings of the mausoleum are examples of traditional Uighur architecture. Abakh Hoja (Aba Hezhuo), who died in 1695, was an outstanding political and Muslim religious leader in Kashi. His sarcophagus, one of 57 in the mausoleum that houses his descendants, lies on an elevated pedestal in the centre of the central building's

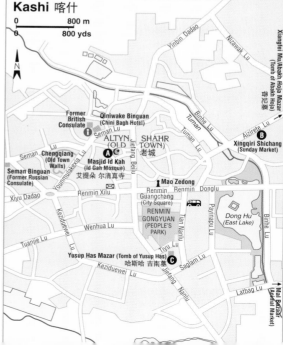

Kashi 喀什

0 — 800 m
0 — 800 yds

N

Yinbin Dadao

Nizavak Lu

Xiangfei Mu/Abakh Hoja Mazar
(Tomb of Abakh Hoja)
香妃墓

Binhe Lu

Tuman Lu

Azirete Lu

Former British Consulate
Qiniwake Binguan (Chini Bagh Hotel)
Seman Lu

ALTYN (OLD TOWN)

SHAHR 老城

Jiefang Beilu

Xingqiri Shichang (Sunday Market) **B**

Seman Chengqiang (Old Town Walls)
Youmulakexia

Masjid Id Kah (Id Gah Mosque) **A C**
艾提朵尔清真寺

Seman Binguan (Former Russian Consulate)

Mao Zedong

Xiyu Dadao

Renmin Xilu

Kezidujewei Lu

Renmin Guangchang (City Square)
Renmin Donglu

RENMIN GONGYUAN (PEOPLE'S PARK)

Tian Nanlu

Paymapu Lu

Dong Hu (East Lake)

Binhe Lu

Wenhua Lu

Tuanjie Lu

Tiyu Lu

Saglam Lu

Yusup Has Mazar (Tomb of Yusup Has) **C**
哈斯哈 吉南墓

Kezidujewei Lu

Jiefang Nanlu

Latbag Lu

Mal Bazaar (Animal Market)

Recommended Restaurants on page 413

main hall, which is reminiscent of a mosque (but not facing Mecca), and is flanked by a slightly leaning minaret. In the near left corner is the sarcophagus of Xiangfei (Fragrant Concubine), the daughter of the last Hoja, Ali Hoja, and the great-granddaughter of Abakh Hoja, and source of the mausoleum's popular name. According to legend, Xiangfei is said to have refused to sleep with the emperor Qianlong, who had abducted and taken her to Beijing after the repression of a rebellion here in 1758. Since she would not consummate the relationship, she was forced to commit suicide by the empress dowager, the emperor's mother. Her body was taken back to Kashi in a carriage, the remnants of which are exhibited in the small mosque.

Around Kashi

About 35km (21 miles) northeast of town lie the remains of **Ha Noi Ancient City** (罕诺依故城; Hanuoyi Gucheng) and **Mor Pagoda** (莫尔佛塔; Muer Fota), both dating from the pre-Islamic period when Buddhism flourished in Xinjiang, and contemporaneous with other abandoned cities in the Taklamakan Desert such as Niya and Karahoja. Thought to have flourished between the 7th and 12th centuries AD, there's little enough to see nowadays, though the well-preserved remains of the Mor Pagoda are clearly indicative of the Buddhist civilisation that once flourished here.

More interesting (and harder to get to) is the natural phenomenon known as "**Shipton's Arch**" (天洞; Tiandong). Remote, unique and astonishing – yet only 40km (25 miles) from downtown Kashgar – this is considered to be by far the largest natural rock arch anywhere in the world. Discovered by British mountaineer and Kashgar-based diplomat Eric Shipton (1907–77), it is located in the heart of the remote canyons of the inaccessible Kara Tagh or Black Mountains. Known in Turkic as Tushuk Tash or "Pierced Rock", and in Chinese as Tiandong or "Heavenly Gap", its location was completely forgotten in the troubled years following the Chinese Communist seizure of power in 1949, and the arch was only rediscovered (and permanently located using GPS technology) by a National Geographic expedition as recently as May 2000.

TIP

Travelling overland between Kashi and Lhasa via western Tibet remains technically illegal, but is becoming increasingly easy. Still, the route is officially closed, and more than one foreigner has been heavily fined for trying to cross it.

FAR LEFT: Xiangfei Mu, the tomb of Abakh Khoja, Kashi.
BELOW: Uighur men in Kashi.

The Great Game

During the late 19th and early 20th centuries, Kashgar was at the very centre of the "Great Game", with both the British and the Russians maintaining consulates in the remote but strategically significant oasis. The **former British Consulate**, known as Chini Bagh or "Chinese Garden", is located behind the Chini Bagh Hotel (Qiniwake Binguan) on Seman Lu, while the **former Russian Consulate** survives at the Seman Binguan, also on Seman Lu. The diplomatic representatives of the two great powers lived and competed with each other in this distant locale, plotting and planning each other's downfall while at the same time meeting for dinner and drinks on a regular basis, driven to friendship by isolation, while at the same time serving the interests of their masters in London and Moscow.

Map on page 398

TIP

The Khunjerab Pass, at precisely 4,693 metres (15,397ft), is the highest paved international frontier crossing in the world. Completed in 1982, it takes its name from the local Wakhi language, meaning "Valley of Blood" – though it is more often snow-covered.

BELOW: the shores of Karakul Lake surrounded by the High Pamirs.

The **Mausoleum of Mahmud al Kashgari** (马哈茂德陵墓; Mahamaode Lingmu; 1008–1105) was built outside Kashi. The building, which is about 45km (28 miles) away along the road to Pakistan, towers over a mosque once destroyed in an earthquake. Mahmud came from the house of the ruling Karachanid family and was one of the most important scholars of his time. Exiled from Xinjiang after the clan's overthrow in 1058, he returned to Kashi shortly before his death.

About 20km (12 miles) north of Kashi, the Buddhist **Sanxian Dong** (三先洞; Caves of the Three Immortals), on a sheer rock face by the Qiakmak River, are not only less interesting than those of Bezeklik or Dunhuang, but are relatively inaccessible and not worth the effort.

Further to the southwest, 200km (125 miles) from Kashi at the beginning of the high peaks of the Pamir range, is **Karakul Lake** (卡拉库尔湖; Kalakuer Hu). The ice-covered peaks of Muztagata (7,546 metres/24,755ft) and Kongur (7,719 metres/25,324ft), the second- and third-highest peaks in the Pamirs, can be seen from Kashi on clear days.

Taxkorgan

About 250km (155 miles) south of Kashi on the **Karakoram Highway** en route to Pakistan is **Taxkorgan**  (塔什库尔干; Tashikuergan), 3,600 metres (11,800ft) above sea level and the last outpost in China before the Pakistan border. The town is the capital of an autonomous district of the same name. A majority of Tajik people live here. According to accounts by Ptolemy (around AD 140), traders from East and West used to trade goods in this area.

Continuing south from Taxkorgan leads to Pakistan's **Karakoram range** (喀拉昆仑山; Kalakunlun Shan), whose awesome craggy peaks contrast markedly with the more rounded Pamirs. The 750km (460-mile) long track across the 4,700-metre (15,420ft) high **Khunjerab Pass** (红其拉甫山口; Hongqilafu Shankou) ⑮ is sometimes difficult due to weather or sometimes to sectarian unrest. About 270km (170 miles) south of the pass is the nearest airport in Pakistan, at Gilgit. Along the road are numerous wall murals, engravings and sculptures from the era of the Silk Road, and the scenery en route is some of the most dramatic on earth. ❑

RESTAURANTS

Restaurants

Prices for a meal for one, with one drink:

$ = under Rmb 50
$$ = Rmb 50–100
$$$ = Rmb 100–150
$$$$ = over Rmb 150

GANSU

Gansu is famous for its beef noodles or *niurou chaomian*, known locally *Lanzhou lamian*. Street food tends to be good, with Muslim vendors selling a delicious array of kebabs and filling breads.

Dunhuang

Some cafés, such as **John's** and **Charley Johng's**, both on Mingshan Lu, provide a good travel service.

Feng Yi Ting 丰宜庭

Silk Road Dunhuang Hotel, Dunyue Lu. $$–$$$
Feng Yi Ting means Chamber of Grandeur, and that's certainly what this excellent restaurant is. It serves a bewildering number of Cantonese and Sichuan specialities.

Shazhou Night Market 沙洲夜市

Off Yangguan Donglu. $
This night market sells Han Chinese, Hui Muslim and Uighur food in a pedestrian area in the northern part of town.

Lanzhou

A good supply of restaurants and street stalls make Lanzhou a great place for eating out.

Boton Coffee Shop, Bodun Canting 佰頓餐厅

Nongmin Xiang and Tianshui Lu. $–$$
Conveniently located next to the Lanzhou Hotel, this is a place to go if you're seeking Western food with English menus and friendly service.

Fengshan Jiudian 凤山酒店

Nongmin Xiang. $
The Fengshan, near the CITS office, serves some excellent local Gansu dishes, including desserts such as stuffed melon or steamed lily.

Hezheng Lu Night Market 和政路夜市

Tianshui Nanlu. $
An excellent and extensive night market.

Mingde Gong 明德宫

191 Jiuquan Lu. $–$$
Serves a variety of Gansu dishes in an elaborate environment. Each of the floors becomes progressively more sophisticated, and consequently more expensive, the higher you go.

Xiahe

Everest Café [English sign]

Renmin Xijie. $
Attached to the Overseas Tibetan Hotel (Huaqiao Fandian), this Nepali-run establishment serves Nepali curries with naan or chapati, steak dishes and Tibetan specialities.

Snowland Restaurant (Xuecheng Canting) 雪城餐厅

Renmin Xijie. $
Good Tibetan cuisine. Try the *momo* (dumplings) and the *tsampa*.

Tsewong's Café [English sign]

Renmin Xijie. $
This is an enduringly popular Xiahe choice offering an eclectic mixture of Tibetan, Muslim and international travellers' fare.

XINJIANG

Uighur cuisine, found throughout Xinjiang, is characterised by mutton, beef, tomatoes, onions, aubergines, naan bread and a variety of dairy products.

Kashgar (Kashi)

Caravan Café [English sign]

120 Seman Lu. $
Good Western breakfasts and coffee, plus kebabs, pizzas and sandwiches. Staff can help with most travel enquiries and arrange excursions.

Jiefang Beilu Night Market 解放北路夜市

Jiefang Beilu, opposite Id Kah Mosque. $
A busy and picturesque night market facing the open square opposite the central mosque.

Lao Chayuan Jiudian 老茶园酒店

251 Renmin Xi Lu. $
Regarded by locals as the finest restaurant in Kashgar, with a variety of Uighur food including *polo* (a Uighur rice speciality), lamb shish kebabs and beef noodle soup.

Turpan (Tulufan)

Turpan Bazaar (Shi Maoyi Shichang) 老城路市场

Off Laocheng Lu. $
Numerous food stalls selling local Muslim cuisine and variants of Chinese cuisine from distant provinces in China proper.

Xin Shiji 新世纪

Xinzhan Dingzi Lukou. $–$$
The Xin Shiji is a great place to sample a Uighur banquet and it's also famous for its kebabs and *sangshen jiu* (mulberry wine). It's also a lively favourite for group tours and locals out for an evening of Xinjiang-style entertainment.

Ürümqi

Try some of the Muslim restaurants on Xinhua Lu or the night market on Changjiang Lu with its lamb kebabs, naan, *laghman* (noodles in a thick stew) and samsa (samosa).

Fubar [English sign]

Gongyuan Beijie. $–$$
Ürümqi's very own sports bar, with regular live football, rugby and cricket coverage from around the world as well as a pool table and darts. The management (Irish and Japanese) are perhaps the best source of information on travel in Xinjiang for Westerners.

Kashgari's 新疆大酒店

168 Xinhua Beilu. $$–$$$
Kashgari's serves probably the best Uighur Muslim cuisine to be found anywhere in Ürümqi. The restaurant is a part of the Xinjiang Grand Hotel and consequently the prices are quite high, but the overall service and interior decoration are outstanding.

CHINA

The Guides That Are Streets Ahead

INSIGHT GUIDES

PARIS

INSIGHT GUIDES

LONDON
CITY GUIDE

UNDERGROUND

KNOW THE CITY LIKE A LOCAL

INSIGHT GUIDES

LONDON

KNOW THE CI...

INSIGHT GUIDES

...STON
CITY GUIDE

CITY LIKE A LOCAL

INSIGHT GUIDES
www.insightguides.com

Insight Guides to every major country are also available.

TRAVEL TIPS

Transport

Getting There **418**
  On Arrival........................**418**
  By Air **418**
  Airline Offices **419**
  Overland Routes..............**420**
  By Sea **421**
Getting Around **421**
  Orientation.....................**421**
  Road Names **421**
  Domestic Travel **421**
  Rail Journey Times **423**
  Group Travel **424**
  Individual Travel **425**

Accommodation

Choosing a Hotel................**427**
Guesthouses......................**427**
Other Accommodation **427**
Hotel Listings **427**
  Anhui.............................**427**
  Beijing...........................**428**
  Chongqing Shi **429**
  Dongbei.........................**429**
  Fujian **429**
  Gansu **430**
  Guangdong **430**
  Guangxi **431**
  Guizhou.........................**431**
  Hainan Island.................**432**
  Hebei **432**
  Henan **432**
  Hong Kong.....................**433**
  Hubei **434**
  Hunan **435**
  Inner Mongolia **435**
  Jiangsu **436**
  Jiangxi..........................**436**
  Macau **436**
  Qinghai **437**
  Shaanxi **437**
  Shandong **438**
  Shanxi **438**
  Shanghai **439**
  Sichuan **440**
  Tibet **441**
  Xinjiang **441**
  Yunnan **442**
  Zhejiang **443**

Shopping

Shopping **444**
  Bargaining **444**
  Import and Export **444**
Where to Shop **444**
  Beijing...........................**445**
  Fujian **445**
  Guangdong **445**
  Guangxi **446**
  Guizhou.........................**446**
  Hainan Island.................**447**
  Hong Kong.....................**447**
  Jiangxi..........................**448**
  Macau **448**
  Shanghai **448**
  Sichuan **449**
  Silk Road.......................**449**
  Tibet **449**
  Xi'an **449**
  Yunnan **449**

Activities

Festivals...........................**450**
  Local Festivals for Deities **451**
  Other Religious Festivals..**451**
The Arts **451**
  Chinese Opera **451**
  Acrobatics **451**
  Concerts **452**
  Museums **452**
Nightlife **452**
  Bars, Discos & Karaoke ..**452**
Outdoor Pursuits **452**
  Spectator Sports **452**
  Participant Sports **452**
Tours and Agencies **453**
  Tour Operators **453**

A – Z

Admission Charges **454**
Budgeting for Your Trip **454**
Business Hours..................**454**
Climate.............................**454**
  Typhoons.......................**454**
Disabled Travellers **455**
Electricity **455**
Embassies & Consulates **455**
Emergencies **455**
Entry Regulations **456**
Gay Travellers **456**
Health & Medical Services ..**456**
Media...............................**458**
Money Matters **459**
Photography **459**
Postal/Courier Services **459**
Public Holidays **459**
Public Toilets.....................**460**
Religious Services..............**460**
Student Travellers **460**
Telecommunications **460**
Time Zone.........................**460**
Tipping **460**
Tour and Travel Agents.......**461**
Travelling with Children **461**
Useful Addresses **461**
Visitor Hotlines **461**
Weights & Measures **461**
What to Bring **461**
What to Wear **461**

Language

General.............................**462**
Language and Writing **462**
Names & Forms of Address..**462**
Pronunciation **463**
Tones **463**
Grammar **463**
Styles of Calligraphy **463**
Words & Phrases...............**463**

Further Reading

History **468**
Biography **468**
Current Affairs **468**
Travel Writing **469**
Philosophy **469**
Fiction **469**
Other Insight Guides **469**

T RANSPORT

GETTING THERE AND GETTING AROUND

GETTING THERE

On Arrival

On arrival you will have to fill in a form with details of your health, and an entry card, on which you fill in details about the length of your stay in China. It will be put with your passport.

There are exchange bureaux at the arrival halls of airports, railway stations and ports where you can change money. The Chinese airlines provide buses that for a modest fare will take travellers from the airport, which is often a long way outside the city, to the airline offices in town.

You can also find taxis to your hotel, but be wary of people offering taxis away from taxi ranks. Before setting off in a taxi, agree on a price for the journey, or ensure that the driver agrees to use the meter.

By Air

The following airports handle international flights:

Beijing

Beijing's Capital Airport, 25km (16 miles) from the centre, connects the city to all parts of China and to the world's major cities (for information, tel: 010-6454 1100). The journey into the city centre takes 30–60 minutes depending on traffic. Airport bus services (Rmb 16) operate regularly to downtown Beijing, and many hotels offer car or minibus services.

Plentiful taxis are on hand, with security guards to ensure licensed drivers accept all passengers.

The Airport Line of Beijing's subway connects Terminals 2 and 3 with Dongzhimen (interchange for lines 2 and 13) and Sanyuanqiao (interchange for line 10).

Chongqing

Chongqing's Jiangbei Airport is 25km (16 miles) north of the city. CAAC (tel: 023-6386 5824) operates shuttle buses every half-hour between its offices on Zhongshan Sanlu and the airport. Metered taxis from the airport to town cost around Rmb 45.

International routes available into Chongqing include Macau, Nagoya, Seoul, Singapore and Bangkok.

Guangzhou

Guangzhou's Baiyun International Airport (www.baiyunairport.com) is 28km (17 miles) north of town and handles flights from various Asian cities as well as Los Angeles, Honolulu, Melbourne, Sydney, Amsterdam, Frankfurt, Paris and Addis Ababa.

Shuttle buses connect the city with the airport (45 minutes), leaving from immediately outside both the domestic and international arrivals terminals. Buy tickets after boarding. A taxi to or from the airport will cost around Rmb 110. Passengers must pay any road or bridge tolls.

Guilin

Liangjiang International Airport (tel: 0773-284 5359) is 28km (17 miles) from Guilin. It has direct flights from Japan, Korea and Thailand. The airport shuttle bus connects with flight arrivals and takes passengers to the Minhang Dasha building on Shanghai Road in Guilin at a cost of around Rmb 20. The taxi fare will be Rmb 80–100.

Hainan Island

Direct flights operate between the resort of Sanya and Seoul, Moscow and Singapore. There are also flights between the provincial capital Haikou and Singapore.

Hong Kong

Hong Kong is a major international air-traffic hub for the region, so there is no shortage of flights. Flight time between London and Hong Kong is 10–12 hours.

Hong Kong's international airport (www.hongkongairport.com) is at Chek Lap Kok, a small island to the north of Lantau Island and about 34km (21 miles) from Central (the main shopping and banking area).

The Airport Express (AEL) is a comfortable train service that runs every 12 minutes and takes 24 minutes into town, offering the most convenient and cost-effective way to get to and from the airport (the journey by road via taxi or bus takes around 40 minutes and costs about HK$270 to Kowloon; HK$340 to Hong Kong Island).

There are numerous buses linking the airport to the city and to destinations in Guangdong. The Airbus services (prefixed "A") run at regular intervals from 6am to midnight and cost around HK$35. Slower commuter buses are prefixed "E", and there are shuttle buses to Tung Chung MTR station. There are also direct ferry services from the airport to Macau and Shenzhen.

Kunming and Jinghong

Kunming's Wujiaba International Airport, just 7.5km (4½ miles) from the city centre, is connected with Bangkok, Chiang Mai, Hanoi, Singapore, Vientiane and Yangon (Rangoon). The taxi fare to most of the city's hotels is about Rmb 25. Jinghong, in southern Yunnan, has flights from Bangkok and Chiang Mai.

Macau

Macau International Airport (tel: 853-861 111) is on the east side of Taipa Island, and is linked by bridges to the downtown area. It generally takes less than 30 minutes to get from the airport to anywhere in Macau.

For transport to and from the airport there are authorised taxis and the regular AP1 bus, which serves major hotels, the ferry terminal and the border gate.

There are regularly scheduled flights between Macau and several cities in Asia, including Bangkok, Jakarta, Kaohsiung, Kota Kinabalu, Kuala Lumpur, Male, Manila, Seoul, Singapore and Taipei.

Shanghai

Shanghai is one of China's main transport hubs, connected to a number of foreign destinations and almost all domestic locations, and is the only city in China to have two airports. Most domestic and some international flights use the old airport at Hongqiao (tel: 021-5260 4620), about 15km (9 miles) west of the city centre. The international airport (tel: 021-9608 1388) in Pudong is 70km (43 miles) east of downtown. It has two terminals and the number of destinations served is steadily increasing.

From Hongqiao Airport it takes 30 minutes to the city. Most hotels have shuttle buses available. Otherwise, plenty of taxis are available right outside both terminals. Don't hire drivers who tout their services at the terminal entrances; their cars don't have meters, and they'll try to charge you exorbitant rates. To get into the city, most drivers use the expressway that connects to the ring road.

From Pudong a taxi will take you approximately an hour (reckon on Rmb 130–50) to the city, but the high-speed MAGLEV train can rocket you into town in under 8 minutes for Rmb 50 (single fare). There are five airport bus lines. Airport Shuttle No. 1 connects Hongqiao and Pudong airports. A new metro line will eventually run east–west between Hongqiao and Pudong airports, and numerous stops in between.

Shenzhen

Shenzhen Bao'an International Airport (www.szairport.com; tel: 0755-9500 0666) is one of China's busiest and handles flights to/from Bangkok, Ho Chi Minh City, Kuala Lumpur, Nagoya (Japan), New York, Seoul, Singapore and Tokyo.

The airport is 35km (20 miles) west of downtown Shenzhen. Hotel (and other) shuttle buses take around 30 minutes, and also go to Hong Kong Airport. There is also a direct ferry link to Hong Kong Airport.

Line One of the city's metro is presently being extended in phases from Shijie Zhi Chuang (the current western terminus) to the airport, with the final section to the airport scheduled to be completed at the end of 2010.

Ürümqi

The airport (tel: 0991-380 1453) is 17km (11 miles) north of the city. China Southern Airlines has its main office at 62 Youhao Nanlu, tel: 0991-451 4668, and is open daily 7am–5pm. The airline has a number of booking offices around the city.

A taxi from the airport will cost around Rmb 30–40, or you can take either the airport bus (Rmb 18) or bus No. 51 (Rmb 5) or No. 2.

Ürümqi is connected via international flights to Almaty (Kazakhstan), Bishkek (Kyrgyzstan), Islamabad (Pakistan), Novosibirsk, Moscow (Russia), Tashkent (Uzbekistan) and Tehran (Iran).

Xiamen and Fuzhou

Xiamen's international airport handles international flights to/from Bangkok, Jakarta, Kuala Lumpur, Manila, Nigata, Osaka, Penang, Seoul, Singapore, Taipei and Tokyo. Xiamen's airport is a 10-minute taxi hop from the city.

Fuzhou has a smaller airport, connected to Bangkok, Kuala Lumpur, Osaka and Singapore.

Xi'an

The airport is about 40km (25 miles) northwest of Xi'an at Xianyang. Most major hotels offer limousine or bus transfers, which have to be arranged ahead of time. China Southern Airlines runs a shuttle bus (6am–6pm) between the airport and Melody Hotel (86 Xi Dajie) just to the west of the Bell Tower, which is timed to its arriving and departing flights.

Otherwise, a taxi will cost you around Rmb 90–100 to go into the city, but you may have to bargain hard as overcharging is common. The trip takes around 50 minutes.

Xi'an's airport connects it to most of the big cities in China, as well as to Nagoya and Hiroshima in Japan.

Airline Offices

Beijing

Air China, 15 Chang'an Xidajie, Xicheng, tel: 010-6656 9226.
Air France, Room 1606–1611, 16/F, Building 1, Kuntai International Mansion, 12A Chaoayangmenwai Dajie, tel: 400-880 8808.
Austrian Airlines, Unit C604, Kempinski Hotel, 50 Liangmaqiao Lu, tel: 010-6464 5999.
British Airways, Room 2112, Building 1, Kuntai International Mansion, 12A Chaoayangmenwai Dajie, tel: 400-650 0073.
Canadian Airlines, Room C201, Lufthansa Centre, 50 Liangmaqiao Lu, tel: 010-6468-2001.
Cathay Pacific, 28/F, East Tower, Twin Towers, B-12 Jiangguomenwai Dajie, tel: 010-5905 7777.
China Eastern Airlines, 1/F, Minhang Building, Xidan, tel: 95808 (national number).
Dragonair, 28/F, East Tower, Twin Towers, B-12 Jiangguomenwai Dajie, tel: 010-5905 7730.
Finnair, Room 204, Scitech Tower, 22 Jianguomenwai Dajie, tel: 010-6512 7180.
Japan Airlines, Hotel New Otani Changfugong, 26 Jianguomenwai Dajie, tel: 400-888 0808.
KLM, 1609, Building 1, Kuntai International Mansion, 12A Chaoyangmenwai Dajie, tel: 400-880 8222.
Korean Air, 1602, 16/F, Hyundai Motor Building, 38 Xiaoyun Lu, tel: 400-658 8888, 8453 8137.
Lufthansa, Room S101, Lufthansa Centre, 50 Liangmaqiao Lu, tel: 010-6468 8838.

Northwest Airlines, Room 501, China World Trade Centre, 1 Jianguomenwai Dajie, tel: 400-814 0081.
Qantas, 7–8 10/F, West Building, Twins Tower, 12 Jianguomenwai Dajie, tel: 010-6567 9006.
Singapore Airlines, 8/F, China World Tower 2, 1 Jianguomenwai Dajie, tel: 010-6505 2233.
Swiss International Airlines, S101 Lufthansa Centre, 50 Liangmaqiao Lu, tel: 010-8454 0180.
Thai Airways, Units 303–4, Level 3 Tower W3, Oriental Plaza, 1 East Chang'anjie, tel: 010-8515 0088.
United Airlines, 15/F, Tower A, Gateway Plaza, Sanyuanqiao, tel: 800-810 8282.

Hong Kong

Air Canada, Rm 1612, Tower 1, New World Tower, 18 Queen's Rd Central, tel: 852-2867 8111.
Air China, 2/F, CNAC Group Building, 10 Queen's Rd Central, tel: 852-3102 3030.
Air France, 18/F, Vicwood Plaza, 199 Des Voeux Road Central, tel: 852-2501 9433.
Air New Zealand, 17/F, Jardine House, 1 Connaught Rd, Central, tel: 852-2862 8988.
American Airlines, 10/F, Peninsula Office Tower, 18 Middle Rd, Tsim Sha Tsui, tel: 852-2826 9269.
British Airways, 24/F, Jardine House, 1 Connaught Place, Central, tel: 852-2822 9000.
Cathay Pacific Airways, 10/F, Peninsula Office Tower, 18 Middle Rd, Tsim Sha Tsui, tel: 852-2747 1888.
Dragonair, 46/F, Cosco Tower, 183 Queen's Road, Sheung Wan, tel: 852-3193 3888.
KLM Royal Dutch, 22/F, World Trade Centre, 280 Gloucester Road, Causeway Bay, tel: 852-2808 2111 (res); 852-2116 8730 (flight info).
Lufthansa, 11/F, Nan Fung Tower, 193 Des Voeux Road, Sheung Wan, tel: 852-2868 2313 (res); 852-2769 6560 (flight info).
Northwest Airlines, 18/F, Cosco Tower, 183 Queen's Rd, Sheung Wan, tel:852-2810 4288.
Qantas Airways, 24/F, Jardine House, 1 Connaught Place, Central, tel: 852-2842 1438.
Singapore Airlines, 17/F, United Centre, 95 Queensway, Admiralty, tel: 852-2520 2233 (res); 852-2769 6387 (info).
Virgin Atlantic Airways, 18/F, Alexandra House, 15–20 Chater Rd, Central, tel: 852-2532 3030.

Shanghai

Air Canada, 1468 Nanjing Rd (W), tel: 021-6279 2999.

Air China, Rm 307, Kerry Center, 1515 Nanjing Rd (W), tel: 400-810 0999.
Air France, Ciro's Plaza Room 3901, 388 Nanjing Rd (W), tel: 400-880 8808.
All Nippon Airways, Shanghai Centre, 1376 Nanjing Rd (W), tel: 021-5696 2525.
China Eastern Airlines, 258 Wei Hai Rd, tel: 95808 (national number).
Dragonair, Room 2103, Shanghai Square, 138 Huaihai Rd (Middle), tel: 021-6375 6375.
Japan Airlines, 7/F, Huaihai Plaza, No. 1045, Huaihai Rd (W), tel: 021-5467 4530.
Lufthansa, 3/F, No.1 Building, Corporate Avenue 222, Hubin Road, tel: 021-5352 4999.
Northwest Airlines, Rm 1007, Kerry Center, 1515 Nanjing Rd (W), tel: 400-814 0081.
Qantas, Room 3202, K Wah Centre, 1010 Huaihai Rd (middle), tel: 021-6145 0188.
Shanghai Airlines, 212 Jiangning Rd, tel: 021-6255 8888.
Singapore Airlines, Room 1106–1110 Plaza 66, 1266 Nanjing Rd, tel: 021-6288 7999.
United Airlines, 3301-17 Central Plaza, 381 Huaihai Rd (Middle), tel: 021-3311 4567.
Virgin Atlantic, Suite 221, 12 Zhongshan No. 1 Rd (E), tel: 021-5353 4600.

Overland Routes

Several of China's international borders are open for crossing by rail or road. Some frontiers, such as those with India and Bhutan, are restricted areas.

Burma (Myanmar)

A border crossing with Burma (Myanmar) opened in 1996, but the Burmese discourage foreigners from using it.

Kazakhstan

There is a daily bus service and a twice-weekly train service between Ürümqi and Almaty in Kazakhstan (you will need to obtain a visa in advance).

Kyrgyzstan

It is, in theory, possible to take a bus to Kashi from Bishkek in Kyrgyzstan over the Torugut Pass, but foreigners are sometimes refused seats.

Laos

From Laos, travellers can enter Mengla County in southern Yunnan at Boten in Luang Nam Tha province. When heading into China from Laos you'll need to arrange your visa in

advance as they are available at the border. There are also passenger boats along the Mekong River between Jinghong and Chiang Saen in Thailand.

Mongolia

It is possible to travel by train between China and Mongolia. There are also buses, but they tend to be slower and far less convenient than the rail links. (For details on trains between Moscow and Beijing which pass through Mongolia, see below.)

Nepal

You can cross the border between Tibet and Nepal at Zhangmu/Kodari. It's possible to travel by road between Kathmandu and Lhasa, but it requires considerable time, not only for travel, but for bureaucracy as well. You cannot obtain a Chinese visa at the border, and the most convenient approach is to join a tour to Lhasa in Kathmandu. Independent travellers should note that transport on the Nepal side is good, but scarce on the Tibetan side. Most travellers must plan on a vehicle hire/share to Lhasa.

Pakistan

It is possible to travel the Karakorum Highway between Islamabad and Kashi. Officially the border is open between April and October, though even those dates are weather-dependent. During this time, there are daily buses, weather permitting, between Taxkorgan and Kashi (5 hours). On both the Pakistani and Chinese sides of the border the roads may be blocked by landslides, and you may have to walk a fair distance, carrying your luggage.

Russia/Mongolia

The 5- or 6-day odyssey on the Trans-Mongolian/Trans-Manchurian railways between Moscow and Beijing is one of the world's classic rail journeys. If arriving from Europe via the Trans-Manchurian or Trans-Mongolian railways (often called the Trans-Siberian, which in fact goes to Siberia's Pacific Coast, not China), all the same health and customs

Plane Tickets

Domestic plane tickets (usually very easy to obtain) are generally sold as one-way tickets, with return fares simply being twice the one-way fare. Ask for discounts, which are generally available from travel agents and airline offices.

procedures apply as if arriving via an international flight.

There is a choice of two routes. The Chinese train – which is better-equipped and maintained – takes five days via Ulan Bator (Ulaanbaatar) through Mongolia, entering China via Erlian. The Russian train, which goes through Manchuria (Dongbei), takes a day longer, and enters China at Manzhouli. Both leave once a week from Moscow.

Depending on the type of train, there are two or three classes. Food on board is not included in the ticket price. If you want to interrupt the train journey in Russia for longer than 24 hours, you need a tourist visa and will have to produce proof that you have a hotel booking.

Vietnam

A twice-weekly train service connects Hanoi and Beijing (38 hours), via the so-called "Friendship Gate" between Pingxiang in China's Guangxi province and Dong Dang in Vietnam. It is also possible to cross the border here on foot and connect with bus routes on either side. The train stops at a number of cities in China, including Nanning, Changsha and Guilin.

You can also cross the border on foot at Hekou in the southeast of Yunnan province. There is a twice-weekly rail service (15 hours) between Kunming and the border post.

Neither Vietnamese nor Chinese visas are available at these border posts – you will need to obtain a Chinese visa in advance from the embassy in Hanoi.

By Sea

Japan

A weekly ship sales between Shanghai and Osaka, Japan, and a less regular service exists to Kobe. There is also a weekly boat between Kobe and Tianjin/Tanggu; trips take two days and can be booked through CITS.

South Korea

A ferry service is available from Inchon, South Korea, to Weihai, Qingdao, Tianjin and Dalian. The voyage between Inchon and Weihai takes about 18 hours, departing thrice weekly. Between Inchon and Qingdao the journey takes 15 hours, departing three times weekly. Between Inchon and Tianjin takes nearly 24 hours, operating every five days. Ferries between Dalian and Inchon sail three times weekly and take around 18 hours; tickets can be booked through CITS.

Getting Around

Orientation

All main cities can be reached by plane, train and buses. The road network has been improved in recent years, even in the remote northern provinces, and in many places buses offer a quicker alternative to trains.

Road Names

Street names are determined by the traditional chequerboard of Chinese urban design. The most important traffic arteries are divided into sectors and laid out in a grid typically based upon the compass points.

Suffixes are added to the primary name to indicate north (bei), south (nan), east (dong) or west (xi) and, additionally, to indicate the middle (zhong) section. A major urban high-way is likely to be labelled da dao' (avenue) or lu (road). Slightly smaller roads may be known as jie (street). A small lane is nong or xiang.

In 2003 Shanghai changed all of its pinyin street names into English. Lu became Road, and the suffixes zhong, nan, bei, dong and xi became Centre, South, North, East and West respectively. These appear in all listings in this book.

Domestic Travel

Air

All of China's major cities are connected by domestic flights and the Chinese government are investing huge amounts of money to improve existing airports and add many new ones. Buying a return ticket on some routes is difficult, except to cities such as Beijing and Shanghai. For shorter journeys within China, the train is generally more enjoyable than travelling by plane, and saves the airport tax of Rmb 50 that is levied at all domestic airports.

Air China (CAAC; tel: 400-810 0999, global sales hotline) flies to more than 200 destinations within China; other major domestic airlines are China Eastern Airlines (tel: 95808) and China Southern Airlines (tel: 020-412 3120), both of which operate on around 120 domestic routes.

For domestic departures you need to check in about 30 minutes before the flight, although Shanghai demands arrival one hour in advance. Beijing, Shanghai and Hong Kong are the major transport hubs. Additional details are listed below.

Luggage

Take sturdy, strong luggage, which should be lockable; sometimes it won't be transported unless it is locked.

For further details of airport locations, public transport and airline information, see pages 418–20.

Chengdu

Chengdu Shangliu Airport is the busiest airport in western China. All of China's major airlines operate out of Chengdu, making it possible to fly to almost any city in China, as well as 20 international destinations.

Chongqing

Chongqing's Jiangbei Airport is an important hub for Air China, Sichuan Airlines and Chongqing Airlines, offering frequent connections with Hong Kong, every major city in China and many minor ones.

Guangzhou

Domestic flights operate between Guangzhou and major cities in China. Tickets for internal flights are sold at the offices of the Chinese carriers and also at the China Southern Airlines main office at 181 Huanshi Donglu (tel: 020-8668 2000), near the main train station.

Guilin

As the tourism hub of Guanxi province, Guilin has flights to almost every major city, including three flights a day to Hong Kong and at least six to Guangzhou and Beijing. The airport is about 28km (17 miles) from the city centre and there's a shuttle bus to the downtown area.

Kashi (Kashgar)

The airport is 11km (7 miles) north of the city. There is a shuttle bus between the airport and the CAAC office on 95 Jiefang Nanlu (tel: 0998-282 2113). China Southern Airlines and Hainan Airlines have daily flights between Kashi and Ürümqi, and seats are not usually difficult to come by.

Kunming

Kunming is the home base for Yunnan Airlines and for Lucky Air, which between them operate flights to destinations around Yunnan province, notably Dali, Mangshi (now known as Pu'er) and Jinghong in Xishuangbanna.

Lanzhou

Lanzhou Airport is inconveniently located some 70km (43 miles) north of town. CAAC (tel: 0931-888 9666) runs an infrequent shuttle bus (Rmb 30) to and from its office on Donggang Xilu. Unfortunately, there are no fixed times for the buses, so be sure to check with the office ahead of time. In Lanzhou Air China is known as China Northwest (Xibei Hangkong), and its office is at 46 Donggang Xilu (tel: 0931-882 1964; 8am–9pm).

Taxi drivers charge between Rmb 200–300 for the trip, and bargaining is expected. Beware of taxi drivers who mill around the CAAC office and offer to take you to the airport for significantly less. Travellers with early-morning flights may want to spend the night before at one of the airport hotels, such as the Zhongchuan Hotel (tel: 0931-841 5926).

Lhasa (Tibet)
Gongar Airport (tel: 0891-624 3446, 0891-682 2393), with flights to a number of major Chinese cities, is nearly 100km (60 miles) from Lhasa. The bus ride (Rmb 20) takes about 2 hours.

Macau
There are regular scheduled flights between Macau and 14 cities in China. Passengers pay a tax of MOP$80 (MOP$50 for under-13s).

Nanchang
The capital of Jiangxi is growing fast, as is its role as a transport hub. There are daily flights to Beijing, Guangzhou, Shanghai and Shenzhen, and several flights a week to other mainland cities.

Nanjing
Nanjing Lukou International Airport is about 35km (22 miles) from downtown Nanjing (tel: 025-5248 0488).

Shanghai
Most domestic flights use Shanghai's old airport at Hongqiao (tel: 021-5260 4620), about 15km (9 miles) west of the city centre. Domestic connections can be booked through China Eastern Airlines' travel agency (tel: 021-6247 5953).

Ürümqi
Within Xinjiang, there are flights from Ürümqi to Yining, Tacheng, Kelamayi (Karamai), Kashi (Kashgar), Akesu (Aksu), Hetian (Hotan), Kuche (Kuqa), Kuerle (Korla), Qiemo (Jumo) and Aletai (Altai). Ürümqi is connected via domestic flights to Beijing, Shanghai, Guangzhou, Changsha, Chengdu, Guilin, Xi'an, Zhengzhou, Tianjin, Fuzhou, Lanzhou and Chongqing.

Xi'an
In Xi'an, CAAC is known as China Northwest Airlines (Xibei Hangkong). It has a number of ticket offices dotted around the city. One of its main offices is located at the corner of Laodong Nanlu and Xiguan Zhengjie, 1km (¾ mile) outside the west gate of the old city (tel: 029-8870 2299). Other airlines flying to Xi'an daily include Air China, China Eastern Airlines, Hainan Airlines and Shanghai Airlines

Chinese Railways
With the opening of the China–Tibet railway (see page 424) the Chinese rail network has extended to almost 55,000km (more than 34,000 miles), of which 4,400km (2,700 miles) are electrified. Average train speed is not very high, although increasing rapidly, due to modernisation and investment programmes. The new D trains are high-speed bullet trains, which are much quicker but up to 50 percent more expensive than T express trains.

Tickets and Reservations
Demand for train tickets is usually high, so, wherever you want to travel to, it is advisable to buy your ticket as soon as reservations open. This varies between types of train and destinations. The usual maximum advance period is 10 days, but may be as long as 20 days for Z trains (high-speed long-distance trains), or as short as three days for local services. During the main travel season (Chinese New Year, and the 1 May and 1 October holiday periods; see also Public Holidays, page 459) it becomes nearly impossible to buy tickets to and from major cities.

There are special ticket counters for foreigners at railway stations. The price also depends on both the class and the speed of the train; there are slow trains, fast trains, express trains and inter-city trains. Reservations can be made at ticket offices downtown, through travel agencies or at your hotel, and this is the easiest option in many places, particularly if you want to travel at short notice. When boarding a train, allow plenty of time, as finding the platform and your allocated coach can be tricky.

In Hong Kong, tickets can be purchased through travel agents, hotels, CITS offices or at the Intercity Passenger Services Centre at Hung Hom railway station (daily 6.30am–7.30pm; tel: 852-2947 7888). In provincial cities, large hotels and the CITS office (for a list of these, see page 453) can help get train tickets.

Berth and seating options
There is no first or second class on Chinese trains, but four categories or classes: *ruanwo* or soft-sleeper, *ruanzuo* or soft-seat, *yingwo* or hard-sleeper, and *yingzuo* or hard-seat. The soft-seat class is usually only available for short journeys.

Long-distance trains normally only have soft-sleeper or hard-sleeper facilities. The soft-sleeper class has four-bed compartments with soft beds, and is recommended, particularly for long journeys. The hard-sleeper class has open, six-bed compartments. The beds are not really hard, but are cramped and not very comfortable. While you can reserve a place for the first three classes (you always buy a ticket with a place number), this is not always essential for the hard-seat category.

There is always boiled water available on the trains. There are washrooms in the soft-sleeper and hard-sleeper classes. The toilets, regardless of which class, are usually not very hygienic, and it is a good idea to bring your own toilet paper. There are dining cars on long-distance trains.

Beijing
There are two main railway stations, Beijing station (Beijing zhan) and Beijing West (Xi zhan). Some trains to other parts of China run from the city's three smaller railway stations. The best place to buy tickets is the foreigners' booking office (open 5.30–7.30am, 8am–6.30pm, 7–11pm) to the left of the main concourse inside Beijing station, where you can also buy tickets for trains leaving from Beijing West; Beijing West also has a foreigners' booking office (open 24 hours). If you want a sleeper berth, especially in summer, it is best to buy your ticket at least two or three days in advance. Return tickets can be purchased for Hong Kong–Beijing, but not for other routes.

Chongqing
Chongqing is connected via direct trains to Beijing (30 hours), Shanghai (43 hours), Chengdu (10 hours), Kunming (17 hours), Guangzhou, Zhengzhou, Yangzhou, Wuchang, Guiyang, Nanning and Zhejiang. Sleeper tickets can be bought at hotels and ticket agencies, but can be hard to come by. The train station is next to the long-distance bus station at the southwestern end of the main peninsula on Nanqu Lu.

Guangzhou
Trains arrive in Guangzhou either at the central Guangzhou railway station

(Guangzhou Huoche Zhan) or at Guangzhou East railway station (Guangzhou Dong Zhan) in Tianhe, Guangzhou's thriving new district in the city's eastern reaches. There are trains to and from most large cities in China, though all Hong Kong-bound trains depart from Guangzhou East.

In Guangzhou, most hotels and the CTS office can help get train tickets. There are approximately two departures every hour on the express trains between Shenzhen and Guangzhou. Travelling time is 55 minutes.

Guilin
Guilin has two railway stations: the South station in the city centre and North station, inconveniently out in the suburbs. There are services to all main cities in China, and trains between Beijing and Vietnam pass through twice a week.

Hong Kong
Hung Hom station (tel: 852-2947 7888) in Kowloon has 12 departures a day to Guangzhou (see above), with a journey time of just under 2 hours. There is also a daily train to Foshan (just over 2 hours). Tickets can be bought through travel agents, hotels, CTS offices or at the lobby of the station. A much cheaper alternative, or if tickets to Guangzhou are sold out, is to take the MTR to the border terminus of Lo Wu (a 40-minute

Rail Journey Times

The distance and approximate travelling time from Beijing. (D) = bullet train:

Beijing to:	Distance miles (km)	Time hours
Chengdu	1,273 (2,048)	25
Chongqing	1,586 (2,552)	24
Datong	249 (400)	6
Dalian	770 (1,239)	10
Guangzhou	1,437 (2,313)	21.5
Guilin	1,326 (2,134)	22
Hangzhou	1,026 (1,651)	13
Harbin	862 (1,388)	8 (D)
Hohhot	423 (680)	10.5
Kunming	1,975 (3,179)	38
Lanzhou	1,169 (1,882)	19.5
Lhasa	2,525 (4,064)	46
Luoyang	509 (819)	8
Nanjing	719 (1,157)	9.5
Qingdao	551 (887)	6 (D)
Shanghai	908 (1,462)	10 (D)
Suzhou	855 (1,376)	8.5
Taiyuan	319 (514)	8.5
Ürümqi	2,345 (3,774)	40
Wuhan	764 (1,229)	9 (D)
Wuxi	829 (1,334)	10.5
Xi'an	724 (1,165)	11

journey, with three departures an hour from 5.30am–10.19pm). Shenzhen station is right across the border.

Kunming
The main (Nanyao) railway station is just 4km (2½ miles) from the city centre, with connections to all major cities in China.

Lanzhou
From Lanzhou, there are long-distance trains to Beijing, Shanghai, Xining, Ürümqi, Xi'an, Chengdu, Golmud and Lhasa (Tibet). Going west to Ürümqi (24 hours), trains stop at Jiayuguan (10 hours), Liuyuan, the train station serving Dunhuang (14 hours), and Daheyan, the station serving Turpan (22 hours).

Sleepers can be hard to come by if you try to reserve them yourself at the station. You'd do better to go to a travel agency or through your hotel.

Lhasa (Tibet)
In 2006 the China–Tibet rail line became the highest railway in the world (topping the Andean former title-holder). The line is not without controversy, with concerns over its effects on the ecology of the Himalayas and the cultural integrity of the Tibet Autonomous Region. Nevertheless, it is a stunning feat of engineering and offers a breathtaking trip – both scenically and literally, since an extra oxygen supply has to be provided. The 48-hour journey from Beijing to Lhasa covers 4,064km (2,525 miles) and attains an altitude of more than 5,000 metres (16,650ft). Ticket prices range from Rmb 389 for a hard seat to Rmb 1,262 for a soft sleeper, and tourist trains will offer sleeping carriages, full dining services and observation cars. Trains run daily from the following stations: Beijing West (tel: 010-9510 5105),

Shanghai (tel: 021-820 7890), Chengdu (028-8332 2088 or 8333 2499), Lanzhou (tel: 0931-492 2222), Chongqing (tel: 023-6386 2607) and Xining (tel: 0971-819 2832). Various stops are made along the way.

Shanghai
Most southbound trains (to Hangzhou, Fujian province, Guangdong province and so on) leave from the new Shanghai South railway station, in the Xuhui district, reachable on metro line 1, tel: 021-6317 9090 or 969-690 000. There are several trains a day to Suzhou, Hangzhou, Nanjing and other nearby destinations. The best train to catch to Beijing is the overnight express that leaves around 7pm and arrives in Beijing the next morning. The express train to Hong Kong runs every day and takes 20 hours. Daily express trains run to Guangzhou and Shenzhen.

Train tickets can be purchased without a surcharge at either of the train stations, or at any of the official outlets that are scattered throughout town, with blue-and-white signs that say, in English: Booking Office for Train Tickets. Alternatively, you can acquire tickets through CITS or any other travel agency, or at a number of hotels, for a small surcharge.

Ürümqi
The railway station is located at the southwestern end of town. From Ürümqi, domestic trains head east and south to Beijing, Shanghai, Zhengzhou, Chengdu and Xi'an, all of which stop at Lanzhou. Heading further west, a stretch of track links Ürümqi with Kashgar, via Kuqa, and the trip takes around 23 hours.

Between Ürümqi and Lanzhou, the stops include Daheyan (Turpan railway station), Hami, Liuyuan

Group Travel

The simplest and most comfortable way of travelling to China at a reasonable price is in a group. Participants will have their passage, hotel accommodation, meals and sightseeing programme booked in advance. There are hardly any additional costs apart from drinks and shopping. Sometimes, additional excursions may be on offer once you have arrived, but they are generally not too expensive. Some places charge for taking photographs.

The pitfalls of a journey through China have increased rather than diminished in recent years; an experienced tour operator can avoid many difficulties.

Each group with more than 10 participants is allocated a permanent Chinese guide. In addition, a local tour guide is supplied by the Chinese tourist office and is in charge of taking you to the sights in his or her local area. Specialists should have detailed knowledge of places of special interest, which can greatly enhance your enjoyment and understanding of China. The qualifications of the local guides vary considerably in terms of their knowledge of the country and its sights and their ability to communicate and organise. The importance of the quality of guide employed by the tour operator shouldn't be underestimated.

A number of tour operators offer trips both along traditional routes and around a theme, such as tai chi *(taijiquan)*, calligraphy, acupuncture and language courses.

(serving Dunhuang) and Jiayuguan. As with rail travel out of Lanzhou, sleepers are difficult to come by.

Xi'an

There are trains from Xi'an to many large cities in China, including Beijing (14 hours express), Shanghai (17–24 hours), Guangzhou, Chengdu, Hefei, Wuhan, Qingdao, Lanzou and Ürümqi. In Xi'an most hotels, travel agencies and CITS can help get train tickets with at least two days' notice, though some places might be able to wangle tickets in less time. You can try to get your own tickets at the railway station on Huancheng Beilu Dongduan just outside the northeast corner of the Old City, but don't expect to get tickets for sleepers on overnight trains at short notice.

Xining

The railway station is on the eastern edge of the city, across the Huangshui River. It's about 3km (2 miles) into the city centre from here – take bus 2 or 28. There are rail links to major cities in eastern China.

Long-Distance Buses

Overland buses are the most important means of transport in many parts of China, especially where there is no railway line. In most towns and settlements there are main bus stations for overland buses. They are the cheapest means of transport, but are also correspondingly slow and dangerous. There are regular breaks during bus journeys; on journeys lasting several days you will usually find simple restaurants and overnight accommodation near the bus stations. Some buses have numbered seats, but it is not usually necessary to book a ticket or seat in advance. Modern buses with air conditioning operate in tourist areas.

Beijing

Long-distance buses connect Beijing with many cities, including Tianjin, Chengde, Beidaihe, Taiyuan and Hohhot. On some routes buses are faster, but generally less comfortable, than trains.

Sleeper buses operate on longer routes. Buses are recommended for relatively short journeys to places such as Tianjin (2 hours) or Chengde (4 hours). Beijing's main long-distance bus stations are at Dongzhimen (for the northeast), Deshengmen (for Chengde), Zhaogongkou and Haihutun (for Tianjin and various cities in southern Hebei province).

Chengdu

Chengdu has numerous long-distance bus stations, and which one you use will depend on where in town you are staying. Most are close to one of the old – and now long gone – city gates, as in the North, South, East or West Gate stations. Chongqing is just 4 hours away by bus, but for other destinations outside Sichuan, buses tend to be time-consuming and uncomfortable.

Chongqing

There are buses connecting Chongqing to many towns in Sichuan province, including Emei, Dazu, Leshan, Shazhou, Yibin and Neijiang.

Buses to Dazu (2 hours) and Chengdu (4 hours) are frequent. The long-distance bus station is next to the train station at the southwestern end of the peninsula on Nanqu Lu, and is relatively clean and user-friendly.

Guilin

The tourism hub of Guangxi province, Guilin is served by frequent and inexpensive buses to destinations within the province. Of Guilin's three bus stations, the main one is on Zhongshan Zhonglu.

Kashi (Kashgar)

The long-distance bus station is on Tiannan Lu, just south of Renmin Lu. There are daily buses from Kashi to Korla, Kuqa, Aksu, Hotan, Daheyan, Ürümqi and Yengisar.

Kunming

The Gaokuai bus station (known locally as *qiche nanzhan*), at 663 Minhang Lu, is served by Yunnan Express buses that run to many Yunnan cities, notably Dali/Xiaguan (4½ hours) and Lijiang (7–8 hours).

Lanzhou

Travelling east from Lanzhou, there are long-distance buses going to Xi'an, Yinchuan and Guyuan. The long-distance bus station serving points east is on Pingliang Lu between Minzhu Lu and Jiuda Lu. Going west, buses serve Linxia, Xiahe and Hezuo.

The west bus station is at the western edge of town on Xijin Donglu. There are several buses a day serving Linxia and Hezuo, but only one direct bus to Xiahe, in the early morning. If you miss that service, you can always take one of the many buses going to Linxia, and change there for one of the many minibuses going to Xiahe.

Foreigners travelling in southern Gansu are required to buy travel insurance (even if they have their own travel insurance), and are not usually allowed to board the bus without it. You can purchase insurance at PICC, 150 Qingyang Lu (tel: 0931-841 6421), at travel agencies or directly at the bus stations.

Lhasa

The long-distance bus station is at the junction of Jinzhuzhong and Minzu roads. Services ply the Sichuan and Qinghai highways and destinations include Golmud, Lanzhou, Chengdu. Tongmai and Chongqing.

Nanchang

In Jiangxi, the regular, well-maintained buses provide the best means of transport within the province. This is particularly true on the modern high-speed expressways, where buses outperform trains in both speed and ease of buying tickets.

Shanghai
It's generally more convenient to take a train to Shanghai rather than a bus, although the city is connected to Suzhou, Nanjing and Hangzhou by modern highways that have made travel immeasurably easier. The North District bus station on Gongxing Lu has buses to destinations in surrounding provinces, and buses to Nanjing, Suzhou and Hangzhou depart from the Hengfeng Lu station, just south of the main Shanghai railway station. Regular, less comfortable buses arrive and depart from the long-distance bus station on Qiujiang Lu, west of Henan Bei Lu. There are several buses each day to closer destinations such as Hangzhou and Suzhou.

Tianjin
Most long-distance buses terminate at the main railway station north of the river, some 2km (1½ miles) from downtown.

Ürümqi
Ürümqi is the hub of bus travel throughout Xinjiang, though trying to figure out which station to leave from can be confusing, and buying tickets at the wrong station can incur additional charges. For most destinations in Xinjiang, buses leave from the long-distance bus station on Heilongjiang Lu. For Turpan, buses leave from the Urumqi–Turpan bus station, near Erdaoqiao Market at the southern end of town. Buses to Turpan take around 3 hours on the freeway.

Buses to Kashi leave from the long-distance bus station on Heilongjiang Lu or from the Nanjiao bus station in the south of Ürümqi. They leave regularly and take around 30 hours. Luxury express sleeper coaches are also available. Be aware beforehand that if you get a sleeper seat, you are confined to the same position for the whole ride. Foreign women travelling alone have reported being harassed on these bus trips.

Buses to Tianchi depart mid-morning from the north gate of People's Park (Renmin Gongyuan) west of the Hongshan intersection and return in the late afternoon. The journey to Tianchi takes around 2–3 hours. Unlike in Gansu, it is not necessary to purchase PICC travel insurance when travelling in Xinjiang.

Xi'an
There are long-distance buses connecting Xi'an with Zhengzhou, Yichang and Luoyang, as well as to Yan'an, Lanzhou, Hanzhong and Huashan. However, the majority of foreign travellers appear to prefer taking the train. The long-distance bus station is near the railway station in the northeastern corner of the Old City.

Xining
The city's long-distance bus station is across the river from the railway station, and the same city bus routes will get you into town. Bus routes include Lanzhou, Golmud, Tongren, Zhangye and Maduo. Foreigners are not permitted to take the Lhasa bus from here.

Water Transport
With a few exceptions, passenger transport on China's extensive river network has given way to commercial shipping. However, there are regular ferry and boat connections between the large coastal cities in China. The same is true for some of the big rivers, particularly the Chang Jiang (Yangzi; *see below*) and the Zhu Jiang (Pearl River), but not the Huang He (Yellow River). Services on the Grand Canal are limited, although boats still run from Hangzhou in Zhejiang province to Suzhou and Wuxi in Jiangsu province. Information on routes and timetable are available from travel agents or shipping agencies.

Chongqing and the Three Gorges
This is China's most popular river trip. The most spectacular scenery on the Chang Jiang (Yangzi) is to be found downstream from Chongqing as far as Yichang (only a few boats go as far as Wuhan, and beyond). This stretch takes anything from 11 hours on a hydrofoil to 2 or 3 days on a cruise ship. There are also boats departing daily from Wuhan going upstream to Chongqing; this journey takes around 3 days. From Yichang it is possible to board boats in either direction.

Since the construction of the Three Gorges Dam the water level on the Chang Jiang has risen by some 175 metres (575ft), which has made the landscape a little less dramatic.

When planning a river trip, there are two main things to bear in mind: when to go and the type of vessel. High season is May–October and for travel during this time you will need to reserve well in advance. The river is very busy at this time, so you may prefer to go off-season, for a more peaceful experience.

Individual Travel
There are three ways of travelling in China for the individual traveller. The most comfortable, and of course, most expensive way is to book a full package tour through a travel agent. Everything is pre-booked and the traveller can choose a tailor-made route. The same is the case for sightseeing: a guide from a China travel agency is available in each town and will help put together and arrange a sightseeing programme.

The second possibility is booking a mini-package tour. The agent pre-books the flights, accommodation with breakfast, transfers and transport of luggage in China, while the traveller is responsible for organising sightseeing. The traveller is met at the airport or railway station on arrival at each town and taken to the hotel. Each hotel has a travel-agency counter, where you can discuss your plans for sightseeing and have them arranged for a fee.

The mini-package option is a good idea. The most essential bookings have been made (to make them yourself requires a lot of time and strong nerves), and with thorough preparation, you have a good chance of getting to know China beyond the usual tourist routes. You should get a definite booking with an experienced travel agent at least three months before departure.

Then there is completely independent travel, without any pre-booking. You'll have to arrange your own air and train tickets at each place you visit. Unless you speak Chinese, you will probably find it easiest to do this through a travel agency, where it is more likely you will find English-speaking staff. At airports and stations, you will often find that information about destinations is given in pinyin, but off the beaten track it will usually be in Chinese characters only.

Last-minute plans can often fall through: you may have to wait several days for your railway or air ticket, or abandon your chosen destination and choose a different one. Reserve air or rail tickets as soon as you arrive; your hotel can do this for you, for a small commission. This can be very useful for hard-to-obtain tickets.

Travel agencies will book hotels for a small fee, but are geared towards the expensive ones.

It is important to know exactly the kind of boat you are buying a ticket for. There are three basic types of vessels plying the Chang Jiang: hydrofoils, passenger boats/Chinese cruise ships, and international cruise ships. There is no standard classification for categories of accommodation on the boats, so make sure you understand exactly what, for example, "first-class" means before you pay for it.

Hydrofoils are the fastest way to travel along the river, but you obviously cannot savour the scenery or stop along the way.

Passenger boats and Chinese cruise ships ferry everything from passengers to cargo. These usually have cabins ranging from first class (two bunks in a room with private shower) to fourth class (communal bunking). Passengers are left to fend for themselves at mealtimes, and hygiene and sanitation are poor. These boats may suit those on a tight budget, but are devoid of all amenities, and only stop at towns, not tourist sights, along the way.

Tickets for these boats can be purchased at Chaotianmen Docks, but it is far easier to book through a hotel in town (which generally have English-speaking staff), or at one of the agencies around town (which generally do not).

Luxury **international cruise ships** are the preferred option for most tourists. But even here, there can be a great deal of difference in facilities and quality, so be clear about the kind of ship you're booking yourself on. Trips booked from outside China are often much more expensive than booking a comparable ship through a local travel agent, but the former often provide added amenities, ranging from casinos to daily movies to mah-jong lessons. Cruise ships make stops along the river at sites of interest; entrance fees to these may be included in the price of your ticket.

Hainan
Ferries to Haikou's Xiuying and Xingang ports operate from the Guangdong cities of Haian, Xuwen, Zhanjiang and Shenzhen.

Hong Kong
There is a wide choice of services on ferries and fast hydrofoils between Hong Kong and many Guangdong cities – including Guangzhou (2 hours by hydrofoil), Shekou (near Shenzhen Airport), Zhongshan and Zhuhai. There are also longer routes in operation – to Shantou (14 hours; daily); to Xiamen (20 hours; five weekly), and to Shanghai (60 hours; weekly service). Most departures are from the China Ferry Terminal at the China Hong Kong City Building, Canton Road, Tsim Sha Tsui.

Travellers heading to Macau will find a variety of rapid craft speeding throughout the day and night from the Hong Kong Macau Ferry Terminal in the Shun Tak Centre, Sheung Wan, on Hong Kong Island. Jetfoils and catamarans make the journey in around an hour (but allow longer for queues at immigration in Macau). There are also (much less frequent) services from Hong Kong Airport, and between Macau and various cities in Guangdong province. It is now possible to go straight from Hong Kong to Taipa on Cotai Jet Ferries (tel: 852-2859 1588), which depart for the new Taipa Ferry Terminal on the hour 7am–5pm and from the Shun Tak Centre on Hong Kong Island.

A variety of ferry companies manage these routes. For information on ferry schedules from Hong Kong, call 852-2859 3333 or 2736 1387/2516 9581.

Shanghai
Shanghai is connected to ports elsewhere in China. Vessels also travel up the Chang Jiang (Yangzi) to destinations along the river, including Nanjing, Wuhan and Chongqing. Destinations along China's coastline include a once-every-four-days boat to Dalian and a daily boat to Putuoshan that leaves at 8pm for the overnight trip. Tickets to all destinations can be booked at the foreigner ticket booth at the Boat Ticket Booking Office, 1 Jinling Rd (E), which sells domestic tickets from first to fourth class. Tickets can also be purchased at the Shiliupu Wharf ticket office, where boats to most domestic destinations depart. The wharf is situated on the Huangpu River on Zhongshan Rd (C), just south of the Bund. International departures are from the international ferry terminal on Taiping Lu.

City Transport
The visitor can choose between taxis, buses or bicycles for transport in the cities. In Beijing, Hong Kong, Guangzhou, Tianjin, Shanghai and Shenzhen there are also underground metro systems.

Taxis are certainly the most comfortable form of transport, and drivers will agree a fixed rate for longer journeys and excursions, with prices usually starting at around Rmb 300–400. In smaller cities this can be bargained down considerably. Taxis are plentiful in all cities, and if you don't speak the language, it is a good idea to carry details of your destination written in Chinese.

Buses in Chinese towns are almost always overcrowded. The fare depends on distance, and should be paid to the conductor. Buses are not easy for foreigners to use, as information is almost exclusively in Chinese script. In some cities such as Beijing, there are also minibuses for certain routes; these carry a maximum of 16 people. They are a bit more expensive, but will stop at any point you want along the route. Drivers pack in as many people as they can, and you may end up standing or sitting next to the driver.

You can hire **bicycles** practically everywhere in China, either at hotels or at bike-hire shops. However, with the recent huge increase in road traffic, cycling is less pleasant than it once was: Beijing has retained its cycle lanes, but in some cities – notably Shanghai – travelling on two wheels is decidedly hazardous.

Rental rates should be around Rmb 5 per hour and up to Rmb 40 per day. Shop around, as these can vary widely. You will usually be required to leave a deposit of up to Rmb 500 and some form of ID. Ask for a receipt, try to avoid leaving your passport, and make sure you have checked your bicycle's brakes, gears and tyre pressure before renting. You must use the designated parking areas, where your bike will be kept safe for a small fee. Cycle helmets can be hard to find, and night-time cycling can be hazardous due to a lack of cycle lights.

Another option is to choose a specialised bike tour. Riding a bike comes into its own when exploring an area of natural beauty. The area around Yangshuo in Guangxi is fantastic for cycling– the extraordinary karst landscape (the terrain between the peaks is actually very flat) is just minutes by bike from the town centre, along quiet roads and trails.

ACCOMMODATION

HOTELS, YOUTH HOSTELS, BED & BREAKFAST

Choosing a Hotel

China's large cities have numerous modern hotels, most of them at the high end of the market, including many of world-class calibre. Many belong to international hotel chains, and their prices are in line with the West. Tour groups usually stay in well-appointed tourist hotels.

Finding rooms at hotels in the middle and lower price ranges can be difficult, particularly during Chinese New Year (a week or two in January or February), and during the May and October holiday periods, when hotels are often completely full.

Worth mentioning are a few well-preserved hotels built by the colonial powers in a few cities. These include the Peace Hotel (Heping Fandian) in Shanghai, the Astor (Lishunde Dafandian) in Tianjin and the Raffles Beijing Hotel (Beijing Fandian) in the nation's capital.

In some of the more far-flung provinces, you may still come across some hotels that will not allow foreigners – usually because of rules imposed by Chinese travel agencies or the local police, who often determine where foreigners may stay. This is not a problem in the main tourist areas.

Rates at all but the cheapest hotels are subject to 10–15 percent service surcharge.

The following hotels are listed by province, then town/city in alphabetical order. Rates for each price category are shown in the yellow boxes in the listings and are for a standard room.

Guesthouses

Individual travellers may be able to find cheap lodgings in guesthouses in smaller towns off the tourist track. They usually have rooms with two or more beds, or dormitories, shower and washing facilities.

Other Accommodation

It is difficult for foreigners to find accommodation outside of hotels and guesthouses, although some universities and institutes have guesthouses where foreign visitors can find good, cheap lodging.

Youth hostels in China can be viewed, and sometimes booked, online at www.iyhf.org.

If you are going on a long trip or hike in the countryside, especially in Tibet or in areas around the sacred mountains of China, you will come across a variety of "long-distance travellers' lodgings". It is advisable to carry your own sleeping bag.

BELOW: Beijng is full of smart hotels.

ANHUI

PRICE CATEGORIES

Prices for a standard double room in peak season:
$$$$$ = over US$200
$$$$ = US$150–200
$$$ = US$100–150
$$ = US$50–100
$ = below US$50

Hefei

$$$
Holiday Inn
1104 Changjiang Dong Lu
Tel: (0551) 220 6666
The towering Holiday Inn is a smart option, with well-equipped rooms, four restaurants and an indoor swimming pool.

$$
Anhui Hotel
18 Meishan Lu
Tel: (0551) 221 8888
It's 3km (2 miles) from the city centre, but is worth the journey. An international-standard hotel located in the scenic Xishan area.

Huaqiao Fandian
98 Changjiang Lu
Tel: (0551) 265 2221
Good budget option in a central location. Get a room in Building B if you can.

BEIJING

$$$$$

China World Hotel
1 Jianguomenwai Dajie
Tel: (010) 6505 2266
One of the capital's best
hotels, offering top-notch
service and rooms, and a
health club, swimming
pool, shopping and
business centres, plus
Western and Asian
restaurants.

Grand Hyatt Beijing
1 Dong Chang'an Jie
Tel: (010) 8518 1234
An enormous but stylish
five-star hotel, right on the
edge of Wangfujing Dajie
and embedded within the
Oriental Plaza complex.

Hilton Beijing Wangfujing
8 Wangfujing Dajie
Tel: (010) 5812 8888
A chic and classy 21st-
century Hilton, with
designer touches at every
turn. Rooms are spacious
with luxurious amenities.
Facilities include an
excellent Portuguese
restaurant.

Peninsula Beijing
8 Jinyu Hutong,
Wangfujing Dajie
Tel: (010) 8516 2888
Just off Wangfujing Dajie,
the Palace is an
impeccable hotel with a
fine spread of restaurants
and luxury brand shopping.

Radisson SAS Royal Hotel
6A Beisanhuan Donglu
Tel: (010) 5922 3388
Scandinavian style
distinguishes this hotel,
in a good location next to
the China International
Exhibition Centre. It has a
complete range of facilities
and three restaurants
offering Chinese and
International cuisine.

The St Regis
21 Jianguomenwai Dajie
Tel: (010) 6460 6688
This very impressive,
centrally located hotel
offers sophistication and
indisputable luxury.
Foreign correspondents
meet at the elegant Press
Club Bar.

$$$$

Grand Mercure
6 Xuanwumennei Dajie
Tel: (010) 6603 6688
This recently opened
four-star hotel is the best
in the Xidan area in the
west of town, with a good
indoor pool.

**Hotel New Otani
Changfugong**
26 Jianguomenwai Dajie
Tel: (010) 6512 5555
Japanese joint venture to
the east of the city centre
and close to the embassy
district.

Novotel Peace Hotel
3 Jinyu Hutong,
Wangfujing Dajie
Tel: (010) 6512 8833
Opposite the Peninsula
Palace Hotel, a short
stroll from Wangfujing
shopping street. Good
facilities and spacious
rooms.

Raffles Beijing Hotel
33 Dong Chang'an Jie
Tel: (010) 6526 3388
Dating from 1917, the
period features lend the
Beijing an air of tradition
lacking in the city's other
five-star hotels. Located
very close to the
Forbidden City and main
shopping areas.

Swissotel Beijing
Hong Kong–Macau Centre,
2 Chaoyangmen Beidajie
Tel: (010) 6553 2288
A semicircular, mirrored
facade dominates one of
Beijing's busy inter-
sections. Popular with
business travellers.

Traders' Hotel
(China World Trade Centre),
1 Jianguomenwai Dajie
Tel: (010) 6505 2277
Reliable service, food and
accommodation. Well
located for business in the
east of the city.

$$$

Beijing International Hotel
9 Jianguomennei Dajie
Tel: (010) 6512 6688
In a good location near
Beijing railway station,
this vast hotel has a full
range of facilities,
including booking offices
for international flights
and trains.

**Holiday Inn Crowne Plaza
Beijing**
48 Wangfujing Dajie, Dengshikou
Tel: (010) 6513 3388

On one of central Beijing's
busiest shopping streets,
close to the Forbidden
City, this hotel has a
health club and small
indoor swimming pool.

Jianguo Hotel
5 Jianguomenwai Dajie
Tel: (010) 6500 2233
Convenient for the
Friendship Store, silk
market and most
embassies, this is a
favourite with long-term
business visitors.

Scitech Hotel
22 Jianguomenwai Dajie
Tel: (010) 6512 3388
Large, modern hotel in the
central commercial district,
with all the usual facilities.

Shangri-La Hotel
29 Zizhuyuan Lu, Haidian District
Tel: (010) 6841 2211
On the western edge of
the city, the Shangri-La
provides a shuttle-bus
service to downtown
areas.

$$

**Beijing Bamboo Garden
Hotel**
24 Xiaoshiqiao Hutong,
Jiugulou Dajie
Tel: (010) 5852 0088
Simple, clean rooms that
open onto a classical
Chinese garden. Close to
the Drum Tower and
Deshengmen gate in the
old city wall.

Fragrant Hills Hotel
inside Fragrant Hills Park
Tel: (010) 6259 1166
Modern sanctuary from
urban noise, in the lush
hills northwest of Beijing,
beyond the Summer
Palace. There is a
swimming pool, and
Chinese and Western
restaurants.

Friendship Hotel
3 Baishiqiao Lu, Haidian District
Tel: (010) 6849 8888
This huge state-run hotel
is spread out among
pleasant grounds close to
the Summer Palace and
university district.

Haoyuan Guesthouse
53 Shijia Hutong, Dongsinan Dajie
Tel: (010) 6512 5557
In a historic and central
part of the city, this is a
charming courtyard hotel

with a small range of
pleasant rooms.

Holiday Inn Lido
Jiangtai Lu
Tel: (010) 6437 6688
This Holiday Inn provides a
kind haven for foreigners.
Just 20 minutes from the
airport, it contains several
shops, including a deli, a
bakery and a supermarket,
plus offices and
apartments.

Lu Song Yuan Hotel
22 Banchang Hutong
Tel: (010) 6401 1116
Housed in a historic
hutong – a style of
architecture that's unique
to Beijing – this well-
located courtyard
guesthouse offers an
atmospheric alternative to
Beijing's plethora of
modern hotels.

Qianmen Jianguo Hotel
175 Yongan Lu
Tel: (010) 6301 6688
This elegant hotel is set
in the old outer city, near
Tiantan. It has 410 rooms
and suites, all newly
decorated, a good range
of eating options, and
nightly Beijing Opera
performances.

$

Fangyuan Hotel
36 Dengshikou Xijie
Tel: (010) 6525 6331
A cheap, simple and
well-located hotel off
Wangfujing Dajie.
Breakfast included.

Youyi Youth Hostel
43 Beisanlitun, Sanlitun
Tel: (010) 6417 2632
Excellently located hostel
in the middle of the
Sanlitun bar area, but with
a noisy (and very popular)
bar attached; breakfast is
included in the price.

**Zhaolong International
Youth Hostel**
2 Gongti Beilu
Tel: (010) 6597 2299
Located behind the hotel
of the same name, this
well-equipped place has
clean accommodation and
a friendly atmosphere.
Self-catering dining room,
reading room, laundry
room, 24-hour hot water
and bike rentals.

CHONGQING SHI

$$$$$
InterContinental Chongqing
101 Minzu Rd, Yuzhong District
Tel: (023) 8906 6888
This 42-storey, 338-room luxury hotel is probably the best choice for business travellers, with features such as private meeting rooms and free Wi-Fi. Leisure amenities include a swimming pool and spa.

$$$$
Hilton Chongqing
139 Zhongshan San Lu
Tel: (023) 8903 9999
Centrally located just minutes from Renmin Square, the Hilton has all the comforts and amenities you would expect of this name chain. Four

restaurants offer a choice of café cuisine, a grill and Cantonese and Sichuan cuisines. The hotel is particularly suited to business travellers, with a host of services that include office rental.
JW Marriott Hotel Chongqing
77 Qingnian Lu
Tel: (023) 6388 8888
The most impressive hotel in Chongqing, the Marriott has four restaurants, an indoor pool, an elegant lobby, several bars, high standards of service and a good location in the downtown area.

$$$
Harbour Plaza
Wuyi Lu
Tel: (023) 6370 0888

Renovated five-star hotel with impressive rooms and a central location.
Holiday Inn Yangtze Chongqing
87 Nanping Beixin Jie, Nan'an District
Tel: (023) 6280 3380
The Holiday Inn, with its views over the Yangzi River and of the skyline of China's fastest-growing city, is a good and slightly more economical choice than some of Chongqing's other brand-name hotels. The hotel has a riverside swimming pool, the perfect place to cool off in the city's notoriously hot summers, with an adjoining barbecue restaurant, along with excellent Sichuan and Cantonese food at the Golden Sand Restaurant.

$
Chung King Hotel
41–43 Xin Hua Lu
Tel: (023) 6383 8888/6384 9301
Located near the Chaotianmen Docks, this modern three-star hotel, reminiscent of dull, old Soviet-style monoliths, offers standard mid-range rooms and facilities including banking, tour and travel bookings. All rooms are en suite and have central air conditioning. Popular with foreigners.
Huixian Lou Hotel
186 Minzu Lu
Tel: (023) 6383 7495
Centrally located and within walking distance of the docks, this is one of the few budget options in town. However, it is still overpriced.

ACCOMMODATION

DONGBEI (HEILONGJIANG AND LIAONING PROVINCES)

Dalian
$$
Dalian Hotel
4 Zhongshan Square
Tel: (0411) 8263 3111
Dalian's most impressive historical hotel, built in 1914 by Japanese occupiers.

Harbin
$$$$
Shangri-La Hotel
555 Youyi Lu
Tel: (0451) 8485 8888
First-class service and comfort. Offers views of the Songhua River and CBD.

$$
Songhuajiang Gloria Inn Harbin
257 Zhongyang Avenue
Tel: (0451) 8463 8855
Decent three-star hotel with a great location near Zhaolin Park and the Songhua River. All rooms have air conditioning.

Shenyang
$
Haiyue City Plaza Hotel
83 Zhongshan Lu
Tel: (024) 6250 1888
Modern four-star hotel in the city centre offering very competitive rates for its spacious rooms.

SHOPPING

FUJIAN

Fuzhou
$$$
Lakeside Hotel
158 Hubin Lu
Tel: (0591) 8783 9888
This hotel is beautifully set between West Lake and West Lake Park. Reasonable rates include breakfast and free internet and long-distance calls.

Xiamen
$$$
Marco Polo Xiamen
8 Jianye Rd (nr Hubin Beilu)
Tel: (0592) 509 1888
Growing old very gracefully indeed, this fine old hotel is at the heart of the

scenic and historic trading port. On the lake front, it offers international standards, including a choice of restaurants, leisure facilities and business services.
Sofitel Plaza Xiamen
19 Hubin Beilu
Tel: (0592) 507 8888
Sofitel was the first Western hotel chain to land in Xiamen, with this swish five-star palace in the city's financial district. Rooms either face the city or the sea, and there's a spa, fitness centre and pool.

$$
Xianglu Grand
18 Changhao Rd, Huli

Tel: (0592) 263 8888
Opened in 2006, this splendid, 1,500-room hotel has as its centrepiece a massive landscaped atrium. Rooms are luxurious, and amenities include a huge spa and fitness centre, a swimming pool and entertainment.
Lujiang Harbourview Hotel
54 Lujiang Lu
Tel: (0592) 202 2922
Attractively set in an old colonial-style building by the waterfront, this hotel is handy for boats to Gulangyu Island. Some rooms have sea views and modern amenities, while retaining the original ambience.

Xiamen Yongshun Hotel
12 Lujiao Lu, Gulangyu Island
Tel: (0592) 206 0920
This mini-chain's main hotel on the charming island of Gulangyu is located in the former British Consulate. There is another small guesthouse on the seafront. Both are comfortable and offer good value for money.

ACTIVITIES

A – Z

PRICE CATEGORIES

Prices for a standard double room in peak season:
$$$$$ = over US$200
$$$$ = US$150–200
$$$ = US$100–150
$$ = US$50–100
$ = below US$50

LANGUAGE

GANSU

Dunhuang

$$$–$$$$

Silk Road Dunhuang Hotel (Dunhuang Shanzhuang)
Dunyue Lu
Tel: (0937) 888 2088
www.the-silk-road.com
Easily Dunhuang's finest property, perhaps even Gansu province's supreme hotel. Located in an incredible setting amid the giant sand dunes south of town, the hotel blends flawlessly with its environment. All bedrooms and suites are elegantly decorated and sport warm desert colours. Certain guest rooms even copy the long-established Silk Road caravanserai style of accommodation. Activities arranged by the hotel include camel-riding over the dunes, sand-sledging down the dunes and archery.

$$$

Grand Sun Hotel (Taiyang Dajiudian)
5 Shazhou Beilu
Tel: (0937) 882 9998
Friendly, hospitable and doubtless the pre-eminent place in downtown Dunhuang. The new wing's rooms are very good, but are more expensive than those in the old wing. Those in the old wing do,

however, have a certain character to them, but are not so well maintained. Tours and expeditions can be arranged at the hotel's tour desk.

$$

Feitian Hotel
Mingshan Lu
Tel: (0937) 882 2008
Very conveniently located close by the long-distance bus station, this is a clean and friendly hotel without a restaurant, but right next to the best selection of English-language menus in Dunhuang on either side of downtown Mingshan Lu. Private bedrooms and dormitory accommodation are both available.

Lanzhou

$$$

JJ Sun Hotel (Jinjiang Yangguang Jiudian)
589 Donggang Xi Lu, Lanzhou
Tel: (0931) 880 5511
www.jinjianghotels.com
The JJ Sun Hotel, a 24-storey, three-star hotel, is situated in the city's busy commercial district. Guest rooms are pleasantly furnished and provide cable television, internet access, mini bar and refrigerator. It's also well placed for some of Lanzhou's best restaurants.

Lanzhou Legend Hotel (Lanzhou Feitian Dajiudian)
599 Tianshui Lu
Tel: (0931) 888 2876
Probably the best hotel in Lanzhou, with all the modern facilities one might expect. There's internet service, cable TV, a choice of several good restaurants, a money exchange and English-speaking staff who can arrange local sightseeing trips and onward reservations. Located in the southeastern part of town, it's well located for both the train station and the long-distance bus station.

$$

Lanzhou Hotel (Lanzhou Fandian)
434 Donggang Xilu
Tel: (0931) 841 6321
A pleasant, reasonably priced establishment set in a nondescript Soviet-style building which has recently been renovated. The hotel is conveniently located for both the train station and long-distance bus station; it offers easy access to downtown Lanzhou, as well as a range of facilities including internet access and travel agencies for onward bookings.

Xiahe

$

Labrang Baoma Hotel (Labuleng Baoma Binguan)
Renmin Xijie
Tel: (0941) 712 1078
This is a well-run and friendly Tibetan-oriented establishment, with pleasing décor and two restaurants serving good Sichuan and Tibetan food. Most rooms have en suite bath. It is reasonably priced and, for travellers on a tight budget, it also offers fairly comfortable dormitory beds. Services available include bicycle hire, which is the ideal way to explore Xiahe and Labrang Monastery.

Overseas Tibetan Hotel (Huaqiao Fandian)
77 Renmin Xijie
Tel: (0941) 712 2642
Situated right next door to Xiahe's major attraction, the Labrang Monastery, this hotel has undergone steady improvement in its general facilities, to the point where the rooms are now really quite comfortable. Unfortunately some guest rooms still do not have their own bathroom. Nevertheless, this is a good, reliable choice if staying in Xiahe.

GUANGDONG

Note: Prices at all of Guangzhou's hotels will rise to full rack rates around the time of the Canton Fair (second half of April and October). For the leisure traveller, this is not a good time to visit the city.

Guangzhou

$$$$$

The Ritz-Carlton, Guangzhou
3 Xing'an Lu (nr Xiancun Lu)
Tel: (020) 3813 6688
With its aristocratic European fittings, fantastic restaurants and top-notch

service, the Ritz-Carlton has strong claims on being the best hotel in Guangzhou. Its location in the sprouting Zhujiang New City is slightly out the way, but will be perfect by 2009–10.

$$$$

China Marriott Hotel
122 Liuhua Lu
Tel: (020) 8666 6888
This huge five-star hotel has a large range of restaurants and bars, a luxury shopping mall and direct metro access. It's centrally located, but the

Guangzhou Trade Fair has now moved from its old spot, just across the street, to the eastern suburbs. It's still easy to reach by metro.

Garden Hotel
368 Huanshi Donglu
Tel: (020) 8333 8989
One of China's three five-star Platinum hotels, the Garden Hotel is a Guangzhou institution. The lobby is regal, and there's a waterfall in its lovely garden.

The Westin Guangzhou
6 Linhe Zhonglu
Tel: (020) 2886 6868

Top new hotel in the thick of the Tianhe district, Guangzhou's smart new shopping and business district. It's just around the corner from the Zhongxin Tower, as well as Guangzhou East Station.

$$$

Asia International Hotel
326 Huanshi Dong
Tel: (020) 6128 8888
A modern high-rise hotel with spacious rooms, a swimming pool and gym, and free high-speed internet. Atop its tower is the Sky Café revolving

restaurant, with panoramic views.

Holiday Inn City Centre Guangzhou
28 Guangming Lu
(nr Huanshi Donglu)
Tel: (020) 6128 6868
Reliable international name that's been grounded in this excellent central location for several years. It's just beside one of the city's most famous bar streets.

Shangri-La Pazhou
Suite 2001, North Tower,
The Hub, 1068 Xingang Donglu,
Hai Zhu District
Tel: (020) 8923 1188
Opened in late 2006, this huge hotel is the only choice in town for travellers attending the Canton Fair. The new Guangzhou International Convention Centre is a five-minute walk away. For everyone else, the suburban location is unattractive.

White Swan Hotel
1 Shamian Nanjie
Tel: (020) 8188 6968
This fine 843-room hotel sits by itself on Shamian Island with a gallery of high-class boutiques and restaurants. Still a prestigious address, the White Swan was the first five-star hotel in China.

$
Shamian Hotel
52 Shamian Nanjie
Shamian Island
Tel: (020) 8121 8288
Popular with foreign visitors, this budget hotel is situated on the picturesque islet of Shamian, opposite the White Swan Hotel.

Shenzhen

$$$$$
Intercontinental Shenzhen
9009 Shennan Dadao, Chinese Overseas Town

Tel: (0755) 3399 3388
With 540 guest rooms and eight themed restaurants – including a venue inside a full-sized galley – the new Intercontinental Shenzhen is eccentric enough to feel at home among the surrounding wacky theme parks. However, this is probably the best hotel in town, and the rooms are quite fantastic. There is a health suite and outdoor swimming pool.

$$$
Crowne Plaza Hotel and Suites Landmark
3018 Nanhu Lu
Tel: (0755) 8217 2288
A solid five-star hotel in the heart of the shopping and business area of Luohu. It recently came under Crowne Plaza management, and offers good facilities including swimming pool, fitness

centre, business services and restaurant.

Shangri-La Shenzhen
East Side, Railway Station,
1002 Jianshe Road
Tel: (0755) 8233 0888
Immediately opposite the Hong Kong border, this is the most popular business-traveller option in town. Having been around for a decade, the rooms and facilities feel slightly jaded, but service is top-notch, and the public areas and restaurants – 360 Bar and Restaurant, in particular – are as luxurious as ever.

$$
Days Hotel Luohu
1021 Yanhe Nanlu
Tel: (0755) 2585 9988
Smart new mid-range hotel located above a shopping mall. Good amenities, and convenient location close to the railway station and Hong Kong border.

GUANGXI

Guilin

$$$
Hotel of Modern Art HOMA
Dabu Town, Yanshan District
Tel: (0773) 386 5555
The star of this uber-kooky design hotel, located beside the Yuzi Paradise sculpture park south of the city, is HOMA Libre – a 46-room building nestled beneath a limestone peak and featuring a sloping roof covered with grass.

Lijiang Waterfall Hotel
1 Shanhu Bei Lu
Tel: (0773) 282 2881

Central hotel overlooking the Li River and facing Elephant Trunk Hill. Rooms are large and facilities, including an indoor pool, sauna and gym, are modern. The hotel has Chinese, Japanese, Korean and Western restaurants.

Sheraton Guilin Hotel
15 Bin Jiang Lu
Tel: (0773) 282 5588
One of the best hotels in Guilin, with a superb riverfront location.

$$
Guilin Fubo Hotel
27 Bin Jiang Lu

Tel: (0773) 256 9898
Friendly mid-range choice, with comfortable rooms and a fine location next to the Li River. Facilities include two restaurants, a health club and business centre.

Nanning

$
Phoenix Hotel
63 Chaoyang Lu
Tel: (0771) 211 9666
Grand and imposing hotel with large, well-furnished

rooms, yet offering great value for money.

Yangshuo

$–$$
Yangshuo Mountain Retreat
Wang Gong Shan Jiao, Feng Lou Cun Wei, Gao Tian
Tel: (0773) 877 7091
The name says it all – a peaceful haven in glorious surroundings on a bank of the Yulong River. Of the 22 rooms, those with a balcony overlooking the river are the best choice.

GUIZHOU

Guiyang

$$
Guizhou Park Hotel
66 Beijing Rd
Tel: (0851) 682 3888
This four-star hotel, beside Quinling Park, has a bowling alley, disco and billiard room. Restaurants offer both Chinese and Western cuisine.

$
Motel 168
2 Sheng Fu Road
Tel: (0851) 816 8168
Swish, modern, central hotel with good restaurant.

Kaili

$
Gui Tai Hotel
Beijing Donglu

Tel: (0855) 826 9888
In the heart of the city. Complimentary breakfast and satellite TV.

Zhaoxing

$
Lulu's Homestay
Tel: (0855) 613 0112
Proprietor Mr Lu is very helpful, food is interesting

and public balconies on each floor have fine views.

PRICE CATEGORIES

Prices for a standard double room in peak season:
$$$$$ = over US$200
$$$$ = US$150–200
$$$ = US$100–150
$$ = US$50–100
$ = below US$50

HAINAN ISLAND

Haikou

$$$$

Sheraton Haikou Resort
199 Binhai Lu
Tel: (0898) 6870 8888
Fronting a sandy coastline, near Holiday Beach and not far from the city centre, this relaxing resort offers fine dining. Amenities include a spa and swimming pool.

$$

HNA Hotel
38 Datong Lu
Tel: (0898) 6679 6999
Central to financial and shopping districts, this hotel has spacious rooms and a landscaped garden.

Nanshan

$$

Nanshan Leisure Villas and Tree House
Nan Shan Park
Tel: (0898) 8883 7936
This great little resort has pleasant sea-view villas, plus more unusual accommodation built into tamarind trees amid sand dunes behind a beautiful beach. Rooms in the treehouse are spartan and bathrooms are shared, but it's all well kept... and fun.

Qixianling

$$$–$$

Paradise Rainforest Spa and Resort
Qixianling National Forest Reserve, Baoting County
Tel: (0898) 8388 8888
This is a superb spa hotel, nestling beneath the jagged peaks of Mount Qixianling. Private balconies have hot-spring-fed hot tubs and there are lovely landscaped public pools. The hotel's Chinese restaurant is exceptionally good and offers some interesting local specialities.

Yalong Wan

$$$$$–$$$$

Hilton Sanya Resort and Spa
Tel: (0898) 8858 8588
In a row of several international resort hotels on Yalong Bay, this one stands out as the most stylish, with chic décor and a spacious spa.

HEBEI

Chengde

$$

Pu Ning Hotel
West Courtyard of Puning Temple
Tel: (0314) 205 8888
Located in the Puning Temple complex and featuring staff in costume, nightly performances and Buddhist-style vegetarian food.

$

Qian Yang Hotel
18 Fule Lu, Shuangqiao District
Tel: (0314) 205 7188
A pleasant, modern tourist hotel, facing the Mountain Resort, with swimming pool, sauna and tennis.

Shanhaiguan

$

The First Pass Hotel (Diyiguan Binguan)
1 Dong Dajie
Tel: (0335) 513 2188
The reproduction Qing architecture of the First Pass tries to blend in with the Great Wall just to the east. Shanhaiguan has only a few hotels and this is your best bet, but the double rooms are average and the staff somewhat indifferent. Breakfast included.

Tianjin

$$$

Astor
33 Tiaer Zhuang Lu
Tel: (022) 2331 1688
In a historic building overlooking the river, this plush hotel offers nice rooms and good amenities.

$$

Huibinyuan Hotel
46 Shuishang Beilu
Tel: (022) 2336 9486
Pleasant three-star hotel located in a scenic area. Rooms have TV, refrigerator and bathroom. Staff speak only very basic English.

$

Super 8 Hotel
5 Jinping Lu
Tel: (022) 5829 8988
Reliable budget option near the long-distance bus station and metro.

HENAN

Dengfeng

$$

Shaolin International Hotel
20 Shaolin Lu
Tel: (0371) 6286 6188
www.shaolinhotel.com
Dengfeng's highest-calibre hotel – and the one used for most inter-national package tours to the Shaolin area – this four-star abode has a vast lobby area and a wide range of rooms, as well as a handful of restaurants specialising in regional Chinese cuisines. Business centre, gym and sauna all available to guests.

Kaifeng

$

Dajintai Hotel
23 Gulou Jie
Tel: (378) 6255 2888
Located in the heart of the Old Town, astride the amazing night market, the Dajintai is the best value in Kaifeng, featuring large, comfortable doubles with attached bathrooms and an inclusive Chinese breakfast.

Kaifeng Hotel
66 Ziyou Lu
Tel: (378) 6595 5589
Another conveniently located option, unmistakable for the Chinese-style flying eaves of its roofs (which were actually built by a Russian group) – the pleasing aesthetics are how the management justify rates that are significantly higher than the Dajintai's.

Luoyang

$$

Peony Hotel
15 Zhongzhou Xilu
Tel: (0379) 6468 0000
Luoyang's most expensive hotel, often full of international package tourists visiting the nearby Longmen Shiku, with cosy but clean rooms befitting the Peony's four-star designation. The city's main CITS office is located on the ground floor, just to the right of the main entrance.

$

Tianxiang Hotel
56 Jinguyuan Lu
Tel: (0379) 6393 5439
Convenient budget option for independent travellers, just a few minutes' walk south of the railway station and offering an array of economically priced rooms – many of them recently renovated. The reasonably priced Sichuan restaurant downstairs is very popular and usually packed out for lunch and dinner.

Zhengzhou

$$$

Crowne Plaza Zhengzhou
115A Jinshui Lu
Tel: (0371) 6595 0055
www.crowneplaza.com/zhengzhou-cp
Situated in the east of Zhengzhou, amid the city's

other five-star accommodation, this well-managed hotel has plush rooms and a wide range of facilities, including a well-maintained pool.
Sofitel Zhengzhou
289 Chengdong Lu
Tel: (0371) 6595 0088
www.sofitel.com/asia

Just edging out the Crowne Plaza as Zhengzhou's poshest lodgings, the nearby Sofitel has all the modern comforts of an international five-star hotel, including a café, two restaurants, two bars, a nightclub, fitness centre, swimming pool and sauna.

$$

Holiday Inn Express
115 Jinshui Lu
Tel: (0371) 6595 6600
Jointly run by the adjacent Crowne Plaza, this offers more affordable, down-to-earth accommodation, with immaculately clean rooms. Rates include breakfast.

HONG KONG

$$$$$

Conrad Hong Kong
Pacific Place, 88 Queensway, Central
Tel: (852) 2521 3838
A European-style de luxe boutique hotel on floors 40 to 61. Understated elegance; spacious rooms and good location adjacent to Pacific Place shopping, Admiralty MTR and trams.
Four Seasons
8 Finance Street, Central
Tel: (852) 3196 8899
Raising the bar for luxury, this glamorous hotel uses light and harbour views to maximum effect. Its French and Cantonese restaurants have won international aclaim.
Grand Hyatt
1 Harbour Road, Wan Chai
Tel: (852) 2261 0222
Luxury on a truly palatial level, particularly its huge Plateau spa; overlooking the harbour and only a short walk to the Convention and Exhibition Centre and Arts Centre.

InterContinental Hong Kong
18 Salisbury Road, Tsim Sha Tsui
Tel: (852) 2721 1211
Breathtaking views across Victoria Harbour. Full range of facilities, including a poolside spa, nightclub and top-notch restaurants. Superb location on the waterfront, close to the Star Ferry and Kowloon's prime entertainment district.
Island Shangri-La
Pacific Place, Supreme Court Road, Central
Tel: (852) 2877 3838
This gracious oasis lives up to its name: elegant décor, helpful staff, exceptional restaurants and beautiful, spacious rooms with stunning panoramic views of the harbour or Peak. Adjacent to Hong Kong Park, Pacific Place shopping and Admiralty MTR and tramlines.
Kowloon Shangri-La
64 Mody Road, Tsim Sha Tsui East
Tel: (852) 2721 2111
Opulence and great harbour views, with a full range of de luxe facilities including indoor pool and highly rated

restaurants. Across from Tsim Sha Tsui East waterfront with easy access to Central.
Langham Place Hotel
555 Shanghai Street, Mong Kok
Tel: (852) 3552 3388
This classy hotel offers sumptuous rooms fitted out with state-of-the-art technology, offset by stunning works of art that reflect the Chinese heritage.
Mandarin Oriental
5 Connaught Road, Central
Tel: (852) 2522 0111
This classy hotel, established in 1963 and consistently rated among the world's best, offers impeccable service and quality, plus a full range of facilities including an indoor pool. Very convenient location.
Marco Polo Hong Kong Hotel
Harbour City, 3 Canton Road, Tsim Sha Tsui
Tel: (852) 2113 0088
This hotel has many rooms with magnificent harbour views. De luxe facilities include an outdoor pool

and five restaurants. Almost unlimited shopping opportunities: it's inside the enormous mall stretching from Ocean Terminal up to the Gateway.
The Peninsula
Salisbury Road, Tsim Sha Tsui
Tel: (852) 2920 2888
Hong Kong's oldest and most prestigious hotel has been a byword for impeccable service and colonial-style grandeur since 1928. Extended to incorporate a 30-storey tower, it has eight top restaurants and a superb location in the heart of Kowloon.
Ritz-Carlton
3 Connaught Road, Central
Tel: (852) 2877 6666
Postmodernist exterior gives way to classy traditionalist interior decorated with period art and antiques. Facilities include a fantastic outdoor pool and good Italian and Japanese restaurants. Convenient location close to Star Ferry.
Sheraton Hong Kong Hotel and Towers
20 Nathan Road, Tsim Sha Tsui
Tel: (852) 2369 1111
Swish hotel on corner of Nathan and Salisbury roads with full range of deluxe facilities, including an outdoor pool and five excellent restaurants. Good location close to museums, shopping, MTR

BELOW: the bright lights of Victoria Harbour, Hong Kong.

TRANSPORT

ACCOMMODATION

SHOPPING

ACTIVITIES

A – Z

LANGUAGE

and Kowloon's prime entertainment district.

The Excelsior
281 Gloucester Road,
Causeway Bay
Tel: (852) 2894 8888
Overlooking the colourful Causeway Bay typhoon shelter, the hotel offers efficient service and a pleasant environment. Close to Causeway Bay's shopping and commercial district and MTR.
Kimberley Hotel
28 Kimberley Road, Tsim Sha Tsui
Tel: (852) 2723 3888
Contemporary décor and furnishings enhance the range of rooms and suites. There are Chinese and Japanese restaurants and recreational amenities include a health spa, gym and golf-driving nets.
Majestic
348 Nathan Road, Yau Ma Tei
Tel: (852) 2781 1333
Well-appointed business hotel offering larger-than-average rooms. It is close to Temple Street night market, shops, cinema and Jordan MTR; also well served by buses.
Marco Polo Gateway
Harbour City, 13 Canton Road, Tsim Sha Tsui
Tel: (852) 2113 0888
Elegant, Continental-style hotel forming part of Harbour City complex; cheaper than its sister-property, the Marco Polo

Hong Kong Hotel, but lacking views and pool.
Marco Polo Prince
Harbour City, 23 Canton Road
Tsim Sha Tsui
Tel: (852) 2113 1888
Similar standard to the Marco Polo Gateway, with relaxed restaurants and an outdoor pool; convenient for China Ferry Terminal and Kowloon Park.
Miramar
118–130 Nathan Road,
Tsim Sha Tsui
Tel: (852) 2368 1111
Completely lacking in pretentions, this is a large but friendly hotel in easy reach of the best restaurants and bars of Tsim Sha Tsui.
Novotel Century Hong Kong
238 Jaffe Road, Wan Chai
Tel: (852) 2598 8888
Hotel with good facilities, including an outdoor pool and health club. Convenient for HK Exhibition and Convention Centre.
Regal Airport
9 Cheong Tat Road
Chek Lap Kok, Lantau
Tel: (852) 2286 8888
Five minutes by covered walkway from the international airport, this light, airy hotel makes the most of its location with views over the runway.
Wharney Guangdong Hotel
57–73 Lockhart Road, Wan Chai
Tel: (852) 2861 1000
Smart modern hotel with good facilities including

rooftop pool. In the heart of Wan Chai's commercial and nightlife district.

Hotel Concourse
22 Lai Chi Kok Road, Mong Kok
Tel: (852) 2397 6683
Modern hotel in vibrant Mong Kok; popular with Asian business travellers. Bargain shopping nearby in Fa Yuen St factory-outlets. Close to MTR.
The Minden
7 Minden Avenue, Tsim Sha Tsui
Tel: (852) 2739 7777
European-style boutique hotel, with original art works enhancing the comfortable rooms.
New Cathay Hotel
17 Tung Lo Wan Road,
Causeway Bay
Tel: (852) 2577 8211
Good option for single travellers. Close to tram, Hong Kong Stadium, Victoria Park and Causeway Bay commercial, dining and shopping districts.
The Salisbury (YMCA)
41 Salisbury Road, Tsim Sha Tsui
Tel: (852) 2268 7000
Book ahead to be sure of a room at this very upscale YMCA. All rooms are well equipped, and many enjoy panoramic views of the harbour. Large indoor pool and other sports facilities.

Caritas Bianchi Lodge
4 Cliff Road, Yau Ma Tei
Tel: (852) 2388 1111

Clean, spacious rooms in well-run Roman Catholic hostel close to Temple Street night market, shops and Yau Ma Tei MTR.
Eaton Hotel
380 Nathan Road, Kowloon
Tel: (852) 2782 1818
The Eaton offers well-equipped rooms; good-value restaurants with regular clientele. Close to Temple Street night market, shops, cinema and Jordan MTR.
Evergreen Hotel
48 Woo Sung St, Yau Ma Tei
Tel: (852) 2780 4222
Clean, tidy rooms. Triples and four-bed rooms are good value. Near Temple Street night market and Jordan MTR.

Anne Black Guest House (YWCA)
5 Man Fuk Road, Kowloon
Tel: (852) 2713 9211
Clean, simple rooms, including one floor exclusively for female guests. A short walk away from the Ladies' Market and Mong Kok MTR.
Cosmic Guesthouse
12/F, Block A1, A2, F1 and F4, Mirador Mansion, 54–64 Nathan Road, Tsim Sha Tsui, Kowloon
Tel: (852) 2369 6669
This clean guesthouse is much loved by travellers for its large rooms and friendly atmosphere. One-to four-bed rooms have phone and TV, mostly with en suite bathrooms.

HUBEI

Wudang Shan

Xuanwu Hotel
Taihe Dadao
(opposite the bus station)
Tel: (0717) 566 5526
This is Wudang Shan town's nicest hotel, which is centrally located along the main avenue (where the street running from the train station dead-ends, and opposite the bus station). Its affordable double rooms are clean and spacious, while cheaper double rooms are

available in the more modest annexe.

Wuhan (Hankou)

Novotel Xinhua Wuhan
558 Jianshe Dadao
Tel: (027) 8555 1188
www.accorhotels.com/asia
Located near the New World Department Store (and an HSBC branch with a 24-hour ATM), this four-star hotel caters to business travellers and has international-standard rooms and facilities. It is recommended

to book online as you get a better rate.

Best Centurial Hotel
131 Yanjiang Dadao
Tel: (027) 8277 7798
Conveniently located near the corner of Jianghan Lu and the riverfront road, with good-value rooms in a recently renovated Renaissance-style building constructed in 1913.
Dahua Hotel
708 Zhongshan Dadao
Tel: (027) 8533 7333
Situated on one of Wuhan's

main thoroughfares, the Dahua is easy to find and has a wide range of affordable, clean rooms in a stately historic building.
Zhufeng Hotel
23 Qianjin Xilu
Tel: (027) 8586 2561

This centrally located budget hotel offers some of downtown Wuhan's cheapest doubles (with or without bathrooms) and is a reasonably clean option for backpackers.

Wuhan (Wuchang)

$

Marine Hotel
530 Zhongshan Lu
Tel: (027) 8874 0122
A short walk across the

road from Wuchang's eternally busy railway station, the Marine Hotel has decent-value doubles with en suite bathrooms and is a reliable option for travellers arriving or departing by train from Wuchang.

Yichang

$$

Taohualing Hotel
29 Yunji Lu

Tel: (0717) 623 6666
www.taohualing-hotel.com
One of Yichang's best hotels, the Taohualing has spacious double rooms with attached bath that represent great value during the non-peak summer months. A small annexe to the main building offers cheaper double rooms for travellers on a budget. A CITS office with helpful staff is a few doors to the north.

$

Yunji Hotel
8 Yunji Lu
Tel: (0717) 605 7888
A short walk from both the train station and the CITS office on Yunji Lu, this spartan hotel has basic doubles and twins (with or without bathrooms) and is one of Yichang's only budget options during the summer cruise-season crunch.

HUNAN

Changsha

$$$

Sheraton Changsha
478 Furong Zhonglu
Tel: (0731) 488 8888
Located within the Yunda International Plaza, a twin-towered office complex with an attached six-storey shopping mall, this new Sheraton probably ranks as the best hotel in the city.

$$

Crowne Plaza City Centre Changsha
868 Wuyi Dadao
Tel: (0731) 288 8888

Taking residence in a new high-rise building bang in the middle of the city, the Crowne Plaza appeals mainly to business travellers, but represents a comfortable and relatively inexpensive option for tourists too.
Huatian Hotel
300 Jiefang Donglu
Tel: (0731) 444 2888
The first five-star in town has kept itself in reasonable trim, even expanding into a second high-rise. With 700 rooms, this is a big, impersonal option, but the Chinese

management is reasonably good, and dining options are excellent.

Fenghuang

Facilities in this popular but remote tourist town are modest, but great river views are available on minuscule tariffs for those willing to look around. When looking for accommodation, head towards the waterside roads either side of Hongqiao Bridge and ask to inspect rooms before you agree to stay.

Zhangjiajie

$$

Xiangdian International Hotel
Zhangjiajie Forest Park
Tel: (0744) 571 2999
This comfortable four-star, decorated in 2008, lies a few minutes' walk from the southern entrance to Hunan's famous scenic reserve. Rooms are based around a series of peaceful courtyards and the glass-domed roof of the restaurant even has views of the mountain peaks. There's also free internet.

INNER MONGOLIA

Baotou

$

Baotou Hotel
33 Gangtie Dajie
Tel: (0472) 536 5199
www.baotouhotel.com.cn
Located alongside the main traffic artery of Baotou's busy Kundulun district, this sizeable hotel is comfortable, affordable and convenient. It also houses the city's main CITS office. Several good restaurants serving local specialities are located nearby.

Hohhot

$$

Holiday Inn Hohhot
33 Zhongshan Xilu
Tel: (0471) 635 1888

www.holidayinn.com/hihohhot
Located in the heart of Hohhot's shopping district, this business hotel has 198 rooms on nine floors, all with satellite television. In addition to having a well-equipped business centre and health suite, the hotel's Jade Vine Restaurant serves tasty Cantonese, Sichuan and Hunan dishes.
Inner Mongolia Hotel
31 Wulanchabu Xilu
Tel: (0471) 693 8888
www.nmghotel.com
Located on the city's east side, this five-star hotel has 344 rooms with all modern conveniences, including satellite TV and high-speed broadband internet access. Hohhot's main CITS office is on the ground floor.

Inner Mongolia International Hotel
66 Xinhua Dajie
Tel: (0471) 666 6688
www.nmgj.cn
This ultra-modern four-star hotel hovers over the west side of Xinhua Square and has spacious, well-lit rooms and suites with satellite TV and high-speed broadband internet. In addition to offering a choice of restaurants, there are ample health and leisure amenities, including billiards and a chess room.
Xincheng Hotel
40 Hulun Nan Lu
Tel: (0471) 666 1888
www.xincheng-hotel.com.cn
Certainly one of Hohhot's smartest hotels, set off the main road in a leafy compound on the city's

eastern side. Pleasant staff preside over Chinese and Western restaurants, a business centre, swimming pool, health spa, tennis courts, bowling alley and indoor miniature golf course.

$

Zhaojun Hotel
53 Xinhua Dajie
(at corner of Xilin Guole)
Tel: (0471) 666 8888
A high-rise three-star hotel in a convenient location, about a 15-minute walk south of the train station. Its 260 rooms and suites have satellite TV and high-speed internet, and amenities include a swimming pool, health and fitness centre, and business facilities.

JIANGSU

Nanjing

$$$
Jinling Hotel
2 Hanzhong Lu
Tel: (025) 8471 1888
For many years the Jinling was the only Chinese-run five-star hotel in China. It has a prime location in the city centre, and offers guests a full complement of facilities including a swimming pool.

$$
Crowne Plaza Nanjing Hotel and Suites
89 Han Zhong Rd
Tel: (025) 8471 8888
A city-centre location in the heart of Nanjing, with modern amenities including in-room safes, and a nice location atop a 60-storey building that provides good views of the ancient capital.

Jingli Hotel
7 Beijing Xilu
Tel: (025) 8331 0818
This fairly smart hotel offers great value for money in a good location in the centre of the city.

Nanjing Grand Hotel
208 Guangzhou Lu
Tel: (025) 8331 1999
Pretty good Japanese joint-venture hotel with pool and roof garden with great views.

Suzhou

$$$$$
Shangri-La Hotel
168 Ta Yuan Rd
Tel: (0512) 6808 0168
Set in the industrial zone, this is one of the tallest buildings in the province. It offers five-star trimmings.

Sheraton Suzhou Hotel and Towers
259 Xinshi Lu
Tel: (0512) 6510 3388
Suzhou's finest hotel, in the southeast of the city by the Panmen scenic area.

$$$
Hotel One
379 Chang Jiang Rd,
New District, Suzhou
Tel: (512) 6878 1111
www.hotelone.com.cn
A business-friendly boutique hotel that opened in 2007 with postmodern décor, free mobile telephone service, and excellent, English-speaking staff, along with pool, spa, and other five-star features.

$
Suzhou Overseas Chinese Hotel
188 Sanxiang Rd
Tel: (0512) 8888 0008
A clean and affordable hotel between the New District and the Old Town.

JIANGXI

Lu Shan

$$
Lushan Hotel
70 He Xilu, Guling
Tel: (0792) 828 2060
This smart hotel is conveniently located in the heart of Guling and combines traditional Chinese and European style. Regional cuisine is offered in the restaurant, and other amenities include a sauna and beauty salon.

Nanchang

$$
Gloria Plaza Hotel
9 Yanjiang Beilu
Tel: (0791) 673 8855
Part of a well-established Chinese hotel group, the Gloria is a reliable hotel overlooking the Gan Jiang River. It is one of the closest hotels to Nanchang's main tourist sight, the Tengwang Pavilion. Facilities include an indoor pool.

Jiangxi Hotel
368 Bayi Dadao
Tel: (0791) 620 6666
This reasonably priced five-star hotel has been open since 1961 and has a slightly antique feel in its public areas. The central location is great, though the guest rooms are also a little tired.

MACAU

$$$$$
Westin Resort
1918 Entrada de Hac Sá
Coloane Island
Tel: (853) 2887 1111
Peaceful seclusion at the southeast of Coloane Island. Eight-storey resort hotel with 208 spacious rooms each with private outdoor terraces overlooking the beach. Adjacent to an 18-hole golf course.

$$$$
Lisboa
2–4 Avenida de Lisboa
Tel: (853) 2837 7666
Famous for its casino, the Lisboa offers 1,000 grand rooms with ornate décor, 18 restaurants and superb entertainment.

Mandarin Oriental Macau
956–1110 Avenida Amizade
Tel: (853) 2856 7888
Still the finest hotel in Macau for comfort and facilities, including the excellent Mezzaluna restaurant and a casino. The area between the hotel and the Cultural Centre offers a full range of resort-style facilities.

Pousada de São Tiago
Avenida da Republica
Tel: (853) 2837 8111
Macau's most romantic hotel, a Portuguese-style inn built within the walls of the 17th-century Barra fort. The 23 rooms feature dark wood, white linen, chandeliers and marble. Book well ahead.

$$$
Hotel Royal
2–4 Estrada de Vitoria
Tel: (853) 2855 2222
Value-for-money hotel in the city centre; facilities include an indoor swimming pool.

BELOW: the Sheraton Suzhou.

QINGHAI

Xining

$$$

Yinlong Hotel
38 Huanghe Lu
Tel: (0971) 616 6666
www.ylhotel.net
The first international-standard, five-star hotel in Qinghai province, the 21-storey Yinlong is Xining's top hotel, with 316 luxurious suites, several Chinese and Western restaurants, seven conference rooms and a fitness centre and sauna. There are also plenty of opportunities for shopping in the nearby mall.

$$

Qinghai Hotel
20 Huanghe Lu
Tel: (0971) 614 4888
www.qhhotel.com
Once Xining's leading hotel, the four-star Qinghai now plays second fiddle to the Yinlong, although it is still the city's largest, with 395 rooms, all with air conditioning, satellite TV and high-speed internet connections. Restaurants serve Chinese and Western cuisine, and there are business services as well as a gym, sauna and beauty salon. Xining's main CITS office is located next door.

$

Meining Hotel
1 Qilian Lu
Tel: (0971) 819 1288
Conveniently located on the southwest corner of the train station square, the Meining is the best of the city's budget options, with bright, airy rooms at bargain-basement prices. The only caveat is that hot water is usually only available in the evenings.

SHAANXI

Xi'an

$$$$$

Sofitel Xi'an on Renmin Square
319 Dongxin Jie
Tel: (029) 8792 8888
www.sofitel.com/asia
A massive new five-star complex that appears to occupy most of what was once the People's Square, the hotel that locals like to call a "six-star" is itself a sprawling symbol of the rapid pace of change in China. Eclipsing the attractive Russian-built Renmin Hotel to the rear, the Sofitel's steep rates earn guests all manner of luxury. There also are several restaurants and a hopping nightclub on the premises.

$$$$

Howard Johnson Plaza Hotel
18 Huancheng Nanlu, West Section
Tel: (029) 8842 1111
www.hojochina.com
Positioned just southwest of Xi'an's South Gate, this gleaming 19-storey tower constitutes one of the city's finest hotels, offering all the usual five-star amenities and flaunting an unapologetically post-modern interior design scheme.

Hyatt Regency Xi'an
158 Dong Dajie
Tel: (029) 8769 1234
A top-of-the-range hotel in an elegant setting, located alongside busy Dong Dajie in the heart of Xi'an's shopping district. In addition to Western and Asian restaurants, the hotel also has a business centre and health club.

$$$

Bell Tower Hotel Xi'an
110 Nan Dajie
(southwest corner of Bell Tower)
Tel: (029) 8760 0000
www.belltowerhtl.com
Its excellent location within easy walking distance of Xi'an's main tourist sites, friendly service and reasonably priced rooms have made this three-star hotel a perennial favourite. In addition to its business centre and mini-mart, it also houses the city's most useful CITS office.

$$

Hotel Royal Garden
334 Dong Dajie
Tel: (029) 8769 0000
This Japanese-Chinese joint-venture hotel is nicely located and has spotlessly clean rooms, offering good value for the price range. Popular with Asian tour groups.

Xi'an Hotel
58 Chang'an Beilu
Tel: (029) 8766 6666
This ageing Chinese-standard four-star is reasonably priced and conveniently located for excursions to the sights in the south of the city.

$

May First Hotel
351 Dong Dajie
Tel: (029) 8768 1098
A popular, mid-range option, with clean and character-filled rooms in a central location. The ground floor comprises a busy cafeteria-style restaurant, while the hotel reception is on the first floor.

Melody Hotel
86 Xi Dajie
Tel: (029) 8728 8888
A no-frills mid-range hotel opposite the Drum Tower and periodically packed out with Chinese tour groups. The staff are experienced in organising tours of Xi'an's eastern and western circuits.

Shuyuan Youth Hostel
2 Shuncheng Xixiang Nan Jie
Tel: (029) 8728 7721
www.hostelxian.com
One of Xi'an's first full-service hostels – essentially an atmospheric budget hotel popular with backpackers – the Shuyuan is tucked away on a quiet lane about 20 metres (66ft) west of the South Gate, in the shadow of the city wall. The appealing rooms are kept spotlessly clean, but many of the reception staff appear jaded compared to those of some of the newer hostels.

Xiangzimen Youth Hostel
16 Xiangzimen Jie
Tel: (029) 6286 7888
About 20 metres (66ft) west of the Shuyuan Youth Hostel is the Xiangzimen, far and away the city's finest youth hostel and an aesthetically appealing accommodation option that puts many of Xi'an's hotels to shame. Set in a beautifully restored three-storey building, the hostel has a wide range of rooms, from romantic doubles with comfortable kang-style beds to clean dormitories. The attached restaurant serves excellent Chinese and Western food, and the bar stays open as long as there are patrons.

Yan'an

$

Silver Seas International Hotel
Daqiao Jie
Tel: (0911) 213 9999
Looming high above the city centre, Yan'an's newest and nicest hotel is impossible to miss. Doubles are large and clean with comfortable beds and modern bathroom fixtures. From here it is a short walk to the bus stops for the former revolutionary headquarters sites.

PRICE CATEGORIES

Prices for a standard double room in peak season:
$$$$$ = over US$200
$$$$ = US$150–200
$$$ = US$100–150
$$ = US$50–100
$ = below US$50

SHANDONG

Qingdao

$$$$

Shangri-La Hotel
9 Xianggang Zhonglu
Tel: (0532) 8388 3838
Situated in the east of
town, an excellent hotel
offering first-class service
and absolute comfort.

$$

Haitian Hotel
48 Xianggang Xilu

Tel: (0532) 8387 1888
Nice, quiet location
opposite the No. 3 Beach.
Sophia International Hotel
217 Xianggang Donglu
Tel: (0532) 8897 1111
Well-priced four-star hotel
with city and ocean views
near Lao Shan.

$

**Qingdao Old Observatory
Hostel (YHA)**
21 Guanxianger Lu

Tel: (0532) 8282 2626
This clean, well-managed
hostel is located in a
renovated observatory and
offers great views of the city.
Helpful English-speaking
staff and fast internet
access are on hand.

Qufu

$$

Queli Hotel
1 Queli Jie

Tel: (0537) 486 6818
Traditional courtyard
building with modern
facilities, close to most of
Qufu's tourist sites.

$

**Qufu International Youth
Hostel**
Gulou Beijie
Tel: (0537) 5165 9660
Hostel close to all the main
sights, with dormitories,
twin and family rooms.

SHANXI

Datong

$$

Garden Hotel
59 Danan Jie
Tel: (0352) 586 5825
www.huayuanhotel.com.cn
By far Datong's most
stylish hotel, a four-star
with unique rooms
featuring carved pear-
wood reproductions of
Ming- and Qing-dynasty
furniture, internet and TV.
Located just to the north
of the main Bank of China
and the Yonghe Shifu
restaurant.

BELOW: hotel lobby in typically flamboyant style.

$

Feitian Hotel
1 Zhanqian Jie
Tel: (0352) 281 5117
Datong's best budget
accommodation, offering
doubles with bath. Situated
opposite the train station,
to the left as you exit.
Hongqi Grand Hotel
11 Zhanqian Jie
Tel: (0352) 536 6666
www.hongqihotel.com
Convenient mid-range option
opposite the train station
and next to the Tonghe
Restaurant. Its rooms are
clean and comfortable.

Pingyao

$$$

Yunjincheng Hotel
56 Xi Dajie
Tel: (0354) 568 9123
www.pibc.cn
The Yunjincheng – also
known as the Pingyao
International Financier Club
– is the most upmarket
hotel in town, with stylish
rooms surrounding
beautiful courtyards.

$

Harmony Guesthouse
165 Nan Dajie
Tel: (0354) 568 4952
Email: harmonyguesthouse@asia.com
With a fantastic location
on idyllic Nan Dajie, near
the city's South Gate, the
Harmony is the most
peaceful of Pingyao's
many traditional guest-
houses. It offers a variety
of tastefully restored
rooms centred on an
elegant courtyard. The
English-speaking owners
are excellent sources of
information on local
history. Free pick-up from
the train or bus station
with a reservation.
Tianyuankui Hotel
73 Nan Dajie
Tel: (0354) 568 0069
Another nicely located
traditional guesthouse
with a wide range of
reasonably priced rooms
and an attractive court-
yards Also offers free
pick-up from the train or
bus station for those
with reservations.

Yamen Hostel
69 Yamen Jie
Tel: (0354) 568 3539
www.yamenhostel.com
Popular with young
backpackers, the Yamen
has a hip atmosphere,
with a Western-style café,
a book exchange and a
DVD room. Free pick-up
with a reservation.

Taiyuan

$$$

**Longcheng International
Hotel**
2 Bingzhou Beilu
Tel: (0351) 820 8888
A sprawling, five-star hotel
at the south end of Wuyi
Square – about a 15-minute
walk from the train station –
excellent value and close
to a few restaurants.

$$

Sanjin International Hotel
108 Yingze Dajie
Tel: (0351) 882 7777
Near the Longcheng at the
south side of Wuyi Square,
this four-star hotel offers
good facilities for the
price, often offering good
discounts off its rack rates.

$

Changtai Hotel
38 Yingze Dajie
Tel: (0351) 223 0888
Good budget to mid-range
option near the train
station, with clean rooms
and modern furnishings;
the friendly staff can help
tourists book railway
tickets.

SHANGHAI

$$$$$

Grand Hyatt Shanghai
Jin Mao Tower, 88 Century Blvd, Pudong
Tel: (021) 5049 1234
A luxury hotel with several excellent restaurants and great views from the 87th-floor bar.

Hyatt on the Bund
199 Huangpu Rd
Tel: (021) 6393 1234
When it opened in 2007, this riverfront property became the first five-star hotel in the up-and-coming Hongkou district, just north of the Bund.

JW Marriott Shanghai at Tomorrow Square
399 Nanjing W Rd
Tel: (021) 5359 4969
The JW Marriott hotel occupies the top floors of Tomorrow Square tower, a uniquely recognisable landmark that dominates the northwest corner of People's Square.
It is a superb hotel with an excellent location: most of Shanghai and parts of Pudong are within 15 minutes' walk.

Marriott Executive Apartments Union Square
506 Shang Cheng Rd, Pudong
Tel: (021) 2899 8888
This newly opened serviced apartment offers short-term stays. The price is similar to a competing hotel, but guests also get a bedroom, kitchen, living room, and other apartment-style perks.

Portman Ritz-Carlton
Shanghai Centre
1376 Nanjing Rd (W)
Tel: (021) 6279 8888
Shanghai's most popular hotel due to its quality facilities and great location. Situated in the Shanghai Centre, it seems to be in the midst of everything – an American

PRICE CATEGORIES

Prices for a standard double room in peak season:
$$$$$ = over US$200
$$$$ = US$150–200
$$$ = US$100–150
$$ = US$50–100
$ = below US$50

office and housing complex including Western shopping, airline offices, foreign restaurants and theatre. The 600 rooms are comfortable; the gym is the best-equipped in town.

Pudong Shangri-La
33 Fucheng Rd
Tel: (021) 6882 8888
Elegant hotel directly opposite the Bund in Pudong. Friendly staff and good facilities. Popular with business travellers.

St Regis
889 Dong Fang Rd, Pudong
Tel: (021) 5050 4567
An elegant hotel in a corner of Pudong that is growing up rapidly around it. The hotel's personal-ised, 24-hour personal butler service is a key selling point.

Shanghai Hilton
250 Huashan Rd
Tel: (021) 6248 0000
This beautifully appointed five-star 43-storey hotel has some of the best dining in town, top-rate, luxurious accommodation and a great location in the city centre.

Westin Shanghai
88 Henan Rd (M)
Tel: (021) 6335 1888
This fabulous new five-star hotel, situated in the area of the Bund, is the most impressive recent addition to Shanghai's hotel scene. Rooms and bathrooms are lavishly presented, and the restaurants are top-notch.

$$$$

Crowne Plaza Shanghai
400 Panyu Rd
Tel: (021) 6145 8888
Email: hicpsha@uninet.com.cn
This 496-room, four-star hotel on the western side of the French Concession is known for its friendly service, quality facilities and good food outlets.

Hotel Sofitel Hyland
505 Nanjing Rd (E)
Tel: (021) 6351 5888
Located right in the middle of the downtown action, this four-star hotel has 400 tastefully decorated rooms and comprehensive

facilities and is convenient for walking on Nanjing Rd and the Bund.

Jinjiang Hotel
59 Maoming Rd (S)
Tel: (021) 3218 9888
Built before 1935, the Jinjiang's buildings were some of the old French Concession's most popular addresses. Rooms are comfortable, traditionally furnished and homely but not luxurious, with the exception of the Grosvenor House, which offers the most decadent suites at the most decadent prices.

Le Royal Meridien Shanghai
789 Nanjing Rd (E)
Tel: (021) 3318 9999
In late 2006, Le Royal Meridien Shanghai became the newest luxury hotel in Shanghai. It sits atop the Shimao Tower at the northeast corner of People's Park, a location that serves most of Shanghai effortlessly. The 789 bar at the summit of the hotel is one of the best places in Shanghai for a nightcap; the views are superb.

Okura Garden Hotel
58 Maoming Rd (S)
Tel: (021) 6415 1111
This beautiful 33-storey five-star hotel in the old French Concession is managed by the Japanese Okura Group and built atop the former French Club of old Shanghai. The hotel is beautifully appointed but has a rather cold atmosphere.

Ruijin Guesthouse
118 Ruijin No. 2 Rd
Tel: (021) 6472 5222
The Morris Estate, now Ruijin Guesthouse, was built by a Western news-paper magnate during pre-Liberation times. Today, five state-run villas in the old French Concession house 47 rooms amid huge lawns and trees. Chinese and Western cuisine served.

Urbn Hotel
183 Jiaozhou St,
near Beijing Rd (W)

Tel: (021) 5153 4600
www.urbnhotels.com
A stylish little boutique property that opened in 2008 as the first carbon-neutral hotel in China.

$$$

City Hotel
5–7 Shaanxi Rd (S)
Tel: (021) 6255 1133
Three-star hotel with great location, business facilities, Chinese and Western cuisine and a disco.

Hengshan Hotel
534 Hengshan Rd
Tel: (021) 6437 7050
Formerly the Picardie Mansions, this Art Deco-style hotel is located on fashionable Hengshan Rd. Adequate rooms, Western and Chinese restaurants, a business centre and a health club.

Howard Johnson Plaza Hotel
595 Jiu Jiang Rd
Tel: (021) 3313 4888
An international-standard business hotel with reasonable rates and a good location between People's Park and the Bund.

Metropole Hotel
180 Jiangxi Rd (C)
Tel: (021) 6321 3030
Over 60 years old, this hotel has seen better days, but offers reasonably priced rooms close to the Bund, as well as a Chinese restaurant, health club and bar.

Park Hotel
170 Nanjing Rd (W)
Tel: (021) 6327 5225
This historic structure overlooking People's Park was once the tallest hotel in Shanghai. Today the 208-room state-run hotel isn't as glamorous, but the rooms have been tastefully refurbished.

Shanghai JC Mandarin
1225 Nanjing Rd (W)
Tel: (021) 6279 1888
Situated in a perfect location in the heart of the city centre, this five-star 30-storey hotel is Singapore-managed with good Southeast Asian food.

Shanghai Mansions
20 Suzhou Rd (N)
Tel: (021) 6324 6260
This Art Deco building located on the Bund right on Suzhou Creek has simple but comfortable rooms with great views of the river.
Yangtze New World Hotel
2099 Yan'an Rd (W)
Tel: (021) 6275 0000
Email: gm_ynwh@online.sh.cn
This four-star hotel in Hongqiao is especially noted for its excellent Chinese restaurants. The 553 rooms are modern and comfortably furnished, with good facilities.

$$

Pacific Hotel
108 Nanjing Rd
Tel: (021) 6327 6226
This older Shanghai hotel is a faded echo of a bygone era. A gold-plated dome with a clock tower crowns the roof, and the entrance leads into an Art Deco lobby.
Pujiang Hotel
15 Huangpu Rd
Tel: (021) 6324 6388
One of Shanghai's oldest – and cheapest – hotels. It has retained a likeable old-fashioned feel and has an excellent location just north of the Bund.

SICHUAN

Chengdu

$$$$

Amara Hotel
2 Taisheng Bei Lu
Tel: (028) 8692 2233
The 232-room Amara is the perfect escape from Chengdu's bustle, with its Balinese-themed décor that extends all the way to the relaxing swimming pool area. The Sichuan and Cantonese dishes at the Xinya Restaurant are highly rated, while the Café Oriental is one of the few places in Chendu to dine on authentic Singaporean cuisine.
Holiday Inn Chengdu West Century City
198-1 Century City Boulevard
Tel: (028) 8534 8888
This sprawling Holiday Inn, with some 780 guest rooms, is geared more to business travellers than to holidaymakers, but it has a wide range of amenities along with five international-standard restaurants.
Kempinski Hotel Chengdu
42 Renmin Nan Lu, Section 4
Tel: (028) 8526 9999
The 483-room all-modern Kempinski is excellently situated in the heart of Chengdu's dining and nightlife area, five minutes south of the Central Business District by taxi.

$$$–$$$$

Holiday Inn–Crowne Plaza
31 Zong Fu Lu
Tel: (028) 8678 6666
Modern hotel with full facilities, in an excellent location.
Sheraton Chengdu Lido
15 Section 1, Renmin Zhonglu
Tel: (028) 8676 8999
This luxurious and highly impressive hotel offers the most outstanding service and facilities in town, with attractive rooms, three restaurants and indoor pool.

$

Mix Hostel
23 Xinghui Xi Lu, Renjia Wan
Tel: (028) 8322 2271
With its cheery décor and very helpful staff, Mix has become a popular choice for budget travellers in Chengdu. The rooms are extremely well appointed and clean – almost bearing out the hostel's claim that it has three-star standards at backpacker prices.
Traffic Hotel
6 Linjiang Zhong Lu
Tel: (028) 8545 1017
On the JinJiang (Golden River), next to the Xinnan-men intercity bus station, the Traffic Hotel is eco-nomical and enjoys a good reputation among travellers for its cleanliness, helpful staff and overall value. There are 170 rooms, which can be rented individually or by the bed (dormitory-style).

ABOVE: the Westin Hotel, Shanghai.

Emei Shan

$$

Golden Summit Hotel
Jinding Area, Mount Emei
Tel: (0833) 509 8045
The Golden Summit doesn't quite reach the standards of comfort it aspires to, and the service is hit and miss, but nobody can fault its breathtaking setting atop Mount Emei.

$

Teddy Bear Youth Hostel
43 Baoguo Lu, Mount Emei
Tel: (0833) 559 0135
This hostel has superb rooms, excellent food, and is the perfect spot to plan an assault on Sichuan's most famous mountain – the staff can help you plan the trip.

Jiuzhaigou

$$$$

Holiday Inn Jiuzhai Jarpo
Ganhaizi Zhangzha, Jiuzhaigou
Tel: (0837) 778 8888
Another Tibetan-themed hotel, the Holiday Inn offers guests well-appointed rooms with high-speed internet access, and superb valley views from its café, which serves a wide range of international, Chinese and Tibetan dishes.

PRICE CATEGORIES

Prices for a standard double room in peak season:
$$$$$ = over US$200
$$$$ = US$150–200
$$$ = US$100–150
$$ = US$50–100
$ = below US$50

Sheraton Jiuzhaigou Resort
Jiuzhaigou Scenic Spot
Tel: (0837) 773 9988
With the appearance of a Tibetan palace, the Sheraton is the perfect place to relax in comfort in one of the most beautiful

corners of China. The 482 guest rooms combine Tibetan décor with all-modern features, such as high-speed, in-room internet access. The hotel has three restaurants offering both international and Chinese cuisine.

Leshan
$–$$
Jiazhou Hotel (Jiazhou Binguan)
19 Baita Jie
Tel: (0833) 213 9888
Located on the Dadu River west of Dafo, the

Jiazhou offers three-star facilities; rooms are equipped with bathroom and satellite TV. The hotel restaurant has river views, and there is a selection of local restaurants on the street near the hotel. Breakfast included.

TIBET

Lhasa
$
Diren Hotel
Junction of Xuexincun and North Linguo roads
Tel: (0891) 627 8888
In a central location, close to Potala Palace, this modern hotel overlooks the La Lu protected wetlands to the rear.

Kyichu
19 Beijing Zhong Lu
Tel: (0891) 633 8824
A friendly, family-run hotel between the Jokhang Temple and Potala Palace. Rooms are in Tibetan style and have bathrooms. Good restaurant and a garden.
Lhasa Century Hotel
6 Beijing Zhong Lu
Tel: (0891) 681 9111

Hotel close to the Zhe Band Temple and Potala Palace. Rooms have private bathrooms.

Shigatse
$$
Shigatse Hotel
13 Shanghai Zhong Lu
Tel: (0892) 882 2525
Modern city-centre hotel

with ornate, Tibetan-style décor and four restaurants.

Tsetang
$$
Tsetang Hotel
21 Naidong Lu
Tel: (0893) 682 9364
Large hotel with air-conditioned rooms, sports facilities and restaurants.

XINJIANG

Kashi (Kashgar)
$–$$$
Chini Bagh Hotel (Qiniwake Binguan)
144 Seman Lu
Tel: (0998) 282 2103
An unattractive and functional hotel built in the grounds of the old British Consulate; nevertheless the rooms are spacious and comfortable. Rooms in the old wing at the back of the hotel are cheaper than in the new wing. Facilities include internet, sauna and a rather run-down karaoke lounge. The old consulate building has been converted into a restaurant but is often closed. A good Chinese restaurant on the premises serves reasonably priced, tasty fare. Western breakfasts and other dishes are available at John's Information Café in the hotel grounds.
Seman Hotel (Seman Binguan)
337 Seman Lu
Tel: (0998) 258 2150
www.semanhotel.com
The large Seman compound with its numerous buildings sits on the grounds of the old

Russian Consulate. It offers fairly comfortable guest rooms, although some rooms are not great. The old consulate building still stands and has the best rooms. By no means the best lodgings in Kashi, but it does still manage to radiate a little 19th-century "Great Game" ambience.

$–$$
Qianhai Hotel (Qianhai Binguan)
48 Renmin Xilu
Tel: (0998) 282 2922
The Qianhai is a peaceful, relaxed, if somewhat anonymous hotel with a few amenities including two pretty good restaurants. Guest rooms include refrigerators, an absolute must in the hot summer season. Occasionally the service can be a little lacking, but the staff do try their best to make an impact.

Turpan (Tulufan)
$$–$$$
Oasis Hotel (Luzhou Binguan)
41 Qingnian Beilu
Tel: (0995) 852 2491

www.the-silk-road.com
Another member of the Silk Road chain which stretches across much of Gansu and Xinjiang, the Oasis is an attractive hotel with a variety of rooms. A unique feature of the Oasis are the Central Asian-style rooms with their *kang* beds or sleeping platforms originally heated by internal flues, though here they are just for style. Services include an internet café, sauna room and an excellent Muslim restaurant serving Xinjiang specialities.

$–$$
Grand Turpan Hotel (Tulufan Dafandian)
20 Gaochang Lu
Tel: (0995) 855 3668
www.xjturpanhotel.com
The Grand is probably the most comfortable budget option in town, with a new wing added in 2001. The newer guest rooms are large and boast mini-bar, satellite television and internet access. The hotel also houses a karaoke lounge and sauna. The friendly tour desk can arrange all manner of local tours.

Turpan Hotel (Tulufan Binguan)
2 Qingnian Lu
Tel: (0995) 852 2301
This is a long-established budget-traveller favourite, with a choice of private rooms and dormitory beds. It's also well located for the enduringly popular John's Information Café (closed in winter months) offering bicycle rental, local tours and Western breakfasts. There are also Uighur song and dance shows each evening during the summer season.

Ürümqi (Wulumuqi)
$$$$–$$$$$
Hoi Tak Hotel (Haide Jiudian)
1 Dong Feng Lu
Tel: (0991) 232 2828
www.hoitakhotel.com
The city's top accommodation, this centrally positioned 36-storey hotel is a genuine five-star option. The upper floors provide wonderful views of the Tian Shan mountain range surrounding Ürümqi. Oddly, the facilities include an eight-lane bowling alley. Other

amenities include snooker tables, sauna and whirlpool.

$$$–$$$$
Hongfu Hotel (Hongfu Dafandian)
26 Huanghe Lu
Tel: (0991) 588 1588
www.hongfuhotel.com
Mainly a business hotel, however, the high-rise Hongfu does offer some

great bargains on its excellent four- to five-star rooms. Guest rooms are enormous and the bathrooms lavish. Amenities include an indoor swimming pool, spa, sauna and massage rooms.

$$–$$$
Bogda Binguan
10 Guangming Lu

Tel: (0991) 886 3910
Centrally located, not far from both Hongshan Park and People's Park, this reasonably priced three-star option is clean, friendly, and within easy walking distance of City Square and the bustling area around Zhongshan Lu and Minzhu Lu.

$–$$
Xinjiang Fandian
107 Changjiang Lu
Tel: (0991) 585 2511
Situated some way from downtown Ürümqi, this is perhaps the best budget option in the city. It's also well located for nearby Ürümqi train station in the southwest of town. Popular with Pakistani travellers.

YUNNAN

Dali

$$
Asia Star Hotel Dali
South Gate, Dali Old Town
Tel: (0872) 267 9999
Relatively luxurious accommodation is offered here, just 15 minutes' walk from the Old Town. The well-appointed rooms have either mountain or lake views.
Landscape Hotel
96 Yuer Lu, Dali Old Town
Tel: (0872) 266 6188
A refurbished, historic Bai minority house in the heart of the Old City is the setting for this atmospheric boutique hotel. It has a lovely courtyard, which is illuminated with lanterns at night.

$
Dali San Ta Yuan Hotel
San Ta Yuan
Tel: (0872) 267 6521
A picturesque location, relaxing ambience and a degree of charm compensate for the minimal English spoken here and the rather neglected look of the décor and fittings. It's a 10-minute taxi ride into town.
Jade Emu International Hostel
West Gate Village, Dali Old Town
Tel: 1388 723 2726
www.jade-emu.com
This new guesthouse, just a minute's walk from Dali's West Gate, is superb value for money, and has all the amenities anyone could ask for, including a pool table and wireless internet.

Manwan Hotel
Canglang Road, Xiaguan
Tel: (0872) 218 8188
If you don't mind too much about location, this is one of Dali's best options, and popular with tour groups. The Manwan offers relatively luxurious accommodation but is, however, located in Dali's rather dismal sister city, a 20-minute taxi ride away to the south of the Old Town.

Jinghong

$$$
Dai Garden Hotel
8 Nonglin Nanlu, Jinghong
Tel: (0691) 212 3888
Nicely sited beside the Liusha River. Three-star facilities with Dai-influenced architecture; pool and nearby lake and park; Cantonese and Western restaurants, also Yunnanese and Dai cuisine in the Peacock Flavour Restaurant, with Dai dance show.

Kunming

$$
Harbour Plaza Kunming
20 Honghuaqiao
Tel: (0871) 538 6688
Located near Green Lake Park, this impressive five-star 21-storey hotel has well-presented, bright and unfussy rooms, some with the benefit of park views. There are excellent facilities here, including three restaurants, deli, outdoor pool, a children's play area and business services.

Kai Wah Plaza International Hotel
157 Beijing Lu
Tel: (0871) 356 2828
www.kaiwahplaza.com
Formerly the Westin, the Kai Wah is the Harbour Plaza's leading competitor, with similar rates and services, and for golfers the added attraction of an out-of-town 71-par golf course (free shuttle-bus services are provided). A gleaming 525-room tower in the heart of the downtown area (not far from the railway station and around 15 minutes by taxi from the airport), the hotel has five executive floors and a good selection of de luxe and superior rooms, along with "panorama suites" that have good views of a rather less than overwhelming cityscape.
Kunming Green Lake Hotel
6 Cuihu Nanlu
Tel: (0871) 515 8888
In a beautiful lakeside location, this former state guesthouse has been tastefully refurbished to retain much of its character. Though there is some room for improvement, it remains one of Kunming's more charming options.

$
Camellia Hotel
154 Dongfeng Donglu
Tel: (0871) 316 3000
Moderately priced, quiet yet well-located hotel close to the heart of the city. Rooms are basic, but clean and comfortable, and there is also

dormitory accommodation for impecunious backpackers. Most of the staff speak at least some English and are very helpful.
Kunming Hotel
145 Dongfeng Donglu
Tel: (0871) 316 2063
Long-established, recently refurbished hotel in a good location, close to the station. Staff are used to dealing with foreign visitors.

Lijiang

$$$$$
Banyan Tree Lijiang
Yuerong Lu, Shuhe, Gucheng District
Tel: (0888) 533 1111
www.banyantree.com
Five-star luxury comes to northwestern Yunnan. Situated north of Lijiang on the way to Shuhe village, this resort property has 55 individual pavilions, a spa, swimming pool and a view of the Jade Dagon Snow Mountain. Tasteful, immaculate, exclusive.

$$
Grand Lijiang Hotel
Xinyi Jie
Tel: (0888) 512 0888
Well located next to the waterwheel square on the

ABOVE: soothing simplicity at the Banyan Tree, Lijiang.

way to the Black Dagon Pool, the four-star Grand Lijiang is a modern, well-equipped hotel with fine views across to the mountains and the old town. Good service and a pleasant restaurant beside the stream.

Jian Nan Chun Hotel
8 Guang Yi Jie
Tel: (0888) 510 2222
Email: hotel@jnchotel.com
www.jnchotel.com

A four-star hotel located in the centre of the Old Town. Favoured by visiting dignitaries, it is built in traditional Chinese style, although the rooms are decidedly modern.

$
First Bend Inn
43 Mishi Xiang, Xinyi Jie
Tel: (0888) 518 1688
The First Bend Inn is a budget hotel with character

in the centre of Lijiang's Old Town. The rooms are comfortable, there's a lovely courtyard and helpful, informative staff, making it particularly good value.

Tengchong

$
Tengchong Hotel
12 Guanting Xiang
Tel: (0875) 512 5634

The Tengchong is a relatively high-standard Chinese *bingguan*, or guesthouse, that offers substantial discounts on its already reasonable room rates on request. Rooms are on par with three-star hotels elsewhere in China, and the friendly staff do their best to accommodate foreign visitors – who have become more frequent in recent years.

ZHEJIANG

Hangzhou

$$$$$
Fuchun Resort
Fuyang Section,
Hangfu Yanjiang Rd
Tel: (0571) 6346 1111
www.fuchunresort.com
A beautifully designed, very upscale resort with a serene ambiance, excellent Hangzhou cuisine, an adjoining 18-hole golf course, and one of the most memorable swimming pools in Asia. Accommodation choices include hilltop villas.
Sofitel Westlake Hangzhou
333 West Lake Ave
Tel: (0571) 8707 5858

A spotless new five-star located a stone's throw from the eastern shores of the famous lake, not far from the Central Business District.

$$
Holiday Inn Hangzhou
289 N Jianguo Rd
Tel: (0571) 8527 1188
A downtown hotel with pool, workout room and other amenities, located 2km (1 mile) from West Lake, and about 1km (²⁄₃ mile) from the Hangzhou Silk Market.
Lakeview Hotel
2 Huancheng Rd (W)
Tel: (0571) 8707 8888

A Chinese-managed hotel with a downtown location two blocks from West Lake, and standard three-star amenities including swimming pool. As with all Chinese hotels, be sure to ask for a non-smoking room if you don't smoke.

Moganshan

$$$–$$$$$
Naked Retreats
Shanghai address:
Lane 248 Taikang Rd
Shanghai tel: (021) 5465 9577
www.nakedretreats.cn
The "Naked" group offers a selection of eight lodges on Moganshan. They come

in different sizes and locations, and all have maid service and kitchens. Prices vary, but none of them are a bargain.

Putuo Shan

$$$
Putuoshan Hotel
93 Meicen Lu
Tel: (0580) 609 2828
Email: htpts@mail.zsptt.zj.cn
Set in attractive and spacious grounds a short walk southwest of Puji Chansi, all rooms at this modern four-star hotel are equipped with air con and satellite TV. The hotel has a medical clinic and shops.

S HOPPING

WHAT TO BUY AND WHERE TO BUY IT

INTRODUCTION

Mainland China today is awash with quality goods, and they can be found in any major city in any of the countless department stores that litter the downtown areas. Typically "Chinese" goods such as silk, jade and porcelain are of a better quality in Hong Kong than elsewhere in China, but not necessarily cheaper. Away from the sleek, air-conditioned shopping malls, it is worth looking in the smaller towns or in the places where ethnic minorities live for local products, which will be difficult to find anywhere else in China. The most usual articles on offer are craft objects for everyday use or specially worked or embroidered garments.

Shoppers are also tempted by low prices for everyday items and clothing. Be warned that low prices are often matched by low quality, and that pirated DVDs and fake "designer" labels are on sale in many places.

Bargaining

Generally speaking, bargaining is acceptable (and expected) in free markets and souvenir stands but not in state-operated stores and modern shops. In busy tourist areas, foreigners are constantly overcharged for both goods and services, so haggling is an essential strategy for buying goods at a reasonable price.

It's advisable to check prices first at state-operated stores, such as the Friendship Store, before buying a similar item in a hotel shop or on the free market. And in the free market, bargain, and be stubborn – but friendly – if interested in an item. Avoid drawn-out haggling just for the sport.

Bargaining usually begins with the shopkeeper suggesting a price and the buyer responding with a lower one. In Beijing, the starting price is generally 30 to 50 percent higher than the price that shopkeepers will eventually accept, so be persistent. Look for missing buttons, stains and other flaws, keep smiling, and don't be afraid to walk away if you find the price unacceptable.

In Hong Kong the once common practice of bargaining for goods is a dying art. Price differences are usually so marginal that it is hardly worth it, and it is a complete waste of time in department stores and modern shops. Elsewhere, shopkeepers who are not used to bargaining will probably react rather impatiently to your efforts. However, you might get a better deal by paying in cash rather than a credit card. Small, family-run shops might be more amenable to bargaining. In markets you should certainly attempt to use your bargaining skills, but even here it is highly unlikely that you'll be able to reduce the asking price by more than about 10 to 20 percent.

WHERE TO SHOP

Department stores: In every town there is a department store selling products for everyday use, from toothpaste to bicycles. However, the quality of clothing fabric (synthetic), the cut and the sizes are usually disappointing.

Some big department stores are state-owned institutions, but there are many privately owned small shops where you will often find products from Hong Kong, including

Import and Export

Antiques that date from before 1795 may not be legally exported. Those that can be taken out of China must carry a small red seal or have one affixed by the Cultural Relics Bureau. All other antiques are the property of the Peoples' Republic of China and, without the seal, will be confiscated without compensation. Beware of fakes: factories producing "antiques" (and the seal) are thriving.

Foreign currency can be freely imported and exported, the only restriction being that you may not export more foreign currency than you imported, except with a special permit.

You should not export, or even buy in the first place, objects made from wild animals, especially ivory. The majority of Western countries ban the import of ivory objects, and will confiscate them without compensation.

higher-quality clothing. There are many luxury shopping malls in China, where you can find designer labels and a wealth of choice. Oriental Plaza in Beijing is a vast, glittering mall where consumers can spend the entire day shopping. Shoppers will likewise be spoilt for choice in the large cities of Shanghai, Guangzhou and Shenzhen.

Friendship Stores: Though something of an anomaly in the frenetic modern Chinese market-place, state-run Friendship Stores still offer a reasonable selection of wares for export. Visitors will probably be mainly interested in their silk fabrics, crafts, traditional paper cuttings (cheap and easy to pack), jade carvings, kites and chopsticks, and the generally good range of books and magazines. Some large Friendship Stores have a delivery section that will send purchases to your home country. Shops and department stores generally open around 9am and close as late as 10pm.

Markets: Food items such as fruit, vegetables, fish and meat are sold at markets. In the free markets, where prices are more flexible, and sometimes higher (offsetting better quality and availability), you may also find wicker baskets, metalwork and clothes, and even tailors. Well worth looking out for are antiques/curio markets where you can sift through a cornucopia of memorabilia and knick-knacks. Perhaps the best-known of these is Panjiayuan Market in Beijing (see below), but many other cities and towns (eg Tianjin) have their own antiques markets. Be on your guard against being fleeced.

Beijing

Beijing is one of the few cities in China where large-sized clothes and shoes are available. English-speaking tailors also provide services at very competitive prices, though the most reliable ones are to be found away from tourist areas. The capital's contemporary art scene is currently one of the most dynamic and exciting in the world. Successful artists' works are "reproduced" days after they appear in public or print, which may provide a bargain-priced wall decoration, provided you are aware of what you are buying.

Speciality Markets

Panjiayuan Market, in the southeast of town off Dongsanhuan Nanlu (Sat–Sun dawn–mid-afternoon), is a hectic sprawl of "antiques" (mostly reproductions) and memorabilia. It is rather distant from the city centre, but is the best place to go for a large number of vendors in one place – if you don't get the price you want just move on to the next seller. Permanent stores sell art, calligraphy and furniture during the week.

About half a kilometre (⅓ mile) north of Panjiayuan is the **Chaowai Market** (daily 10am–6pm), a jumble of reasonably priced classical-style furniture and curios over four floors.

Hongqiao Market, on Hongqiao Lu (daily 8.30am–7pm), has the best collection of antique clocks, Mao statues and the three floors of pearl stalls that give it the nickname "Pearl Market".

For traditional Chinese paintings, calligraphy supplies and rare books, poke around at **Liulichang** (daily 9am–5.30pm), just west of Qianmen district.

If your thirst for Chinese tea remains unquenched, then a visit to **Maliandao** (daily 8.30am–6pm) is an absolute must. Just south of Beijing West railway station, the hundreds of stalls on this dedicated tea street stretch into the distance with vendors from around China offering you a seat and a highly ritualised sample of their wares. Teapots, caddies and other paraphernalia can be picked up at wholesale prices.

Yashow Market (daily 9.30am–9pm) in Sanlitun is a Beijing institution. Larger-sized clothing can be found along with bags, shoes, tableware, MP3 players and gifts. Determined bargaining is essential for the best prices.

Shopping Areas

Wangfujing Dajie is Beijing's premier shopping street, a part-pedestrianised gala of luxury shopping malls, restaurants, food streets and shops. At 200 Wangfujing Dajie, check out the **Beijing Arts & Crafts Central Store** for jade, jewellery, lacquer and silks. Dongdan Beidajie and Xidan Dajie, perpendicular to Chang'an Jie, are also popular shopping streets.

Further north, along the west side of Wangfujing, is the **Foreign Languages Bookstore**. The first floor has a wide range of books on China in English, and perhaps the city's best selection of imported English novels and children's books. The upper floors have everything from Chinese art to computers and a music store.

One-stop Shopping

Capitalism's answer for one-stop shoppers is the glossy joint-venture

Birds and Flowers

Situated just southeast of Tiantan is the **Yuting Flower and Bird Market**, which is open 7am–6pm. Come here for birds and animals of every description and a plethora of other items. It's probably a good idea to tie this in with a visit to Tiantan.

shopping centres that draw China's nouveaux riches, as well as tourists and mobs of window-shoppers. On the southeast corner of Wangfujing Dajie is the huge and glitzy **Oriental Plaza** retail complex, the last word on shopping in Beijing. You can spend the whole day here, perusing the shops and eating at its numerous restaurants.

The **Youyi Shopping City** in the Beijing Lufthansa Centre (52 Liangmaqiao Lu, Chaoyang District; daily 9am–9pm) carries products with a broad price range. The city's best silk selection – sold by the yard – is offered at reasonable prices.

Joy City is Xidan's newest and most impressive mall. The 13-storey illuminated glass building contains fashion and gifts from around Asia, international brands and numerous snack shops and restaurants.

Fujian

The number-one souvenir in Fujian is the local tea, with masses of outlets to choose from. **Ten Fu Tea**'s flagship store in **Fuzhou** is a good place to buy, with lots of nice packages.

Guangdong

Guangzhou

Don't expect the glitz and variety of goods available in Hong Kong. Still, Guangzhou offers both variety and

good value. The main shopping areas in Guangzhou are Zhongshan Wulu, Beijing Lu, Renmin Nanlu, Zhongshan Silu and Xiajiu Lu-Shangjiu Lu. The main open-air market is at Qingping Lu, near Shamian Island.

There are several large **department stores** and **wholesale markets** in Guangzhou with a wide array of merchandise, at prices lower than in Hong Kong. **Teemall** (Tianhe Cheng) at 208 Tianhe Lu, just opposite the Tianhe Sports Centre (Tianhe Tiyu Zhongxin), is one of the most popular malls in town, located in the smart, trendy new district of Tianhe. **China Plaza** (Zhonghua Guangchang), at 33 Zhongshan San Lu, is a more centrally located equivalent.

The pedestrianised streets of **Xiajiu Lu** and **Shangjiu Lu**, even further west, have more organic charm thanks to the traditional 1920s architecture which envelops a range of young, funky shops. Just north of here, around **Changshou Lu**, are alleys filled with jade stalls. South is the once notorious **Qingping Market**, still the best place in town to pick up Chinese herbs and medicines.

The government-owned **Guangzhou Friendship Store**, at 369 Huanshi Donglu, opposite the Garden Hotel, offer a wide selection of goods, though you'll find cheaper merchandise elsewhere.

Antiques
The largest private market for antiques is the **Kangwang Lu (formerly Daihe Lu) Market**, which sprawls over several lanes. There are smaller antique markets nearby, most notably at the **Xiguan Antique City** on Lizhiwan Lu, just north of Changshou Lu, a few blocks west.

Despite the pitfalls, there is still much to buy: *kam muk* (gilded sculptured wood panels), vintage watches, tiny embroidered shoes for Chinese women with bound feet, and a wide range of beautiful Shiwan porcelain from nearby **Foshan**.

For serious collectors, antiques with authentic red-wax seals authorising export can be bought from government shops. Try the **Guangzhou Antique Shop** (146/162/170 Wende Beilu, tel: 8333 0175, fax: 8335 0085) for *kam muk*, calligraphy works, jewellery boxes, paintings, porcelain and silver.

Birdcages
The Chinese love songbirds and show them off in splendidly decorated cages at public parks. Antique cages cost from Rmb 100–700; newer ones can be bought at the **Bird Market**, located at the Dongfeng Lu entrance of Liuhua Park.

Clothing and textiles
Of special interest to visitors is Guangdong black-mud silk, which is painstakingly handmade and dyed as many as 30 times, using the red extract of the gambier root and the iron-rich river mud from the Pearl River. The material stays cool and dry in humid weather. The silk is available from the **Xin Da Xin** department store, at the corner of Beijing Lu and Zhongshan Wulu.

Guangdong province is a major production centre for off-the-peg clothes and shoes. **Haizhu Square** (Haizhu Guangchang), on the north bank of the Pearl River (Zhu Jiang) in western Guangzhou, is arguably the top spot in town to take advantage. This has long been a popular place to pick up clothes and accessories, and is peppered with large wholesale markets, selling everyting from shoes to curtain fabric. Close by is Guangzhou's most famous, though not necessarily best, shopping street – **Beijing Lu**.

Jade
Be wary about buying from open-air private markets, as there are plenty of imitations around. Buy from established shops like **Jade Shop** (12–14 Zhongshan Wulu), **Baoli Yuqi Hang** (220 Zhongshan Silu), **Guangzhou Antique Shop** (696 Wende Lu) and the jewellery shops of the China, Garden and White Swan hotels.

Mao memorabilia
The industry in Mao memorabilia continues to supply an enthusiastic market with a range of kitsch items in dubious taste. The **Kangwang Lu** antique market has a reasonable variety of Mao artefacts, while the Friendship Stores sell diamond-studded medals. For badges, the **stamp market** in People's Park has the best pieces. Choose with care, however, as prices can be steep.

Paper cuts
The **Renshou Temple** in Foshan, previously famous for its paper cuts of scenes from the Cultural Revolution, has remained the major production centre for this delicate craft. However, its production nowadays focuses on farm scenes.

Pearls
Most of the pearls on sale in Guangzhou are saltwater southern pearls called *hepu*, cultured in silver-lipped oysters. The largest of these lustrous pearls can have a diameter of 1.2–1.6cm (½–⅔in). Recommended shops: **Guangzhou Gold and Silver Jewellery Centre** (109 Dade Lu) and **Sun Moon Hall** (Equatorial Hotel, Renmin Beilu).

Seals (chops)
You can have your name engraved in Chinese characters on a seal, called a chop in colonial English, at the basement floor of the **White Swan Hotel**. The material used can be hard wood, soapstone, crystal or agate. The shop will also sell you the special red ink *(hong yau)* that goes with the seal. Do not buy from side-street sellers, as the seals they sell are made of bakelite and resin imitations of stone.

Shenzhen
This city is seen by many in Hong Kong as one giant shopping suburb. There is a wide variety of merchandise at prices much lower than you will ever find in Hong Kong, Europe or North America, but there aren't as many jaw-dropping discounts these days, as prices rise to reflect the new affluence of China's middle classes.

Lo Wu Commercial City, immediately on the right as you emerge from customs, is the place everyone heads to, a vast shopping mall packed with electronics, jewellery, clothes and all kinds of chinoiserie. Shops are generally open daily 10am–8 or 9pm. Most people venture no further, but there are also some great bargains to be had in the main shopping area of **Dongmen** in the centre of Shenzhen (take Line 1 of the subway to Laojie, and head in the direction of Jiefang Lu). You'll also find the best tailors here, clustered together in **Bu Cheng**.

Whatever you are buying, remember to bargain hard!

Guangxi

Caligraphy and classic landscape paintings are popular items, as well as the traditional crafts and fashions of the dominant Zhuang ethnic group. Yangshuo can be a good place to buy clothing and some unusual souvenirs.

Guizhou

In Guiyang, Qiancuihang, located on Beijing Lu in front of the Guishou Park Hotel, has good-quality batik, paintings, masks and minority handicrafts. It's a large shop catering to tourists, but is well worth a visit. Miao women occasionally sell embroidered textiles in a courtyard near the CITS office in Kaili. There are also a couple of shops selling minority wares near the entrance. Miao traders also operate throughout the region, although you may need to go to their home to view their merchandise. Machine-produced items will obviously be cheaper than those that have been meticulously sewn. Check the stitching to reveal the production method used. Beware of buying silver jewellery on the street, since much of it is fake.

Hainan Island

Tea is a popular choice in Hainan, as are pearls. High-quality jewellery can be found fairly easily, especially around Sanya. Hawkers sell pearl necklaces cheaply around Dadonghai. Also, check out the food products at Sanya's **No. 1 Market** (Diyi Shichang) centred around Xinjian Jie, east of Jiefang Lu.

Hong Kong

Hong Kong people are insatiable shoppers, and the territory is a shopper's paradise, although no longer the bargain basement it once was. Venues range from colourful night markets and pungent emporiums to glitzy malls.

Prime shopping areas are Central, Admiralty and Causeway Bay on Hong Kong Island, and Tsim Sha Tsui in Kowloon. Shopping hours vary, but the good news is that shopping basically goes on until late seven days a week. Even during public holidays, shops are almost always open – the one exception being during Chinese New Year in January/February. As a guide, shops in Central close earlier, around 7pm, but the other main areas tend to stay open until 10pm, sometimes later.

Malls

Hong Kong has some of the world's most glitzy and glamorous shopping malls. The best-known are **The Landmark** and the **IFC Mall** in Central, **Pacific Place** in Admiralty, **Times Square** in Causeway Bay, and **City Plaza** in Taikoo Shing. In Kowloon the linked **Ocean Terminal** and **Harbour Centre** complexes plus **Festival Walk** in Kowloon Tong will keep you busy.

Department Stores

Upmarket stores such as **Lane Crawford** in the IFC building in Central, or Japanese store **Seibu**, in Pacific Place, are the local equivalents of Bloomingdale's

HKTB Shopping Guide

Before browsing, pick up a copy of the HKTB's official shopping guide – available at the HKTB Information Centres in Central and Tsim Sha Tsui – an invaluable free booklet with many useful tips. An important thing to note about shopping in Hong Kong is that goods purchased are not normally returnable or refundable; don't make expensive purchases if uncertain.

Tourists have clout in Hong Kong: if you run into significant problems with merchants that you cannot resolve, call the HKTB's multilingual hotline: 852-2807 6177. If the offending shop is an HKTB member, the tourist board will try to resolve the matter.

or Harrods – classy and very expensive. For more down-to-earth prices, try long-established local department stores like **Sincere** and **Wing On** (211 Des Voeux Road, Central), where local people shop.

Also extremely popular are the Japanese department stores **Mitsukoshi** and **Sogo** in Causeway Bay. Marks & Spencer, a little piece of England in the tropics, has several stores in Central, Kowloon and Causeway Bay, though prices are higher than in the UK stores.

However, it's the mainland Chinese department stores that are most worthy of exploration, even if you don't intend to buy. **Chinese Arts & Crafts** is the most upmarket of all and concentrates on high-quality handicrafts, antiques, clothing and jewellery. **Yue Hwa** (301–309 Nathan Road, Kowloon and Des Voeux Road, Central) and **Chung Kiu Chinese Products** emporiums stock arts and crafts, and a whole range of consumer items produced across the border. **PRC department stores** sell Chinese foodstuffs as well as inexpensive household items, ceramics and handicrafts. And finally, don't miss out on 1930s-style **Shanghai Tang** department store (Pedder Building, Central), which has retro-nostalgia Chinese fashions and gift items.

Markets

Hong Kong has a number of lively and interesting shopping markets. **Cat Street**, off Hollywood Road in Central, is a flea market offering inexpensive trinkets and bric-a-brac. **Stanley Market**, on the south side of the island and open daily 10am–7pm, sells clothes, linen and tableware. **Temple Street**, Hong

Kong's most popular night market, runs from Jordan to Yau Ma Tei in Kowloon. Cheap clothing, watches, pens, sunglasses, CDs, electronic gadgets and luggage abound in its colourfully lit stalls. There are also Chinese fortune-tellers and Chinese opera singers practising. It's open in the daytime too, but only really gets going after 7pm. The so-called **Ladies' Market** on Tung Choi Street in Mong Kok is less tourist-oriented than Temple Street. Specialities include local women's fashions, jewellery and accessories. Open 3–10pm. Jewellery fans may like to check out the **Jade Market**, located under the flyover near Kansau Street in Yau Ma Tei. Open daily 10am–6pm.

What to Buy
Art, antiques and crafts

Hong Kong is a centre for Asian arts and crafts, with some superb antique furniture, ceramics, sculptures, textiles and traditional paintings from China, Tibet, Japan and Southeast Asia. More affordable are modern Chinese and Vietnamese paintings, Chinese-style rugs, reproduction Korean chests, "antique" Chinese furniture and ceramics, Thai Buddha figurines, Balinese woodwork, Chinese folk paintings and other ethnic handicrafts.

The greatest concentration of antique and carpet dealers is along Hollywood Road in Central, but there are also a number of top-quality shops in Pacific Place, and at Harbour City in Kowloon. Fine-art galleries are clustered around Hollywood Road, but you may want to check exhibition listings in the newspapers, the free *HK*, *BC* and *Time Out* magazines.

The **Chinese Arts & Crafts** and other **PRC department stores** are great places to look for Chinese arts and crafts. The **Hong Kong Museum of Art** shop is a good place to pick up smaller gift items and cards.

Wan Chai is the best place to try for customised rattan and reproduction rosewood furniture, but **Luk's Furniture Warehouse** in Aberdeen also has a very good range of reproduction "antiques" and Korean chests.

Your best bet for Chinese ceramics is a local factory like **Wah Tung China** in Aberdeen (which also has a small outlet on Hollywood Road) and **Overjoy Porcelain Factory** in Kwai Chung, New Territories.

Cameras and electronic goods

If you are prepared to shop around, these are still good buys in Hong

Custom Tailors

Having your own suit made to measure is still a popular luxury for visitors to Hong Kong. The territory has some of the legendary tailors of Old Shanghai, who have passed on their skills to the next generation. The speed and quality of craftsmanship and the range of fabrics here are all excellent. Such personal tailoring is no longer a massive bargain, but still worthwhile. A few places can produce your suit within 24 hours, but you won't usually see the best-quality results. Expect your tailor to take about a week if you want a high-quality garment. There are a lot of tailors in Tsim Sha Tsui and a few in Wan Chai and Causeway Bay. The Shanghai Tang store in Central also offers a Shanghainese tailoring service for either Western- or Mandarin-style suits.

Kong. Electronics shops cluster in **Causeway Bay** and **Tsim Sha Tsui**, especially along Nathan, Peking, Mody and Carnarvon roads. Merchants can spot a sucker at 50 paces, so bargain hard; the fixed-price retail chains **Broadway Photo Supply** and **Fortress** are reliable alternatives. When buying electronic goods, remember to check for correct voltage, adaptors etc.

Computers
Hong Kong is a major exporter of computers, components and accessories, and you will find the most up-to-date models at great prices. There are a number of arcades devoted solely to selling computers and accessories – most notably in the **Sham Shui Po** district of Kowloon. If you are buying a computer, make sure that the keyboard is in English and not English with Cantonese symbols.

Fashion
All the big names are here – Armani, Chanel, DKNY, Issey Miyake and dozens more. They are most easily located in the classier corridors of **The Landmark**, **Pacific Place**, **Prince's Building** and **Times Square Galleria** in Central District and Admiralty. The top-flight hotel arcades – **New World Centre** and **Harbour City complex** – are along Canton Road in Tsim Sha Tsui. Don't expect lower prices than in Europe or US.
   Inspiring work by up-and-coming Hong Kong designers can be found in the **TDC's Design Gallery** (Level 1, Convention Plaza, Harbour Road,

Wan Chai). More traditional are the quintessential Chinese *cheongsam*, Mao suits and Tang jackets available off-the-peg, or custom-tailored, from **Shanghai Tang** (Pedder Building; tel: 2525 7333).
   For real bargains, head for the **street markets** and factory outlets in Wan Chai, Tsim Sha Tsui and Mong Kok. For a fraction of the price back home, these sell over-runs and slightly damaged "seconds" of locally manufactured clothes designed for the export market. As a general guide, bargain-priced womenswear, menswear, T-shirts and jeans, and children's clothes can be found in the **factory outlets** along Haiphong and Granville roads in Tsim Sha Tsui, **Spring Garden Lane** and **Johnston Road** in Wan Chai, **Stanley Market** on the south of Hong Kong Island, **Jardine's Bazaar** in Causeway Bay, and the **Ladies' Market** and **Fa Yuen Street** in Mong Kok.

Jewellery, watches and gemstones
Hong Kong is a magnet for precious stones from all over Asia and pearls from the Pacific Rim, and there is a wide range of jewellery available in retail outlets. Because Hong Kong is a free port and there is no tax on the import or export of precious metals, prices are competitive.
   There are gold and jewellery **factory outlets in Hung Hom** but better bargains can be found in the shops along **Queen's Road Central**. **Chinese Arts & Crafts** and other **PRC department stores** offer good deals on gold and jade, and these should come with a written guarantee.
   Popular jewellery items include jade (though you should avoid buying expensive items without expert advice) and bright-yellow 24-ct gold, called *chuk kam* in Cantonese. Jewellery stores specialising in *chuk kam* are usually very crowded, and the atmosphere resembles a betting shop more than a shop. These items are sold by the weight of the gold only, so you pay no premium for the design.
   Another good buy in Hong Kong is pearls, which come in all shapes, sizes

and colours. The practice of bargaining is much less common in jewellery stores these days, but you can try your luck by asking for a discount.

Jiangxi
Jiangxi's famous porcelain is available all over the province, but for the best deals Jingdezhen, China's porcelain capital, is the place to buy. The city centre is full of shops, but the best selection and best prices can be found at the **Guomao Shichang** (International Trade Market) next to Jiefang Lu.

Macau
Macau is good for Chinese antiques and artefacts, and an excellent place to buy well-crafted Asian furniture in wood or wicker. Many Hong Kong expats buy their furniture here and have it delivered to Hong Kong. Shipping prices may be lower than expected. Many antiques stores are clustered in **Rua de São Paulo**, the busy lane which leads up to the facade of São Paulo. You are free to bargain hard here. Otherwise, Macau is rarely thought of as a shopping mart, except for its magnificently priced wines, brandies and ports, which are restricted upon return to Hong Kong. Though it is a duty-free port like Hong Kong, the array of goods available is not nearly as extensive and some items are more expensive.

Shanghai
Shanghai is one of China's commercial capitals, and the number of both foreign and domestic goods available to the consumer has skyrocketed in the past few years. The best streets to shop on are Nanjing Rd and Huaihai Rd. Pedestrianised Nanjing Rd is usually mobbed by local and out-of-town Chinese shoppers at weekends, while Huaihai Rd offers a more refined experience that attracts foreigners and Shanghai's nouveaux riches.

Department Stores and Malls
Shanghai is full of Western-style malls and departments stores selling everything from local goods to foreign-name brands.
   The **Shanghai No. 1 Department Store**, 800–830 Nanjing Rd (E), tel: 6322 3344, is the largest and most famous state-owned store in town, and specialises in domestic goods. **Plaza 66**, 1266 Nanjing Rd (W), tel: 3210 4566, is an exclusive mall offering top-brand names, while **Westgate Mall**, 1038 Nanjing Rd (W), tel: 6272 1111, has an

excellent range of shops. In Xujiahui, **Grand Gateway** (tel: 6407 0111) is a vast department store with an excellent range of sporting goods and loads of restaurants.

Middle- to high-level shopping can be found at the **Hongqiao Parkson** on Zunyi Rd. Meanwhile, in Pudong, the giant **SuperBrand Mall**, 168 Lu Ji Zu Rd, in the shadow of the Pearl Oriental Tower, is moving steadily upscale, and is now one of the city's prime malls. Some of its indoor-outdoor restaurants offer unbeatable views of the Bund, just across the river. Otherwise you can find almost all you may need from shoes to food and toys on the multiple floors of Carrefour, Shuisheng Rd, Gubei.

Meanwhile, American electronics retailer **Best Buy** has a huge outlet in downtown Xujiahui, bringing fixed prices, English-speaking staff, great bargains, and clean, well-lit interiors to the city's often chaotic retail experience.

What to Buy

Arts and crafts
The consistently reliable state-owned department store, the **Friendship Store**, at 1188 Changshou Rd, sells Chinese arts and crafts and silk.

You can watch Shanghai artisans at work at the **Arts and Crafts Research Institute** (also known as Shanghai Arts and Crafts Museum), 79 Fenyang Rd.

Porcelain and other wares can be purchased at the Shanghai **Jingdezhen Porcelain Store**, 212 Shanxi North Road, while tea and Yixing pots are plentiful at the **Shanghai Huangshan Tea Company**, 605 Huaihai Rd (C).

Clothing and fabrics
Custom tailor shops abound in Shanghai. One of the very best – with top-drawer prices to match – is **Phonepha Custom Tailor**, at 7 Dong Ping Road, tel: 5465 2468. The proprietor, Guillaume Rousseau, is a craftsman with European tastes who offers sound fashion advice to go with the suits and shirts. Equally fine threads can be form-fitted at **Dave's Custom Tailoring**, 6 Lane 288, Wuyuan Road, tel: 5404 0001.

At the other end of the spectrum – the cheap-and-cheerful end – is the new **South Bund Fabric Market**, at 399 Lu Jia Bang Road. This vast warren of stalls is for the adventurous, people who can venture into the hawker stalls and emerge with inexpensive custom-made suits and jackets and dresses. The cloth is from China, not Europe, but is of reasonable quality, and tailors stand ready with scissors and thread once

you've made your choice. Garments can be ready in 24 hours.

Shop for silk at the **Golden Dragon Silk and Wool Company**, 145 Maoming Rd, which has the widest selection in town.

Sichuan
Both Chengdu and Chongqing are modern cities that offer a wealth of shopping opportunities. For quality goods and any essentials, the **Pacific Department Store**, 12 Zongfu Lu, Jinjiang District, and **Isetan**, Lido Square, Chunxi Lu, in Chengdu are the best options. For traditional souvenirs, the alleys around Chengdu's **Wuhou Temple** have some great buys.

Silk Road
Kashi
Laocheng Shichang (Old Town Bazaar), on Jiefang Beilu and the surrounding streets, offers a multitude of shopping opportunities, with Uighur-style carpets, shoes, clothing, spices, herbs and many, many other items. Heavy competition among traders means you ought to be able to find some bargains. Xingqitian Shichang (Sunday Market), across the river from central Kashgar, off Aizirete Lu, is the town's main attraction, a huge market selling everything from clothing, knives, household goods and food to a variety of domestic animals.

Turpan
Turpan Shichang (Turpan Bazaar), on Laocheng Lu, is a modest affair in comparison with other larger cities in the Xinjiang region. It's mainly a Uighur market selling an array of fancy hats and clothing as well as silk. Most of the market, however, is turned over to fresh produce, with a variety of exotic fruits, dried fruits, spices and nuts.

Ürümqi
Erdaoqiao Shichang (Erdaoqiao Market), between Xinhua Nanlu and Jiefang Lu is Ürümqi's largest bazaar. It's mainly a local place, so prices are competitive. Look out for traditional handicrafts, hats, clothing and silk. Fine-quality silk carpets from Xinjiang and other parts of Central Asia are available on the second floor.

Xiahe
Xiahe's main street leading to the Labrang Monastery is overflowing with shops and stalls selling all manner of Tibetan items, including prayer wheels, bells, silver ornaments, handicrafts, hats and shawls. Bargaining is essential. It's a great place to browse

and also to watch the continuous flow of Tibetan pilgrims searching for the perfect item to take back to their homes in Tibet.

Tibet
In Tibet there are lots of unusual items that make excellent souvenirs, such as woven rugs, *thangka* (a kind of scroll painting), traditional clothing and knitwear, silver jewellery, singing bowls, Buddha figures and incense. Check out the markets in Lhasa, but be aware that many of these "local" products are actually mass-produced in Nepal. Visit foundation stores, like the **Dropenling Handicraft Development Centre** on Chak Tsal Gang Lu, to be sure your purchase is assisting the Tibetan economy.

Xi'an
In Xi'an, **Shuyuanmen**, sometimes know as the Arts Street, runs between the South Gate and the Forest of Stelae Museum. It's a collection of Ming- and Qing-style buildings with shops selling all manner of stuff including calligraphy, jade ornaments, the infamous terracotta warrior reproductions and ink paintings. Prices are a little higher than other shopping areas in Xi'an. **Rongshengzhai Tourist Shopping Centre**, 42 Chang'an Lu, is a huge showroom offering an array of handicrafts. **Kaiyuan Shopping Centre**, Dong Dajie (East Street), near the Bell Tower intersection, is a good place to find clothes, and it stocks a wide range of well-known brands.

Yunnan
In **Kunming**, for a comprehensive selection of Yunnan's traditional arts and crafts, Zhenqing Cultural Square, 82 Baita Lu, is the best place to visit. For imported goods and essentials, the **Kunming Department Store**, Jinri Park, and the **Southwest Commercial Building**, 18 Renmin Zhong, are the city's best.

Alternatively, head to **Dali** for marble, which has patterns that strongly resemble the traditional Chinese brush landscapes. **Boai Lu** is a good place to shop for marble, while stores on **Huguo Lu** (Foreigners' Street) have a good selection of batiks, as fabric or ready-made items. In the northwest of the province there are some interesting art galleries showing Dongba-inspired paintings in modern style. Copies of these are available inexpensively and make a unique gift or souvenir.

ACTIVITIES

FESTIVALS, THE ARTS, NIGHTLIFE AND OUTDOOR PURSUITS

FESTIVALS

Holidays such as **National Day** and **International Labour Day** are fixed on the modern calendar, but most traditional festivals and events are determined by the lunar calendar, which means the date varies slightly from year to year. The following calendar of events highlights the major national festivals, but each region has its own special days and events.

January/February

The most important festival time is the **Lunar New Year**, or **Spring Festival**, which usually falls in late January or early February. Public buildings are festooned with coloured lights, people from all over China travel to reunite with family and friends, debts are settled, and food is consumed – lots of it. In recent years, a more relaxed atmosphere has brought the revival of old Spring Festival traditions, such as giving *hongbao* – small red envelopes containing money – to children and young adults. Temple fairs feature martial-arts demonstrations, stand-up comedy, home-made toys and, of course, food. One slightly less traditional activity that has become common during this time is shopping. As with the post-Christmas period in the West, the week following Spring Festival sees the streets of every town and city heaving with pedestrians looking for a bargain.

Northerners, who have amazing resilience to the bitter winters, partake with gusto in ice-sculpting competitions and winter swimming. The time and duration of the festivals depend on the weather. Both Beijing and Harbin are noted for their ice-sculpting festivals.

April

On the 12th day of the third lunar month, at the beginning of April, the Chinese honour their deceased ancestors by observing **Qingming**, sometimes referred to as the "grave-sweeping" day. It is much less impressive nowadays, as people are cremated instead of being buried. Qingming is a time for remembering ancestors and for age-old ritualistic ceremonies, but also for revelling on a warm spring day. Qingming was made a one-day public holiday in 2008, and it's become common for workers and students to head home to mark the occasion.

May/June

International Labour Day on 1 May has once again reverted to being a single one-day holiday after several years spent as one of China's three "Golden Week" holidays. Following hot on its heels is **Youth Day**, a commemoration of the May 4 Movement of 1919, reflected by large editorials and government hoopla in the official press.

International Children's Day is celebrated in earnest on 1 June by letting classes out early and treating children to outings at public parks.

July/August

1 July is the **Anniversary of the Communist Party**, which was founded in Shanghai in 1921. This means very little to the average citizen, but is plenty of fun for high-level party members.

The fifth day of the fifth lunar month (in June or July) brings the **Dragon Boat Festival**, with dragon-boat races in many cities. It commemorates the memory of Qu Yuan (340–278 BC), a poet in the days of the Kingdom of Chu, who, rather than submit to political pressure, drowned himself in the Miluo River, in Hunan. To prevent the fish from eating his body, the people threw glutinous rice cakes (*zongzi*) into the river. Nowadays, these *zongzi* are simply eaten to mark the occasion.

1 August is the **Anniversary of the People's Liberation Army**. Inaugurated in 1927 and formerly marked by enormous parades, it is now celebrated mainly in the media.

September/October

The timing of the **Mid-Autumn Festival** again depends on when the moon reaches its fullest, usually around mid-September. The shops do great business in "mooncakes" – pastries filled with gooey sesame paste, red-bean and walnut filling. *Tang yuan*, glutinous rice-flour balls with sweet fillings in sugar syrup, and

Travel during Festivals

If you wish to see or take part in any of these festivals, you will need to travel to your destination well in advance, particularly for the Lunar New Year, 1 May and 1 October holidays. At these times of year, many attractions become impossibly overcrowded and tickets on any form of transport are extremely difficult to obtain, as millions of people hit the road for family reunions.

Acrobatics

Acrobatics – a mixture of proper acrobatics, magic and animal acts and clowns – are popular throughout China. Almost every large town has its own troupe of acrobats, many of which tour the country. In big cities such as Beijing, Shanghai and Guangzhou, there are several venues dedicated to the genre.

Chaoyang Theatre, Beijing
36 Dongsanhuan Bei Lu
Tel: 6507 2421.
Performances daily at 7.15pm.

ERA Intersection of Time
Shanghai Circus World,
2266 Gonghexin Rd
Tel: 6630 0000.
This permanent circus is fast-paced and professional, with dozens of breathtaking acts of balance and magic. Its most famous act must be seen to be believed.

Wan Sheng Theatre, Beijing
95 Tianqiao Market (west of the Temple of Heaven)
Tel: 6303 7449.
Performances daily at 7.15pm.

yue bing, a cake baked specifically for this occasion, are also eaten. In the tradition of poets, this is the time to drink a bit of wine and toast the moon. It is now a one-day public holiday. *See page 459 for a full list of public holidays.*

Late September is normally the time when Chinese communities celebrate the memory of **Confucius**.

1 October is the PRC's birthday, **National Day**, celebrated with a one-week public holiday. Government buildings, road intersections and hotels are decked out in lights, and flower arrangements and Sun Yatsen's portrait are displayed in Tiananmen Square. Tens of thousands turn out on the square for picture-taking and general merry-making.

November/December

November and December are quiet months in China, but **Christmas** is gaining momentum as a consumer celebration. Christian churches hold special services that draw thousands of spectators. In Beijing, for example, it is fashionable to exchange greeting cards and presents, while Santa Claus makes the odd shop appearance.

Local Festivals for Deities

Various deities in the Chinese Daoist and Buddhist pantheon are honoured in festivals across China. Some are local concerns, but three of the most widespread are the birthdays of Confucius (September 28), Guanyin (19th day of the 2nd lunar month) and Tin Hau (23rd day of the 3rd lunar month).

Other Religious Festivals
Islam

In Xinjiang and other predominantly Muslim areas, two main festivals are celebrated: **Id al-Fitr** (Turkish: Bayram, the "Festival of the Breaking the Fast"), held at the end of Ramadan, and **Id al-Adha** (Turkish: Kurban, the "Festival of the Sacrifice", held to mark the culmination of the Hajj pilgrimage to Mecca. Ramadan – observed by many Muslims in China – is easier on the non-Muslim visitor than it would be, for example, in Iran or Saudi Arabia, as Han Chinese restaurants remain open everywhere.

Tibetan Buddhism

Labrang Monastery, at Xiahe in Gansu province, is one of the six great monasteries of the Tibetan Yellow Hat sect, and is the most important Tibetan monastery in China outside the Tibetan Autonomous region. Major festivals are held here each year involving merit-making, *sutra*-chanting and devil-dancing. The most important of all, **Monlan** or "Great Prayer", falls sometime in February or March, with pilgrims dressed in their finest clothes visiting from all over the Tibetan-speaking world.

THE ARTS

Chinese Opera

There are more than 300 types of opera in China, the most famous being Beijing Opera. You can attend performances of traditional opera in virtually every town – obtain the address of theatre and opera venues from your hotel or from travel agencies. A visit to the Chinese opera is a relaxed affair and occasionally quite noisy, and normal day clothes are quite acceptable.

Beijing
Chang'an Grand Theatre
7 Jiangguomennei Dajie (next to the International Hotel)
Tel: 6510-1309
Huguang Guildhall
3 Hufang Qiao, Xuanwu
Tel: 6351-8284
Houses an opera museum as well as nightly performances.
Lao She Teahouse
3/F, 3 Qianmen Xidajie
Tel: 6303 6830
Performances vary, but usually include Beijing Opera and other folk arts such as acrobatics, magic or comedy. Performances nightly.
Zhengyici Theatre
220 Xiheyan Dajie, Xuanwu District
Tel: 8315 1649
The only surviving Beijing Opera Theatre built entirely of wood, the Zhengyici Theatre preserves the traditional intimate layout of a roofed stage surrounded on three sides by tea tables. Ticket prices here are significantly higher than elsewhere: Rmb 380–680. Performances are every night.
Liyuan Theatre
Qianmen Hotel, 175 Yongan Lu
Tel: 6301 6688 ext. 8860
Nightly performances in the most popular Beijing Opera venue for tourists.
Short Beijing Opera performances are held at the **Palace of Prince Gong** (Gong Wang Fu), generally available for tour groups only.

Guangzhou (Guangdong)
Sun Yatsen Memorial Hall
Yuexiu Hill
Occasional performances of opera from all over China are held in this grand traditional octagonal building.
Huang Hua Gang Theatre
96 Xianlie Zhong Lu
Tel: 020-8776 0445
One of the best venues in Guangzhou for mainstream performing arts, including traditional operatic shows.
Xinghai Concert Hall
33 Qingbo Lu, Ersha Island
Tel: 020-8735 2222

TRANSPORT
ACCOMMODATION
SHOPPING
ACTIVITIES
A – Z
LANGUAGE

A new world-class concert facility on moneyed Ersha Island. Hosts Guangzhou's own symphony orchestra, as well as visiting philharmonics, and occasionally stages domestic opera performances.

Shanghai

Yifu Theatre
701 Fuzhou Rd
Tel: 6351 4668
Regular performances of Beijing Opera, as well as the regional Huju, Kunju and Shaoxing operas.
Shanghai Grand Theatre
Renmin (People's) Square
Tel: 6372 8701
World-class theatre complex. Large auditorium shows operas and classical concerts, smaller theatres have Beijing Opera and chamber music. Tours available daily.

Concerts

There are regular performances of Western classical and Chinese music in various cities. Dance performances are also common. In many areas – particularly in those of the national minorities – you can see performances of local dances and songs on the stage. Ballet is also performed, while young people are very keen on pop concerts. You can find out about the time and place of performances in each town from the hotel or through travel agencies. Local English-language magazines such as *That's Shanghai/Beijing/PRD*, *City Weekend* and *City Talk* also give up-to-date listings for the major cities.

Museums

There are a great variety of museums in China. From the revolution to natural history, everything is captured in exhibitions at various places. Many Chinese museums are not very well administered and not easy for the visitor to appreciate. English labelling is the exception rather than the rule. Opening hours are usually between 9am and 5pm,

Hong Kong Holidays

In Hong Kong, the Christian **Good Friday** and **Easter Monday** are public holidays, as are **Christmas** and **Boxing Day**. There are also days off for the Chinese ancestor-worshipping festivals of **Qing Ming** (April) and **Chung Yeung** (October), as well as **Buddha's Birthday** (May) and **SAR Establishment Day** (1 July)

and there is almost always a small admission fee, though Shanghai experimented with a free-entry policy in 2008, and there are indications that China may move towards extending this. Most museums are open weekends but may close for one day during the week. Individual museums are described in the Places section of the book.

NIGHTLIFE

Bars, Discos and Karaoke

Nightlife is increasingly a feature of modern China, especially in Beijing, Shanghai and Guangzhou. In southern Chinese towns, there tends to be more life at night than in the north of the country, with restaurants, bars and cafés generally remaining open until midnight or even later.

In the larger cities, many bars and pubs have opened in recent years, and are now meeting places for affluent young professionals. Also common are karaoke bars. The Japanese-style singalong swept China in the 1990s, increasing the planet's off-key harmonies considerably. Most are easily recognised by the letters "OK" amongst the characters for their names. Some of these are pricey, with the clientele being rich businessmen, and some are fronts for prostitution; such hostess-style bars are illegal, and can fleece customers, so beware. Stick to major chains such as Partyworld.

Discos are popular throughout China. Many hotels have their own, frequented by well-off local youths and open until the early hours. Some of the newer hotels are also developing the lobby bar-lounge concept.

Check the monthly English-language magazines in Beijing, Shanghai, Guangzhou and other large cities for the latest listings on nightclubs around town. These cater to the large expat communities and are excellent sources of information.

OUTDOOR PURSUITS

Spectator Sports

The Olympic Games

The 2008 Olympics in Beijing was a huge success for the Chinese government, both in terms of enhancing China's image abroad and of promoting sports among its own

people. The country won a record 51 gold medals in various disciplines, including badminton, table tennis, gymnastics, judo, weightlifting and diving. One legacy of the US$43 billion investment will be a clutch of world-class sporting facilities to help ensure that China performs well in the medal table at the next games.

Football

Despite the dismal (and much criticised) performance of the Chinese football team at the Olympics, soccer is a hugely popular spectator sport in China, although relatively few people play it. *Bamboo Goalposts* is an entertaining account of British football journalist Rowan Simon's efforts to establish the game at grass-roots level despite the many obstacles.

Participant Sports

Golf

Golf is booming in China. It is extremely popular with well-heeled businessmen, their expat friends and the burgeoning middle classes. There are about 350 courses in the country, mainly in the south, with many more planned (a controversial issue, given the pressure on land resources in the country). An estimated 1 million Chinese people play golf, although it is still considered an elite sport, out of reach for most of the population. The most famous course is probably Mission Hills (www.missionhillsgroup.com) north of Shenzhen, ranked as the world's largest, with 216 holes – and a membership fee of over US$100,000.

Hiking

Hong Kong is good for hiking, with the ridge walk along the spine of Hong Kong Island and numerous trails in the New Territories and outlying islands. On the mainland, the holy Daoist and Buddhist mountains such as **Emei Shan** in Sichuan and **Tai Shan** in Shandong make for fabulous hikes. **Heng Shan** in Hunan is another highlight, but avoid weekends and holidays as it is very popular with tour groups. The Wulingyuan area of Hunan is also very scenic, as are the Wuyi Shan mountains of **Fujian**. The dramatic karst scenery of **Guangxi** province surrounding Guilin (excluding individual climbs such as the ascent of Moon Hill) is more usually explored by cyclists or rock-climbers. **Guizhou** is recommend for hikes between villages in the province's east and south. Up in the northeast the **Changbai Shan**

close to the North Korean border is a more remote hiking area, while over in Xinjiang the area around **Tianchi** (Heaven Lake) near Ürümqi is simply beautiful. The wilds of **western Sichuan** and **Tibet** will appeal to the more adventurous hiker and require proper preparation and equipment.

In **Yunnan**, tropical Xishuangbanna also offers village treks as well as more hardcore jungle treks; these are best organised through tour operators in Jinghong. The **Cangshan Mountains** west of Dali and **Tiger Leaping Gorge** near Lijiang are also excellent hiking country. Tours can be arranged through hotels/guesthouses, but it is possible to explore the area independently.

Other Activities

Adventure sports

In **Guangxi** province, Yangshuo is a good base from which to try out a wealth of outdoor activities amid some stunning landscapes. Cycling can be followed by rafting down the Li River, or combined with a hike accompanied by tour guides. Bikes, tandems and mountain bikes can all be hired in the town. Bamboo rafting and kayaking are offered by various companies. Rock-climbing over the limestone crags is a popular pastime. Caving around Yangshuo can be arranged by a travel agent or with a freelance guide. Hot-air balloon flights are operated by Guilin Yangshuo Flying Balloon Club – a wonderful way to enjoy the landscape.

Skiing

The Window of the World theme park in Shenzhen (**Guangdong** province) has an indoor ski centre.

Watersports

In **Guangdong** – watersports are available at the Xiaomeisha resort to east of Shenzhen. In **Fujian**, you can try white-water rafting, trekking and kayaking in Wuyishan. **Hainan** Island's warm, white-sand beaches have facilities for scuba-diving, fishing and paragliding.

TOURS AND AGENCIES

Tour Operators

There are countless travel agencies within and outside China that handle domestic travel arrangements. Prominent among the agencies is **China International Travel Services** (**CITS**), formerly virtually the sole agency handling overseas tourists. It has branches throughout China. **China Travel Services** (**CTS**) is a similar organisation, originally responsible for domestic tourists and overseas Chinese, but now also catering to foreigners. The efficiency of both organisations still leaves a lot to be desired, however, and standards of spoken English are generally poor. Offices do not usually help with standard tourist information.

Agencies may also have business interests extending beyond simply arranging tours and bookings; they may own or partly own hotels. An agency that arranges a tour may contact agencies in places you will visit, and ask them to deal with local bookings.

Sometimes agencies such as CITS may hold tickets for rail journeys, operas, acrobatic performances and concerts, even when events are sold out. Prices will be higher, however.

There are also small-scale, unlicensed tour operators. Use discretion when choosing one of these: some use unroadworthy vehicles, take their customers to shops and restaurants that give the guides "backhanders" (though this probably also happens with licensed operators), and demand mark-ups of 100 percent or more for tickets to tourist sites. Others may be trustworthy, and cheap.

It is, of course, quite possible to travel in China without using any agency. See pages 424 and 425 for the merits of group and individual travel.

CITS Offices

Beijing: 1 Dongdan Beijadie, tel: 010-8522 8888 (phone service 24 hours); 8.30–11.30am and 1.30–5pm. Also try Beijing Tourist Information Centre at Capital Airport

(tel: 6459 8137) and 11 Gongti Beilu (tel: 6417 6627).
Changsha: 11/F, Xiaoyuan Building, Wuyi Donglu, Changsha, tel: add area code 0731-228 0442
Chengdu: 65, Sec 2, Renmin Nan Lu, tel: 028-8665 8731.
Chongqing: 8th Floor, Building A, Zourong Square, 151 Zourong Lu, Yuzhong; tel: 023- 6385 0196.
Dalian: 1 Changtong Jie, tel: 0411-8368 7843.
Guangzhou: 618 Jiefang Beilu, tel: 020-2201 3333.
Guilin: 19 Binjiang Lu, Guilin, tel: 0773-288 2727.
Hangzhou: 1 Shihang Rd, tel: 0571-8505 9109 or 8515 2888.
Hong Kong: CTS, G/F, CTS House, 78–83 Connaught Road, Central, tel: 852-2853 3888; fax: 2541 9777; the main Hong Kong Tourism Board is at the Star Ferry Pier in Tsim Sha Tsui, tel: 852-2508 1234.
Kashi (Kashgar): Chini Bagh Hotel, 93 Seman Road, tel: 0998-298 3156. Daily 9.30am–1.30pm, 4–8pm.
Kunming: 285 Huancheng Nan Lu, tel: 0871-355 4283.
Lanzhou: Tourism Building, Nongmin Xiang, tel: 0931-883 5566.
Luoyang: Changjiang Lu, tel: 0379-432 3212.
Nanchang: 368 Bayi Dadao (behind the Jiangxi Hotel); tel: 0791-620 2259.
Nanjing: 202-1 Zhongshan Beilu, tel: 025-8353 8735 or 8353 8737; Mon–Sat 9am–5pm.
Ningbo: Suite 48, Lane 130 Kaiwing St, tel: 0574-8719 3068.
Qingdao: Yuyuan Building, 73 Xianggang Xilu, tel: 0532-389 3066.
Shanghai: Shanghai Guangming Building, 2 Jinling Rd (E), tel: 021-6323 8770.
Shenzhen: 2 Chuanbu Jie, Heping Lu, Luohu District, tel: 0755-8247 7050.
Suzhou: 18 Dajing Xiang, tel: 0512-6515 5207.
Tianjin: 22 Youyi Lu, tel: 022-2810 9985; Mon–Fri 9am–5pm; Sat 9am–noon.
Ürümqi: 38 Xinhua Nanlu, tel: 0991-282 1428.
Wuhan: 692 Jiefang Dadao, Hankou, tel: 027-8585 5622.
Wuxi: 18 Zhongshan Rd, tel: 0510-8270 5369 or 8272 4077.
Xiamen: 22A Huangda Dasha, 28 Houdi Xilu; tel: 0592-518 9110. Daily 8am–5.30pm.
Xi'an: 48 (N) Changan Lu, tel: 029-8524 1864; Bell Tower Hotel, tel: 029-727 9200, ext. 2842; Mon–Fri 8.30am–noon, 2.30–5.30pm.
The **Macau Government Tourist Office** is at 9 Largo do Senado, tel: 853-315 566, fax: 510 104.

A – Z

A HANDY SUMMARY OF PRACTICAL INFORMATION, ARRANGED ALPHABETICALLY

A Admission Charges 454
B Budgeting for Your Trip 454
   Business Hours 454
C Climate 454
D Disabled Travellers 455
E Electricity 455
   Embassies and
      Consulates 455
   Emergencies 455

   Entry Regulations 456
G Gay Travellers 456
H Health and Medical Services 456
M Media 458
   Money Matters 459
P Photography 459
   Postal/Courier Services 459
   Public Holidays 459
   Public Toilets 460

R Religious Services 460
S Student Travellers 460
T Telecommunications 460
   Time Zone 460
   Tipping 460
   Travelling with Children 461
U Useful Addresses 461
W What to Bring 461
   What to Wear 461

A dmission Charges

Not at all pricey, by international standards, admission charges vary from Rmb 10 for a state-run museum to Rmb 100 or so for larger theme parks and around Rmb 200 for some nature parks. In 2007, many museums stopped charging admission. Most temples charge only a few kuai. In some places, such as Jinggangshan and Lushan, visitors are required to buy a multiple-attraction pass (around Rmb 150).

B udgeting for Your Trip

In a vast country such as this prices will vary considerably, not only between city and countryside but also between provinces. You might need as little as US$40–50 a day in, say, Yunnan province, to cover accommodation, meals, attractions and transport, but in Hong Kong you could pay four times that amount just for your hotel. Allowing for a reasonably good standard of accommodation away from the city hotspots, you would need around US$120 a day. Transport and food are very reasonably priced everywhere (see also Admission Charges above).

Business Hours

Shops are open every day, including public holidays – the one major exception being at Chinese New Year. Opening hours are usually from 8.30am or 9am to 8pm, but may extend to 10pm in places. Government offices and banks are usually open Mon–Fri, from 8.30 or 9am, and close at 5, 5.30 or 6pm, with a lunch break from noon to 1.30pm. Many banks, notably the Bank of China, are now open seven days a week from 8am to 6pm. Times are approximate; allow for local variations. In western China, for example, offices often open later, as they are on Beijing time.

Typhoons

July to October is typhoon season in southern China. In Hong Kong, storm warnings are graded as 1, 3, 8, 9 and 10 – 1 signalling a mild possibility, 10 indicating a head-on, life-threatening storm. Never underestimate a typhoon.
● **To get a storm warning update, tel: 852-2835 1473 (Hong Kong).**

C limate

China is a huge country, covering 35 degrees of latitude, with a great variety of climates. It is generally warm and humid in southeastern and central China, but the west, the north and northeast are quite dry. Most of China has a summer rainy season and a winter dry season. The best times for travelling are generally spring (Apr/May) and autumn (Sept/Oct).

Northern China, north of the Chang Jiang (Yangzi River), has cold, dry winters – particularly cold in the northeast where temperatures remain well below freezing for months on end. Summers are warm or hot with variable humidity and some torrential rain. Beijing and Xi'an can be affected by sand blowing in from the Gobi Desert in spring.

In **Central China** summers are hot and humid, with a lot of rain. In low-lying regions around the Yangzi and along the coasts, winters are fairly mild but often damp (Shanghai is often grey and cool from December to March). The cities of Chongqing, Wuhan and Nanjing are notorious for their summer heat and humidity.

Most of **Southern China** has a

CLIMATE CHART

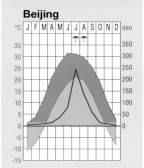

Beijing

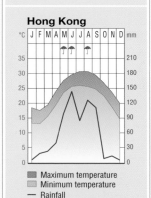

Hong Kong

■ Maximum temperature
□ Minimum temperature
— Rainfall
☂ Rainy months

subtropical climate, with long, hot summers and short, cool winters. There are spells of heavy rain in the summer, and typhoons can affect the coasts between July and September. Upland areas inland tend to get a lot of rain throughout the year and can be cold in winter. The exception is Yunnan, which has warmer, drier winters. Southern Yunnan (Xishuangbanna) and Hainan island have true tropical climates with year-round warmth.

In **Western China**, the Tibet-Qinghai Plateau has moderately warm summers, while winters can get very cold; there is little rainfall throughout the year. Most of Xinjiang is arid and fiercely hot in summer (Turpan is the hottest of all), frigid in winter. Northern areas are less hot in summer.

D isabled Travellers

Only in recent years have the needs of disabled people received attention in China. Regulations regarding rooms and other facilities for the disabled must be met by new hotels. In

general, though, towns, institutions, public transport and sights offer little accessibility.

Travelling in a group for the disabled certainly reduces these problems considerably. The China National Tourist Offices and CITS *(see page 453)* have information about special trips for the disabled.

E lectricity

Electricity in China is 220 volts, 50 cycles AC. Don't forget to take an international adaptor, to accommodate different-style plugs. If travelling away from tourist centres, it is worth taking battery-operated equipment.

Embassies and Consulates

Beijing

Australia, 21 Dongzhimenwai Dajie, tel: 010-5140 4111.
Canada, 19 Dongzhimenwai Dajie, Chaoyang District, tel: 010-5139 4000.
Ireland, 3 Ritan Donglu, tel: 010-6532 2691.
Mongolia, 2 Xiushui Bei Jie, Jianguomenwai, tel: 010-6532 1203.
Nepal, 1 Xiliujie, Sanlitun Lu, tel: 010-6532 1795.
New Zealand, 1 Ritan Dong Erjie, tel: 010-8532 7000.
Singapore, 1 Xiushui Bei Jie, Jianguomenwai, tel: 010-6532 1115.
United Kingdom, 11 Guanghua Lu, Jianguomenwai, tel: 010-5192 4000, fax: 010-6532 1937.
United States, Jianwai Xiushui Bei Jie No. 3, tel: 010-6532 3831, fax: 010-6532 2483.

Shanghai

Australia, 22/F, CITIC Square, 1168 Nanjing Road (W), tel: 021-5292 5500.
Canada, Shanghai Centre, Suite 604, 1376 Nanjing Rd (W), tel: 021-6279 8400, fax: 021-6279 8401.
Japan, 8 Wanshan Rd, tel: 021-5257 4766.
New Zealand, 989 Chang Le Rd, tel: 021-5407 5858.

Singapore, 89 Wanshan Rd, tel: 021-6278 5566.
United Kingdom, Shanghai Ctr, Suite 301, 1376 Nanjing Rd (W), tel: 021-6279 7650, fax: 021-6279 7651.
United States, 1469 Huaihai Rd (C), tel: 021-6433 6880, fax: 021-6433 4122.

Hong Kong

Australia, 21–24/F, Harbour Ctr, 25 Harbour Road, Wan Chai, tel: 852-2827 8881.
Canada, 11/F, Tower One, Exchange Square, 8 Connaught Place, Central, tel: 852-2810 4321.
Japan, 46/F, Tower One, Exchange Square, Central, tel: 852-2522 1184.
New Zealand, Rm 6505, Central Plaza, 18 Harbour Road, Wan Chai, tel: 852-2877 4488.
Singapore, Unit 901, 9/F, Tower One, Admiralty Centre, 18 Harcourt Road, Admiralty, tel: 852-2527 2212.
United Kingdom, 1 Supreme Court Road, Admiralty, tel 852-2901 3000.
United States, 26 Garden Road, Central, tel: 852-2523 9011.

Emergencies

Security and Crime

There is still less crime in China than in many other countries but, as vigorous crime crackdowns by the government (in the form of thousands of executions per year) attest, crime is an increasing problem.

Take the same precautions applicable anywhere, on the street and with valuables in hotels and on public transport. Pickpockets and bag-slashers can be a problem, especially on crowded trains and buses, and in stations. Because of the influx of poor migrant workers, cities such as Guangzhou tend to have more crime than elsewhere, and muggings have been reported in some areas, notably Shenzhen. Still, one needn't worry in most towns and cities. Women should dress discreetly and avoid going out alone at night, though generally they are

Overseas Chinese Embassies

Australia, 15 Coronation Drive, Yarralumla, ACT 2600, Canberra, tel: (61-2) 6273 4780; www.chinaembassy.org.au
Canada, 515 St Patrick Street, Ottawa, Ontario KIN 5H3, tel: (1-613) 789 3434; www.chinaembassycanada.org
New Zealand, 2–6 Glenmore Street, Wellington, tel: (64-4) 472 1382; www.chinaembassy.org.nz

Singapore, 150 Tanglin Road, Singapore 247969, tel: (65) 6471 2117; www.chinaembassy.org.sg
United Kingdom, 31 Portland Place, London W1B 1QD, tel: (44-20) 7636 5637; 0891 880 808. www.chinese-embassy.org.uk
United States, 2201 Wisconsin Avenue NW, Washington DC 20007, tel: (1-202) 338 6688; www.china-embassy.org

Important Numbers

Police: 110
Fire: 119
Ambulance: 120
Local directory assistance: 114
Domestic directory assistance: 116
International directory assistance (English): 114
Time: 117
Weather: 12121
For emergency services in Hong Kong, tel: 999. In Macau, tel: 919.

safer in China than in many other parts of the world. It is a good idea to carry the telephone number of your hotel concierge on a piece of paper, or loaded into a mobile phone, as few police officers speak English.

The **Public Security Bureau** (Gongan Ju) is the ever-present police force responsible for everything – chasing murderers, quenching dissent, issuing visa extensions. They are usually friendly towards foreigners, even if the rules that they are strictly enforcing seem illogical at times. Also, with serious travel-related disputes – for example, with taxi drivers or hotels – they are usually able to resolve the problem. To stay in their good books, don't be caught trying to travel in restricted areas or on an expired visa. Throughout China, visitors who are not staying in hotels must register with the local Public Security Bureau (see page 461 for contact details).

Luggage

Luggage should be sturdy and lockable – sometimes a requirement for transport. Avoid taking shiny designer luggage, which is an obvious target for thieves.

Entry Regulations

Visas and Passports

All foreigners must acquire an entry visa before arrival in China, although those visiting Hong Kong or Macau only do not usually require one. If you are part of a group, the tour operator will often obtain it; group visas will usually be issued for groups of at least 10, and the guide accompanying your group will keep the visas. Individual travellers can apply at any Chinese embassy. The procedure is straightforward, taking about a week, depending on current regulations and on your own country's rules for visiting Chinese citizens. A 30-day single-entry visa is usually issued. Your passport must

be valid for six months after the expiry date of the entry visa.

It used to be much quicker and easier to obtain or renew visas in Hong Kong than elsewhere in China, but the difference is less marked these days.

If your visa expires while you are in China, it can be extended by the local Public Security Bureau (see above). However, make sure you visit them before it expires, because fines for overstaying can be steep, and it may be a long and frustrating process getting the stamp you need.

Nowadays, most of the country is open to foreigners, except some border areas and military zones. A permit is still required for Tibet.

Customs

On arrival, each traveller must complete a health declaration form.

Tourists can freely import two bottles of wine or spirits and 400 cigarettes, as well as foreign currency and valuables for personal use without restrictions. The import of weapons, ammunition, drugs and pornographic literature is prohibited.

On departure, antiques such as porcelain, paintings, calligraphy, carvings and old books must carry the red lacquer seal of an official antique shop. Otherwise, they can be confiscated by the customs officials without compensation. (See also Shopping, page 444)

Gay Travellers

Between the establishment of the People's Republic in 1949 and economic liberalisation in the 1990s, homosexuality was considered a psychological illness and severely circumscribed. China, though, has a long tradition of gay sexuality –

known as the "way of the cut sleeve" in traditional literature – and in the past two decades gay people of both sexes have increasingly reasserted their presence and rights, especially in go-ahead cities such as Shanghai, Beijing and Guangzhou. Don't expect a scintillating gay scene elsewhere, however.

H ealth and Medical Services

The most frequently reported health problem in Eastern Asia is diarrhoea. The best prevention is to ensure maximum hygiene while travelling, especially in restaurants and roadside snack bars. Never eat raw, uncooked, or partially cooked food, including salads, other than in the top hotels. Animal or human excrement is still frequently used as fertiliser, so bacteria on uncooked vegetables can easily be ingested. Also suggested if travelling outside of a tour group: acquire chopsticks and a tin bowl with a lid for train journeys and meals in small roadside restaurants. Drink only boiled or bottled water, even though the tap water is drinkable in some places, and reduce exposure to insects as far as possible.

Adjustment to a different climate and different food frequently leads to minor colds or digestive problems. Keep well hydrated in the heat and humidity.

Tibet, the northwest, and the tropical province of Yunnan make particularly high demands on the body. Heart disease and high blood pressure can both lead to serious problems in Tibet because of high altitude. Temperatures are high and conditions dry along the Silk Road.

If planning to visit areas outside of Beijing, Shanghai, Guangzhou and Hong Kong, you should take out emergency evacuation insurance.

Two of the largest emergency evacuation companies are SOS Assistance and Asia Emergency Assistance. They have offices in many major cities worldwide (see page 457 for the Hong Kong address).

Insect-Transmitted Illnesses

Malaria
Transmitted to humans by mosquitoes, which are most active from dusk to dawn.
Symptoms: fever and flu-like symptoms, chills, aches and tiredness. Up to one year after returning home, travellers should consult a physician for any kind of flu-like illness.
Risk: little or no risk in urban areas and popular tourist destinations;

there is no risk in provinces bordering Mongolia or in Heilongjiang, Ningxia, Qinghai, Hong Kong or Macau. The highest risk exists in rural areas not visited by most travellers. In these areas, transmission is most common from May to December; in the south, transmission occurs year-round. Whether taking preventative drugs or not, travellers in risk areas should avoid being bitten by mosquitoes: use mosquito repellents, wear long-sleeved shirts and long trousers and ask at your hotel for a mosquito net or an electronic mosquito repellent device *(quwenqi)* or coil *(wenxiang)*.

Taking drugs to prevent malaria is recommended only for travellers to rural areas and those who expect to have outdoor exposure during evening hours. Deciding which medicine to take is not easy. Consult medical authorities or a physician in travel medicine for advice before you travel.

Dengue fever
Primarily an urban viral infection transmitted by mosquitoes in or around human habitations. The mosquitoes are typically at their most active around dawn and dusk.
Symptoms: sudden onset of high fever, severe headaches, joint and muscle pain, and a rash, which shows up 3–4 days after the fever.
Risk: occurs in parts of southern China and Taiwan. The risk is minimal for most travellers. Those who have lived several years in high-risk areas are more susceptible than short-term visitors. There is no vaccine or specific treatment available.

Japanese encephalitis
A mosquito-borne viral disease prevalent in rural areas, often in rice-growing areas.
Symptoms: none, or headache, fever and other flu-like symptoms. Serious complications can lead to a swelling of the brain (encephalitis).
Risk: low or minimal risk. Occurs in rural China and Korea; very rarely in Hong Kong and Taiwan. Mosquitoes bite in the late afternoon and early evening. Transmission is usually during the rainy season. There is no specific drug for treatment, but there is a preventative vaccine, which should be considered for those who plan visits of four weeks or more to rural areas.

Emergency Evacuation

International SOS (HK) Limited, 16/F, World Trade Centre, 280 Gloucester Road, Causeway Bay, Hong Kong, tel: 852-2528 9998, fax: 852-2528 9933.

Contamination
Hepatitis A
A viral infection of the liver transmitted by faecal-contaminated food or drink, or through direct person-to-person contact.
Symptoms: fatigue, fever, loss of appetite, nausea, dark urine and/or jaundice, vomiting, aches. There is currently no specific treatment for Hepatitis A, although an effective vaccine is available and highly recommended, especially for those who plan to travel repeatedly or at length in China. Immune globulin is recommended only for short-term protection.

Hepatitis B
All countries in Asia, including China, report high levels of infection. Hepatitis B is a viral infection of the liver transmitted through the exchange of blood or blood-derived fluids, or through sexual activity with an infected person. Unscreened blood and unsterilised needles, or contact with potentially infected people with open skin lesions, are sources of infection. Inoculations for this type of hepatitis should be started six months prior to travel.

Typhoid fever
A bacterial infection transmitted by contaminated food and/or water, or directly between people. Travellers to East Asia are susceptible to typhoid fever, particularly in rural areas.
Symptoms: fever, headaches, tiredness, loss of appetite and constipation. Be cautious in selecting food and water. Drinking bottled or boiled water and eating only well-cooked food lowers the risk of infection. Typhoid fever is treated with antibiotics. Vaccination is recom-mended for travellers off the tourist routes, especially if staying for six weeks or more. Available vaccines protect 70–90 percent of users.

Cholera
An acute intestinal infection caused by bacteria, most often through contaminated water or food. The risk is virtually non-existent in China.
Symptoms: abrupt onset of watery diarrhoea, dehydration, vomiting and muscle cramps. Medical care must be sought quickly when cholera is suspected. The available vaccine is not recommended for most travellers.

Schistosomiasis (bilharzia)
An infection from a flatworm larvae that penetrates the skin, including unbroken skin.

Avoiding Illness

To reduce the risk of infection on your travels:
- reduce exposure to insects
- ensure decent quality of food and water
- be aware of potential diseases in the regions that you visit
- avoid high-risk activities linked with HIV/Aids, such as drug-taking using suspect needles and unprotected sex

Risk: schistosomiasis is found in some areas of China, including rivers and lakes of southeastern and eastern China, especially along the Chang Jiang (Yangzi River) and tributaries. The risk comes from bathing, wading or swimming in contaminated fresh water.

There is no easy way to identify infested water. If exposed, immediate and vigorous drying with a towel or rubbing alcohol on the exposed areas can reduce risk. Water treated with chlorine or iodine is virtually safe; salt water poses no risk.

Medical Services
There is a big difference in China between urban and rural medical services. If travelling in the countryside, there may be no appropriate medical services beyond primary healthcare, which is good in China. Some hospitals in cities have special sections for foreigners where English is spoken.

Many of the large hotels have their own doctors. Payment must be made on the spot for treatment, medicine and transport. If planning to visit areas outside Beijing, Shanghai, Guangzhou and Hong Kong, consider emergency evacuation insurance.
International SOS (HK) Limited, 16/F, World Trade Centre, 280 Gloucester Road, Causeway Bay, tel: 852-2528 9998; fax: 852-2528 9933; alarm tel: 852-2528 9900.
Asia Emergency Assistance (AEA), 9/F, Allied Resources Bldg, 32 Ice House St, Central, Hong Kong, tel: 852-2810 8898, fax: 852-2845 0395. Beijing: 010-6462 9100.

Beijing
Emergency/evacuation
MEDEX Assistance Corporation, Beijing Lufthansa Centre, Regus Office 19, tel: 010-6465 1264, fax: 010-6465 1240.
International SOS Clinic, Building C, BITIC Jing Yi Building, 1 Xingfu Sancun Beijie, tel: 010-6462 9199; 24-hour alarm tel: 010-6462 9100.

Emergency/general

The best hospitals for foreigners are the **Sino-Japanese Friendship Hospital**, Heping Donglu, Chaoyang District, tel: 010-6422 1122; and **Capital Hospital**, 53 Dongdanbei Dajie, tel: 010-6529 6114.

More expensive, but the best place for treatment of serious illness, is the private **Beijing United Family Health Centre**, 2 Jiangtai Lu (close to Lido Hotel), tel: 010-6433 3960, fax: 010-6433 3963, 24-hour Emergency Hotline 010-6433 2345. All staff speak excellent English.

Chengdu

Global Doctors, Kelan Building, Bangkok Garden, 21 Renmin Nan Lu, Section 4, tel: 028-8522 6058.

Chongqing

Chongqing First People's (Diyi Renmin) Hospital, 40 Daomenkou Jie, tel: 023-6384 1324.

Fujian

Fujian Provincial Hospital, 134 Dong Dajie, Fuzhou, tel: 0591-8755 7768.
City Medical Consultancy, 123 Xidi Villa, Hubin Beilu, Xiamen City, tel: 0592-532 3168 (24 hours).

Guangzhou

Emergencies
Sun Yatsen Memorial Hospital, 107 Yanjiang Xilu, tel: 020-8133 2199.
Guangzhou No. 1 Hospital, 1 Panfu Lu, tel: 020-8104 8888.
Can-Am International Medical Centre, 5/F, Garden Hotel, 368 Huangshi Dong Lu, tel: 020-8387 9057 or 020-8386 6988 (24-hour hotline).
Kai Yi International Dental Care, tel: 020-3886 4821.

Guilin

Guilin People's Hospital (Guilin Shi Renmin Yiyuan), 12 Wenming Lu, tel: 0773-282 5116.

Hangzhou

Chinese Medicine Hospitals
Shengzhong Hospital, 57 Youdian Lu, tel: 0571-8706 8001 or 8701 0630.
Hangzhou City Central Hospital, 453 Tiyuchang Lu, tel: 0571-8582 7888 or 8582 7502.

Western Medicine Hospitals
Run Run Shao Hospital, 3 Qingchun Road, Hangzhou, tel: 0571-8609 0073.
No. 1 Hospital of Zhejiang University, No. 79 Qingchun Road, Hangzhou, tel: 0571-8723 6111/ 6114/6666.

Hong Kong

Though many Chinese people still prefer traditional cures for minor ills, modern Western practices dominate, and most doctors did much of their training overseas. There are also numerous expatriate doctors and dentists.

Hospitals

No Hong Kong hospital is cheap, but all have good specialists and facilities. The most notable hospitals are:
Central Medical Practice, 1501 Prince's Bldg, Central, tel: 852-2521 2567.
Hong Kong Adventist Hospital, 40 Stubbs Road, Happy Valley, tel: 852-2574 6211. Operates an expat-staff outpatient department Sun–Fri noon, and also has a **dental clinic** with 24-hour emergency service.
Hong Kong Central Hospital, 1B Lower Albert Road, Central, tel: 852-2522 3141.
Prince of Wales Hospital, 30–32 Ngan Shing St, Sha Tin, New Territories, tel: 852-2632 2211.
Queen Elizabeth Hospital, 30 Gascoigne Rd, Kowloon, tel: 852-2958 8888.
Queen Mary Hospital, Pokfulam Rd, Hong Kong, tel: 852-2816 6366.

Clinics

Clinics are an economical alternative.
Anderson & Partners, tel: 852-2523 8166, **Vio & Partners**, tel: 852-2521 3302 and **Dr Oram & Partners**, tel: 852-2525 1730, have clinics on both sides of the harbour.

Kaifeng

Kaifeng No. 1 People's Hospital, 85 Hedao Lu, tel: 0378-595 8812.

Kashi (Kashgar)

People's Hospital (Renmin Hospital), Jichang Lu, tel: 0998-282 2338.

Kunming

Hospital of the Kunming Medical College, 153 Xichang Lu, tel: 0871-532 4888/532 4590 (emergency hotline).
Yunnan First People's Hospital, 172 Jinbi Lu, tel: 363 4031.
Richland International Hospital, Beijing Lu extension, Shangdu Guoji Xiaoqu, tel: 574 1988.

Lanzhou

Gansu Province People's Hospital, 96 Donggang Donglu, tel: 0931-841 6801.

Lhasa

Number One People's Hospital, 18 Linkuo Beilu, tel: 0891-6332 462.

Macau

Kiang Wu Hospital, Estrada Coelho do Amaral, tel: 853-2837 1333.
S. Januário Hospital, Estrada do Visconde de S. Januário. Tel: 853-2831 3731.

Nanchang

Nanchang No. 1 Hospital, 128 Xiangshan Beilu, tel: 0791-886 2299.

Nanjing

Gulou Hospital, 321 Zhongshan Lu, tel: 025-8330 4616 or 8361 1838.

Qingdao

People's Hospital, 17 Dexian Lu, tel: 0532-285 2154.

Shanghai

Emergency/evacuation
SOS International Assistance, tel: 021-5298 9538; alarm tel: 021-6295 0099.

Emergency/general
Shanghai Emergency Centre, 638 Yishan Lu, 24-hour hotline tel: 021-3414 0030.
Huashan Hospital, 12 Ürümqi Rd (C), 15/F, Foreigners' Clinic, tel: 021-6248 3986/6248 9999, ext. 1921.
World Link Medical Centre, Shanghai Centre, 1376 Nanjing Rd (W), tel: 021-6445 5999.

Shenzhen

Shenzhen People's Hospital, Dongmen Bei Lu, tel: 0755-2553 3018.

Ürümqi

Xinjiang People's Hospital, 91 Tianchi Lu, tel: 0991-282 2927.
Ürümqi Chinese Medical Hospital, 60 Youhao Nanlu, tel: 0991-452 0963.

Xi'an

Xi'an Shaanxi Province People's Hospital, 214 Youyi Xilu, tel: 029-525 1331 ext. 2283/2284.

Zhengzhou

Hospital No. 1, Henan Medical University, Daxue Lu, tel: 0371-696 4992.

Ⓜ edia

An English-language newspaper, the *China Daily*, is published every day except Sunday. It is informative but toes the party line. It is often obtainable from the big hotels for free. Same-day editions are available only in large cities; elsewhere, it'll probably be several days late.

In Shanghai, two other English-language publications, the *Shanghai Star* and *Shanghai Daily*, are free, and there are plenty of free listing magazines, including *That's Shanghai*, *City Weekend* and *City Talk*. Throughout China, large hotels sell foreign-language newspapers and journals, including the *International Herald Tribune, The Times, Asian Wall Street Journal, Time, Newsweek* and many more. Foreign online newspapers are not generally jammed, except for the BBC online news in Chinese.

Money Matters

The Chinese currency is called *renminbi* (people's currency) and is often abbreviated **RMB**. The basic unit is the *yuan* (colloquially, *kuai*). Ten *jiao* (colloquially, *mao*) make one yuan; ten *fen* make one jiao. Thus, 100 fen make one yuan. Notes are currently issued for 1, 2, 5, 10, 20, 50 and 100 yuan. Coins come in 1 yuan, 5 jiao, 1 jiao and 5 fen.

Hong Kong and Macau have retained their separate currencies, the Hong Kong dollar (HKD) and pataca (MOP), respectively. The former is pegged to the US dollar at a rate of 7.8; the pataca is pegged to the Hong Kong dollar. Hong Kong dollars are also widely accepted in Guangzhou and Shenzhen, but if you are staying more than a day in mainland China it is worth changing your money to Chinese currency.

Major currencies are accepted in banks and hotels. Global network-connected ATM machines (Cirrus, Plus) can be found in major cities and tourist towns – try branches of the Bank of China, major hotels and department stores. **Citibank** also has a presence in Beijing, Shanghai and Guangzhou, and its ATMs usually accept lots of different cards.

Many places frequented by foreigners take the usual **credit cards** such as American Express, Visa, Diners Club and MasterCard. Don't expect to use them much outside of the major cities, however. Train and bus tickets must be purchased in cash, but plane tickets can be bought with credit cards.

Cash advances may be obtained from major branches of the Bank of China, including, in Beijing, the Bank of China at 410 Fuchengmennei Dajie, tel: 010-6601 6688, or 19 Donganmen Dajie, tel: 010-6519 9114.

P hotography

Taking photographs of or filming military installations is prohibited. As in other countries, some museums, palaces or temples will not allow

Domestic Area Codes

Add 0 to the codes below if dialling from within China:

Beijing	10
Chengdu	28
Chongqing	23
Guangzhou	20
Guilin	773
Hangzhou	571
Harbin	451
Kashi	998
Kunming	871
Luoyang	379
Nanjing	25
Sanya	898
Shanghai	21
Shenyang	24
Shenzhen	755
Suzhou	512
Qingdao	532
Tianjin	22
Ürümqi	991
Wuhan	27
Xi'an	29
Xiamen	592
Zhengzhou	371

The international dialling code for Hong Kong is 852; for Macau it is 853; these are used when dialling from elsewhere in China.

photographs to be taken, or will charge a fee. At other times, photography is allowed, but without using a flash.

No special permit is necessary for a movie camera, as long as it is clearly not for professional use.

Postal/Courier Services

Domestic mail delivery is exceedingly fast and cheap in China, and it puts most Western postal services to shame. Within some cities, there is often same-day delivery; between large cities, delivery is usually overnight. International mail, too, is efficient.

Express mail (EMS) is available to the majority of international destinations, as are private international courier services. Note that large parcels must be packed and sealed at the post office.

For general delivery or *poste restante* services, you should visit the central post office. Card members can also use American Express offices for receiving mail.

Courier Services

Beijing
DHL: tel: 010-6466 2211, fax: 010-6436 5767.
Federal Express: tel: 800-988 1888 (toll free), 400-886 1888 (mobile users toll free), fax: 010-6467 3725.

TNT: tel: 800-820 9868, fax: 010-6462 4018.
UPS: tel: 800-820 8388, fax: 010-6593 2941.

Hong Kong
DHL: tel: 852-2400 3388 (24-hour hotline), fax: 2400 2388.
Federal Express: tel: 852-2730 3333.
TNT: tel: 852-2331 2663/2266
UPS: tel: 852-2738 5000, fax: 2738 5070.

Shanghai
DHL: tel: 800-810 8000.
Federal Express: tel: 800-988 1888 (international service), 400-889 1888 (domestic service).
UPS: tel: 800 820 8388.

Xi'an
DHL: tel: 029-731 8313.
Federal Express: tel: 029-328 2754/322 7713.
UPS: tel: 029-742 0830/0141.

Public Holidays

Traditional festivals, such as the Spring Festival (Lunar New Year), follow the lunar calendar and thus dates vary annually (within a four-week range). Important official holidays follow the Gregorian calendar. This calendar does not apply to Hong Kong or Macau.
1 January: New Year's Day
January/February: variable. Lunar New Year (Spring Festival)
8 March: International Women's Day
1 May: International Labour Day
4 May: Youth Day (May 4th Movement)
1 June: Children's Day
1 July: Founding of the Communist Party

Dialling Codes

Country codes: China: 86; **Hong Kong**: 852; **Macau:** 853
Direct-dial international calls: dial 00, then the country code and telephone number.
Home country direct-dial: dial 108, then the country's international area code. For example, to call Britain, dial 108-44, then the domestic area code and number. For the United States and Canada, dial 108-1 (NB in Hong Kong, this is Directory Assistance number).
AT&T: 108-11 (from Hong Kong: 800 96 1111)
MCI: 108-12 (from Hong Kong: 800 96 1121)
Sprint: 108-13 (from Hong Kong: 800 96 1877)

1 August: Founding of People's Liberation Army
1 October: National Day
1–7 May and **1–7 October** are also week-long public holidays for the majority of Chinese. Most shops are open on holidays. School/university holidays in China are between 1 August and 30 September.

Don't plan on travel or border crossings during holidays unless reservations have been made and confirmed a long time in advance. It is especially wise not to make any travel plans during the Spring Festival, when everyone is travelling to their hometown.

In Hong Kong, the Christian Good Friday, Easter Monday and Christmas Day are public holidays, and there are several other holidays (see also page 452).

Public Toilets

Except for Hong Kong, where facilities are generally clean and well-maintained, public toilets in China are best avoided. Squat toilets are the norm, privacy cannot always be counted upon, toilet paper is rarely provided and standards of hygiene and sanitation are generally low. Some international fast-food chains provide Western-style facilities, but by far the most pleasant option is to head for a good hotel.

R eligious Services

Officially, the People's Republic encourages atheism. However, there are Buddhist and Daoist temples and places of worship throughout the country, as well as mosques in the Muslim areas and in all large cities, which have regular prayers at the prescribed times. Catholic and Protestant churches can also be found in most big cities.

S tudent Travellers

There are no special rules for foreign students in China. Taking an ISIC card may get you discounts off sights, however, so take one along with you.

T elecommunications

Telephone/fax

Domestic long-distance calls are cheap; international calls are expensive. Local calls in China from hotels are usually free of charge. International calls made from hotels typically have high surcharges added to China's already high IDD rates. IP (Internet Phone) cards are the cheapest way to phone abroad; these can be purchased at news-stands and hotels in large cities. You call a local number, enter a PIN code and then the number you wish to dial abroad. Calls are typically much cheaper than standard phone cards and can be used for long-distance calls within China as well.

Like many nations expanding their domestic telephone networks, China's telephone numbers can change at short notice. If you hear a peculiar ringing sound on the line and can't get through, the number may have changed.

Most of the big hotels have fax facilities for business people. Alternatively, central telegraph and post offices provide fax services.

Hong Kong is known for having one of the most advanced telecommunications systems in the world. It also has one of the highest rates of mobile phone penetration. Mobile phones can be rented at Hong Kong International Airport, To avoid roaming charges on your own mobile, pick up a prepaid SIM card, widely available in telephone company shops and convenience stores.

Email and Internet

Many hotels will provide in-room internet access, or contain a business centre where you can get online. Even budget hostels will often have free wireless service, and high-speed (broadband) is taken for granted everywhere. In larger cities you will find cafés and bars that provide free wireless internet for those with laptops.

Beijing

Once ubiquitous, numbers of internet cafés in Beijing and other large cities in China have fallen in recent years as the authorities cracked down on licences. Internet cafés can also be difficult to locate as many do not have English signs. A convenient but

Time Zone

All of China is officially on Beijing time: GMT +8 hours, EST +16 hours. There is no daylight-saving time. In the far west of China (Xinjiang), an unofficial time zone exists which is, sensibly, 2 hours behind Beijing time. Be warned that this can cause confusion.

pricey choice is the Qianyi internet café (3rd floor, Old Station Building, Qianmen; tel: 010-6705 1722; 9am–midnight) just to the southeast of Tiananmen Square. Look in the vicinity of universities for cheaper places; youth hostels also have cheap internet access, and you will be able to log on at most hotels.

Hong Kong

Internet access is available in all hotel business centres. More and more hotels offer broadband connections in their rooms for guests with laptops. Internet cafés are not common in Hong Kong, but free internet access is available at many coffee shops around the SAR. Branches of the Pacific Coffee, Starbucks and Mix chains offer computers for free use by their customers – although you may have to wait at busy times.

Shanghai

Shanghai has plenty of internet cafés and other places to get online, including hostels and hotels. Try the ground floor of the Shanghai Library (tel: 021-6445 5555) at 1555 Huaihai Rd (C) or China Telecom at 30 Nanjing Road (E).

Tipping

Officially, it is still illegal to accept tips in China (but not in Hong Kong and Macau, see below). Moreover, for a long time, it has been considered patronising. Tourism has changed attitudes in areas such as Guangzhou and Shanghai, and it has become the custom for travel groups to give a tip to Chinese travel guides and bus drivers. If you are travelling with a group, ask the guide, who is responsible for the "official" contacts of the group, whether a tip is appropriate and how much.

Tipping is still uncommon in most restaurants and hotels, although it is accepted in the top-class ones. As part of the ritual any gift or tip will, at first, be firmly rejected.

Hong Kong and Macau

Tipping is customary in Hong Kong bars, restaurants and hotels. Though a 10 percent service charge is often added to restaurant bills, a further 5 percent is usually added, to go direct to the staff. Taxi drivers do not expect to be tipped, but rounding up the fare to the nearest dollar or two is appreciated. In Macau, Shenzhen and Guangzhou tipping is increasingly common practice.

Tour and Travel Agents

See Activities page 453.

Travelling with Children

The Chinese are very fond of children, so travelling with a family in China can be a great pleasure. Facilities are mostly good. If you have toddlers or babies, note that disposable nappies and baby food in jars are available in all of the larger cities, but plan to pick up sufficient supplies for trips to more remote areas. Children travel at reduced cost on trains and planes, and some hotels will allow one or two children under 12 to stay in their parents' room for no extra charge. Larger hotels usually offer some form of childcare, but expect to pay a fee.

U seful Addresses

Public Security Bureaus

Beijing: (deals with customs/visa matters only) 2 Andingmen Dongdajie, tel: 010-6404 7799 (main), 010-8401 5292 (visa enquiries). Mon–Sat 8.30am–4.30pm.
Chengdu: 144 Wenwu Lu, tel: 028-8640 7074.
Chongqing: 555 Huangnipang Huanglonglu Yubei District, tel: 023-6396 1916. Mon–Fri 9–11.30am, 2–5pm.
Guangzhou: 155 Jiefang Nanlu, tel: 020-9611 0110.
Hangzhou: 35 Guanghua Rd, tel: 0571-8728 0300.
Kaifeng: 86 Zhongshan Lu, tel: 0378-532 2242. 8.30am–noon and 3–6pm.
Kashi (Kashgar): 111 Yunmulakexia Lu or 67 Renmin Donglu, tel: 0998-282 2048.
Kunming: 82 Renmin Donglu, tel: 0871-316 6191.

Visitor Hotlines

Beijing: tel: 6513 0828
Shanghai: tel: 6252 0000
Shanghai Visitor Association: tel: 6272 0000
Guangzhou: tel: 8667 7422

Weights and Measures

Both the local and international standards for weights and measures are used in China:

feet	chi	metre
3.28	03.00	1.00
1.09	01.00	0.33
1.00	00.91	0.31
acre	**mu**	**hectare**
2.47	15.00	1.00
0.16	01.00	0.07
1.00	03.22	1.61
pound	**jin**	**kilo**
2.20	02.00	1.00
1.10	01.00	0.50
1.00	00.91	0.45
gallon	**sheng**	**litre**
0.22	1.00	1.00
1.00	4.55	4.55

Lanzhou: 310 Wudu Lu, tel: 0931-846 2851. Mon–Fri 8am–noon, 2.30–6.30pm.
Luoyang: 1 Tiyuchang Lu, tel: 0379-393 8397.
Nanjing: 1 Honggongci, tel: 025-8442 0114 or 8442 0005.
Nanning: Keyuan Dadao, tel: 0771 289 1260. Mon–Fri 9am–4.30pm.
Qingdao: (deals with customs/visa matters only) 272 Ningxia Lu, tel: 0532-8579 2555.
Shanghai: 1500 Minsheng Rd, Pudong, tel: 021-6854 1199. Mon–Sat 9am–5pm.
Tai'an: Corner of Dongyue Lu and Qingnian Lu, tel: 0538-827 5264.
Ürümqi: Corner of Minzhu Lu and Jiankang Lu, tel: 0991-281 0452 ext. 3614. Mon–Fri 9.30am–1.30pm, 4–8pm.
Xi'an: 138 Xi Dajie, tel: 029-723 4500 ext. 51810. Mon–Fri 8am–noon, 3–6pm.
Zhengzhou: 70 Erqi Lu, tel: 0371-622 2023.

China National Tourism Offices

Australia, 19/F, 44 Market St, Sydney, NSW 2000, tel: 02-9299 4057, fax: 9290 1958.
Singapore, 7 Temasek Blvd, 12-02 Suntec Tower One, Singapore 038987, tel: 337 2220, fax: 338 0777.
United Kingdom, 4 Glenworth St, London NW1 5PG, tel: 020 7935 9787, fax: 020 7487 5842.
United States, 350 Fifth Avenue, Suite 6413, Empire State Building, New York, NY 10118, tel: 1-760 9700, fax: 1-760 8809.

American Express Offices

Beijing, Room 2101, L115D West Wing Building, China World Trade Centre, Beijing 100004, tel: 010-

6505 2888. Mon–Fri 9am–5pm, Sat 9am–noon.
Guangzhou, 339 Huanshi Dong Lu, Guangzhou 510060, tel: 020 8331 1771. Mon–Fri 9am–5pm, Sat 9am–noon.
Shanghai, 206 East Tower, Shanghai Centre; 1376 Nanjing Rd (W), Shanghai 200040, tel: 021-6279 8082. Mon–Fri 9am–5pm, Sat 9am–noon.
Xiamen, Rm 27, 2/F, Holiday Inn Crowne Plaza Harbour View, 12-8 Zhenhai Lu, Xiamen 361001, tel: 0592 212 0268.

W hat to Bring

Nowadays, if you are travelling to the major cities of Shanghai, Beijing or Guangzhou, you will probably be able to find most basic items, and then some. However, if you plan to spend much time travelling outside of the main centres and in the countryside, then it's worth bringing your own gear: hotel shops will have a limited choice of Western goods, but in small towns and rural areas, items such as tampons and deodorant are still difficult to find. It's always a good idea to bring your own medication.

It is prudent to bring a set of well-fitting earplugs as travel and even accommodation can be extremely noisy in China. Westerners may have difficulty finding suitably sized clothes, so be sure to bring adequate clothing if you are tall or well built.

An electrical adaptor may be useful, too; many of the older hotels have sockets which require a three-pin plug and hotels often only have a limited number of adaptors available.

What to Wear

In the summer months, take light cotton clothes that are easily washed and not too delicate. Something warm is useful, even in the hottest season, as the air conditioning in hotels and shopping malls is often vigorous. Footwear should be comfortable and strong.

Most Chinese wear ordinary clothes to evening performances at the Beijing Opera, the theatre or the circus. It is best to follow this custom, especially at some of the venues in rural areas: the floor is often of compressed mud, making high-heeled shoes an unwise option. In contrast, urban discos and clubs call for more formal dress.

Rainwear is useful, especially during the summer months. China's rainy season is from May to August.

TRANSPORT

ACCOMMODATION

SHOPPING

ACTIVITIES

A – Z

LANGUAGE

LANGUAGE

UNDERSTANDING THE LANGUAGE

General

The use of English is steadily increasing in China, but on the whole you will still find it difficult to meet people away from the big hotels and business and tourist centres who speak any English, never mind German or French. Group travellers generally have translators with them in case of communication problems. But if you are travelling on your own, it is worth taking a dictionary and learning some standard Chinese (known in the West as Mandarin Chinese and in China as *putonghua*, meaning common language).

Over a billion people in China, and many other Chinese in Southeast Asia and North America, speak Mandarin Chinese. Yet within China itself the situation is complicated by the fact that in many parts of the country – particularly in the south – a dialect form of the language is spoken which bears little relation to Mandarin. The Cantonese spoken in Hong Kong and Guangzhou is one such dialect, and is almost completely incomprehensible to Mandarin speakers. A native of Guangzhou or Hong Kong cannot understand someone from Beijing or vice versa. The different dialects have the same grammar and vocabulary; it's the pronunciation that differs, as well as the use of seven tones *(see following page)* instead of the usual four, which makes Cantonese particularly difficult for Westerners to master. Other regional dialects include Fujianese and Shanghainese.

The mutual incomprehension is, however, eased by the fact that the Chinese character script remains the same for all dialects and can be understood by all literate Chinese. People can understand each other by simply writing the symbols.

Minority languages include Tibetan, Mongolian and Uighur, although many people in these areas have at least some knowledge of Mandarin Chinese.

Language and Writing

Written Chinese is a language of symbols or images. Each symbol represents a one-syllable word. There are in total more than 47,000 symbols, though modern Chinese uses only a fraction of these. For a daily newspaper, between 3,000 and 4,000 symbols are sufficient. Scholars know between 5,000 and 6,000. Many symbols used to be quite complicated, but reforms were introduced in the People's Republic in 1949 to simplify the written language. Today, these simplified symbols are used throughout mainland China, though in Hong Kong and Taiwan, the complex ones are still used.

Many Chinese words are composed of two or more symbols or single-syllable words. For instance, the Chinese word for film is *dian-ying*, and is made up of the two words: *dian* for electricity and *ying* for shadow. To make reading easier, the pinyin system joins syllables which together form words.

Pinyin

Standard Chinese is based on the pronunciation of the northern dialects, particularly the Beijing dialect. There is an officially approved roman writing of standard Chinese, called Hanyu Pinyin (the phonetic transcription of the language of the Han people). Pinyin is used throughout the People's Republic; many shops and public facilities show names both in symbols and in pinyin.

Most modern dictionaries use the pinyin system. (Taiwan, however, usually uses the older Wade-Giles transliteration system.) This transcription may at first appear confusing: the city of Qingdao, for example, is pronounced *chingdow*. It would definitely be useful to familiarise yourself a little with the pronunciation of pinyin *(see below)*. Even when asking for a place or street name, you need to know how it is pronounced, otherwise you won't be understood. This guide uses the pinyin system throughout for Chinese names and expressions.

Names and Forms of Address

Chinese names usually consist of three, or sometimes two, syllables, each with its own meaning. Traditionally, the first syllable is the family name, the second or two others are personal names. For instance, in Deng Xiaoping, Deng is the family name, Xiaoping the personal name. The same is true for Fu Hao, where Fu is the family name, Hao the personal name.

Until the 1980s, the address *tongzhi* (comrade) was common, but today *xiansheng* and *furen*, the Chinese equivalent of Mr and Mrs, are more usual. A young woman, as well as female staff in hotels and restaurants, can be addressed as *xiaojie* (Miss). Address older men, especially those in important positions, as *xiansheng* or *shifu* (Master).

Pronunciation

The pronunciation of the consonants is similar to English *(see below)*. The i after the consonants ch, c, r, sh, s, z, zh is not pronounced; it indicates that the preceding sound is lengthened.

Pinyin/Phonetic/Sound
a/a/f**a**r
an/un/r**un**
ang/ung /l**ung**
ao/ou/l**oud**
b/b/**b**ath
c/ts/ra**ts**
ch/ch/**ch**ange
d/d/**d**ay
e/er/d**ir**t
e (after i, u, y)/a/tr**a**m
ei/ay/m**ay**
en/en/wh**en**
eng/eong/**ng** has a nasal sound
er/or/h**o**nour
f/f/**f**ast
g/g/**g**o
h/ch/lo**ch**
i/ee/k**ee**n
j/j/**j**eep
k/k/ca**k**e
l/l/**l**ittle
m/m/**m**onth
n/n/**n**ame
o/o/b**o**nd
p/p/tra**pp**ed
q/ch/**ch**eer
r/r/**r**ight
s/s/me**ss**
sh/sh/**sh**ade
t/t/**t**on
u/oo/sh**oo**t
u (after j, q, x, y)/as German ü/**ü**ber
w/w/**w**ater
x/sh/as in **sh**eep
y/y/**y**ogi
z/ds/re**ds**
zh/dj/**j**ungle

Tones

It is sometimes said that Chinese is a monosyllabic language. At first sight, this seems to be true, since each character represents a single syllable that generally indicates a specific concept. However, most words are made up of two or three syllables, sometimes more. In the Western sense, spoken Chinese has only 420 single-syllable root words, but tones are used to differentiate these basic sounds, which often makes it very difficult for foreigners to learn the language. For instance, if one pronounces the syllable *mai* with a falling fourth sound (mài) it means to sell; if it is pronounced with a falling-rising third sound, it means to buy. The meaning of a word is given by the symbol, but the tone is not.

Mandarin has four tones and a fifth, "neutral" sound: The first tone

Styles of Calligraphy

In the history of Chinese calligraphy, there are four basic styles of writing. The first is the archaic *xiao zhuan* (small-seal script), established in the Qin dynasty (221–206 BC) and which is meticulous and laborious.

The square *li shu*, with its clear brushstrokes, was established in the Han dynasty and used in official writing. Many of the inscriptions on steles of ancient Chinese classics are done in this style.

Cao shu ("grass" or cursive style), in which brushstrokes are often joined together in one continuous flow, was developed as a quicker and simpler alternative to the more formal scripts. More so than any other style, the flamboyance of *cao shu* is a form of individual expression.

Finally, *kai shu* is a combination of the more formal *li shu* and the more expressive *cao shu*, and is the basis of today's standard calligraphic script.

Calligraphy is still highly esteemed, practised by housewives and politicians alike. Even the old masters will claim they are but students of this fine art.

is spoken high-pitched and even, the second rising, the third falling and then rising, and the fourth sound falling.

first sound ma: **mother**
second sound má: **hemp**
third sound mǎ: **horse**
fourth sound mà: **to complain**

Grammar

The Chinese sentence structure is simple: subject, predicate, object. The simplest way of forming a question is to add the question particle "ma" to the end of a statement. It is usually not possible to know from a Chinese word whether it is a noun, adjective or another form, singular or plural: it depends on the context.

Words and Phrases

The following pages contain useful words and phrases translated into pinyin and Chinese characters.

English	Pinyin	Characters
Hello	Nǐ hǎo	你好
How are you?	Nǐ hǎo ma?	你好吗？
Thank you	Xièxie	谢谢
Goodbye	Zài jiàn	再见
My name is...	Wǒ jiào...	我叫...
My last name is...	Wǒ xìng...	我姓...
What is your name?	Nín jiào shénme míngzi?	您叫什么名字？
What is your last name?	Nín guìxìng?	您贵姓？
I am very happy...	Wǒ hěn gāoxìng...	我很高兴...
All right	Hǎo	好
Not all right	Bù hǎo	不好
Can you speak English?	Nín huì shuō Yīngyǔ ma?	您会说英语吗？
Can you speak Chinese?	Nín huì shuō Hànyǔ ma?	您会说汉语吗？
I cannot speak Chinese	Wǒ bù huì Hànyǔ	我不会汉语
I do not understand	Wǒ bù dǒng	我不懂
Do you understand?	Nín dǒng ma?	您懂吗？
Please speak a little slower	Qǐng nín shuō màn yìdiǎnr	请您说慢一点儿
What is this called?	Zhège jiào shénme?	这个叫什么？
How do you say...	... zěnme shuō?	...怎么说？
Please	Qǐng	请/谢谢

English	Pinyin	Characters
Never mind	Méi guānxì	没关系
Sorry	Duìbùqǐ	对不起

PRONOUNS

English	Pinyin	Characters
Who/who is it?	Shéi?	谁?
My/mine	Wǒ/wǒde	我/我的
You/yours (singular)	Nǐ/nǐde	你/你的
He/his	Tā/tāde	他/他的
She/hers	Tā/tāde	她/她的
We/ours	Wǒmen/wǒmende	我们/我们的
You/yours (plural)	Nǐmen/nǐmende	你们/你们的
They/theirs	Tāmen/tāmende	他们/他们的
You/yours (respectful)	Nín/nínde	您/您的

TRAVEL

English	Pinyin	Characters
Where is it?	zài nǎr?	...在哪儿?
Do you have it here?	Zhèr... yǒu ma?	这儿有... 吗?
No/it's not here/there aren't any	Méi yǒu	没有
Hotel	Fàndiàn/bīnguǎn	饭店/宾馆
Restaurant	Fànguǎnr	饭馆
Bank	Yínháng	银行
Post Office	Yóujú	邮局
Toilet	Cèsuǒ	厕所
Railway station	Huǒchē zhàn	火车站
Bus station	Qìchē zhàn	汽车站
Embassy	Dàshíguǎn	大使馆
Consulate	Lǐngshìguǎn	领事馆
Passport	Hùzhào	护照
Visa	Qiānzhèng	签证
Pharmacy	Yàodiàn	药店
Hospital	Yīyuàn	医院
Doctor	Dàifu/yīshēng	大夫/医生
Translate	Fānyì	翻译
Bar	Jǐubā	酒吧
Do you have...?	Nín yǒu... ma?	您有... 吗?
I want/I would like	Wǒ yào/wǒ xiǎng yào	我要/我想要
I want to buy...	Wǒ xiǎng mǎi...	我想买...
Where can I buy it?	Nǎr néng mǎi... ma?	哪儿能买吗?
This/that	Zhège/nèige	这个/那个
Green tea/black tea	Lǜchá/hóngchá	绿茶/红茶
Coffee	Kāfēi	咖啡
Cigarette	Xiāngyān	香烟
Film (for camera)	Jiāojuǎnr	胶卷儿
Ticket	Piào	票
Postcard	Míngxìnpiàn	明信片
Letter	Yì fēng xìn	一封信
Air mail	Hángkōng xìn	航空信
Postage stamp	Yóupiào	邮票

SHOPPING

English	Pinyin	Characters
How much?	Duōshǎo?	多少
How much does it cost?	Zhège duōshǎo qián?	这个多少钱?
Too expensive, thank you	Tài guì le, xièxie	太贵了, 谢谢
Very expensive	Hěn guì	很贵
A little (bit)	Yìdiǎnr	一点儿
Too much/too many	Tài duō le	太多了
A lot	Duō	多
Few	Shǎo	少

MONEY MATTERS, HOTELS, TRANSPORT, COMMUNICATIONS

English	Pinyin	Characters
Money	Qián	钱
Chinese currency	Rénmínbì	人民币
One yuan/one kuai (10 jiao)	Yì yuán/yī kuài	一元/一块
One jiao/one mao (10 fen)	Yì jiāo/yì máo	一角/一毛
One fen	Yì fēn	一分
Traveller's cheque	Lǚxíng zhīpiào	旅行支票
Credit card	Xìnyòngkǎ	信用卡
Foreign currency	Wàihuìquàn	外汇券

English	Pinyin	Characters
Where can I change money?	Zài nǎr kěyǐ huàn qián?	在哪儿可以换钱?
I want to change money	Wǒ xiǎng huàn qián	我想换钱
What is the exchange rate?	Bǐjià shì duōshǎo?	比价是多少?
We want to stay for one (two/three) nights	Wǒmen xiǎng zhù yì (liǎng/sān) tiān	我们想住一(两，三)天
How much is the room per day?	Fángjiān duōshǎo qián yì tiān?	房间多少钱一天?
Room number	Fángjiān hàomǎ	房间号码
Single room	Dānrén fángjiān	单人房间
Double room	Shuāngrén fángjiān	双人房间
Reception	Qiántái/fúwùtái	前台/服务台
Key	Yàoshi	钥匙
Clothes	Yīfu	衣服
Luggage	Xínglǐ	行李
Airport	Fēijīchǎng	飞机场
Bus	Gōnggòng qìchē	公共汽车
Taxi	Chūzū qìchē	出租汽车
Bicycle	Zìxíngchē	自行车
Telephone	Diànhuà	电话
Long-distance call	Chángtú diànhuà	长途电话
International call	Guójì diànhuà	国际电话
Telephone number	Diànhuà hàomǎ	电话号码
Telegram	Diànbào	电报
Computer	Diàn nǎo/jìsuànjī	电脑/计算机
Check email	Chá diànxìn	查电信
Use the internet	Shàng wǎng	上网

TIME

When?	Shénme shíhou?	什么时候?
What time is it now?	Xiànzài jǐdiǎn zhōng?	现在几点种?
How long?	Duōcháng shíjiān?	多长时间?
One/two/three o'clock	Yì diǎn/liǎng diǎn/sān diǎn zhōng	一点/两点/三点钟
Early morning/morning	Zǎoshang/shàngwǔ	早上/上午
Midday/afternoon/evening	Zhōngwǔ/xiàwǔ/wǎnshang	中午/下午/晚上
Monday	Xīngqīyī	星期一
Tuesday	Xīngqīèr	星期二
Wednesday	Xīngqīsān	星期三
Thursday	Xīngqīsì	星期四
Friday	Xīngqīwǔ	星期五
Saturday	Xīngqīliù	星期六
Sunday	Xīngqītiān/xīngqīrì	星期天/星期日
Weekend	Zhōumò	周末
Yesterday/today/tomorrow	Zuótiān/jīntiān/míngtiān	昨天/今天/明天
This week/last week/ next week	Zhègexīngqī/shàngxīngqī/ xiàxīngqī	这个星期/上星期/ 下星期
Hour/day/week/month	Xiǎoshí/tiān/xīngqī/yuè	小时/天/星期/月
January/February/March	Yīyuè/èryuè/sānyuè	一月/二月/三月
April/May/June	Sìyuè/wǔyuè/liùyuè	四月/五月/六月
July/August/September	Qīyuè/bāyuè/jiǔyuè	七月/八月/九月
October/November/December	Shíyuè/shíyīyuè/shíèryuè	十月/十一月/十二月

EATING OUT

Restaurant	Cāntīng/fànguǎn'r	餐厅/饭馆儿
Attendant/waiter	Fúwùyuán	服务员
Waitress	Xiǎojiě	小姐
Eat	Chī fàn	吃饭
Breakfast	Zǎofàn	早饭
Lunch	Wǔfàn	午饭
Dinner	Wǎnfàn	晚饭
Menu	Càidān	菜单
Chopsticks	Kuàizi	筷子
Knife	Dāozi	刀子
Fork	Chāzi	叉子
Spoon	Sháozi	勺子
Cup/glass	Bēizi/bōlíbēi	杯子/玻璃杯
Bowl	Wǎn	碗
Plate	Pán	盘
Paper napkin	Cānjīn zhǐ	餐巾纸
I want...	Wǒ yào...	我要
I do not want...	Wǒ bú yào...	我不要

English	Pinyin	Characters
I did not order this	Zhège wǒ méi diǎn	这个我没点
I am a vegetarian	Wǒ shì chī sù de rén	我是吃素的人
I do not eat any meat	Wǒ suǒyǒude ròu dōu bù chī	我所有的肉都不
I do not eat any meat or fish	Wǒ suǒyǒude ròu hé yú, dōu bù chī	我所有的肉和鱼都不吃
Please fry it in vegetable oil	Qīng yòng zhíwù yóu chǎo chǎo	请用植物油炒炒吃
Beer	Píjiǔ	啤酒
Red/white wine	Hóng/bái pútaojiǔ	红/白葡萄酒
Liquor	Bái jiǔ	白酒
Mineral water	Kuàngquánshuǐ	矿泉水
Soft drinks	Yǐnliào	饮料
Cola	Kělè	可乐
Tea	Cháshuǐ	茶水
Fruit	Shuǐguǒ	水果
Bread	Miànbāo	面包
Toast	Kǎomiànbāo	烤面包
Yoghurt	Suān nǎi	酸奶
Fried/boiled egg	Chǎo/zhǔ jīdàn	炒/煮鸡蛋
Rice	Mǐfàn	米饭
Soup	Tāng	汤
Stir-fried dishes	Chǎo cài	炒菜
Beef/pork/lamb/chicken	Niú/zhū/yáng/jī ròu	牛肉/猪肉/羊肉/鸡肉
Fish	Yú	鱼
Vegetables	Shūcài	蔬菜
Spicy/sweet/sour/salty	Là/tián/suān/xián	辣/甜/酸/咸
Hot/cold	Rè/liáng	热/凉
Can we have the bill, please	Qīng jié zhàng/mǎidān	请结帐/买单

Specialities

Peking Duck	Běijīng kǎoyā	北京烤鸭
Hot pot	Huǒ guō	火锅
Phoenix in the Nest	Fèng zài wōli	凤在窝里
Mandarin fish	Tángcù guìyú	糖醋鳜鱼
Thousand layer cake	Qiān céng bǐng	千层饼
Lotus prawns	Ǒu piàn'r xiārén	藕片儿虾仁
Home-style cooking	Jiā cháng cài	家常菜

Appetizers

Deep-fried peanuts	Zhá huāshēngmǐ	炸花生米
Boiled peanuts	Zhǔ huāshēngmǐ	煮花生米
Soft beancurd	Bàn dòufu	拌豆腐
"Hairy" green beans	Máo dòu	毛豆
Mashed cucumber	Pái huǎnggguā	排黄瓜
Pressed beancurd strips	Dòufu sī	豆腐丝
Thousand-year-old eggs	Sōnghuā dàn	松花蛋
Smoked beancurd with celery	Qíncài dòufu gān'r	芹菜豆腐干儿

Meat dishes

Aubergine/eggplant fritters stuffed with minced pork	Qié hé	茄盒
Spicy chicken with chillies	Làzi jīdīng	辣子鸡丁
Spicy chicken with peanuts	gōngbào jīdīng	宫爆鸡丁
Pork with egg and "tree ear" fungus	Mùxū ròu	木须肉
Shredded pork with bamboo shoots	Dōngsǔn ròusī	冬笋肉丝
Beef in brown sauce	Hóngshāo niúròu	红烧牛肉
Sizzling "iron plate" beef	Tiěbǎn niúròu	铁板牛肉
Beef with potatoes	Tǔdòu niúròu	土豆牛肉

Seafood

Prawns with cashew nuts	Yāoguǒ xiārén	腰果虾仁
Carp in brown sauce	Hóngshāo lǐyú	红烧鲤鱼
Boiled prawns	Shuǐzhǔ xiārén	水煮虾仁
Stir-fried prawns	Qīngchǎo xiārén	清炒虾仁
Sweet and sour mandarin fish	Tángcù guìyú	糖醋鳜鱼
Hot and sour squid	Suānlà yóuyú juàn	酸辣鱿鱼卷

Vegetable dishes

Sweetcorn with pine kernels	Sōngrén yùmǐ	松仁玉米
Mangetout/snowpeas	Hélán dòu	荷兰豆

English	Pinyin	Characters
Spicy "dry" green beans	Gānbiān biǎndòu	干煸扁豆
Spicy "fish flavour" aubergine	Yúxiāng qiézi	鱼香茄子
Greens with dried mushrooms	Xiānggū yóucài	香菇油菜
Spicy beancurd with chilli	Málà dòufu	麻辣豆腐
Stir-fried egg and tomato	Xīhóngshì chǎo jīdàn	西红柿炒鸡蛋
Fried shredded potato	Tǔdòu sī	土豆丝
Clay pot with beancurd soup	Shāguō dòufu	沙锅豆腐
Sour cabbage with "glass" noodles	Suāncài fěnsī	酸菜粉丝
Potato, aubergine and green pepper	Dì sān xiān	地三鲜

Staple food

Steamed bread	Mántou	馒头
Cornbread	Wōtou	窝头
Fried rice	Dàn chǎo fàn	蛋炒饭
Plain rice	Bái fàn	白饭
Sizzling rice crust	Guōbā	锅巴
Noodles	Miàntiáo	面条
Pancakes	Bǐng	饼

Soups

Hot and sour soup	Suānlà tāng	酸辣汤
Egg and tomato soup	Xīhóngshì jīdàn tāng	西红柿鸡蛋汤
Beancurd soup	Dòufu tāng	豆腐汤
Lamb and marrow soup	Yángròu dōngguā tāng	羊肉冬瓜汤
Fish-head soup	Yútóu tāng	鱼头汤

Fast food

Noodles	Miàntiáo	面条
Stuffed pasta parcels	Jiǎozi	饺子
Meat/vegetable filling	Ròu xiàn/sù xiàn	肉馅/素馅
Steamed meat buns	Bāozi	包子
"Potstickers" (fried jiaozi)	Guōtiē	锅贴
Egg pancake	Jiān bǐng	煎饼
Wonton soup	Húndùn	混沌
Soy milk	Dòu jiāng	豆浆
Deep-fried dough sticks	Yóutiáo	油条

NUMBERS

One	Yī	一
Two	Èr	二
Three	Sān	三
Four	Sì	四
Five	Wǔ	五
Six	Liù	六
Seven	Qī	七
Eight	Bā	八
Nine	Jiǔ	九
Ten	Shí	十
Eleven	Shíyī	十一
Twelve	Shíèr	十二
Twenty	Èrshí	二十
Thirty	Sānshí	三十
Forty	Sìshí	四十
Fifty	Wǔshí	五十
Sixty	Liùshí	六十
Seventy	Qīshí	七十
Eighty	Bāshí	八十
Ninety	Jiǔshí	九十
One hundred	Yìbǎi	一百
One hundred and one	Yìbǎi língyī	一百零一
Two hundred	Liǎng bǎi	两百
Three hundred	Sān bǎi	三百
Four hundred	Sì bǎi	四百
Five hundred	Wǔ bǎi	五百
One thousand	Yìqiān	一千

FURTHER READING

History

Behind the Wall (Colin Thubron). Written in the mid-eighties, it is a reminder of what China was then, and – Thubron being as prescient as he is – there many fascinating insights into the China of today.
China: A New History (John King Fairbank). A definitive general account of China's long history by a doyen of American Sinologists.
Foreign Devils on the Silk Road: The Search for the Lost Treasures of Central Asia (Peter Hopkirk). Essential reading for anyone en route to Dunhuang and China's northwest.
The Great Chinese Revolution, 1800–1985 (John King Fairbank). A concise and thorough summary of two turbulent centuries, by a leading China scholar.
Life along the Silk Road (Susan Whitfield). A fascinating and erudite collection of historical "short stories" based on characters – the merchant, the soldier, the courtesan, etc – chiefly based on first-hand information derived from the archives and murals of Dunhuang.
Mao: The Unknown Story (Jung Chang, Jon Halliday). Thought-provoking and searingly critical appraisal of the Mao era. Essential reading for anyone interested in the evolution of modern China.
Oracle Bones: A Journey Between Past and Present (Peter Hessler). The follow-up to the New Yorker correspondent's 2001 River Town interweaves his experience as a journalist in China with explorations of the country's history.
Red Star Over China (Edgar Snow). First-hand account of the birth and early years of Chinese Communism by an American journalist and sympathiser who was a personal friend of Mao Zedong and Zhou Enlai.
The Search for Modern China (Jonathan Spence). Definitive history of China from the establishment of the Ming dynasty to the modern day.
Trespassers on the Roof of the World: The Race for Lhasa (Peter Hopkirk). Engaging and painstakingly researched account of the major 19th-century attempts by Westerners to reach this long-forbidden city.

Biography

China Remembers (Li Jia and Calum MacLeod). Vivid personal accounts of China's 20th century, with scene-setting background history.
God's Chinese Son (Jonathan Spence). Spence's masterly grasp of storytelling and historical research makes this an enthralling biography of Hong Xiuquan, leader of the Christian Taiping.
The Hermit of Peking: the Hidden Life of Sir Edmund Backhouse (Hugh Trevor-Roper). Marvellous piece of investigative spadework from the famed historian on the trail of forger and eccentric Wykehamist Edmund Backhouse.
The Man Who Loved China (Simon Winchester). The story of Joseph Needham, the Cambridge professor who devoted 60 years of his life to researching and chronicling the History of Science and Civilization in China in more than 20 encylopaedic volumes.
The Private Life of Chairman Mao (Dr Li Zhisui). A gossipy, erudite and highly amusing look at the depravities, personal habits and disastrous policies of Chairman Mao, by his Western-educated personal physician.
The Soong Dynasty (Sterling Seagrave). The story of China's most influential family, including Chiang Kaishek, his wife, Soong Mayling, and her brother, T.V. Soong – for a time China's richest man – during the first half of the 20th century.
Wild Swans: Three Daughters of China (Jung Chang). The turbulence of the Cultural Revolution in China as seen through the eyes of three generations of women – grandmother, mother and daughter.

Current Affairs

China Shakes The World (James Kynge). This is primarily a piece of highly readable economics by the Financial Times' former Beijing Bureau chief, but it goes far beyond statistics to deliver a superb snapshot of life in 21st-century China.

China Wakes: The Struggle for the Soul of a Rising Power (Nicholas D. Kristof and Sheryl WuDunn). A captivating collection of vignettes from the experiences of these former New York Times correspondents.
The China Dream: The Elusive Quest for the Greatest Untapped Market on Earth (Joe Studwell). Salutary observations and cautionary tales for those contemplating doing business in China.
China's New Confucianism: Politics and Everyday Life in a Changing Society (Daniel A. Bell). How China's traditional past is influencing and changing contemporary realities.
The Chinese (Jasper Becker). Fine analysis of contemporary China and what makes the country tick, from a former correspondent of the South China Morning Post.
The Coming Collapse of China (Gordon Chang). Strong on polemic, Chang's book may seem opinionated, but it is backed up by solid research and ultimately convinces.
The Dragon in the Land of Snows: A History of Modern Tibet since 1947 (Tsering Shakya). A painstakingly researched yet highly readable account of modern Tibet – the best yet published.
The Search for a Vanishing Beijing, a Guide to China's Capital through the Ages (M.A. Aldrich). A deeply informed exploration of China's history, legends and culture, as seen through the window of its fast-changing capital city.
The Ugly Chinaman and the Crisis of Chinese Culture (Bo Yang, translated by Don Cohn). A controversial and scathing indictment of many aspects of traditional Chinese culture, which has sparked intense debate in the Chinese-speaking world.
Wild Grass, Three Portraits of Change in Modern China (Ian Johnson). The book tells the stories of three ordinary Chinese people who, in their own small ways, challenge the system.
Wild West China: The Taming of Xinjiang (Christian Tyler). An important book tackling China's Islamic northwestern region and its aspirations for independence.

Travel Writing

Bamboo Goalposts (Rowan Simons). Highly amusing account of British journalist and football enthusiast's attempts to persuade the Chinese to embrace the beautiful game.

My Life as an Explorer (Sven Hedin, with a prologue and epilogue by Peter Hopkirk). The epic memoirs of the legendary Swedish explorer, adventurer and archaeologist give a fascinating insight into aspects of the Silk Road and Tibet that no longer exist.

News from Tartary (Ian Fleming). Classic travelogue across northwest China and Xinjiang in the 1930s.

Red Dust, a Path Through China (Ma Jian). It begins as a travel-adventure article by a disillusioned Beijing native, but soon evolves into a sweeping appraisal of modern China.

Riding the Iron Rooster: By Train Through China (Paul Theroux). Highly readable and informed account of China on the cusp of opening to the outside world.

The River at the Centre of the World: A Journey up the Yangtze and back in Chinese Time (Simon Winchester). Fascinating account of the author's voyage from the mouth of China's longest river to its source in Tibet, masterfully weaving travel prose with historical narrative.

River Town: Two Years on the Yangtze (Peter Hessler). Hessler's celebrated tale of two years in Fuling on the Yangtze River.

Seven Years in Tibet (Heinrich Harrer). The evocative account of a German national trapped in Tibet by World War II who became friends with the Dalai Lama.

Shadow of the Silk Road (Colin Thubron). Although Thubron follows the Silk Road from Xi'an all the way to its western terminus in Turkey, his account of contemporary Chinese Central Asia in the first half of this book is unsurpassed.

The Travels of Marco Polo (Ronald Latham). Tried and tested English translation of Polo's *Il Milione*, including his travels through 13th-century China.

Philosophy

Art of War (Sun Tzu, translated by Ralph D. Sawyer). Though there are dozens of English translations of this ancient Chinese military treatise, this is one of the most highly acclaimed.

Bardo Thodol (known in the West as *The Tibetan Book of the Dead*, discovered by Karma Lingpa). The classic text detailing what Tibetans believe the human consciousness experiences in the interim period between death and rebirth.

Daode Jing (Tao Te Ching) (Laozi). Both profound and accessible, the Classic of the Way and its Power is a keystone to understanding Daoist philosophy.

Understanding Confucianism: Origins, Beliefs, Practices, Holy texts, Sacred Places (Jennifer Oldstone-Moore). Learned yet very readable account of the principals of the philosophical system that made traditional China tick and laid the foundations of Chinese culture.

Fiction

A Case of Two Cities, by Qui Xiaolong. One of a series of wonderfully gritty detective novels featuring the gentle and poetic Inspector Chen Cao, and his investigations into the seamy, crime-ridden underworld of modern Shanghai.

The True Story of Ah Q, by Lu Xun. A scathing but engaging look at the deep endemic flaws in the Chinese character, by China's most famous 20th-century novelist.

Other Insight Guides

Insight Guides cover destinations all over the world, providing information on culture and all the top sights, as well as superb photography.

Send Us Your Thoughts

We do our best to ensure the information in our books is as accurate and up-to-date as possible. The books are updated on a regular basis, using local contacts, who painstakingly add, amend and correct as required. However, some mistakes and omissions are inevitable, and we are ultimately reliant on our readers to put us in the picture.

We would welcome your feedback on any details related to your experiences using the book on the road, and will acknowledge all contributions. We'll offer an Insight Guide to the best letters received.

Please write to us at:
  Insight Guides
  PO Box 7910
  London SE1 1WE
  United Kingdom
Or email us at:
  insight@apaguide.co.uk

Other Insight Guides to China include: *Southern China* (covering the southern provinces from Fujian to Yunnan and including Hong Kong) and *The Silk Road* (covering all the main sights along the historic route between China and the Mediterranean). The smaller-format city guides cover *Beijing, Shanghai* and *Hong Kong*.

Insight Step by Step guides offer an itinerary-based approach to destinations, with recommendations from a local expert to make the most of a short stay. Titles in this region include *Beijing* and *Hong Kong* as well as *Tokyo, Singapore* and *Kuala Lumpur*.

Insight Smart Guides provide comprehensive information in an easy-to-carry and innovative format, with lavish illustrations, in-depth listings and an indexed street atlas. There are Smart Guides to *Beijing and Hong Kong, Hanoi & Ho Chi Minh City* and *Tokyo*.

Insight Fleximaps combine clear, detailed cartography with essential travel information. The laminated finish makes the maps durable, weatherproof and easy to fold. Titles covering this region include *Beijing, Xi'an, Shanghai, Nanjing, Guangzhou, Shenzhen, Hong Kong, Macau, Ho Chi Minh City* and *Vietnam, Cambodia & Laos*.

TRANSPORT

ACCOMMODATION

EATING OUT

ACTIVITIES

A – Z

LANGUAGE

Art & Photo Credits

PICTURE SPREADS

© 2009 Apa Publications GmbH & Co.
Verlag KG (Singapore branch)

Production: Linton Donaldson

INDEX

Numbers in bold refer to main entries

A

Aberdeen (Hong Kong) 279
Academy for Performing Arts (Hong Kong) 278
accommodation 427–43
acrobatics 213, 451
acupuncture 86
admission charges 454
adventure sports 337, 453
agriculture 52, 54
air travel
  domestic 421
  international 418–20
Aksu 409
ancestor worship 75–6
Ancient Observatory (Beijing) 138
Anhui province 262, 427
Anshan 161
Anting 221
antiques 98, 444
Anyang 196
architecture 100–3
art 94–9
  see also museums & galleries; rock art
arts, performing 91–3, 451–2
astronomy 42
ATM machines 459
Avenue of Stars (Hong Kong) 281

B

Bai people 344–5, 366
Baidi Cheng 255
Baishui 369
Bank of China Tower (Hong Kong) 275
Baoding Shan 254
Baotou 168, 435
Barkhor (Lhasa) 383
beaches
  Bangchuido Jingqu 162
  Beidaihe 154–5
  Clearwater Bay (Hong Kong) 283
  Dameisha & Xiaomeisha (Shenzhen) 304
  Fujiazhuang 162
  Hac Sa (Coloane) 294
  Hainan Island 308–9
  Hung Shing Ye (Lamma) 287
  Laohu Tan 162
  Qingdao 177
  Repulse Bay (Hong Kong) 279–80
  Silver Beach (Beihai) 338
  Silvermine Bay (Lantau) 286
Bei Shan 254
Beidaihe 154–5
Beihai 338, 343
Beijing 129–45
  accommodation 428
  Ancient Observatory 138
  Baita Si 140
  Beihai Park 140
  CCTV Tower 145

Chairman Mao Mausoleum 134–5
  cuisine 111
  Dashanzi Art District 144–5
  excursions 148–55
  Forbidden City 130–2
  Haidian District 144
  history 129
  Houhai Lake 136, 140–1
  hutong 136
  Jing Shan 132
  Kong Miao 139
  Olympics 28–9, 72–3, 129, 145
  restaurants, cafés & bars 146–7
  shopping 138–9, 445
  Summer palaces 142–4
  Sun Yatsen Park 132–3
  Temple of Heaven 137–8
  Tiananmen Square 134–5
  transport 133, 418, 422, 424
  Underground City 137
  Xiang Shan (Fragrant Hills) 143, 144
  Yonghe Gong 139
  Zhongnanhai 140
bicycle hire 426
birdwatching
  Caohai Hu 342
  Lake Zhalong 165
  Qinghai Hu 393
Black Stone Forest 363
Bodhidharma 192, 193
Bon religion 79, 80
Boxer Rebellion 47, 133
Britain 45–7
  and Hong Kong 273–4
Bronze Square (Shaoshan) 321
Buddhism 40, 41, 78–80
  sacred peaks 264–5
  temples 104–5
budgeting 454
the Bund (Shanghai) 213–15
Bupan Aerial Walkway 372
Burma (Mayanmar) 372, 420
bus travel
  city 426
  long-distance 424
business hours 454

C

calligraphy 94–5, 463
Cangshan mountain range 366
Canton system 45
Cantonese cuisine 109
Caohai Hu 342
carpets & rugs 153
casinos, Macau 293, 294
Castle Peak (Hong Kong) 284
castles & fortifications
  city gates & walls (Dali) 365
  city walls (Fenghuang) 323
  city walls (Nanjing) 229, 330
  diaolou watchtowers (Kaiping) 305

dzong (Gyantse) 386
  Fortaleza da Barra (Macau) 293
  Fortaleza do Monte (Macau) 291
  fortress of Shajio (Humen) 304
  Great Wall 148–51, 155, 156–7, 401
  Gu Nanmen (Guilin) 333
  Guia Fortress & Lighthouse (Macau) 294
  Gulou (Beijing) 136, 140
  Gulou (Nanjing) 231–2
  Gulou (Xi'an) 185
  Huanghe Lou (Wuhan) 259
  Huli Shan Fort (Xiamen) 311
  Jiayuguan fort 402–3
  Juyongguan Fortress 149–50
  Kam Tin walled villages (Hong Kong) 284
  Ming wall (Xi'an) 184
  Old City Wall (Chaozhou) 307
  Overhanging Great Wall (Jiayuguan) 403
  Shang-era walls (Zhengzhou) 194–5
  Shipaotai (Shantou) 306
  tulou roundhouses 102, 312, 314
  Tung Chung (Lantau) 285
  Zhenchenglou (Hukeng) 312, 314
  Zhonglou (Beijing) 136, 140
  Zhonglou (Nanjing) 231–2
  Zhonglou (Xi'an) 184–5
cathedrals
  Dongtang (Beijing) 139
  Harbin 164
  St John's (Hong Kong) 277
  Xujiahui (Shanghai) 222
Causeway Bay (Hong Kong) 278, 279
caves
  Bezeklik 406
  Bingling Si (Linxia) 399–400
  cave houses (Henan province) 190
  Dazu 254
  Heifo Xinshui (Yangshuo) 337
  Heilong Dong (Yangshuo) 337
  Heilong Dong (Zhenyuan) 340
  Kezier Qianfodong 409
  Lianhuayan (Xingping) 336
  Longgong Dong 342
  Longmen Shiku 191–3
  Ludiyan (Guilin) 335
  Mogao Caves 403–4
  Sanxian Dong 412
  Yungang Shiku (Datong) 172
  Zhijin Dong 342
CCTV Tower (Beijing) 145
censorship 56
Chang Jiang 34–5, 227, 251
  boat trips 253
Chang Jiang (Yangzi) region 251–63
Changbai Shan Scenic Area 163

Changchun 163–4, 165
Changsha 320–1, 323, 435
Chaotianmen (Chongqing) 252
Chaozhou 306–7
Chek Lap Kok (Hong Kong) 284
Chengde 153–4, 155, 432
Chengdu 348–52, 357
  accommodation 440
  transport 349, 421, 424
**Chengyang Wind and Rain Bridge
  (Sanjiang)** 338
Cheung Chau (Hong Kong) 287
Chiang Kaishek 49–51, 254
children 461
Chinese Communist Party (CCP)
  49–53, 57–8
Chinese New Year 83
Chinese opera 92–3, 451–2
Chishui 342
Chiu Chow
  cuisine 109
  people 306
cholera 457
Chong'an 340
Chongqing 251–4, 263
  accommodation 429
  transport 253, 418, 421, 422,
    424
Chongye 385
Chongzhen, Emperor 132
Christianity 80–1
churches
  see also **cathedrals**
  Catholic (Dali) 365
  Mu'en Tang (Shanghai) 218
  Portuguese Catholic (Ningbo)
    248
  Sacred Heart (Guangzhou) 299
  St Michael's Catholic (Qingdao)
    177
  Santo Agostinho (Macau) 293
  São Domingos (Macau) 290
  São Lourenço (Macau) 293
  São Paulo (Macau) 290–1
cinema 91
Ciping 320
Civil War 51
Cixi, Empress Dowager 132
  Yiheyuan (Beijing) 143
Clearwater Bay (Hong Kong) 283
Clearwater Pool (Changsha) 321
climate 31–2, 454–5
clothing 461
Colina da Guia (Macau) 294
Colina da Penha (Macau) 293
Coloane (Macau) 294
concerts 452
Confucianism 77–8, 104
Confucius 38, 88
  birthplace 179
  Confucius Six Arts City (Qufu)
    180–1
  grave (Kong Lin) 180
  Kong Family Mansion (Qufu)
    180
Conghua 307
conservation 325
consulates 455
corruption 58
costumes, minority 345

Cotai strip (Macau) 294
courier services 459
crafts 94–9
credit cards 459, 461
crime 455–6
  Guangzhou 301
  Shanghai 217
Cuandixia 155
Cui Hu (Kunming) 361
Cuiheng 305
cuisines 106–13
Cultural Revolution 50, **53**, 74
currency 459
Customs House (Shanghai) 214
customs regulations 456

D

Dadonghai 309
***dafo* (Leshan)** 355
Dagu Shan 162
Dai people 344, 370, 371
  Dai Minority Park (Ganlanba)
    372
Dalai Lama 79–80, 380
  Norbulingka (Lhasa) 383
  Potala Palace (Lhasa) 381–2
Dali 364–6, 373, 442
Dali, Kingdom of 359
Dalian 160–2, 165, 429
Damenglong 372
Dandong 161, **162**, 165
Danxia Shan 307
Daoism 76–7, 264–5
  temples 104–5
Darchen 391
Datong 172, 181, 438
Dazu 254
Dehong 372
Democracy Wall Movement 54
Deng Xiaoping 50, 53–5, 58, 67
Dengfeng 193, 433
Dengue fever 457
Deqin 370
Des Voeux Road (Hong Kong)
  276
dialling codes 459
Dian Kingdom 359
Dianchi 362
Diecai Shan (Guilin) 335
Dinghu Shan 305, 325
Dingri 389
Dingshan 240
disabled travellers 455
Disneyland (Hong Kong) 285–6
Dong people 340, 344–5
Dongbei 159–69
  accommodation 429
  transport 160
Dragon Boat Festival 82, 112,
  340, 341, 450
dragons 105, 131
Du Fu 88–9, 350–1
Dujiangyan 353
Dunhuang 403, 413
  accommodation 430
  transport 399
Duolun Street (Shanghai) 216
Dutch East India Company 45
Duxiu Feng (Guilin) 335

E

earthquakes 33
  2008 33, 59, 353
economy 55, 59, **67–71**
education 71
electricity 455
Elliot, Captain Charles 46
embassies 455
Emei Shan 264, **353–5**, 440
Emeishan 353–4
emergencies 455–6
  medical 456–8
emigration 316–17
entry regulations 418, **456**
environmental issues 35, 70–1
Er Hai 366
etiquette 112
Everest, Mount 33, **388**
  Base Camp 388–9
Exchange Square (Hong Kong)
  274
exercise 86

F

Falun Gong movement 56, 58, 81
family values 26–7
Fanjing Shan 341
Feixia Scenic Area 307
feng shui 75, 100
Fengdu 254
Fenghuang 323, 435
Fenghuangshan (Yan'an) 189
festivals & events 82–3, **450–1**
  Bun Festival (Cheung Chau) 287
  Dragon Boat Festival 82, 112,
    340, 341, 450
  festival food 112
  Ice Lantern Festival (Harbin)
    165
  Lunar New Year 82, **83**
  Miao *lusheng* festivals 340
  Mid-Autumn Festival 82
  Turpan Grape Festival 405
film *see* **cinema**
**First National Congress of the
  Communist Party of China
  (Shanghai)** 221
Five Phoenix Hall (Lijiang) 368
Flagstaff House (Hong Kong) 277
Flint, James 45
food and drink
  beer (Qingdao) 176–7, 178
  cuisines of China **106–13**
  Guangzhou 300
  medicinal 85
  Mongolian 169
Forbidden City (Beijing) 130–2
foreign affairs 56–7
**Former Revolutionary Headquarters
  (Ciping)** 320
fortune-telling 74–5, 283
Foshan 304
Four Modernisations 54
Four Treasures of the Study 95
Friendship Pass 338–9
Friendship Stores 139, **444–5**
frontiers 420
Fubo Shan (Guilin) 335

Fujian province 310–15
  accommodation 429
  shopping 445
  transport 309
Fushun 162
Fuzhou 314, 429
  transport 309, 419

G

Ganlanba 372
Gansu province 397–404, 413
  accommodation 430
  transport 399
Gaochang 406
Gaozong, Emperor 188
gay travellers 456
GDP 67, 71
Gegentala 169
geography 31–5
geomancy 130
Germany 49, 176–7
Ghengis Khan 43
  Mausoleum 169
golf 452
Golmud 387
Gong, Prince 140
Gonggashan, Mount 357
Government House (Hong Kong)
  277
governor's residence (Qingdao)
  177
Grand Canal 141, 227, **237–40**
Great Game 395, **411**
Great Hall of the People (Beijing)
  134
Great Hall of the People
  (Chongqing) 253
Great Leap Forward 50, **52**
Great Wall 148–51, 155, 401
  building of 156–7
  Museum (Jiayuguan) 403
  walking 155, **157**
group travel 424
Gu Shan 314
Guangdong province 297–307
  accommodation 430–1
  transport 303
Guangji Bridge (Chaozhou) 307
Guangxi province 331–9, 343
  accommodation 431
  shopping 446
  transport 333
Guangzhou 297–302
  accommodation 430–1
  history 297–8
  restaurants 315
  Shamian & old city 298–9
  shopping 445–6
  Sun Yatsen 301
  transport 303, 418, 421, 422–3
  waterfront 299
Guanxing Tai 194
guesthouses 427
Guge 391
Gugong see **Forbidden City**
Guilin 332–5, 343
  accommodation 431
  transport 333, 418, 421, 423,
    424

Guiyang 339–40, 343, 431
Guizhou province 331, **339–42**
  accommodation 431
  restaurants 343
  shopping 446–7
  transport 341
Gulangyu 311–12
gunpowder 42
Guomindang see **Nationalist Party**
Guozijian (Beijing) 139–40
Gyantse 386–7

H

Ha Noi Ancient City 411
Haikou 308, 432
Hailuogou Glacier 357
Hainan Island 308–9, 315
  accommodation 432
  shopping 447
  transport 309, 418, 426
Hakka people 306, 307
  tulou roundhouses 102, **312**,
    314
Han Chinese 21, 344
Han dynasty 39–40
Hangzhou 243–7
  accommodation 443
  restaurants 249
Hankou (Wuhan) 259, 434
Hanyang (Wuhan) 260–1
Happy Valley (Hong Kong) 279
Harbin 164–5, 429
health 456–8
Hebei province 152–5, 171, **176**
  accommodation 432
Heihe 165
Henan province 183–4, **189–97**
  accommodation 432
  transport 190
Heng Shan (Hunan) 264, **321–2**
Heng Shan (Shanxi) 173, 264–5
hepatitis A & B 457
hiking 157, **452–3**
Himalaya 33, 388
history 37–71
Hohhot 166–8, 169, 435
Hollywood Road (Hong Kong)
  276
Hong Ge (Wuhan) 260
Hong Kong 273–87
  accommodation 433–4
  Central District 274–8
  Cheung Chau 287
  Disneyland 284–5
  history 273
  Kowloon 280–3
  Lamma 286–7
  Lantau 285–6
  New Territories 283–4
  public holidays 452
  restaurants & bars 288–9
  shopping 447–8
  south side 279–80
  transport 275, 286, 418, 423,
    426
  Victoria Peak 277–8
  Wan Chai & Causeway Bay
    278–9
  Western District 278

Hong Kong Arts Centre 278
Hong Kong Convention & Exhibition
  Centre 278–9
Hong Kong Cultural Centre 281
Hong Shan (Ürümqi) 408
Hong Wu, Emperor 233
Hong Xiuquan 230
Hongkong & Shanghai Bank
  Building (Hong Kong) 275
Hongkou district (Shanghai)
  215–17
Hongqi Yunhe 196
Hongyan 254
hospitals 457–8
hot springs
  Conghua 307
  Huaqing 187
  Tirthapuri 391
hotels 427–43
Houhai (Beijing) 140
Hu Jintao 58, 59
Hu Yaobang 55
Hua Guofeng 53–4
Hua Shan 188–9, 264–5
Huaihai Road (Shanghai) 221
Huaiyang cuisine 110
Huang He 34, 171, 183, 397, 398
  unpredicability of 172
Huang Shan 262
Huanghuacheng 151
Huanglongxi 353
Huangpo River 210
Huangyaguan 151
Huaqiao see **Overseas Chinese**
Hubei province 258–62
  accommodation 434–5
  transport 258
Hudie Quan 366
Hui 29, 401
Huitengxile 169
Hukeng 312, 314
hukou **system** 25
human rights 56, 59
Humen 304
Hunan province 258, **320–3**
  accommodation 435
  cuisine 110
  transport 323
Hundred Flowers Movement 52
Huoyan Shan 405–6
hutong 130, **136**
Huxinting Teahouse (Shanghai)
  219

I

Id Gah Square (Kashi) 409–10
Impression Liu Sanjie (Yangshuo)
  337
individual travel 425
industry 55
infrastructure 69, 71
Inner Mongolia 166–9
  accommodation 435
  transport 167
International Finance Centre Two
  (IFC-2) (Hong Kong) 274
internet access 460
inventions 42
Islam 80, 142

J

jade 97–8
Jade Dragon Snow Mountain 368–9
Jade Hill (Fuzhou) 314
Japan
  ferry from 421
  occupation of Manchuria 51, 161
  occupation of Qingdao 49, 176–7
  relations with 56
  Unit 731 Japanese Germ Warfare
    Experimental Base (Pingfang)
    165
  World War II 51
Japanese encephalitis 457
Jardine House (Hong Kong) 275
Jesuits 44, 81
Jews, Kaifeng 196
Ji'an 162–3
Jiang Zemin 50, 55, 57
Jiangsu province 227–41
  accommodation 436
  transport 231
Jiangxi province 318–20, 323
  accommodation 436
  shopping 448
  transport 319
Jianshui 364
Jiao Shan 155
Jiaohe Gucheng 407
Jiayuguan 402–3
Jiefang Bei (Chongqing) 252
Jieyin Dian (Emei Shan) 354
Jilin City 163
Jinan 181
Jing Shan (Beijing) 132
Jingdezhen 320
Jinggangshan 320
Jinghong 371, 373
  accommodation 442
  transport 361, 418
Jingling Hotel (Nanjing) 229
Jingpo Hu 163
Jinshanling 151
Jiuhua Shan 262, 264–5
Jiujiang 320
Jiuquan 402
Jiuzhaigou 356–7, 440–1
Journey to the West Statues
  (Lanzhou) 398

K

Kaifeng 195–6, 197, 432
Kailash, Mount 390–1
Kaili 340, 431
Kaiping 305
Kam Tin (Hong Kong) 284
Kampa La 386
Kangding 357
Karakoram range 412
Karakul Lake 412
Karo La 386
karst 334, 335
Kashi (Kashgar) 408, 409–11, 413
  accommodation 441
  shopping 449
  transport 399, 421, 424
Kazaks 29
Kazakstan 420

Khotan 409
Khunjerab Pass 412
Kirghiz 29
Kong Fuzi see Confucius
Koolhaas, Rem 145
Korla 409
Kowloon Peninsula (Hong Kong)
  280–3
Koxinga
  Memorial Hall (Xiamen) 312
  statue (Xiamen) 311
Kuan Xiangzi (Chengdu) 350
Kublai Khan 43, 129
  Beihai Park (Beijing) 140
Kubuqi Desert 169
Kunming 360–2, 373
  accommodation 442
  excursions from 362–3
  transport 361, 418, 421, 423,
    424
Kuqa 409
Kyrgyzstan 420

L

lacquerware 98–9
lamaseries see monasteries
Lamma (Hong Kong) 286–7
Lan Kwai Fong (Hong Kong) 276
Lancang Jiang 35, 360
land issues 70
The Landmark (Hong Kong) 276
The Lanes (Hong Kong) 276
Lang Liwei 59
Langmusi 356–7
language 462–7
Lantau (Hong Kong) 284–5
Lanzhou 397–8, 413
  accommodation 430
  transport 399, 422, 423, 424
Lao Long Tou 155
Lao Shan 177–8
Laos 420
Laozi 76–7
Largo do Senado (Macau) 290
Leal Senado (Macau) 290
Legislative Council (Legco)
  Building (Hong Kong) 275
Leshan 355, 441
Lhasa 381–3, 393
  accommodation 441
  transport 383, 387, 421–2, 423,
    424
Lhatse 388, 390
Li Bai 88–9
Li Hongzhi 81
Li people 309, 369
Li River 335–6
  riverboat trips 337
Li Yuen Street East & West (Hong
  Kong) 276
Lijiang 367–8, 373, 442–3
Lin Zexu 46, 304
Linggang New City 221
Linxia 398–400
Linzhou 196
Litang 357
literature 88–90
Liu Shaoqi 53
Liulichang (Beijing) 135

Lo Wu Commercial City (Shenzhen)
  303, 446
Lockhart Road (Hong Kong) 279
Long March 50, 51, 189
  Museum (Zunyi) 342
Longji Titian 337
Longjing 247
Longsheng 337
Lu Xun 90
  former home (Shanghai) 216
  Former Residence (Shaoxing)
    247
  Memorial Hall (Shaoxing) 247
  museum (Beijing) 141
Luchan 364
lucky numbers 75
Luding 357
luggage 421, 456
Lugu Lake 369
Luhuitou 308
Lunar New Year 82, 83
Luoyang 189–91, 197, 432
Lushan 320, 436

M

Ma Ying-jeou 57
Macartney, Lord 45
Macau 44, 290–4
  accommodation 436
  casinos 293
  historic centre 290–1
  restaurants & bars 295
  shopping 448
  Taipa and Coloane 294
  transport 291, 419, 422
Macau Tower 291, 293
malaria 456–7
Manasarovar, Lake 390
Manchuria see Dongbei
Manchus 44, 159
Mao Zedong 50–3
  Ancestral Temple (Shaoshan)
    321
  Clearwater Pool (Changsha) 321
  cult of 320
  Former Residence (Shaoshan)
    321
  Hongyan 254
  Mausoleum (Beijing) 134
  Museum (Shaoshan) 321
  Portrait (Beijing) 133
  Yan'an 189
  Zunyi Conference Site 341–2
markets 445
  Animal Market (Kashi) 410
  Beijing speciality 445
  Bird Market (Hong Kong) 282
  Cat Street (Hong Kong) 447
  Central Market (Hong Kong) 278
  Flower Market (Hong Kong) 282
  Fuyou Road Sunday antique
    market (Shanghai) 220
  Fuzi Miao (Nanjing) 230
  Goldfish Market (Hong Kong) 282
  Jade Market (Hong Kong) 282,
    447
  Jade Market (Ruili) 372
  Jinsha Night Market (Jinghong)
    371, 373

Ladies' Market (Hong Kong) 282, 447
Nationalities' Square night market (Linxia) 399
night market (Kaifeng) 195
Panjiayuan (Beijing) 138
Qingping Shichang (Guangzhou) 299
Silk Alley (Beijing) 139
Stanley Market (Hong Kong) 280, 447
Temple Street night market (Hong Kong) 282, 447
martial arts 192, 193
Marxism 49
Matang 340
May Fourth Movement 48–9
media 28, 458–9
medical services 456–8
medicine, traditional 84–7
Meijiawu 247
Meizhou 307
Mekong river see **Lancang**
Memorial to the Nanjing Massacre 229–30
Mencius (Mengzi) 38, 77, 181
Mengla 372
Menglun 372
Miao people 309, 339, 344
festivals 340, 345
Mid-Autumn Festival 82
migrant workers 23–5
Ming dynasty 43
tombs 150, **151–2**
Mingsha Hill 403
minority groups 29, 58–9, **344–5**
China Folk Culture Village (Shenzhen) 304
Dai Minority Park (Ganlanba) 372
National Minorities Park (Jinghong) 371
Yunnan Nationalities Village (Kunming) 363
missionaries, Christian 43–4, 80–1
Mochou Hu (Nanjing) 229
Moganshan 248, 443
monasteries
see also **temples**
Baoguang Si (Xindu) 352
Baoguo Si (Emei Shan) 354
Bezeklik 406
Chi Lin Nunnery (Hong Kong) 283
Dabeichan Yuan (Tianjin) 153
Dazhao (Hohhot) 168
Drepung (near Lhasa) 384
Ganden (near Lhasa) 384
Labrang (Xiahe) 357, **400–1**
Lingyin Si (Hangzhou) 246
Mindroling 385
Nechung (near Lhasa) 384
Palkhor Chode 386
Po Lin (Lantau) 285
Ramoche (Lhasa) 383
Rongbuk 388
Sakya 388
Samye 385
San Ta Si (Dali) 365
Sera (near Lhasa) 384
Shaolin Si 192, **193**
Songsenling (Songzhanling) 370

Ta'er Si 392–3
Tashilhunpo (Shigatse) 387
Tholing 391
Trandruk 384–5
Wat Manting (Jinghong) 371
Wudangzhao (Baotou) 168
Xiangguo Si (Kaifeng) 195
Xilituzhao (Hohhot) 168
Yin Hing (Lantau) 285
Zhongyue Miao 194
money 459
Mong Kok (Hong Kong) 282
Mongolia 420
see also **Inner Mongolia**
Mongols 29, 136
Monument to the People's Heroes (Beijing) 134
Monument to the Revolutionary Martyrs (Beishan) 320
mosques
Ashab Mosque (Quanzhou) 313
Dongguan Great Mosque (Xining) 392
Huaisheng Si (Guangzhou) 300
Id Gah Mosque (Kashi) 410
Kowloon Mosque (Hong Kong) 281
Ox Street Mosque (Beijing) 142
Qingzhen Dasi (Hohhot) 168
Qingzhen Dasi (Xi'an) 186
Sugong Ta (Turpan) 405
Mosuo people 369
mountain sickness 380
Mudanjiang 163
museums & galleries 452
1 August Uprising Museum (Nanchang) 319
9.18 History Museum (Shenyang) 161
Banpo Museum 187
Beijing Planning Exhibition Hall 137
Dali Museum 364–5
Dashanzi Art District (Beijing) 144–5
Dongba Research Institute (Lijiang) 368
Dr Sun Yatsen Residence Memorial Museum (Cuiheng) 305
Du Fu Caotang (Chengdu) 350–1
Forest of Stelae Museum (Xi'an) 186
Gansu Provincial Museum (Lanzhou) 398
Grand Prix Museum (Macau) 294
Great Wall Museum (Jiayuguan) 403
Guangdong Museum of Art (Guangzhou) 302
Hebei Provincial Museum (Shijiazhuang) 176
Henan Provincial Museum (Zhengzhou) 195
History Museum (Shanghai) 215
Hong Ge (Wuhan) 260
Hong Kong Heritage Museum 283
Hong Kong Museum of Art 281

Hong Kong Museum of History 282
Hong Kong Racing Museum 279
Hong Kong Railway Museum 284
Hong Kong Science Museum 182
Hong Kong Space Museum 281
Hubei Provincial Museum (Wuhan) 260
Hunan Provincial Museum (Changsha) 321
Inner Mongolia Museum (Hohhot) 167
Kaifeng Museum 196
Kong Family Mansion (Qufu) 180
Koxinga Memorial Hall (Xiamen) 312
Long March Museum (Zunyi) 342
Lu Xun Former Home (Shanghai) 216
Lu Xun Former Residence (Shaoxing) 247
Lu Xun Museum (Beijing) 141
Luoyang Museum 190–1
Macau Museum of Art 294
Madame Tussaud's (Hong Kong) 278
Mao's Former Residence (Shaoshan) 321
Maritime Museum (Hong Kong) 280
Maritime Museum (Macau) 293
Maritime Museum (Quanzhou) 313
Minority Nationalities Museum (Wuzhishan) 309
Municipal Museum (Guangzhou) 301
Museum of Comrade Mao (Shaoshan) 321
Museum of Contemporary Art (Shanghai) 218
Museum of Macau 291
Museum of Taipa & Coloane History 294
Nanjing Museum 232
New Suzhou Museum 236
Ningxia Museum (Yinchuan) 401
Opium War Museum (Humen) 304
Overseas Chinese Museum (Xiamen) 310
Palace Museum (Beijing) 132
Piano Museum (Xiamen) 312
Provincial Museum (Guiyang) 339
Provincial Museum (Nanning) 338
Sam Tung Uk Museum (Hong Kong) 284
Sanxingdui Museum 352–3
Shaanxi History Museum (Xi'an) 186–7
Shanghai Art Museum 218
Shanghai Duolun Museum of Modern Art 216
Shanghai Museum 217–18
Sichuan University Museum (Chengdu) 351
Song Qingling Former Residence (Chongqing) 253
Stilwell Museum (Chongqing) 253

Sun Yatsen Residence (Shanghai) 222
Taipa Houses Museum 294
Taiping Museum (Nanjing) 230
Tea Ware Museum (Hong Kong) 277
Tianjin Museum 153
Unit 731 Japanese Germ Warfare Experimental Base (Pingfang) 165
West Lake Museum (Hangzhou) 245
Wine Museum (Macau) 294
Xiamen Museum 312
Xi'an Museum 186
Xianyang Museum 188
Xihan Nanyue Wangmu (Guangzhou) 302
Xinjiang Sheng Bowuguan (Ürümqi) 408
Yan'an Revolutionary Museum 189
Yantai Museum 178
Yin Ruins Museum 196
Yunnan Provincial Museum (Kunming) 361
Yuzi Paradise 336
Zhu De's Former Residence (Nanchang) 319
muslims 80, 142
Mutianyu 150
Muyu Zhen 261
mythological creatures 105

N

names 22, 462–3
Nanchang 318–19, 323
accommodation 436
transport 319, 422, 424–5
Nanfeng Ancient Kiln (Shiwan) 305
Nanjing 227, **228–33**
accommodation 436
restaurants & bars 241
transport 231, 422
Nanjing Massacre 51, 230–1
Nanjing Road (Shanghai) 217, 219
Nanjing, Treaty of 47, 228
Nanluoguxiang (Beijing) 141
Nanning 338, 343, 431
Nanshi (Old City) (Shanghai) 219–20
Nanyue 321
Nanzhao Dao 366
Nanzhao Kingdom 359, 364
NAPE waterfront (Macau) 293
Nathan Road (Hong Kong) 281
National Day 82
Nationalist Party 49–51, 57
nationalist sentiment 28–9
natural resources 35
nature reserves
Changbai Shan 163
Chebaling National 307
Dinghu Shan **305**, 325
Fanjing Shan 341
Jianfeng Ling Primeval Forest Reserve 309
Jiuzhaigou 356
Lake Zhalong 165

Nanling National Forest Park 307
Poyang Lake National 320
Qinghai Lake Natural Protection Zone 393
Sanchahe 371
Shennongjia Forest Reserve 261
Wolong 353
Wulingyuan Scenic Reserve 322–3
Wuyi Shan 314
Naxi people 344–5, 367
Neo-Confucianism 78
Neolithic period 37
Nepal 386, 389–90, 420
New Kowloon (Hong Kong) 283
New Territories (Hong Kong) 283–4
nightlife 452
Nine Bend Stream 314
Ningbo 248
Ningming 338
Ningxia Hui Autonomous Region 401
No. 1 Department Store (Shanghai) 217
North Korea 161, 162–3
Nyalam 389
Nyatri Tsenpo 379

O

oil fields 165
Old Film Café (Shanghai) 216
Olympic Games (2008) 28–9, 59, **72–3**, 129, 452
Olympic Stadium (Beijing) **72–3**, 145
one-child policy 23, 26
Opium Wars 46–7
Museum (Humen) 304
outdoor pursuits 452–3
overland routes 420–1
Overseas Chinese 310, **316–17**

P

packing 461
pagodas
108 Dagobas (Qingtongxia) 401
architecture 101
Bai Ta (Beijing) 140
Bai Ta (Fuzhou) 314
Baita Shan (Lanzhou) 398
Bamboo Shoot Pagoda (Damenglong) 372
Bao Ta (Yan'an) 189
Baochu (Hangzhou) 245
Beisi Ta (Suzhou) 237
Chongxi Ta (Zhaoqing) 305
Dayan Ta (Xi'an) 186
Dongsi Ta (Kunming) 360
Fan Ta (Kaifeng) 195
Futu Pagoda (Dali) 366
Gongtang Ta (Xiahe) 401
Guang Ta (Guangzhou) 300
Hua Ta (Guangzhou) 300
Kumbum (Palkhor Chode) 386
Linggu Ta (Nanjing) 233
Lone Pagoda (Dali) 365–6
Mor Pagoda 411
Mu Ta (Yingxian) 173–4

Riyue Shuangta (Guilin) 333
Songyuesi Ta 101, **193–4**
Talin (Stupa Forest) (Shaolin) 101, **193**
Three Pagodas (Dali) 365
Tie Ta (Kaifeng) 195
Tiger Hill (Suzhou) 237–8
Wenfeng Ta (Anyang) 196
Wu Ta (Fuzhou) 314
Xi Ta (Yinchuan) 401
Xiaoyan Ta (Xi'an) 101, **186**
Xisi Ta (Kunming) 360
Xixiu Shan Ta 342
Xuanwen Ta (Taiyuan) 175
painting 94–6
Pakistan 420
palaces
Bishu Shanzhuang (Chengde) 153–4
Chaotian Gong (Nanjing) 229
Forbidden City (Beijing) 130–2
Imperial Palace (Shenyang) 160–1
Jinjiang Princes' Palace (Guilin) 334
Ming Imperial Palace (Nanjing) 232
Mu Family Mansion (Lijiang) 368
Ningshou Gong (Beijing) 132
Norbulingka (Lhasa) 383
Potala (Lhasa) 381–2
Qianqing Gong (Beijing) 131–2
Summer palaces (Yuanming Yuan & Yiheyuan) (Beijing) 133, **142–4**
Weihuang Gong (Changchun) 164
Working People's Cultural Palace (Beijing) 133
Pamir range 412
Panchen Lama 79–80, 380
Tashilhunpo Monastery (Shigatse) 387
pandas, giant 325, 352
paper manufacture 42
Park Hotel (Shanghai) 218–19
parks & gardens
see also **nature reserves; theme parks**
Beihai Park (Beijing) 140
Black Dragon Pool Park (Lijiang) 368
Botanical Gardens (Beijing) 144
Camies Grotto (Macau) 291
Canglang Ting (Suzhou) 235–6
Classical Chinese gardens 103
Dong Hu (Wuhan) 260
Flora Garden (Macau) 294
Garden of Seclusion and Meditation (Tongli) 239
Great Bridge Park (Nanjing) 228
Hong Kong Park 277
Hongkou Park (Shanghai) 216
Huangpu Park (Shanghai) 215
Jiangxin Dao (Wenzhou) 249
Kowloon City Walled Park 283
Kowloon Park (Hong Kong) 281
Lieshi Lingyuan (Guangzhou) 302
Liu Yuan (Shuzhou) 237
May Fourth Square (Qingdao) 177

Mei Yuan (Tai Hu) 240
People's Park (Chengdu) 349–50
People's Park (Shanghai) 217
Qianling Park (Guiyang) 339–40
Qinghui Yuan (Shunde) 305
Qixing Gongyuan (Guilin) 335
Sai Kung Country Park (Hong
   Kong) 284
Shamian Gongyuan (Guangzhou)
   299
Shouxihu Gongyuan (Yangzhou)
   240
Shuzhuang Garden (Xiamen) 312
Summer palaces (Beijing) 143–4
Sun Yatsen Park (Beijing) 132–3
Tie Ta Gongyuan (Kaifeng) 195
Tropical Botanical Gardens
   (Menglun) 372
Tropical Flower and Plants
   Garden (Jinghong) 371
Wangjianglou (Chengdu) 351
Wangshi Yuan (Suzhou) 235
Water Wheel Park (Lanzhou) 398
World Horticultural Garden (near
   Kunming) 362
Xinglong Tropical Botanical
   Garden 308
Xiu Shan Park (Tonghai) 364
Xu Yuan (Nanjing) 231
Xuanwu Hu (Nanjing) 233
Yu'er Park (Dali) 365
Yuexiu Gongyuan (Guangzhou)
   301
Yuhua Yuan (Beijing) 132
Yuyuan Garden (Shanghai) 219
Yuzi Paradise 336
Zhaolin Park (Harbin) 165
Zhongshan Park (Qingdao) 177
Zhongxin Park (Tianjin) 153
Zhuozheng Yuan (Suzhou) 236
Zoological & Botanical Gardens
   (Hong Kong) 277
passports 456
pavilions
   Kuixing Lou (Zhenyuan) 341
   Penglai (Yantai) 178–9
   Sanqing (Qingdao) 178
   Tengwang (Nanchang) 318–19
   Wangjianglou (Chengdu) 351
   Yueyang Lou 258–9
Peace Hotel (Shanghai) 214
Peak Tower (Hong Kong) 277–8
Pearl Oriental TV Tower (Shanghai)
   223
Pearl River Delta (PRD) 68, **304–5**
**Peasant Movement Training
   Institute (Guangzhou)** 302
Pei, I.M. 236
Peking University (Beijing) 144
Peninsula Hotel (Hong Kong) 281
people 21–9
   minority groups 29, 58–9,
     344–5
   Overseas Chinese 310, **316–17**
People's Republic 51–2
People's Square (Chongqing) 253
People's Square (Shanghai)
   217–18
pharmacies 85
photography 459

Pingshiku (Guilin) 335
Pingyao 175–6, 181, 438
Pinyin 462
Pipa Shan 254
poetry 88–9
pollution 35, 70–1
Polo, Marco 43–4, 227, 240
population 21, **22–3**
porcelain 96–7
Portugal 44
   return of Macau 290
postal services 459
Poyang Hu 320
printing 42
property law 58, 70
public holidays 452, **459–60**
Public Security Bureaux 461
**Pudong International Airport
   (Shanghai)** 210
Pudong Xinqu (Shanghai) 223
Pujiang 221
Pujiang Hotel (Shanghai) 216
Putao Gou (Turpan) 405
Putuo Shan 249, 264, 443
Puyi, Emperor 48, 51, 164

Q

Qian Shan 161
Qiandaohu 247
Qianlong, Emperor 45–6, 142–3
Qianmen Gate (Beijing) 135
Qiantang River 247
Qiao Jia Dayuan 175
qigong 86
Qin dynasty 38–9
Qin Shi Huangdi, Emperor 39, 183,
   184, 199
Qing dynasty 44–8
   Chengde 153–4
   tombs 150, 151, 161
Qingcheng Hou Shan 352
Qingcheng Shan 352
Qingdao 176–8, 181, 438
Qingfeng hutong (Beijing) 136
Qinghai Hu 393
Qinghai province 379, **392–3**, 437
Qinglan 308
Qixing Yan (Zhaoqing) 305
Qu Yuan 112, 257
Quanzhou 312–13, 315
Queen's Road (Hong Kong) 276
Qufu 179–81, 438
Qutang Xia 255

R

rail travel 422–4
   China–Tibet 29, **387**
   Ürümqi–Almaty **395**, 399
Red Army 51
Red Guard 53
religion 74–81
religious services 460
Renmin Daqiao (Guangzhou) 299
Republican Revolution, 1911 48
Repulse Bay (Hong Kong) 279–80
Ricci, Matteo 44, 80
rivers 34–5
road names 421

road travel 420
rock art
   Bingling Si (Linxia) 399–400
   Dazu 254
   Khunjerab Pass 412
   Longmen Shiku 191
   Mogao Caves 403–4
   Yungang Shiku (Datong) 172
Ruili 372
Russia 164–5, 420–1

S

sacred peaks 264–5
   see also **Emei Shan**; **Heng Shan**;
     Hua Shan; **Jiuhua Shan**; **Putuo
     Shan**; **Song Shan**; **Tai Shan**;
     Wudang Shan; **Wutai Shan**
Sai Kung (Hong Kong) 284
Sakya 387–8
Sandouping 257
Sanjiang 337, 338
**Santa Casa da Misericórdia
   (Macau)** 290
Sanxia 255–8
   river trips 425–6
Sanxindui 200–1
Sanya 308
Satellite Launch Centre (Jiuquan)
   402
schistosomiasis 457
sea travel 421
Sha Tin (Hong Kong) 283
Shaanxi province 183–9, 197
   accommodation 437
   transport 185
Shamian (Guangzhou) 298–9
Shandong province 171, **177–81**
   accommodation 438
   transport 178
Shang dynasty 38, 194, 196, 200
Shanghai 209–23
   accommodation 439–40
   Art District 222
   the Bund 213–15
   economy 68–9
   history 212
   Hongkou (Shanghai) 215–16
   Huaihai Road & Xuhui 221–2
   Jing An 219
   Nanjing Road 217, 219
   Old City (Nanshi) 219–20
   Pearl Oriental TV Tower 223
   People's Square 217–18
   Pudong Xinqu 223
   restaurants & bars 224–5
   satellite cities 221
   shopping 448–9
   transport 211, 419, 422, 423,
     425, 426
   Xintiandi 220–1
   Yufuo Si 217
**Shanghai Arts & Crafts Research
   Institute** 222
Shanghai Centre 219
Shanghai Exhibition Centre 219
Shanghai Library 222
Shanghai Railway Station 216
Shanghai Urban Planning Centre
   218

Shangri-La 357, **370**
Shanhaiguan **155**, 432
Shanshangan Huiguan (Kaifeng) 196
Shantou **306**, 315
Shanxi province **171–6**, 181
  accommodation 438
  transport 175
Shao Hao, Emperor 181
Shaolin Si 192–3
Shaoshan 321
Shaoxing 247
Shapotou 401
Shashi 258
She Shan (Wuhan) 259
Shennong 84
Shenyang **159–61**, 429
Shenzhen **302–4**, 315
  accommodation 431
  shopping 446
  transport 303, 419
Shibing 341
Shibing (Miao hamlet) 340
Shigatse **387**, 441
Shijiazhuang 176
shikumen 220–2
Shimei Wan 308
Shipton's Arch 411–12
Shitoucheng (Nanjing) 229
Shiwan 305
shopping **444–9**
Shuanglang 366
Shunan Bamboo Sea 355
Shunde 305
Sichuan province **347–57**
  accommodation 440–1
  cuisine 109–10
  shopping 449
  transport 349
silk **96**, 237, **240**
Silk Road **394–5**, **397–413**
  accommodation 430, 441–2
  shopping 449
  transport 395, **399**
Simatai 150–1
skiing 163, 165, 453
sky burials 356
soccer 452
social issues 58–9, 70–1
SoHo (Hong Kong) 276
Sok Kwu Wan (Lamma) 286
Song dynasty 41–3
Song Qingling
  former residence (Chongqing) 253
  house (Beijing) 140
Song Shan 193, 264
Songpan 356
Songsten Gampo 379, 385
Songyang Shuyuan 193
Songzhanling 370
South Korea, ferry from 421
space programme 59, 402
Special Economic Zones (SEZ) 55, 68
Spring Festival *see* **Lunar New Year**
Stanley (Hong Kong) 280
Star Ferry (Hong Kong) 274
Statue Square (Hong Kong) 275
Stilwell, General Joseph 253

Stone Forest 363
student travellers 460
stupas see **pagodas**
Sui dynasty 40
Sun Yatsen 48–50
  Hong Ge (Wuhan) 260
  Mausoleum (Nanjing) 232–3
  Memorial Hall (Guangzhou) 301
  Monument (Guangzhou) 301
  Residence Memorial Museum (Cuiheng) 305
  Song Qingling house (Beijing) 140
  Sun Yatsen Residence (Shanghai) 222
  Zhongshan Gongyuan (Beijing) 132–3
Sunlight Rock (Gulangyu) 312
Suzhou 227, **233–8**
  accommodation 436
  restaurants 241
Suzhou No. 1 Silk Mill 237
Suzhou Science & Cultural Arts Centre 234

T

Tai Hu 239–40
Tai O (Lantau) 285
Tai Po (Hong Kong) 284
Tai Shan 179, 264
Tai'an 179
Taihuai 174
tailors, custom 448
Taipa (Macau) 294
Taiping Rebellion 47
  Taiping Museum (Nanjing) 230
Taishi Shan Scenic Area 194
Taiwan 51, 57, 310
Taiyuan 174–5, 181, 438
Taklamakan desert 33, 409, 411
Tang dynasty 40–1
Tanggula Pass 387
Taoism *see* **Daoism**
taxis 426
Taxkorgan 412
tea production, Longjing 247
technology 42
telecommunications 28, 460
temples 104–5
  see also **monasteries**
  architecture 101–2
  Baima Si (Luoyang) 191
  Baita Si (Beijing) 136, **141**
  Baiyun Guan (Lanzhou) 398
  Baiyunguan (Beijing) 142
  Baxian An (Xi'an) 187
  Beishan Si (Xining) 392
  Bingling Si (Linxia) 399–400
  Biyun Si (Beijing) 144
  Changchun Guan (Wuhan) 259–60
  Chenghuang Miao (Zhengzhou) 195
  Chenjia Si (Guangzhou) 301
  Ching Chung Koon (Hong Kong) 284
  Chongshan Si (Taiyuan) 175
  Chunman Dasi (Ganlanba) 372
  Dafo Si (Zhangye) 402

Dafo Si (Zhengding) 176
Dai Miao (Tai'an) 179
Daming Si (Yangzhou) 240
demon temples (Mount Mingshan) 254
Famen Si 188
Fayu Si (Putuo Shan) 249
Fayuan Si (Beijing) 142
Fengxian Si 191–3
Gantong Si 366
Guangxiao Si (Guangzhou) 300–1
Guiyuan Si (Wuhan) 260–1
Heilongtan (near Kunming) 362
Hongfu Si (Guiyang) 340
Hualin Si (Guangzhou) 299
Huating Si (near Kunming) 362
Huayan Si (Datong) 172–3
Jiangnan Suspended Temple (Tonglu) 247
Jin Dian (near Kunming) 362
Jinding Si (Emei Shan) 354
Jing' An Si (Shanghai) 219
Jokhang (Lhasa) 382–3
Kaiyuan Si (Quanzhou) 313
Kong Miao (Beijing) 139
Kong Miao (Qufu) 180
Kong Miao (Zhengzhou) 194
Lidai Diwang Miao (Beijing) 144
Linggu Si (Nanjing) 233
Liurong Si (Guangzhou) 300
Longhua Gu Si (Shanghai) 222
Luohan Si (Chongqing) 253
Maitreya (Shigatse) 387
Man Mo (Hong Kong) 278
Mao's Ancestral Temple (Shaoshan) 321
Nanputuo Si (Xiamen) 311
Nanshan Si (Taihuai) 174
Pak Tai (Cheung Chau) 287
Pak Tai (Hong Kong) 279
Penglai Pavilion (Yantai) 178–9
Puji Chansi (Putuo Shan) 249
Puning Si (Chengde) 154
Pusa Ding (Taihuai) 174
Putuozongcheng (Chengde) 154
Qingyang Gong (Chengdu) 351
Qiongzhu Si (near Kunming) 362
Sanqing Ge (Kunming) 363
Shibaozhai 254
Shuanglin Si 176
Shuangta Si (Taiyuan) 175
Sigong Si (Zhenyuan) 341
Taihua Si (Kunming) 362–3
Tanhua Si (Kunming) 362
Tanzhe Si 155
Tayuan Si (Taihuai) 174
Temple of 10,000 Buddhas (Hong Kong) 283
Temple da A-Ma (Macau) 293
Temple of Heaven (Beijing) 102, 133, **137–8**
Tianhou Gong (Shantou) 306
Tianhou Gong (Tianjin) 152
Tin Hau (Yung Shue Wan) 286–7
Waiba Miao (Chengde) 154
Wannian Si (Emei Shan) 355
Wanshou Si (Beijing) 141
Wenshu Yuan (Chengdu) 351
Wofu Si (Beijing) 144